Engineering Mathematics
for
Technicians

Anthony Nicolaides
B.SC. (Eng), C.Eng, M.I.E.T.

P.A.S.S. PUBLICATIONS
Private Academic & Scientific Studies Ltd

ii ━ Prelims

© A. Nicolaides
First Edition 2009

ISBN-13   978-1-872684-74-1
£19.95

Printed and bound in Great Britain by
CPI Antony Rowe, Chippenham and Eastbourne

1. Mathematics I/II   ISBN-13   978-1-872684-50-5
                                    Second Edition

2. Analytical Mathematics II   ISBN-13   978-1-872684-51-2
                                    Second Edition

3. Algebra III   ISBN-13   978-1-872684-52-9
                                    Second Edition

4. Calculus III   ISBN-13   978-1-872684-64-2
                                    Second Edition

which can be purchased separately on a CD for £3/CD, minimum number 25.

P.A.S.S. PUBLICATIONS

Mathematics for Technicians

Mathematics I/II

Anthony Nicolaides
B.SC. (Eng), C.Eng, M.I.E.T.

P.A.S.S. PUBLICATIONS
Private Academic & Scientific Studies Ltd

© A. Nicolaides
Second Edition 2009

ISBN-13   978-1-872684-50-5

Mathematics I/II

First Published in 1991 by Private Academic & Scientific Studies Ltd

P.A.S.S. PUBLICATIONS

Preface

This book covers adequately the following:

- The law of indices.

- The laws of logarithms.

- The plotting of a straight line graph using experimental data and use it to deduce the gradient, intercept and equation of the line.

- The solution of circular and triangular measurement problems involving the use of radian, sine, cosine and tangent functions.

- The sketching and drawing of the three trigonometric functions over a complete cycle.

- Solving problems involving the sine and cosine rules.

- Solving algebraically and graphically two linear and linear/non linear equations.

- Collecting data and producing statistical diagrams, histograms and frequency curves.

- Determining the mean, median and mode for two statistical problems and explain the relevance of each average as a measure of central tendency.

- Evaluating standard deviations for grouped and ungrouped data.

- Transposing formulae used in Engineering, Physics and Electronics.

The author was a Full Time Senior Lecturer and course Tutor for the BTEC National Diploma in Engineering for many years at a Prestigeous Further Education College which at one time was The Technical College of Europe (SELTEC).

The Full solutions of all the exercises are fully worked out.

Anthony
Nicolaides
B.Sc. (Eng.),
C.Eng. M.I.E.T.

Contents

Mathematics I (First Mathematics)

1

Mathematics I (First Mathematics) Arithmetic

1. Positive integer indices

Evaluates expressions involving integer indices and uses standard form:

- base, index, power, reciprocal in terms of a^n
- $a^m a^n = a^{m+n}$, $\frac{a^m}{a^n} = a^{m-n}$, $(a^m)^n = a^{mn}$, $a^o = 1$, $a^{-n} = \frac{1}{a^n}$
- standard form eg 1.234×10^5
- four basic operations using standard forms.

(a) Negative and positive integer numbers

ARITHMETIC is a Greek word derived from the word 'arithmos' which means 'number', and arithmetic is the study of the Mathematics of numbers.

The aim is to provide the student with a basic understanding of the fundamental concepts of arithmetic and to help develop mental calculation and logical thinking.

INTEGER NUMBERS are whole numbers and there are positive and negative integer numbers.

POSITIVE INTEGER NUMBERS are denoted as $+1, +2, +3, +5, +8, +17, +125$ or $1, 2, 3, 5, 8, 12, 17, 125$ without the plus sign in front of the number.

NEGATIVE INTEGER NUMBERS are denoted as $-1, -2, -3, -4, -6, -7, -9, -15$, the minus sign in front of the number is essential to denote that the number in negative.

(b) Base and index (power)

The number 2^3, which is read as 'two to the power three' or 'two is raised to the power or index three' and it means

$$2^3 = 2 \times 2 \times 2 = 8.$$

The 2 is called the **base** and the 3 is called the index or power.

2^3 means the base two is raised to the index three. Other examples of base and index are:

$$2^5 = 2 \times 2 \times 2 \times 2 \times 2 = 32$$
$$3^4 = 3 \times 3 \times 3 \times 3 = 81$$
$$10^7 = 10 \times 10 \times 10 \times 10 \times 10 \times 10 \times 10$$
$$= 10,000,000 \text{ which reads ten million.}$$

The indices in the above examples are positive. The following numbers read

$$1 = 10^0 \quad \text{Unit}$$
$$10 = 10^1 \quad \text{Ten}$$
$$100 = 10^2 \quad \text{Hundred}$$
$$1000 = 10^3 \quad \text{Thousand}$$
$$10,000 = 10^4 \quad \text{Ten Thousand}$$
$$100,000 = 10^5 \quad \text{Hundred Thousand}$$
$$1,000,000 = 10^6 \quad \text{Million}$$
$$10,000,000 = 10^7 \quad \text{Ten Million}$$
$$100,000,000 = 10^8 \quad \text{Hundred Million}$$
$$1,000,000,000 = 10^9 \quad \text{Billion}$$
$$1,000,000,000,000 = 10^{12} \quad \text{Trillion}$$

Several of the above numbers have many digits and become tedious to write them fully out. These numbers can be written in abbreviation as shown adjacently:

$$10^6 = 1,000,000$$
$$= 10 \times 10 \times 10 \times 10 \times 10 \times 10$$
$$10^9 = 1,000,000,000 = 10 \times 10 \times 10 \times 10$$
$$\times 10 \times 10 \times 10 \times 10 \times 10.$$

WORKED EXAMPLE 1

(a) Write down three positive integers

   (i) one with one digit

   (ii) one with two digits and

   (iii) one with three digits

(b) Write down three negative integers

   (i) one with one digit

   (ii) one with two digits and

   (iii) one with three digits

Solution 1

(a) (i) 3   (ii) 25   (iii) 987 or

   (i) +3   (ii) +25   (iii) +987

(b) (i) −7   (ii) −64   (iii) −823.

WORKED EXAMPLE 2

(a) Write down the number 32 as a power of 2.

(b) Write down the number 81 as a power of 3.

(c) Write down the number 10,000,000,000,000 as a power of 10.

Solution 2

(a) $32 = 2^1 \times 2^1 \times 2^1 \times 2^1 \times 2^1 = 2^5$.

Since the base of each number is the same and is equal to 2, we write this base down and add the indices

$$1+1+1+1+1 = 5, \text{ therefore } 32 = 2^5$$

(b) $81 = 3^1 \times 3^1 \times 3^1 \times 3^1 = 3^4$.

Similarly since the base is the same and is equal to 3, we write this base and count the indices

$$1+1+1+1 = 4 \text{ therefore } 81 = 3^4$$

(c) $10,000,000,000,000 = 10^1 \times 10^1 \times 10^1 \times 10^1 \times 10^1 \times 10^1 \times 10^1 \times 10^1 \times 10^1 \times 10^1 \times 10^1 \times 10^1 \times 10^1 = 10^{13}$.

The base of this number is 10 which is multiplied thirteen times, we write 10 as the common base and add the indices to give the total or final index of the number.

WORKED EXAMPLE 3

Write the answers of the following numbers

  (i) 2^4 (ii) 3^5 (iii) 4^3

(iv) 5^2 (v) 6^3 (vi) 7^2

(vii) 8^3 (viii) 2^7 (ix) 9^3

  (x) 10^5.

Solution 3

Work out the following numbers mentally.

  (i) $2^4 = 2 \times 2 \times 2 \times 2 = 16$

 (ii) $3^5 = 3 \times 3 \times 3 \times 3 \times 3 = 243$

(iii) $4^3 = 4 \times 4 \times 4 = 64$

(iv) $5^2 = 5 \times 5 = 25$

 (v) $6^3 = 6 \times 6 \times 6 = 216$

(vi) $7^2 = 7 \times 7 = 49$

(vii) $8^3 = 8 \times 8 \times 8 = 512$

(viii) $2^7 = 2 \times 2 \times 2 \times 2 \times 2 \times 2 \times 2 = 128$

(ix) $9^3 = 9 \times 9 \times 9 = 729$

 (x) $10^5 = 100,000$.

WORKED EXAMPLE 4

State the base and the index or power of the number 5^7. Evaluate this number without the use of an electronic calculator, and name the result.

Solution 4

The base of the number 5^7 is 5 and the index or power of this number is 7.

$$
\begin{array}{r}
625 \quad \times \\
125 \\
\hline
3125 \\
1250 \\
625 \\
\hline
78,125
\end{array}
$$

$5^7 = 5 \times 5 \times 5 \times 5 \times 5 \times 5 \times 5 = 25 \times 25 \times 25 \times 5$
$= 625 \times 125 = 78, 125$ by long multiplication, seventy eight thousand and one hundred and twenty five.

WORKED EXAMPLE 5

State the base and the power of the number 3^5 and evaluate this number without the use of a calculator and name the result.

Solution 5

The base of this number is 3 and the power or index is 5.

$3^5 = 3 \times 3 \times 3 \times 3 \times 3 = 9 \times 9 \times 3 = 81 \times 3 = 243$, two hundred and forty three.

Indices

To multiply numbers having the same base but the same or different indices, we write the base down and add the indices.

$2^5 \times 2^3 \times 2^2 \times 2^{11} \times 2^{52} = 2^{5+3+2+11+52}$
$$= 2^{73}.$$

All the five numbers have the same base (two), then the result has the same base (two), and the new index is the sum of the indices, i.e.,

$5 + 3 + 2 + 11 + 52 = 73.$

WORKED EXAMPLE 6

Express as a single power of 3 the product of the following numbers:
$$3^1, 3^2, 3^3, 3^4, 3^5.$$

Solution 6

$3^1 \times 3^2 \times 3^3 \times 3^4 \times 3^5 = 3^{1+2+3+4+5} = 3^{15}.$

WORKED EXAMPLE 7

Express the product of the following numbers $5^4, 5^3, 5^2, 5^1$ as a single power of 5 and find its value without a calculator by long multiplication.

Solution 7

$5^4 \times 5^3 \times 5^2 \times 5^1 = 5^{4+3+2+1} = 5^{10}$
observe that $5 = 5^1$.

To find the value of 5^{10}, we multiply 5 ten times
$$
\begin{aligned}
5^{10} &= 5 \times 5 \times 5 \times 5 \times 5 \times 5 \times 5 \times 5 \times 5 \times 5 \\
&= 25 \times 25 \times 25 \times 25 \times 25 \\
&= 625 \times 625 \times 25 \\
&= 390,675 \times 25 \\
&= 9,765,625
\end{aligned}
$$

$$
\begin{array}{r}
625 \quad \times \\
625 \\
\hline
3125 \\
1250 \\
3750 \\
\hline
390,625
\end{array}
\qquad
\begin{array}{r}
390,625 \quad \times \\
25 \\
\hline
1953125 \\
781250 \\
\hline
9,765,625
\end{array}
$$

nine million seven hundred and sixty five thousand six hundred and twenty five.

The powers of 2

$2^1 \times 2^1 = 2^2 = 4$
$2^1 \times 2^1 \times 2^1 = 2^3 = 8$
$2^1 \times 2^1 \times 2^1 \times 2^1 = 2^4 = 16$
$2^1 \times 2^1 \times 2^1 \times 2^1 \times 2^1 = 2^5 = 32$
$2^1 \times 2^1 \times 2^1 \times 2^1 \times 2^1 \times 2^1 = 2^6 = 64$
$2^1 \times 2^1 \times 2^1 \times 2^1 \times 2^1 \times 2^1 \times 2^1 = 2^7 = 128$
$2^1 \times 2^1 \times 2^1 \times 2^1 \times 2^1 \times 2^1 \times 2^1 \times 2^1 = 2^8 = 256$
$2^1 \times 2^1 \times 2^1 \times 2^1 \times 2^1 \times 2^1 \times 2^1 \times 2^1 \times 2^1$
$\qquad = 2^9 = 512$
$2^1 \times 2^1 \times 2^1 \times 2^1 \times 2^1 \times 2^1 \times 2^1 \times 2^1 \times 2^1 \times 2^1$
$\qquad = 2^{10} = 1024$.

The powers of 3

$3^1 \times 3^1 = 3^2 = 9$
$3^1 \times 3^1 \times 3^1 = 3^3 = 27$
$3^1 \times 3^1 \times 3^1 \times 3^1 = 3^4 = 81$

$3^1 \times 3^1 \times 3^1 \times 3^1 \times 3^1 = 3^5 = 243$
$3^1 \times 3^1 \times 3^1 \times 3^1 \times 3^1 \times 3^1 = 3^6 = 729$
$3^1 \times 3^1 \times 3^1 \times 3^1 \times 3^1 \times 3^1 \times 3^1 = 3^7 = 2,187$
$3^1 \times 3^1 \times 3^1 \times 3^1 \times 3^1 \times 3^1 \times 3^1 \times 3^1$
$\qquad = 3^8 = 6,561$
$3^1 \times 3^1 \times 3^1 \times 3^1 \times 3^1 \times 3^1 \times 3^1 \times 3^1 \times 3^1$
$\qquad = 3^9 = 19,683$
$3^1 \times 3^1 \times 3^1 \times 3^1 \times 3^1 \times 3^1 \times$
$3^1 \times 3^1 \times 3^1 \times 3^1 = 3^{10} = 59,049.$

The powers of 5

$5^1 \times 5^1 = 25 = 5^2$
$5^1 \times 5^1 \times 5^1 = 125 = 5^3$
$5^1 \times 5^1 \times 5^1 \times 5^1 = 625 = 5^4$
$5^1 \times 5^1 \times 5^1 \times 5^1 \times 5^1 = 3125 = 5^5$
$5^1 \times 5^1 \times 5^1 \times 5^1 \times 5^1 \times 5^1 = 15,625 = 5^6$
$5^1 \times 5^1 \times 5^1 \times 5^1 \times 5^1 \times 5^1 \times 5^1 = 78,125 = 5^7$
$5^1 \times 5^1 \times 5^1 \times 5^1 \times 5^1 \times 5^1 \times 5^1 \times 5^1$
$\qquad = 390,625 = 5^8$
$5^1 \times 5^1 \times 5^1 \times 5^1 \times 5^1 \times 5^1 \times 5^1 \times 5^1 \times 5^1$
$\qquad = 1,953,125 = 5^9$
$5^1 \times 5^1 \times 5^1 \times 5^1 \times 5^1 \times 5^1 \times 5^1 \times 5^1 \times 5^1 \times 5^1$
$\qquad = 9,765,625 = 5^{10}.$

So far we have considered indicial numbers with bases and indices as numbers. We can now represent the bases and indices of numbers by letters. Let the base be a and the index be m then the number can be represented by

If the base is b and the index n then the number is represented by b^n.

In general we can write $\boxed{a^m \times a^n = a^{m+n}}$

since the bases of the two numbers are the same, the result has the same base and the index is the sum of the two indices m plus n.

What does a^m mean? It means that a is multiplied by itself m times.
What does x^y mean? It means that x is multiplied by itself y times.
What does 10^4 mean? It means that 10 is multiplied by itself 4 times,

$10^4 = 10^1 \times 10^1 \times 10^1 \times 10^1$
$\qquad = 10^{1+1+1+1} = 10^4.$

Exercises 1

1. Express the following numbers as powers of 2.

   (i) 16   (ii) 32   (iii) 64   (iv) 4

   (v) 2   (vi) 128   (vii) 8   (viii) 256

   (ix) 512   (x) 1024   (xi) 1.

2. Express the following numbers as powers of 3.

   (i) 81   (ii) 243   (iii) 3   (iv) 9

   (v) 729   (vi) 27   (vii) 1   (viii) 2187.

3. Express the following numbers as powers of 5.

   (i) 125   (ii) 625   (iii) 5

   (iv) 25   (v) 1   (vi) 3125.

4. (a) Write down a few positive integer numbers.

   (b) Write down a few negative integer numbers.

5. Evaluate the following indicial number

   (i) 2^6 (ii) 3^4 (iii) 4^4

   (iv) 5^3 (v) 7^3 (vi) 10^5.

6. (a) State the base and index for the following indicial numbers

   (i) 3^7 (ii) 27^3 (iii) 375^3

   (iv) 99^3 (v) 101^{35}.

7. Evaluate the following:

   (a) $2^1 \times 2^2 \times 2^3 \times 2^4$ (b) $\dfrac{2^1 \times 2^3 \times 3^4 \times 3^5}{2^5 \times 3^6}$

   (c) $3^3 \times 3^2 \times 3^1 \times 3^0$ (d) $\dfrac{5 \times 5^3 \times 5^5}{5^4}$

   (e) $\dfrac{2 \times 3^2 \times 4 \times 5^2}{2^3 \times 3 \times 5}$.

8. (a) Express the product of the following numbers $3^5, 3^3, 3^7, 3^9$ as a single power of 3.

   (b) Express the product of the following numbers $2^2, 2^5, 2^7$ as a single power of 2.

   (c) Express the result of (b) to the result of (a) as a ratio of powers.

2

The reciprocal of a positive number

The reciprocal of the number 2 is $\frac{1}{2}$,

the reciprocal of the number 3 is $\frac{1}{3}$,

the reciprocal of the number 15 is $\frac{1}{15}$.

In other words, the reciprocal of a number is one over the number.

How can we write these numbers $\frac{1}{2}$, $\frac{1}{3}$ and $\frac{1}{15}$ in index form?

$$\frac{1}{2} = 2^{-1}, \frac{1}{3} = 3^{-1}, \frac{1}{15} = 15^{-1}.$$

In general the reciprocal of x is $\frac{1}{x}$ which can be written as

$$\boxed{\frac{1}{x} = x^{-1}}$$

The base is x and the index is negative one.

This notation is extremely useful when we wish to write a very small number in index form.

The electronic charge, is $e = 1.6 \times 10^{-19}$ C what does this mean?

$$1.6 \times 10^{-19} = \frac{1.6}{10^{19}} = 0.00000000000000000016$$

the decimal point is shifted to the left nineteen places.

Another useful example is the electronic mass

$m = 9.11 \times 10^{-31}$ kg

$= 0.000000000000000000000000000000911$

As it can be seen it has many digits and it is rather clumsy.

This number is written in the indicial form 9.11×10^{-31}, and fewer digits are used to express the same quantity.

The radius of an atom, the smallest indivisible particle is of the order of 10^{-10} m, what does this length mean?

$$10^{-10} = \frac{1}{10^{10}} = \frac{1}{10,000,000,000}$$

this is the reciprocal of ten billion or

$1 \times 10^{-10} = 0.0000000001$, the decimal point is shifted to the left ten places

$1 \times 10^{10} = 10,000,000,000$, the decimal point is shifted to the right ten places

$$\frac{10^{-10}}{1} = \frac{1}{10^{10}} = 10^{-10}.$$

Note that under the number 10^{-10} there is a one to make the index positive we displace the number from the numerator to the denominator. If the number is 10^{10} in the denominator and we wish to take up to the numerator we merely change the sign of the index

$$\frac{1}{10^{10}} = 10^{-10}.$$

Distinguish between the negative integer index and the positive integer index. The radius of the nucleus of an atom is of the order of 1.0×10^{-15} m i.e., 1.0×10^{-15} m $= 0.000000000000001$ m, the decimal point is shifted to the left fifteen places, this length is extremely small.

In general if a is the base and the index or power is $-n$ then

$$a^{-n} = \frac{1}{a^n}$$

a^{-n} is the reciprocal of a^n and a^n is the reciprocal of a^{-n}

$$a^n = \frac{1}{a^{-n}}$$

what is the significance of a base when raised to a negative index?
It means that the reciprocal of the base when raised to a positive index and vice-versa.
In general numbers are expressed in positive indices.

WORKED EXAMPLE 8

Express the following numbers as positive indices:

(i) a^{-n} (ii) 2^{-5}

(iii) 3^{-3} (iv) $\dfrac{1}{2^{-5}}$

(v) $\dfrac{2^3}{2^{-3}}$ (vi) $\dfrac{3^5}{3^{-1}}$

(vii) $\dfrac{2^5 \times 5^2}{2^{-3} \times 5^{-3}}$ (viii) $7^{-1} \times 8^{-1}$

(ix) $2^{-1} \times 3^{-1} \times 4^{-1}$ (x) $\dfrac{1}{6^{-2}5^{-3}7^{-4}}$.

Solution 8

(i) $a^{-n} = \dfrac{1}{a^n}$

(ii) $2^{-5} = \dfrac{1}{2^5}$

(iii) $3^{-3} = \dfrac{1}{3^3}$

(iv) $\dfrac{1}{2^{-5}} = 2^5$

(v) $\dfrac{2^3}{2^{-3}} = 2^3 \times 2^3 = 2^6$

(vi) $\dfrac{3^5}{3^{-1}} = 3^5 \times 3^1 = 3^{5+1} = 3^6$

(vii) $\dfrac{2^5 \times 5^2}{2^{-3} \times 5^{-3}} = 2^5 \times 5^2 \times 2^3 \times 5^3 = 2^8 \times 5^5$

(viii) $7^{-1} \times 8^{-1} = \dfrac{1}{7} \times \dfrac{1}{8} = \dfrac{1}{56}$

(ix) $2^{-1} \times 3^{-1} \times 4^{-1} = \dfrac{1}{2} \times \dfrac{1}{3} \times \dfrac{1}{4} = \dfrac{1}{24}$

(x) $\dfrac{1}{6^{-2} \times 5^{-3} \times 7^{-4}} = 6^2 \times 5^3 \times 7^4$.

WORKED EXAMPLE 9

Find the value of
(i) 10^{-2} (ii) 9^{-3} (iii) 7^{-4}

(iv) 11^{-2} (v) 100^{-3}.

Solution 9

(i) $10^{-2} = \dfrac{1}{10^2} = \dfrac{1}{100} = 0.01$

(ii) $9^{-3} = \dfrac{1}{9^3} = \dfrac{1}{729}$

(iii) $7^{-4} = \dfrac{1}{7^4} = \dfrac{1}{2401}$

(iv) $11^{-2} = \dfrac{1}{11^2} = \dfrac{1}{121}$

(v) $100^{-3} = \dfrac{1}{100^3}$

$$= \frac{1}{100 \times 100 \times 100} = \frac{1}{1000000}.$$

To show that $\dfrac{a^m}{a^n} = a^{m-n}$

$$\frac{a^m}{a^n} = a^m \cdot a^{-n} = a^{m-n} \quad \text{therefore}$$

$$\boxed{\frac{a^m}{a^n} = a^{m-n}}$$

Simplify the following:

(i) $\dfrac{x^3 x^2 y^2 y^{-3}}{x y^3}$ (ii) $\dfrac{a^3 b^1 b^4}{a^5}$

Solution 10

(i) $\dfrac{x^3 x^2 y^2 y^{-3}}{x y^3} = x^3 x^2 y^2 y^{-3} x^{-1} y^{-3}$

$= x^{3+2-1} y^{2-3-3}$

$= x^4 y^{-4} = \frac{x^4}{y^4}$

(ii) $\dfrac{a^3 b^1 b^4}{a^5} = a^3 b^{1+4} a^{-5} = a^{3-5} b^5$

$= a^{-2} b^5 = \dfrac{b^5}{a^2}$

WORKED EXAMPLE 11

Simplify (i) $\dfrac{x^3 y^4 z^5}{x y^{-4} z}$ and

(ii) $\dfrac{w^3 u^3 v^3}{wuv}$.

Solution 11

(i) $\dfrac{x^3 y^4 z^5}{x y^{-4} z} = x^3 y^4 z^5 x^{-1} y^4 z^{-1}$

$= x^{3-1} y^{4+4} z^{5-1}$

$= x^2 y^8 z^4$

(ii) $\dfrac{w^3 u^3 v^3}{wuv} = w^3 w^{-1} u^3 u^{-1} v^3 v^{-1}$

$= w^{3-1} u^{3-1} v^{3-1} = w^2 u^2 v^2$

The superpowers

$(\mathbf{a^m})^\mathbf{n}$ $(a^m)^n$ means that a^m is the base and n is the index and therefore a^m is multiplied by itself n times

$(a^m)^n = a^m \cdot a^m \cdot a^m \cdot a^m \cdot a^m \ldots$

$= a^{m+m+m+\ldots(n \text{ times})}$

$= a^{nm}$ $\boxed{(a^m)^n = a^{mn}}$

note that the powers or indices are multiplied.

WORKED EXAMPLE 12

Determine as a single power the following:

(i) $(2^3)^2$ (ii) $(3^2)^5$ (iii) $(4^2)^3$

(iv) $(5^2)^5$ (v) $(7^3)^7$

Solution 12

(i) $(2^3)^2 = 2^{3\times2} = 2^6$

(ii) $(3^2)^5 = 3^{2\times5} = 3^{10}$

(iii) $(4^2)^3 = 4^{2\times3} = 4^6$

(iv) $(5^2)^5 = 5^{2\times5} = 5^{10}$

(v) $(7^3)^7 = 7^{3\times7} = 7^{21}$.

WORKED EXAMPLE 13

Evaluate the following:

(i) $(2^{-3})^3$ (ii) $(3^3)^{-2}$ (iii) $(5^{-1})^5$

(iv) $(3^{-2})^{-2}$ (v) $(5^{-2})^2$.

Solution 13

(i) $(2^{-3})^3 = 2^{-9} = \frac{1}{2^9}$

(ii) $(3^3)^{-2} = 3^{-6} = \frac{1}{3^6}$

(iii) $(5^{-1})^5 = 5^{-5} = \frac{1}{5^5}$

(iv) $(3^{-2})^{-2} = 3^{(-2)(-2)} = 3^4$

(v) $(5^{-2})^2 = 5^{-4} = \frac{1}{5^4}$.

Suppose now that we have to raise to a certain power the product of certain numbers such as $(2^1 \times 3^1 \times 4^1)^3 = 2^3 \times 3^3 \times 4^3$ each number is raised to the power 3 or such as

$(2^2 \times 3^3 \times 4^5)^2 = 2^{2\times2} \times 3^{3\times2} \times 4^{5\times2}$

$= 2^4 \times 3^6 \times 4^{10}$.

The rule is extended to

$(a^n b^m c^p)^x = a^{nx} b^{mx} c^{px}$

WORKED EXAMPLE 14

Simplify the following

(i) $(2^2 \times 3^2 \times 5^3)^4$ (ii) $(1 \times 4^3 \times 6^7)^{-2}$

(iii) $(2 \times 3 \times 4)^{-3}$.

Solution 14

(i) $(2^2 \times 3^2 \times 5^3)^4 = 2^{2\times4} \times 3^{2\times4} \times 5^{3\times4}$
$$= 2^8 \times 3^8 \times 5^{12}$$

(ii) $(1 \times 4^3 \times 6^7)^{-2} = 1^{-2} \times 4^{3\times(-2)} \times 6^{7\times(-2)}$
$$= \frac{1}{1^2} \times 4^{-6} \times 6^{-14}$$
$$= 1 \times \frac{1}{4^6} \times \frac{1}{6^{14}} \times = \frac{1}{4^6 \times 6^{14}}$$

(iii) $(2\times3\times4)^{-3} = 2^{1\times(-3)} \times 3^{1\times(-3)} \times 4^{1\times(-3)}$
$$= 2^{-3} \times 3^{-3} \times 4^{-3}$$
$$= \frac{1}{2^3} \times \frac{1}{3^3} \times \frac{1}{4^3} = \frac{1}{8} \times \frac{1}{27} \times \frac{1}{64}$$
$$= \frac{1}{8 \times 27 \times 64} = \frac{1}{216 \times 64} = \frac{1}{13{,}824}.$$

To show that any number raised to the power zero is unity.

$$x^0 = 1$$

$$\frac{x^1}{x^1} = x^1 \cdot x^{-1} = x^{1-1} = x^0 = 1 \text{ since } \frac{x}{x} = 1.$$

Therefore $\boxed{x^0 = 1}$ or (ANY NUMBER)$^0 = 1$

$2^0 = 3^0 = 1^0 = 4^0 = 5^0 = 6^0 = 7^0$
$\quad = 8^0 = 9^0 = 10^0 = x^0 = 1$

$\frac{2^1}{2^1} = 1 = 2^1 \times 2^{-1} = 2^0 \quad$ therefore $\quad 2^0 = 1$

$\frac{3^1}{3^1} = 1 = 3^1 \times 3^{-1} = 3^{1-1} = 3^0$ and $3^0 = 1.$

Summary of the rules of indices

(i) $a^m \cdot a^n = a^{m+n}$ (ii) $\frac{a^m}{a^n} = a^{m-n}$

(iii) $(a^m)^n = a^{mn}$.

WORKED EXAMPLE 15

Evaluate n from the following equations:
(i) $2^n = 1$ (ii) $2^n = \frac{1}{8}$ (iii) $2^n = 128$.

Solution 15

(i) $2^n = 1 = 2^0$ therefore $\boxed{n = 0}$

since the bases are the same then the indices must be the same if the two indicial numbers are to be the same.

(ii) $2^n = \frac{1}{8} = \frac{1}{2^3} = 2^{-3} \quad 2^n = 2^{-3} \quad \boxed{n = -3}$

(iii) $2^n = 128 = 2 \times 2 \times 2 \times 2 \times 2 \times 2 \times 2 = 2^7$
$2^n = 2^7 \quad$ therefore $\quad \boxed{n = 7}$

WORKED EXAMPLE 16

Simplify

(i) $\frac{x^0}{y^0 z^0}$ (ii) $\frac{x}{xy^{-1}}$ (iii) $(xyz)^0$ (iv) $(x^2 y^3 z)^5$.

Solution 16

(i) $\frac{x^0}{y^0 z^0} = \frac{1}{1 \times 1} = 1 \quad \left(\frac{x}{yz}\right)^0 = 1$

(ii) $\frac{x}{xy^{-1}} = x^1 x^{-1} y^{+1} = x^0 y^1 = y$

$\frac{x}{xy^{-1}} = y$

(iii) $(xyz)^0 = x^0 y^0 x^0 = 1 \times 1 \times 1 = 1$
$$(xyz)^0 = 1$$

(iv) $(x^2 \cdot y^3 \cdot z)^5 = x^{2\times5} y^{3\times5} z^{1\times5} = x^{10} y^{15} z^5$

note when we have product of numbers and all these numbers are raised to a certain power then each number is raised to this power.

Exercises 2

1. Find the reciprocals of the following integer numbers:

(i) 2 (ii) 25 (iii) 7 (iv) 35
(v) 5 (vi) 47 (vii) 52 (viii) 8
(ix) 77 (x) 10.

2. Find the reciprocals of the following:

    (i) x (ii) y (iii) z

    (iv) xy (v) xyz.

3. Explain the significance of the following negative indices:

    (i) x^{-1} (ii) y^{-2} (iii) 3^{-5}

    (iv) z^{-3} (v) $(xy)^{-2}$ (vi) $(xyz)^{-1}$.

4. Express the following numbers as positive indices:

    (i) x^{-3} (ii) 3^{-5} (iii) $\dfrac{1}{2^{-4}}$

    (iv) $\dfrac{2^5}{2^{-5}}$ (v) x^{-n}.

5. Express the following as negative indices:

    (i) x (ii) xy (iii) 3^5

    (iv) 2^7 (v) 3^4.

6. Simplify

    (i) $\dfrac{2^3 x^4 y^3}{8xy}$ (ii) $\dfrac{a^2 b^2 c^2}{4b^4 c}$ (iii) $\dfrac{x^2 y^3 z^4}{xyz^2}$.

7. Simplify the following superpowers:

    (i) $(2^2)^2$ (ii) $(3^3)^3$ (iii) $(3^{-3})^{-4}$

    (iv) $(5^2)^{-5}$.

8. Write as a single number in index form:

    (i) $7^5 \div 7^{-4}$ (ii) $5^{-2} \div 5^2$

    (iii) $5^3 \div 5^3$.

9. Find the values

    (i) 5^{-1} (ii) 10^{-3} (iii) 7^{-2}

    (iv) 13^{-2} (v) 16^{-2}.

10. Simplify

    (a) $(2^3 5^2 x^2)^2$ (b) $(3^4 3^{-2} y)^3$.

11. Evaluate n from the following equations:

    (i) $2^n = 256$ (ii) $2^n = 2$

    (iii) $2^n = 8$ (iv) $2^n = \dfrac{1}{8}$

    (v) $2^n = \dfrac{1}{64}$ (vi) $2^n = 4$

    (vii) $2^n = 128$ (viii) $2^n = \dfrac{1}{2}$

    (ix) $2^{-n} = \dfrac{1}{4}$ (x) $2^{-n} = 2^5$

    (xi) $2^{-n} = 2^6$ (xii) $2^{-n} = \dfrac{1}{128}$.

12. Evaluate n from the following equations:

    (i) $3^{-n} = \dfrac{1}{3}$ (ii) $3^{-n} = \dfrac{1}{9}$

    (iii) $3^{-n} = \dfrac{1}{27}$ (iv) $3^n = 243$

    (v) $3^{-n} = \dfrac{1}{2187}$ (vi) $3^{-n} = 9^{-2}$

    (vii) $3^n = 9$ (viii) $3^{-n} = \dfrac{1}{81}$

    (ix) $3^n = 1$ (x) $3^n = \dfrac{1}{27}$

    (xi) $3^n = 3$ (xii) $3^{-n} = 3^3$.

13. Evaluate x from the following equations:

    (i) $5^x = 1$ (ii) $5^{-x} = \dfrac{1}{125}$

    (iii) $5^x = 5$ (iv) $5^x = 125$

    (v) $5^x = 625$ (vi) $5^x = \dfrac{1}{125}$

    (vii) $5^x = 3125$ (viii) $5^x = 25$

    (ix) $5^x = 25^{-5}$ (x) $5^{-3x} = 5^{-1}$.

3

To express numbers in standard form.

Four basic operations using standard forms

Any number may be expressed in **standard form**

$$A \; 10^n$$

where A is any number between 1 and 10, this is denoted as $1 \leq A < 10$, it can be equal to 1 but it must be less than 10, i.e. 1.0×10^{-3} and 9.99×10^5 indicate the following numbers 0.001 and 999000 respectively where $A = 1.0$ and $A = 9.99$ and n is a positive or a negative integer.

For example 1.234×10^5 is the standard form of the number 123,400 where

$A = 1.234$ and $n = 5$.

The electronic mass $m = 9.11 \times 10^{-31}$ kg where $A = 9.11$ and $n = -31$.

The electronic charge $e = 1.6 \times 10^{-19}$ kg where $A = 1.6$ and $n = -19$.

The velocity of electromagnetic waves is $c = 3 \times 10^8$ m/s where $A = 3.0$ and $n = 8$.

The radius of an atom is of the order of $r = 1.0 \times 10^{-10}$ m where $A = 1.0$ and $n = -10$.

All the above physical quantities are given in standard form, they are neater and are expressed in fewer digits, thus saving a great deal of space.

WORKED EXAMPLE 17

Write the following numbers in standard form:

(i) 2   (ii) 25

(iii) 365   (iv) 7890

(v) 55,300   (vi) 2.35

(vii) 29.35   (viii) 0.375

(ix) 0.0035   (x) 0.50015

(xi) 79.7

(xii) 0.000000001

(xiii) 25,000,000,000

(xiv) 0.00000000000000000016

(xv) 0.000000000000001.

Solution 17

(i) $2 = 2.0 \times 10^0$

(ii) $25 = 2.5 \times 10^1$

(iii) $365 = 3.65 \times 10^2$

(iv) $7890 = 7.89 \times 10^3$

(v) $55,300 = 5.53 \times 10^4$

(vi) 2.35×10^0

(vii) $29.35 = 2.935 \times 10^1$

(viii) $0.375 = 3.75 \times 10^{-1}$

(ix) $0.0035 = 3.5 \times 10^{-3}$

(x) $0.50015 = 5.0015 \times 10^{-1}$

(xi) $79.7 = 7.97 \times 10$

(xii) $0.000000001 = 1.0 \times 10^{-9}$

(xiii) $25,000,000,000 = 2.5 \times 10^{10}$

(xiv) $0.0000000000000000016 = 1.6 \times 10^{-19}$

(xv) $0.000000000000001 = 1.0 \times 10^{-15}$.

Significant figures

The number 3,795,899 has seven significant figures this number can be expressed in five significant figures, 3,795,900 or in four significant figures is 3,796,000 and in three significant figures is 3,800,000 which is also in two significant figures and 4,000,000 is the number in one significant figure.

The number 3.795899 is expressed in seven significant figures or six decimal places, the same number can be expressed in

3.796   four significant figures or three decimal places

3.8   two significant figures or one decimal place

4.0   one significant figure.

The number 3.795899 expressed correct to one significant figure is 4.

Therefore the number 3,795,899 in one significant figure is 4,000,000 or better still **correct to one significant** figure.

WORKED EXAMPLE 18

Write the numbers in the standard form and indicate the first, second, third and so on significant figures:

(i) 235600   (ii) 0.000235600

Solution 18

(i) $235600 = 2.356 \times 10^5$

First Second Third Fourth significant figure

(ii) $0.000235600 = 2.356 \times 10^{-4}$

First Second Third Fourth significant figure

For number less than one such as 0.000235600, the zeros at the beginning do not count, thus

0.0002356 is in four significant figures or 0.000236 is in three significant figures.

WORKED EXAMPLE 19

Calculate the area of a rectangle whose sides are 0.253 m and 375 mm and give your answer correct to three significant figures and in standard form.

Solution 19

$$0.253 \text{ m} = 0.253 \times 10^3 \text{ mm} = 253 \text{ mm}$$
Area of rectangle $= 0.253 \times 10^3 \times 375 \text{ mm}^2$
$$= 253 \times 375 \text{ mm}^2 = 94,875 \text{ mm}^2$$

```
 375
 253
----
1125
1875
 750
------
94,875
```

94,875   this number is expressed in five significant figures $= 9.49 \times 10^4 \text{ mm}^2$ to 3 s.f. the fifth significant figure is 5, the fourth figure is written as 7

94,880   the third significant figure is written as nine and the number in three significant figures is ninety four

94,900   thousands and nine hundred and in standard form is written as 9.49×10^4.

WORKED EXAMPLE 20

Write down the significant figure indicated in the brackets for each of the following numbers:

(i) 75.39 (3)   (ii) 888.5 (2)

(iii) 0.00777 (3)   (iv) 0.00159 (2)

(v) 35,675 (4)   (vi) 0.0525 (2)

(vii) 39,995 (4)   (viii) 39.75 (1)

(ix) 598 (1)   (x) 59.8 (2).

Solution 20

(i) 75.39 (3)   (ii) 888.5 (2)
   $75.39 \approx 75.4$ $888.5 \approx 890$

(iii) 0.00777 (3)   (iv) 0.00159 (2)
   $0.00777 = 0.00777$ $0.00159 \approx 0.0016$

(v) 35,675 (4)   (vi) 0.0525 (2)
   $35,675 \approx 35,680$ $0.0525 \approx 0.053$

(vii) 39,995 (4)   (viii) 39.75 (1)
   $39,995 \approx 40,000$ $39.75 \approx 40.00$

(ix) 598 (1)   (x) 59.8 (2)
   $598 \approx 600$ $59.8 \approx 60.0$.

WORKED EXAMPLE 21

Give the following numbers correct to three significant figures and in standard form:

(i) 799,875   (ii) 0.00799875

(iii) 7.99875   (iv) 799.875

(v) 799,875,000.

Solution 21

(i) $799,875 = 799,880$
           to five significant figures
        $= 799,900$
           to four significant figures
        $= 800,000$
           to three significant figures
        $= 8.00 \times 10^5$
           correct to three significant
           figures and in standard form

(ii) $0.00799875 \approx 0.00799880 \approx 0.0079990$
           $\approx 0.008 = 8.00 \times 10^{-3}$

(iii) $7.99875 \approx 8.00 \times 10^0$

(iv) $799.875 \approx 800 \approx 8.00 \times 10^2$

(v) $799,875,000 \approx 8.00 \times 10^8$.

WORKED EXAMPLE 22

(a) Express correct to 3 significant figures

   (i) 25,872   (ii) 2.5872   (iii) 0.025872

   (iv) 900.5   (v) 0.050065.

(b) Evaluate correct to 3 significant figures

   (i) $(0.625)^{-\frac{1}{2}}$ (ii) $(0.625)^3$

   (iii) $(0.625)^{\frac{1}{2}}$ (iv) $(0.625)^4$

   (v) $(0.625)^{1.5}$.

Solution 22

(a) (i) 25,900   (ii) 2.59   (iii) 0.0259

   (iv) 901   (v) 0.0501.

(b) Use the calculator to evaluate the following

   (i) $(0.625)^{-\frac{1}{2}} = 1.264911064$
              $= 1.26$ to 3 s.f.

   (ii) $(0.625)^3 = 0.244140625$
              $= 0.244$ correct to 3 s.f.

   (iii) $(0.625)^{\frac{1}{2}} = 0.790569415$
              $= 0.791$ to 3 s.f.

   (iv) $(0.625)^4 = 0.152587889$
              $= 0.153$ to 3 s.f.

   (v) $(0.625)^{1.5} = 0.494105884$
              $= 0.494$ to 3 s.f.

Four basic operations using standard forms

There are four basic operations: Addition, Subtraction, Multiplication and Division.

Addition

$$A + B = \text{Sum}$$
Augend   Addend

$$2 + 3 = 5$$
Augend Addend Sum

$$A + B = B + A$$
$$B + A = A + B$$

Addition of positive integers
$35 + 77 = 112$ or $77 + 35 = 112$

Add the following numbers

$3,755 + 2,999 + 1,175 + 978 + 887 + 536 + 632 + 445 + 125 = 11,532$

Add the following decimal numbers

$0.001234 + 5.351234 = 5.352468$

Addition of numbers expressed in standard forms

$3.5 \times 10^3 + 1.9 \times 10^2 = 3,500 + 190$

$$= 3,690 = 3.69 \times 10^3.$$

WORKED EXAMPLE 23

Add the following numbers and express the result in standard form and correct to three significant figures.

3,956,000, 3,595, 727, 100, 0.0035.

Solution 23

$3,956,000 + 3,595 + 727$

$\quad + 100 + 0.0035 = 3,960,422.0035$

$$= 3.96 \times 10^6 \text{ to 3 s.f.}$$

WORKED EXAMPLE 24

Add the following numbers 3.67×10^{-3}, 1.99×10^{-2} and 2.67×10^{-2} and give the result correct to three significant figures and in standard form.

Solution 24

$$3.67 \times 10^{-3} = 0.00367$$

$$1.99 \times 10^{-2} = 0.0199$$

$$2.67 \times 10^{-2} = 0.0267$$

$0.00367 + 0.0199 + 0.0267 = 0.05027$

$$= 5.03 \times 10^{-2} \text{ to 3 s.f.}$$

Subtraction

$$A - B = C \text{ (difference)}$$

$\quad\quad \downarrow \quad\quad \downarrow$

$\text{minuend} \quad \text{subtrahend}$

WORKED EXAMPLE 25

Express the difference of the numbers 2.50×10^{-5} and 2.50×10^{-3} in standard form where 2.50×10^{-3} is the minuend and 2.50×10^{-5} is the subtrahend and vice-versa.

Solution 25

$2.50 \times 10^{-3} - 2.50 \times 10^{-5}$

$\quad = 0.0025 - 0.000025$

$\quad = 0.002475 = 2.475 \times 10^{-3}$

$2.50 \times 10^{-5} - 2.50 \times 10^{-3}$

$\quad = 0.000025 - 0.0025$

$\quad = -0.002475 = -2.475 \times 10^{-3}.$

The difference in the first case is positive and equal to 2.475×10^{-3} and in the second case the difference is negative and equal to -2.475×10^{-3}.

Multiplication

$$A \times B$$

$A \times B = C \text{ (product)}$

$\quad\quad \downarrow \quad\quad \downarrow$

$\text{multiplicand} \quad \text{multiplier}$

$375 \quad \times \quad 25 \quad = \quad 9,375$

$\quad \downarrow \quad\quad\quad \downarrow \quad\quad\quad \downarrow$

$\text{multiplicand} \quad \text{multiplier} \quad \text{product}$

$25 \quad \times \quad 375 \quad = \quad 9,375$

$\quad \downarrow \quad\quad\quad \downarrow \quad\quad\quad \downarrow$

$\text{multiplicand} \quad \text{multiplier} \quad \text{product}$

WORKED EXAMPLE 26

Multiply the following numbers

$3.75 \times 10^{-9}, 2.07 \times 10^5, 1.956 \times 10^{-2}$

and express the result correct to three significant figures.

Solution 26

$3.75 \times 10^{-9} \times 2.07 \times 10^5 \times 1.956 \times 10^{-2} =$
$0.000015183 = 15.2 \times 10^{-6} = 1.52 \times 10^{-5}$ to
3 s.f. and in standard form.

Use a calculator to multiply the numbers 3.75, 2.07, 1.956

$3.75 \times 2.07 \times 1.956 = 15.18345$
$= 15.2$ to 3 s.f.

Insert the result above, then use the rule of indices to obtain the value 10^{-6}

$10^{-9} \times 10^5 \times 10^{-2} = 10^{-9+5-2} = 10^{-6}$
1.52×10^{-5} to 3 s.f. and in standard form.

Division

$\dfrac{A}{B} = C \text{(quotient)}$ $\dfrac{\text{Divident}}{\text{Divisor}} = \text{QUOTIENT}$

$C = $ quotient $A = $ divident $B = $ divisor

WORKED EXAMPLE 27

(a) Find the quotient by dividing 395,675 by 0.0125 correct to three significant figures.

(b) Express the result correct to three significant figures $\dfrac{3.957 \times 10^{-7}}{0.125 \times 10^{-9}}$.

Solution 27

Use a calculator to obtain the divident

(a) $\dfrac{395,675}{0.0125} = 31,654,000$

$= 3.17 \times 10^7$ to 3 s.f.

(b) $\dfrac{3.957 \times 10^{-7}}{0.125 \times 10^{-9}} = 31.656 \times 10^2$

$= 3.17 \times 10^3$ to 3 s.f. and standard form.

WORKED EXAMPLE 28

Calculate the area of a rectangular plate correct to three significant figures, the length of the plate in mm is 25.16 ± 0.005 and the breadth in mm 13.69 ± 0.005.

Solution 28

$A = $ Area of rectangular plate
$= $ length $\times$ breadth $= l \times b$.

The length of the plate is 25.16 ± 0.005, i.e. 25.165 or 25.155 and the breadth of the plate is 13.69 ± 0.005 i.e 13.695 or 13.685.

The quantity plus or minus ($\pm$) 0.005 is the tolerance

$A = l \times b = 25.165 \times 13.695$
$= 344.63467 = 345$ mm^2 to 3 s.f.

$A = l \times b = 25.165 \times 13.685$
$= 344.38302 = 344$ mm^2 to 3 s.f.

$A = l \times b = 25.155 \times 13.695$
$= 344.49772 = 345$ mm^2 to 3 s.f.

$A = l \times b = 25.155 \times 13.685$
$= 344.24617 = 344$ mm^2 to 3 s.f.

If initially we take the length correct to three significant figures as 25.2 and that of the breadth as 13.7, then the area is $25.2 \times 13.7 = 345.24 = 345$ mm^2 correct to three significant figures.

Exercises 3

1. Write the following numbers in standard form 1.234×10^n
   (i) 23   (ii) 123
   (iii) 2354   (iv) 25,399
   (v) 27,920,000   (vi) 0.1
   (vii) 0.0025   (viii) 0.000035
   (ix) 0.0000000099   (x) 0.00003503.

2. Indicate the first, second, third, fourth and so on significant figures in the following numbers:
   (i) 95,000   (ii) 675,300
   (iii) 0.0039   (iv) 37.3
   (v) 390.005.

3. Calculate the area of the following rectangular areas:
   (i) $l = 35.35$ mm, $b = 21.9$ mm
   (ii) $l = 39.99$ cm, $b = 25.0$ cm.

4. Write down the significant figure indicated in the brackets for each of the following numbers:
   (i) 25.95 (3)   (ii) 0.0003599 (2)
   (iii) 25,945 (3).

5. Express the following numbers correct to three significant figures and in standard form.

   (i) 77,777   (ii) 29,005

   (iii) 25.975   (iv) 0.003567

   (v) 9,567.

6. Evaluate correct to three significant figures

   (i) $(25.95)^3$

   (ii) $(0.0625)^5$

   (iii) $(0.00125)^{-5}$.

7. Express the following results in standard form and correct to three significant figures:

   (i) $395.300 \times 10^{-5} + 29.65 \times 10^{-4}$

   (ii) $1.234 \times 10^{-9} + 37.95 \times 10^{-8}$

   (iii) $259.35 - 36.39$

   (iv) $\dfrac{25.99 \times 10^{-5}}{3.75 \times 10^{-4}}$.

8. A square plate has an area of 256.95 mm^2. Calculate the side of the plate correct to three significant figures.

4

Evaluates expressions involving negative and fractional indices and relates indices and logarithms.

- index rules for negative and fractional indices
- combination of positive, negative and fractional indices
- inverse of $a^x = y$ as $x = \log_a y$
- logarithms of numbers

Index rules for negative and fractional indices

We have already seen the following indicial rules

$a^m a^n = a^{m+n}$

$\dfrac{a^m}{a^n} = a^{m-n}$

$(a^m)^n = a^{mn}$.

The indices are now negative and fractional. What is the meaning of $4^{\frac{1}{2}}$?

$4^{\frac{1}{2}}$ means $\sqrt[2]{4^1}$ or the square root of four to the power one as shown or merely $\sqrt{4} = \pm 2$ do not forget the plus or minus in this case since $(-2) \times (-2) = 4$ or $(2) \times (2) = 4$.

What is the meaning of $4^{\frac{3}{5}}$?

$4^{\frac{3}{5}}$ means $\sqrt[5]{4^3}$ or the fifth root of four raised to the power 3.

We have noticed in these two examples, when we raise a number to a fractional index, the

denominator of the fraction is the root and the numerator of the fraction is the power.

In general, $a^{\frac{p}{q}}$ is $\sqrt[q]{a^p}$, i.e. the q th root of a raised to the power p.

$$7^{\frac{3}{5}} = \sqrt[5]{7^3} \qquad 2^{\frac{1}{4}} = \sqrt[4]{2^1}$$

$$2^{\frac{2}{3}} = \sqrt[3]{2^2} \qquad 2^{\frac{1}{6}} = \sqrt[6]{2^1}$$

$$\boxed{x^{\frac{p}{q}} = \sqrt[q]{x^p}}$$

what is the meaning of $2^{-\frac{3}{4}}$?

$2^{-\frac{3}{4}} = \dfrac{1}{2^{\frac{3}{4}}}$ i.e. the reciprocal of 2 raised to the power $\frac{3}{4}$

$$2^{-\frac{3}{4}} = \dfrac{1}{2^{\frac{3}{4}}} = \dfrac{1}{\sqrt[4]{2^3}}.$$

WORKED EXAMPLE 29

Express the following indicial numbers in the root form:

(i) $2^{\frac{1}{2}}$ (ii) $5^{\frac{3}{4}}$ (iii) $7^{\frac{1}{3}}$ (iv) $4^{\frac{3}{7}}$

(v) $3^{\frac{1}{4}}$ (vi) $2^{-\frac{1}{2}}$ (vii) $5^{-\frac{3}{4}}$ (viii) $7^{-\frac{1}{3}}$

(ix) $4^{-\frac{3}{7}}$ (x) $3^{-\frac{1}{4}}$.

Solution 29

(i) $2^{\frac{1}{2}} = \sqrt[2]{2^1} = \sqrt{2}$ notice that there is no need to write the square root (it is implied) and also 2^1 means 2 so also in this case the power 1 is implied.

(ii) $5^{\frac{3}{4}} = \sqrt[4]{5^3}$

(iii) $\sqrt[3]{7} = 7^{\frac{1}{3}}$

(iv) $\sqrt[7]{4^3} = 4^{\frac{3}{7}}$

(v) $3^{\frac{1}{4}} = \sqrt[4]{3}$

(vi) $2^{-\frac{1}{2}} = \dfrac{1}{2^{\frac{1}{2}}} = \dfrac{1}{\sqrt{2}}$

(vii) $5^{-\frac{3}{4}} = \dfrac{1}{5^{\frac{3}{4}}} = \dfrac{1}{\sqrt[4]{5^3}}$

(viii) $7^{-\frac{1}{3}} = \dfrac{1}{7^{\frac{1}{3}}} = \dfrac{1}{\sqrt[3]{7}}$

(ix) $4^{-\frac{3}{7}} = \dfrac{1}{4^{\frac{3}{7}}} = \dfrac{1}{\sqrt[7]{4^3}}$

(x) $3^{-\frac{1}{4}} = \dfrac{1}{3^{\frac{1}{4}}} = \dfrac{1}{\sqrt[4]{3}}$.

WORKED EXAMPLE 30

Express the following root numbers in the indicial form:

(i) $\sqrt[7]{5}$ (ii) $\sqrt[3]{3}$ (iii) $\sqrt[4]{3^2}$

(iv) $\sqrt{5^2}$ (v) $\sqrt{15}$ (vi) $\sqrt[3]{27}$

(vii) $\sqrt[3]{8}$ (viii) $\sqrt[5]{64}$ (ix) $\sqrt[3]{125}$

(x) $\dfrac{1}{\sqrt[5]{625}}$.

Solution 30

(i) $\sqrt[7]{5} = 5^{\frac{1}{7}}$

(ii) $\sqrt[3]{3} = 3^{\frac{1}{3}}$

(iii) $\sqrt[4]{3^2} = 3^{\frac{2}{4}} = 3^{\frac{1}{2}}$

(iv) $\sqrt{5^2} = 5^{\frac{2}{2}} = 5$

(v) $\sqrt{15} = 15^{\frac{1}{2}}$

(vi) $\sqrt[3]{27} = 27^{\frac{1}{3}} = (3^3)^{\frac{1}{3}} = 3$

(vii) $\sqrt[3]{8} = 8^{\frac{1}{3}} = (2^3)^{\frac{1}{3}} = 2$

(viii) $\sqrt[5]{64} = 64^{\frac{1}{5}} = (2^6)^{\frac{1}{5}} = 2^{\frac{6}{5}}$

(ix) $\sqrt[3]{125} = 125^{\frac{1}{3}} = (5^3)^{\frac{1}{3}} = 5^{\frac{3}{3}} = 5^1 = 5$

(x)
$$\dfrac{1}{\sqrt[5]{625}} = \dfrac{1}{(625)^{\frac{1}{5}}} = \dfrac{1}{\left[(25)^2\right]^{\frac{1}{5}}}$$
$$= \dfrac{1}{25^{\frac{2}{5}}} = \dfrac{1}{(5^2)^{\frac{2}{5}}} = \dfrac{1}{5^{\frac{4}{5}}}.$$

Index rules for positive negative and fractional indices

WORKED EXAMPLE 31

Write down in their simplest form

(i) $25^{\frac{1}{2}}$ (ii) $36^{\frac{1}{2}}$

(iii) $49^{\frac{1}{2}}$ (iv) $125^{\frac{1}{3}}$

(v) 3^{-3} (vi) $25^{\frac{1}{2}} \times 25^{\frac{1}{2}}$

(vii) $81^{\frac{1}{2}} \times 81^{\frac{1}{2}}$ (viii) $121^{0.5}$

(ix) $169^{-0.5}$ (x) $9^{\frac{1}{3}} \times 3^{\frac{1}{3}} \times 27^{\frac{1}{3}}$

(xi) $25^{-0.25}$ (xii) $8^{\frac{2}{3}}$

(xiii) $625^{-\frac{1}{2}}$ (xiv) $16^0 \times 16^{\frac{1}{2}} \times 2$

(xv) $\left(\dfrac{1}{25^2}\right)^{-1}$.

Solution 31

(i) $25^{\frac{1}{2}} = \sqrt{25} = 5$ (ii) $36^{\frac{1}{2}} = \sqrt{36} = 6$

(iii) $49^{\frac{1}{2}} = \sqrt{49} = 7$

(iv) $125^{\frac{1}{3}} = \sqrt[3]{125} = (5^3)^{\frac{1}{3}} = 5^1 = 5$

(v) $3^{-3} = \dfrac{1}{3^3} = \dfrac{1}{27}$

(vi) $25^{\frac{1}{2}} \times 25^{\frac{1}{2}} = (5^2)^{\frac{1}{2}} \times (5^2)^{\frac{1}{2}} = 5 \times 5$
$\qquad = 25$ or $25^{\frac{1}{2}} \times 25^{\frac{1}{2}} = (25 \times 25)^{\frac{1}{2}}$
$\qquad = 625^{\frac{1}{2}} = 25.$

(vii) $81^{\frac{1}{2}} \times 81^{\frac{1}{2}} = (81 \times 81)^{\frac{1}{2}}$
$$= (81^2)^{\frac{1}{2}} = 81^1 = 81$$

(viii) $121^{0.5} = (11 \times 11)^{0.5}$
$$= (11^2)^{\frac{1}{2}} = 11^1 = 11$$

(ix) $169^{-0.5} = \dfrac{1}{169^{0.5}} = \dfrac{1}{(13 \times 13)^{\frac{1}{2}}}$
$$= \dfrac{1}{(13^2)^{\frac{1}{2}}} = \dfrac{1}{13}$$

(x) $9^{\frac{1}{3}} \times 3^{\frac{1}{3}} \times 27^{\frac{1}{3}} = (3^2)^{\frac{1}{3}} \cdot \left(3^{\frac{1}{3}}\right) \cdot (3^3)^{\frac{1}{3}}$
$$= 3^{\frac{2}{3}} \cdot 3^{\frac{1}{3}} \cdot 3^{\frac{3}{3}} = 3^{\frac{2}{3}+\frac{1}{3}+1}$$
$$= 3^2 = 9$$

(xi) $25^{-0.25} = \dfrac{1}{25^{0.25}} = \dfrac{1}{(5^2)^{\frac{1}{4}}} = \dfrac{1}{5^{\frac{1}{2}}} = \dfrac{1}{\sqrt{5}}$

(xii) $8^{\frac{2}{3}} = (2^3)^{\frac{2}{3}} = 2^2 = 4$

(xiii) $625^{\frac{-1}{2}} = \dfrac{1}{625^{\frac{1}{2}}} = \dfrac{1}{(25^2)^{\frac{1}{2}}}$
$$= \dfrac{1}{25^{\frac{2}{2}}} = \dfrac{1}{25^1} = \dfrac{1}{25}$$

(xiv) $16^0 \times 16^{\frac{1}{2}} \times 2 = 1 \times (2^4)^{\frac{1}{2}} \times 2$
$$= 1 \times 2^{\frac{4}{2}} \times 2 = 1 \times 2^2 \times 2 = 2^3 = 8$$

(xv) $\left(\dfrac{1}{25^2}\right)^{-1} = \dfrac{1}{\frac{1}{25^2}}$
$$= 1 \div \tfrac{1}{25^2} = 1 \times 25^2 = 625.$$

INVERSE OF $a^x = y$ as $x = \log_a y$

To express an indicial expression to a logarithmic expression

$y = a^x$ can be written in logarithmic form as follows $x = \log_a y$, x is equalled to the logarithm of y to the base a.

This statement may be a little bit difficult.

Let us consider the following example.

$8 = 2^3$ then $3 = \log_2 8$, in other words 3 equals to the logarithm of 8 to the base 2.

Express $5^4 = 625$ in logarithmic form

Solution 32

$$625 = 5^4, \quad \text{or} \quad 4 = \log_5 625$$

base

5 is the base in both the indicial and logarithmic forms, 625 is the number whose logarithm is required.

Express the following numbers in logarithmic form:

(i) 3^3 (ii) 5^3 (iii) 10^4 (iv) 2^{-4} (v) 3^{-2}.

Solution 33

(i) $3^3 = 27$ in logarithmic form $\log_3 27 = 3$

(ii) $5^3 = 125$ in logarithmic form $\log_5 125 = 3$

(iii) $10^4 = 10{,}000$ in logarithmic form
$$\log_{10} 10{,}000 = 4$$

(iv) $2^{-4} = \dfrac{1}{2^4} = \dfrac{1}{16}$ in logarithmic form
$$\log_2 \dfrac{1}{2^4} = -4$$

(v) $3^{-2} = \dfrac{1}{3^2} = \dfrac{1}{9}$ in logarithmic form
$$\log_3 \dfrac{1}{9} = -2.$$

Definition of a logarithm

What is a logarithm of a number?
The logarithm of 100 to the base 10 is written as

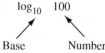

$$\log_{10} \quad 100$$

Base   Number

So what does it mean $\log_{10} 100$?

Let us denote the result with n, then $\log_{10} 100 = n$.

The definition is the base 10 raised to the result n equals the number 100

$$10^n = 100 \qquad 10^n = 10^2$$

since the equation has the same base then $n = 2$, therefore $\log_{10} 100 = 2$

check $10^2 = 100$ correct.

What is the $\log_{10} 10,000$?

$$\log_{10} 10,000 = n$$

$$10^n = 10,000 = 10^4$$

$$10^n = 10^4$$

therefore $n = 4$.

WORKED EXAMPLE 34

Use the definition of a logarithm of a number to find the value x in the following:

(i) $\log_2 8 = x$ (ii) $\log_3 81 = x$

(iii) $\log_5 125 = x$ (iv) $\log_{10} 1000 = x$

(v) $\log_3 243 = x$.

Solution 34

(i) $\log_2 8 = x$ by the definition of a logarithm of a number, we have $2^x = 8 = 2^3$

$$2^x = 2^3$$

since the base of the number on the left hand side of the equation is the same as the base of the number on the right hand side (2) then the indices x and 3 must be equal.

$$x = 3$$

$$\log_2 8 = 3$$

check $\quad 2^3 = 8$, correct.

(ii) $\log_3 81 = x$, by definition $3^x = 81 = 3^4$ and therefore $x = 4$

(iii) $\log_5 125 = x$, $5^x = 125 = 5^3$, then $x = 3$

(iv) $\log_{10} 1000 = x$, $10^x = 1000 = 10^3$, then $x = 3$

(v) $\log_3 243 = x$, $3^x = 243 = 3^5$, then $x = 5$.

WORKED EXAMPLE 35

Use the definition of a logarithm of a number to find the value of x in the following:

(i) $\log_4 x = 2$ (ii) $\log_{16} x = 1$

(iii) $\log_{10} x = 5$ (iv) $\log_5 x = 3$

(v) $\log_{64} x = \frac{1}{2}$ (vi) $\log_{125} x = \frac{1}{3}$

(vii) $\log_{\frac{1}{2}} x = 3$ (viii) $\log_{\frac{1}{8}} x = 3$

(ix) $\log_a x = 0$ (x) $\log_t x = 1$.

Solution 35

(i) $\log_4 x = 2$, by the definition of a logarithm of a number, $4^2 = x$, therefore $x = 4 \times 4 = 16$

(ii) $\log_{16} x = 1$, $16^1 = x$, therefore $x = 16$

(iii) $\log_{10} x = 5$, $10^5 = x = 100,000$, therefore $x = 100,000$

(iv) $\log_5 x = 3$, $5^3 = x$ or $x = 125$

(v) $\log_{64} x = \frac{1}{2}$, $64^{\frac{1}{2}} = x$ or $x = 8$

(vi) $\log_{125} x = \frac{1}{3}$, $(125)^{\frac{1}{3}} = x$ or $x = (5^3)^{\frac{1}{3}} = 5$

(vii) $\log_{\frac{1}{2}} x = 3$, $\left(\frac{1}{2}\right)^3 = x$, then $\boxed{x = \frac{1}{8}}$

(viii) $\log_{\frac{1}{8}} x = 3$, $\left(\frac{1}{8}\right)^3 = x$

$$= \frac{1}{8^3} = \frac{1}{64 \times 8} = \frac{1}{512}$$

(ix) $\log_a x = 0$, $a^0 = x$ or $x = 1$

(x) $\log_t x = 1$, $t^1 = x$ then $x = t$.

WORKED EXAMPLE 36

Use the definition of a logarithm of a number to find the value of x in the following:

(i) $\log_x 1000 = 3$

(ii) $\log_x 10^{25} = 25$

(iii) $\log_x 8 = 3$

(iv) $\log_x 16 = 4$

(v) $\log_x 0.00001 = -5$.

Solution 36

(i) $\log_x 1000 = 3$.

by the definition of a logarithm of a number, $x^3 = 1000 = 10^3$, since the indices of the left hand and right hand sides are the same then the bases must be the same therefore $\boxed{x = 10}$

(ii) $\log_x 10^{25} = 25$, $x^{25} = 10^{25}$ therefore $x = 10$

(iii) $\log_x 8 = 3$, $x^3 = 8 = 2^3$, $\boxed{x = 2}$

(iv) $\log_x 16 = 4$, $x^4 = 16 = 2^4$, $x = 2$

(v) $\log_x 0.00001 = -5$, $x^{-5} = 0.00001$
$= 10^{-5}$, $\boxed{x = 10}$.

Exercises 4

A. Find the values of x in the following:

1. $\log_2\left(\frac{1}{8}\right) = x$ 2. $\log_2\left(\frac{1}{16}\right) = x$

3. $\log_3\left(\frac{1}{27}\right) = x$ 4. $\log_3\left(\frac{1}{81}\right) = x$

5. $\log_4\left(\frac{1}{64}\right) = x$ 6. $\log_2\left(\frac{1}{32}\right) = x$

7. $\log_{\frac{1}{2}} 2 = x$ 8. $\log_{\frac{1}{2}} 4 = x$

9. $\log_3 27 = x$ 10. $\log_3 9 = x$

11. $\log_3 81 = x$ 12. $\log_{\frac{1}{3}} 81 = x$

13. $\log_{\frac{1}{3}} 27 = x$ 14. $\log_{\frac{1}{3}} 9 = x$

15. $\log_{10} 10 = x$ 16. $\log_{10} 100 = x$

17. $\log_{\frac{1}{5}} 25 = x$ 18. $\log_{\frac{1}{5}} 125 = x$

19. $\log_3 3 = x$ 20. $\log_{\frac{1}{3}} 9 = x$

21. $\log_{\frac{1}{3}} 27 = x$ 22. $\log_{27} 3 = x$

23. $\log_{27} 9 = x$

B. Find the values of x in the following:

24. $\log_{\frac{1}{4}} 16 = x$ 25. $\log_{\frac{1}{3}}\left(\frac{1}{27}\right) = x$

26. $\log_{\frac{1}{3}}\left(\frac{1}{9}\right) = x$ 27. $\log_9 3 = x$

28. $\log_9 9 = x$ 29. $\log_9 27 = x$

30. $\log_9 81 = x$ 31. $\log_{10} 1000 = x$

32. $\log_{10} 0.1 = x$ 33. $\log_{10} 0.01 = x$

34. $\log_{10} 0.001 = x$ 35. $\log_5 25 = x$

36. $\log_{25} 25 = x$ 37. $\log_5 125 = x$

C. Check that the answer in the bracket is the correct answer of x

1. $\log_{10} x = 1 (10)$

2. $\log_3 x = 2 (9)$

3. $\log_5 x = 3 (125)$

4. $\log_{\frac{1}{7}} x = 1\left(\frac{1}{7}\right)$

5. $\log_{\frac{1}{9}} x = 2\left(\frac{1}{81}\right)$

6. $\log_3 x = -5\left(\frac{1}{243}\right)$

7. $\log_{\frac{1}{3}} x = -1 (3)$

8. $\log_{\frac{1}{27}} x = -3 (3^9)$

9. $\log_{10} x = -5 (10^{-5})$

10. $\log_7 x = 3 (7^3)$

11. $\log_3 x = -3\left(\frac{1}{27}\right)$

12. $\log_2 x = -1\left(\frac{1}{2}\right)$

13. $\log_x 10 = 1 (10)$

14. $\log_x 0.001 = 3\left(\frac{1}{10}\right)$

15. $\log_x 27 = 3 (3)$

16. $\log_x 343 = 3 (7)$

17. $\log_x\left(\frac{1}{10,000}\right) = 4\left(\frac{1}{10}\right)$

18. $\log_x 8 = \frac{1}{2} (64)$

19. $\log_x 4 = 64\left(2^{\frac{1}{32}}\right)$

20. $\log_x 3 = 1 (3)$

5

Mathematics II
Formulae and Laws

5.1 Determines a logical sequence of steps to evaluate an expression containing at least two variables/constants, eg ax^b, ab^x, $(a+x)^n$ with and without the use of a calculator

To evaluate ax^b

For different values of a and b, the calculations are evaluated as shown in the table

x	$3x^2$
0	$3(0)^2 = 0$
1	$3(1)^2 = 3$
2	$3(2)^2 = 12$
3	$3(3)^2 = 27$
-1	$3(-1)^2 = 3$
-2	$3(-2)^2 = 12$
-3	$3(-3)^2 = 27$

$5x^3$	$-2x^4$
$5(0)^3 = 0$	$-2(0)^4 = 0$
$5(1)^3 = 5$	$-2(1)^4 = -2$
$5(2)^3 = 40$	$-2(2)^4 = -32$
$5(3)^3 = 135$	$-2(3)^4 = -162$
$5(-1)^3 = -5$	$-2(-1)^4 = -2$
$5(-2)^3 = -40$	$-2(-2)^4 = -32$
$5(-3)^3 = -135$	$-2(-3)^4 = -162$

without the use of a calculator, the variable value of x is raised to the power two and the result

is then multiplied as shown in the above table, similarly the variable value of x is raised to the power three and the result is multiplied by 5.

The above can be evaluated with the use of a calculator.

The value of x is entered on the display,

5, then press $\boxed{AC}$ $\boxed{INV}$ $\boxed{\times}$ $\boxed{7}$ $\boxed{=}$ and the answer will be $5^7 = 78125$.

Determine the value $5x^7$ when $x = 9$

$\boxed{AC}$ $\boxed{9}$ $\boxed{INV}$ $\boxed{\times}$ $\boxed{7}$ $\boxed{=}$ $\boxed{\times}$ $\boxed{5}$ the answer on the display is $5x^7 = 5(9)^7 = 23,914,845$. The number is raised to the power 7 and the result is then multiplied by 5.

WORKED EXAMPLE 37

Evaluate the following with the use a calculator

(i) $-5(5)^3$ (ii) $3(7)^4$

(iii) $3(-9)^6$ (iv) $5(10)^7$.

Solution 37

(i) 5 is raised to the power 3

   5 $\boxed{INV}$ $\boxed{\times}$ $\boxed{3}$ $\boxed{=}$ the result on the display is 125, this is multiplied by (-5) the answer is -625.

   125 $\boxed{\times}$ $\boxed{9}$ $\boxed{+/-}$ $\boxed{=}$

(ii) Similarly check for the other evaluations
   $3(7)^4 = 7203$

21

(iii) $3(-9)^6 = 1,594,323$

(iv) $5(10)^7 = 50,000,000$

| AC | 1 | 0 | INV | × | 7 | = | × | 5 | = |

To evaluate ab^x

x	$3(2)^x$	$5(4)^x$
0	$3(2)^0 = 3$	5
1	$3(2)^1 = 6$	20
2	$3(2)^2 = 12$	80
3	$3(2)^3 = 24$	320
−1	$3(2)^{-1} = 1.5$	1.25
−2	$3(2)^{-2} = 0.75$	0.3125
−3	$3(2)^{-3} = 3.375$	0.078125

With a use of calculator $5(4)^{-3} = 0.078125$

| AC | 4 | INV | × | 3 | +/− | = | × | 5 |

To evaluate $(a + x)^n$

x	$(5+x)^7$
0	$(5+0)^7 = 78125$
1	$(5+1)^7 = 279,936$
2	$(5+2)^7 = 823,543$
3	$(5+3)^7 = 2,097,152$
−1	$(5-1)^7 = 16,384$
−2	$(5-2)^7 = 2,187$
−3	$(5-3)^7 = 128$

$(5+2)^7 = 823,543$

| AC | 5 | + | 2 | = | INV | × | 7 | = |

Table of values

5.2 Draws up a table of values by carrying out repeated calculated from an equation or formula for different values of the variables.

To draw up a table of values for $y = 3x^2 - 5x + 2$

x	x^2	$3x^2$	$-5x$	2	y
0	0	0	0	2	2
1	1	3	−5	2	0
2	4	12	−10	2	4
3	9	27	−15	2	14
−1	1	3	5	2	10
−2	4	12	10	2	24
−3	9	27	15	2	44

To draw up a table of values for the formula
$$A_2 = \frac{A_1}{1 + \beta A_1}.$$
If $A_1 = 1000$, find A_2 for $\beta = 0, 0.1, 0.2, 0.5, 1.0$

A_1	β	βA_1	$1 + \beta A_1$	A_2
1000	0	0	1	1000
1000	0.1	100	101	9.901
1000	0.2	200	201	4.975
1000	0.5	500	501	1.996
1000	1.0	1000	1001	0.999

Transposition of formulae

Consider the linear equation $y = mx + c$

y is the subject of the equation above, that is, y is expressed in terms of m, x and c. If x is required to be the subject of the equation, then we have to transpose the equation

$$y = mx + c$$

subtracting c from both side of the equation, we have

$$y - c = mx + c - c$$
$$y - c = mx$$
$$mx = y - c$$

or dividing both sides by m

$$\frac{mx}{m} = \frac{y-c}{m}$$
$$x = \frac{y-c}{m}$$

then x is the subject of the equation.

WORKED EXAMPLE 38

Make x the subject of the following equations:

(i) $3x + 5 = 1$

(ii) $y = 5x - 7$

(iii) $y = \frac{1}{x} + 30$

Solution 38

(i) $3x + 5 = 1$ subtract 5 from each side

$$3x + 5 - 5 = 1 - 5$$

then $\quad 3x = -4$

divide both sides by 3

$$\frac{3x}{3} = -\frac{4}{3} \qquad \boxed{x = -\frac{4}{3}}$$

(ii) $y = 5x - 7$

adding 7 on both sides

$$y + 7 = 5x - 7 + 7$$

$$y + 7 = 5x \qquad \text{or} \qquad 5x = y + 7$$

dividing each side by 5

$$\frac{5x}{5} = \frac{y+7}{5} \qquad x = \frac{y+7}{5}$$

(iii) $y = \dfrac{1}{x} + 30$

subtracting 30 from each side

$$y - 30 = \frac{1}{x} + 30 - 30$$

$$y - 30 = \frac{1}{x}$$

or $\quad \dfrac{1}{x} = y - 30$

taking the reciprocals of each side

$$\frac{x}{1} = \frac{1}{y - 30} \qquad x = \frac{1}{y - 30}$$

5.3 Transposes formulae which contain a root or a power e.g.

$$T = 2\pi\sqrt{\frac{l}{g}} \text{ for } l, \ A = \pi r^2 \text{ for } r.$$

Make l, the subject of the formula $\quad T = 2\pi\sqrt{\dfrac{l}{g}}$.

In order to get rid of the square root, we have to square both sides of the equation

$$T = 2\pi\sqrt{\frac{l}{g}}$$

$$T^2 = 4\pi^2\left(\frac{l}{g}\right)$$

observe that the square root has disappeared but the quantity under the root is placed in brackets of course in this example it does not matter.

$$\frac{T^2}{1} = \frac{4\pi^2 l}{g}$$

cross multiplying we have $T^2 g = 4\pi^2 l$ or $4\pi^2 l = T^2 g$

dividing both sides by $4\pi^2$, we have

$$\frac{4\pi^2 l}{4\pi^2} = \frac{T^2 g}{4\pi^2}$$

therefore $\qquad \boxed{l = \dfrac{T^2 g}{4\pi^2}}$

and l now is the subject of the equation, in other words, l is expressed in forms of T, g and π.

WORKED EXAMPLE 39

Make r the subject of the equation $\quad A = \pi r^2$.

Solution 39

$$A = \pi r^2$$

$$\text{or} \quad \pi r^2 = A$$

since we would like to make r the subject of the equation, we bring the term containing r on the left of the equation

$$\pi r^2 = A$$

dividing both sides by π, we have $\dfrac{\pi r^2}{\pi} = \dfrac{A}{\pi}$

π cancels on the left hand side leaving $r^2 = \dfrac{A}{\pi}$

square rooting both sides, we have $\boxed{r = \sqrt{\dfrac{A}{\pi}}}$

r is expressed in terms of A and π.

WORKED EXAMPLE 40

Make g the subject of the equation

$$T = 2\pi\sqrt{\frac{l}{g}} \qquad \qquad \dots (1)$$

Solution 40

Squaring up both sides of equation (1)

we have, $T^2 = \left(2\pi\sqrt{\dfrac{l}{g}}\right)^2$

$$T^2 = 2^2\pi^2\left(\sqrt{\dfrac{l}{g}}\right)^2$$

$$\frac{T^2}{1} = 4\pi^2\frac{l}{g}$$

Cross multiplying $\qquad T^2g = 4\pi^2l$

dividing each form by T^2 $\dfrac{T^2g}{T^2} = \dfrac{4\pi^2l}{T^2}$

$$\boxed{g = \frac{4\pi^2l}{T^2}}$$

WORKED EXAMPLE 41

Transpose the formula $\qquad f = \dfrac{1}{2\pi\sqrt{LC}}$

to make (i) C the subject of the formula
(ii) L the subject of the formula.

Solution 41

(i) $f = \dfrac{1}{2\pi\sqrt{LC}}$

squaring up both sides of the equation

$$(f)^2 = \left(\frac{1}{2\pi\sqrt{LC}}\right)^2$$

$$\frac{f^2}{1} = \frac{1}{4\pi^2LC}$$

note that each quantity is squared up
Cross multiplying

$$f^24\pi^2LC = 1$$

dividing by $f^24\pi^2$ L each side

$$\frac{f^24\pi^2LC}{f^24\pi^2L} = \frac{1}{f^24\pi^2L}$$

$$\boxed{C = \frac{1}{4\pi^2Lf^2}}$$

(ii) $f^24\pi^2LC = 1$

and dividing by $f^24\pi^2C$ each side

$$\frac{f^24\pi^2LC}{f^24\pi^2C} = \frac{1}{f^24\pi^2C}$$

$$\boxed{L = \frac{1}{4\pi^2Cf^2}}$$

WORKED EXAMPLE 42

Express π in terms of f , L and C

$$f = \frac{1}{2\pi\sqrt{LC}} \qquad\qquad \dots(2)$$

Solution 42

Cross multiplying equation (2) and dividing both sides by $2f\sqrt{LC}$

$$\frac{2\pi f\sqrt{LC}}{2f\sqrt{LC}} = \frac{1}{2f\sqrt{LC}}$$

we have $\qquad \pi = \dfrac{1}{2f\sqrt{LC}}.$

WORKED EXAMPLE 43

The volume of a sphere of radius r is given by the formula

$$V = \frac{4}{3}\pi r^3$$

make r the subject of the equation

Solution 43

$$V = \frac{4}{3}\pi r^3$$

Cross multiplying

$$3V = 4\pi r^3 \qquad \text{or} \qquad 4\pi r^3 = 3V$$

dividing both sides by 4π

$$\frac{4\pi r^3}{4\pi} = \frac{3V}{4\pi} \qquad r^3 = \frac{3V}{4\pi}$$

taking the cube roots on both sides

$$r = \sqrt[3]{\frac{3V}{4\pi}}.$$

WORKED EXAMPLE 44

$V = \frac{1}{3}\pi r^2 h$ is the volume of cylinder with base radius r and height h.

Make r the subject of the equation.

Solution 44

$$V = \frac{1}{3}\pi r^2 h \qquad \text{or} \qquad \frac{1}{3}\pi r^2 h = V$$

if $A = B$ then $B = A$

dividing by $\frac{1}{3}\pi h$ each side

$$\frac{\frac{1}{3}\pi r^2 h}{\frac{1}{3}\pi h} = \frac{V}{\frac{1}{3}\pi h}$$

$$r^2 = \frac{3V}{\pi h}$$

taking the square roots $r = \sqrt{\dfrac{3V}{\pi h}}$.

WORKED EXAMPLE 45

(a) Make x the subject of the following equations:

   (i) $x^2 + y^2 = 9$ (ii) $\sqrt{xy} = c$

   (iii) $\dfrac{x^2}{4} + \dfrac{y^2}{9} = 1$

(b) Make y the subject of these equations.

Solution 45

(a) (i) $x^2 + y^2 = 9$

    To make x the subject of this equation, we keep the term x^2 on the left hand side of the equation and take everything else on the right hand side of the equation

    $x^2 + y^2 = 9 \qquad x^2 = 9 - y^2$

    taking the square roots

    $x = \pm\sqrt{9 - y^2} \qquad x = \sqrt{9 - y^2}$

    the positive value of x.

(ii) $\sqrt{xy} = c$

squaring up both sides of this

$$(\sqrt{xy})^2 = c^2$$

$$xy = c^2$$

dividing both sides by y $\dfrac{xy}{y} = \dfrac{c^2}{y}$

$$\boxed{x = \frac{c^2}{y}}$$

(iii) $\dfrac{x^2}{4} + \dfrac{y^2}{9} = 1$

$$\frac{x^2}{4} = 1 - \frac{y^2}{9}$$

$$\frac{x^2}{4} = \frac{9 - y^2}{9}$$

multiplying both sides by 4

$$x^2 = \frac{4}{9}(9 - y^2)$$

taking the square roots on both sides

$$x = \pm\left[\frac{4}{9}(9 - y^2)\right]^{\frac{1}{2}}$$

$$= \pm\frac{2}{3}(9 - y^2)^{\frac{1}{2}}$$

the positive value of

$$\boxed{x = \frac{2}{3}(9 - y^2)^{\frac{1}{2}}}$$

(b) (i) $x^2 + y^2 = 9$

    $y^2 = 9 - x^2$

    $y = \pm\sqrt{9 - x^2} \qquad y = \sqrt{9 - x^2}$

(ii) $\sqrt{xy} = c$

    $xy = c^2 \qquad y = \dfrac{c^2}{x}$

(iii) $\dfrac{x^2}{4} + \dfrac{y^2}{9} = 1$

    $\dfrac{y^2}{9} = 1 - \dfrac{x^2}{4}$

    $y^2 = 9\left(1 - \dfrac{x^2}{4}\right)$

$$y = \pm 3 \left(1 - \frac{x^2}{4}\right)^{\frac{1}{2}}$$

$$y = 3 \left(1 - \frac{x^2}{4}\right)^{\frac{1}{2}}$$

$$y = \frac{3}{2} \left(4 - x^2\right)^{\frac{1}{2}}.$$

WORKED EXAMPLE 46

$$A = \frac{1}{2}r^2\theta.$$

Find r in terms of A and θ. If $\theta = \frac{\pi}{3}$, $A = 10$ then calculate r.

Solution 46

$$A = \frac{1}{2}r^2\theta$$

$$2A = r^2\theta$$

$$r^2\theta = 2A$$

$$r^2 = \frac{2A}{\theta}$$

$$r = \sqrt{\frac{2A}{\theta}}$$

$$r = \sqrt{\frac{2(10)}{\frac{\pi}{3}}} = \sqrt{\frac{60}{\pi}}$$

$$r = 4.37.$$

5.4 Transposes formulae in which the subject is contained in more than one term, e.g.

$$I = \frac{iR}{R+r} \quad \text{for} \quad R.$$

cross multiplying, we have

$$I(R + r) = iR \times 1$$

observe that there is a one under I and that $R + r$ must be bracketed as shown

multiplying out the brackets

$$IR + Ir = iR$$

taking IR to the right of the equation

$$Ir = iR - IR$$

taking R as the common factor

$$Ir = R(i - I)$$

or $R(i - I) = Ir$

dividing both sides by $(i - I)$

$$\frac{R\cancel{(i-I)}}{\cancel{(i-I)}} = \frac{Ir}{i-I}$$

$$\boxed{R = \frac{Ir}{i-I}}$$

R is expressed in terms of I, i, and r.

WORKED EXAMPLE 47

Make I the subject of the equation

$$R = \frac{Ir}{i - I}.$$

Solution 47

$$R = \frac{Ir}{i - I}.$$

Cross multiplying $R(i - I) = Ir \times 1$

observe there is a one under R and $i - I$ must be bracketed

multiplying out the bracket $Ri - RI = Ir$

taking $-RI$ to the other side of the equation

$$Ri = Ir + RI$$

or $Ir + RI = iR$

dividing each side by $(r + R)$, we have

$$\frac{I\cancel{(r+R)}}{\cancel{(r+R)}} = \frac{iR}{r+R}$$

we are back to the original form of the equation where I is expressed in terms of R, i and r.

WORKED EXAMPLE 48

Make t the subject of the equation $\dfrac{1+t}{1-t} = \dfrac{a}{b}$ and find the value of t if $a = 5$ and $b = 2$.

Solution 48

$$\frac{1+t}{1-t} = \frac{a}{b}$$

cross multiply $(1+t)b = a(1-t)$

multiply out the brackets $b + bt = a - at$

collect the terms on one side containing t

$$bt + at = a - b$$

factorise the left hand side by taking t as a common factor $t(b + a) = a - b$

divide each term by $b + a$

$$\frac{t(b+a)}{b+a} = \frac{a-b}{b+a}$$

$$\boxed{t = \frac{a-b}{a+b}}$$

$$t = \frac{5-2}{5+2} = \frac{3}{7}$$

$$t = \frac{3}{7}.$$

WORKED EXAMPLE 49

Make y the subject of the equation

$$\sqrt{\frac{1-y}{1+y}} = \frac{a}{b}.$$

Solution 49

$$\sqrt{\frac{1-y}{1+y}} = \frac{a}{b}$$

square both sides $\dfrac{1-y}{1+y} = \dfrac{a^2}{b^2}$

cross multiply $b^2(1 - y) = a^2(1 + y)$

$$b^2 - b^2 y = a^2 + a^2 y$$

collect the terms containing y on the right hand side

$$b^2 - a^2 = a^2 y + b^2 y$$

swap the right hand side by the left hand side

$$a^2 y + b^2 y = b^2 - a^2$$

take y common factor on the left hand side

$$y(a^2 + b^2) = b^2 - a^2$$

divide each side by $a^2 + b^2$

$$y = \frac{b^2 - a^2}{b^2 + a^2}.$$

5.5 Demonstrates the effects of rounding and truncation errors

Rounding off numbers

π correct to sixteen significant figures is 3.141592653589793. Numbers may be written correct to any number of significant figures.

For example the five significant number 25,375 may be written as 25,380 correct to four significant figures or it may be written as 25,400 correct to three significant figures or it may be written as 25,000 correct to two significant figures.

As a general rule if the figure is less than five then the previous figure is not altered, if the figure is five or greater than five then the previous figure is increased by one.

In Engineering, the numbers in general are quoted correct to three significant figures unless they are stated otherwise.

The value of π in ten significant figures is given as 3.141592654, in eight significant figures is given as 3.1415927, in four significant figures is 3.142 and correct to three significant figures π is 3.14.

π is an irrational number, that is, it cannot be expressed exactly by a rational number such as $\frac{p}{q}$ where p and q are integers.

But if we require to express π correct to three significant figures, then it can be expressed as a rational number such as $\frac{22}{7}$ which is equal to 3.1428571 or correct to three significant figures 3.14.

A better rational number is $\frac{355}{113}$ which is remembered from the number 113355 by dividing the last three figures by the first three figures, but

$$\frac{355}{113} = 3.1415929 \approx 3.141593$$

$\frac{355}{113}$ correct to seven significant figures, is 3.141593.

What are the effects of rounding off numbers in addition, subtraction, multiplication and division?

A number correct to two significant figures is 5.3 but this number may lie between 5.25 and 5.35 which implies that this number may be 5.3 ± 0.05.

If $A = 72.6$ and $B = 24.5$
then $A + B = 72.6 + 24.5 = 97.1$
and $A - B = 72.6 - 24.5 = 48.1$

but $72.55 \leq A \leq 72.65$, that is, A lies between 72.55 and 72.65 and also $24.45 \leq B \leq 24.55$, that is, B lies between 24.45 and 24.55.
$A = 72.6 \pm 0.05$ and $B = 24.5 \pm 0.05$.

Adding the maximum errors, the addition becomes $72.65 + 24.55 = 97.20$ subtracting the maximum errors, the subtraction becomes $72.65 - 24.55 = 48.1$, unaltered, but $72.65 - 24.45 = 48.2$ therefore the accuracy in subtracting and adding is clearly shown.

The accuracy of multiplication and division may be illustrated.

Multiply the numbers $29 \times 33 = 957$

If the product of the least value is taken as $28.5 \times 32.5 = 926.25$ and if the product of the greatest value is taken $29.5 \times 33.5 = 988.25$

If can be clearly seen that the results deviate from the original product of 957.

Truncation

To 'truncate' means to 'cut off' figures from a number so that we can approximate or check roughly the results of calculations.

If $\pi = \frac{22}{7}$, calculate the area of a circle to three significant figures if the radius is $r = 5$ cm. Recalculate the area of the circle if π is taken as $\frac{335}{113}$.

What is the area of the circle if the π is the value 3.1415927?

Solution 50

$$A = \pi r^2 = \frac{22}{7}(5^2) = \frac{22}{7}(25) = 78.6$$

$$A = \pi r^2 = \frac{355}{113}(25) = 78.5$$

$$A = \pi r^2 = 3.1415927 \times 25 = 78.539816$$

$$A_2 = \frac{A_1}{1 + \beta A_1}$$

Solution 51

$$\frac{1 + \beta A_1}{A_1} = \frac{1}{A_2}$$

(a) If $A_1 = 10,000$ and $A_2 = 9,000$ find β.

$$\frac{1}{A_1} + \beta = \frac{1}{A_2}$$

$$\beta = \frac{1}{A_2} - \frac{1}{A_1} = \frac{1}{9,000} - \frac{1}{10,000}$$

$$= 0.00011111 - 0.0001$$

$$= 0.00001111111 = 1.11 \times 10^{-5}.$$

(b) If $A_2 = 9,000$, $\frac{1}{A_2} = 0.00011 \approx 0.0001$

then $\beta \approx 0$

(c) If $A_2 = 100$

$$\beta = \frac{1}{100} - \frac{1}{10,000} = 0.01 - 0.0001$$

$$= 0.0099$$

Exercises 5

Transpose the following formulae and make the symbol adjacent to each formula, the subject of the formula.

1. $T = 2\pi\sqrt{\dfrac{l}{g}}$, for l

2. $A = \pi r^2$, for r

3. $V = \dfrac{4}{3}\pi r^3$, for r

4. $S = \pi rl + \pi r^2$, for l

5. $S = 4\pi r^2$, for r

6. $I = \dfrac{V}{r+R}$, for V

7. $s = r\theta$, for θ

8. $A = \dfrac{1}{2}r^2\theta$, for r

9. $A = \dfrac{1}{2}r^2\sin\alpha$, for $\sin\alpha$

10. $A = \dfrac{1}{2}r^2\theta - \dfrac{1}{2}r^2\sin\theta$, for r

11. $F = mg$, for g

12. $v = u + at$, for t

13. $v^2 = u^2 + 2as$, for s

14. $A_f = \dfrac{A}{1+\beta A}$, for A

15. $A_v = \dfrac{-\mu R_L}{r_{ds} + R_L}$, for R_L

16. $A_v = \dfrac{h_{fe}R_L}{h_{ie}}$, for hie

17. $r = \sqrt{\dfrac{2A}{\theta}}$, for θ

18. $R_L = -\dfrac{A_v hie}{h_{fe}}$, for A_v

19. $R_L = -\dfrac{r_{ds}A_v}{\mu + A_v}$, for A_v

20. $s = \dfrac{v^2 - u^2}{2a}$, for u

21. $\theta = \dfrac{2A}{r^2} + \sin\theta$, for r

22. $l = \dfrac{gT^2}{4\pi^2}$, for T

23. $r = \sqrt{\dfrac{A}{\pi}}$, for A

24. $l = \dfrac{S}{\pi r} - r$, for S

25. $r = \sqrt{\dfrac{2A}{\sin\theta}}$, for $\sin\theta$

26. $g = \dfrac{4\pi^2 l}{T}$, for l

27. $r = \dfrac{V}{I} - R$, for R

28. $E = \dfrac{1}{2}mv^2$, for v

29. $r = \sqrt{\dfrac{2A}{\theta - \sin\theta}}$, for A

30. $r^3 = \dfrac{3V}{4\pi}$, for V

31. $r = \sqrt{\dfrac{2A}{\theta}}$, for θ

32. $r = \sqrt{\dfrac{2A}{\theta}}$, for A

33. $\dfrac{t+a}{t-a} = \dfrac{A}{B}$, for a

34. $\dfrac{t+a}{t-a} = \dfrac{A}{B}$, for t

35. $f = \dfrac{1}{2\pi}\sqrt{\dfrac{1}{LC}}$, for L

36. $f = \dfrac{1}{2\pi}\sqrt{\dfrac{1}{LC}}$, for C

37. $f = \dfrac{1}{2\pi}\sqrt{\left(\dfrac{1}{LC} - \dfrac{R^2}{L^2}\right)}$, for R

38. $ax^2 + bx + c = 0$, for x

39. $f = \dfrac{1}{2\pi}\sqrt{\left(\dfrac{1}{LC} - \dfrac{R^2}{L^2}\right)}$, for L

40. $\dfrac{x+y}{x-y} = \dfrac{1}{l}$, for y

41. $T = \dfrac{1}{f}$, for f

42. $T = \dfrac{2\pi}{w}$, for w

43. $\rho = \dfrac{RA}{l}$, for l

44. $\alpha = \dfrac{R_\theta - R_o}{R_o\theta}$, for R_θ

45. $X_c = \dfrac{1}{2\pi f C}$, for C

46. $Z = \sqrt{R^2 + \left(\omega L - \dfrac{1}{\omega C}\right)^2}$, for R

47. $\eta = \dfrac{T_2 - T_1}{T_2}$, for T_2

48. $W = \dfrac{1}{2}LI^2$, for I

49. $W = \dfrac{1}{2}IW_2^2 - \dfrac{1}{2}IW_1^2$, for I

50. $W = \dfrac{1}{2}CV^2$, for V

51. $F = \dfrac{Q_1 Q_2}{4\pi \varepsilon r^2}$, for r

52. $hf = \phi + \dfrac{1}{2}mv\mathrm{max}^2$ for $v\mathrm{max}$

53. Make x the subject of the following:

   (i) $A = \pi x^2$

   (ii) $V = \dfrac{4}{3}\pi x^3$

   (iii) $S = 4\pi x^2$

   (iv) $V = \pi x^2 h$

   (v) $S = \pi x^2 + 2\pi x h$

   (vi) $x^2 + y^2 = r^2$

   (vii) $T = 2\pi\sqrt{\dfrac{x}{g}}$

   (viii) $v = \sqrt{2gx}$

   (ix) $E = \dfrac{1}{2}mx^2$

   (x) $x^2 + R^2 = Z^2$

54. $\dfrac{R_{t_1}}{R_{t_2}} = \dfrac{R_0(1 + \alpha t_1)}{R_0(1 + \alpha t_2)}$ (α)

55. $\dfrac{1}{C} = \dfrac{1}{C_1} + \dfrac{1}{C_2} + \dfrac{1}{C_3}$ (C)

56. $X_L = 2\pi f_0 L$ and $X_c = \dfrac{1}{2\pi f_0 C}$

If $X_L = X_C$ show that $f_0 = \dfrac{1}{2\pi\sqrt{LC}}$

57. If $\dfrac{1}{X^2} = \dfrac{1}{X_1^2} + \dfrac{1}{X_2^2}$ find a formula for X_1 in terms of X and X_2.

58. If $I = \dfrac{nE}{r+nR}$, make n the subject of the equation and find its value if $I = 5$, $R = 100, r = 1{,}000, E = 10{,}000$

59. $\beta = \dfrac{\alpha}{1 - \alpha}$ (α)

60. $\alpha = \dfrac{\beta}{(1 + \beta)}$ (β)

61. $\gamma = \dfrac{1}{1 - \alpha}$ (γ)

62. $Z = \sqrt{R^2 + (X_L - X_c)^2}$ (R)

63. $Q = \dfrac{1}{R}\sqrt{\dfrac{L}{C}}$ (C)

64. $\dfrac{1}{R} = \dfrac{1}{R_1} + \dfrac{1}{R_2}$ (R_1)

65. $\dfrac{1}{f} = \dfrac{1}{u} + \dfrac{1}{v}$ (v).

6

Determines linear laws from experimental data

6.1 Plots coordinates from a set of experimental data which obey a linear law, e.g. Hooke's Law, Ohm's Law.

The Plotting of points.

The coordinates of a point.

Two perpendicular axes intersect at a point which is called **the origin** and the perpendicular axes are called **the cartesian axes**, the **y-axis** and the x-axis. Fig. 1 shows the coordinate system of axes. To plot a set of a point $A(x_1, y_1)$, mark x_1 along the x-axis and y_1 along the y-axis and draw vertical and horizontal lines as shown in Fig. 1.

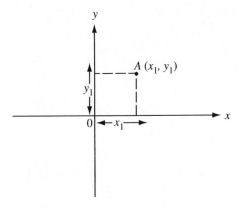

Fig. 1

WORKED EXAMPLE 52

Plot the following sets of points:

(i) $A(0, 0)$	(ii) $B(0, 2)$	(iii) $C(0, -3)$
(iv) $D(1, 0)$	(v) $E(-2, 0)$	(vi) $F(1, 1)$
(vii) $G(1, 3)$	(viii) $H(2, -2)$	(ix) $I(-2, 3)$
(x) $J(-4, +4)$	(xi) $K(-4, -4)$	

Solution 52

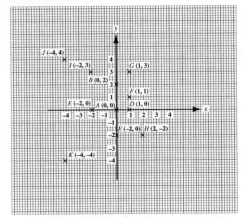

Fig. 2

Hooke's law states that the extension of a uniform wire (an elastic material) is directly proportional to the applied load, provided the limit of proportionality has not been exceeded.

The following experimental data are shown in the table.

x (extension in mm)	1	2	3	4	5
F (load in kg)	5	10	15	20	25

It is required to plot the load along the y-axis and the extension along the x-axis. The graph of F against x is a perfect straight line through all the points, see graph Fig. 3.

Ohm's law states that the potential difference across a linear resistor is directly proportional to the current flowing through the resistor provided the temperature is kept constant.

The above statement can be written as follows

$$V \propto I$$

where $\propto$ is the sign of proportionality, in order to replace this sign by the equal sign of the equation, we have

$V = RI$ where R is the resistance of the resistor, a constant $R = \frac{V}{I}$.

For different values of current, I, there are different values of voltages, V

$$R = \frac{V_1}{I_1} = \frac{V_2}{I_2} = \frac{V_3}{I_3} = \frac{V_4}{I_4} \text{ and so on}$$

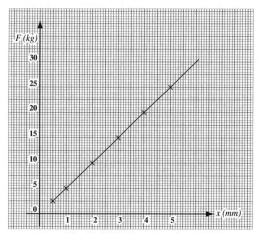

Fig. 3

6.2 Draws the best straight line by eye to fit the points

WORKED EXAMPLE 53

A length of 80 cm of mild steel wire of uniform diameter was loaded, and the following results were obtained.

Load F(N)	Extension x (mm)
20	0.2
60	0.54
82	0.8
108	1.0
140	1.3
160	1.47
180	1.72
225	2.07
242	2.3
274	2.56
320	3

Plot the points and draw the best fit straight line. Determine the gradient of the line.

Hooke's law states that the extension of a uniform wire (an elastic material) is directly proportional to the applied load, provided the limit of proportionality has not been exceeded.

Note that when the applied load is zero, the extension is zero so that the best fit straight line should pass through the origin $(0, 0)$.

The gradient is given by drawing a dotted line from 300 N to 2.8 mm

$$m = \frac{300 \text{ N}}{2.8 \text{ mm}} \approx 107 \text{ N/mm}$$

Solution 53

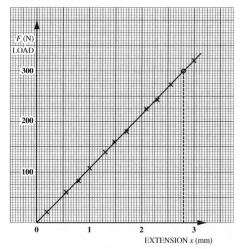

Fig. 4

WORKED EXAMPLE 54

The current through a resistor is measured by an ammeter placed in series with the resistor and the voltage or potential difference across the resistor is measured by a voltmeter placed in parallel with the resistor.

In an experiment, the following set of readings were recorded for different voltage adjustments:

$I(\mu A)$	$V(mV)$	$I(\mu A)$	$V(mV)$
20	100	75	400
30	170	80	450
43	250	90	500
55	300	100	570
60	350		

Plot V against I and hence estimate the value of the resistance of the resistor.

Solution 54

The points (I, V) are plotted as shown in the graph. When the current is zero, the potential difference should be zero, another point is included $(0, 0)$, the origin.

The best fit straight line is drawn through the origin and the points are as shown.

The gradient, m is estimated as shown.

$$m = \frac{(500 - 0)\text{mV}}{(90 - 0)\mu A} = \frac{500 \times 10^{-3}}{90 \times 10^{-6}}$$

$$= \frac{500}{90} \times 10^{-3} \times 10^{6}$$

$$R = \frac{500}{90} \times 10^{3} \, \Omega \approx 5.56 \, k\Omega$$

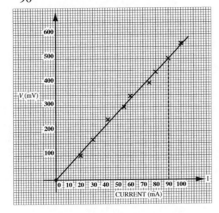

Fig. 5

The best fit straight line

It is required to determine the resistance of a linear resistor by recording the readings of the current through the resistor and the voltage across the resistor.

The data are as follows:

$I(A)$	$V(V)$	$I(A)$	$V(V)$
0.3	7.5	3	35
0.8	3	3.5	40
1	10	4	50
2	23	4.5	45
2.8	25		

Draw a graph of V against I, draw the best straight line that can be fitted through these experiment points.

$$R = \frac{46}{4} = 11.5 \, \Omega$$

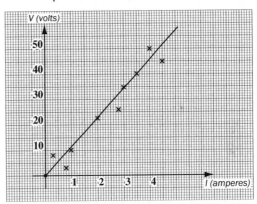

Fig. 6

6.3 Deduces the equation of the straight line from gradient and intercept

The equation of the straight line having a gradient, m, and an intercept, c, on the y-axis is given

$$\boxed{y = mx + c}$$

This equation is known as the gradient/intercept form of a straight line.

The gradient of a straight line

Let $A(x_1, y_1)$, $B(x_2, y_2)$ be two points in the coordinate system, find the gradient of the line joining A and B

$$m = \text{gradient} = \frac{y_2 - y_1}{x_2 - x_1}$$

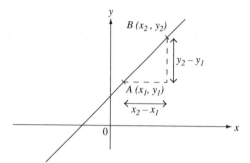

Fig. 7

▬▬▬▬▬▬▬▬▬

WORKED EXAMPLE 55

Straight lines are drawn through the set of points of the previous example 52, A and B, B and D, E and J, D and E, F and H, I and J, A and H and C and J. Determine in each case the gradient of the lines, AB, BD, EJ, DE, FH, IJ, AH and CJ.

Solution 55

$A(0, 0)$ and $B(0, 2)$

gradient of $AB = \dfrac{2 - 0}{0 - 0} = \dfrac{2}{0} = \text{infinite.}$

$B(0, 2)$ and $D(1, 0)$

gradient of $BD = \dfrac{0 - 2}{1 - 0} = \dfrac{-2}{1} = -2.$

$E(-2, 0)$ and $J(-4, -4)$

gradient of $EJ = \dfrac{-4 - 0}{-4 - (-2)} = \dfrac{-4}{-2} = 2.$

$D(1, 0)$ and $E(-2, 0)$

gradient of $DE = \dfrac{0 - 0}{-2 - 1} = \dfrac{0}{-3} = 0.$

$F(1, 1)$ and $H(2, -2)$

gradient of $FH = \dfrac{-2 - 1}{2 - 1} = \dfrac{-3}{1} = -3.$

$I(-2, 3)$ and $J(-4, 4)$

gradient of $IJ = \dfrac{4 - 3}{-4 - (-2)} = \dfrac{1}{-2} = -\dfrac{1}{2}.$

$A(0, 0)$ and $H(2, -2)$

gradient of $AH = \dfrac{-2 - 0}{2 - 0} = \dfrac{-2}{2} = -1.$

$C(0, -3)$ and $J(-4, -4)$

gradient of $CJ = \dfrac{-4 - (-3)}{-4 - 0}$

$$= \dfrac{-4 + 3}{-4} = \dfrac{-1}{-4} = \dfrac{1}{4}.$$

Intercepts

When a straight line cuts the x-axis and y-axis as shown in Fig 8, the values a and b are called the intercepts, that is, the length from the origin to the point of intersection between the line and axes.

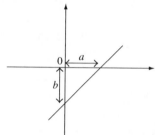

Fig. 8

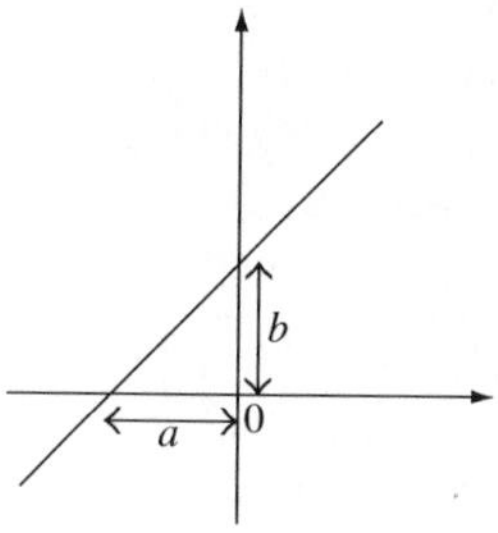

Fig. 9

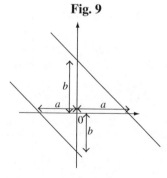

Fig. 10

The length along the x-axis is a and length along the y-axis is b.

The intercept form of a straight line

$$\frac{x}{a} + \frac{y}{b} = 1$$

If $x = 0$ then $y = b$ and if $y = 0$ then $x = a$ that shows clearly that the intercept along the x and y-axis are a and b respectively.

WORKED EXAMPLE 56

Plot the following sets of points on a linear graph paper. Draw the line through these points: $A(-4, -2.6)$, $B(-3, -1.4)$, $C(-2, 0)$, $D(0, 2.6)$ $E(2, 5.2)$ and $F(4.1, 8)$.

Determine the slope and the intercepts, hence write down the equation of the straight line.

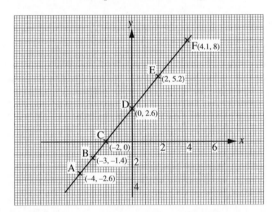

Fig. 11

Solution 56

The graph of the sets of points is shown and it is observed that all the points lie exactly on the line. Consider the extreme sets of points $(4.1, 8)$ and $(-4, -2.6)$

$$m = \frac{8 - (-2.6)}{4.1 - (-4)} = \frac{10.6}{8.1} = 1.31.$$

The intercepts along the x-axis and y-axis are respectively -2 and 2.6.

$$-\frac{x}{2} + \frac{y}{2.6} = 1 \quad \text{multiplying each term by 2.6}$$

$$y = 2.6 + x\frac{2.6}{2} \quad y = 1.3x + 2.6.$$

The gradient/intercept form of a straight line

$$y = mx + c$$

where m is the gradient and c is the intercept along the y-axis since if $x = 0$ then $y = c$.

$$y = 1.31x + c$$

but c is 2.6 therefore $y = 1.31x + 2.6$

is the gradient/intercept form of a straight line.

WORKED EXAMPLE 57

Draw the graph:

x	y
11	26
30	22.4
50	18.6
70	16
90	13.2
110	10.4
130	7.8
150	5

Hence find the equation of the straight line obtained in the following forms:

(a) Gradient/intercept (b) General (c) Intercept.

Solution 57

The graph of y against x is plotted.

The equation of a straight line is given $y = mx + c$ where m is the gradient and c is the y intercept.

The gradient $m = \dfrac{27.6 - 6}{0 - 136} = -\dfrac{21.6}{136}$

when $x = 0$, $y = c = 27.6$

therefore $y = -\dfrac{21.6}{136}x + 27.6$

(a) $y = -0.159x + 27.6$

(b) $y + 0.159x - 27.6 = 0$

(c) $\dfrac{x}{\dfrac{27.6}{0.159}} + \dfrac{y}{27.6} = 1$

$$\dfrac{x}{174} + \dfrac{y}{27.6} = 1$$

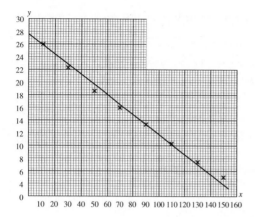

Fig. 12

The equation of a straight line

The general form

The general form of the equation of a straight line is given by

$$ax + by + c = 0$$

The coefficients of x and y are constants and c is another constant.

This form although is general is not useful in assessing the position of the straight line at a glance.

The intercept/gradient form

The intercept/gradient form of a straight line is given by $y = mx + c$

The coefficient of x gives the gradient of the straight line and c is the intercept on the y-axis?

This form is extremely useful in assessing the position of the straight line at a glance.

The intercept form of a straight line

The intercept form of a straight line is given by

$$\frac{x}{a} + \frac{y}{b} = 1$$

where a and b are the intercepts on the x-axis and y-axis respectively.

WORKED EXAMPLE 58

Sketch the straight line $\dfrac{x}{2} + \dfrac{y}{3} = 1$

Solution 58

$$\frac{x}{2} + \frac{y}{3} = 1$$

If $x = 0$ then $y = 3$ and if $y = 0$, $x = 2$, the set of points are drawn. The straight line is drawn through A and B.

Therefore, two units are marked on the positive axis and three units are marked on the y-axis, the points A and B are then joined by a straight line.

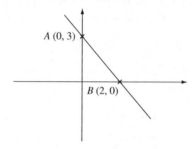

Fig. 13

WORKED EXAMPLE 59

Sketch the straight line

$$y = 2x - 1$$

Solution 59

The gradient of the line is 2, the coefficient of x and the intercept on the y-axis is -1, since if $x = 0$, $y = -1$. A positive gradient line passing through $A(0, -1)$ is drawn with a gradient 2.

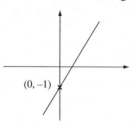

Fig. 14

WORKED EXAMPLE 60

Sketch the straight line graph $2x - y + 5 = 0$

Solution 60

$2x - y + 5 = 0$ If $y = 0, 2x = -5$ or $x = -2.5$
if $x = 0, y = 5$.

From these two points a graph is drawn, through
the points $A(-2.5, 0)$ and $B(0, 5)$.

A straight line is drawn if **two** points are known.

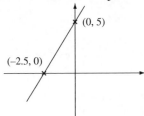

Fig. 15

WORKED EXAMPLE 61

Draw the following straight line by drawing
tables of values for values of
$x = -3, -2, -1, 0, 1, 2, 3$.

(i) $y = -\dfrac{1}{2}x + 3$　(ii) $2x + 4y - 1 = 0$

(iii) $\dfrac{x}{-1} + \dfrac{y}{2} = 1$

Solution 61

(i) $y = -\dfrac{1}{2}x + 3$

x	$\dfrac{-1}{2}x$	3	y
-3	$\dfrac{3}{2}$	3	4.5
-2	1	3	4
-1	$\dfrac{1}{2}$	3	3.5
0	0	3	3
1	$\dfrac{-1}{2}$	3	2.5
2	-1	3	2
3	$\dfrac{-3}{2}$	3	1.5

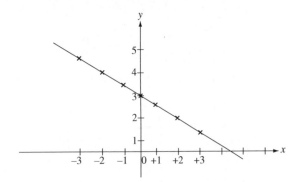

Fig. 16

Although we need only two points to draw
accurately a straight line several points are
plotted for practice.

(ii) $2x + 4y - 1 = 0$

$4y = -2x + 1$　$y = -\dfrac{1}{2}x + \dfrac{1}{4}$

x	$\dfrac{-1}{2}x$	$\dfrac{1}{4}$	y
-3	$\dfrac{3}{2}$	$\dfrac{1}{4}$	1.75
-2	1	$\dfrac{1}{4}$	1.25
-1	$\dfrac{1}{2}$	$\dfrac{1}{4}$	0.75
0	0	$\dfrac{1}{4}$	0.25
1	$\dfrac{-1}{2}$	$\dfrac{1}{4}$	-0.25
2	-1	$\dfrac{1}{4}$	-0.75
3	$\dfrac{-3}{2}$	$\dfrac{1}{4}$	-1.25

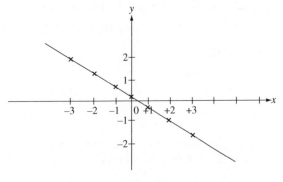

Fig. 17

(iii) $\dfrac{x}{-1} + \dfrac{y}{2} = 1$

$\dfrac{y}{2} = \dfrac{x}{1} + 1$

$y = 2(x + 1) \quad y = 2x + 2$

x	$2x$	2	y
-3	-6	2	-4
-2	-4	2	-2
-1	-2	2	0
0	0	2	2
1	2	2	4
2	4	2	6
3	6	2	8

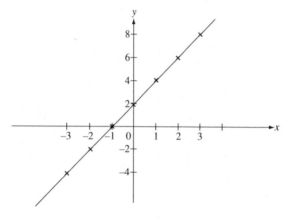

Fig. 18

6.4 Determine the law of the straight line graph from the coordinates of two points on the line

Consider the points $A(x_1, y_1)$ and $B(x_2, y_2)$ as shown in Fig. 19, the gradient m is given by

$m = \dfrac{y_2 - y_1}{x_2 - x_1}$ $\qquad \ldots (1)$

Taking any point $A(x, y)$ as shown we can deduce the gradient m as follows

$m = \dfrac{y - y_1}{x - x_1}$ $\qquad \ldots (2)$

Therefore equations (1) and (2) are the same the equation of a straight line through A and B is

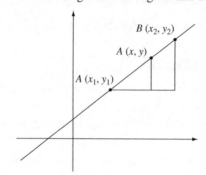

Fig. 19

$$\dfrac{y_2 - y_1}{x_2 - x_1} = \dfrac{y - y_1}{x - x_1}$$

WORKED EXAMPLE 62

Find the equation of a straight line passing through the points $A(1, 3)$ and $B(-2, 4)$.

Solution 62

Consider that $A(x_1, y_1)$ and $B(x_2, y_2)$

$\dfrac{y_2 - y_1}{x_2 - x_1} = \dfrac{4 - 3}{-2 - 1} = \dfrac{1}{-3} = \dfrac{y - 3}{x - 1}$

$\dfrac{-1}{3} = \dfrac{y - 3}{x - 1} \qquad -x + 1 = 3y - 9$

$3y + x - 10 = 0 \qquad 3y = -x + 10$

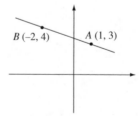

Fig. 20

The gradient/intercept form of the straight line

$$y = \dfrac{-1}{3}x + \dfrac{10}{3} \qquad 3y + x = 10$$

The intercept form of the straight line

$$\dfrac{y}{\frac{10}{3}} + \dfrac{x}{10} = 1$$

The general form of the straight line

$$x + 3y - 10 = 0$$

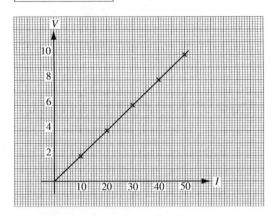

Fig. 21

Exercises 6

1. Plot the following sets of points:
   (i) $A(-1, -1)$ (ii) $B(0, -3)$

   (iii) $C(-2, 3)$ (iv) $D(1, 2)$ (v) $E(3, 4)$

2. The voltage across a resistor and the current through the resistor, I are given as follows: (see graph Fig. 2l)

V (volts)	10	8	6	4	2
I (amperes)	50	40	30	20	10

   Plot a graph through the set of points. Comment on the result.

3. Write down the straight line equation giving the gradient of the line and the intercept on the y-axis.

4. A straight line graph passes through the origin, state the value of the intercept.

5. The intercept on the x-axis is -3, and intercept on the y-axis is -4. Write down the equation of the line.

6. The gradient of a straight tine is -1 and the intercept on the y-axis is 3, write down the equation of the line.

7. Show that the gradient of a straight line passing through two points (x_1, y_1) and (x_2, y_2) is $(y_2 - y_1)/(x_2, x_1)$.

8. Sketch the graph $x + y = 1$

9. Sketch the line $y = 2x + 3$.

10. Write down three different forms for a straight line.

Graphical solutions of equations

Identifies points of intersections of two graphs and recognises their significance.

7.1 Solves a pair of simultaneous equations in two unknowns graphically.

To find the solutions of two linear equations such as
$$ax + by + c = 0 \quad dx + ey + f = 0$$

we draw each linear equation separately, the intersection of the two line graphs gives the solution of these equations simultaneously.

The point P, the intersection, of the lines has a common point to these two equations (x_1, y_1) and satisfies the equations

$$ax_1 + by_1 + c = 0 \text{ and } dx_1 + ey_1 + f = 0.$$

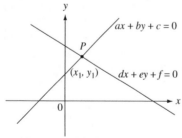

Fig. 22

WORKED EXAMPLE 63

Solve the linear equations
$$x - y = -2 \quad x + y = 12$$
simultaneously using a graphical method. Check your answer with an algebraic method.

40

Solution 63

Draw the linear equations $x - y = -2$

If $y = 0$, $x = -2$; If $y = 1$, $x = -1$ $x + y = 12$
If $y = 0$, $x = 12$; If $x = 0$, $y = 12$.

The points $(-2, 0)$, $(-1, 1)$ and $(12, 0)$, $(0, 12)$ are plotted on a graph paper, a line through the sets of points $(-2, 0)$ and $(-1, 1)$ is drawn and another line through the sets of points $(12, 0)$, $(0, 12)$ is drawn. The intersection of these lines give coordinates of $(5, 7)$

therefore $x = 5$, $y = 7$.

To check these results algebraically
$$x - y = -2 \quad \ldots (1) \qquad x + y = 12 \quad \ldots (2)$$

adding equations (1) and (2) we have

$$2x = 10 \quad \boxed{x = 5}$$

substituting $x = 5$ in equation (1)
$$5 - y = -2 \quad 5 + 2 = y \quad \boxed{y = 7}$$

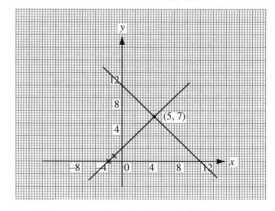

Fig. 23

WORKED EXAMPLE 64

Draw the lines $3x - y - 5 = 0$ and $-2x + 3y + 1 = 0$. Hence find the point of intersection. Check that each equation is satisfied.
Solve the two equations simultaneously by means of an algebraic method.

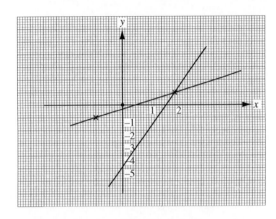

Fig. 24

Solution 64

$3x - y - 5 = 0$,　choose convenient values,

if $x = 0, -y - 5 = 0, y = -5$; if $y = 1, 3x = 6$, $x = 2$; therefore,

we have two sets of points when
$x = 0, y = -5$　$y = 1, x = 2$
$-2x + 3y + 1 = 0$

If $y = 1, -2x = -4, x = 2$;
If $x = -1, 3y = -3, y = -1$;

therefore, we have two other sets of points
$x = 2, y = 1$　$x = -1, y = -1$.

Algebraically　$3x - y = 5$ ... (1)
$\qquad\qquad -2x + 3y = 1$ ... (2)

Multiplying equation (1) by 3,
we have　$9x - 3y = 15$ ... (3)

re-writing (2)　$-2x + 3y = -1$ ... (4)

adding (3) and (4) $7x = 14$　$x = 2$.

Substituting $x = 2$ in (1), we have
$3(2) - y = 5$　$-y = 5 - 6$　$-y = -1$　$y = 1$

therefore the point of intersection is $(2, 1)$.

Verify $3x - y - 5 = 0$, if $x = 2$, and $y = 1$

L.H.S. $3(2) - 1 - 5 = 6 - 6 = 0$

R.H.S. $= 0$

therefore　L.H.S. $=$ R.H.S.

If $x = 2, y = 1$

$-2x + 3y + 1 = 0$

L.H.S. $= -2x + 3y + 1 = -2(2) + 3(1) + 1$
$\qquad = -4 + 3 + 1 = 0$

R.H.S. $= 0$　therefore　L.H.S. $=$ R.H.S.

WORKED EXAMPLE 65

Solve the equations below simultaneously by a graphical method, make a table for values of x equal to 0, 2, 5, 7, 12.

$\qquad 9x - 10y = -10$ ... (1)

$\qquad 10x - 12y = -20$ ... (2)

Solution 65

Re-arranging (1), $9x + 10 = 10y, 0.9x + 1 = y$

x	$0.9x$	$+1$	y
0	0	+1	1
2	1.8	+1	2.8
5	4.5	+1	5.5
7	6.3	+1	7.3
12	10.8	+1	11.8

Plot the values of y against the values of x.

Re-arranging (2), $10x + 20 = 12y$

$$y = \frac{10}{12}x + \frac{20}{12} = \frac{5}{6}x + \frac{5}{3}$$

x	0	2	5	7	12
$\frac{5}{6}x$	0	$\frac{5}{3}$	$\frac{25}{6}$	$\frac{35}{6}$	10
$\frac{5}{3}$	$\frac{5}{3}$	$\frac{5}{3}$	$\frac{5}{3}$	$\frac{5}{3}$	$\frac{5}{3}$
y	$\frac{5}{3}$	$\frac{10}{3}$	$\frac{35}{6}$	$\frac{45}{6}$	$\frac{35}{3}$
$y \approx$	1.67	3.33	5.8	7.5	11.7

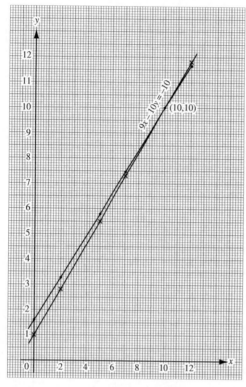

Fig. 25

7.2 Determines the roots of a quadratic equation by the intersection of the graph with the x-axis

WORKED EXAMPLE 66

Draw the graph of the quadratic function $y = x^2 - 2x - 5$ for values of x between -4 and 5, and hence find the values of x when $y = 10$.

Solution 66

x	x^2	$-2x$	-5	y
-4	16	8	-5	19
-3	9	6	-5	10
-2	4	4	-5	3
-1	1	2	-5	-2
0	0	0	-5	-5
1	1	-2	-5	-6
2	4	-4	-5	-5
3	9	-6	-5	-2
4	16	-8	-5	3
5	25	-10		10

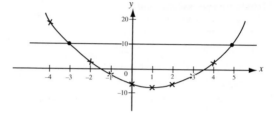

Fig. 26

The curve shows the function $y = x^2 - 2x - 5$ and the straight line $y = 10$, the intersection is $x = 5$ and $x = -3$.

7.3 Solves a linear and a quadratic equation by the intersection of their graphs.

Quadratic functions and quadratic equations

Quadratic function

The general form of the quadratic function is $y = ax^2 + bx + c$.

Observe that the highest degree in x is 2. The shape of the graph is a parabola with either a minimum or a maximum value as shown in Fig. 27 and Fig. 28

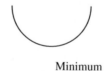

Minimum

Fig. 27

Maximum

Fig. 28

WORKED EXAMPLE 67

Draw the graph for $y = -2x^2 + 5x - 3$ between the values $x = 0$ and $x = 2$, at intervals of 0.2. State the coordinates of the maximum point.

Solution 67

x	$-2x^2$	$+5x$	-3	y
0	0	0	-3	-3
0.2	-0.08	1.00	-3	-2.08
0.4	-0.32	2.00	-3	-1.32
0.6	-0.72	3.00	-3	-0.72
0.8	-1.28	4.00	-3	-0.28
1.0	-2	5.00	-3	0
1.2	-2.88	6.00	-3	0.12
1.4	-3.92	7.00	-3	0.08
1.6	-5.12	8.00	-3	-0.12
1.8	-6.48	9.00	-3	-0.48
2.0	-8	10.00	-3	-1.00

y max $= 0.12$ when $x = 1.2$

see graph Fig. 29.

WORKED EXAMPLE 68

Solve graphically the simultaneous equations
$$y = x^2 - 2x - 2$$
$$x - y + 2 = 0$$

(i) by drawing one graph

(ii) by drawing two graphs

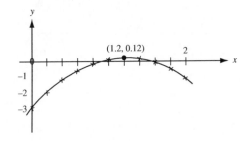

Fig. 29

Solution 68

(i) $y = x^2 - 2x - 2 = x + 2$

$y = x^2 - 3x - 4 = 0$

Draw the graph y against x and $y = 0$.

x	x^2	$-3x$	-4	y
-3	9	9	-4	14
-2	4	6	-4	6
-1	1	3	-4	0
0	0	0	-4	-4
1	1	-3	-4	-6
2	4	-6	-4	-6
3	9	-9	-4	-4
4	16	-12	-4	0

$x = -1$ and $x = 4$ are the solutions, the intersection of the function $x^2 - 3x - 4$ and $y = 0$. See graphs Fig. 32 and Fig. 30.

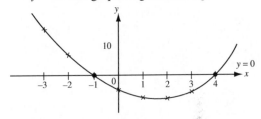

Fig. 30

From Fig. 30 $x = 4$, $x = -1$; when $x = 4$, $y = 6$ and when $x = -1$, $y = 1$.

(ii) $y = x^2 - 2x - 2$

x	x^2	$-2x$	-2	y
-3	9	6	-2	13
-2	4	4	-2	6
-1	1	2	-2	1
0	0	0	-2	-2
1	1	-2	-2	-3
2	4	-4	-2	-2
3	9	-6	-2	1
4	16	-8	-2	6

$y = x + 2$

x	x	2	y
-3	-3	2	-1
-2	-2	2	0
-1	-1	2	1
0	0	2	2
1	1	2	3
2	2	2	4
3	3	2	5
4	4	2	6

see graph Fig. 31. The intersections of the graphs give the solutions: $x = -1$, $y = 1$; $x = 4$, $y = 6$.

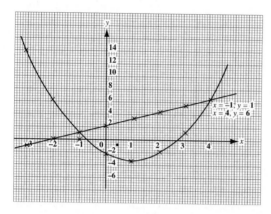

Fig. 31

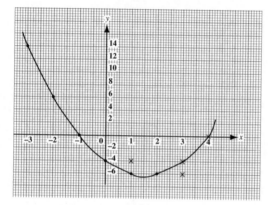

Fig. 32

Cubic functions and cubic equations.

7.4 Plots the graph of a cubic equation with specified interval and range.

The general form of a cubic equation is given $ax^3 + bx^2 + cx + d = 0$ where a, b, c and d are constants and x is a variable.

WORKED EXAMPLE 69

Plot the graph of the cubic function $y = 2x^3 - 3x^2 - 11x - 12$ between the values $x = -4$ and $x = 4$, at intervals of 0.5. Give your answers correct to **two** decimal places, for the equation $2x^3 - 3x^2 - 11x + 8 = 0$.

Solution 69

Use the following scales on the x-axis 1 cm = 0.5 and the y-axis 1 cm = 10.

y is plotted against x and a smooth curve is obtained with a maximum point at $x = -1$ and a minimum point at $x = 2$, the graph cuts the x-axis at $x = 3.55$ and the y-axis at $y = -12$.

In order to solve the equation $2x^3 - 3x^2 - 11x + 8 = 0$, we make $y = -20$, a horizontal line

x	-4	-3.5	-3.0	-2.5	-2.0	-1.5	-1	-0.5	0
	0.5	1	1.5	2	2.5	3	3.5	4	
-12	-12	-12	-12	-12	-12	-12	-12	-12	-12
	-12	-12	-12	-12	-12	-12	-12	-12	
$-11x$	44	38.5	33	27.5	22	16.5	11	5.5	0
	-5.50	-11	-16.5	-22	-27.5	-33	-38.5	-44	
$-3x^2$	-48	-36.75	-27	-18.75	-12	-6.75	-3	-0.75	0
	-0.75	-3	-6.75	-12	-18.75	-27	-36.75	-48	
$-2x^3$	-128	-85.75	-54	-31.25	-16	-6.75	-2	-0.25	0
	0.25	2	6.75	16	31.25	54	85.75	128	
y	-144	-96	-60	-34.5	-18	-9	-6	-7.5	-12
	-18.00	-24	-28.5	-30	-27	-18	-1.5	24	

intersects the graph at $x = -2.08$, $x = 0.68$ and $x = 2.93$.

Check whether these values satisfy the cubic eqn.
$2x^3 - 3x^2 - 11x + 8 = 0$ $x = -2.08$

L.H.S $2(-2.08)^3 - 3(-2.08)^2 - 11(-2.08) + 8$
$= -17.998 - 12.98 + 22.88 + 8$
$= -0.098$ (this is nearly zero)

   $x = 0.68$

L.H.S. $2(0.68)^3 - 3(0.68)^2 - 11(0.68) + 8$
$= 0.629 - 1.387 - 7.48 + 8 = -0.238$ (this is nearly zero)

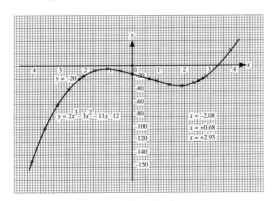

Fig. 33

   $x = 2.93$

L.H.S. $2(2.93)^3 - 3(2.93)^2 - 11(2.93) + 8$
$= 50.31 - 25.76 - 32.23 + 8$
$= 0.32$ (this is nearly zero)

━━━━━━━━━━━━━━
WORKED EXAMPLE 70

Plot the graph of the cubic function $y = x^3 + 3x + 8$ between the values $x = -3$ and $x = 2$ at intervals of 0.5, hence solve the equation

   (i) $x^3 + 3x + 8 = 5$ (ii) $x^3 + 3x = 0$
(iii) $x^3 + 3x + 8 = -20$.

Solution 70

The graph is plotted according the table shown, taking the following scales x-axis, $0.5 \equiv 1$ cm and $5 \equiv 1$ cm on the y-axis.
   (i) If $y = 5$, a straight line is drawn which intersects the curve at $x = -0.75$ therefore

$x^3 + 3x + 8 = 5$
or $x^3 + 3x + 3 = 0$ has only one solution $x = -0.75$

  (ii) If $x^3 + 3x = 0$ $x(x^2 + 3) = 0$
   $x = 0$, or $x^2 + 3 = 0$ (no solution)
   therefore $x = 0$ when $y = 8$
   $x^3 + 3x + 8 = 8$
   therefore the solution $x^3 + 3x = 0$
   is at $x = 0$

 (iii) $x^3 + 3x + 8 + 20 = 0$ $x^3 + 3x + 28 = 0$
   $x = -2.7$ the intersection of
   $y = -20$ and $y = x^3 + 3x + 8$.

   $y = x^3 + 3x + 8$

x	8	$3x$	x^3	y
-3	8	-9	-27	-28
-2.5	8	-7.5	-15.625	-15.125
-2.0	8	-6	-8	-6
-1.5	8	-4.5	-3.375	0.125
-1.0	8	-3	-1	4
-0.5	8	-1.5	-0.125	6.375
0	8	0	0	8
0.5	8	1.5	0.125	9.625
1.0	8	3	1	12
1.5	8	4.5	3.375	15.875

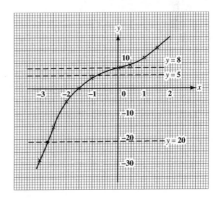

Fig. 34

Exercises 7

Solve the following linear simultaneous equations algebraically.

1. $6x + 5y = 5 \quad 5x + 7y = 3$
   (Ans. $x = 1.18$, $y = -0.41$)

2. $26x - 25y = 50 \quad -25x + 25.1y = 40$
   (Ans. $x = 81.7$, $y = 82.97$)

3. $4x + 3y = 8 \quad 75x + 77y = 50$
   (Ans. $x = 5.61$, $y = -4.82$)

4. $1.1x + y = 2 \quad x + 1.2y = 3$
   (Ans. $x = -1.87$, $y = 4.06$)

5. $0.5x - 0.3y = 6 \quad 15x + 15.3y = 12$
   (Ans. $x = 7.84$, $y = -6.93$)

6. $2x - 5y = -1 \quad 10x + 15y = -2$
   (Ans. $x = -0.3125$, $y = 0.075$)

7. $0.5x - 3y = 5 \quad 0.1x + y = -7$
   (Ans. $x = -20$, $y = -5$)

8. $15y - 13.5x = 2.5 \quad 15x - 13.5y = 3.5$
   (Ans. $x = 2.02$, $y = 1.99$)

9. $x - 5y = 30 \quad 6.1x + 5.10y = 80$
   (Ans. $x = 15.5$, $y = -2.9$)

10. $23x + 20y = 600 \quad 20x + 26y = 300$
    (Ans. $x = 48.5$, $y = -25.8$)

11. $5.5x + 4.5y = 5 \quad 4.5x + 10y = 10$
    (Ans. $x = 0.144$, $y = 0.935$)

12. $3x - 4y = 23 \quad -x + y = -6$
    (Ans. $x = 1$, $y = -5$)

13. $5x + 2y = -4 \quad 4x + 5y = 7$
    (Ans. $x = -2$, $y = 3$)

14. $5x + 4y = -5 \quad -4x - 3y = 5$
    (Ans. $x = -5$, $y = 5$)

15. $5x + 7y = -30 \quad 4x - 3y = -2.5$
    (Ans. $x = -2.5$, $y = -2.5$)

16. $x + 7y = -19 \quad 4x - 5y = 23$
    (Ans. $x = 2$, $y = -3$)

Solve graphically the simultaneous equations

17. $-3x + 4y = -23 \quad x - y = 6$

18. $5x + 2y = -4 \quad -4x - 5y = -7$

19. $5x + 4y = -5 \quad 4x + 3y = -5$

20. $5x + 7y = -30, -4x + 3y = 2.5$

21. $x + 7y = -19, -4x + 5y = -23$

Draw the following quadratic functions for the range of values of x shown adjacently.

22. $y = 6x^2 + 7x - 5$ for x between -2 and 1

23. $y = x^2 + x - 2$ for x between -3 and 2

24. $y = x^2 - x - 6$ for x between -3 and 3

25. $y = -x^2 - 3x - 2$ for x between -3 and 0

26. $y = -x^2 + 6x - 5$ for x between 0 and 6 and hence find the values of x for which $y = 0$.

Solve graphically the following simultaneous equations:

27. $4x + 2 - y = 0 \quad$ Take values of x
    $y = -4x^2 + 5x + 7$ between -1 and 2.

28. $y = x^2 + 5x + 4 \quad y = 0$ Take values of x between 0 and -5.

29. $y = x^2 - 8x + 1$ and $y = -14$
    Take values of x between $x = 1$ and $x = 6$.

Solve the cubic equations graphically

30. $y = x^3 - 2x^2 - 5x + 6 = 0$
    for values of x between $x = -3$ and $x = 4$

31. $y = x^3 - x^2 + x - 1 = 0$
    for values of x between $x = -2$ and $x = 3$

32. $y = x^3 - 4x^2 + 4x = 0$
    for values of x between $x = -2$ and $x = 3$

33. Draw the graph of $y = 2x^2 - 4x - 5$ for values of x between -3 and 5.

x	$2x^2$	$-4x$	-5	y
-3	18	12	-5	25
-2	8	8	-5	11
-1	2	4	-5	1
0	0	0	-5	-5
1	2	-4	-5	-7
2	8	-8	-5	-5
3	18	-12	-5	1
4	32	-16	-5	11
5	50	-20	-5	25

(a) What is the value of y when $x = -2.3, 1.3, 3.7$?

(b) What are the values of x when
$y = 18, 5, -3$ and -7?

(c) What is the least value of y and for what value of x does it occur?

(d) For what value of x is $y = -7$ and why have you only one answer?

(e) About what line is the curve symmetrical?

(f) For what range of values of x is y negative?

(g) Solve graphically the equation
$2x^2 - 4x - 5 = 0$.

(h) Solve graphically the equation
$2x^2 - 4x = 0$.

(i) Find from your graph the gradient when $x = -2$ and when $x = 2$.

(j) What name is given to curves of the type
$y = 2x^2 - 4x - 5 = 0$?

(k) State whether y has a maximum or minimum value and what that value is.

(l) If $y = -2x^2 + 4x + 5$, state whether y has a maximum or minimum value.

Geometry.

Geometry.

Defines the radian and calculates areas and arc lengths of circles.

8.1 Defines the radian.

Let s be the length of arc subtending an angle θ. If $s = r$, then the angle subtended θ is one radian. Therefore, a radian is the angle subtending a length of arc which is equal to the length of radius r.

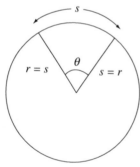

Fig. 35

8.2 Converts degrees measure to radians and vice versa.

One complete revolution of the circle describes an angle equal of 360 degrees or 2π radians, therefore

$$(2\pi)^c = 360°$$

^{c} denotes radians $°$ denotes degrees

1 degree = 60 minutes or $1° = 60'$

$'$ denotes minutes

1 minute = 60 seconds or $1' = 60''$

$''$ denotes seconds

$$(2\pi)^c = 360° \ldots (1)$$
2π radians is equal to 360 degrees

$$x^c = y° \ldots (2) \quad x \text{ radians is equal to } y \text{ degrees}$$

dividing equation (1) by equation (2)

$$\frac{2\pi}{x} = \frac{360}{y} \text{ or } y° = \frac{360x}{2\pi} = \left(\frac{180x}{\pi}\right)^c$$

$$\boxed{y° = \frac{180x^c}{\pi}}$$

Similarly
$$(2\pi)^c = 360° \ldots (3) \qquad y^c = x° \ldots (4)$$

dividing equation (3) by equation (4)

$$\frac{2\pi}{y} = \frac{360}{x} \qquad y = \frac{2\pi x}{360}$$

$$\boxed{y° = \frac{\pi x°}{180}}.$$

WORKED EXAMPLE 71

Convert the following angles to radians:

(i) 30°   (ii) 60°   (iii) 90°

(iv) 38°   (v) 49°   (vi) 87°

(vii) 367°   (viii) 3,000°   (ix) 5,000°

(x) 10,000°

to three decimal places.

Solution 71

Using the formula $y^c = \left(\dfrac{\pi x^\circ}{180}\right)$

(i) $y^c = \left(\dfrac{\pi \, 30^\circ}{180}\right) = 0.523598775 \approx 0.524^c$

$30^\circ = 0.523598775^c \approx 0.524^c$

(ii) $y^c = \left(\dfrac{\pi \, 60^\circ}{180}\right) = \dfrac{\pi}{3}$

$= 1.047197551 \approx 1.047^c$

$60^\circ = 1.047197551^c \approx 1.047^c$

(iii) $y^c = \left(\dfrac{\pi \, 90^\circ}{180}\right) = \dfrac{\pi}{2}$

$= 1.570796327 \approx 1.571^c$

$90^\circ = 1.570796327 \approx 1.571^c$

(iv) $y^c = \left(\dfrac{\pi \, 38^\circ}{180}\right) = 0.663225115 \approx 0.663^c$

$38^\circ = 0.663225115^c \approx 0.663^c$

(v) $49 \times \dfrac{\pi}{180} = 0.855^c$

(vi) $87 \times \dfrac{\pi}{180} = 1.518^c$

(vii) $367 \times \dfrac{\pi}{180} = 6.405^c$

(viii) $3{,}000 \times \dfrac{\pi}{180} = 52.360^c$

(ix) $5{,}000 \times \dfrac{\pi}{180} = 87.266^c$

(x) $10{,}000 \times \dfrac{\pi}{180} = 174.533^c$.

Convert the following angles to degrees:

(i) π^c (ii) $\left(\dfrac{\pi}{2}\right)^c$ (iii) 1^c

(iv) 0.05^c (v) 5^c (vi) $(3\pi)^c$

(vii) $-\left(\dfrac{\pi}{4}\right)^c$ (viii) $\left(\dfrac{2\pi}{3}\right)^c$

(ix) $\left(\dfrac{11\pi}{6}\right)^c$ (x) $\left(\dfrac{1}{5}\right)^c$

to three significant figures.

Solution 72

$y^\circ = \left(\dfrac{180 x^c}{\pi}\right)$

general formula to convert x radians to y degrees.

(i) $y^\circ = \left(\dfrac{180 x^c}{\pi}\right) = \dfrac{180\pi^c}{\pi} = 180^\circ$

$\pi^c = 180^\circ$

(ii) $\left(\dfrac{\pi}{2}\right)^c = \dfrac{180^\circ}{2} = 90.0^\circ$

(iii) $1^c = \dfrac{180}{\pi} = 57.29577951^\circ = 57.3^\circ$

(iv) $0.05^c = \dfrac{180 \times 0.05}{\pi}$

$= 2.864788976^\circ = 2.87^\circ$

(v) $5^c = \dfrac{180 \times 5}{\pi} = 286.48^\circ = 287^\circ$

(vi) $(3\pi)^c = 3 \times 180^\circ = 540^\circ$

(vii) $-\left(\dfrac{\pi}{4}\right)^c = -\dfrac{180^\circ}{4} = -45.0^\circ$

(viii) $\left(\dfrac{2\pi}{3}\right)^c = 2 \times \dfrac{180^\circ}{3} = 120^\circ$

(ix) $\left(\dfrac{11\pi}{6}\right)^c = 11\dfrac{180^\circ}{6} = 330^\circ$

(x) $\left(\dfrac{1}{5}\right)^c = \dfrac{1}{5}\dfrac{180^\circ}{\pi} = 11.46^\circ \approx 11.5^\circ$.

Length of arc

Consider a circle of radius r as shown in Fig. 36

Fig. 36

The circumference of the circle, C is given by the formula

$C = 2\pi r = \pi D$

where $D = 2r =$ diameter.

The length of arc, s, can be found as follows: If the angle subtending the arc s, θ then is

$s = 2\pi r \times \dfrac{\theta}{2\pi}$ which states that the length of arc s is a portion of the total perimeter

therefore $\boxed{s = r\theta}$ where θ must be expressed in radians.

WORKED EXAMPLE 73

Find the length of arc of a circle of 10 mm diameter subtending an angle 30°.

Solution 73

The angle must be first converted into radians,

$$30° = \left(\frac{\pi}{6}\right)^c = \frac{3.14159}{6} = 0.5236^c.$$

The length of arc subtending this angle is

$$s = r\theta = \frac{10}{2} \times 0.5236 = 2.618 \text{ mm}$$

$$s = 2.618 \text{ mm}$$

WORKED EXAMPLE 74

The length of arc of a circle of 50 cm radius is 25 cm, find the angle subtended by this arc in degrees.

Solution 74

$$s = r\theta \quad \text{the length of arc}$$

$$s = 25 \text{ cm}, r = 50 \text{ cm, then } 25 = 50\,\theta$$

$$\theta = \frac{25}{50} = 0.5^c = 0.5 \times \frac{180°}{\pi} = 28.65°$$

WORKED EXAMPLE 75

An arc of 35 cm long subtends an angle 179°, find the radius of the circle.

Solution 75

The length of arc is given by the formula $s = r\theta$ where s and r are given in cm and θ in radians

$$r = \frac{s}{\theta} = \frac{35}{3.124} \text{ where}$$

$$179° \times \frac{\theta}{180°} = 3.124^c = 179°$$

$$r = \frac{35}{3.124} = 11.2 \text{ cm}$$

WORKED EXAMPLE 76

A chord divides the circumferences of a circle of diameter 30 mm in the ratio $\frac{s_1}{s_2} = \frac{1}{5}$ where s_1 and s_2 are the minor and major lengths of arcs. Determine the angles subtending the minor and major lengths of arcs and the corresponding lengths of arcs.

Solution 76

$$s = r\theta$$

$$\frac{s_1}{s_2} = \frac{1}{5} = \frac{r\theta}{r(2\pi - \theta)} = \frac{\theta}{2\pi - \theta}$$

$$2\pi - \theta = 5\theta$$

$$6\theta = 2\pi$$

$$\theta = \frac{\pi}{3}$$

the angle of the minor arc $= \frac{\pi}{3}$ or 60°

the angle of the major arc $= \frac{5\pi}{3}$ or 300°

$$s_1 = r\theta = 15\left(\frac{\pi}{3}\right) = 5\pi = 15.71 \text{ mm}$$

the length of the minor arc

$$s_2 = r(2\pi - \theta)$$
$$= 15\left(\frac{5\pi}{3}\right) = 25\pi = 78.54 \text{ mm}$$

the length of the major arc.

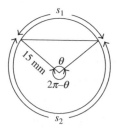

Fig. 37

WORKED EXAMPLE 77

A chord, *AB*, of 25 cm is drawn parallel to the diameter, *CD*, of a circle of radius 20 cm. Determine the angle subtended by the chord at the centre, *AÔB* and hence calculate the perimeter *ABDCA*.

Solution 77

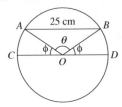

Fig. 38

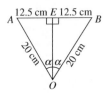

Fig. 39

$AB = 25$ cm $\quad CD = 40$ cm

Draw a perpendicular line from the centre O to the side AB, this line bisects $A\hat{O}B$ and the side AB

$$\sin \alpha = \frac{AE}{AO} = \frac{12.5}{20} = 0.625$$

using the calculator with mode 5 (thus working in radians) gives $\alpha = 0.675\,131532^c$ or $\boxed{\theta = 1.35^c}$

The length of arc AC = the length of arc $BD = r\phi = 20(0.896) = 17.9$ cm

where $\phi = \frac{\pi}{2} - \alpha = \frac{\pi}{2} - 0.675^c = 0.896^c$.

The perimeter $= AB$ (chord) $+ BD$ (length or arc) $+ CD$ (diameter) $+ CA$ (length of arc)

$$= 25 + 17.9 + 40 + 17.9 = 100.8 \text{ cm}$$

Area of a sector

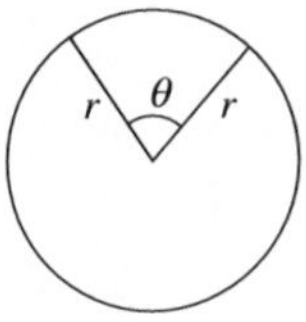

Fig. 40

A circle of radius r has an area equal to πr^2

$$A = \pi r^2$$

the area of a sector is a portion of the area of a circle in a ratio $\dfrac{\theta}{2\pi}$

$$A_1 = \pi r^2 \times \frac{\theta}{2\pi} = \frac{1}{2}r^2\theta$$

Area of a sector $= \dfrac{1}{2}r^2\theta$

where θ must be expressed in radians.

$$\boxed{A_1 = \frac{1}{2}r^2\theta}$$

Calculate the area of a sector, if $\theta = \frac{\pi}{3}$ and $r = 1$ m.

Solution 78

$$A_1 = \frac{1}{2}(1)^2\frac{\pi}{3} = \frac{\pi}{6} = 0.524 \text{ m}^2.$$

WORKED EXAMPLE 79

The area of a sector is 5 cm^2 and $r = 4$ cm, find the angle θ.

Solution 79

$$A_1 = \frac{1}{2}r^2\theta = 5$$

$$r^2\theta = 10 \quad \theta = \frac{10}{4^2} = 0.625^c$$

$$\theta = 0.625 \times \frac{180°}{\pi} = 35.81°.$$

WORKED EXAMPLE 80

A chord divides the area of a circle into a minor and major segments.
If $\theta = \frac{\pi}{6}$ is the angle of the minor segment, find the ratio of the major segment to that of the minor segment to the nearest whole number.

Solution 80

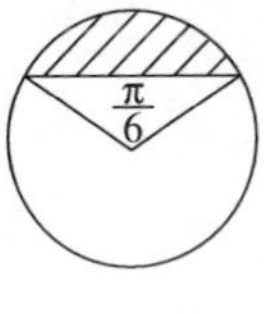

Area of segment = area of sector − area of triangle

Fig. 41

Fig. 42

Area of segment $= \dfrac{1}{2}r^2\theta - \dfrac{1}{2}r^2 \sin \theta$

Fig. 43

Area of sector $= \dfrac{1}{2}r^2\theta$

Fig. 44

Area of triangle $= \dfrac{1}{2}r^2 \sin \theta$

$\dfrac{\text{Area of minor segment}}{\text{area of major segment}}$

$= \dfrac{\frac{1}{2}r^2\theta - \frac{1}{2}r^2 \sin \theta}{\frac{1}{2}r^2(2\pi - \theta) - \frac{1}{2}r^2 \sin(2\pi - \theta)}$

$= \dfrac{\frac{1}{2}r^2(\theta - \sin \theta)}{\frac{1}{2}r^2[(2\pi - \theta) - \sin(2\pi - \theta)]}$

$= \dfrac{\theta - \sin \theta}{(2\pi - \theta) - \sin(2\pi - \theta)}$

$= \dfrac{\frac{\pi}{6} - \sin \frac{\pi}{6}}{2\pi - \frac{\pi}{6} - \sin(2\pi - \frac{\pi}{6})}$

$= \dfrac{\frac{\pi}{6} - \frac{1}{2}}{11\frac{\pi}{6} - \sin 11\frac{\pi}{6}}$

$= \dfrac{\frac{\pi}{6} - \frac{1}{2}}{11\frac{\pi}{6} - (-\frac{1}{2})} = \dfrac{\frac{\pi}{6} - \frac{1}{2}}{11\frac{\pi}{6} + \frac{1}{2}}$

$= \dfrac{0.023598775}{6.259586532} = 3.77 \times 10^{-3}$

$\dfrac{\text{area of major segment}}{\text{area of minor segment}} = 265.25 \approx 265.$

Exercises 8

1. A chord divides the circumference of a circle of diameter 30 mm in the ratio $\frac{s_1}{s_2} = \frac{1}{5}$, determine the angles subtending the minor and major lengths of arcs and the corresponding lengths of arcs.

2. A chord of 25 mm is drawn parallel to the diameter of a circle of radius 20 mm calculate the area between the chord and diameter in three significant figures.

3. A chord divides the circumference of a circle in the ratio $\frac{s_1}{s_2} = \frac{1}{3}$, determine the length of the chord if the radius is 45 mm.

4. A circle of 15 mm radius has a chord of 5 mm, determine the major length of the arc.

5.

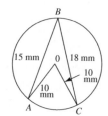

Fig. 45

Two chords of length 15 mm and 18 mm are drawn in a circle as shown in Fig. 45, the radius is 10 mm. Determine the area of the sector AOC.

6. Find the area hatched. Two concentric circles are shown in Fig. 46 of radii 10 mm and 25 mm.

Fig. 46

7. The annular area between two circles is 100 mm². If the larger radius of the circles is 20 mm, find the smaller radius.

9

Trigonometry

Develops some properties of Trigonometric functions.

Trigonometry is a Greek word and means the measurement of a triangle (trigono).

Consider a right angled triangle as shown (see Fig. 47)

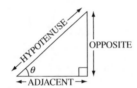

Fig. 47

the side opposite to the right angle (90°) is called **hypotenuse** and is the largest side, if θ is an acute angle then the side next to it is the **adjacent** and the side opposite is the **opposite**.

Pythagoras theorem

$(\text{HYPOTENUSE})^2 = (\text{ADJACENT})^2 + (\text{OPPOSITE})^2$.

The hypotenuse squared is equal to the sum of the squares of the adjacent and opposite sides.

sine θ is abbreviated to $\sin \theta$

cosine θ is abbreviated to $\cos \theta$

tangent θ is abbreviated to $\tan \theta$.

Definitions

$\sin \theta = \dfrac{\text{opposite}}{\text{hypotenuse}}$

$\cos \theta = \dfrac{\text{adjacent}}{\text{hypotenuse}}$

$\tan \theta = \dfrac{\text{opposite}}{\text{adjacent}}$

$$\boxed{\sin \theta = \frac{a}{c}} \qquad \dots (1)$$

$$\boxed{\cos \theta = \frac{b}{c}} \qquad \dots (2)$$

$$\boxed{\tan \theta = \frac{a}{b}} \qquad \dots (3)$$

Sohcahtao

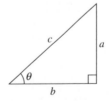

Fig. 48

dividing the numerator and denominator of equation (3) by c we have

$$\tan \theta = \frac{\frac{a}{c}}{\frac{b}{c}} = \frac{\sin \theta}{\cos \theta}$$

$$\boxed{\tan \theta = \frac{\sin \theta}{\cos \theta}}$$

Using Pythagoras theorem $a^2 + b^2 = c^2$ dividing each term by c^2

$$\frac{a^2}{c^2} + \frac{b^2}{c^2} = \frac{c^2}{c^2}$$

or $\left(\dfrac{a}{c}\right)^2 + \left(\dfrac{b}{c}\right)^2 = 1$

$$\sin^2\theta + \cos^2\theta = 1$$

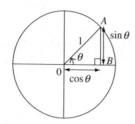

Fig. 49

Consider a circle of unit radius, that is, $OA = 1$, $A\hat{O}B = \theta$

$\sin\theta = \dfrac{AB}{OA} = \dfrac{AB}{1}$ therefore $AB = \sin\theta$

$\cos\theta = \dfrac{OB}{OA} = \dfrac{OB}{1}$ therefore $OB = \cos\theta$.

From the right angled triangle we have

$$OB^2 + BA^2 = OA^2$$

$$\boxed{\cos^2\theta + \sin^2\theta \equiv 1}$$

the fundamental identity.

Consider the set squares

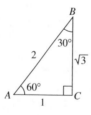

Fig. 50

From the triangle ABC

$$\sin 30° = \frac{1}{2} = 0.5$$

$$\tan 30° = \frac{1}{\sqrt{3}} \times \frac{\sqrt{3}}{\sqrt{3}} = \frac{1}{3}\sqrt{3} = \frac{1.732}{3} = 0.577$$

$$\tan 60° = \frac{\sqrt{3}}{1} = 1.732$$

$$\cos 30° = \frac{\sqrt{3}}{2} = \frac{1.732}{2} = 0.866$$

$$\cos 60° = \frac{1}{2} = 0.5$$

$$\sin 60° = \frac{\sqrt{3}}{2} = \frac{1.732}{2} = 0.866$$

therefore $\cos 30° = \sin 60°$

$$\sin 30° = \cos 60°.$$

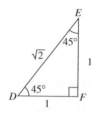

Fig. 51

From the triangle DEF

$$\sin 45° = \frac{1}{\sqrt{2}}$$

$$\tan 45° = \frac{1}{1} = 1 \quad \cos 45° = \frac{1}{\sqrt{2}}$$

therefore $\sin 45° = \cos 45° = \dfrac{1}{\sqrt{2}} = 0.707.$

9.1 Sketches a sine wave over one complete cycle by relating the angle of a rotating unit radius to the vertical projection.

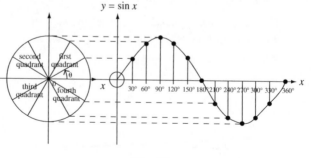

Fig. 52

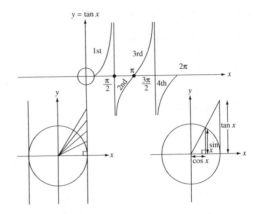

Fig. 54

The positive angles are measured from the reference line *ox* in an anticlockwise direction and the negative angles are measured from the reference line *ox* in a clockwise direction.

There are four quadrants, first quadrant $\theta = 0 - 90°$, second quadrant, $\theta = 90° - 180°$ third quadrant $180° - 270°$, and fourth quadrant $270° - 360°$. The sines in the first and second quadrants are positive and the sines in the third and fourth quadrants are negative, above the *x*-axis are positive and below the *x*-axis are negative.

9.2 Sketches a cosine wave over one complete cycle by relating the angle of a rotating unit radius to the horizontal projection.

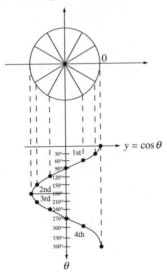

Fig. 53

Defines $\tan A = \dfrac{\sin A}{\cos A}$ and sketches the graph of $\tan A$ as *A* varies from $0°$ to $360°$.

WORKED EXAMPLE 81

If $\sin x = \frac{2}{9}$, find the values of $\cos x$ and $\tan x$ by using a right angled triangle.

Solution 81

$$\sin x = \frac{2}{9} = \frac{\text{opposite}}{\text{hypotenuse}} \text{ by definition}$$

construct a right angled triangle and apply this definition, the opposite of *x* is 2 and the hypotenuse is 9, therefore $\sin x = \dfrac{2}{9}$.

Using pythagoras theorem

$$AB^2 + BC^2 = AC^2$$
$$AB^2 = AC^2 - BC^2 = 9^2 - 2^2 = 81 - 4 = 77$$
$$AB = \sqrt{77} = 8.77 \quad \cos x = \frac{8.77}{9} = \frac{877}{900}$$
$$\tan x = \frac{2}{8.77} = \frac{200}{877} = 0.228.$$

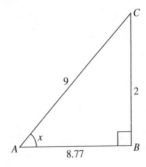

Fig. 55

If $\tan x = \dfrac{1}{5}$, find the values of $\sin x$ and $\cos x$.

Solution 82

$\sin x = \dfrac{1}{5}$

the opposite side of x is 1 and the adjacent side of x is 5.

$AC^2 = AB^2 + BC^2 = 5^2 + 1^2 = 25 + 1 = 26$

$AC = \sqrt{26}$ and $\cos x = \dfrac{5}{\sqrt{26}}$

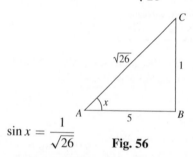

$\sin x = \dfrac{1}{\sqrt{26}}$

Fig. 56

If $\cos x = \dfrac{5}{13}$, find $\tan x$ and $\sin x$.

Solution 83

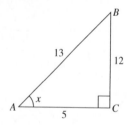

Fig. 57

$\cos x = \dfrac{5}{13}$

$AB^2 = AC^2 + BC^2$

$BC^2 = AB^2 - AC^2$

$\quad = 13^2 - 5^2 = 169 - 25 = 144$

$BC = \sqrt{144} = 12$

$\sin x = \dfrac{12}{13}, \quad \tan x = \dfrac{12}{5}.$

If $\cos x = \dfrac{3}{4}$ and $\sin y = \dfrac{4}{5}$ evaluate

(i) $\sin x \cos y + \sin y \cos x$

(ii) $\cos x \cos y - \sin x \sin y$

(iii) $\cos x \cos y + \sin x \sin y$

(iv) $\sin x \cos y - \sin y \cos x$

(v) $\dfrac{\tan x + \tan y}{1 - \tan x \tan y}.$

Solution 84

$\sin x = \dfrac{\sqrt{7}}{4}$

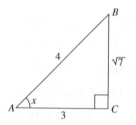

Fig. 58

$BC^2 = AB^2 - AC^2$

$BC = \sqrt{4^2 - 3^2} = \sqrt{16 - 9} = \sqrt{7}$

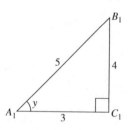

Fig. 59

$A_1C_1^2 = A_1B_1^2 - B_1C_1^2$

$\quad\quad = 5^2 - 4^2 = 25 - 16 = 9$

$A_1C_1 = 3$

(i) $\sin x \cos y + \sin y \cos x$

$= \left(\dfrac{\sqrt{7}}{4}\right)\left(\dfrac{3}{5}\right) + \left(\dfrac{4}{5}\right)\left(\dfrac{3}{4}\right)$

$= \dfrac{3\sqrt{7}}{20} + \dfrac{12}{20} = \dfrac{3\sqrt{7} + 12}{20} = 0.997$

(ii) $\cos x \cos y - \sin x \sin y$

$$= \left(\frac{3}{4}\right)\left(\frac{3}{5}\right) - \left(\frac{\sqrt{7}}{4}\right)\left(\frac{4}{5}\right)$$

$$= \frac{9 - 4\sqrt{7}}{20} = -0.0792$$

(iii) $\cos x \cos y + \sin y \cos x$

$$= \frac{9 + 4\sqrt{7}}{20} = 0.9792$$

(iv) $\sin x \cos y - \sin x \sin y$

$$= \frac{3\sqrt{7} - 12}{20} = -0.203$$

(v) $\dfrac{\tan x + \tan y}{1 - \tan x \tan y} = \dfrac{\dfrac{\sqrt{7}}{3} + \dfrac{4}{3}}{1 - \dfrac{\sqrt{7}}{3}\dfrac{4}{3}}$

$$= \frac{\dfrac{\sqrt{7} + 4}{3 - 4\sqrt{7}}}{3} = \frac{6.646}{-0.528} = -12.6$$

From the triangle ABC $\tan x = \dfrac{\sqrt{7}}{3}$

From the triangle $A_1 B_1 C_1$ $\tan y = \dfrac{4}{3}$

Sine rule

Let ABC be any triangle as shown in Fig. 60

The sides a, b and c are shown as opposite to the angles $\hat{A}$, $\hat{B}$ and $\hat{C}$ respectively.

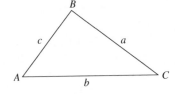

Fig. 60

Let R be the radius of the circumscribing circle of the triangle ABC as shown in Fig. 61

Draw the diameter from B, BD and construct the dotted line DC, so that the triangle BCD is a right angled triangle where $B\hat{C}D$ is $90°$ since BD is a diameter. Angles $B\hat{A}C = \hat{A} = B\hat{D}C$ since they

subtend the same arc BC.

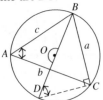

Fig. 61

From the triangle BDC we have

$$\sin B\hat{D}C = \frac{BC}{BD} = \frac{a}{2R}$$

$$\sin \hat{A} = \frac{a}{2R} \qquad \frac{a}{\sin \hat{A}} = 2R$$

Similarly it can be proved that

$$\frac{b}{\sin \hat{B}} = 2R \quad \text{and} \quad \frac{c}{\sin \hat{C}} = 2R$$

Therefore $\boxed{\dfrac{a}{\sin A} = \dfrac{b}{\sin B} = \dfrac{c}{\sin C}}$

This proof is not required for this level.

WORKED EXAMPLE 85

If $A = 45°$ and $C = 95°$ $a = 25$ mm, find the third angle and the other two sides.

Solution 85

The third angle $B = 180° - (45° + 95°)$
$$= 180° - 140° = 40°$$

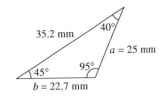

Fig. 62

Using the sine rule

$$\frac{a}{\sin A} = \frac{c}{\sin 95°} \qquad \frac{25}{\sin 45°} = \frac{c}{\sin 95°}$$

$$c = \frac{25 \sin 95°}{\sin 45°} = 35.2 \text{ mm}$$

Using the sine rule again

$$\frac{b}{\sin B} = \frac{a}{\sin A}$$

$$b = a\frac{\sin B}{\sin A} = 25 \times \frac{\sin 40°}{\sin 45°} = 22.7 \text{ mm.}$$

Therefore the third angle is 40° and the other sides are 22.7 mm and 35.2 mm.

WORKED EXAMPLE 86

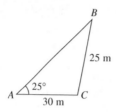

Fig. 63

Fig. 63 shows the given data:

(a) Determine the two angles B and C in degrees, minutes and seconds.

(c) The third side in three significant figures.

Solution 86

Using the sine rule $\dfrac{a}{\sin A} = \dfrac{b}{\sin B}$

$$\frac{25}{\sin 25°} = \frac{30}{\sin B}$$

$$\sin B = \frac{30\sin 25°}{25} = 0.507141914$$

$$B = 30° 28' 25''$$

$$C = 180° - (25° + 30° 28' 25'')$$

$$= 180° - 55° 28' 25''$$

$$C = 124° 31' 35''$$

$$\frac{c}{\sin C} = \frac{a}{\sin A}$$

$$c = a\frac{\sin C}{\sin A} = 25\frac{\sin 124° 31' 35''}{\sin 25°} = 48.7 \text{ m.}$$

Cosine rule

The cosine rule is used when we would like to solve a triangle knowing (i) three sides only, or (ii) two sides and the angle between them.

$$a^2 = b^2 + c^2 - 2bc\cos A \qquad \ldots (1)$$

$$b^2 = a^2 + c^2 - 2ac\cos B \qquad \ldots (2)$$

$$c^2 = a^2 + b^2 - 2ab\cos C \qquad \ldots (3)$$

WORKED EXAMPLE 87

Determine the angles of the triangle with sides $a = 12$ cm, $b = 7$ cm and $c = 13$ cm.

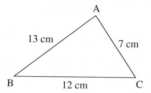

Solution 87

From equation (1) $a^2 = b^2 + c^2 - 2bc\cos A$

$$2bc\cos A = b^2 + c^2 - a^2$$

$$\cos A = \frac{b^2 + c^2 - a^2}{2bc}$$

$$= \frac{7^2 + 13^2 - 12^2}{2 \times 7 \times 13} = \frac{218 - 144}{182} = \frac{74}{182}$$

$$A = 66° 0' 32''.$$

From equation (2) $b^2 = a^2 + c^2 - 2ac\cos B$

$$2ac\cos B = a^2 + c^2 - b^2$$

$$\cos B = \frac{a^2 + c^2 - b^2}{2ac}$$

$$= \frac{12^2 + 13^2 - 7^2}{2 \times 12 \times 13} = \frac{264}{312}$$

$$B = 32° 12' 15''$$

$$C = 180° - (A + B)$$

$$= 180° - (32° 12' 15'' + 66° 0' 32'')$$

$$= 180° - 98° 12' 47'' \quad C = 81° 47' 13''.$$

Exercises 9

1. Write down the values of the sine 0°, 30°, 60°, 90°, 120°, 180°.

2. Write down the values of the cosine 45°, 90°, 135°, 150°, 210°.

3. Write down the values of the tangent 0°, 45°, 60°, 90°, 120°, 135°, 180°.

4. Write down the values of the sine.

$$\left(\frac{\pi}{3}\right)^c, \left(\frac{\pi}{4}\right)^c, \left(\frac{\pi}{2}\right)^c, \left(\frac{\pi}{6}\right)^c, (\pi)^c, \left(\frac{3\pi}{2}\right)^c,$$

$$\left(\frac{11\pi}{6}\right)^c, (2\pi)^c, (5\pi)^c.$$

5. Write down the values of the cosine

$$0^c, \left(\frac{\pi}{6}\right)^c, \left(\frac{\pi}{2}\right)^c, \left(\frac{4\pi}{3}\right)^c, \left(\frac{7\pi}{4}\right)^c.$$

6. write down the values of the tangent

$$\left(\frac{\pi}{6}\right)^c, \left(\frac{\pi}{3}\right)^c, \pi^c, \left(\frac{3\pi}{2}\right)^c, \left(\frac{11\pi}{4}\right)^c.$$

7. Use a calculator to find the values of the sine, cosine and tangent of the following angles:

   $15°, 25°, 32°, 65°, 88°, 93°, 99°, 136°, 178°, 200°, 320°.$

8. Evaluate the following using a calculator to 3 significant figures:

   (i) $3\sin 25° + 5\cos 35° + 7\tan 39°$

   (ii) $\cos 35° - \sin 79° + \tan 44°$

   (iii) $5\cos 35° + 6\sin 90° - 7\tan 82°.$

9. Find all the values of θ between $0°$ and $360°$

   (i) $\sin x = \frac{1}{2}$ (ii) $\cos x = -0.866$

   (iii) $\tan x = 1$ (iv) $\sin x = -\frac{\sqrt{3}}{2}$

   (v) $\tan x = -\sqrt{3}$ indicate these values
                      on a simple graph sketch.

10. If $\sin x = \frac{4}{7}$. Find $\cos x$ and $\tan x$.

    (i) If x is an acute angle
    (ii) If x is an obtuse angle

11. Sketch the sine wave if the angle, θ lies between $-360°$ and $360°$.

12. Sketch the cosine wave if the angle, θ lies between $-360°$ and $360°$.

13. Sketch the tangent wave if the angle, θ lies between $-360°$ and $360°$.

14. Draw neatly

    (i) $y = \sin x$ $-360° \le x \le 360°$

    (ii) $y = \cos x$ $-360° \le x \le 360°$

    (iii) $y = \tan x$ $-360° \le x \le 360°$

    (a) Find the values of the angles x if

      (i) $y = \frac{1}{4}$ (ii) $y = -\frac{2}{3}$

      (iii) $y = -0.8.$

    (b) Find the value of y if

      (i) $x = 125°$ (ii) $x = 39°$
      (iii) $x = 275°.$

15. Draw a unit radius circle and indicate in which quadrant the sine of an angle is negative and in which quadrant the sine of an angle is positive.

16. Repeat question 15 for the cosine.

17. Repeat question 15 for the tangent.

10

Statistics

10 Determines and measures the location for ungrouped data and for data grouped in equal interval classes.

10.1 Defines the arithmetic mean, median and mode and explains where each is an appropriate measure of central tendency.

Arithmetic mean

A number of observations are made, the arithmetic mean is found to be the ratio of the sum of the observations divided by the number of observations.

ARITHMETIC MEAN

$$= \frac{\text{sum of the observations}}{\text{number of the observations}}$$

10.2 Calculates the arithmetic mean for ungrouped data.

WORKED EXAMPLE 88

Find the mean height of fifteen male students whose heights are:

1.85 cm, 1.79 m, 1.75 m, 1.76 m, 1.75 m, 1.68 m, 1.90 m, 1.82 m, 1.55 m, 1.92 m, 1.86 m, 1.83 m, 1.75 m, 1.75 m, 1.74 m.

The answer should be given in three significant figures.

Solution 88

MEAN HEIGHT

$$= \frac{\begin{array}{c}(1.85 + 1.79 + 1.75 + 1.76 + 1.75 + 1.68 \\ + 1.90 + 1.82 + 1.55 + 1.92 + 1.86 \\ + 1.83 + 1.75 + 1.75 + 1.74)\end{array}}{15}$$

$$= \frac{26.7}{15} = 1.78 \text{ m.}$$

10.3 Places ungrouped data in rank order and determines the median and modal values.

The median

Numbers can either be arranged in ascending or descending order, **the median** is the value which lies half-way. If we write the heights of the previous example in ascending order, we have

1.55, 1.68, 1.74, 1.75, 1.75, 1.75, 1.75, 1.76, 1.79, 1.82, 1.83, 1.85, 1.86, 1.90, 1.92.

The median is the value which lies half-way, and this is 1.76 m. The median of the set of numbers is 1.76 m.

If the numbers are arranged in a descending order,

1.92, 1.90, 1.86, 1.85, 1.83, 1.82, 1.79, 1.76, 1.75, 1.75, 1.75, 1.75, 1.74, 1.68, 1.55.

The median is again 1.76 m.

The above example considers an odd number of observations, if the number of the observations are even.

WORKED EXAMPLE 89

Find the median of the following heights:

1.55, 1.68, 1.74, 1.75, 1.75, 1.75, 1.75, 1.76 , 1.79, 1.82, 1.83, 1.85, 1.86 and 1.90.

Solution 89

The number of the observations above is even, the median is therefore the mean of the two numbers half-way: $\frac{1}{2}(1.75 + 1.76) = 1.755$ m

The mode

The mode is the most frequently occuring value.

WORKED EXAMPLE 90

Find the mode of the heights:

1.85, 1.79, 1.75, 1.76, 1.75, 1.68, 1.90, 1.82, 1.55, 1.92, 1.86, 1.83, 1.75, 1.75, 1.74 m.

Solution 90

The most frequently occuring value of height is 1.75 m, it occurs four times in the above observations, all the other heights occur once.
The mode is 1.75 m.

10.4 Calculates the arithmetic mean for grouped data.

The collection and analysis of large quantities of data.
POPULATION is the set of individuals or elements on which a measure is to be made.
VARIATE or VARIABLE is the measure or attribute which is to be measured on the population.

There are two types of variables: quantitative and qualitative.
A QUALITATIVE is a non-numerical variate, that is, the colour of the eyes or of the hair, the brand of the washing powder, the grade in an examination.
A QUANTITATIVE is a variate which has a numerical value.

There are two types of Quantitative:

(i) **Discrete.** It takes only specific values in a given range, that is, sizes of shoes 36, 38,41,43, ...

(ii) **Continuous.** It may take any value within a given range

(a) Length of rods produced to a nominal value.

(b) Weight of males in a city.

(c) Time it takes to arrive at a destination.

The continuous type of variate is the most common.

10.5 Estimates the mode of grouped data using a histogram.

Frequency tables or frequency distributions

The values of the variate as obtained from measurement or observation are called the RAW DATA.

This can be reduced to a more manageable size by counting the number of times a particular value occurs, called the FREQUENCY, f.

The counting is performed by means of a TALLY CHART and the table so formed is called a FREQUENCY TABLE.

Example

Consider a sample batch of 104 carbon resistors of nominal value 68 Ω.

67.4	67.5	67.3	68.1	68.2	68.3	68.3	69.0
67.3	68.1	68.2	68.0	67.9	67.4	68.1	67.0
67.5	68.2	68.0	67.9	67.8	67.3	67.3	67.5
68.0	68.1	67.9	68.2	67.5	67.5	68.1	68.2
68.2	68.3	68.1	68.2	67.8	67.8	67.9	67.9
68.9	68.8	68.8	69.0	67.0	67.1	67.2	67.3
68.6	68.7	68.6	68.7	68.6	68.7	68.7	67.7
68.4	68.5	68.4	68.5	68.6	68.5	68.5	68.4
68.2	68.3	68.0	68.1	68.0	68.0	68.1	68.2
68.3	68.0	67.9	67.5	67.9	67.8	67.8	69.0
67.5	67.6	67.5	67.8	67.8	68.0	68.1	68.2
68.0	68.2	68.4	68.5	68.4	68.6	68.4	68.5
68.4	68.6	68.7	68.6	67.7	67.7	67.7	68.7

THE TALLY CHART FREQUENCY TABLE

Value of resistor	Number of resistors of this size	Frequency f
67.0	//	2
67.1	/	1
67.2	/	1
67.3	//////	5
67.4	//	2
67.5	/////////	8
67.6	/	1
67.7	////	4
67.8	///////	7
67.9	///////	7
68.0	//////////	9
68.1	//////////	9
68.2	///////////	11
68.3	//////	5
68.4	///////	7
68.5	//////	6
68.6	///////	7
68.7	//////	6
68.8	//	2
68.9	/	1
69.0	///	3

The histogram

This is a diagrammatic representation of a frequency table or frequency distribution. In its simplest form it consists of series of rectangles all of the same width, erected over the value and whose height represents the frequency of that value.

The histogram for the example of the sample batch of 104 carbon resistors is shown below

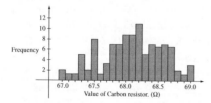

Fig. 64: The histogram shows clearly the pattern of variation with most values being grouped near the centre of 68.2 Ω.

Grouped frequency tables

The data can be even further condensed by grouping values into classes or categories. The classes are obtained by dividing the RANGE of values of the variate into a number of intervals of equal width.

The RANGE for the data is the difference between the greatest and the least values $69.0 - 67.0 = 2.00$.

The number of classes used is usually between 5 and 15.

A convenient number of classes is 7 then the grouped frequency table is as follows:

	Class	Frequency
first	67.0 to 67.2	4
second	67.3 to 67.5	15
third	67.6 to 67.8	12
fourth	67.9 to 68.1	25
fifth	68.2 to 69.4	23
sixth	68.5 to 68.7	19
seventh	68.8 to 69.0	6

For the first class there are **four** resistors whose value falls between 67.0 and 67.2 Ω, therefore the class frequency is 4.

67.0 Ω is the lower class limit

67.2 Ω is the upper class limit

For the second class there are **fifteen** resistors whose value falls between 67.3 to 67.5 Ω the lower class limit is 67.3 Ω and the upper class limit is 67.5 Ω.

For the third class, the class frequency is 12, and so on.

Class boundaries

For the first class interval $67.0 - 67.2$ Ω there are 4 resistors whose value is greater than 66.95 but less than or equal to 67.2 Ω, 66.95 is the lower class boundary and 67.25 is the upper class boundary. Its class width is therefore $67.25 - 66.95 = 0.3$. This is true for all the classes.

A grouped frequency table based on class boundaries is as follows for the above example.

Class	Frequency
66.95 − 67.25	4
67.25 − 67.55	15
67.55 − 67.85	12
67.85 − 68.15	25
68.15 − 68.45	23
68.45 − 68.75	19
68.75 − 69.05	6

Note

Once the data has been grouped into classes any individual value loses its identity and it is then taken that the values in any one class are spread evenly within it.

The Histogram for the grouped frequency distribution may be drawn using the lower and upper boundary values for each class as the extreme values for each rectangle representing the corresponding class frequency.

Thus each rectangle starts where the preceeding one ends and there are no gaps.

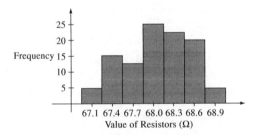

Fig. 65

10.6 Determines the median, quartiles and percentiles from cumulative frequency data.

Cumulative frequency tables

A cumulative frequency table is obtained by adding the frequencies of each class. At each stage the total frequency obtained is that which occurs at the upper class boundary.

Cumulative frequency table for the above data.

Upper class boundary	Cumulative Frequency
67.25	4
67.55	19
67.85	31
68.15	56
68.45	79
68.75	98
69.05	104

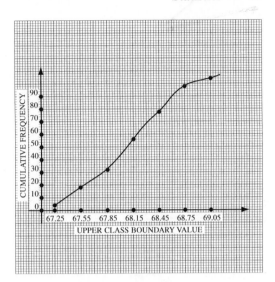

Fig. 66

Cumulative frequency curve or ogive

This is obtained by plotting the graph of the cumulative frequency against the corresponding upper class boundary values.

Measures of central tendency

The frequency distribution table the histogram show the way in which a distribution behaves together with some of its more important features. To summarise the data a single number is found which serves to be representative of the data. Such a number is called an AVERAGE and since it usually close to where the values tend to cluster, towards the middle when the values are arranged according to size it is also known as a MEASURE OF CENTRAL TENDENCY.

There are three such averages which are the most commonly used.

1. THE ARITHMETIC MEAN

   If the data values are x_1, x_2, x_3, ..., x_n occuring with frequencies f_1, f_2, f_3, ..., f_n respectively then the arithmetic mean, denoted by $\bar{x}$ is given by

   $$\bar{x} = \frac{\sum fx}{\sum f} \quad \text{where } \sum fx \text{ denoted } f_1x_1 + f_2x_2 + f_3x_3 + \ldots + f_nx_n \text{ and}$$

$\sum f$ denoted $f_1 + f_2 + f_3 + ... + f_n$ for an ungrouped distribution.

For a grouped distribution the same formula applies but $x_1, x_2, ... , x_n$ are the values at the centre of each class or interval.

2. THE MODE

The mode is the most frequently occuring value. The procedure for ungrouped data is to form a frequency distribution table then the mode or modal value will become obvious.

For a grouped data an estimation of the mode is obtained using a histogram.

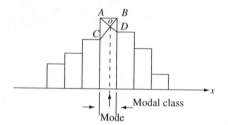

Fig. 67

Draw the diagonals AD and BD in the modal class rectangle, they intersect at O. The value of x at O is then an estimation of the mode.

3. THE MEDIAN

This is the centre value when the data is arranged in order of size or rank. If there is an even number of data values and hence two middle values then the median is the value mid-way between these two.

WORKED EXAMPLE 91

Find the values of the mean, median and mode of the set of numbers

125, 123, 125, 120, 122, 123, 121, 125, 124

Solution 91

Placing the numbers in ascending order 120, 121, 122, 123, $\boxed{123}$, 124, 125, 125, 125

Mean value

$$= \frac{120 + 121 + 122 + 2(123) + 124 + 3(125)}{9}$$

$$= \frac{1108}{9} = 123.1 \text{ to 4 significant figures.}$$

Medium value = middle term = 123

Mode = 125.

WORKED EXAMPLE 92

The average mark obtained by 24 students in an examination were

55, 49, 53, 75, 36, 40, 45, 72, 65, 70, 50, 48, 42, 35, 28, 80, 75, 71, 41, 37, 50, 51, 43, 30.

Determine the mean mark and the median mark.

Solution 92

Placing the marks in rank, we have

28, 30, 35, 36, 37, 40, 41, 42, 43, 45, 48, $\boxed{49, 50,}$ 50, 51, 53, 55, 65, 70, 71, 72, 75, 75, 80.

Mean value $= \bar{x} = \dfrac{1241}{24} = 51.7$ to 3 significant figures.

Median value = arithmetic mean of middle terms

$$= \frac{49 + 50}{2} = 49.5.$$

WORKED EXAMPLE 93

The value of inductance of a sample of coils is determined correct to the nearest mH. The results are shown below:

Inductance mH	Frequency
25	5
26	12
27	15
28	40
30	35
31	20

Determine the mean value of inductance for this sample.

Solution 93

Mean value

$$= \frac{\begin{array}{l} 5 \times 25 + 12 \times 26 + 15 \times 27 \\ + 40 \times 28 + 35 \times 30 + 20 \times 31 \end{array}}{5 + 12 + 15 + 40 + 35 + 20}$$

$$= \frac{3632}{127} = 28.6 \text{ mH} \quad \text{to 3 significant figures.}$$

WORKED EXAMPLE 94

500 students have taken an examination in Mathematics.

The frequency distribution of the examination marks is shown in the table below.

Cumulative frequency table

Marks	Frequency	Marks	Cumulative Frequency
1–10	5	≤ 10	5
11–20	20	≤ 20	25
21–30	30	≤ 30	55
31–40	50	≤ 40	105
41–50	80	≤ 50	185
51–60	100	≤ 60	285
61–70	120	≤ 70	405
71–80	79	≤ 80	484
81–90	10	≤ 90	494
91–100	6	≤ 100	500

Construct the cumulative frequency table and hence draw the cumulative frequency curve for this distribution.

Estimate from your curve

   (i) the number of students who got 40 mark or less

   (ii) the number of students who got more than 70 marks

   (iii) the pass mark, if 150 students must fail the examination

   (iv) the mark that 50 students must be given a grade A.

   (v) the median

   (vi) the lower quartile

   (vii) the upper quartile

(viii) 90th percentile.

Solution 94

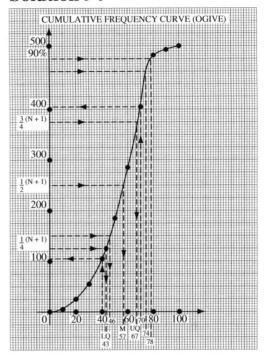

Fig. 68

Answers: (i) 105 (ii) 95 (iii) 46 (iv) 72 (v) 57 (vi) 43 (vii) 67 (viii) 72.

WORKED EXAMPLE 95

The table below shows the frequency distribution of the heights of 450 male students between 16 and 25 years of age.

Frequency distribution	
Heights	Frequency
1.40–1.50 m	50
1.51–1.60 m	90
1.61–1.70 m	140
1.71–1.80 m	90
1.81–1.90 m	70
1.91–2.00 m	10

Cumulative Frequency Distribution	
Heights	Cumulative Frequency
1.40–1.50 m	50
1.51–1.60 m	140
1.61–1.70 m	280
1.71–1.80 m	370
1.81–1.90 m	440
1.91–2.00 m	450

Construct a cumulative frequency table for this frequency distribution. Take the first value as less than 1.50 m.

Draw the cumulative frequency curve (ogive) from the computed cumulative frequency table. Use a scale of 1 cm to represent 5 cm on the height axis and 2 cm to represent 100 students on the cumulative frequency axis.

Use your cumulative frequency curve to estimate
 (i) the median height
 (ii) the lower and upper quartiles
 (iii) the number of students that measure more than 1.75 m
 (iv) the interquartile range and the semi interquartile range.

Solution 95

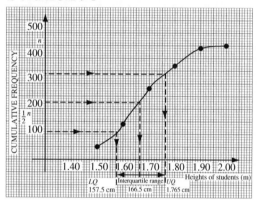

Fig. 69

Exercises 10

1. Find the mean weight of twelve female ballet dancers whose weight are:
 45 kg, 43 kg, 48 kg, 44 kg, 45 kg, 49 kg, 45.5 kg, 46.5 kg, 47 kg, 45 kg, 48.5 kg, 50 kg.

2. Find the median of the weights in the exercise 1.

3. Find the mode of the observations in the exercise 1.

4. A batch of carbon resistors is given:
 1.2 kΩ, 1.15 kΩ, 1.25 kΩ, 1.23 kΩ, 1.18 kΩ, 1.2 kΩ, 1.21 kΩ, 1.19 kΩ, 1.26 kΩ.

 Determine: (i) the mean value (ii) the median (iii) the mode to three significant figures.

5. Determine the arithmetic mean, the median and the mode of the terms given in metres:
 25, 28, 29, 24, 25, 28, 29, 30, 25, 23.

6. The value of resistance of a sample of resistors is determined correct to the nearest 1 Ω. The results are shown below:

Resistance (Ω)	Frequency
470	4
472	17
473	29
474	29
477	41
475	34
476	32

Determine the mean value of resistance for this sample in 3 significant figures.

7. The yield of 105 roots of potatoes had the following masses:

Mass (kg)	Number of roots
0.1–0.9	12
1.0–1.9	18
2.0–2.9	20
3.0–3.9	25
4.0–4.9	15
5.0–5.9	10
6.0–6.9	5

Construct a histogram and hence determine the modal value of the distribution. (3.25 kg).

8. Draw up cumulative frequency distributions shown in the table below:

Resistance Ω	f	Inductance mH	f
325	5	24	10
326	6	25	12
327	8	26	16
328	9	27	18
329	14	28	28
330	20	29	40
331	15	30	30
332	7	31	14
333	4	32	8

Capacitance (μF)	f
10	5
11	7
12	15
13	25
14	40
15	35
16	30
17	28
18	14

9. The values of a batch of resistors were measured and the results noted as follows:

$R(\Omega)$	f
46	9
47	11
48	22
49	31
50	19
51	6
52	2

Draw a histogram and hence determine the modal value and the median value of resistance.

10. Screws were packed in boxes, the nominal number in each box being 150. 100 boxes were checked and the number recorded in the table below:

Number of screws	Frequency
147	3
148	6
149	9
150	14
151	15
152	20
153	18
154	10
155	5

Find the mean of the distribution.

11

Calculates standard deviation of given data

11.1 Describes the concepts of variability of data and the need to measure scatter.

11.2 Define the standard deviation.

11.3 Calculate the standard deviation for ungrouped data.

11.4 Calculate the standard deviation for grouped data with equal intervals.

Dispersion or spread or scatter of data.

The mean, mode and median give some idea about the position of the distribution, the measure of central tendency.

The most important measure of the scatter or spread or dispersion of data is the **range** and **the standard deviation**.

Range is equal to the difference of the largest observation minus the smallest observation

range = maximum observation − minimum observation.

The standard deviation is denoted by the Greek letter σ (sigma) and is defined as the Root Mean Square Deviation.
For ungrouped Data

(a) The arithmetic mean, $\bar{x}$, is calculated using

$$\bar{x} = \frac{x_1 f_1 + x_2 f_2 + x_3 f_3 + \ldots + x_n f_n}{f_1 + f_2 + f_3 + \ldots + f_n} \ldots (1)$$

where x_1, x_2, x_3, ..., x_n are the measured observations which have frequencies f_1, f_2, f_3, ..., f_n respectively. Equation (1) is written more condensely as

$$\bar{x} = \frac{\sum\limits_{r=1}^{r=n} x_r f_r}{\sum\limits_{r=1}^{n} f_r}$$

where $\sum$ means the 'sum of' $x_r f_r$ from $r = 1$ to $r = n$.

(b) the differences of the value of the set of items from $\bar{x}$ (that is, the deviation of each value from the mean are calculated

$(x_1 - \bar{x})$, $(x_2 - \bar{x})$, $(x_3 - \bar{x})$, ..., $(x_n - \bar{x})$

(c) these differences are squared,

$(x_1 - \bar{x})^2$, $(x_2 - \bar{x})^2$, $(x_3 - \bar{x})^2$, ..., $(x_n - \bar{x})^2$

(d) these squared terms are added together

$(x_1 - \bar{x})^2 + (x_2 - \bar{x})^2 + (x_3 - \bar{x})^2 + \ldots + (x_n - \bar{x})^2$

(e) the mean value of the sum of the squared terms

$$\frac{(x_1 - \bar{x})^2 + (x_2 - \bar{x})^2 + (x_3 - \bar{x})^2 + \ldots + (x_n - \bar{x})^2}{n}$$

(f) the square root of the mean value of the sum

of the squares gives σ,

σ = standard deviation

$$\sigma = \sqrt{\frac{\sum_{r=1}^{n}(x_r - \bar{x})^2}{n}}$$

WORKED EXAMPLE 96

Calculate the standard deviation of the set of resistors

12.15 Ω, 12.85 Ω, 12.00 Ω, 12.65 Ω, 12.40 Ω, 12.25 Ω, 12.37 Ω.

Solution 96

$\bar{x}$ = mean value

$$= \frac{12.15 + 12.85 + 12.00 + 12.65 + 12.40 + 12.25 + 12.37}{7}$$

$$= 12.38 \text{ Ω}$$

$(12.15 - 12.38)^2$, $(12.85 - 12.38)^2$, $(12.00 - 12.38)^2$, $(12.65 - 12.38)^2$, $(12.40 - 12.38)^2$, $(12.25 - 12.38)^2$, $(12.37 - 12.38)^2$, the square of difference from mean, 0.0529, 0.2209, 0.1444, 0.0729, 0.0004, 0.0169, 0.0001.

The sum of the differences squared

$0.0529 + 0.2209 + 0.1444 + 0.0729 + 0.0004 + 0.0169 + 0.0001 = 0.5085$.

The Mean value of the squares $= \dfrac{0.5085}{7} = 0.0726$

standard deviation $= \sqrt{0.0726} = \pm 0.2695$.

The range $= 12.85 - 12.65 = 0.20$, this is of the same order as the standard deviation 0.269.

WORKED EXAMPLE 97

Calculate the mean and standard deviation for the following frequency distribution.

resistance (Ω)	frequency
12.15	7
12.85	15
12.00	5
12.65	25
12.40	30
12.25	8

Solution 97

x	f	xf	x^2f
12.00	5	60.00	720
12.15	7	85.05	1033.36
12.25	8	98.00	1200.5
12.40	30	372.00	4612.8
12.65	25	316.25	4000.56
12.85	15	192.75	2476.84

$$\bar{x} = \frac{x_1 f_1 + x_2 f_2 + \dots}{f_1 + f_2 + \dots}$$

$$= \frac{60 + 85.05 + 98.00 + 372 + 316.25 + 192.75}{5 + 7 + 8 + 30 + 25 + 15}$$

$$= \frac{1124.05}{90} = 12.4894.$$

$$\sum x^2 f = 720 + 1033.36 + 1200.5 + 4612.8 + 4000.56 + 2476.84$$

$$= 14044.06$$

$$\sigma = \sqrt{\frac{\sum x^2 f}{\sum f} - \bar{x}^2}$$

$$= \sqrt{\frac{14044.06}{90} - 12.4894^2}$$

$$= \sqrt{156.05 - 155.985} = 0.235.$$

WORKED EXAMPLE 98

Calculate the standard deviation of the set of heights

1.78 m, 1.79 m, 1.78 m, 1.80 m, 1.69 m, 1.85 m, 1.82 m, 1.81 m.

Solution 98

$\bar{x}$ = mean value of height in m.

$$
\begin{aligned}
&= \frac{\begin{array}{c}1.78 + 1.79 + 1.78 + 1.80 \\ + 1.69 + 1.85 + 1.82 + 1.81\end{array}}{8} \\
&= 1.79 \text{ m.}
\end{aligned}
$$

The square of differences from mean are

$(x_1 - \bar{x})^2$, $(x_2 - \bar{x})^2$, $(x_3 - \bar{x})^2$, $(x_4 - \bar{x})^2$, $(x_5 - \bar{x})^2$, $(x_6 - \bar{x})^2$, $(x_7 - \bar{x})^2$, $(x_8 - \bar{x})^2$, respectively $(1.78 - 1.79)^2$, $(1.79 - 1.79)^2$, $(1.78 - 1.79)^2$, $(1.80 - 1.79)^2$, $(1.69 - 1.79)^2$, $(1.85 - 1.79)^2$, $(1.82 - 1.79)^2$, $(1.81 - 1.79)^2$, respectively 0.0001, 0, 0.0001, 0.0001, 0.01, 0.0036, 0.0009, 0.0004.

Therefore the sum of the differences squared is equal to 0.0152.

The mean squares $= \dfrac{0.0152}{8} = 1.9 \times 10^{-3}$.

The standard deviation σ is given

$$
\sigma = \sqrt{1.9 \times 10^{-3}} = \pm 0.0436.
$$

Standard deviation for grouped data

The standard deviation is found in a similar way to the ungrouped data.

The mean value $\bar{x}$ is given

$$
\bar{x} = \frac{\sum(\text{frequence} \times \text{class mid-point values})}{\sum \text{frequency}}
$$

and for the calculation of $(x - \bar{x})$, the x values are the class mid-point values.

The standard deviation, σ is given

$$
\sigma = \sqrt{\frac{\sum[\text{frequency} \times (x - \bar{x})^2]}{\sum \text{frequency}}}
$$

WORKED EXAMPLE 99

The heights of 150 people are measured correct to the nearest cm and the frequency distribution is as shown

Height (cm)	Class mid point	Frequency
155–159	157	10
160–164	162	30
165–169	167	80
170–174	172	20
175–179	177	10

Calculate the mean height and the standard deviation, to one decimal and three decimal places respectively.

Solution 99

Mean height

$$
\bar{x} = \frac{\begin{array}{c}10 \times 157 + 30 \times 162 + 80 \\ \times 167 + 20 \times 172 + 10 \times 177\end{array}}{150} = \frac{25000}{150}
$$

$= 166.7$ cm to one decimal place.

$\bar{x} = 166.7$ cm

Standard deviation

x cm	$x - \bar{x}$ cm	$(x - \bar{x})^2$ cm^2	f	$f(x - \bar{x})^2$ cm^2
157	−9.7	94.09	10	940.9
162	−4.7	22.04	30	662.7
167	0.3	0.09	80	7.2
172	5.3	28.09	20	561.8
177	10.3	106.09	10	1060.9

$$
\sum f(x - \bar{x})^2 = 3233.5
$$

$$
\sigma = \sqrt{\frac{3733.5}{150}} = \pm 4.643 \text{ cm.}
$$

WORKED EXAMPLE 100

The capacitance in microfarads of a sample of 100 similar capacitors drawn from a batch was measured and results are tabulated as shown.

Capacitance (μF)	Class mid point	Frequency
50–54	52.5	10
55–59	57.5	18
60–64	62.5	25
65–69	67.5	22
70–74	72.5	16
75–79	77.5	9

Calculate the mean value of the capacitance and the standard deviation of the sample.

Solution 100

Mean value of capacitance $= \bar{x}$

$$\bar{x} = \frac{\begin{array}{c}10 \times 52.5 + 18 \times 57.5 + 25 \times 62.5 \\ +22 \times 67.5 + 16 \times 72.5 + 9 \times 77.5\end{array}}{100}$$

$$\bar{x} = \frac{6465}{100} = 64.65$$

x	f	fx	$x - \bar{x}$	$f(x - \bar{x})^2$
52.5	10	525	−12.15	1476.2250
57.5	18	1035	−7.15	920.2050
62.5	25	1562.5	−2.15	115.5625
67.5	22	1485	2.85	178.6950
72.5	16	1160	7.85	985.9600
77.5	9	697.5	12.85	1486.1025

$$\sum fx = 6465 \qquad \sum f(x - \bar{x})^2 = 5162.75$$

standard deviation, $\sigma = \sqrt{\dfrac{5162.75}{100}} = \pm 7.185$.

Use the data of example 100, calculate the standard deviation of capacitance to 3 decimal places.

The standard deviation $s = \sqrt{\dfrac{\sum fx^2}{\sum f} - \bar{x}^2}$ must be used. If a is working then $\bar{u} = \bar{x} - a$ and standard deviation of $u =$ standard deviation of x.

Solution 101

x	x^2	f	fx^2
52.5	2756.25	10	27562.5
57.5	3306.25	18	59512.5
62.5	3906.25	25	97656.25
67.5	4556.25	22	100237.50
72.5	5256.25	16	84100
77.5	6006.25	9	54056.25
		$\sum f$	$\sum fx^2$
		$= 100$	$= 423125.00$

$$S = \sqrt{\frac{423125.00}{100} - 64.65^2}$$

$$= \sqrt{4231.2475 - 41796225}$$

$$= \pm 7.185$$

Assignments

Phase test 1

Duration: 1 hour

1. $y = \dfrac{x}{1 + bx}$

   make b the subject of the equation.

   If $x = 100$ and $y = 5$, what is the value of b?

2. $\dfrac{1}{R} = \dfrac{1}{R_1} + \dfrac{1}{R_2}$

   make R_1 the subject of the equation.

   If $R = 100$ and $R_2 = 500$, what is the value of R_1?

3. $f = \dfrac{1}{2\pi \sqrt{LC}}$

   (a) if $L = 5 \times 10^{-3}$, $C = 20 \times 10^{-6}$, what is the value of f?

   (b) if $f = 1,000,000$ and $C = 50 \times 10^{-9}$, what is the value of L?

4. (a) Draw the straight line $\quad 2x + y = 1$

   if $y = 3$ what is x?

   if $x = 2$ what is y?

   (b) Draw the straight line $\quad 5x + 4y = 2$

   if $y = 3$ what is x?

   if $x = 2$ what is y?

   Hence find the intersection of these two straight lines.

   (c) Check your solution by solving the simultaneous equations

   $2x + y = 1 \qquad 5x + 4y = 2$

   algebraically.

Phase test 2

Duration: 1 hour

1. Draw the quadratic

   $y = 2x^2 + x - 6$

   for value of $x = -3, -2, -1, 0, 1, 2$, hence find the two values of x for which $y = 0$.

2. Draw the cubic equation

   $y = x^3 - 2x^2 - 5x + 6$

   for value of $x = -3, -2, -1, 0, 1, 2, 3, 4$,

   hence find the values of x for which $y = 0$.

3. $A_1 = \dfrac{A_2}{1 + \beta A_2}$

   make A_2 the subject of the equation
   if $A_1 = 10$ and $A_2 = 1000$. what is the value of β?

4. $R = \dfrac{R_1 R_2}{R_1 + R_2}$

   make R_2 the subject of the equation.

   If $R = 10$ and $R_1 = 50$, what is the value of R_2?

Phase test 3

Duration: 1 hour

1. If $\sin x = \frac{2}{3}$, find $\tan x$ and $\cos x$ without the use of the calculator. Construct a right angle triangle from the definition of the sine.

2. A circle has radius 5 mm and an arc subtends an angle $\frac{\pi}{3}$.

(a) find the length of arc and the area of the sector

(b) show that the area of a sector is $\frac{1}{2}r^2\theta$ where θ is in radians.

3. A triangle has sides $a = 9$ cm, $b = 7$ cm and the angle $A = 100°$ determine the value of the angle B and the third side c, use the sine rule.

4. The following measurements were noted in a sample:

Diameter (mm)	Frequency
115	4
116	7
117	15
118	20
118	12
120	3

Draw a cumulative frequency graph to represent this distribution, and from your graph determine the median diameter, to 2 decimal places.

Phase test 4

Duration: $1\frac{1}{2}$ hour

1. Convert the following angles to radians
   (a) $20°$ (b) $162.54°$ (c) $321°31'02''$

2. Convert the following radian angles to degrees
   (a) 0.9823 (b) $\frac{13\pi}{5}$ (c) 5.6072

3. An arc AB of a circle of radius 20 cm subtends an angle of $50°$ at the centre of the circle. Find the length of AB correct to 2 decimal places.

4. The area of the sector of a circle of diameter 80 mm is 1250 mm^2. Calculate the value of the angle that the arc of the sector subtends at the centre of the circle in (a) radians (b) degrees.

5. Find the values of θ between $0°$ and $360°$ for which
   (a) $\sin \theta = 0.7312$
   (b) $\cos \theta = -0.3425$
   (c) $\tan \theta = -3.1852$

6. If $\sin A = \frac{4}{5}$ and A is an acute angle use the identity $\cos^2 A + \sin^2 A = 1$ to find the value of $\cos A$ and hence find the value of $\tan A$.

   If also $\cos B = \frac{-5}{13}$ and B is an obtuse angle find the value of $\sin A \cos B - \cos A \sin B$.

7. In the triangle PQR, angle $Q = 50°$, angle $R = 72°$ and $QR = 7.4$ cm. Use the sine rule to solve the triangle.

Phase test 5

Duration: $1\frac{1}{2}$ hour

1. (a) Solve algebraically the simultaneous equations using the elimination and substitution methods
   $$y = 2x + 2$$
   $$3y + x = 20$$ **10 Marks**

   (b) Solve the above simultaneous equations graphically.
                                        10 Marks

2. Make f the subject of the equation
   $$\frac{P}{Q} = \sqrt{\frac{f + x}{f - x}}$$ **10 Marks**

3. Draw the graph of $y = 4x^2 - 3x - 2$
   for values of x $-1, -0.5, 0, 0.5, 1.0, 1.5$
   and hence find the value of x when $y = 1$, check your answer with an algebraic method.
                                        10 Marks

4. (a) A straight line passes through the points $A(2, -4)$ and $B(-3, 5)$, determine the gradient of the line and hence find the equation of the line in the general form.

(b) Sketch the lines

(i) $2y = x$ (ii) $3x - 5y + 1 = 0$

20 Marks

5. Draw the graph $y = x^3 - 4x^2 - x + 4$

for values of x $-2, -1, 0, 1, 2, 3, 4, 5, 6$

Find the values of x when

(i) $y = 30$ (ii) $y = 4$ and $y = -6$

10 Marks

6. (i) Express $x°$ in radians.

(ii) Express y^c in degrees.

(iii) Show that the area of a sector is $A = \frac{1}{2}r^2\theta$.

(iv) Show that the length of an arc subtending and angle Ψ is $r\Psi$ where r is the radius of the circle.

(v) The radius of a circle is $r = 25$ cm and the area of the sector is 30 cm^2, find the angle θ.

20 Marks

7. (a) Sketch (i) $y = 3\sin\theta$ (ii) $y = 2\cos\theta$

(b) Define (i) $\sin x$ (ii) $\cos x$ (iii) $\tan x$

using a right angled triangle.

(c) If the hypotenuse is unity show that $\sin^2 x + \cos^2 x = 1$

10 Marks

Phase test 6

Duration: $1\frac{1}{2}$ hour

1. The volume of a sphere of radius r is given by the formula

$$V = \frac{4}{3}\pi r^3.$$

Make r the subject of this equation and hence find the value of the radius if the volume of a spherical baloon is 100 m^3.

20 Marks

2. (i) Write down the values of the angles in degrees for the following:

(a) $\theta = \frac{\pi}{4}$ (b) $\theta = \frac{\pi}{10}$ (c) $\theta = 1^c$.

(ii) Write down the values of the angles in radians for the following:

(a) $\theta = 35°$ (b) $\theta = 720°$

(c) $\theta = 350°$.

20 Marks

3.

(i) Determine the hatched area

(ii) The length of arc subtending the 30° angle.

20 Marks

4. (a) Sketch the following graphs:

(i) $y = \sin x$ (ii) $y = -\cos x$

(iii) $y = \tan x$.

(b) (i) If $\tan x = \frac{\sin x}{\cos x}$

show that $\tan x = \frac{a}{b}$ by considering the definitions of $\sin x$ and $\cos x$.

(ii) Write down pythagoras theorem for the triangle shown and hence show that $\sin^2 x + \cos^2 x = 1$

20 Marks

5. (i) Find r

(ii) If $\sin x = \dfrac{3}{5}$.

Find $\cos x$ and $\tan x$

(iii) If $C = 2\pi r$,

find the length of arc subtending an angle $\dfrac{\pi}{3}$.

(iv) $f = \sqrt{\dfrac{x-1}{x+2}}$

express x in terms of f.

20 Marks

Phase test 7

Duration $1\frac{1}{2}$ hour

1. A straight line passes through the points $A(-1, -3)$ and $B(5, -7)$, determine the gradient of the straight line.

2. The intercepts of a straight line are -3 on the x-axis and 5 on the y-axis, write down the intercept form of the straight line.

3. Sketch the lines

   (i) $y = 0$ (ii) $x = 0$

  (iii) $y = -x$ (iv) $y = x + 1$

   (v) $y = 3x$.

4. The experimental data on a linear resistor are as follows:

$I(A)$	$V(V)$
0.3	7.5
0.8	3
1	10
2	23
2.8	25
3	35
3.5	40
4	50
4.5	45

Draw a graph of V against I and draw the best fit straight line through the points and find an estimate for the slope.

5. Prove that the points $(0.1, 5)$, $(0.2, 10)$, $(0.3, 15)$ lie in a straight line.

6. Show that the lines are parallel

$$y + x - 1 = 0 \quad 2y = -2x + 9.$$

7. What are the gradients of the lines?

   (i) $y = -3x - 5$ (ii) $3x + y - 7 = 0$

  (iii) $\dfrac{x}{-1} + \dfrac{y}{2} = 1$.

Phase test 8

1. The area of the sector of a circle of radius r, subtended by an angle θ degrees at the centre of the circle is given by

$$A = \frac{\pi r^2 \theta}{360}.$$

(a) If the radius of the circle is 2 cm and the angle $\theta = 73°12'$, assuming $\pi = 3.1416$, calculate a value for A to 2 decimal places.

(b) Rearrange the expression to make r the subject of the formula.

2. The data shows the force F newtons which, when applied to a lifting machine, overcomes a corresponding load of L newtons.

F newtons	L newtons
19	40
35	120
50	230
93	410
125	540
147	680

Verify that the equation relating F and L is of the form $F = kL + c$ by plotting a graph of F (y-axis) against L (x-axis) and determine the value of k and c. State the law.

Assuming the law to be valid outside the range given, find the force necessary to lift a load of 1000 N.

3. Sketch a graph of $\cos\theta$ against θ between $0°$ and $360°$ stating the maximum and minimum values of $\cos\theta$.

State all the values of θ, to the nearest degree, between $0°$ and $360°$ that satisfy the equation $\cos\theta = -0.342$.

4. State the sine rule.

Use the sine rule to find a, $\hat{A}$ and $\hat{C}$ in triangle ABC given that

$\hat{B} = 83°16'$,

$b = 16.48$ mm, and

$c = 12.92$ mm.

5. In a series of tests the distance to take-off for a number of aircraft of the same type with equal loads was measured to the nearest five metres. Calculate the mean distance to take-off to the nearest metre.

Distance to take-off (m)	No. of aircraft
240	2
245	1
250	5
255	8
260	7
265	3
270	5
275	2
280	1

Phase test 9

1. Given the relationship

$$A = \frac{V}{100}\left[Q - \frac{mV^2}{g}\right]$$

determine a value for A, to 3 decimal places, given $Q = 50.28$, $m = 17$, $V = 5.0$ and $g = 9.81$

2. Draw on the same axes graphs of $3y - 2x = 0$ and $4y = -x - 11$.

From the graphs, determine the solution of the pair of simultaneous equations $3y - 2x = 0$ and $4y = -x - 11$.

(Consider equations over range $x = -4$ to $x = +4$).

3. Make a free-hand sketch of the graph of $\sin\theta$ against θ between $0°$ and $720°$.

State

(i) the maximum and minimum values of $\sin\theta$

(ii) the period of the sine function.

4. For a triangle ABC in which $A = 37°$, $B = 73°$ and $b = 4.30$ m, state the Sine Rule and use it to calculate values of a and c.

5. The heights of a group of children were measured to the nearest centimetre and the results were as follows:

Height (cm)	Frequency
158	10
159	14
160	16
161	23
162	27
163	18
164	7
165	2

Find the mean height of the children, correct to 2 decimal places.

Phase test 10

1. Given the formula

   $C = 2\sqrt{2rh - h^2}$

   evaluate C correct to 2 decimal places if $r = 1.87$ m and $h = 2.09$ m.

2. Draw on the same axes the graphs of $y = x^2 + 3x + 4$,

   for values of x from -5 to $+2$, and $y = 4 - x$.

   Hence determine the values of x and y which satisfy the pair of equations $y = x^2 + 3x + 4$ and $y = 4 - x$.

3. Make a free-hand sketch of the graph of $\cos\theta$ against θ for θ between $0°$ and $720°$.

   State

   (i) the maximum and minimum values of $\cos\theta$

   (ii) the period of the cosine function.

4. For a triangle ABC in which $b = 63.7$ cm, $c = 29.6$ cm and $C = 27°22'$, state the Sine Rule and use it to find the two possible values of B.

5. Screws were packed in boxes, the nominal number in each box being 150. 100 boxes were checked and the numbers recorded in the table below:

Number of screws	Frequency
147	3
148	6
149	9
150	14
151	15
152	20
153	18
154	10
155	5

Find the mean of the distribution.

Phase test 11

1. In the formula $\dfrac{1}{R} = \dfrac{1}{R_1} + \dfrac{1}{R_2} + \dfrac{1}{R_3}$

   make R_1 the subject

2. If $Z = \sqrt{R^2 + \left(\dfrac{1}{\omega c}\right)^2}$ express ω in terms of Z, R and C.

   Calculate the value of ω when $Z = 1300$, $R = 500$ and $C = 2.3148 \times 10^{-12}$.

3. Two D.I.Y. companies make the following charges for delivery of their goods.

   Company A £40 and 20p per mile.

   Company B £35 and 30p per mile.

   (i) Show this information graphically by drawing two straight lines on the same axes of Total cost, C, against distance, d.

   (ii) From your graph determine the distance for which the total cost is the same for each company.

   (iii) For company B determines the cost – distance equation in the form $C = ad + b$ and hence calculate the distance for which a delivery charge of £50 is made.

4. (i) Complete the following table of values for the quadratic function

   $y = 2x^2 + 5x - 4$

x	$2x^2$	$+5x$	-4	$y = 2x^2$ $+5x - 4$
-5	50	-25	-4	21
-4		-20	-4	
-3	18	-15	-4	-1
-2	8	-10	-4	-6
-1	2	-5	-4	-7
0			-4	
1	2		-4	
2	8	10	-4	14

(ii) Plot the graph of the function in (i) and hence determine the values of x, which are the solutions of the equation $2x^2 + 5x - 4 = 0,$ to 2 decimal places.

(iii) On the same axes draw the line whose equation is $x - 2y + 2 = 0$. Hence find the solutions of the equations

$$y = 2x^2 + 5x - 4$$

and

$$x - 2y + 2 = 0$$

5. Plot the graph of $y = 5x^3 - 9x^2 + 3x + 1$ from $x = -0.4$ to $x = 1.4$ at intervals of 0.2 units, and hence find the values of the roots of the equation

$$5x^3 - 9x^2 + 3x + 1 = 0.$$

First Mathematics and Mathematics II Solutions 1

1.   (i) $16 = 2^1 \times 2^1 \times 2^1 \times 2^1 = 2^4$

   (ii) $32 = 2^1 \times 2^1 \times 2^1 \times 2^1 \times 2^1 = 2^5$

  (iii) $64 = 2^1 \times 2^1 \times 2^1 \times 2^1 \times 2^1 \times 2^1 = 2^6$

  (iv) $4 = 2^1 \times 2^1 = 2^2$

  (v) $2 = 2^1$

  (vi) $128 = 64 \times 2 = 2^6 \times 2^1 = 2^7$

  (vii) $8 = 2^1 \times 2^1 \times 2^1 = 2^3$

  (viii) $256 = 128 \times 2 = 2^7 \times 2^1 = 2^8$

  (ix) $512 = 2^8 \times 2^1 = 2^9$

  (x) $1024 = 512 \times 2 = 2^9 \times 2^1 = 2^{10}$

  (xi) $1 = 2^0$.

Any number raised to nought or zero is unity $2^0 = 1$.

2.   (i) $81 = 3^1 \times 3^1 \times 3^1 \times 3^1 = 3^4$

  (ii) $243 = 3^1 \times 3^1 \times 3^1 \times 3^1 \times 3^1 = 3^5$

  (iii) $3 = 3^1$

  (iv) $9 = 3^1 \times 3^1 = 3^2$

  (v) $729 = 243 \times 3 = 3^5 \times 3^1 = 3^6$

  (vi) $27 = 3^1 \times 3^1 \times 3^1 = 3^3$

  (vii) $1 = 3^0$

  (viii) $2187 = 729 \times 3 = 3^7$.

3.   (i) $125 = 5^1 \times 5^1 \times 5^1 = 5^3$

  (ii) $625 = 25 \times 25 = 5^1 \times 5^1 \times 5^1 \times 5^1$
$= 5^4$

  (iii) $5 = 5^1$

  (iv) $25 = 5^1 \times 5^1 = 5^2$

  (v) $1 = 5^0$

  (vi) $3125 = 625 \times 5 = 5^4 \times 5^1 = 5^5$.

4.   (a) $3, 25, 37, +125, 729$

  (b) $-5, -32, -49, -7, -295$.

5.   (i) $2^6 = 2 \times 2 \times 2 \times 2 \times 2 \times 2 = 8 \times 8 = 64$

  (ii) $3^4 = 3 \times 3 \times 3 \times 3 = 9 \times 9 = 81$

  (iii) $4^4 = 4 \times 4 \times 4 \times 4 = 16 \times 16 = 256$

  (iv) $5^3 = 5 \times 5 \times 5 = 125$

  (v) $7^3 = 7 \times 7 \times 7 = 49 \times 7 = 343$

  (vi) $10^5 = 100,000$.

6.   (a)   (i) 3^7 the base is 3 and the index is 7

       (ii) 27^3 the base is 27 and the index is 3

      (iii) 375^3 the base is 375 and the index is 3

      (iv) 99^3 the base is 99 and the index is 3

      (v) 101^{35} the base is 101 and the index is 35.

7.   (a) $2^1 \times 2^2 \times 2^3 \times 2^4 = 2^{1+2+3+4} = 2^{10}$

  (b) $\dfrac{2^1 \times 2^3 \times 3^4 \times 3^5}{2^5 \times 3^6} = \dfrac{2^{1+3} \times 3^{4+5}}{2^5 \times 3^6}$

$= \dfrac{2^4 \times 3^9}{2^5 \times 3^6} = \dfrac{3^3}{2^1}$

  (c) $3^3 \times 3^2 \times 3^1 \times 3^0 = 3^{3+2+1+0} = 3^6$

  (d) $\dfrac{5 \times 5^3 \times 5^5}{5^4} = \dfrac{5^{1+3+5}}{5^4} = \dfrac{5^9}{5^4}$

$= 5^5$ (see next lesson)

79

(e) $\dfrac{2 \times 3^2 \times 4 \times 5^2}{2^3 \times 3 \times 5}$

$= \dfrac{2^1 \times 2^2 \times 3^2 \times 5^2}{2^3 \times 3^1 \times 5^1}$

$= \dfrac{2^3 \times 3^2 \times 5^2}{2^3 \times 3^1 \times 5^1}$

$= 3 \times 5 = 15$ (see next lesson)

8.   (a) $3^5 \times 3^3 \times 3^7 \times 3^9 = 3^{5+3+7+9}$

$= 3^{24}$

(b) $2^2 \times 2^5 \times 2^7 = 2^{2+5+7}$

$= 2^{14}$

(c) $\dfrac{2^{14}}{3^{24}}$.

Solutions 2

1. (i) the reciprocal of 2 is $\dfrac{1}{2}$

   (ii) the reciprocal of 25 is $\dfrac{1}{25}$

   (iii) the reciprocal of 7 is $\dfrac{1}{7}$

   (iv) the reciprocal of 35 is $\dfrac{1}{35}$

   (v) the reciprocal of 5 is $\dfrac{1}{5}$

   (vi) the reciprocal of 47 is $\dfrac{1}{47}$

   (vii) the reciprocal of 52 is $\dfrac{1}{52}$

   (viii) the reciprocal of 8 is $\dfrac{1}{8}$

   (ix) the reciprocal of 77 is $\dfrac{1}{77}$

   (x) the reciprocal of 10 is $\dfrac{1}{10}$.

2. (i) $x^{-1} = \dfrac{1}{x}$

   (ii) $y^{-1} = \dfrac{1}{y}$

   (iii) $z^{-1} = \dfrac{1}{z}$

   (iv) $(xy)^{-1} = \dfrac{1}{xy}$

   (v) $(xyz)^{-1} = \dfrac{1}{xyz}$.

3. (i) x^{-1} means $\dfrac{1}{x}$ is the reciprocal of x

   (ii) y^{-2} means $\dfrac{1}{y^2}$ is the reciprocal of y^2

   (iii) 3^{-5} means $\dfrac{1}{3^5}$ is the reciprocal of 3^5

   (iv) z^{-3} means $\dfrac{1}{z^3}$ is the reciprocal of z^3

   (v) $(xy)^{-2}$ means $\dfrac{1}{(xy)^2} = \dfrac{1}{x^2y^2}$ is the reciprocal of x^2y^2

   (vi) $(xyz)^{-1}$ means $\dfrac{1}{(xyz)^1}$ is the reciprocal of xyz.

4. (i) $x^{-3} = \dfrac{1}{x^3}$

   (ii) $3^{-5} = \dfrac{1}{3^5}$

   (iii) $\dfrac{1}{2^{-4}} = 2^4$

   (iv) $\dfrac{2^5}{2^{-5}} = 2^5 2^5 = 2^{10}$

   (v) $x^{-n} = \dfrac{1}{x^n}$

5. (i) $x = \dfrac{1}{x^{-1}}$

   (ii) $xy = \dfrac{1}{(xy)^{-1}} = \dfrac{1}{x^{-1}y^{-1}}$

   (iii) $3^5 = \dfrac{1}{3^{-5}}$

   (iv) $2^7 = \dfrac{1}{2^{-7}}$

   (v) $3^4 = \dfrac{1}{3^{-4}}$.

6. (i) $\dfrac{2^3 x^4 y^3}{8xy} = 2^3 \times 2^{-3} x^4 x^{-1} y^3 y^{-1}$
$$= x^3 y^2$$

(ii) $\dfrac{a^2b^2c^2}{4b^4c} = \dfrac{1}{4}a^2b^2b^{-4}c^2c^{-1}$

$\qquad = \dfrac{1}{4}a^2b^{-2}c^1 = \dfrac{1}{4}\dfrac{a^2c}{b^2}$

(iii) $\dfrac{x^2y^3z^4}{xyz^2} = x^2x^{-1}y^3y^{-1}z^4z^{-2}$

$\qquad = x^{2-1}y^{3-1}z^{4-2} = x^1y^2z^2.$

7.   (i) $(2^2)^2 = 2^4$

     (ii) $(3^3)^3 = 3^9$

     (iii) $3^{(-3)(-4)} = 3^{12}$

     (iv) $(5^2)^{-5} = 5^{-10}$

8.   (i) $7^5 \div 7^{-4} = \dfrac{7^5}{7^{-4}} = 7^57^4 = 7^9$

     (ii) $5^{-2} \div 5^2 = \dfrac{5^{-2}}{5^2} = 5^{-2}5^{-2}$

$\qquad\qquad = 5^{-4} = \dfrac{1}{5^4}$

     (iii) $5^3 \div 5^3 = \dfrac{5^3}{5^3} = 5^35^{-3}$

$\qquad\qquad = 5^{3-3} = 5^0 = 1.$

9.   (i) $5^{-1} = \dfrac{1}{5}$

     (ii) $10^{-3} = \dfrac{1}{10^3} = \dfrac{1}{1000}$

     (iii) $7^{-2} = \dfrac{1}{7^2} = \dfrac{1}{49}$

     (iv) $13^{-2} = \dfrac{1}{13^2} = \dfrac{1}{169}$

     (v) $16^{-2} = \dfrac{1}{16^2} = \dfrac{1}{256}.$

10.   (a) $(2^35^2x^2)^2 = 2^65^4x^4$

     (b) $(3^43^{-2}y)^{-3} = 3^{-12}3^{(-2)(-3)}y^{(1)(-3)}$

$\qquad\qquad = 3^{-12}3^{+6}y^{-3}$

$\qquad\qquad = 3^{-12+6}y^{-3}$

$\qquad\qquad = 3^{-6}y^{-3} = \dfrac{1}{3^6y^3}.$

11.   (i) $2^n = 256 = 2^8$

$\qquad 2^n = 2^8 \quad \boxed{n = 8}$

     (ii) $2^n = 2^1 \quad \boxed{n = 1}$

     (iii) $2^n = 8 \quad 2^n = 2^3 \quad \boxed{n = 3}$

     (iv) $2^n = \dfrac{1}{8} = \dfrac{1}{2^3} = 2^{-3}$

$\qquad 2^n = 2^{-3} \quad \boxed{n = -3}$

     (v) $2^n = \dfrac{1}{64} = \dfrac{1}{2^6} = 2^{-6}$

$\qquad 2^n = 2^{-6} \quad \boxed{n = -6}$

     (vi) $2^n = 4 \quad 2^n = 2^2 \quad \boxed{n = 2}$

     (vii) $2^n = 2^7 = 128 \quad n = 7 \quad \boxed{n = 7}$

     (viii) $2^n = \dfrac{1}{2} \quad 2^n = 2^{-1}$

$\qquad 2^n = 2^{-1} \quad \boxed{n = -1}$

     (ix) $2^{-n} = \dfrac{1}{4} \quad 2^{-n} = \dfrac{1}{2^2} = 2^{-2}$

$\qquad 2^{-n} = 2^{-2} \quad -n = -2 \Rightarrow \boxed{n = 2}$

     (x) $2^{-n} = 2^5 \quad -n = 5 \quad \boxed{n = -5}$

     (xi) $2^{-n} = 2^6 \quad \boxed{n = -6}$

     (xii) $2^{-n} = \dfrac{1}{128} = \dfrac{1}{2^7} = 2^{-7}$

$\qquad -n = -7 \Rightarrow \boxed{n = 7}$

12.   (i) $3^{-n} = \dfrac{1}{3} = 3^{-1}$

$\qquad -n = -1 \quad \boxed{n = 1}$

     (ii) $3^{-n} = \dfrac{1}{9} = \dfrac{1}{3^2} = 3^{-2}$

$\qquad 3^{-n} = 3^{-2} \quad -n = -2 \quad \boxed{n = 2}$

     (iii) $3^{-n} = \dfrac{1}{27} = \dfrac{1}{3^3} = 3^{-3}$

$\qquad -n = -3 \Rightarrow \boxed{n = 3}$

     (iv) $3^n = 243 = 3^5 \quad \boxed{n = 5}$

     (v) $3^{-n} = \dfrac{1}{2187} = \dfrac{1}{3^7} = 3^{-7}$

$\qquad -n = -7 \Rightarrow \boxed{n = 7}$

(vi) $3^{-n} = 9^{-2} = (3^2)^{-2} = 3^{-4}$

$\boxed{-n = -4}$ or $n = 4$

(vii) $3^n = 9 = 3^2$ $\boxed{n = 2}$

(viii) $3^{-n} = \dfrac{1}{81}$ $-n = -4$ $\boxed{n = 4}$

(ix) $3^n = 1 = 3^0$ $\boxed{n = 0}$

(x) $3^n = \dfrac{1}{27} = 3^{-3}$ $\boxed{n = -3}$

(xi) $3^n = 3^1$ $\boxed{n = 1}$

(xii) $3^{-n} = 3^3$ $\boxed{n = -3}$

13.　(i) $5^x = 1 = 5^0$ $\boxed{x = 0}$

(ii) $5^{-x} = \dfrac{1}{125} = \dfrac{1}{5^3} = 5^{-3}$

$-x = -3$ $\boxed{x = 3}$

(iii) $5^x = 5^1$ $\boxed{x = 1}$

(iv) $5^x = 125 = 5^3$ $\boxed{x = 3}$

(v) $5^x = 625 = 5^4$ $\boxed{x = 4}$

(vi) $5^x = \dfrac{1}{125} = \dfrac{1}{5^3} = 5^{-3}$

$\boxed{x = -3}$

(vii) $5^x = 3125 = 5^5$ $\boxed{x = 5}$

(viii) $5^x = 25 = 5^2$ $\boxed{x = 2}$

(ix) $5^x = 25^{-5} = (5^2)^{-5} = 5^{-10}$

$5^x = 5^{-10}$ $\boxed{x = -10}$

(x) $5^{-3x} = 5^{-1}$

$-3x = -1 \Rightarrow$ $\boxed{x = \dfrac{1}{3}}$.

Solutions 3

1.   (i) $23 = 2.3 \times 10^1$

    (ii) $123 = 1.23 \times 10^2$

    (iii) $2,354 = 2.354 \times 10^3$

    (iv) $25,399 = 2.540 \times 10^4$

    (v) $27,920,000 = 2.792 \times 10^7$

    (vi) $0.1 = 1.0 \times 10^{-1}$

    (vii) $0.0025 = 2.500 \times 10^{-3}$

    (viii) $0.000035 = 3.500 \times 10^{-5}$

    (ix) $0.0000000099 = 9.900 \times 10^{-9}$

    (x) $0.00003503 = 3.503 \times 10^{-5}$.

2.   (i)   95,000   (five significant figures)

    (ii)   675,300   (six significant figures)

    (iii)   0.0039   (two significant figures)

    (iv)   37.3   (three significant figures)

    (v)   390,005   (six significant figures).

3.   (i) $l = 35.35$ mm $b = 21.9$ mm

    Area of rectangle $= l \times b = 35.35 \times 21.9 = 774$ mm^2 to three significant figures

    (ii) $l = 39.99$ cm $b = 25.0$ cm

    Area of rectangle $= l \times b = 39.99 \times 25.0 = 999.8$ cm^2 to four significant figures

4. (i) 26.0   (ii) 0.000 36   (iii) 25,900

5.   (i) 7.78×10^4 (ii) 2.90×10^4

    (iii) 2.60×10^1 (iv) 3.57×10^{-3}

    (v) 9.57×10^3

6.   (i) 17,500   (ii) 9.54×10^{-7}

    (ii) 3.28×10^{14}.

7.   (i) $395.300 \times 10^{-5} + 29.65 \times 10^{-4}$

$$= 39.53 \times 10^{-4} + 29.65 \times 10^{-4}$$

$$= 69.18 \times 10^{-4} = 6.92 \times 10^{-3}$$

    to three significant figures

    (ii) $1.234 \times 10^{-9} + 37.95 \times 10^{-8}$

$$= 1.234 \times 10^{-9} + 379.5 \times 10^{-9}$$

$$= 380.734 \times 10^{-9}$$

$$= 3.81 \times 10^{-7}$$

    to three significant figures

    (iii) $259.35 - 36.39$

$$= 2.5935 \times 10^2 - 0.3639 \times 10^2$$

$$= 2.2296 \times 10^2 = 2.23 \times 10^2$$

    (iv) $\dfrac{25.99 \times 10^{-5}}{3.75 \times 10^{-4}} = 6.93 \times 10^{-5} \times 10^4$

$$= 6.93 \times 10^{-1}.$$

8. $256.95 = a^2$ where a is the side of the square plate

    $a = 16.03$ mm $a = 16.0$ mm.

Solutions 4

A.

1. $\log_2\left(\dfrac{1}{8}\right) = x,$

   $2^x = \dfrac{1}{8} = 2^{-3}, \quad x = -3$

2. $\log_2\left(\dfrac{1}{16}\right) = x,$

   $2^x = \dfrac{1}{16} = \dfrac{1}{2^4} = 2^{-4}, \quad x = -4$

3. $\log_3\left(\dfrac{1}{27}\right) = x,$

   $3^x = \dfrac{1}{27} = \dfrac{1}{3^3} = 3^{-3}, \quad x = -3$

4. $\log_3\left(\dfrac{1}{81}\right) = x,$

   $3^x = \dfrac{1}{81} = \dfrac{1}{3^4} = 3^{-4}, \quad x = -4$

5. $\log_4\left(\dfrac{1}{64}\right) = x,$

   $4^x = \dfrac{1}{64} = \dfrac{1}{4^3} = 4^{-3}, \quad x = -3$

6. $\log_2\left(\dfrac{1}{32}\right) = x,$

   $2^x = \dfrac{1}{32} = \dfrac{1}{2^5} = 2^{-5}, \quad x = -5$

7. $\log_{\frac{1}{2}} 2 = x,$

   $\left(\dfrac{1}{2}\right)^x = 2, (2^{-1})^x = 2^1,$

   $2^{-x} = 2^1, x = -1$

8. $\log_{\frac{1}{2}} 4 = x,$

   $\left(\dfrac{1}{2}\right)^x = 4 = 2^2, 2^{-x} = 2^2, x = -2$

9. $\log_3 27 = x, 3^x = 27 = 3^3, x = 3$

10. $\log_3 9 = x, \quad 3^x = 9 = 3^2, x = 2$

11. $\log_3 81 = x, \quad 3^x = 3^4, x = 4$

12. $\log_{\frac{1}{3}} 81 = x,$

    $\left(\dfrac{1}{3}\right)^x = 81 = 3^4, 3^{-x} = 3^4, x = -4$

13. $\log_{\frac{1}{3}} 27 = x,$

    $\left(\dfrac{1}{3}\right)^x = 27 = 3^3, 3^{-x} = 3^3, x = -3$

14. $\log_{\frac{1}{3}} 9 = x,$

    $\left(\dfrac{1}{3}\right)^x = 9 = 3^2, 3^{-x} = 3^2, x = -2$

15. $\log_{10} 10 = x, \quad 10^x = 10^1, x = 1$

16. $\log_{10} 100 = x,$

    $10^x = 100 = 10^2, x = 2$

17. $\log_{\frac{1}{5}} 25 = x,$

    $\left(\dfrac{1}{5}\right)^x = 25, 5^{-x} = 5^2, x = -2$

18. $\log_{\frac{1}{5}} 125 = x,$

    $\left(\dfrac{1}{5}\right)^x = 125 = 5^3, 5^{-x} = 5^3, x = -3$

19. $\log_3 3 = x, \quad 3^x = 3^1, x = 1$

20. $\log_{\frac{1}{3}} 9 = x,$

    $\left(\dfrac{1}{3}\right)^x = 9 = 3^2, 3^{-x} = 3^2, x = -2$

21. $\log_{\frac{1}{3}} 27 = x,$

    $\left(\dfrac{1}{3}\right)^x = 27 = 3^3, 3^{-x} = 3^3, x = -3$

22. $\log_{27} 3 = x, 27^x = 3^1, 3^{3x} = 3^1, x = \dfrac{1}{3}$

23. $\log_{27} 9 = x$,

$$27^x = 9, 3^{3x} = 3^2, x = \frac{2}{3}.$$

B.

24. $\log_{\frac{1}{4}} 16 = x$,

$$\left(\frac{1}{4}\right)^x = 16 = 4^2, 4^{-x} = 4^2, x = -2$$

25. $\log_{\frac{1}{3}} \left(\frac{1}{27}\right) = x$,

$$\left(\frac{1}{3}\right)^x = \frac{1}{27}, 3^{-x} = \frac{1}{3^3} = 3^{-3}, x = 3$$

26. $\log_{\frac{1}{3}} \left(\frac{1}{9}\right) = x$,

$$\left(\frac{1}{3}\right)^x = \frac{1}{9} = \frac{1}{3^2} = 3^{-2}, 3^{-x} = 3^{-2},$$
$$x = 2$$

27. $\log_9 3 = x$, $\quad 9^x = 3, 3^{2x} = 3^1, x = \frac{1}{2}$

28. $\log_9 9 = x$, $\quad 9^x = 9^1, x = 1$

29. $\log_9 27 = x$,

$$9^x = 27, 3^{2x} = 3^3, x = \frac{3}{2}$$

30. $\log_9 81 = x$, $\quad 9^x = 81 = 9^2, x = 2$

31. $\log_{10} 1000 = x$, $10^x = 1000 = 10^3, x = 3$

32. $\log_{10} 0.1 = x$,

$$10^x = 0.1 = \frac{1}{10} = 10^{-1}, x = -1$$

33. $\log_{10} 0.01 = x$,

$$10^x = 0.01 = \frac{1}{100} = 10^{-2}, x = -2$$

34. $\log_{10} 0.001 = x, 10^x = 0.001 = 10^{-3}$,
$x = -3$

35. $\log_5 = 25x$, $\quad 25^x = 25^1, x = 1$

36. $\log_{25} 25 = x$, $\quad 25^x = 25^1, x = 3$

37. $\log_5 125 = x$, $\quad 5^x = 125 = 5^3, x = 3$

C.

1. $10^1 = x, x = 10$

2. $\log_3 x = 2, x = 3^2 = 9$

3. $\log_5 x = 3, x = 5^3 = 125$

4. $\log_{\frac{1}{7}} x = 1, \left(\frac{1}{7}\right)^1 = x$

5. $\log_{\frac{1}{9}} x = 2, \left(\frac{1}{9}\right)^2 = x = \frac{1}{81}$

6. $\log_3 x = -5, \quad 3^{-5} = x = \frac{1}{243}$

7. $\log_{\frac{1}{3}} x = -1, \left(\frac{1}{3}\right)^{-1} = x, x = 3$

8. $\log_{\frac{1}{27}} x = -3$,

$$\left(\frac{1}{27}\right)^{-3} = x = \left(\frac{1}{3^3}\right)^{-3}$$
$$= (3^{-3})^{-3} = 3^9$$

9. $\log_{10} x = -5, 10^{-5} = x$

10. $\log_7 x = 3, 7^3 = x$

11. $\log_3 x = -3, 3^{-3} = x = \left(\frac{1}{3^3}\right) = \frac{1}{27}$

12. $\log_2 x = -1, 2^{-1} = x = \frac{1}{2}$

13. $\log_x 10 = 1, x^1 = 10, x = 10$

14. $\log_x 0.001 = 3$,

$$x^3 = 0.001 = 10^{-3}, x = \frac{1}{10}$$

15. $\log_x 27 = 3, x^3 = 27 = 3^3, x = 3$

16. $\log_x 343 = 3$,

$$x^3 = 343 \Rightarrow x = 343^{\frac{1}{3}} = 7$$

17. $\log_x \frac{1}{10,000} = 4$,

$$x^4 = \frac{1}{10,000} = \frac{1}{10^4} = 10^{-4}, x = \frac{1}{10}$$

18. $\log_x 8 = \frac{1}{2}, \quad x^{\frac{1}{2}} = 8, x = 64$

19. $\log_x 4 = 64, x^{64} = 4, x = 4^{\frac{1}{64}} = 2^{\frac{1}{32}}$

20. $\log_x 3 = 1, x^1 = 3$.

Mathematics II
Solutions 5

1. $T = 2\pi \sqrt{\dfrac{l}{g}}$

   squaring up both sides

   $T^2 = 4\pi^2 \left(\dfrac{l}{g} \right)$

   cross multiplying

   $T^2 g = 4\pi^2 l \quad 4\pi^2 l = T^2 g$

   dividing by $4\pi^2$ both sides

   $\dfrac{4\pi^2 l}{4\pi^2} = \dfrac{T^2 g}{4\pi^2} \quad l = \dfrac{T^2 g}{4\pi^2}$

2. $A = \pi r^2 \quad \pi r^2 = A$

   dividing by π both sides

   $\dfrac{\pi r^2}{\pi} = \dfrac{A}{\pi} \quad r^2 = \dfrac{A}{\pi}$

   square rooting both sides

   $r = \sqrt{\dfrac{A}{\pi}}$

3. $V = \dfrac{4}{3}\pi r^3$

   cross multiplying

   $3V = 4\pi r^3$

   dividing both sides by 4π

   $\dfrac{3V}{4\pi} = r^3 \quad r^3 = \dfrac{3V}{4\pi}$

   cube rooting both sides

   $r = \sqrt[3]{\dfrac{3V}{4\pi}}$

4. $S = \pi rl + \pi r^2 \quad S - \pi r^2 = \pi rl$

   $\pi rl = S - \pi r^2$

   dividing both sides by πr

   $\dfrac{\pi rl}{\pi r} = \dfrac{S - \pi r^2}{\pi r}$

$l = \dfrac{S - \pi r^2}{\pi r} = \dfrac{S}{\pi r} - \dfrac{\pi r^2}{\pi r}$

$l = \dfrac{S}{\pi r} - r$

5. $S = 4\pi r^2 \quad 4\pi r^2 = S$

   dividing both sides by 4π

   $\dfrac{4\pi r^2}{4\pi} = \dfrac{S}{4\pi} \quad r^2 = \dfrac{S}{4\pi}$

   square rooting both sides

   $r = \sqrt{\dfrac{S}{4\pi}}.$

6. $I = \dfrac{V}{r + R}$

   cross multiplying

   $I(r + R) = V \text{ or } V = I(r + R).$

7. $s = r\theta \quad r\theta = s \quad \theta = \dfrac{s}{r}.$

8. $A = \dfrac{1}{2}r^2 \theta$

   cross multiplying

   $2A = r^2 \theta \quad r^2 = \dfrac{2A}{\theta} \quad r = \sqrt{\dfrac{2A}{\theta}}$

9. $A = \dfrac{1}{2}r^2 \sin \alpha$

   $2A = r^2 \sin \alpha \quad \sin \alpha = \dfrac{2A}{r^2}$

10. $A = \dfrac{1}{2}r^2 \theta - \dfrac{1}{2}r^2 \sin \theta$

    $2A = r^2 \theta - r^2 \sin \theta$

    $\quad = r^2(\theta - \sin \theta)$

    $r^2 = \dfrac{2A}{\theta - \sin \theta} \quad r = \sqrt{\dfrac{2A}{\theta - \sin \theta}}$

11. $F = mg \quad mg = F \quad g = \dfrac{F}{m}$

12. $v = u + at \quad u + at = v$

$at = v - u \quad t = \dfrac{v - u}{a}$

13. $v^2 = u^2 + 2as \quad v^2 - u^2 = 2as$

$2as = v^2 - u^2 \quad s = \dfrac{v^2 - u^2}{2a}$

14. $A_f = \dfrac{A}{1 + \beta A} \qquad A_f(1 + \beta A) = A$

$A_f + A_f \beta A = A \quad A_f = A - A_f \beta A$

$A - A_f \beta A = A_f \quad A(1 - A_f \beta) = A_f$

$A = \dfrac{A_f}{1 - A_f \beta}$

15. $A_v = \dfrac{-\mu R_L}{r_{ds} + R_L}$

$A_v(r_{ds} + R_L) = -\mu R_L$

$A_v r_{ds} + A_v R_L = -\mu R_L$

$A_v r_{ds} = -\mu R_L - A_v R_L$

$\qquad = -R_L(\mu + A_v)$

$R_L = \dfrac{-A_v r_{ds}}{\mu + A_v}$

16. $A_v = \dfrac{-h_{fe} R_L}{h_{ie}} \quad$ for h_{ie}

$hie = \dfrac{-h_{fe} R_L}{A_v}$

17. $r = \sqrt{\dfrac{2A}{\theta}} \quad r^2 = \dfrac{2A}{\theta} \quad \theta = \dfrac{2A}{r^2}$

18. $R_L = \dfrac{-A_v hie}{h_{fe}} \quad A_v = \dfrac{-R_L h_{fe}}{hie}$

19. $R_L = \dfrac{-r_{ds} A_v}{\mu + A_v}$

$R_L(\mu + A_v) = -r_{ds} A_v$

$R_L \mu + A_v R_L = -r_{ds} A_v$

$A_v(R_L + r_{ds}) = -\mu R_L$

$A_v = \dfrac{-\mu R_L}{R_L + r_{ds}}$

20. $s = \dfrac{v^2 - u^2}{2a} \quad 2as = v^2 - u^2$

$u^2 = v^2 - 2as \quad u = \sqrt{v^2 - 2as}$

21. $\theta = \dfrac{2A}{r^2} + \sin\theta \quad \theta - \sin\theta = \dfrac{2A}{r^2}$

$r^2 = \dfrac{2A}{\theta - \sin\theta} \quad r = \sqrt{\dfrac{2A}{\theta - \sin\theta}}$

22. $l = \dfrac{gT^2}{4\pi^2} \quad gT^2 = l4\pi^2$

$T^2 = \dfrac{l4\pi^2}{g} \quad T = \sqrt{4\pi^2 \dfrac{l}{g}} = 2\pi\sqrt{\dfrac{l}{g}}$

23. $r = \sqrt{\dfrac{A}{\pi}} \quad r^2 = \dfrac{A}{\pi} \quad A = \pi r^2$

24. $l = \dfrac{S}{\pi r} - r \quad l + r = \dfrac{S}{\pi r} \quad S = \pi r(l + r)$

25. $r = \sqrt{\dfrac{2A}{\sin\theta}} \quad r^2 = \dfrac{2A}{\sin\theta} \quad \sin\theta = \dfrac{2A}{r^2}$

26. $g = \dfrac{4\pi^2 l}{T} \quad 4\pi^2 l = gT \quad l = \dfrac{gT}{4\pi^2}$

27. $r = \dfrac{V}{I} - R \quad R = \dfrac{V}{I} - r \quad R = \dfrac{V - Ir}{I}$

28. $E = \dfrac{1}{2}mv^2 \quad 2E = mv^2$

$v^2 = \dfrac{2E}{m} \quad v = \sqrt{\dfrac{2E}{m}}$

29. $r = \sqrt{\dfrac{2A}{\theta - \sin\theta}} \quad r^2 = \dfrac{2A}{\theta - \sin\theta}$

$2A = r^2(\theta - \sin\theta) \quad A = \dfrac{r^2}{2}(\theta - \sin\theta)$

30. $r^3 = \dfrac{3V}{4\pi} \quad 3V = 4\pi r^3 \quad V = \dfrac{4\pi r^3}{3}$

31. $r = \sqrt{\dfrac{2A}{\theta}} \quad r^2 = \dfrac{2A}{\theta} \quad \theta = \dfrac{2A}{r^2}$

32. $r = \sqrt{\dfrac{2A}{\theta}} \quad r^2 = \dfrac{2A}{\theta} \quad A = \dfrac{r^2\theta}{2}$

33. $\dfrac{t+a}{t-a} = \dfrac{A}{B} \quad (t+a)B = A(t-a)$

$tB + aB = At - Aa \quad a(B+A) = At - Bt$

$a = \dfrac{t(A-B)}{A+B}$

34. $\dfrac{t+a}{t-a} = \dfrac{A}{B}$

$(t+a)B = A(t-a)$

$tB + aB = At - aA$

$tB - At = -aB - Aa$

$t(B-A) = -a(B+A)$

$t = \dfrac{-a(A+B)}{B-A} \qquad t = \dfrac{a(A+B)}{A-B}$

35. $f = \dfrac{1}{2\pi}\sqrt{\dfrac{1}{LC}} \qquad f^2 = \dfrac{1}{2\pi^2}\cdot\dfrac{1}{LC}$

$L = \dfrac{1}{4\pi^2 C f^2}$

36. $f = \dfrac{1}{2\pi}\sqrt{\dfrac{1}{LC}} \qquad f^2 = \dfrac{1}{4\pi^2}\cdot\dfrac{1}{LC}$

$C = \dfrac{1}{4\pi^2 L f^2}$

37. $f = \dfrac{1}{2\pi}\sqrt{\dfrac{1}{LC} - \dfrac{R^2}{L^2}}$

$f^2 = \dfrac{1}{4\pi^2}\left(\dfrac{1}{LC} - \dfrac{R^2}{L^2}\right)$

$\qquad = \dfrac{1}{4\pi^2 LC} - \dfrac{R^2}{4\pi^2 L^2}$

$\dfrac{R^2}{4\pi^2 L^2} = \dfrac{1}{4\pi^2 LC} - f^2$

$R^2 = 4\pi^2 L^2\left(\dfrac{1}{4\pi^2 LC} - f^2\right)$

$R^2 = \dfrac{L}{C} - f^2 4\pi^2 L^2$

$R = \sqrt{\dfrac{L}{C} - f^2 4\pi^2 L^2}$

38. $ax^2 + bx + c = 0$

$x = \dfrac{-b \pm \sqrt{b^2 - 4ac}}{2a}$

39. $f = \dfrac{1}{2\pi}\sqrt{\left(\dfrac{1}{LC} - \dfrac{R^2}{L^2}\right)}$

$f^2 = \dfrac{1}{4\pi^2}\left(\dfrac{1}{LC} - \dfrac{R^2}{L^2}\right)$

$4\pi^2 f^2 = \dfrac{1}{LC} - \dfrac{R^2}{L^2} \qquad 4\pi^2 f^2 L^2 = \dfrac{L}{C} - R^2$

$4\pi^2 f^2 L^2 - \dfrac{L}{C} + R^2 = 0$

$a = 4\pi^2 f^2 \quad b = -\dfrac{1}{C} \quad C = R^2$

$L = \dfrac{\frac{1}{C} \pm \sqrt{\left(-\frac{1}{C}\right)^2 - 16\pi^2 f^2 R^2}}{8\pi^2 f^2}$

40. $\dfrac{x+y}{x-y} = \dfrac{1}{l} \qquad (x+y)l = x - y$

$xl + yl = x - y \qquad yl + y = x - xl$

$y(l+1) = x(1-l) \qquad y = \dfrac{x(1-l)}{(1+l)}$

41. $T = \dfrac{1}{f} \qquad f = \dfrac{1}{T}$

42. $T = \dfrac{2\pi}{w} \qquad w = \dfrac{2\pi}{T}$

43. $\rho = \dfrac{RA}{l} \qquad l = \dfrac{RA}{\rho}$

44. $\alpha = \dfrac{R_\theta - R_0}{R_0 \theta} \qquad \alpha R_0 \theta = R_\theta - R_0$

$R_0 + \alpha R_0 \theta = R_\theta \qquad R_\theta = R_0(1 + \alpha\theta)$

45. $X_c = \dfrac{1}{2\pi f C} \qquad C = \dfrac{1}{2\pi f X_c}$

46. $Z = \sqrt{R^2 + \left(wL - \dfrac{1}{wC}\right)^2}$

$Z^2 = R^2 + \left(wL - \dfrac{1}{wC}\right)^2$

$R^2 = Z^2 - \left(wL - \dfrac{1}{wC}\right)^2$

$R = \sqrt{Z^2 - \left(wL - \dfrac{1}{wC}\right)^2}$

47. $\eta = \dfrac{T_2 - T_1}{T_2}$ $\eta T_2 = T_2 - T_1$

    $T_1 = T_2 - \eta T_2$ $T_1 = T_2(1 - \eta)$

    $T_2(1 - \eta) = T_1$ $T_2 = \dfrac{T_1}{1 - \eta}$

48. $W = \dfrac{1}{2}LI^2$ $2W = LI^2$ $LI^2 = 2W$

    $I^2 = \dfrac{2W}{L}$ $I = \sqrt{\dfrac{2W}{L}}$

49. $W = \dfrac{1}{2}IW_2^2 - \dfrac{1}{2}IW_1^2$

    $2W = IW_2^2 - IW_1^2$ $2W = I(W_2^2 - W_1^2)$

    $I(W_2^2 - W_1^2) = 2W$ $I = \dfrac{2W}{W_2^2 - W_1^2}$

50. $W = \dfrac{1}{2}CV^2$ $2W = CV^2$

    $CV^2 = 2W$ $V^2 = \dfrac{2W}{C}$ $V = \sqrt{\dfrac{2W}{C}}$

51. $F = \dfrac{Q_1 Q_2}{4\pi \varepsilon r^2}$ $r^2 = \dfrac{Q_1 Q_2}{4\pi \varepsilon F}$

    $r = \sqrt{\dfrac{Q_1 Q_2}{4\pi \varepsilon F}}$

52. $hf = \phi + \dfrac{1}{2}m\,\vartheta\text{max}^2$

    $m\,\vartheta\text{max}^2 = 2hf - 2\phi$

    $\vartheta\text{max}^2 = \dfrac{2hf - 2\phi}{m}$

    $\vartheta\text{max} = \sqrt{\dfrac{2hf - 2\phi}{m}}$

53.   (i) $A = \pi x^2$, $\pi x^2 = A$, $x^2 = \dfrac{A}{\pi}$,

        $x = \sqrt{\dfrac{A}{\pi}}$

    (ii) $V = \dfrac{4}{3}\pi x^3$, $4\pi x^3 = 3V$,

        $x^3 = \dfrac{3V}{4\pi}$, $x = \sqrt[3]{\dfrac{3V}{4\pi}}$

    (iii) $S = 4\pi x^2$, $4\pi x^2 = S$, $x^2 = \dfrac{S}{4\pi}$,

        $x = \sqrt{\dfrac{S}{4\pi}}$

    (iv) $V = \pi x^2 h$, $\pi x^2 h = V$, $x^2 = \dfrac{V}{\pi h}$,

        $x = \sqrt{\dfrac{V}{\pi h}}$

    (v) $S = \pi x^2 + 2\pi x^2 h$,

        $\pi x^2 + 2\pi x^2 h = S$

        $x^2(\pi + 2\pi h) = S \Rightarrow x = \sqrt{\dfrac{S}{\pi + 2\pi h}}$

    (vi) $x^2 + y^2 = r^2$, $x^2 = r^2 - y^2$,

        $x = \sqrt{r^2 - y^2}$

    (vii) $T = 2\pi\sqrt{\dfrac{x}{g}}$, $T^2 = 4\pi^2\dfrac{x}{g}$,

        $x = g\dfrac{T^2}{4\pi^2}$

    (viii) $v = \sqrt{2gx}$, $2gx = v^2$, $x = \dfrac{v^2}{2g}$

    (ix) $E = \dfrac{1}{2}mx^2$,

        $2E = mx^2$, $mx^2 = 2E$, $x = \sqrt{\dfrac{2E}{m}}$

    (x) $x^2 + R^2 = Z^2$, $x^2 = Z^2 - R^2$,

        $x = \sqrt{Z^2 - R^2}$

Note that in all the above we have taken the positive root of x. Make the subjects of the formulae, the symbol adjacent.

54. $\dfrac{R_{t_1}}{R_{t_2}} = \dfrac{R_0(1 + \alpha t_1)}{R_0(1 + \alpha t_2)}$

    $R_{t_1}(1 + \alpha t_2) = R_{t_2}(1 + \alpha t_1)$

    $R_{t_1} + \alpha R_{t_1} t_2 = R_{t_2} + R_{t_2}\alpha t_1$

    $\alpha(R_{t_1} t_2 - R_{t_2} t_1) = R_{t_2} - R_{t_1}$

    $\alpha = \dfrac{R_{t_2} - R_{t_1}}{R_{t_1} t_2 - R_{t_2} t_1}$

55. $\dfrac{1}{C} = \dfrac{1}{C_1} + \dfrac{1}{C_2} + \dfrac{1}{C_3} \Rightarrow$

    $C = \dfrac{1}{\dfrac{1}{C_1} + \dfrac{1}{C_2} + \dfrac{1}{C_3}}$

56. $X_L = 2\pi f_o L = X_c = \dfrac{1}{2\pi f_o C}$

$(2\pi f_o L)(2\pi f_o C) = 1 \quad 4\pi^2 f_o^2 LC = 1$

$f_o^2 = \dfrac{1}{4\pi^2 LC} \quad f_o = \dfrac{1}{2\pi\sqrt{LC}}$

57. $\dfrac{1}{X^2} = \dfrac{1}{X_1^2} + \dfrac{1}{X_2^2}, \quad \dfrac{1}{X^2} - \dfrac{1}{X_2^2} = \dfrac{1}{X_1^2}$

$X_1^2 = \dfrac{1}{\dfrac{1}{X_2^2} - \dfrac{1}{X^2}} = \dfrac{X^2 X_2^2}{X_2^2 - X^2}$

$X_1 = \sqrt{\dfrac{X^2 X_2^2}{X_2^2 - X^2}} = \dfrac{X X_2}{\sqrt{X_2^2 - X^2}}$

58. If $I = \dfrac{nE}{r + nR}$

$nE = I(r + nR) \Rightarrow nE - InR = Ir$

$n(E - IR) = Ir$

$n = \dfrac{Ir}{E - IR} = \dfrac{5 \times 1,000}{10,000 - 5 \times 100}$

$= \dfrac{5,000}{9,500} = \dfrac{50}{95} = \dfrac{10}{19}$

59. $ß = \dfrac{\alpha}{1 - \alpha}, \quad \alpha = ß(1 - a), \quad \alpha + ß\alpha = ß$

$\alpha(1 + ß) = ß, \quad \alpha = \dfrac{ß}{(1 + ß)}$

60. $\alpha = \dfrac{ß}{1 + ß} \quad \alpha(1 + ß) = ß \quad \alpha + \alpha ß = ß$

$\alpha = ß - \alpha ß = ß(1 - \alpha) \quad ß = \dfrac{\alpha}{1 - \alpha}$

61. $\gamma = \dfrac{1}{1 - \alpha} \quad \gamma(1 - \alpha) = 1$

$\gamma - \alpha\gamma = 1 \quad \gamma - 1 = \alpha\gamma \quad \alpha = \dfrac{\gamma - 1}{\gamma}$

62. $Z = \sqrt{R^2 + (X_L - X_c)^2}$
$Z^2 = R^2 + (X_L - X_C)^2$
$Z^2 - (X_L - X_C)^2 = R^2$
$R = \sqrt{Z^2 - (X_L - X_C)^2}$

63. $Q = \dfrac{1}{R}\sqrt{\dfrac{L}{C}}, QR = \sqrt{\dfrac{L}{C}},$

$Q^2 R^2 = \dfrac{L}{C}, \quad C = \dfrac{L}{Q^2 R^2}$

64. $\dfrac{1}{R} = \dfrac{1}{R_1} + \dfrac{1}{R_2},$

$\dfrac{1}{R_1} = \dfrac{1}{R} - \dfrac{1}{R_2} = \dfrac{R_2 - R}{RR_2}$

$R_1 = \dfrac{RR_2}{R_2 - R}$

65. $\dfrac{1}{f} = \dfrac{1}{v} + \dfrac{1}{u},$

$\dfrac{1}{v} = \dfrac{1}{f} - \dfrac{1}{u} = \dfrac{u - f}{fu}, \quad v = \dfrac{fu}{u - f}$

Solutions 6

1.

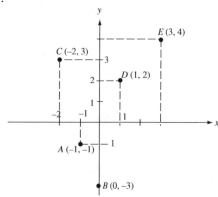

Fig. 70

2. The points lie exactly on the straight line, the ratio $\dfrac{V}{I}$ has the same value for the five sets of points.

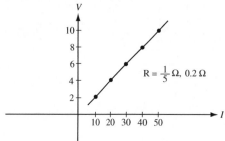

$$R = \tfrac{1}{5}\Omega,\ 0.2\,\Omega$$

Fig. 71

3. $y = mx + c$
   m is the gradient of the straight line and c is the intercept on the y-axis.

4. $y = mx$ is the equation of the line passing through the origin, the intercept is zero, $c = 0$.

5. $\dfrac{x}{-3} + \dfrac{y}{-4} = 1$

   If $x = 0$, $y = -4$ and

   if $y = 0$, $x = -3$.

6. $y = mx + c \qquad y = -x + 3$

7.

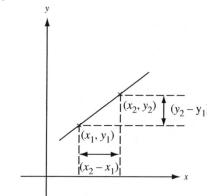

$$m = \text{gradient} = \frac{y_2 - y_1}{x_2 - x_1}$$

Fig. 72

8. $x + y = 1$

   If $x = 0$, $y = 1$;   If $y = 0$, $x = 1$

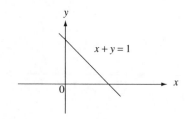

Fig. 73

9. $y = 2x + 3$ If $x = 0, y = 3$;
   If $x = 1, y = 5$

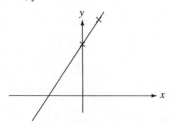

Fig. 74

10.   (i) $y = mx + c$

       the gradient/intercept form

      (ii) $ax + by + c = 0$

       the general form

      (iii) $\dfrac{x}{a} + \dfrac{y}{b} = 1$

       the intercept form.

Solutions 7

1. $6x + 5y = 5$ ... (1)

   $5x + 7y = 3$ ... (2)

   Multiply (1) by 5 and (2) by -6

   $30x + 25y = 25$ ... (3)

   $-30x - 42y = -18$ ... (4)

   adding (3) and (4)

   $-17y = 7 \quad y = \dfrac{-7}{17} = -0.41$

   substituting this value in (1)

   $6x + 5(-0.41) = 5$

   $6x = 5 + 2.06$

   $x = \dfrac{7.06}{6} = 1.18$

   therefore $x = 1.18, \quad y = -0.41$.

2. $26x - 25y = 50$ ... (1)

   $-25x + 25.1y = 40$ ... (2)

   Multiplying (1) by 25 and (2) by 26

   $650x - 625y = 1250$ ... (3)

   $-650x + 652.6y = 1040$ ... (4)

   adding (3) and (4)

   $27.6y = 2290 \qquad y = 82.97$

   substituting in (1)

   $26x - 25(82.97) = 50$

   $26x = 50 + 2074.28$

   $x = 81.7$

3. $4x + 3y = 8$ ... (1)

   $75x + 77y = 50$ ... (2)

   multiplying (1) by 75 and (2) by -4

   $300x + 225y = 600$ ... (3)

   $-300x - 308y = -200$ ... (4)

   adding (3) and (4)

   $-83y = 400 \qquad y = -4.82$

   substituting this value in (1) we have

   $4x - 3(4.82) = 8$

   $4x = 22.46 \qquad x = 5.61$

4. $1.1x + y = 2$ ... (1)

   $x + 1.2y = 3$ ... (2)

   multiplying (1) by 1 and (2) by -1.1

   $1.1x + y = 2$ ... (3)

   $-1.1x - 1.32y = -3.3$ ... (4)

   adding (3) and (4)

   $-0.32y = -1.3$

   $y = 4.06$

   substituting this value in (1)

   $1.1x + 4.06 = 2 \qquad 1.1x = 2 - 4.06$

   $x = -\dfrac{2.06}{1.1} = -1.87$

   $x = -1.87, \ y = 4.06$

5. $0.5x - 0.3y = 6$ ... (1)

   $15x + 15.3y = 12$ ... (2)

   multiplying (1) by 15.3 and (2) by 0.3

   $7.65x - 4.59y = 91.6$ ... (3)

   $4.5x + 4.59y = 3.6$ ... (4)

   adding (3) and (4)

   $12.15x = 95.2 \qquad x = 7.84$

   substituting this value in (1)

   $0.5(7.84) - 0.3y = 6$

   $0.3y = 0.5 \times 7.84 - 6$

   $y = -6.93$

6. $2x - 5y = -1$ ... (1)

   $10x + 15y = -2$ ... (2)

multiplying (1) by 3 and (2) by 1

$6x - 15y = -3$ ... (3)

$10x + 15y = -2$ ... (4)

adding (3) and (4) we have

$16x = -5$

$x = \dfrac{-5}{16} = -0.3125$

substituting in (1)

$2(-0.3125) - 5y = -1$

$-5y = -1 + 0.625 = -0.375$

$y = 0.075$

7. $0.5x - 3y = 5$ ... (1)

$0.1x + y = -7$ ... (2)

multiplying (1) by 1 and (2) by 3

$0.5x - 3y = 5$ ... (3)

$0.3x + 3y = -21$ ... (4)

adding (3) and (4)

$0.8x = -16 \qquad x = -20$

substituting in (1) $0.5(-20) - 3y = 5$

$-3y = 5 + 10, \; y = -5$

8. $15y - 13.5x = 2.5$ ... (1)

$15x - 13.5y = 3.5$ ... (2)

multiplying (1) by 13.5 and (2) by 15

$202.5y - 182.25x = 33.75$ ... (3)

$225x - 202.5y = 52.5$ ... (4)

adding (3) and (4)

$42.75x = 86.25 \qquad x = 2.02$

substituting in (1)

$15y - 13.5(2.02) = 2.5$

$15y = 29.77 \quad y = 1.99$

9. $x - 5y = 30$ ... (1)

$6.1x + 5.1y = 80$ ... (2)

multiplying (1) 5.1 and (2) by 5

$5.1x - 25.5y = 153$ ... (3)

$30.5x + 25.5y = 400$ ... (4)

adding (3) and (4)

$35.6x = 553 \qquad x = 15.5$

substituting in (1)

$15.5 - 5y = 30$

$-5y = 14.5 \quad y = -2.9$

10. $23x + 20y = 600$ ... (1)

$20x + 26y = 300$ ... (2)

multiplying (1) by -20 and (2) by 23

$-460x - 400y = -12,000$ ... (3)

$460x + 598y = 6,900$ ... (4)

adding (3) and (4)

$198y = -5100 \quad y = -25.8$

substituting in (1)

$23x + 20(-25.8) = 600$

$23x = 600 + 516 \quad x = \dfrac{1116}{23} = 48.5$

11. $5.5x + 4.5y = 5$ ... (1)

$4.5x + 10y = 10$ ... (2)

multiplying (1) by 4.5 and (2) by -5.5

$24.75x + 20.25y = 22.5$ ... (3)

$-24.75x - 55y = -55$ ... (4)

adding (3) and (4)

$-34.75y = -32.5 \quad y = 0.935$

substituting in (1)

$5.5x + 4.5(0.935) = 5$

$5.5x = 5 - 4.2075 = 0.7925$

$x = 0.144$

12. $3x - 4y = 23$ ... (1)

$-x + y = -6$ ... (2)

multiplying (1) by 1 and (2) by 3

$3x - 4y = 23$ ... (3)

$-3x + 3y = -18$ ... (4)

adding (3) and (4) $-y = 5, \; y = -5$

substituting in (1)

$3x - 4(-5) = 23$

$3x = 23 - 20 \quad 3x = 3 \; x = 1$

13. $5x + 2y = -4$ ... (1)

$4x + 5y = 7$ ... (2)

multiplying (1) by -5 and (2) by 2

$-25x - 10y = 20$ ... (3)

$8x + 10y = 14$ ... (4)

adding (3) and (4)

$-17x = 34 \quad x = -2$

substituting in (1)

$5(-2) + 2y = -4$

$2y = -4 + 10 \quad y = 3$

14. $5x + 4y = -5$ ... (1)

    $-4x - 3y = 5$ ... (2)

    multiplying (1) by 3 and (2) by 4

    $15x + 12y = -15$ ... (3)

    $-16x - 12y = 20$ ... (4)

    adding (3) and (4)

    $-x = +5 , \quad x = -5$

    substituting in (1)

    $5(-5) + 4y = -5$

    $4y = -5 + 25 \quad 4y = 20 \quad y = 5$

15. $5x + 7y = -30$ ... (1)

    $4x - 3y = -2.5$ ... (2)

    multiplying (1) by 3 and (2) by 7

    $15x + 21y = -90$ ... (3)

    $28x - 21y = -17.5$ ... (4)

    adding (3) and (4)

    $43x = -107.5, \quad x = -2.5$

    substituting in (1)

    $5(-2.5) + 7y = -30$

    $7y = -30 + 12.5 = -17.5, \quad y = -2.5$

16. $x + 7y = -19$ ... (1)

    $4x - 5y = 23$ ... (2)

    multiplying (1) by -4 and (2) by 1

    $-4x - 28y = 76$ ... (3)

    $4x - 5y = 23$ ... (4)

    adding (3) and (4)

    $-33y = 99 \quad y = -3$

    substituting in (1)

    $x - 21 = -19 \quad x = 2$

17. To solve graphically two linear simultaneous equations we need two points. We can, therefore choose two suitable sets of points

    $x - y = 6; \quad$ if $x = 0, y = -6$

    if $y = 0, x = 6$

    $-3x + 4y = -23;$ if $y = 1, x = 9$

    if $x = 5, y = -2$

A straight line through the two sets of points $(0, -6)$ and $(6, 0)$ is drawn and another straight line through the two sets of points $(9, 11)$ and $(5, -2)$ is drawn. The two lines intersect at the point $(1, -5)$. (see Fig. 75)

18. $5x + 2y = -4;$ if $x = 2, y = -7,$

    if $y = 3, x = -2$

    $-4x - 5y = -7;$ if $x = -2, y = 3,$

    if $y = -1, x = 3$

The two lines intersect at $x = -2, y = 3$. (see Figs. 76 & 77)

19. $5x + 4y = -5;$ if $y = 0, x = -1,$

    if $x = 3, y = -5$

    $4x + 3y = -5;$ if $y = 5, x = -5,$

    if $x = 7, y = -11$

The two sets of points are plotted and the lines were drawn. These lines intersect at the point $(-5, 5)$. (see Fig. 78)

20. $5x + 7y = -30 \quad -4x + 3y = 2.5$

    if $y = 0, x = -6 \quad$ if $y = -2.5, x = -2.5$

    if $x = 1, y = -5 \quad$ if $x = 5, y = 7.5$

These two sets of points are plotted and the lines drawn, the point of intersection is at $(-2.5, -2.5)$. (see Fig. 79)

21. $x + 7y = -19 \quad -4x + 5y = -23$

    if $y = 0, x = -19 \quad$ if $y = 1, x = 7$

    if $x = -5, y = -2 \quad$ if $x = 2, y = -3$

The two lines are drawn and intersect at $(2, -3)$. (see Fig. 80)

22.

x	$6x^2$	$7x$	-5	y
-1.5	13.5	-10.5	-5.0	-2.0
-1	6	-7	-5	-6
-0.75	3.375	-5.250	-5.000	-6.875
-0.5	1.5	-3.5	-5.0	-7.0
0	0	0	-5	-5
0.5	1.5	3.5	-5.0	0
1.0	6	7	-5	8
-2	24	-14	-5	5

From the graph when $y = 0$, $x = 0.5$ and $x = -1.8$. (see Fig. 81)

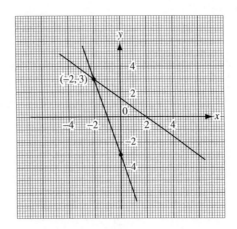

Fig. 77

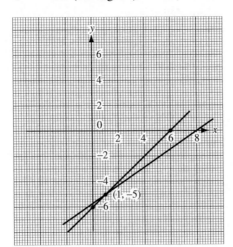

Fig. 75

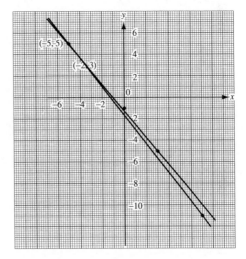

Fig. 78

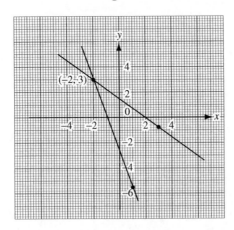

Fig. 76

23.

x	x^2	$+x$	-2	y
-3	9	-3	-2	4
-2.5	6.25	-2.50	-2	1.75
-2.0	4	-2	-2	0
-1.0	1	-1	-2	-2
0	0	0	-2	-2
1	1	1	-2	0
2	4	2	-2	4

From the graph when $y = 0, x = 1, x = -2$. (see Fig. 81a.)

24.

x	x^2	$-x$	-6	y
-3	9	3	-6	6
-2	4	2	-6	0
-1	1	1	-6	-4
0	0	0	-6	-6
1	1	-1	-6	-6
2	4	-2	-6	-4
3	9	-3	-6	0

From the graph when $y = 0$, $x = -2$ and $x = 3$. (see Fig. 82)

25.

x	$-x^2$	$-3x$	-2	y
-3	-9	9	-2	-2
-2.5	-6.25	7.50	-2	-0.75
-2.0	-4	6	-2	0
-1.5	-2.25	4.5	-2	0.25
-1	-1	3	-2	0
-0.5	-0.25	1.50	-2	-0.75
0	0	0	-2	-2

From the graph $x = -2$ and $x = -1$ when $y = 0$. (see Fig. 83)

26.

x	$-x^2$	$+6x$	-5	y
0	0	0	-5	-5
1	-1	6	-5	0
2	-4	12	-5	3
3	-9	18	-5	4
4	-16	24	-5	3
5	-25	30	-5	0
6	-36	36	-5	-5

From the graph $x = 1$ and $x = 5$ for $y = 0$. (see Fig. 84)

27. $4x + 2 - y = 0$ is a straight line

If $y = 0$, $x = -\dfrac{1}{2}$ and if $x = 0$, $y = 2$.

These two sets of points are plotted and a line is drawn through the points

x	$-4x^2$	$5x$	7	y
-1	-4	-5	7	-2
-0.5	-1	-2.5	7	3.5
0	0	0	7	7
0.5	-1	2.5	7	8.5
1	-4	5	7	8
2	-16	10	7	1

The quadratic function $y = -4x^2 + 5x + 7$

is drawn, the intersections of the line and the curve are $(-1, -2)$ and $(1.25, 6.5)$.

Therefore $x = -1$ and $x = 1.25$ solve the graphs simultaneously. (see Fig. 85)

28.

x	x^2	$5x$	4	y
0	0	0	4	4
-1	1	-5	4	0
-2	4	-10	4	-2
-3	9	-15	4	-2
-4	16	-20	4	0
-5	25	-25	4	4

y is plotted against x

$y = 0$ is a straight line representing the x-axis. The intersections of the line and the curve give $(-4, 0)$ and $(-1, 0)$. Therefore $x = -4$ and $x = -1$. (see Fig. 86)

29.

x	x^2	$-8x$	$+1$	y
1	1	-8	1	-6
2	4	-16	1	-11
3	9	-24	1	-14
4	16	-32	1	-15
5	25	-40	1	-14
6	36	-48	1	-11

Plot y against x, a curve is obtained and draw the line $y = -14$

The intersections are: $(3, -14)$, $(5, -14)$

Therefore $x = 3$ and $x = 5$. (see Fig. 87)

30.

x	x^3	$-2x^2$	$-5x$	6	y
-3	-27	-18	15	6	-24
-2	-8	-8	10	6	0
-1	-1	-2	5	6	8
0	0	0	0	6	6
1	1	-2	-5	6	0
2	8	-8	-10	6	-4
3	27	-18	-15	6	0
4	64	-32	-20	6	18

The graph of y against x is plotted when $y = 0$, $x = -2$, $x = 1$, $x = 3$. (see Fig. 88)

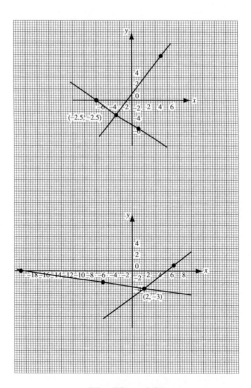

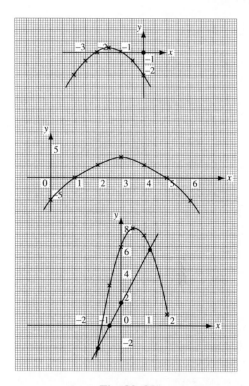

Fig. 79 and 80

Fig. 83–85

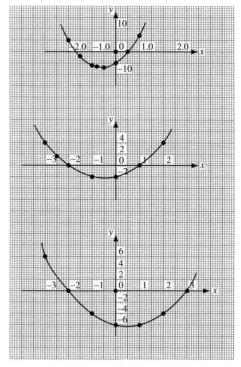

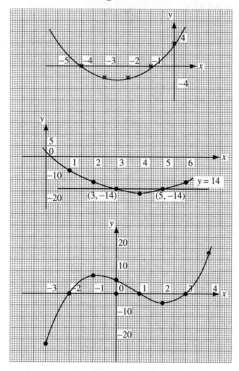

Fig. 81, 81a and 82

Fig. 86–88

31.

x	x^3	$-x^2$	$+x$	-1	y
-2	-8	-4	-2	-1	-15
-1	-1	-1	-1	-1	-4
0	0	0	0	-1	-1
1	1	-1	1	-1	0
2	8	-4	2	-1	5
3	27	-9	3	-1	20

y is plotted against x when $y = 0$, $x = 1$. For values greater than 2, y is large and for values less than -1, y is large and negative. It appears that there is only one solution for $x = 1$ when $y = 0$. (see Fig. 89)

32.

x	x^3	$-4x^2$	$4x$	y
-2	-8	-16	-8	-32
-1	-1	-4	-4	-9
0	0	0	0	0
1	1	-4	4	1
2	8	-16	8	0
3	27	-36	12	3

when $y = 0$, $x = 0$, $x = 2$, there are two solutions. (see Fig. 90)

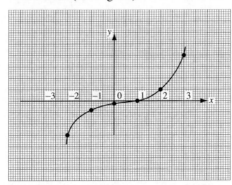

Fig. 89

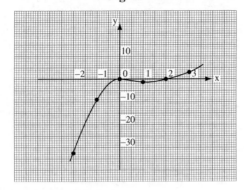

Fig. 90

33. (a) when $x = -2.3$,
$y = 2(-2.3)^2 - 4(-2.3) - 5 = 14.78$
From the graph $y \approx 14.5$

when $x = 1.3$,
$y = 2(1.3)^2 - 4(1.3) - 5 = -6.82$
From the graph $y \approx -6.9$

when $x = 3.7$,
$y = 2(3.7)^2 - 4(3.7) - 5 = 7.58$
From the graph $y \approx 7$

(b) when $y = 18$, $x = -2.55$ and $x = 4.55$
when $y = 5$, $x = -1.4$ and $x = 3.5$
when $y = -3$, $x = -0.35$ and $x = 2.55$ when $y = -7$, $x = 1$

(c) y min $= -7$ when $x = 1$

(d) $x = 1$, since this point lines on the axis of symmetry

(e) $x = 1$

(f) y is negative for the range of x between -0.85 and 3.1

(g) $x = -0.85$ and $x = 3.1$

(h) when $y = -5$, then $2x^2 - 4x - 5 = -5$
$2x^2 - 4x = 0$, then $x = 0$, $x = 2$

(i) when $x = -2$ the gradient is -12
when $x = 2$ the gradient is 4

(j) parabola

(k) y is a minimum when $x = 1$

(l) y is a maximum when $x = 1$ since the curve is a mirror image about $y = -7$.

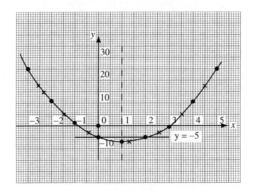

Fig. 91

Solutions 8

Geometry.

1.

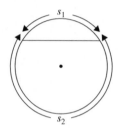

Fig. 92

$$\frac{r\theta}{r(2\pi - \theta)} = \frac{s_1}{s_2} = \frac{1}{5}$$

$$5\theta = 2\pi - \theta \qquad 6\theta = 2\pi$$

$$\theta = \frac{\pi}{3} = 60°$$

$$60° \text{ minor} = \frac{\pi}{3} \qquad 300° \text{ major} = \frac{5\pi}{3}$$

$$s_1 = 15\frac{\pi}{3} = 5\pi = 15.71 \text{ mm}$$

$$s_2 = 75\frac{\pi}{3} = 25\pi = 78.54 \text{ mm}$$

2.

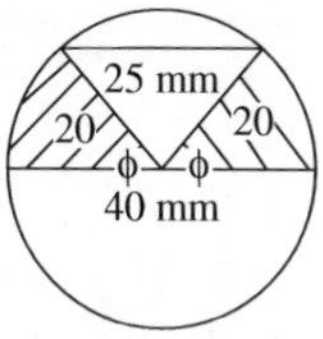

Fig. 93

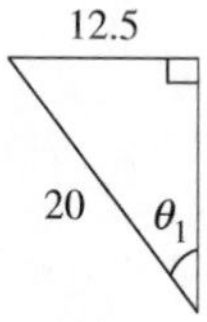

Fig. 94

$$\theta_1 = 0.675131532^c$$
$$2\theta_1 = 1.350263066^c.$$

$$\text{Area of triangle} = \frac{1}{2}20^2 \sin 2\theta_1$$

$$= 200 \sin 1.350263066^c$$

$$= 195.1561875$$

$$\text{Area of sectors} = \frac{1}{2}r^2\phi + \frac{1}{2}r^2\phi = r^2\phi$$

$$= 20^2 \times 0.8957 = 358.27$$

$$2\phi = \pi - 1.3503$$

$$\phi = 0.8957^c$$

$$\text{Total area} = 358.27 + 195.16$$

$$= 553.43 \text{ mm}^2$$

$$\approx 553 \text{ mm}^2$$

3.

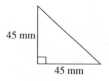

Fig. 95

$$\frac{s_1}{s_2} = \frac{1}{3} = \frac{r\theta}{r(2\pi - \theta)}$$

$$3\theta = 2\pi - \theta$$

$$4\theta = 2\pi$$

$$\theta = \frac{\pi}{2}$$

Fig. 96

$$45^2 + 45^2 = AB^2$$

$$AB = 45\sqrt{2} = 63.64 \text{ mm}$$

4. $\sin \alpha = \dfrac{2.5}{15} = 0.16666$

$\alpha = 0.167448079^c$

$2\alpha = 0.334896158^c$

major length $= (2\pi - 0.334896158)r$

of the arc $= 89.2$ mm

where $r = 15$ mm

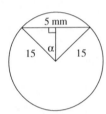

Fig. 97

5.

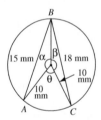

Fig. 98

Fig. 99

$\sin x = \dfrac{7.5}{10}$

$x = 48.6°$

$\alpha = 97.2°$

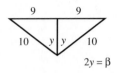

Fig. 100

$\sin y = \dfrac{9}{10}$

$y = 64.16°$

$\beta = 128.32°$

$\theta = 360° - (a + \beta)$

$= 360° - (97.2° + 128.32°)$

$= 134.48° = 2.347^c$

$134.48° \times \dfrac{\pi}{180} = 2.347^c$

The area of the sector $= \dfrac{1}{2}10^2 \, 2.347^c$

$= 117.4 \text{ mm}^2$

$= 117 \text{ mm}^2$ to 3 s.f.

6.

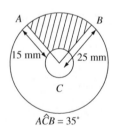

$A\hat{C}B = 35°$

Area of large sector $= \dfrac{1}{2}r_1^2\theta$

$= \dfrac{1}{2} \times 25^2 \times \dfrac{35\pi}{180}$

$= 190.9 \text{ mm}^2.$

Area of small sector

$= \dfrac{1}{2}r_2^2\theta = \dfrac{1}{2}10^2 \times \dfrac{35\pi}{180} = 30.5 \text{ mm}^2.$

Hatched area $= 190.9 - 30.5$

$= 160.4$ mm$^2 = 160$ mm^2 to 3 s.f.

7. Area of circle $= \pi r^2 = \dfrac{\pi d^2}{4}$

where $d = 2r$ or $r = \dfrac{d}{2}$.

Area of circular annulus $= \pi R_1^2 - \pi R_2^2$

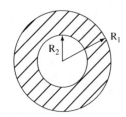

$100 = \pi 20^2 - \pi R_1^2$

$\pi R_1^2 = 400\pi - 100$

$R_1 = 19.2$ mm.

Solutions 9

1. $\sin 0° = 0$
   $\sin 30° = 0.5$
   $\sin 60° = 0.866$
   $\sin 90° = 1$
   $\sin 120° = 0.866$
   $\sin 180° = 0$

2. $\cos 45° = 0.707$
   $\cos 90° = 0$
   $\cos 135° = -0.707$
   $\cos 150° = -0.866$
   $\cos 210° = -0.866$

3. $\tan 0° = 0$
   $\tan 45° = 1$
   $\tan 60° = \sqrt{3}$
   $\tan 90° = \pm\infty$
   $\tan 120° = -\sqrt{3}$
   $\tan 135° = -1$
   $\tan 180° = 0$

4. $\sin\left(\dfrac{\pi}{3}\right)^c = \dfrac{\sqrt{3}}{2}$ $\sin\left(\dfrac{\pi}{4}\right)^c = \dfrac{1}{\sqrt{2}}$
   $\sin\left(\dfrac{\pi}{2}\right)^c = 1$ $\sin\left(\dfrac{\pi}{6}\right)^c = \dfrac{1}{2}$
   $\sin(\pi)^c = 0$ $\sin\left(\dfrac{3\pi}{2}\right)^c = -1$
   $\sin\left(\dfrac{11\pi}{6}\right)^c = -\dfrac{1}{2}$ $\sin(2\pi)^c = 0$
   $\sin(5\pi)^c = 0$

5. $\cos 0^c = 1$ $\cos\left(\dfrac{\pi}{6}\right)^c = 0.866$
   $\cos\left(\dfrac{\pi}{2}\right)^c = 0$ $\cos\left(\dfrac{4\pi}{3}\right)^c = -\dfrac{1}{2}$
   $\cos\left(\dfrac{7\pi}{4}\right)^c = 0.707$

6. $\tan\left(\dfrac{\pi}{6}\right)^c = \dfrac{1}{\sqrt{3}}$
   $\tan\left(\dfrac{\pi}{3}\right)^c = \sqrt{3}$
   $\tan\pi^c = 0$
   $\tan\left(\dfrac{3\pi}{2}\right)^c = \pm\infty$
   $\tan\left(\dfrac{11\pi}{4}\right)^c = -1$

7. $\sin 15° = 0.259$ $\sin 25° = 0.423$
   $\sin 32° = 0.530$
   $\cos 15° = 0.966$ $\cos 25° = 0.906$
   $\cos 32° = 0.848$
   $\tan 15° = 0.268$ $\tan 25° = 0.466$
   $\tan 32° = 0.625$
   $\sin 65° = 0.906$ $\sin 88° = 0.999$
   $\sin 93° = 0.9986$
   $\cos 65° = 0.423$ $\cos 88° = 0.035$
   $\cos 93° = -0.0523$
   $\tan 65° = 2.145$ $\tan 88° = 28.64$
   $\tan 93° = -19.08$
   $\sin 99° = 0.9877$ $\sin 136° = 0.695$
   $\sin 178° = 0.0349$
   $\cos 99° = -0.1564$ $\cos 136° = -0.719$
   $\cos 178° = -0.999$
   $\tan 99° = -6.314$ $\tan 136° = -0.9657$
   $\tan 178° = -0.0349$
   $\sin 200° = -0.342$ $\sin 320° = -0.643$
   $\cos 200° = -0.9397$ $\cos 320° = 0.766$
   $\tan 200° = 0.364$ $\tan 320° = -0.839$

8. (i) $3\sin 25° + 5\cos 35° + 7\tan 39°$

$$= 3(0.4226) + 5(0.8192)$$
$$+7(0.8098)$$

$$= 1.2679 + 4.0958 + 5.6685$$

$$= 11.032$$

$$= 11.0 \text{ to 3 significant figures}$$

(ii) $\cos 35° - \sin 79° + \tan 44°$

$$= 0.803$$

$$= 0.8192 - 0.9816 + 0.9657$$

$$= 0.803$$

(iii) $5\cos 35° + 6\sin 90° - 7\tan 82°$

$$= 4.0958 + 6 - 49.8076 = -39.7$$

9. (i) $\sin x = \dfrac{1}{2}, \quad x = 30° \text{ and } x = 150°$

(ii) $\cos x = -0.866,$

$$x = 150° \quad \text{and} \quad x = 210°$$

(iii) $\tan x = 1, \quad x = 45° \text{ and } x = 225°$

(iv) $\sin x = -\dfrac{\sqrt{3}}{2},$

$$x = 240° \quad \text{and} \quad x = 300°$$

(v) $\tan x = -\sqrt{3},$

$$x = 300° \quad \text{and} \quad x = 120°$$

(i)

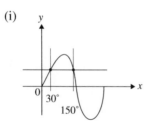

Fig. 101

(ii)

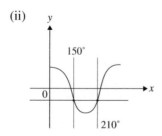

Fig. 102

(iii)

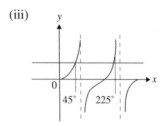

Fig. 103

(iv)

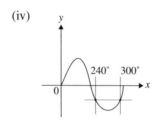

Fig. 104

(v)

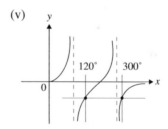

Fig. 105

10. Using Pythagoras theorem

$$AB^2 + 4^2 = 7^2$$

$$AB^2 = 49 - 16$$

$$AB = \sqrt{33}$$

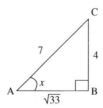

Fig. 106

(i) If x is an acute angle

$$\cos x = \frac{AB}{7} = \frac{\sqrt{33}}{7}$$

$$\tan x = \frac{4}{AB} = \frac{4}{\sqrt{33}}$$

(ii) If x is an obtuse angle

$$\cos x = \frac{-\sqrt{33}}{7}$$

$$\tan x = \frac{-4}{\sqrt{33}}$$

11.

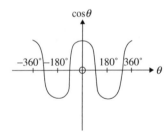

Fig. 107

12.

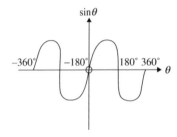

Fig. 108

13.

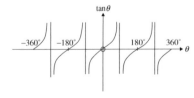

Fig. 109

14. (a)
(i)

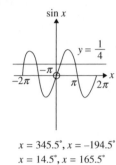

$x = 345.5°, x = -194.5°$
$x = 14.5°, x = 165.5°$

Fig. 110

(ii)

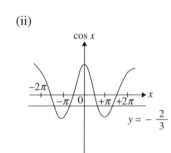

$x = -131.8°$
$x = 131.8°$
$x = 228.2°$
$x = -228.2°$

Fig. 111

(iii)

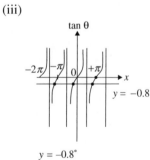

$y = -0.8°$
$x = -38.6°, x = -218.6°$
$x = 38.6°, x = -218.6°$

Fig. 112

(b)

(i) If $x = 125°$

$y = \sin 125° = 0.819$ to 3 s.f.

(ii) If $x = 39°$

$y = \cos 39° = 0.777$ to 3 s.f.

(iii) If $x = 275°$

$y = \tan 275° = -11.4$ to 3 s.f.

15.

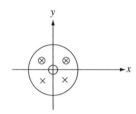

Fig. 113

The sine of an angle is negative in the third and fourth quadrants ($\times$).

The sine of an angle is positive in the first and second quadrants ($\otimes$).

16.

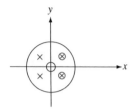

Fig. 114

The cosine of an angle is negative in the second and third quadrants ($\times$).

The cosine of an angle is positive in the first and fourth quadrants ($\otimes$).

17. The tangent of an angle is negative in the second and third quadrants ($\otimes$).

The tangent of an angle is positive in the first and third quadrants ($\times$).

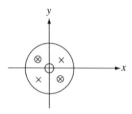

Fig. 115

Solutions 10

1. Mean Weight

$$= \frac{\begin{matrix} 45 + 43 + 48 + 44 + 45 + 49 + 45.5 \\ + 46.5 + 47 + 45 + 48.5 + 50 \end{matrix}}{12}$$

$$= \frac{556.5}{12}$$

$$= 46.375 \text{ kg}$$

2. We write the weights in ascending order

43, 44, 45, 45, 45, $\boxed{45.5, 46.5}$, 47, 48, 48.5, 49, 50

the number of the observations is even, the median is therefore the mean of the two numbers half way:

$$\frac{1}{2}(45.5 + 46.5) = 46 \text{ kg}$$

3. The most frequently occuring value of weight is 45 kg. The mode is 45 kg.

4. (i) The mean value

$$= \frac{\begin{matrix} 1.2 + 1.15 + 1.25 + 1.23 + 1.18 \\ + 1.2 + 1.21 + 1.19 + 1.26 \end{matrix}}{9}$$

$$= \frac{10.87}{9}$$

$$= 1.207777778$$

$$= 1.21 \text{ k}\Omega \qquad \text{to three significant figures.}$$

(ii) writing the values of resistors in ascending order

1.15, 1.18, 1.19, 1.20, $\boxed{1.20}$, 1.21, 1.23, 1.25, 1.26 kΩ

The median value is 1.20 kΩ, the observations are odd.

(iii) The mode = 1.20 kΩ

5. Placing the numbers in rank

23, 24, 25, 25, $\boxed{25, 28}$, 28, 29, 29, 30

Mean value $= \bar{x} = \dfrac{266}{10} = 26.6$

Median value = arithmetic mean of the two middle terms

$$= \frac{25 + 28}{2}$$

$$= 26.5$$

Mode = 25

6. $\bar{x} = \dfrac{\begin{matrix} 4 \times 470 + 17 \times 472 + 29 \times 473 \\ + 29 \times 474 + 41 \times 477 + 34 \\ \times 475 + 32 \times 476 \end{matrix}}{4 + 17 + 29 + 29 + 41 + 34 + 32}$

$$= \frac{88306}{186}$$

$$= 474.8$$

$$\bar{x} = 475 \ \Omega$$

7.

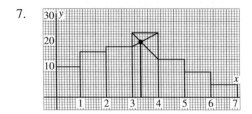

Fig. 116

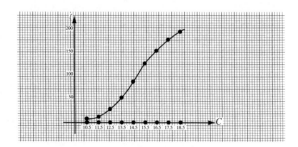

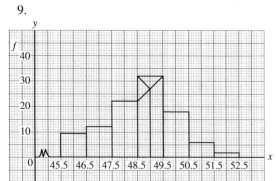

Figs. 117–119

8.

R (Ω)	f	L (mH)	f	C (μF)	f
325.5	5	24.5	10	10.5	5
326.5	11	25.5	22	11.5	12
327.5	19	26.5	38	12.5	27
328.5	28	27.5	56	13.5	52
329.5	42	28.5	84	14.5	92
330.5	62	29.5	124	15.5	127
331.5	77	30.5	154	16.5	157
332.5	84	31.5	168	17.5	185
333.5	88	32.5	176	18.5	199

9.

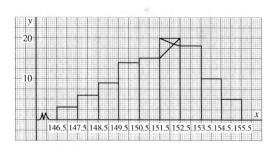

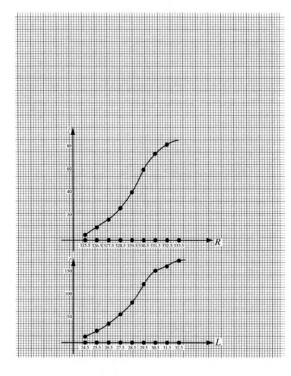

10. $\bar{x} = \dfrac{\Sigma f x}{\Sigma f}$

$$= \frac{\begin{array}{l}(3 \times 147 + 6 \times 148 + 9 \times 149 \\ + 14 \times 150 + 15 \times 151 + 20 \times 152 \\ + 18 \times 153 + 10 \times 154 + 5 + 155)\end{array}}{3 + 6 + 9 + 14 + 15 + 20 + 18 + 10 + 5}$$

$$= \frac{15144}{100} = 151.44$$

Index
Mathematic I/II

Mathematics
for
Technicians

Analytical Mathematics II

Anthony Nicolaides
B.Sc. (Eng.), C. Eng. M.I.E.T.

P.A.S.S. PUBLICATIONS
Private Academic & Scientific Studies Ltd

© A. Nicolaides
Second Edition 2009

ISBN-13 978-1-872684-51-2

Analytical Mathematics II

First Published in Great Britain 1991 by Private Academic & Scientific Studies Ltd

This book is copyright under the Berne Convention.

All rights are reserved. Apart as permitted under the copyright Act, 1956 no part or this publication may be reproduced, stored in a retrieval system, or transmitted in any form of by any means, electrical, mechanical, optical, photocopying, recording or otherwise, without the prior permission of the publishers.

P.A.S.S. PUBLICATIONS

Preface

This book covers adequately the following:

- Factorisation and quadratics; by extraction of a common factor eg $ax + ay, a(x + 2) + b(x + 2)$; by grouping eg $ax - ay + bx - by$; quadratic expressions eg $a^2 + 2ab + b^2$; roots of an equation eg quadratic equations with real roots by factorisation, and by the use of formula. $a^2 - b^2 = (a - b)(a + b)$; by completing the square and splitting the middle term.

- Law of logarithms ($\log A + \log B = \log AB$, $\log A^n = n \log A$, $\log A - \log B = \log \frac{A}{B}$) eg common logarithms (base 10) natural logarithms (base e), exponential growth and decay.

- Determinants and Matrices and Applications to simple technical problems.

- To use elementary calculus techniques. Differentiation: differential coefficient; gradient of a Curve $y = f(x)$; rate of change; Leibnitz notation ($\frac{dy}{dx}$); differentiation of simple polynomial functions; algebraic and trignometric functions; problems involving evaluation eg gradient at a point.

- Integration: integration as reverse of differentiating basic rules for simple polynomial functions, algebraic functions, indefinite integrals; constant of integration; definite integrals; limits; evaluation of simple polynomial functions; area under the curve eg $y = x(x - 3)$, $y = x^2 + x + 4$

- Simple curve sketching, parabolas, rectangular hyperbolas, circles, ellipses

- Non-linear to linear laws

- Uses graphs to determine values and establish power laws.

- Assignments

  All the exercises set in the text are fully worked out, the only book or CD with full solutions. The author was a Full Time senior lecturer at Lewisham College, a grade one Further Education Establishments, Mr. Anthony Nicolaides was a course Tutor for 12 years for the BTEC National Diploma in Engineering and taught for many years Mathematics and Electrical and Electronic Engineering.

Anthony Nicolaides
B.Sc.(Eng.), C.Eng. M.I.E.T.

Contents

Analytical Mathematics II

1

Solves simple quadratic equations by analytical methods

Analytical Mathematics II

1.1 Recognizes factors of quadratic expressions, including $(a+b)^2$, $(a-b)^2$ and $(a+b)(a-b)$.

The square of a binomial expression.

A binomial expression is an expression with two terms such as $(a + b)$.

A trinomial expression is an expression with three terms such as $(a + b + c)$.

The square of a binomial expression is found as follows:

$$(a+b)^2 = (a+b)(a+b) = aa + ab + ba + bb$$
$$= a^2 + 2ab + b^2.$$

The student should learn this identity.

$$(a + b)^2 = a^2 + 2ab + b^2. \qquad \ldots(1)$$

If a is the first term and b is the second term of the binomial expression, equation (1) is read as follows: a plus b all squared is equal to the square of the first term plus twice the product of the first term times the second term plus the square of the second term.

The expression (1) is an identity and an equation, that is, it is valid for all real values of a and b.

If $a = 3$ and $b = 4$

L.H.S. = Left Hand Side = $(a + b)^2$
$$= (3 + 4)^2$$
$$= 7^2 = 49$$

R.H.S. = Right Hand Side = $a^2 + 2ab + b^2$
$$= 3^2 + 2 \times 3 \times 4 + 4^2$$
$$= 9 + 24 + 16 = 49.$$

Therefore the left hand side is equal to the right hand side.

If $a = -5$ and $b = -7$

L.H.S. = $(a + b)^2$
$$= (-5 - 7)^2 = (-12)^2 = 144$$

R.H.S. = $a^2 + 2ab + b^2$
$$= (-5)^2 + 2(-5)(-7) + (-7)^2$$
$$= 25 + 70 + 49 = 144.$$

Again, the left hand side is equal to the right hand side.

WORKED EXAMPLE 1

Write down the identities for the following:

  (i) $(x + y)^2$
 (ii) $(2a + b)^2$
(iii) $(1 + x)^2$
 (iv) $(2a + 3b)^2$
  (v) $(1 + 3x)^2$.

Solution 1

  (i) $(x + y)^2 = x^2 + 2xy + y^2$
 (ii) $(2a + b)^2 = (2a)^2 + 2(2a)b + b^2$
$$= 4a^2 + 4ab + b^2$$

1

(iii) $(1 + x)^2 = 1 + 2x + x^2$

(iv) $(2a + 3b)^2 = (2a)^2 + 2(2a)(3b) + (3b)^2$
$$= 4a^2 + 12ab + 9b^2$$

(v) $(1 + 3x)^2 = 1 + 6x + 9x^2.$

The binomial expression $(a - b)^2$ where,

$$(a - b)^2 = a^2 + 2a(-b) + (-b)^2$$
$$= a^2 - 2ab + b^2$$

hence,

$$(a - b)^2 \equiv a^2 - 2ab + b^2 \qquad ...(2)$$

WORKED EXAMPLE 2

Write down the identities for the following:

(i) $(x - y)^2$

(ii) $(2a - b)^2$

(iii) $(1 - x)^2$

(iv) $(2a - 3b)^2$

(v) $(1 - 3x)^2.$

Solution 2

(i) $(x - y)^2 = x^2 - 2xy + y^2$

(ii) $(2a - b)^2 = 4a^2 - 4ab + b^2$

(iii) $(1 - x)^2 = 1 - 2x + x^2$

(iv) $(2a - 3b)^2 = 4a^2 - 12ab + 9b^2$

(v) $(1 - 3x)^2 = 1 - 6x + 9x^2.$

WORKED EXAMPLE 3

Simplify the following expressions:

(i) $a^2 + 2ab + b^2$

(ii) $a^2 - 2ab + b^2$

(iii) $1 + 2x + x^2$

(iv) $1 - 2x + x^2$

(v) $x^2 + 2xy + y^2$

(vi) $x^2 - 2xy + y^2$

(vii) $1 + 4x + 4x^2$

(viii) $4a^2 - 8ab + 4b^2$

(ix) $4x^2 - 12xy + 9y^2.$

Solution 3

(i) $a^2 + 2ab + b^2 = (a + b)^2$

(ii) $a^2 - 2ab + b^2 = (a - b)^2$

(iii) $1 + 2x + x^2 = (1 + x)^2$

(iv) $1 - 2x + x^2 = (1 - x)^2$

(v) $x^2 + 2xy + y^2 = (x + y)^2$

(vi) $x^2 - 2xy + y^2 = (x - y)^2$

(vii) $1 + 4x + 4x^2 = (1 + 2x)^2$

(viii) $4a^2 - 8ab + 4b^2 = (2a - 2b)^2$

(ix) $4x^2 - 12xy + 9y^2 = (2x - 3y)^2.$

The difference of two squares

$$a^2 - b^2 \equiv (a - b)(a + b) \qquad ... (3)$$

The difference of the two squares, is equal to the product of the difference of the two terms, times the sum of the two terms.

$$(a - b)(a + b) = aa + ab - ba - bb$$
$$= a^2 + ab - ab - b^2$$
$$= a^2 - b^2$$

multiplying out the brackets, we obtain the terms $a^2 + ab - ab - b^2$ and simplifying we have the difference of the two squares.

The student must remember that the factors of $a^2 - b^2$ are $(a - b)$ and $(a + b)$
$a^2 - b^2 \equiv (a - b)(a + b).$

What is the value of $9,999^2 - 9,998^2$?

Applying the formula in (3), we have;

$$9,999^2 - 9,998^2 = (9,999 - 9,998)$$
$$(9,999 + 9,998) = 1 \times (19,997) = 19,997.$$

WORKED EXAMPLE 4

Simplify the following expressions:

(i) $(a - b)(a + b)$

(ii) $(1 - x)(1 + x)$

(iii) $(2x - 3y)(2x + 3y)$

(iv) $(2x - 3)(2x + 3)$

(v) $(8x - 2y)(8x + 2y).$

Solution 4

(i) $(a - b)(a + b) = a^2 - b^2$

(ii) $(1 - x)(1 + x) = 1 - x^2$

(iii) $(2x - 3y)(2x + 3y) = 4x^2 - 9y^2$
(iv) $(2x - 3)(2x + 3) = 4x^2 - 9$
(v) $(8x - 2y)(8x + 2y) = 64x^2 - 4y^2$.

WORKED EXAMPLE 5

Without the use of a calculator, evaluate the expressions:

(i) $99^2 - 98^2$
(ii) $25^2 - 24^2$
(iii) $23^2 - 20^2$
(iv) $99,998^2 - 99,997^2$
(v) $999^2 - 997^2$.

Solution 5

(i) $(99)^2 - (98)^2 = (99 - 98)(99 + 98)$
$= 1 \times (197) = 197$

(ii) $(25)^2 - (24)^2 = (25 - 24)(25 + 24)$
$= 1 \times 49 = 49$

(iii) $(23)^2 - (20)^2 = (23 - 20)(23 + 20)$
$= 3 \times 43 = 129$

(iv) $(99,998)^2 - (99,997)^2$
$= (99,998 - 99,997)(99,998 + 99,997)$
$= 1 \times 199,995 = 199,995$

(v) $(999)^2 - (997)^2 = (999 - 997)(999 + 997)$
$= 2 \times (1,996) = 3,992$.

WORKED EXAMPLE 6

Solve the following equations by using the formula of the difference of the squares.

(i) $x^2 - 1 = 0$
(ii) $4x^2 - 9 = 0$
(iii) $9^2x^2 - 1 = 0$
(iv) $x^2 - 16 = 0$
(v) $9x^2 - 5^2 = 0$.

Solution 6

(i) $x^2 - 1 = (x - 1)(x + 1) = 0$,
$x - 1 = 0$ or $x + 1 = 0$,
therefore $x = 1$ and $x = -1$

(ii) $4x^2 - 9 = (2x - 3)(2x + 3) = 0$,
$2x - 3 = 0$ or $2x + 3 = 0$,
therefore $x = \frac{3}{2}$ or $x = -\frac{3}{2}$

(iii) $9^2x^2 - 1 = (9x - 1)(9x + 1) = 0$,
$9x - 1 = 0$ or $9x + 1 = 0$,
therefore $9x = 1$ or $x = \frac{1}{9}$
and $9x = -1$ or $x = -\frac{1}{9}$

(iv) $x^2 - 16 = 0 = (x - 4)(x + 4)$,
$x - 4 = 0$ or $x = 4, x = -4$

(v) $9x^2 - 5^2 = (3x - 5)(3x + 5) = 0$,
$3x = 5$ or $3x = -5$,
$x = \frac{5}{3}$ and $x = -\frac{5}{3}$.

1.2 Factorises quadratic expressions including perfect squares and the difference of two squares.

To factorise a quadratic expression by splitting the middle term.

Consider the opening of the brackets of two factors by multiplying out:

$$(x - 1)(x + 3) = x^2 + 3x - x - 3$$
$$= x^2 + 2x - 3.$$

Therefore, the product of the factors $(x - 1)$ and $(x + 3)$ is $x^2 + 2x - 3$. What about the reverse process, knowing the quadratic expression $x^2 + 2x - 3$, how can we factorise it by splitting the middle term, $2x$?

$$x^2 + 2x - 3 = x^2 + 3x - x - 3.$$

$2x = 3x - x = $ correct (the sum of $3x$ and $-x$)
$2x = 4x - 2x = $ correct (the sum of $4x$ and $-2x$).

Which type of splitting do we require?
The first, or the second or any other one?
The terms $3x$, and $-x$ give $2x$ when adding the terms $(3x)(-x) = -3x^2$ when multiplied, it is observed that the product of the first term and the third term of the quadratic expression or the trinomial, $x^2 + 2x - 3$ is, $(-3)(x^2) = -3x^2$ and this agrees with the product of the splitted terms $(3x)$ and $(-x)$, therefore the first type of splitting is the only correct one.

$x^2 + 2x - 3 = x^2 + 3x - x - 3$
$$= x(x + 3) - (x + 3)$$
$$= (x + 3)(x - 1)$$
the factors of $x^2 + 2x - 3$ are $(x + 3)$ and $(x - 1)$.

WORKED EXAMPLE 7

Factorise $x^2 + x - 12$ by splitting the middle term.

Solution 7

$x^2 + x - 12 = x^2 + 4x - 3x - 12$.

Note that $x = 4x - 3x$ (the sum of the splitted terms) and $(x^2)(-12)$ (the product of the first and thrid terms of the quadratic expression) should be equal to the product of the splitted terms, $(4x)(-3x) = -12x^2$
$x^2 + x - 12 = x^2 + 4x - 3x - 12$
$$= x(x + 4) - 3(x + 4)$$
$$= (x + 4)(x - 3).$$

Therefore, the factors of $(x + 4)$ and $(x - 3)$ when multiplied give the trinomial $x^2 + x - 12$.

WORKED EXAMPLE 8

Factorise $2x^2 + 5x - 3$ by splitting the middle term.

Solution 8

$2x^2 + 5x - 3 = 2x^2 + 6x - x - 3$
$$= 2x(x + 3) - (x + 3)$$
$$= (x + 3)(2x - 1).$$

WORKED EXAMPLE 9

Factorise $15x^2 - x - 2$ by splitting the middle term.

Solution 9

$15x^2 - x - 2 = 15x^2 - 6x + 5x - 2$
$$= 5x(3x + 1) - 2(3x + 1)$$
$$= (3x + 1)(5x - 2).$$

The perfect Squares

$(a + b)^2 = a^2 + 2ab + b^2 = (a + b)(a + b)$

$(a - b)^2 = a^2 - 2ab + b^2 = (a - b)(a - b)$

$(1 - 2x)^2 = 1 - 4x + 4x^2 = (1 - 2x)(1 - 2x).$

All the above examples are perfect squares.
Factorise $a^2 + 2ab + b^2$, by splitting the middle term.
$a^2 + 2ab + b^2 = a^2 + ab + ab + b^2$
$$= a(a + b) + b(a + b)$$
$$= (a + b)(a + b) = (a + b)^2.$$
Similarly
$1 - 4x + 4x^2 = 1 - 2x - 2x + 4x^2$
$$= (1 - 2x) - 2x(1 - 2x)$$
$$= (1 - 2x)(1 - 2x) = (1 - 2x)^2.$$

WORKED EXAMPLE 10

Factorise the expression $9x^2 - 30x + 25$ by splitting the middle term.

Solution 10

$9x^2 - 30x + 25 = 9x^2 - 15x - 15x + 25$
$$= 3x(3x - 5) - 5(3x - 5)$$
$$= (3x - 5)(3x - 5)$$
$$= (3x - 5)^2.$$

The Difference of two squares

Factorise $x^2 - a^2$.
$x^2 - a^2 = x^2 + ax - ax - a^2 = x(x + a) - a(x + a)$
$$= (x + a)(x - a)$$

$ax - ax = 0$
$(ax)(-ax) = -a^2x^2 = $ product of x^2 and $-a^2$.

WORKED EXAMPLE 11

Factorise $4x^2 - 9$.

Solution 11

$$4x^2 - 9 = 4x^2 + (2x)(3) - (2x)(3) - 9$$
$$= 4x^2 + 6x - 6x - 9$$
$$= 2x(2x + 3) - 3(2x + 3)$$
$$= (2x - 3)(2x + 3).$$

Note the following:

We have created two terms $6x$ and $-6x$ which cancel each other when added, when the terms $6x$ and $-6x$ are multiplied give $-36x^2$, the product of $4x^2$ and -9. The created terms is the product of the square root of $4x^2$ and the square root of 9, $2x$ and 3 respectively.

WORKED EXAMPLE 12

Factorise $25x^2 - 9y^2$.

Solution 12

$$25x^2 - 9y^2 = 25x^2 + (5x)(3y) - (5x)(3y) - 9y^2$$
$$= 25x^2 + 15xy - 15xy - 9y^2$$
$$= 5x(5x + 3y) - 3y(5x + 3y)$$
$$= (5x + 3y)(5x - 3y).$$

Factorisation by the method of completing the squares.

WORKED EXAMPLE 13

Factorise $x^2 + x - 12$ by means of the method of completing the squares.

Solution 13

$$[x^2 + x] - 12 = \left[\left(x + \frac{1}{2}\right)^2 - \frac{1}{4}\right] - 12$$
$$= \left[x^2 + 2\left(\frac{1}{2}\right)x + \frac{1}{4} - \frac{1}{4}\right] - 12$$

$$= \left[x^2 + x + \frac{1}{4} - \frac{1}{4}\right] - 12$$
$$= \left[\left(x + \frac{1}{2}\right)^2 - \frac{1}{4}\right] - 12$$
$$= \left(x + \frac{1}{2}\right)^2 - \frac{1}{4} - \frac{48}{4}$$
$$= \left(x + \frac{1}{2}\right)^2 - \frac{49}{4}$$
$$= \left(x + \frac{1}{2}\right)^2 - \left(\frac{7}{2}\right)^2$$
$$= \left(x + \frac{1}{2} - \frac{7}{2}\right)\left(x + \frac{1}{2} + \frac{7}{2}\right)$$
$$= (x - 3)(x + 4).$$

It is observed, in order to make the first two terms of the quadratic expression a perfect square it is needed to add half of the coefficient of x squared, that is, $\left(\frac{1}{2} \times 1\right)^2 = \frac{1}{4}$, adding and subtracting $\frac{1}{4}$ to the quadratic expression.

The previous expression can also be written as follows and does not alter the quadratic expression.

$$x^2 + x - 12 = x^2 + x + \frac{1}{4} - \frac{1}{4} - 12$$
$$= \left(x + \frac{1}{2}\right)^2 - \frac{1}{4} - 12$$
$$= \left(x + \frac{1}{2}\right)^2 - \frac{49}{4}$$
$$= \left(x + \frac{1}{2}\right)^2 - \left(\frac{7}{2}\right)^2.$$

Thus, creating a difference of two squares, which can be expressed as two factors of the difference and the sum.

$$x^2 + x - 12 = \left[\left(x + \frac{1}{2}\right) - \frac{7}{2}\right]$$
$$\left[\left(x + \frac{1}{2}\right) + \frac{7}{2}\right]$$
$$= (x - 3)(x + 4).$$

WORKED EXAMPLE 14

Factorise $x^2 + 2x - 3$ by means of the method of completing the squares.

Solution 14

$$x^2 + 2x - 3 = x^2 + 2x + \left[\frac{1}{2}(2)\right]^2 - \left[\frac{1}{2}(2)\right]^2 - 3$$

$$= x^2 + 2x + 1^2 - 1^2 - 3$$

$$= (x + 1)^2 - 1 - 3$$

$$= (x + 1)^2 - 4$$

$$= (x + 1)^2 - 2^2.$$

$$x^2 + 2x - 3 = [(x + 1) - 2][(x + 1) + 2]$$

$$= (x - 1)(x + 3).$$

WORKED EXAMPLE 15

Factorise $2x^2 + 5x - 3$ by means of the method of completing the squares.

Solution 15

This example is a little more difficult.

$$2x^2 + 5x - 3 = 2\left(x^2 + \frac{5}{2}x - \frac{3}{2}\right)$$

$$= 2\left\{[x^2 + \frac{5}{2}x + \left[\frac{1}{2}\left(\frac{5}{2}\right)\right]^2\right.$$

$$\left. - \left[\frac{1}{2}\left(\frac{5}{2}\right)\right]^2 - \frac{3}{2}]\right\}$$

$$= 2\left[x^2 + \frac{5}{2}x + \frac{5^2}{4^2} - \frac{5^2}{4^2} - \frac{3}{2}\right]$$

$$= 2\left[\left(x + \frac{5}{4}\right)^2 - \frac{25}{16} - \frac{3}{2}\right]$$

$$= 2\left[\left(x + \frac{5}{4}\right)^2 - \frac{25}{16} - \frac{24}{16}\right]$$

$$= 2\left[\left(x + \frac{5}{4}\right)^2 - \frac{49}{16}\right]$$

$$= 2\left[\left(x + \frac{5}{4}\right)^2 - \left(\frac{7}{4}\right)^2\right]$$

$$= 2\left\{\left(x + \frac{5}{4}\right) - \frac{7}{4}\right\}$$

$$\left\{\left(x + \frac{5}{4}\right) + \frac{7}{4}\right\}$$

$$= 2\left(x - \frac{2}{4}\right)\left(x + \frac{12}{4}\right)$$

$$= (2x - 1)(x + 3).$$

1.3 Recognizes that some simple quadratic expressions do not factorise e.g. $a^2 + b^2$

We have seen how to factorise trinomials or quadratic expressions and difference of squares, but the sum of two squares cannot be factorised, such as $a^2 + b^2$.

1.4 Defines the roots of an equation

There are two roots of a quadratic equation.

If $x = \alpha$ and $x = \beta$ are the roots then $x - \alpha = 0$ and $x - \beta = 0$, also the product $(x - \alpha)(x - \beta) = 0$ or $x^2 - \alpha x - \beta x + \alpha\beta = 0$

$$x^2 - (\alpha + \beta)x + \alpha\beta = 0$$

If $\alpha = -1$ and $\beta = -2$ then the quadratic equations is

$$x^2 - (-1 - 2)x + (-1)(-2) = 0$$
$$x^2 + 3x + 2 = 0$$

1.5 Determines the equation which is satisfied by a given pair of roots

---

WORKED EXAMPLE 16

A quadratic equation has a pair of roots, $x = 1$ and $x = 2$. Determine the quadratic equation.

Solution 16

$x = 1$ or $x - 1 = 0$
$x = 2$ or $x - 2 = 0$
$(x - 1)(x - 2) = 0$
$x^2 - x - 2x + 2 = 0$
$x^2 - 3x + 2 = 0$

WORKED EXAMPLE 17

Determine the quadratic equation whose roots are $x = -3$ and $x = 5$.

Solution 17

$x = -3$ or $x + 3 = 0$,

$x = 5$ or $x - 5 = 0$

$(x + 3)(x - 5) = 0$,

$x^2 + 3x - 5x - 15 = 0$

$x^2 - 2x - 15 = 0$.

1.6 Recognizes (a) a quadratic expression; (b) a quadratic equation

(a) A quadratic expression

A quadratic expression of general form is given as $y = ax^2 + bx + c$ where a, b and c are real constants x is the independent variable and y is the dependent variable. This quadratic expression represents a parabola which may have a maximum or minimum depending on the sign of the constant 'a', if it is negative it is a maximum, if it is positive it is a minimum.

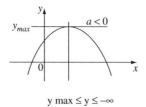

y max $\leq$ y $\leq -\infty$

Fig. 1

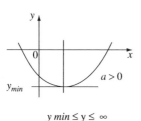

y min $\leq$ y $\leq \infty$

Fig. 2

Fig 1. and Fig 2. represents parabolas with values of y between y max and negative infinity and y min and positive infinity respectively. Therefore, the values of y depend on the various values of x.

An alternative notation for a quadratic expression is given below.

$f(x) = ax^2 + bx + c$

where $f(x)$ is read as 'f of x' and denotes a function in terms of x.

(b) A quadratic equation

When $y = f(x) = 0$ then the quadratic expression becomes a quadratic equation. Therefore a quadratic equation is given as:

$ax^2 + bx + c = 0$.

WORKED EXAMPLE 18

(a) Draw a graph $y = 2x^2 - 5x - 2$ for the values of x, $-2, -1, 0, 1, 2, 3$.

(b) If $y = 0$, find from the graph the values of x.

Solution 18

(a)

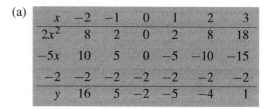

x	-2	-1	0	1	2	3
$2x^2$	8	2	0	2	8	18
$-5x$	10	5	0	-5	-10	-15
-2	-2	-2	-2	-2	-2	-2
y	16	5	-2	-5	-4	1

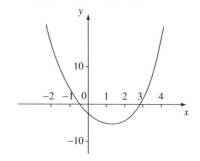

Fig. 3

When $y = 0$ then $x = 2.85$ and $x = -0.35$.

A quadratic expression represents a curve which is a parabola and a quadratic equation represents two points on the parabola, when $y = 0$ then $x = -0.35$ and $x = 2.85$. The coordinates of the points are $(-0.35, 0)$ and $(2.85, 0)$.

1.7 Solves quadratic equations with real roots by factorisation

There are two distinct methods of factorisation of quadratic expressions.

(a) The method of splitting the middle term;

(b) The method of completing the square.

WORKED EXAMPLE 19

Solve the quadratic equation $x^2 - 11x + 30 = 0$ by the two methods of factorisation.

Solution 19

(a) $x^2 - 11x + 30 = 0$

$x^2 - 6x - 5x + 30 = 0$

$x(x - 6) - 5(x - 6) = 0$

$(x - 6)(x - 5) = 0$

$x - 5 = 0$ or $x - 6 = 0$

$x = 5$ or $x = 6.$

(b) $x^2 - 11x + 30 = 0$

$x^2 - 11x + \left(\dfrac{11}{2}\right)^2 - \left(\dfrac{11}{2}\right)^2 + 30 = 0$

$\left(x - \dfrac{11}{2}\right)^2 - \dfrac{121}{4} + 30 = 0$

$\left(x - \dfrac{11}{2}\right)^2 - \dfrac{121}{4} + \dfrac{120}{4} = 0$

$\left(x - \dfrac{11}{2}\right)^2 - \dfrac{1}{4} = 0$

$\left(x - \dfrac{11}{2}\right)^2 - \left(\dfrac{1}{2}\right)^2 = 0$

$\left[\left(x - \dfrac{11}{2}\right) - \dfrac{1}{2}\right]\left[\left(x - \dfrac{11}{2}\right) + \dfrac{1}{2}\right] = 0$

$\left(x - \dfrac{12}{2}\right)\left(x - \dfrac{10}{2}\right) = 0$

$(x - 6)(x - 5) = 0$

$x - 6 = 0$ or $x - 5 = 0$

$x = 6$ or $x = 5.$

WORKED EXAMPLE 20

Solve the quadratic equation $8x^2 - 2x - 15 = 0$ by the two methods of factorisation.

Solution 20

(a) $8x^2 - 2x - 15 = 0$

$8x^2 - 12x + 10x - 15 = 0$

$4x(2x - 3) + 5(2x - 3) = 0$

$(2x - 3)(4x + 5) = 0$

$(2x - 3) = 0$ or $4x + 5 = 0$

$x = \dfrac{3}{2}$ or $x = -\dfrac{5}{4}.$

(b) $8x^2 - 2x - 15 = 0$

$8\left(x^2 - \dfrac{2}{8}x - \dfrac{15}{8}\right) = 0$

$8\left(x^2 - \dfrac{1}{4}x - \dfrac{15}{8}\right) = 0$

$8\left[x^2 - \dfrac{1}{4}x + \left(\dfrac{1}{8}\right)^2 - \left(\dfrac{1}{8}\right)^2 - \dfrac{15}{8}\right] = 0$

$8\left[x^2 - \dfrac{1}{4}x + \dfrac{1}{64} - \dfrac{1}{64} - \dfrac{15}{8}\right] = 0$

$8\left[\left(x - \dfrac{1}{8}\right)^2 - \dfrac{1}{64} - \dfrac{120}{8 \times 8}\right] = 0$

$8\left[\left(x - \dfrac{1}{8}\right)^2 - \dfrac{121}{64}\right] = 0$

$8\left[\left(x - \dfrac{1}{8}\right)^2 - \left(\dfrac{11}{8}\right)^2\right] = 0$

$8\left[\left\{\left(x - \dfrac{1}{8}\right) - \dfrac{11}{8}\right\}\right.$

$\left.\left\{\left(x - \dfrac{1}{8}\right) + \dfrac{11}{8}\right\}\right] = 0$

$8\left(x - \dfrac{12}{8}\right)\left(x + \dfrac{10}{8}\right) = 0$

$8\left(x - \dfrac{3}{2}\right)\left(x + \dfrac{5}{4}\right) = 0$

$$(2x - 3)(4x + 5) = 0$$
$$2x - 3 = 0 \text{ or } 4x + 5 = 0$$
$$x = \frac{3}{2} \text{ or } x = -\frac{5}{4}.$$

1.8 Solves quadratic equations, which provide real roots, by the use of the formula.

The quadratic equation $ax^2 + bx + c = 0$ dividing each term by a, provided that $a \neq 0$, we have

$$x^2 + \frac{b}{a}x + \frac{c}{a} = 0.$$

Using the method of completing the square, we have:

$$x^2 + \frac{b}{a}x + \left(\frac{b}{2a}\right)^2 - \left(\frac{b}{2a}\right)^2 + \frac{c}{a} = 0.$$

By adding and subtracting the squares of the half of the coefficient of x.

$$\left(x + \frac{b}{2a}\right)^2 = \frac{b^2}{4a^2} - \frac{c}{a} = \frac{b^2 - 4ac}{4a^2}.$$

Square rooting both sides, we have:

$$x + \frac{b}{2a} = \pm\sqrt{\frac{b^2 - 4ac}{4a^2}}$$

$$x = -\frac{b}{2a} \pm \frac{\sqrt{b^2 - 4ac}}{2a}$$

$$x = \frac{-b \pm \sqrt{b^2 - 4ac}}{2a}.$$

The formula for solving the quadratic equation.

WORKED EXAMPLE 21

Solve the quadratic equations by means of the formula.

(i) $x^2 + 2x - 3 = 0$
(ii) $x^2 + x - 12 = 0$
(iii) $2x^2 + 5x - 3 = 0$

Solution 21

(i) $x^2 + 2x - 3 = 0$
$a = 1, b = 2, c = -3$

$$x = \frac{-b \pm \sqrt{b^2 - 4ac}}{2a}$$
$$= \frac{-2 \pm \sqrt{2^2 - 4(1)(-3)}}{2 \times 1}$$
$$= \frac{-2 \pm \sqrt{4 + 12}}{2} = \frac{-2 \pm \sqrt{16}}{2}$$
$$= \frac{-2 \pm 4}{2}$$
$$x = \frac{-2 + 4}{2} = 1 \text{ or } x = \frac{-2 - 4}{2} = -3.$$

Therefore $x = 1$ and $x = -3$.

(ii) $x^2 + x - 12 = 0$
$a = 1, b = 1$ and $c = -12$
$$x = \frac{-b \pm \sqrt{b^2 - 4ac}}{2a}$$
$$x = \frac{-1 \pm \sqrt{1^2 - 4 \times 1 \times (-12)}}{2 \times 1}$$
$$= \frac{-1 \pm \sqrt{49}}{2}$$
$$x = \frac{-1 \pm 7}{2}$$
$$x = \frac{-1 + 7}{2} = 3 \text{ or } x = \frac{-1 - 7}{2} = -4.$$

Therefore $x = 3$ or $x = -4$.

(iii) $2x^2 + 5x - 3 = 0$
$a = 2, b = 5$ and $c = -3$
$$x = \frac{-b \pm \sqrt{b^2 - 4ac}}{2a}$$
$$x = \frac{-5 \pm \sqrt{5^2 - 4 \times 2 \times (-3)}}{2 \times 2}$$
$$= \frac{-5 \pm \sqrt{25 + 24}}{4}$$
$$x = \frac{-5 \pm 7}{4}$$
$$x = \frac{-5 + 7}{4} = \frac{1}{2} \text{ or } x = \frac{-5 - 7}{4} = -3$$
$$x = \frac{1}{2} \text{ or } x = -3.$$

1.9 Forms and solves quadratic equations which are mathematical models of practical problems e.g. linear accelerated motion, second order chemical reaction

Forming a quadratic equation

A vehicle with an initial velocity, u, a final velocity, v and a constant acceleration, a, in time, t has a relationship.

$$v = u + at \qquad \qquad ...(1)$$

Fig. 4

The velocity/time graph is shown in Fig. 4.

The distance travelled, s, is given by the area of the trapezium.

$$s = \frac{1}{2}(u + v)t \qquad \qquad ...(2)$$

Substituting (1) in (2) we have:

$$s = \frac{1}{2}(u + u + at)t = ut + \frac{1}{2}at^2.$$

This is a quadratic equation in t, which can be written as $\frac{1}{2}at^2 + ut - s = 0$.

This is a mathematical model of a practical problem of linear accelerated motion.

Solving the quadratic equation of linear accelerated motion

▬ **WORKED EXAMPLE 22**

Determine the time taken for a linear accelerated motion of a vehicle, if the initial velocity is 10 m/s, with a constant acceleration 5 m/s^2 to cover a distance of 1,000 m.

Solution 22

Given the quadratic equation in t, $\frac{1}{2}at^2 + ut - s = 0$ and substituting the values given $a = 5$ m/s^2, $u = 10$ m/s, $s = 1,000$ m;

$\frac{1}{2}5t^2 + 10t - 1000 = 0$ Multiplying each term by 2;

$$5t^2 + 20t - 2,000 = 0$$

$$t = \frac{-20 \pm \sqrt{20^2 - 4 \times 5(-2,000)}}{2 \times 5}$$

$$= \frac{-20 \pm \sqrt{400 + 40,000}}{10}$$

$$= -2 \pm \sqrt{4 + 400} = -2 \pm 20.1$$

$t = 18.1$s and $t = -22.1$s the latter is disregarded since negative time has no significance, therefore, the time taken is 18.1s.

▬ **WORKED EXAMPLE 23**

A square has side 'a' cm and its diagonal is 8 cm longer than its side. Determine the value of the side to the nearest whole centimeter.

Solution 23

Using Pythagoras theorem.

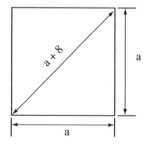

$$(a + 8)^2 = a^2 + a^2$$
$$a^2 - 16a - 64 = 0$$
$$a = \frac{16 \pm \sqrt{16^2 - 4 \times 1 \times (-64)}}{2}$$
$$= \frac{16 \pm 22.6274}{2}$$

$a = 19.3$ cm or $a = -3.31$ cm the negative value of the side is meaningless, therefore the value of the side to the nearest whole centimeter is 19.

1.10 Checks solution of the equation by substitution disregarding irrelevant roots.

This is best illustrated with an example. If the longer side of a rectangle is 3 units more than the shorter side, determine the sides if the area of the rectangle is 4 m^2.

Let x be the shorter side, therefore the longer side is $x + 3$.

The area of the rectangle $= x(x + 3) = 4$, $x^2 + 3x - 4 = 0$.

Applying the quadratic formula:

$$x = \frac{-3 \pm \sqrt{3^2 + 16}}{2} = \frac{-3 \pm 5}{2}$$

$x = -4$ and $x = 1$.

The root $x = -4$ is an irrelevant root since the side or length cannot be negative, therefore we take the solution $x = 1$, the shorter side and hence the longer side will be $x + 3 = 1 + 3 = 4$ m. Area of the rectangle $= 4 \times 1 = 4$ m^2.

1.11 Solves algebraically simultaneous quadratic and linear equations.

WORKED EXAMPLE 24

Solve simultaneously the equations:

(i) $y = 6x + 10$ and $y = x^2 - 5x + 40$
(ii) $y = x^2 - 5x + 7$ and $y = -3x + 10$.

Solution 24

(i) $y = 6x + 10$ ...(1)
$y = x^2 - 5x + 40$ ...(2)

Substituting equation (1) in (2) we have;

$6x + 10 = x^2 - 5x + 40$
$x^2 - 5x - 6x + 40 - 10 = 0$
$x^2 - 11x + 30 = 0$

Applying the quadratic formula;

$$= \frac{-b \pm \sqrt{b^2 - 4ac}}{2a}$$

$$= \frac{-(-11) \pm \sqrt{(-11)^2 - 4 \times 1 \times 30}}{2 \times 1}$$

$$= \frac{11 \pm \sqrt{121 - 120}}{2}$$

$$= \frac{11 \pm 1}{2}$$

$x = \frac{11 + 1}{2} = 6$ or

$x = \frac{11 - 1}{2} = \frac{10}{2} = 5$

$x = 6 \quad x = 5$.

Substituting these values in

(1) $y = 6 \times 6 + 10 = 36 + 10 = 46$ and $y = 6 \times 5 + 10 = 30 + 10$

when $x = 6$, $y = 46$ and when $x = 5$, $y = 40$.

(ii) $y = x^2 - 5x + 7$ ...(1)
$y = -3x + 10$.   ...(2)

Substituting equation (2) in (1) we have;

$-3x + 10 = x^2 - 5x + 7$
$x^2 - 5x + 7 + 3x - 10 = 0$
$x^2 - 2x - 3 = 0$.

Applying the quadratic formula;

$$x = \frac{2 \pm 4}{2}$$

$x = 3$ or $x = -1$.

Substituting these values in (2)

$y = -3(3) + 10 = -9 + 10 = 1$
when $x = 3$, $y = -1$.

$y = -3(-1) + 10 = 3 + 10 = 13$
when $x = -1$, $y = 13$.

Exercises 1

1. Write down the identities for the following:

(i) $(1 - 2x)^2$
(ii) $(2 + y)^2$
(iii) $(b + 3c)^2$
(iv) $(3 - x)^2$
(v) $(4x + 5y)^2$.

2. Simplify the following expressions:

   (i) $z^2 - 2az + a^2$

   (ii) $1 + 2x + x^2$

   (iii) $9x^2 + 6xy + y^2$.

3. Write down the identities for the following:

   (i) $(a + b)^2$

   (ii) $(a - b)^2$

   (iii) $a^2 - b^2$.

4. Evaluate the following without the use of an electronic calculator:

   (i) $(96)^2 - (95)^2$

   (ii) $(101)^2 - (100)^2$

   (iii) $(199)^2 - (197)^2$.

5. Solve the following equations:

   (i) $y^2 - 9^2 = 0$

   (ii) $4t^2 - 1 = 0$

   (iii) $16x^2 - 9 = 0$.

6. Factorise the following quadratic expressions by means of splitting the middle term.

   (i) $x^2 + 3x + 2$

   (ii) $6x^2 + x - 1$

   (iii) $x^2 + 10x - 24$

   (iv) $x^2 - 2x - 80$

   (v) $x^2 - 4x + 3$

   (vi) $x^2 + 9x + 20$

   (vii) $x^2 - 6x + 9$

   (viii) $9x^2 - 9x - 28$

   (ix) $5x^2 + 9x - 2$

   (x) $2x^2 - 3x - 9$.

7. Factorise the following quadratic expressions by means of completing the square:

   (i) $x^2 - 2x + 1$

   (ii) $x^2 - 3x - 4$

   (iii) $x^2 - 2x$

   (iv) $x^2 + 5x$

   (v) $6x^2 - x - 1$.

8. Find the quadratic equations whose roots are given by the following pairs:

   (i) $(-3, -2)$

   (ii) $(1, -4)$

   (iii) $(2, -3)$

   (iv) $(5, 6)$

   (v) $\left(\dfrac{1}{2}, \dfrac{3}{4}\right)$

   (vi) $\left(-\dfrac{3}{5}, \dfrac{6}{7}\right)$

   (vii) $(2, -4)$

   (viii) $(3, 3)$.

9. Solve the following quadratic equations by using the formula:

   (i) $x^2 - 3x + 2 = 0$

   (ii) $x^2 + 3x + 2 = 0$

   (iii) $6x^2 + 5x + 1 = 0$

   (iv) $x^2 - 8x + 15 = 0$

   (v) $x^2 + 5x + 6 = 0$

   (vi) $(x + 1)(x - 3) = x + 2$

   (vii) $x^2 - 0.02x - 0.03 = 0$

   (viii) $x^2 + 7x - 5 = 0$

   (ix) $x^2 - 9x - 15 = 0$.

   (x) $\dfrac{x + 1}{3} + \dfrac{4}{x - 2} = 5$

   (xi) $\dfrac{1}{x - 1} + \dfrac{2}{x + 2} = 7$

   (xii) $0.3x^2 - 2.9x + 2.1 = 0$

   (xiii) $x^2 - 5 = 0$

   (xiv) $x^2 - 3 = 0$

   (xv) $(x - 7)(x + 8) = 0$

   (xvi) $x^2 - 6x + 8.4375 = 0$

   (xvii) $x^2 + 2x + 0.4375 = 0$

   (xviii) $x^2 - 3.9x - 0.1975 = 0$.

10. Distinguish between a quadratic expression and a quadratic equation. Illustrate by giving an example.

11. Draw the graphs of the quadratic functions:

    (i) $y = x^2 - 7x + 10$ (x between 0 and 6)

    (ii) $y = -x^2 - 8x - 7$ (x between -8 and 0).

    Hence solve the quadratic equations $x^2 - 7x + 10 = 0$ and $x^2 + 8x + 7 = 0$

12. If $v = u + at$ and $s = \frac{1}{2}(u + v)t$ show that
$s = ut + \frac{1}{2}at^2$, If $s = 15$ m,
$u = 5$ m/s and $a = 3$m/s^2, determine the
value of time.

13. The diagonal of a square of side x is $x + 3$.
Find the value of x.

14. The height of a right angled triangle is 3 cm
shorter than the base. Find the value of the
height, if the diagonal is 5 cm.

15. Solve the simultaneous equations:

   (i) $y = 9x^2 - 7x - 25$
   $y = 2x + 3$

   (ii) $y = x^2 + 11x + 25$
   $y = 2x + 5$

   (iii) $y = 9x^2 + 7x - 20$
   $y = 7x - 4$

   (iv) $y = 14x^2 - 25x + 1$
   $y = +4x - 11$.

16. The area of the trapezium is 125 m^2, the
longer parallel side is 5 m more than the
shorter parallel line, determine the length of
the longer side if the distance between the
two parallel lines is twice that of the shorter
side.

2

States the laws of logarithms and simplifies logarithmic expressions.

2.1 Defines a logarithm to any base.

The logarithm of a number N to the base b is equal to R and is written as:

$\log_b N = R$ or $\log_{base}$ number = result.

By definition $b^R = N$, (base)^{result} = number.

If N = 1000 and $b = 10$

$\log_{10} 1000 = R$

$10^R = 1000 = 10^3$

R = 3

therefore $\log_{10} 1000 = 3$ (logarithmic form)

or

$10^3 = 1000$ (indicial form).

2.2 Converts a simple indicial relationship to logarithmic relationship and vice versa.

WORKED EXAMPLE 25

Write in logarithmic form the following indicial form numbers.

(i) $2^5 = 32$

(ii) $3^2 = 9$

(iii) $5^3 = 125$.

Solution 25

(i) $2^5 = 32$

$\log_2 32 = 5$

(ii) $3^2 = 9$

$\log_3 9 = 2$

(iii) $5^3 = 125$

$\log_5 125 = 3$.

WORKED EXAMPLE 26

Write in indicial form the following logarithmic form numbers:

(i) $\log_{10} 0.0001 = -4$

(ii) $\log_{10} 1,000,000 = 6$

(iii) $\log_5 625 = 4$

Solution 26

(i) $\log_{10} 0.0001 = -4$

$10^{-4} = 0.0001$

(ii) $\log_{10} 1,000,000 = 6$

$10^6 = 1,000,000$

(iii) $\log_5 625 = 4$

$5^4 = 625$.

WORKED EXAMPLE 27

Determine the values of x for the following:

(i) $\log_{10} x = -7$

(ii) $\log_x 128 = 7$

(iii) $\log_3 243 = x$

(iv) $\log_{\frac{1}{2}} x = 7$

(v) $\log_x 3^{-5} = 5$

(vi) $\log_{\frac{1}{8}} 2 = x$

Solution 27

(i) $\log_{10} x = -7$ or $10^{-7} = x = 0.0000001$

(ii) $\log_x 128 = 7$ or $x^7 = 128 = 2^7$

$x = 2$

(iii) $\log_3 243 = x$ or $3^x = 243 = 3^5$

$x = 5$

(iv) $\log_{\frac{1}{2}} x = 7$ or $\left(\frac{1}{2}\right)^7 = x$

$\left(2^{-1}\right)^7 = x = 2^{-7} = \frac{1}{2^7}$

$x = \frac{1}{128} = 0.0078125$

(v) $\log_x 3^{-5} = 5$ or $x^5 = 3^{-5} = \left(3^{-1}\right)^5$

$x = 3^{-1} = \frac{1}{3} = 0.333$

(vi) $\log_{\frac{1}{8}} 2 = x$ or $\left(\frac{1}{8}\right)^x = 2$

$\left(\frac{1}{2^3}\right)^x = 2$

$\left(2^{-3}\right)^x = 2^1$

$2^{-3x} = 2^1$

$-3x = 1$

$x = -\frac{1}{3}.$

2.3 Deduces the laws of logarithms in the following terms where b is any base

(a) $\log_b MN = \log_b M + \log_b N$

(b) $\log_b \frac{M}{N} = \log_b M - \log_b N$

(c) $\log_b N^a = a \log_b N$

To deduce;

(a) $\log_b MN = \log_b M + \log_b N$

let $\log_b MN = x$, $\log_b M = x_1$,

$\log_b N = x_2$

by definition

$b^x = MN$, $b^{x_1} = M$,

$b^{x_2} = N$, $b^{x_1} b^{x_2} = MN$,

$b^{x_1 + x_2} = MN = b^x$

hence $x = x_1 + x_2$

therefore $\log_b MN = \log_b M + log_b N$.

To deduce;

(b) $\log_b \frac{M}{N} = \log_b M - \log_b N$

let $x = \log_b \frac{M}{N}$

by definition $b^x = \frac{M}{N}$

let $x_1 = \log_b M$ and   let $x_2 = \log_b N$

by definition $b^{x_1} = M$

by definition $b^{x_2} = N$

$\frac{M}{N} = \frac{b^{x_1}}{b^{x_2}} = b^{x_1 - x_2} = b^x$

hence $x_1 - x_2 = x$

therefore $\log_b M - \log_b N = \log_b \frac{M}{N}$.

To deduce;

(c) $\log_b N^a = a \log_b N$

$\log_b N^a = \log_b NNNN \dots (a \text{ times})$

$= \log_b N + \log_b N + \dots (a \text{ times})$

$\log_b N^a = a \log_b N.$

2.4 States that $\log_b 1 = 0$, $\log_b b = 1$ and the limit as x tends to 0 $\log_b 0 \to -\infty$

The logarithm of unity to any base is zero.

$\log_b 1 = 0$ since by definition $b^0 = 1$.

The logarithm of a number b to the same base b is unity.

$\log_b b = 1$ since by definition $b^1 = b$

$\log_b x \to -\infty$ as x tends to zero since, by definition $b^{-\infty} = x = \frac{1}{b^\infty} = \frac{1}{\infty} = 0$.

2.5 Applies the laws to simplify expressions

WORKED EXAMPLE 28

Simplify the following expressions:

(i) $2 \log a - \log b + \log c$

(ii) $\log M + 2 \log N - 3 \log P$

(iii) $\log Q^{\frac{1}{2}} - \log P^{\frac{1}{3}} + \frac{1}{5} \log R^{\frac{1}{4}}$.

Solution 28

(i) $2 \log a - \log b + \log c$

$= \log a^2 - \log b + \log c$

$= \log a^2 \frac{c}{b}$

(ii) $\log M + 2 \log N - 3 \log P$

$= \log M + \log N^2 - \log P^3$

$= \log \frac{MN^2}{P^3}$

(iii) $\log Q^{\frac{1}{2}} - \log P^{\frac{1}{3}} + \frac{1}{5} \log R^{\frac{1}{4}}$

$= \frac{\log Q^{\frac{1}{2}} R^{\frac{1}{4} \times \frac{1}{5}}}{P^{\frac{1}{3}}}$

$= \frac{\log Q^{\frac{1}{2}} R^{\frac{1}{20}}}{P^{\frac{1}{3}}}$.

WORKED EXAMPLE 29

Simplify the following logarithms.

(i) $2 \log b + \log b^3 - \log b^{\frac{1}{2}}$

(ii) $\log a - \log 4a + \log a^5$

(iii) $\log c^2 - \log c + 5 \log c^3$.

Solution 29

(i) $2 \log b + \log b^3 - \log b^{\frac{1}{2}}$

$= \log \frac{b^2 b^3}{b^{\frac{1}{2}}}$

$= \log \frac{b^5}{b^{\frac{1}{2}}} = \log b^{\frac{9}{2}}$

(ii) $\log a - \log 4a + \log a^5$

$= \log \left(\frac{a}{4a} \right) a^5 = \log \frac{a^5}{4}$

(iii) $\log c^2 - \log c + 5 \log c^3$

$= \log \left(\frac{c^2}{c} \right) c^{15} = \log c^{16}$.

WORKED EXAMPLE 30

Evaluate the following logarithms.

(i) $\log \sqrt{1000} - \log 10^3 + \log \sqrt{1000}$

(ii) $\log_2 8 + \log_2 128 + 5 \log_2 2 + 7$

(iii) $\log_3 243 + \log_3 3 + \log_3 9$.

Solution 30

(i) $\log \sqrt{1000} - \log 10^3 + \log \sqrt{1000}$

$= \frac{1}{2} \log 1000 - \log 1000 + \frac{1}{2} \log 1000$

$= \log 1000 - \log 1000 = 0$

(ii) $\log_2 8 + \log_2 128 + 5 \log_2 2 + 7$

$= \log_2 2^3 + \log_2 2^7 + 5 \log_2 2 + 7$

$= 3 \log_2 2 + 7 \log_2 2 + 5 \log_2 2 + 7$

$= 3 + 7 + 5 + 7 = 22$

(iii) $\log_3 243 + \log_3 3 + \log_3 9$

$= \log_3 3^5 + 1 + \log_3 3^2$

$= 5 \log_3 3 + 1 + 2 \log_3 3$

$= 5 + 1 + 2 = 8$.

WORKED EXAMPLE 31

Evaluate the following expressions:

(i) $\log_{100} 1$

(ii) $\log_{300} 0$

(iii) $\log_I I$

Solution 31

(i) $\log_{100} 1 = x$

$100^x = 1$

therefore $x = 0$

(ii) $\log_{300} 0 = x$

$300^x = 0$

$x \to -\infty$

(iii) $\log_I I = x$

$I^x = I$

$x = 1$.

2.6 Applies the laws to solve equations

WORKED EXAMPLE 32

Solve, for x, the equations:

(i) $5^{(3x+1)} = 625$

(ii) $3^{(2x-1)} = 243$

(iii) $2^{(7x+2)} = 1024$.

Solution 32

(i) $5^{(3x+1)} = 625$.

Taking logarithms to the base 5 on both sides.

$\log_5 5^{(3x+1)} = \log_5 625$

$(3x + 1) \log_5 5 = \log_5 5^4 = 4 \log_5 5$

$3x + 1 = 4$ or $3x = 3$ or $x = 1$.

Alternatively;

$5^{(3x+1)} = 625$

$5^{(3x+1)} = 5^4$

$3x + 1 = 4$

$3x = 3$

$x = 1$.

(ii) $3^{(2x-1)} = 243$.

Taking logarithms to the base 3 on both sides.

$\log_3 3^{(2x-1)} = \log_3 243$

$(2x - 1) \log_3 3 = \log_3 3^5 = 5 \log_3 3$

but $\log_3 3 = 1$

$2x - 1 = 5$

$2x = 6$

$x = 3$.

Alternatively;

$3^{(2x-1)} = 243$

$3^{(2x-1)} = 3^5$

$2x - 1 = 5$

$2x = 6$

$x = 3$.

(iii) $2^{(7x+2)} = 1024$.

Taking logarithms to the base 2 on both sides.

$2^{(7x+2)} = 1024$

$\log_2 2^{(7x+2)} = \log_2 1024$

$(7x + 2) \log_2 2 = \log_2 2^{10} = 10 \log_2 2$

$7x + 2 = 10$

$7x = 8$

$x = \dfrac{8}{7}$.

Alternatively;

$2^{(7x+2)} = 2^{10}$

$7x + 2 = 10$

$7x = 8$

$x = \dfrac{8}{7}$.

Exercises 2

1. Write $\log_x y = n$ in the indicial form.

2. Write $z^y = N$ in the logarithmic form.

3. What is the meaning of $\log_{10} 0.00001$?

4. What is the meaning $10^5 = 100,000$?

5. Show that $\log_N N = 1$.

6. Evaluate $\log_{10} 10 \times 10 \times 10 \times 10 \times 10$.

7. Evaluate $\log_{\frac{1}{2}} \dfrac{1}{2}$.

8. Show that $\log_{10} \dfrac{1}{10^5} = -5$.

9. Write in logarithmic form the following numbers:

   (i) $6^2 = 36$ (ii) $7^3 = 343$

   (iii) $\left(\dfrac{1}{2}\right)^{\frac{1}{2}} = \dfrac{1}{\sqrt{2}}$ (iv) $9^3 = 729$.

10. Write in indicial form the following numbers:

   (i) $\log_3 x = y$ (ii) $\log_5 z = N$

   (iii) $\log_b N = R$ (iv) $\log_5 125 = 3$

   (v) $\log_2 1024 = 10$.

11. Determine the values of x for the following:

   (i) $\log_2 x = 5$

   (ii) $\log_{\frac{1}{2}} x = \dfrac{1}{2}$

   (iii) $\log_x 512 = 9$

   (iv) $\log_x 3^5 = 5$

   (v) $\log_3 \dfrac{1}{3} = x$.

12. Find the values:

   (i) $\log_{100} 10$

   (ii) $\log_{\frac{1}{2}} 2$

   (iii) $\log_2 \dfrac{1}{2}$

   (iv) $\log_1 1$

   (v) $\log_{100} 1000$

   (vi) $\log_{10} 10^{-23}$

   (vii) $\log_3 \dfrac{1}{3^3}$

   (viii) $\log_M M$.

13. If $\log_{10} x = -\infty$ what is x?

14. If $x \to \infty$, find $\dfrac{1}{x}$.

15. If $x \to -\infty$, find $\dfrac{1}{x}$.

16. If $\log_{\frac{1}{1000}} 1000 = x$, what is the value of x.

17. Simplify:
   $$\log_b x - 2\log_b x + \log_b x^5.$$

18. Simplify:
   $$\sqrt{\log_{\frac{1}{x}} x - \log_x \dfrac{1}{x} + 2}$$

19. Simplify:
   $$\log_{10} 20 - \log_{10} 200 + \log_{10} 80 - \log_{10} 8.$$

20. Simplify:
   $$\log a - \log ab + \log b.$$

21. Expand:
   $$\log Q^{\frac{1}{3}} P^{\frac{1}{4}} R^{\frac{1}{5}}.$$

3

Plots and evaluates solutions of exponential growth and decay problems.

3.1 States that the derivative of the exponential function is equal to the function.

The exponential function.

When a constant is raised to the power which is a variable such as $y = a^x$ the base is a constant and the exponent is a variable.

$y = 2^x$ and $y = 3^x$ are exponential functions.

$$e = 1 + \frac{1}{1!} + \frac{1}{2!} + \frac{1}{3!} + \ldots$$

a sum of infinite terms.

$$e = 1 + 1 + \frac{1}{2} + \frac{1}{6} + \frac{1}{24} + \frac{1}{120} + \frac{1}{720} + \ldots$$

where $6! = 1 \times 2 \times 3 \times 4 \times 5 \times 6$ (factorial 6)

$e = 2.718281828$ to nine decimal places e is a number between 2 and 3.

$$y = e^x$$

This is a special exponential function whose derivative is the same as the function. $\frac{dy}{dx} = e^x =$ the derivative or the gradient.

This is the only function whose derivative is the same as the function.

3.2 Plots the graphs of $y = e^{ax}$ and $y = e^{-ax}$ using tables/calculators

The graphs of $y = e^x$ and $y = e^{-x}$

x	e^x	e^{-x}
−2.5	0.08	12.1
−2.0	0.13	7.36
−1.5	0.22	4.48
−1	0.36	2.71
−0.5	0.60	1.64
0	1	1
0.5	1.64	0.60
1	2.71	0.36
1.5	4.48	0.22
2	7.36	0.13
2.5	12.1	0.08

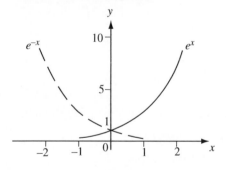

Fig. 6

The graphs of $y = e^{\frac{1}{2}x}$ and $y = e^{-\frac{1}{2}x}$

x	$e^{\frac{x}{2}}$	$e^{-\frac{x}{2}}$
−2	0.368	2.718
−1.5	0.472	2.117
−1	0.607	1.649
−0.5	0.779	1.284
0	1	1
0.5	1.284	0.779
1	1.649	0.607
1.5	2.117	0.472
2.0	2.718	0.368

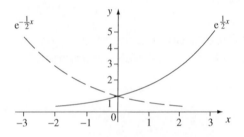

Fig. 7

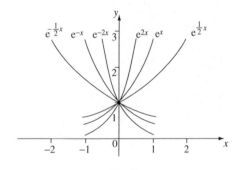

Fig. 8

$y = e^{ax}$ when $a = \dfrac{1}{2}, a = 1, a = 2$ as a increases the graph increases more abruptly.

$y = e^{ax}$ shows growth

$y = e^{-ax}$ shows decay.

3.3 Draws graphs of experimental data of decays and growths which are exponential functions.

A capacitor is charged via a resistor.

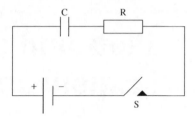

Fig. 9

When S is closed, the voltage across a capacitor is given by the expression.

$v = V\left(1 - e^{-\frac{t}{RC}}\right)$ where t is the time at any instant and the current through the capacitor is given by $i = \left(\frac{V}{R}\right) e^{-\frac{t}{RC}}$ where t is the time at any instant.

The growth curve.

<hr>

WORKED EXAMPLE 33

If $V = 100$ volts, $R = 10 \text{ K}\Omega, C = 100 \ \mu\text{F}$ determine the voltage v at the following times $t(s)$ 0.1, 0.2, 0.5, 0.8, 1, 1.2, 1.5, 1.8, 2, and 5.

Solution 33

$$v = V(1 - e^{-\frac{t}{RC}})$$
$$v = 100(1 - e^{-\frac{t}{1}})$$
$$RC = 10 \times 10^3 \times 100 \times 10^{-6} = 1 \ s$$
$$v = 100(1 - e^{-t})$$
$$t = 0$$
$$v = 100(1 - e^0) = 100(1 - 1) = 0 \text{ volts}$$
$$t = 0.1 \text{ s} \quad v = 100(1 - e^{-0.1})$$
$$= 9.52 \text{ volts}$$

$t = 0.2$ s $\quad v = 100\,(1 - e^{-0.2})$

$\qquad\qquad = 18.1$ volts

$t = 0.5$ s $\quad v = 100\,(1 - e^{-0.5})$

$\qquad\qquad = 39.4$ volts

$t = 0.8$ s $\quad v = 100\,(1 - e^{-0.8})$

$\qquad\qquad = 55.1$ volts

$t = 1$ s, $\quad v = 100\,(1 - e^{-1})$

$\qquad\qquad = 63.2$ volts

$t = 2$ s $\quad v = 100\,(1 - e^{-2})$

$\qquad\qquad = 86.5$ volts

$t = 5$ s $\quad v = 100\,(1 - e^{-5})$

$\qquad\qquad = 99.3$ volts.

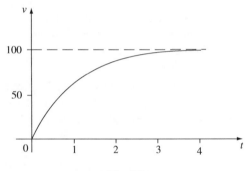

Fig. 10

WORKED EXAMPLE 34

Determine the current i for the previous example with the same values of time.

Solution 34

$$i = le^{-\frac{t}{RC}}$$

$RC = 1$ s $\quad i = \left(\dfrac{V}{R}\right)e^{-\frac{t}{1}}$

$\qquad\qquad = \dfrac{100}{(10 \times 10^3)}\,e^{-t}$

$\qquad\qquad = 10 \times 10^{-3}\,e^{-t}$

$t = 0$ $\qquad i = 10 \times 10^{-3}\,e^0 = 10$ mA

$t = 0.1$ s $\quad i = 10 \times 10^{-3}\,e^{-0.1} = 9.05$ mA

$t = 0.2$ s $\quad i = 10 \times 10^{-3}\,e^{-0.2} = 8.19$ mA

$t = 0.5$ s $\quad i = 10 \times 10^{-3}\,e^{-0.5} = 6.07$ mA

$t = 0.8$ s $\quad i = 10 \times 10^{-3}\,e^{-0.8} = 4.49$ mA

$t = 1$ s $\qquad i = 10 \times 10^{-3}\,e^{-1} = 3.68$ mA

$t = 2$ s $\qquad i = 10 \times 10^{-3}\,e^{-2} = 1.35$ mA

$t = 3$ s $\qquad i = 10 \times 10^{-3}\,e^{-5} = 0.068$ mA

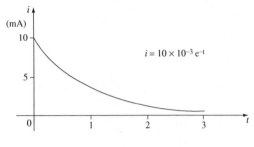

Fig. 11

3.4 Determines the gradients of such curves and recognizes they are proportional to the ordinate.

The gradient of $y = 3e^x$ is the same as the function,

$\dfrac{dy}{dx} = 3e^x$. If $x = 1$,

$y = 3e = 8.15$, the ordinate of the gradient $= 3e^x = 8.15$. The gradient at $x = 1$ is the same as the ordinate.

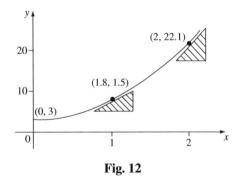

Fig. 12

Exercises 3

1. If $y = 5e^x$, show that the gradients at $x = 1$ and $x = 2$ are the same values as the functions at $x = 1$ and $x = 2$ respectively.

2. What is the gradient of the function
$y = \dfrac{1}{2}e^x$ at $x = 0.5$?

3. What is the gradient of the function $y = 4e^x$ at $x = 0.1$?

4. Sketch the following graphs:

   (i) $y = e^{3x}$

   (ii) $y = \dfrac{1}{5}e^{-3x}$

   (iii) $y = 3e^{-2x}$.

5. The following are growth and decay functions of the charge on a capacitor.

   (i) $q = Q(1 - e^{-\frac{t}{\tau}})$

   (ii) $q = Qe^{-\frac{t}{\tau}}$.

   Sketch these graphs.

6. (a) For values of x from -2 to $+2$ at 0.2 unit intervals draw neatly the graph $y = 3e^x$.

   (i) From the graph, read off the values of x when $y = 15$, $y = 10$, and $y = 5$.

   (ii) from the graph, read off the values of y when $x = -1.9$, $x = -1.1$, $x = 0.3$, $x = 0.9$ and $x = 1.7$.

   (b) Draw neatly the graph $y = 3e^{-x}$ on the same graph paper for the same unit intervals. From the graphs determine the point of intersection of the two graphs $y = 3e^{-x}$ and $y = 3e^x$ and what can you say about the y-axis.

7. Use the calculator to find the values of the following:

   (i) $32.5\, e^{-3.7}$ (ii) $7.5\, e^{3.1}$

   (iii) $25\, e^2$ (iv) $100\, e^{-3}$

   (v) $-1000\, e^{\frac{3}{4}}$

8. Use the calculator to find the value of v in the formula $v = 100\,(1 - e^{-\frac{t}{\tau}})$ where $t = 5 \times 10^{-3}$ s, $\tau = 25 \times 10^{-3}$ s.

9. The charge on a capacitor at time t is given $q = Q(1 - e^{-\frac{t}{\tau}})$, if $q = 2$ coulombs, determine Q if $t = 5$ ms and $\tau = 2$ s.

Understands the notation of matrices and determinants

4.1 Recognizes the notation for a matrix

Notation of a matrix 2×2

$$A = \begin{pmatrix} a_{11} & a_{12} \\ a_{21} & a_{22} \end{pmatrix}$$

Which is an array of numbers consisting of two rows and two columns and the order of the matrix is 2×2 the first 2 denotes the number of rows and the second 2 the number of columns. a_{11}, a_{12}, a_{21} and a_{22} are the elements of the matrix and the subscripts, 11, denotes the first row and the first column, 12, denotes the first row and the second column, 21, denotes the second row and the first column and finally 22, denotes the second row and the second column.

What does a 2×1 matrix represent?

$\begin{pmatrix} 2 \\ 1 \end{pmatrix}$ is 2×1 matrix which represents a vector of 2 units horizontally and one unit vertically.

4.2 Calculates the sum and difference of two matrices (2×2 only).

Sum and difference of two matrices.

Matrices are denoted by single bold capital letters, for example:

$$A = \begin{pmatrix} a_{11} & a_{12} \\ a_{21} & a_{22} \end{pmatrix} \text{ and } B = \begin{pmatrix} b_{11} & b_{12} \\ b_{21} & b_{22} \end{pmatrix}.$$

The sum of two matrices such as $A+B$ or $B+A$. The difference of two matrices such as $A - B$ or $B - A$.

$$A + B = \begin{pmatrix} a_{11} & a_{12} \\ a_{21} & a_{22} \end{pmatrix} + \begin{pmatrix} b_{11} & b_{12} \\ b_{21} & b_{22} \end{pmatrix}$$

$$= \begin{pmatrix} a_{11} + b_{11} & a_{12} + b_{12} \\ a_{21} + b_{21} & a_{22} + b_{22} \end{pmatrix}$$

$$B + A = \begin{pmatrix} b_{11} & b_{12} \\ b_{21} & b_{22} \end{pmatrix} + \begin{pmatrix} a_{11} & a_{12} \\ a_{21} & a_{22} \end{pmatrix}$$

$$= \begin{pmatrix} b_{11} + a_{11} & b_{12} + a_{12} \\ b_{21} + a_{21} & b_{22} + a_{22} \end{pmatrix}.$$

It is observed that $A + B = B + A$ therefore the summation of matrices is associative.

$$A - B = \begin{pmatrix} a_{11} & a_{12} \\ a_{21} & a_{22} \end{pmatrix} - \begin{pmatrix} b_{11} & b_{12} \\ b_{21} & b_{22} \end{pmatrix}$$

$$= \begin{pmatrix} a_{11} - b_{11} & a_{12} - b_{12} \\ a_{21} - b_{21} & a_{22} - b_{22} \end{pmatrix}.$$

WORKED EXAMPLE 35

If $A = \begin{pmatrix} 1 & -1 \\ 2 & 0 \end{pmatrix}$ and $B = \begin{pmatrix} 2 & 3 \\ -1 & 4 \end{pmatrix}$.

Determine:

(i) $A + B$

(ii) $A - B$ and

(iii) $B - A$

Solution 35

(i) $\mathbf{A} + \mathbf{B} = \begin{pmatrix} 1 & -1 \\ 2 & 0 \end{pmatrix} + \begin{pmatrix} 2 & 3 \\ -1 & 4 \end{pmatrix}$

$\qquad = \begin{pmatrix} 1+2 & -1+3 \\ 2-1 & 0+4 \end{pmatrix} = \begin{pmatrix} 3 & 2 \\ 1 & 4 \end{pmatrix}$

$\qquad \mathbf{A} + \mathbf{B} = \begin{pmatrix} 3 & 2 \\ 1 & 4 \end{pmatrix}$

(ii) $\mathbf{A} - \mathbf{B} = \begin{pmatrix} 1 & -1 \\ 2 & 0 \end{pmatrix} - \begin{pmatrix} 2 & 3 \\ -1 & 4 \end{pmatrix}$

$\qquad = \begin{pmatrix} 1-2 & -1-3 \\ 2-(-1) & 0-4 \end{pmatrix}$

$\qquad = \begin{pmatrix} -1 & -4 \\ 3 & -4 \end{pmatrix}$

$\qquad \mathbf{A} - \mathbf{B} = \begin{pmatrix} -1 & -4 \\ 3 & -4 \end{pmatrix}$

(iii) $\mathbf{B} - \mathbf{A} = \begin{pmatrix} 2 & 3 \\ -1 & 4 \end{pmatrix} - \begin{pmatrix} 1 & -1 \\ 2 & 0 \end{pmatrix}$

$\qquad = \begin{pmatrix} 2-1 & 3-(-1) \\ -1-2 & 4 \end{pmatrix}$

$\qquad = \begin{pmatrix} 1 & 4 \\ -3 & 4 \end{pmatrix}.$

4.3 Calculates the product of two matrices (2 × 2 only). Demonstrates that the product of two matrices, in general, is non-commutative.

The product of two matrices.

$\mathbf{A} = \begin{pmatrix} a_{11} & a_{12} \\ a_{21} & a_{22} \end{pmatrix}$ and $\mathbf{B} = \begin{pmatrix} b_{11} & b_{12} \\ b_{21} & b_{22} \end{pmatrix}$

$\mathbf{AB} = \begin{pmatrix} \overrightarrow{a_{11} \quad a_{12}} \\ a_{21} \quad a_{22} \end{pmatrix} \begin{pmatrix} b_{11} & b_{12} \\ b_{21} & b_{22} \end{pmatrix}$

$\qquad = \begin{pmatrix} a_{11}\,b_{11} + a_{12}\,b_{21} & a_{11}\,b_{12} + a_{12}\,b_{22} \\ a_{21}\,b_{11} + a_{22}\,b_{21} & a_{21}\,b_{12} + a_{22}\,b_{22} \end{pmatrix}.$

WORKED EXAMPLE 36

If $\mathbf{A} = \begin{pmatrix} 2 & 1 \\ -1 & 3 \end{pmatrix}$ and $\mathbf{B} = \begin{pmatrix} -1 & 2 \\ 1 & -2 \end{pmatrix}$

Determine: (i) $\mathbf{AB}$ and (ii) $\mathbf{BA}$.

Solution 36

(i) $\mathbf{AB} = \begin{pmatrix} \overrightarrow{2 \quad 1} \\ -1 \quad 3 \end{pmatrix} \begin{pmatrix} -1 & 2 \\ 1 & -2 \end{pmatrix}$

$\qquad = \begin{pmatrix} 2\times(-1)+1\times1 & 2\times2+1\times(-2) \\ (-1)\times(-1)+3\times1 & (-1)\times2+3\times(-2) \end{pmatrix}$

$\qquad = \begin{pmatrix} -2+1 & 4-2 \\ 1+3 & -2-6 \end{pmatrix}$

$\qquad = \begin{pmatrix} -1 & 2 \\ 4 & -8 \end{pmatrix}.$

(ii) $\mathbf{BA} = \begin{pmatrix} \overrightarrow{-1 \quad 2} \\ 1 \quad -2 \end{pmatrix} \begin{pmatrix} 2 & 1 \\ -1 & 3 \end{pmatrix}$

$\qquad = \begin{pmatrix} (-1)\times2+2\times(-1) & (-1)\times1+2\times3 \\ 1\times2+(-2)\times(-1) & 1\times1+(-2)\times3 \end{pmatrix}$

$\qquad = \begin{pmatrix} -2-2 & -1+6 \\ 2+2 & 1-6 \end{pmatrix}$

$\qquad = \begin{pmatrix} -4 & 5 \\ 4 & -5 \end{pmatrix}$

$\qquad \mathbf{AB} = \begin{pmatrix} -1 & 2 \\ 4 & -8 \end{pmatrix}$ and

$\qquad \mathbf{BA} = \begin{pmatrix} -4 & 5 \\ 4 & -5 \end{pmatrix}.$

The product of two matrices, in general, is non-commutative. That is $\mathbf{AB} \neq \mathbf{BA}$.
The product of two matrices is more difficult than the addition and subtraction, therefore consider a few more worked examples in order to master this operation.

Determine MN and MNP if:

$$\mathbf{M} = \begin{pmatrix} 1 & 0 \\ 2 & 1 \end{pmatrix}$$

$$\mathbf{N} = \begin{pmatrix} 2 & -2 \\ 1 & 3 \end{pmatrix}$$

$$\mathbf{P} = \begin{pmatrix} -3 & 1 \\ 1 & -2 \end{pmatrix}.$$

Solution 37

$$\mathbf{MN} = \begin{pmatrix} 1 & 0 \\ 2 & 1 \end{pmatrix} \begin{pmatrix} 2 & -2 \\ 1 & 3 \end{pmatrix}$$

$$= \begin{pmatrix} 1 \times 2 + 0 \times 1 & 1 \times (-2) + 0 \times 3 \\ 2 \times 2 + 1 \times 1 & 2 \times (-2) + 1 \times 3 \end{pmatrix}$$

$$= \begin{pmatrix} 2 & -2 \\ 5 & -1 \end{pmatrix}$$

$$\mathbf{MNP} = \begin{pmatrix} 2 & -2 \\ 5 & -1 \end{pmatrix} \begin{pmatrix} -3 & 1 \\ 1 & -2 \end{pmatrix}$$

$$= \begin{pmatrix} 2 \times (-3) + (-2) \times 1 & 2 \times 1 + (-2)(-2) \\ 5 \times (-3) + (-1) \times 1 & 5 \times 1 + (-1) \times (-2) \end{pmatrix}$$

$$\mathbf{MNP} = \begin{pmatrix} -8 & 6 \\ -16 & 7 \end{pmatrix}.$$

4.5 Defines the unit matrix

Unit matrix

$$\mathbf{I} = \begin{pmatrix} 1 & 0 \\ 0 & 1 \end{pmatrix} \quad \text{is called the unit matrix.}$$

The special property of a unit matrix. Multiplying any matrix by the unit matrix, the matrix remains unaltered.

$$\mathbf{M} = \begin{pmatrix} 3 & 4 \\ -2 & 1 \end{pmatrix} \quad \text{and } \mathbf{I} = \begin{pmatrix} 1 & 0 \\ 0 & 1 \end{pmatrix}$$

$$\mathbf{MI} = \begin{pmatrix} 3 & 4 \\ -2 & 1 \end{pmatrix} \begin{pmatrix} 1 & 0 \\ 0 & 1 \end{pmatrix}$$

$$= \begin{pmatrix} 3 \times 1 + 4 \times 0 & 3 \times 0 + 4 \times 1 \\ -2 \times 1 + 1 \times 0 & -2 \times 0 + 1 \times 1 \end{pmatrix}$$

$$= \begin{pmatrix} 3 & 4 \\ -2 & 1 \end{pmatrix} = \mathbf{M}.$$

Therefore $\mathbf{MI} = \mathbf{M}$

$$\mathbf{IM} = \begin{pmatrix} 1 & 0 \\ 0 & 1 \end{pmatrix} \begin{pmatrix} 3 & 4 \\ -2 & 1 \end{pmatrix}$$

$$= \begin{pmatrix} 1 \times 3 + 0 \times (-2) & 1 \times 4 + 0 \times 1 \\ 0 \times 3 + 1 \times (-2) & 0 \times 4 + 1 \times 1 \end{pmatrix}$$

$$= \begin{pmatrix} 3 & 4 \\ -2 & 1 \end{pmatrix}.$$

$\mathbf{IM} = \mathbf{M}.$

Therefore premultiplying a matrix (**M**) by a **unit matrix** and post multiplying a matrix (**M**) by a **unit matrix**, the matrix is unaltered.

$\mathbf{IM} = \mathbf{MI} = \mathbf{M}.$

4.6 Recognizes the notation for a determinant.

The determinant of an array of elements is denoted as:

$$|A| = \begin{vmatrix} a_{11} & a_{12} \\ a_{21} & a_{22} \end{vmatrix}$$

$$= a_{11} a_{22} - a_{12} a_{21}.$$

4.7 Evaluates a 2 × 2 determinant

Evaluate a determinant.

Evaluate $\begin{vmatrix} 2 & 4 \\ 1 & -3 \end{vmatrix}.$

Solution

$$\begin{pmatrix} 2 & 4 \\ 1 & -3 \end{pmatrix} = 2 \times (-3) - 4 \times 1$$
$$= -6 - 4 = -10.$$

WORKED EXAMPLE 38

Write $ab - cd$ as a determinant.

Solution 38

$$ab - cd = \begin{vmatrix} a & c \\ d & b \end{vmatrix}$$
$$= \begin{vmatrix} b & d \\ c & a \end{vmatrix}$$
$$= \begin{vmatrix} b & c \\ d & a \end{vmatrix}.$$

5

Solves simultaneous equations with two unknowns, using matrices and determinants.

5.1 Solves simultaneous linear equations with two unknowns using determinants.

Solution of simultaneous equations.

$$a_{11}x + a_{12}y = c_1$$
$$a_{21}x + a_{22}y = c_2$$
$$a_{11}x + a_{12}y - c_1 = 0$$
$$a_{21}x + a_{22}y - c_2 = 0$$
$$\frac{x}{\Delta_1} = -\frac{y}{\Delta_2} = \frac{1}{\Delta} \quad \text{Cramer's Rule}$$
$$x = \frac{\Delta_1}{\Delta} \text{ and } y = -\frac{\Delta_2}{\Delta}$$

$$\Delta_1 = \begin{vmatrix} a_{12} & -c_1 \\ a_{22} & -c_2 \end{vmatrix}$$

$$\Delta_2 = \begin{vmatrix} a_{11} & -c_1 \\ a_{21} & -c_2 \end{vmatrix}$$

$$\Delta = \begin{vmatrix} a_{11} & a_{12} \\ a_{21} & a_{22} \end{vmatrix}.$$

WORKED EXAMPLE 39

Solve the simultaneous equations.
$$3x - 4y = 5$$
$$-2x + y = 3$$

Solution 39

$$\Delta_1 = \begin{vmatrix} -4 & -5 \\ 1 & -3 \end{vmatrix}$$

$$\Delta_2 = \begin{vmatrix} 3 & -5 \\ -2 & -3 \end{vmatrix}$$

$$\Delta = \begin{vmatrix} 3 & -4 \\ -2 & 1 \end{vmatrix}.$$

$$x = \frac{\Delta_1}{\Delta} = \frac{\begin{vmatrix} -4 & -5 \\ 1 & -3 \end{vmatrix}}{\begin{vmatrix} 3 & -4 \\ -2 & 1 \end{vmatrix}}$$

$$= \frac{+12 + 5}{3 - 8} = -\frac{17}{5}$$

$$y = -\frac{\Delta_2}{\Delta} = -\frac{\begin{vmatrix} 3 & -5 \\ -2 & -3 \end{vmatrix}}{\begin{vmatrix} 3 & -4 \\ -2 & 1 \end{vmatrix}}$$

$$= \frac{-(-9 - 10)}{3 - 8} = -\frac{19}{5}$$

$$y = -\frac{19}{5} \text{ and } x = -\frac{17}{5}.$$

Solving the simultaneous equations conventionally.

$3x - 4y = 5 \ldots (1) \times 2$

$-2x + y = 3 \ldots (2) \times 3$

$\overline{6x - 8y = 10 \ldots (3)}$

$\underline{-6x + 3y = 9 \ldots (4)}$

$\overline{-5y = 19 \quad (3) + (4)}$

$y = -\dfrac{19}{5}.$

Substituting in $3x - 4y = 5$.

$3x - 4\left(-\dfrac{19}{5}\right) = 5$

$3x = 5 - \dfrac{76}{5} = \dfrac{(25 - 76)}{5} = -\dfrac{51}{5}$

$x = -\dfrac{51}{15} = -\dfrac{17}{5}$

$x = -\dfrac{17}{5}.$

WORKED EXAMPLE 40

Solve the simultaneous equations.

$2x + 3y = -7$

$x - 5y = -15.$

Using the method of determinants and check your solutions by the conventional method.

Solution 40

$2x + 3y + 7 = 0$

$x - 5y + 15 = 0$

$\Delta_1 = \begin{vmatrix} 3 & 7 \\ -5 & 15 \end{vmatrix}$

$\Delta_2 = \begin{vmatrix} 2 & 7 \\ 1 & 15 \end{vmatrix}$

$\Delta = \begin{vmatrix} 2 & 3 \\ 1 & -5 \end{vmatrix}$

$\dfrac{x}{\Delta_1} = -\dfrac{y}{\Delta_2} = \dfrac{1}{\Delta}$

$x = \dfrac{\Delta_1}{\Delta}$ and $y = -\dfrac{\Delta_2}{\Delta}$

$\Delta_1 = \begin{vmatrix} 3 & 7 \\ -5 & 15 \end{vmatrix} = 45 + 35 = 80$

$\Delta_2 = \begin{vmatrix} 2 & 7 \\ 1 & 15 \end{vmatrix} = 30 - 7 = 23$

$\Delta = \begin{vmatrix} 2 & 3 \\ 1 & -5 \end{vmatrix} = -10 - 3 = -13$

$x = -\dfrac{80}{13}$ and $y = \dfrac{-23}{-13}$, therefore

$y = \dfrac{23}{13}$

$2x + 3y = -7 \quad \ldots (1) \times 1$

$\underline{x - 5y = -15 \quad \ldots (2) \times -2}$

$2x + 3y = -7 \quad \ldots (3)$

$\underline{-2x + 10y = 30 \quad \ldots (4)}$

$13y = 23 \quad (3) + (4)$

$y = \dfrac{23}{13}.$

Substituting in $x - 5y = -15$

$x = -15 + 5\left(\dfrac{23}{13}\right) = \dfrac{(-195 + 115)}{13} = -\dfrac{80}{13}$

$x = -\dfrac{80}{13}$ and $y = \dfrac{23}{13}.$

WORKED EXAMPLE 41

Solve the simultaneous equations:

$5x + 4y + 2 = 0$

$2x - 3y - 13 = 0.$

Solution 41

$5x + 4y = -2 \quad \ldots (1) \times -2$

$\underline{2x - 3y = 13 \quad \ldots (2) \times 5}$

$\overline{-10x - 8y = 4 \quad \ldots (3)}$

$\underline{10x - 15y = 65 \quad \ldots (4)}$

$\overline{-23y = 69 \quad (3) + (4)}$

$y = -3.$

Substituting in $2x - 3y = 13$, $2x + 9 = 13$,
$2x = 4$, $x = 2$.

$$\Delta_1 = \begin{vmatrix} 4 & 2 \\ -3 & -13 \end{vmatrix} \qquad \Delta_2 = \begin{vmatrix} 5 & 2 \\ 2 & -13 \end{vmatrix}$$

$$= -52 + 6 = -46 \qquad \Delta_2 = -65 - 4$$

therefore, $\Delta_2 = -69$.

$$\Delta = \begin{vmatrix} 5 & 4 \\ 2 & -3 \end{vmatrix} = -15 - 8 = -23$$

$$\frac{x}{\Delta_1} = -\frac{y}{\Delta_2} = \frac{1}{\Delta}$$

$$x = \frac{\Delta_1}{\Delta} = \frac{-46}{-23} = 2$$

$$y = \frac{-\Delta_2}{\Delta} = \frac{69}{-23} = -3.$$

5.2 Describes the meaning of a determinant whose value is zero and defines a singular matrix.

Consider the determinant whose value is zero.

$$\begin{vmatrix} 1 & 3 \\ 2 & a \end{vmatrix} = 0$$

$1 \times a - 3 \times 2 = 0$.

Therefore, $a = 6$

$$\begin{vmatrix} 1 & 3 \\ 2 & 6 \end{vmatrix} = 0$$

$$M = \begin{pmatrix} 1 & 3 \\ 2 & 6 \end{pmatrix} = \text{singular matrix}$$

because its determinant is zero.

5.3 Obtains the inverse of a 2 × 2 matrix.

The inverse of a matrix.

$$A = \begin{pmatrix} a_{11} & a_{12} \\ a_{21} & a_{22} \end{pmatrix}.$$

The minors of A

$$\begin{pmatrix} a_{22} & a_{21} \\ a_{12} & a_{11} \end{pmatrix}.$$

The cofactor of A

$$\begin{pmatrix} a_{22} & -a_{21} \\ -a_{12} & a_{11} \end{pmatrix}.$$

The transpose of the cofactors of A

$$\begin{pmatrix} a_{22} & -a_{12} \\ -a_{21} & a_{11} \end{pmatrix} = \text{adjoint matrix} = A^{*T}$$

$A^{-1} = \text{inverse matrix}$

$$= \frac{\text{adjoint matrix}}{\text{determinant of matrix}} = \frac{\begin{pmatrix} a_{22} & -a_{12} \\ -a_{21} & a_{11} \end{pmatrix}}{\begin{vmatrix} a_{11} & a_{12} \\ a_{21} & a_{22} \end{vmatrix}}$$

If the determinant of matrix is zero, that is, the matrix is singular then A^{-1} is not defined, since it tends to infinity.

WORKED EXAMPLE 42

Determine the inverse matrix of: $\begin{pmatrix} 5 & 4 \\ 2 & -3 \end{pmatrix}.$

Solution 42

$A = \begin{pmatrix} 5 & 4 \\ 2 & -3 \end{pmatrix}.$ The minors $= \begin{pmatrix} -3 & 2 \\ 4 & 5 \end{pmatrix}$ and

the cofactors $= \begin{pmatrix} -3 & -2 \\ -4 & 5 \end{pmatrix}.$

The transpose of the cofactors $= \begin{pmatrix} -3 & -4 \\ -2 & 5 \end{pmatrix}$

$$A^{-1} = \frac{\begin{pmatrix} -3 & -4 \\ -2 & 5 \end{pmatrix}}{\begin{vmatrix} 5 & 4 \\ 2 & -3 \end{vmatrix}}$$

$$= \frac{1}{(-15 - 8)} \begin{pmatrix} -3 & -4 \\ -2 & 5 \end{pmatrix}$$

$$= -\frac{1}{23} \begin{pmatrix} -3 & -4 \\ -2 & 5 \end{pmatrix}$$

$$A^{-1} = \begin{pmatrix} \dfrac{3}{23} & \dfrac{4}{23} \\ \dfrac{2}{23} & \dfrac{-5}{23} \end{pmatrix}.$$

5.4 Solves simultaneous linear equations with two unknowns by means of matrices.

WORKED EXAMPLE 43

Solve the simultaneous equations.
$5x + 4y = -2 \qquad 2x - 3y = 13$
by means of matrices.

Solution 43

The equations can be written in matrix form as:

$$\begin{pmatrix} 5 & 4 \\ 2 & -3 \end{pmatrix} \begin{pmatrix} x \\ y \end{pmatrix} = \begin{pmatrix} -2 \\ 13 \end{pmatrix} \qquad \ldots (1)$$

Let $A = \begin{pmatrix} 5 & 4 \\ 2 & -3 \end{pmatrix}$ its inverse matrix is

$$A^{-1} = \begin{pmatrix} \dfrac{3}{23} & \dfrac{4}{23} \\ \dfrac{2}{23} & \dfrac{-5}{23} \end{pmatrix}.$$

Pre-multiplying each side of (1) by A^{-1}

$$\begin{pmatrix} \dfrac{3}{23} & \dfrac{4}{23} \\ \dfrac{2}{23} & \dfrac{-5}{23} \end{pmatrix} \begin{pmatrix} 5 & 4 \\ 2 & -3 \end{pmatrix} \begin{pmatrix} x \\ y \end{pmatrix}$$

$$= \begin{pmatrix} \dfrac{3}{23} & \dfrac{4}{23} \\ \dfrac{2}{23} & \dfrac{-5}{23} \end{pmatrix} \begin{pmatrix} -2 \\ 13 \end{pmatrix}$$

$$= \begin{pmatrix} \left(\dfrac{3}{23}\right) \times 5 + \left(\dfrac{4}{23}\right) \times 2 \\ \left(\dfrac{3}{23}\right) \times 4 + \left(\dfrac{4}{23}\right) \times (-3) \\ \left(\dfrac{2}{23}\right) \times 5 + \left(\dfrac{-5}{23}\right) \times 2 \\ \left(\dfrac{2}{23}\right) \times 4 + \left(\dfrac{-5}{23}\right) \times (-3) \end{pmatrix} \begin{pmatrix} x \\ y \end{pmatrix}$$

$$= \begin{pmatrix} -\dfrac{6}{23} & + & \dfrac{52}{23} \\ -\dfrac{4}{23} & & -\dfrac{65}{23} \end{pmatrix} = \begin{pmatrix} \dfrac{46}{23} \\ -\dfrac{69}{23} \end{pmatrix}$$

$$\begin{pmatrix} 1 & 0 \\ 0 & 1 \end{pmatrix} \begin{pmatrix} x \\ y \end{pmatrix} = \begin{pmatrix} \dfrac{46}{23} \\ -\dfrac{69}{23} \end{pmatrix}$$

$$\begin{pmatrix} x \\ y \end{pmatrix} = \begin{pmatrix} 2 \\ -3 \end{pmatrix}$$

$x = 2 \quad y = -3.$

5.5 Relates the use of matrices to simple technical problems.

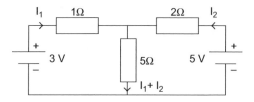

Fig. 13

Applying kirchhoff's laws:

$3 = I_1 \times 1 + 5(I_1 + I_2)$

$5 = I_2 \times 2 + 5(I_1 + I_2)$

or $\quad 6I_1 + 5I_2 = 3$

$\qquad 5I_1 + 7I_2 = 5$

in matrix form:

$$\begin{pmatrix} 6 & 5 \\ 5 & 7 \end{pmatrix} \begin{pmatrix} I_1 \\ I_2 \end{pmatrix} = \begin{pmatrix} 3 \\ 5 \end{pmatrix} \qquad \ldots (1)$$

$A = \begin{pmatrix} 6 & 5 \\ 5 & 7 \end{pmatrix} \quad$ The minors $= \begin{pmatrix} 7 & 5 \\ 5 & 6 \end{pmatrix}.$

The cofactors $= \begin{pmatrix} 7 & -5 \\ -5 & 6 \end{pmatrix}.$

The adjoint matrix $= \begin{pmatrix} 7 & -5 \\ -5 & 6 \end{pmatrix}$

$$A^{-1} = \frac{\begin{pmatrix} 7 & -5 \\ -5 & 6 \end{pmatrix}}{\begin{vmatrix} 6 & 5 \\ 5 & 7 \end{vmatrix}} = \frac{1}{42 - 25} \begin{pmatrix} 7 & -5 \\ -5 & 6 \end{pmatrix}$$

$$= \frac{1}{17} \begin{pmatrix} 7 & -5 \\ -5 & 6 \end{pmatrix} = \begin{pmatrix} \dfrac{7}{17} & \dfrac{-5}{17} \\ \dfrac{-5}{17} & \dfrac{6}{17} \end{pmatrix}.$$

Pre-multiplying (1) by A^{-1}

$$A^{-1}A\begin{pmatrix} I_1 \\ I_2 \end{pmatrix} = A^{-1}\begin{pmatrix} 3 \\ 5 \end{pmatrix}$$

$$I\begin{pmatrix} I_1 \\ I_2 \end{pmatrix} = \begin{pmatrix} \dfrac{7}{17} & \dfrac{-5}{17} \\ \dfrac{-5}{17} & \dfrac{6}{17} \end{pmatrix} \begin{pmatrix} 3 \\ 5 \end{pmatrix}$$

$$\begin{pmatrix} I_1 \\ I_2 \end{pmatrix} = \begin{pmatrix} \dfrac{21}{17} & - & \dfrac{25}{17} \\ \dfrac{-15}{17} & + & \dfrac{30}{17} \end{pmatrix} = \begin{pmatrix} \dfrac{-4}{17} \\ \dfrac{15}{17} \end{pmatrix}.$$

$$I_1 = -\frac{4}{17}$$

$$I_2 = \frac{15}{17}.$$

Alternatively for checking:

$$6I_1 + 5I_1 = 3 \quad \ldots (1) \times -5$$

$$5I_1 + 7I_2 = 5 \quad \ldots (2) \times 6$$

$$\overline{-30I_1 - 25I_2 = -15 \quad \ldots (3)}$$

$$\underline{30I_1 + 42I_2 = 30 \qquad \ldots (4)}$$

$$17I_2 = 15 \qquad (3) + (4)$$

$$I_2 = \frac{15}{17}.$$

Substituting in $6I_1 + 5I_2 = 3$

$$6I_1 + 5\left(\frac{15}{17}\right) = 3$$

$$6I_1 = 3 - \frac{75}{17} = \frac{51 - 75}{17} = \frac{-24}{17}$$

$$I_1 = -\frac{4}{17}.$$

Exercises 4/5

1. Denote an array of elements as a matrix of 2×2. What is the significance 2×2?

2. What does a 2×2 matrix represent? What is 2×1 matrix? Give examples.

3. If $P = \begin{pmatrix} -3 & -1 \\ -4 & -5 \end{pmatrix}$ and $Q = \begin{pmatrix} 2 & 2 \\ 3 & 4 \end{pmatrix}$

   Find $P + Q$ and $Q - P$.

4. If $A = \begin{pmatrix} 1 & 2 \\ 3 & 4 \end{pmatrix}$ $B = \begin{pmatrix} 5 & 6 \\ 7 & 8 \end{pmatrix}$ and

   $$C = \begin{pmatrix} 9 & 10 \\ 11 & 12 \end{pmatrix}$$

   find (i) $A + B + C$

   (ii) $2A + 5B - 3C$.

5. If $A = \begin{pmatrix} 1 & 0 \\ 2 & 3 \end{pmatrix}$ and $B = \begin{pmatrix} 2 & 3 \\ 1 & a \end{pmatrix}$

   determine a if $A + B = \begin{pmatrix} 3 & 3 \\ 3 & 6 \end{pmatrix}$.

6. Show that $A + B = B + A$, that is, associative.

7. If $A = \begin{pmatrix} 3 & -3 \\ 5 & 2 \end{pmatrix}$, $B = \begin{pmatrix} 1 & 2 \\ -2 & 1 \end{pmatrix}$

   Find (i) AB

   (ii) A^2

   (iii) $B^2 A$.

8. If $M = \begin{pmatrix} 2 & 2 \\ 0 & 1 \end{pmatrix}$, $N = \begin{pmatrix} -1 & 3 \\ 2 & 4 \end{pmatrix}$.

   Find MN and NM.

9. If $I = \begin{pmatrix} 1 & 0 \\ 0 & 1 \end{pmatrix}$.

   Find I^3 and $5\,I$.

10. If $A = \begin{pmatrix} 3 & 4 \\ 6 & 9 \end{pmatrix}$ and $I = \begin{pmatrix} 1 & 0 \\ 0 & 1 \end{pmatrix}$.

    Find (i) $A + 3I$

    (ii) IA.

11. Find the determinants.

    (i) $\begin{vmatrix} 2 & 3 \\ 1 & -2 \end{vmatrix}$

    (ii) $\begin{vmatrix} -1 & -1 \\ -1 & 2 \end{vmatrix}$

    (iii) $\begin{vmatrix} -2 & 6 \\ 1 & 3 \end{vmatrix}$

12. Write the following expressions in determinant forms.

    (i) $xy - zt$

    (ii) $ab + cd$

    (iii) $3 \times 2 - 5 \times 1.$

13. Solve the following simultaneous equations by means of the determinant method.

    (i) $3I_1 - 5I_2 = 1$
    $I_1 + I_2 = 11$

    (ii) $-x + y = 9$
    $-2x + 20y = 18.$

14. What is a singular matrix?

    Give an example.

15. Find the inverse matrices of the following and check their accuracy.

    (i) $\begin{pmatrix} 1 & 2 \\ 3 & 4 \end{pmatrix}$

    (ii) $\begin{pmatrix} -1 & 3 \\ 4 & 2 \end{pmatrix}$

    (iii) $\begin{pmatrix} 2 & 5 \\ 6 & -2 \end{pmatrix}.$

16. Solve the following simultaneous equations by means of the matrices method.

    (i) $3a - 5b = 1$
    $a + b = 11$

    (ii) $-I_1 + I_2 = 9$
    $-2I_1 + 20I_2 = 18.$

Determines the rate of change of a function.

6.1 Determines the average and instantaneous gradients, rate of change values, to a simple curve, e.g. $y = ax^2$.

WORKED EXAMPLE 44

Determine the gradient of $y = 3x^2$ at $x = 1$ and $x = 2$.

Solution 44

x	x^2	$y = 3x^2$
0	0	0
0.5	0.25	0.75
1	1	3
1.5	2.25	6.75
2	4	12
2.5	6.25	18.75

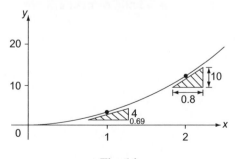

Fig. 14

The gradient at $x = 1$ is approximately

$$= 6 \approx \frac{4}{0.69}.$$

The gradient at $x = 2$ is approximately

$$= 12 \approx \frac{10}{0.8}.$$

The gradient at any point can be determined graphically by drawing a tangent at the point and thus forming a right angled triangle.

This is a rather tedious and inaccurate method for determining gradients.

6.2 Deduces that the process of moving a point on the curve towards a fixed point on the curve causes the gradient of the secant through the points to approach that of the tangent to the curve at the fixed point.

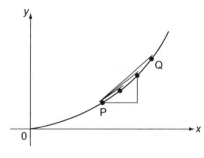

Fig. 15

Consider a fixed point P and a moving point Q towards the fixed point. As Q approaches the fixed point P the chord PQ diminishes gradually and causes the gradient of the secant through the points to approach that of the tangent to the curve at the point P (the fixed point).

6.3 Identifies incremental changes in the x, y directions as $\delta x, \delta y$.

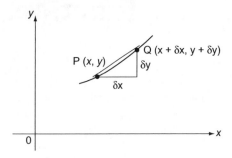

Fig. 16

Consider a fixed point P (x, y) and a moving point Q $(x + \delta x, y + \delta y)$ very close to P.

The gradient of the chord PQ is $\frac{\delta y}{\delta x}$ where δy and δx are infinitecimally small quantities.

6.4 Determines the ratio $\frac{\delta y}{\delta x}$ in terms of x and δx for the function in 6.1.

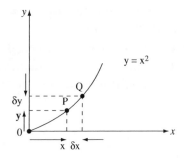

Fig. 17

$At\, P, y = x^2$ ...(1)

$At\, Q, y + \delta y = (x + \delta x)^2$ ...(2)

$(2) - (1)$

$\delta y = (x + \delta x)^2 - x^2$

$= (x + \delta x - x)(x + \delta x + x)$

$\delta y = \delta x(x + \delta x + x)$

$\frac{\delta y}{\delta x} = 2x + \delta x.$

6.5 Derives the limit of $\left(\frac{\delta y}{\delta x}\right)$ as δx tends to zero and defines it as $\left(\frac{dy}{dx}\right)$.

as $\delta x \to 0, \left(\frac{\delta y}{\delta x}\right) \to \left(\frac{dy}{dx}\right),$

$\left(\frac{\delta y}{\delta x}\right) = 2x + \delta x$

$\left(\frac{dy}{dx}\right) = 2x$ the gradient at P of the function $y = x^2.$

$\left(\frac{\delta y}{\delta x}\right)$ represents the gradient of the chord PQ,

$\left(\frac{dy}{dx}\right)$ represents the gradient at **P** of the function $y = x^2.$

6.6 States that the rate of change at a maximum or minimum point of a curve is zero.

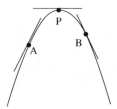

Fig. 18 A maximum point of a curve.

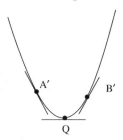

Fig. 19 A minimum point of a curve.

In Fig. 18, at A the gradient is positive that is, $\frac{dy}{dx} > 0$, at B the gradient is negative, that is, $\frac{dy}{dx} < 0$, at P the maximum point $\frac{dy}{dx} = 0$.

In Fig. 19. at A′, the gradient is negative, at B′, the gradient is positive and at Q, the gradient is zero.

Therefore at P and Q the gradients are zero, and *the rate of change at a maximum or minimum point of a curve is zero.*

WORKED EXAMPLE 45

Distinguish between the ratios $\frac{\delta y}{\delta x}$ and $\frac{dy}{dx}$.

Solution 45

δx and δy represent incremental changes in the x and y directions respectively.

The gradient of a chord PQ, where Q is very close to the fixed point, P, is $\frac{\delta y}{\delta x}$.

As Q approaches P, that is δx tends to zero then $\frac{\delta y}{\delta x}$ tends to $\frac{dy}{dx}$ which is the gradient of the tangent at the fixed point P.

Turning points:

A turning point is, as the word suggests, where the curve changes direction. To change direction the gradient of the curve must change sign, either from positive to negative, or from negative to positive. In order to do this the gradient must at some point be zero. It is this point, where the gradient is zero, that is called a *turning point.*

We have seen previously that a quadratic expression has one *turning point* which is either a maximum or a minimum.

To find the turning point, we find first the derivative of the function, $\frac{dy}{dx}$ which we make equal to zero.

$\frac{dy}{dx} = 0$ for turning points of either a maximum or minimum.

Exercise 6

1. Draw accurately on a graph paper the function $y = x^2$ for values of x between 0 and 3 at intervals of 0.5.

   Draw the chord between P(2, 4) and Q_1 (3, 9). Obtain the gradient of the chord PQ_1, Q is allowed to move towards P at Q_2 (2.5, 6.25), determine now the gradient of the chord PQ_2. Q is now moved nearer to P, Q_3 (2.1, 4.41), the new gradient of PQ_3 is now found.

   Q is now moved very close to P without touching it, determine the gradient PQ_4.

   What is the gradient at P, that is, when δx approaches zero?

2. Comment on the expression.

   $$\frac{dy}{dx} = \lim_{\delta x \to 0} \frac{\delta y}{\delta x}.$$

3. What is a turning point?
   With the aid of sketches for a quadratic expression illustrate what is the condition for a turning point.

7

Differentiates simple algebraic and trigonometric functions.

7.1 Derives $\frac{dy}{dx}$ for the functions $y = ax^n$, $n = 0, 1, 2, 3$ from first principles.

First derivatives from first prinicples.

(i) $y = ax^0$

$y = a$ ...(1) where a is a constant.
$y + \delta y = a$ ...(2) giving x an increment δx
then y increases to $y + \delta y$

$$(2) - (1)$$

$\delta y = 0$

dividing by δx both sides

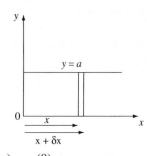

$$\frac{(\delta y)}{(\delta x)} = \frac{(0)}{(\delta x)} = 0$$

Fig. 20

as $\delta x \to 0$ then $\frac{\delta y}{\delta x} \to \frac{dy}{dx}$ therefore $\frac{dy}{dx} = 0$

the first derivative of a constant is zero.

(ii) $y = ax$ ...(1)

$y + \delta y = a(x + \delta x)$ ...(2) − (1)

$y + \delta y - y = ax + a\delta x - ax$

$\delta y = a\delta x$

$\frac{\delta y}{\delta x} = a$ as $\delta x \to 0$, $\frac{\delta y}{\delta x} \to \frac{dy}{dx}$

therefore, $\dfrac{dy}{dx} = a$

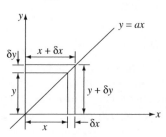

Fig. 21

(iii) $y = ax^2$

$y + \delta y = a(x + \delta x)^2$

$\delta y = ax^2 + 2ax\delta x + a\delta x^2 - ax^2$

$\delta y = 2ax\delta x + a\delta x^2$

$\dfrac{\delta y}{\delta x} = 2ax + a\delta x$

as $\delta x \to 0$ then $\dfrac{\delta y}{\delta x} \to \dfrac{dy}{dx}$

$\dfrac{dy}{dx} = 2ax$

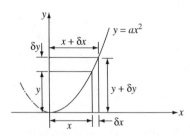

Fig. 22

(iv) $y = ax^3$

$$y + \delta y = a(x + \delta x)^3$$

$$\delta y = a(x + \delta x)^3 - ax^3$$

$$= a(x^3 + 3x^2\delta x + 3x\delta x^2 + \delta x^3) - ax^3$$

$$\delta y = 3ax^2\delta x + 3ax\delta x^2 + a\delta x^3$$

$$\frac{\delta y}{\delta x} = 3ax^2 + 3ax\delta x + a\delta x^2$$

as $\delta x \to 0$, $\dfrac{\delta y}{\delta x} \to \dfrac{dy}{dx}$

$$\frac{dy}{dx} = 3ax^2$$

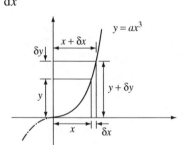

Fig. 23

7.2 Differentiates simple algebraic functions of the form $y = ax^n + bx^{n-1} + \dots$

$$y = ax^n \qquad \frac{dy}{dx} = anx^{n-1}.$$

WORKED EXAMPLE 46

Differentiate the following algebraic functions:

(i) $y = 3x$ (ii) $y = x^2$

(iii) $y = x^5$ (iv) $y = -ax^7$

(v) $y = -x^{-3}$ (vi) $y = \dfrac{1}{x^2}$

(vii) $y = \dfrac{4}{x^4}$ (viii) $y = \sqrt{x}$

(ix) $y = x^{-\frac{1}{5}}$ (x) $y = \left(\dfrac{1}{5}\right)x^{\frac{1}{7}}$.

Solution 46

(i) $y = 3x$, $\dfrac{dy}{dx} = 3$

(ii) $y = x^2$, $\dfrac{dy}{dx} = 2x$

(iii) $y = x^5$, $\dfrac{dy}{dx} = 5x^4$

(iv) $y = -ax^7$, $\dfrac{dy}{dx} = -7ax^6$

(v) $y = -x^{-3}$, $\dfrac{dy}{dx} = (-1)(-3)x^{-4}$

$$= 3x^{-4} = \frac{3}{x^4}$$

(vi) $y = \dfrac{1}{x^2} = x^{-2}$, $\dfrac{dy}{dx} = -2x^{-3} = -\dfrac{2}{x^3}$

(vii) $y = \dfrac{4}{x^4} = 4x^{-4}$,

$$\frac{dy}{dx} = -16x^{-5} = -\frac{16}{x^5}$$

(viii) $y = \sqrt{x}$, $y = x^{\frac{1}{2}}$, $\dfrac{dy}{dx} = \left(\dfrac{1}{2}\right)x^{-\frac{1}{2}}$

(ix) $y = x^{-\frac{1}{5}}$, $\dfrac{dy}{dx} = \left(-\dfrac{1}{5}\right)x^{-\frac{6}{5}}$

(x) $y = \left(\dfrac{1}{5}\right)x^{\frac{1}{7}}$, $\dfrac{dy}{dx} = \left(\dfrac{1}{35}\right)x^{-\frac{6}{7}}$.

WORKED EXAMPLE 47

Find the first derivatives of the following functions:

(i) $y = -7$

(ii) $x = 3t^3 - 3t^2 + t$

(iii) $y = \dfrac{1}{x} + \dfrac{1}{x^2}$

(iv) $y = x^7 - 3x^5 + x^3 - 5$

(v) $y = \dfrac{4}{x^3} - \dfrac{3}{x^4} + \dfrac{1}{x^5}$

(vi) $y = \dfrac{1}{\sqrt[3]{x^4}}$

(vii) $x = 3t^3 - 2t^2 + t - 4$

(viii) $y = \sqrt[5]{x^3}$

(ix) $z = \dfrac{1}{y} - \dfrac{4}{y^2}$

(x) $s = ut + \left(\dfrac{1}{2}\right)gt^2.$

Solution 47

(i) $y = -7$

$\dfrac{dy}{dx} = 0$

(ii) $x = 3t^3 - 3t^2 + t$

$\dfrac{dx}{dt} = 9t^2 - 6t + 1$

(iii) $y = \dfrac{1}{x} + \dfrac{1}{x^2} = x^{-1} + x^{-2}$

$\dfrac{dy}{dx} = -x^{-2} - 2x^{-3}$

(iv) $y = x^7 - 3x^5 + x^3 - 5$

$\dfrac{dy}{dx} = 7x^6 - 15x^4 + 3x^2$

(v) $y = \dfrac{4}{x^3} - \dfrac{3}{x^4} + \dfrac{1}{x^5}$

$y = 4x^{-3} - 3x^{-4} + x^{-5}$

$\dfrac{dy}{dx} = -12x^{-4} + 12x^{-5} - 5x^{-6}$

$= -\dfrac{12}{x^4} + \dfrac{12}{x^5} - \dfrac{5}{x^6}$

(vi) $y = \dfrac{1}{\sqrt[3]{x^4}} = x^{-\frac{4}{3}}$

$\dfrac{dy}{dx} = -\dfrac{4}{3}(x^{-\frac{7}{3}}) = -\dfrac{4}{3x^{\frac{7}{3}}}$

(vii) $x = 3t^3 - 2t^2 + t - 4$

$\dfrac{dx}{dt} = 9t^2 - 4t + 1$

(viii) $y = \sqrt[5]{x^3} \quad y = x^{\frac{3}{5}}$

$\dfrac{dy}{dx} = \left(\dfrac{3}{5}\right)x^{-\frac{2}{5}} = \dfrac{3}{5x^{\frac{2}{5}}}$

(ix) $z = \dfrac{1}{y} - \dfrac{4}{y^2} \quad z = y^{-1} - 4y^{-2}$

$\dfrac{dz}{dy} = -y^{-2} + 8y^{-3} = -\dfrac{1}{y^2} + \dfrac{8}{y^3}$

(x) $s = ut + \left(\dfrac{1}{2}\right)gt^2$

$\dfrac{ds}{dt} = u + \dfrac{1}{2}2gt = u + gt.$

7.3 Demonstrates graphically results for the derivatives sin θ and cos θ.

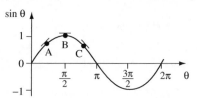

Fig. 24

$y = \sin\theta$

$\dfrac{dy}{d\theta} = \cos\theta$

the derivative at A

$\left(x = \dfrac{\pi}{4}\right)$

$\dfrac{dy}{d\theta} = \cos\dfrac{\pi}{4} = 0.707$

the derivative at B

$\left(x = \dfrac{\pi}{2}\right)$

$\dfrac{dy}{d\theta} = \cos\dfrac{\pi}{2} = 0$

the derivative at C

$\left(x = \dfrac{3\pi}{4}\right)$

$\dfrac{dy}{d\theta} = \cos\dfrac{3\pi}{4} = -0.707$

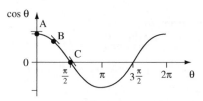

Fig. 25

$y = \cos\theta$

$\dfrac{dy}{d\theta} = -\sin\theta$

the derivative at A

$x = 0$

$\dfrac{dy}{d\theta} = -\sin 0 = 0$

the derivative at B

$x = \dfrac{\pi}{4}$

$\dfrac{dy}{d\theta} = -\sin\dfrac{\pi}{4} = -0.707$

the derivative at C

$x = \dfrac{\pi}{2}$

$\dfrac{dy}{d\theta} = -\sin\dfrac{\pi}{2} = -1.$

7.4 Differentiates functions of the form $y = a\cos\theta$ and $y = b\sin\theta$.

$y = a\cos\theta \qquad \dfrac{dy}{d\theta} = -a\sin\theta$

$y = b\sin\theta \qquad \dfrac{dy}{d\theta} = b\cos\theta.$

Exercises 7

1. Differentiate from first principles the following functions:

    (i) $y = -5$

    (ii) $y = 2x$

    (iii) $y = -3x^2$

    (iv) $y = 4x^3$

2. Differentiate with respect to x:

    (i) $y = 3x^4$

    (ii) $y = 3x^2$

    (iii) $y = 3x^2 - 3x$

    (iv) $y = x^2 + 3x + 5$

    (v) $y = 4x^3 + 4x^2 + 4x + 5$

    (vi) $y = \dfrac{3}{4}x^3 - \dfrac{1}{2}x^2 - \dfrac{1}{5}x + 5$

    (vii) $y = 4x^3 + 2x^2 + 20$

    (viii) $y = 5x^6 - 3x^4 + x + 1$

    (ix) $y = x^3 - x^2 - x + 1$

    (x) $y = 1.9 - 2.5x + 7.4x^2.$

3. Find the gradients of the following curves at the given points.

    (i) $y = 4x^2$ at the point $x = 1$

    (ii) $y = 2x^3$ at the point $x = -2$

    (iii) $y = 3x - 5$

    (iv) $y = 5x^4 - 3x^3 + 2x^2 + 5x - 1$ at the point $x = 0$

    (v) $y = \dfrac{1}{3}x^2 - \dfrac{1}{5}x$ at the point $x = -\dfrac{1}{2}$

4. Differentiate the following:

    (i) $y = 3x$

    (ii) $y = -x^2$

    (iii) $y = 4x^3$

    (iv) $y = 5x^4$

    (v) $y = \dfrac{1}{5}x^4$

    (vi) $y = \dfrac{1}{2}x^{\frac{1}{2}}$

    (vii) $y = -\dfrac{3x^{\frac{3}{2}}}{4}$

    (viii) $y = -\dfrac{1}{x}$

    (ix) $y = \dfrac{1}{x^2}$

    (x) $y = 5\sqrt{x}$

    (xi) $y = \dfrac{4}{\sqrt{x}}$

    (xii) $y = 5\sqrt[3]{x^2}$

    (xiii) $y = 3x^3 + 2x^2 - 5x + 7$

    (xiv) $y = 5x^2 + 5x - \dfrac{3}{x}$

    (xv) $y = \sqrt{x} + \dfrac{1}{\sqrt{x}}$

    (xvi) $s = 10 - 6t - 7t^2 + 2t^3$

    (xvii) $s = 4\pi\tau^2$

    (xviii) $A = \pi\tau^2$

    (xix) $s = \dfrac{3}{5}\sqrt{t}$

    (xx) $k = \dfrac{0.01}{T^2}.$

5. Find the gradient of the curve $y = 3x^2 - 5x - 5$ at the points where $x = 1$ and $x = -2$.

6. Find the gradient of the curve $y = x^3 + x^2 - 5x + 7$ at the points where

   $x = 0, x = 1$ and $x = 2$.

7. Find the values of x for which the gradient of the curve $y = 3x^2 + 1x - 5$ is equal to

   (a) 1 (b) 2 (c) 0.

8. Find the derivatives of the following:

   (i) $y = 3 \sin \theta$

   (ii) $y = -5 \cos \theta$.

9. Determine the gradients of the functions at $x = 0, x = \frac{\pi}{4}$ and $x = \frac{\pi}{2}$

   (i) $t = 4 \sin x$

   (ii) $t = -5 \cos x$.

10. Find the turning points of the following curves:

    (i) $y = x^2 - 6x + 5$

    (ii) $y = 4x^2 + 2x + 7$

    (iii) $y = 6x^2 + 5$

    (iv) $y = x^2 + 3x - 1$

    (v) $y = \frac{1}{3}x^2 - 2x + 2$.

8

Understands the processes of indefinite and definite integration and determines integrals of simple algebraic functions.

8.1 Defines indefinite integration as the reverse process of differentiation.

$$\int ax^n dx = \frac{ax^{n+1}}{n+1} + c, \quad n \neq -1,$$

where c is an arbitrary constant.

$$y = \frac{a}{n+1}x^{n+1} + c$$

$$\frac{dy}{dx} = \frac{a}{n+1}(n+1)x^{n+1-1}$$

$$= ax^n.$$

The differentiation of $\dfrac{ax^{n+1}}{n+1} + c$ is ax^n, the integration of ax^n is $\dfrac{ax^{n+1}}{n+1} + c$, therefore the reverse process of differentiation is indefinite integration.

8.2 Determines indefinite integrals of simple algebraic functions and functions involving $\cos\theta$, $\sin\theta$.

$$\int ax^n dx = \frac{ax^{n+1}}{n+1} + c, \quad n \neq -1.$$

Determine the following indefinite integrals:

(i) $\int 3x^3 dx$

(ii) $\int \left(\dfrac{1}{x^2} - \dfrac{1}{x^3} \right) dx$

(iii) $\int x^{\frac{4}{3}} dx$

(iv) $\int (ax^2 + bx + c) dx$

(v) $\int (3x^2 - 2x + 7) dx.$

Solution 48

(i) $\int 3x^3 dx = \dfrac{3x^4}{4} + c$

(ii) $\int \left(\dfrac{1}{x^2} - \dfrac{1}{x^3} \right) dx$

$$= \int \left(x^{-2} - x^{-3} \right) dx$$

$$= \frac{x^{-2+1}}{-2+1} - \frac{x^{-3+1}}{-3+1} + c$$

$$= -\frac{1}{x} + \frac{1}{2x^2} + c$$

(iii) $\int x^{\frac{4}{3}} dx = \dfrac{x^{\frac{4}{3}+1}}{\frac{4}{3}+1} + c$

$= \left(\dfrac{3}{7}\right) x^{\frac{7}{3}} + c$

(iv) $\int (ax^2 + bx + c) dx$

$= \dfrac{ax^3}{3} + \dfrac{bx^2}{2} + cx + \text{constant}$

(v) $\int (3x^2 - 2x + 7) dx$

$= \dfrac{3x^3}{3} - \dfrac{2x^2}{2} + 7x + c$

$= x^3 - x^2 + 7x + c$

$\int \cos\theta d\theta = \sin\theta + c$

$\int \sin\theta d\theta = -\cos\theta + c.$

8.3 Recognizes the need to include an arbitrary constant of integration.

WORKED EXAMPLE 49

The gradient of a curve is given by $\frac{dy}{dx} = 3x^2 - 5x + 2$. Determine the curve given that is passes through the point $(1, 2)$.

Solution 49

$\dfrac{dy}{dx} = 3x^2 - 5x + 2$

$dy = (3x^2 - 5x + 2) dx$

$\int dy = \int (3x^2 - 5x + 2) dx$

$y = \dfrac{3x^3}{3} - \dfrac{5x^2}{2} + 2x + c$

it passes through the point $(1, 2)$, $x = 1$ when $y = 2$.

$2 = 1 - \dfrac{5}{2} + 2 + c$

$c = 2 - \dfrac{1}{2} = \dfrac{3}{2}$

$y = x^3 - \dfrac{5x^2}{2} + 2x + \dfrac{3}{2}.$

8.4 Defines $\int_a^b y dx$ as the area under the curve between ordinates at $x = a$, and $x = b$.

Definite integral.

Consider a curve $y = f(x)$ as shown in Fig. 26 with an elemental strip of width dx and height y, any point on the curve of coordinates (x, y).

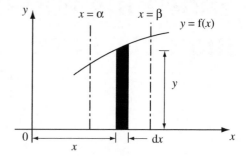

Fig. 26

The area of the elemental strip is ydx, the area of a rectangle. We would like to find the area of all the strips between $x = \alpha$ and $x = \beta$, this is denoted as:

$\int_\alpha^\beta y\, dx$

α and β are the lower and upper limits of x. The definite integral, is the summation of all the elemental strips between the limits between $x = \alpha$ and $x = \beta$.

8.5 Evaluates $\int_a^b y\, dx$ by $[\Phi(x)]_a^b = \Phi(b) - \Phi(a)$ for simple functions, where $\Phi(x)$ is the indefinite integral of (x).

$\int_a^b y\, dx = \int_a^b f(x)\, dx = [\Phi(x)]_a^b$

$= \Phi(b) - \Phi(a)$

where $y = f(x) = a$ function of x and $\Phi(x)$ is the indefinite integral of $f(x)$.

Determine the area of the function $y = x^2$ between $x = 1$ and $x = 2$.

Solution 50

$$\int_{x=1}^{x=2} y \, dx = \int_1^2 y \, dx = \int_1^2 x^2 \, dx$$

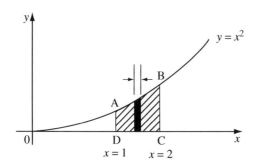

Fig. 27

The definite integral is the hatched area shown in Fig. 27.

Considering an elemental area $y \, dx$ shown, we are summing up all these areas between $x = 1$ and $x = 2$.

$$\int_1^2 y \, dx = \int_1^2 x^2 \, dx = \left[\frac{x^3}{3} + c\right]_1^2$$

$$= \left[\frac{2^3}{3} + c\right] - \left[\frac{1^3}{3} + c\right].$$

$$= \frac{2^3}{3} + c - \frac{1}{3} - c$$

$$= \frac{8}{3} - \frac{1}{3}$$

$$= \frac{7}{3} \text{ square units.}$$

It is observed that the arbitrary constant is cancelled in the definite integral.

$$\int_1^2 x^2 \, dx = \text{area 0ABCD0} - \text{area 0AD0}.$$

8.6 Determines areas by applying definite integral for simple algebraic functions.

WORKED EXAMPLE 51

Evaluate the integral $\int_1^2 (2x^2 - 3x - 1) dx$.

Solution 51

$$\int_{-1}^2 (2x^2 - 3x - 1) \, dx$$

$$= \left[\frac{2x^3}{3} - \frac{3x^2}{2} - x\right]_{-1}^2$$

$$= \left[\frac{2}{3}(2)^3 - \frac{3}{2}(2)^2 - 2\right]$$

$$- \left[\frac{2}{3}(-1)^3 - \frac{3}{2}(-1)^2 - (-1)\right]$$

$$= \left(\frac{2}{3} \times 8 - \frac{3}{2} \times 4 - 2\right) - \left(-\frac{2}{3} - \frac{3}{2} + 1\right)$$

$$= \left(\frac{16}{3} - 6 - 2\right) - \left(-\frac{2}{3} - \frac{1}{2}\right)$$

$$= \frac{16}{3} - 6 - 2 + \frac{7}{6}$$

$$= \frac{32}{6} + \frac{7}{6} - 8$$

$$= \frac{39}{6} - 8$$

$$= 6.5 - 8 = -1.5 \text{ square units.}$$

What is the significance of the negative answer? It is an area below the x-axis. An area should be expressed as a positive number, if it is either below the x-axis or above the x-axis.

WORKED EXAMPLE 52

(a) Sketch the graph of $y = x^2 - x - 2$.

(b) Determine the area enclosed between the curve and the axes in the third quadrant.

Solution 52

(a)

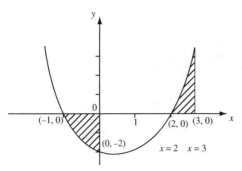

Fig. 28

$$f(x) = x^2 - x - 2$$
$$f(0) = -2$$
$$f(x) = 0, x = -1, x = 2.$$

(b) $\int\limits_{-1}^{0} (x^2 - x - 2)\,dx$

$$= \left[\frac{x^3}{3} - \frac{x^2}{2} - 2x \right]_{-1}^{0}$$

$$= \left[\frac{0}{3} - \frac{0}{2} - 2(0) \right]$$

$$\quad - \left[\frac{(-1)^3}{3} - \frac{(-1)^2}{2} - 2(-1) \right]$$

$$= 0 - \left(\frac{-1}{3} - \frac{1}{2} + 2 \right)$$

$$= -1\frac{1}{6}.$$

The negative sign only indicates that the area is below the x-axis.

The area required is positive and it is equal to $1\frac{1}{6}$ square units.

───────
WORKED EXAMPLE 53

Evaluate $\int\limits_{2}^{3} (x^2 - x - 2)\,dx$ and indicate this area on the graph.

Solution 53

$$\int\limits_{2}^{3} (x^2 - x - 2)\,dx$$

$$= \left[\frac{x^3}{3} - \frac{x^2}{2} - 2x \right]_{2}^{3}$$

$$= \left[\frac{3^3}{3} - \frac{3^2}{2} - 2(3) \right] - \left[\frac{2^3}{3} - \frac{2^2}{2} - 2(2) \right]$$

$$= \left(\frac{27}{3} - \frac{9}{2} - 6 \right) - \left(\frac{8}{3} - 2 - 4 \right)$$

$$= \frac{54 - 27 - 36}{6} + \frac{10}{3}$$

$$= -\frac{9}{6} + \frac{10}{3}$$

$$= \frac{-9 + 20}{6} = \frac{11}{6}$$

$$= \frac{11}{6} \text{ square units.}$$

This area is indicated on the graph of Fig. 28.

WORKED EXAMPLE 54

(a) Sketch the graph $y = -x^2 - x + 2$

(b) Determine the area enclosed by the curve and the axes in the first quadrant.

Solution 54

(a) $f(x) = -x^2 - x + 2, f(0) = 2$

$\quad\;\; f(x) = 0, x = 1 \text{ or } x = -2$

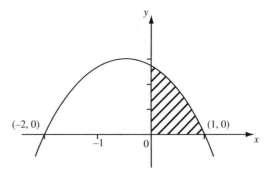

Fig. 29

(b) $\int\limits_0^1 (-x^2 - x + 2)dx$

$= \left[-\dfrac{x^3}{3} - \dfrac{x^2}{2} + 2x \right]_0^1$

$= \left[-\dfrac{1}{3} - \dfrac{1}{2} + 2 \right] - \left[-\dfrac{0}{3} - \dfrac{0}{2} + 0 \right]$

$= 1\dfrac{1}{6}$ square units.

Exercises 8

1. Write down the indefinite integral of the function ax^n and the result.

2. (i) $\int 3t^5 dt$

   (ii) $\int 5y^4 dy$

   (iii) $\int -z^3 dz$

   (iv) $\int 2x^2 dx$

   (v) $\int -3y^3 dy$.

3. integrate the following:

   (i) x (ii) y

   (iii) z (iv) t

   (v) $3x^3$ (vi) $z^{\frac{1}{4}}$

   (vii) $2t^2 - 3t$ (viii) $\dfrac{1}{x^3}$

   (ix) $\dfrac{1}{y^2}$ (x) $x^{\frac{3}{4}}$.

4. (i) $\int (2x^2 + 3x + 5)dx$

   (ii) $\int \left(\dfrac{1}{x^2} + \dfrac{1}{x^3} - \dfrac{1}{x^4} \right) dx$.

5. (i) $\int \dfrac{1}{\sqrt{x}} dx$

   (ii) $\int \left(\sqrt{x} - \dfrac{1}{\sqrt{x}} \right) dx$.

6. (i) $\int 3 \sin x \, dx$

   (ii) $\int 5 \cos x \, dx$.

7. (i) $\int\limits_1^2 (x^2 - 3x)dx$

   (ii) $\int\limits_{-1}^1 (-x^3 - 2x)dx$.

8. (i) $\int\limits_0^1 (ax^2 + bx + c)dx$

   (ii) $\int\limits_{t=1}^{t=2} (3t - 5)dt$.

9. (i) Sketch the graph $y = (x + 2)(x + 3)$.

   (ii) Determine the area enclosed between the curve and the x-axis.

10. Determine the area enclosed between the curve $y = (x - 4)(x - 5)$ and the x-axis.

Integrate the following:

11. $\int 2x \, dx$ 12. $\int 3x^2 dx$

13. $\int 5x^3 dx$ 14. $\int \dfrac{x^4}{4} dx$

15. $\int x^{\frac{1}{2}} dx$ 16. $\int -x^{\frac{3}{2}} dx$

17. $\int \dfrac{dx}{x^2}$ 18. $\int 3\sqrt{x} \, dx$

19. $\int \dfrac{dx}{\sqrt{x}}$ 20. $\int 5\sqrt[3]{x} \, dx$

21. $\int (2x^3 + 2x^2 + 5x + 2)dx$

Evaluate the following:

22. $\int\limits_0^1 \left(\sqrt{x} + \dfrac{1}{\sqrt{x}} \right) dx$

23. $\int\limits_0^1 (10 + 6t + 7t^2 + 2t^3)dt$

24. $\int\limits_1^2 \pi r^2 dr$

25. $\int\limits_1^3 0.2t^{1.2} dt$

26. $\int\limits_0^1 \dfrac{3}{5}\sqrt{t} \, dt$

27. $\int\limits_1^2 \dfrac{0.1}{T^2} dT$

Simple curve sketching.

9.1 Draws up suitable tables of values and plots curves of the type $y = ax^2 + bx + c$, $y = \dfrac{a}{x}$, $y = ax^{\frac{1}{2}}$.

9.2 Recognizes the change in the parabola caused by a change in, a, b or c.

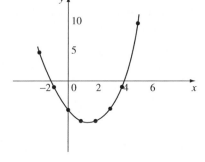

Fig. 30

WORKED EXAMPLE 55

Draw up suitable tables of values and plot the curves.

(a) $y = x^2 - 3x - 5$.

(b) $y = -2x^2 + 3x - 4$.

Solution 55

The curves are parabolas.

(a)

x	x^2	$-3x$	-5	y
-2	4	6	-5	5
-1	1	3	-5	-1
0	0	0	-5	-5
1	1	-3	-5	-7
2	4	-6	-5	-7
3	9	-9	-5	-5
4	16	-12	-5	-1
5	25	-15	-5	5

(b) $y = -2x^2 + 3x - 4$

x	$-2x^2$	$+3x$	-4	y
-2	-8	-6	-4	-18
-1	-2	-3	-4	-9
0	0	0	-4	-4
1	-2	3	-4	-3
2	-8	6	-4	-6
3	-18	9	-4	-13
4	-32	12	-4	-24

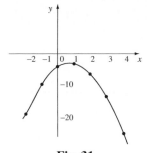

Fig. 31

The quadratic function $y = ax^2 + bx + c$.

Observations

This function has either a maximum or a minimum. If the coefficient of x^2 is negative it is a maximum, if it is a positive it is a minimum, as it can be seen from the two previous examples. In the first example, the curve intersects the x-axis, this implies that the function can be zero,

$y = 0$ or that the discriminant is positive. The discriminant is the quantity under the square root in the formula:

$$x = \frac{-b \pm \sqrt{b^2 - 4ac}}{2a}$$

which is the solution of the quadratic equation.

$$D = b^2 - 4ac = (-3)^2 - 4(1)(-5)$$
$$= 9 + 20 = 29$$

where D = discriminant.

In the second example the discriminant, $D = b^2 - 4ac = (3)^2 - 4(-2)(-4) = 9 - 32 = -21$ is negative which implies that the function cannot be equal to zero, and therefore it does not intersect the x-axis.

If the discriminant is zero, then $x = -\frac{b}{2a}$, this implies that the function touches the x-axis since there is one solution

$$x = \frac{-b}{2a} = \frac{3}{4}.$$

$x = 0.75$, what is then the value of c?. $b^2 - 4ac = 0, 3^2 - 4(-2)c = 0, c = \frac{9}{8}, y = -2x^2 + 3x + \frac{9}{8}.$

As it can be seen, y is always negative for the function $y = -2x^2 + 3x - 4$ ($y < 0$).

Summarizing

If $a < 0$, the curve has a maximum,

If $a > 0$, the curve has a minimum.

If $D = b^2 - 4ac > 0$, the curve intersects the x-axis.

If $D = b^2 - 4ac = 0$, the curve touches the x-axis.

It $D = b^2 - 4ac < 0$, the curve neither intersects not touches the x-axis.

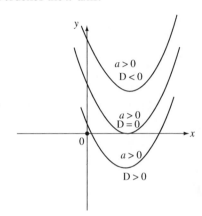

Fig. 32

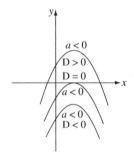

Fig. 33

Hyperbola

$y = \frac{a}{x}$, when x is large, y is small, when x is small, y is large. The curve is a rectangular hyperbola as shown in Fig. 34. The x-axis and y-axis are asymptotes, that is, the curves meet with the axes at infinity.

WORKED EXAMPLE 56

Draw up a suitable table of values and plot the curve $y = \frac{3}{x}$.

Solution 56

Draw up a suitable table of values and plot the curve $y = \frac{3}{x}$.

x	y
12	$\frac{1}{4}$
9	$\frac{1}{3}$
3	1
1	3
-3	-1
-9	$-\frac{1}{3}$
-12	$-\frac{1}{4}$

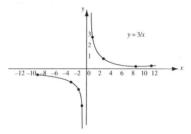

Fig. 34   Rectangular hyperbola.

WORKED EXAMPLE 57

Draw up a suitable table of values and plot the curve $y = -\frac{6}{x}$.

Solution 57

x	y
-12	$\frac{1}{2}$
-9	$\frac{2}{3}$
-6	1
-3	2
-1	6
1	-6
3	-2
6	-1
9	$-\frac{2}{3}$
12	$-\frac{1}{2}$

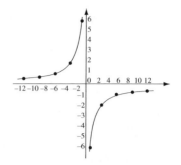

Fig. 35

Therefore we have discontinuous curves.

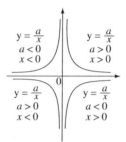

Fig. 36

The function $y = ax^{\frac{1}{2}}$

WORKED EXAMPLE 58

Draw up suitable table of values and plot the curve $y = 4x^{\frac{1}{2}}$.

Solution 58

x	$\sqrt{x} = x^{\frac{1}{2}}$	y
0	0	0
1	± 1	± 4
4	± 2	± 8
9	± 3	± 12
25	± 5	± 20
36	± 6	± 24

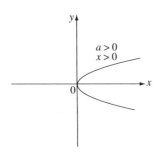

Fig. 37

It is observed that x must be positive so that we can find the square roots. Also we observe that there are two values of y for one value of x.

WORKED EXAMPLE 59

Draw up suitable table of values and plot the curve $y = -2x^{\frac{1}{2}}$.

Solution 59

x	$\sqrt{x} = x^{\frac{1}{2}}$	$y = -2x^{\frac{1}{2}}$
0	0	0
1	± 1	± 2
4	± 2	± 4
9	± 3	± 6
25	± 5	± 10
36	± 6	± 12

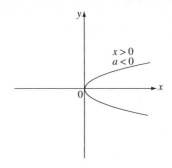

Fig. 38

9.3 Reduces relationships such as $y = ax^2 + b$; $y = a + \frac{b}{x}$ to appropriate straight line graph form.

9.4 Uses the straight line graph form to determine values of constants a and b.

9.5 Uses the graph to determine intermediate values.

$y = ax^2 + b$ is a non-linear graph if we plot y against x; if, however, y is plotted against x^2 then the graph becomes of the linear form, $y = aX + b$ where $X = x^2$.

WORKED EXAMPLE 60

The table below shows the values of the variables x and y which are believed to be related by the equation $y = Ax^2 + B$ where A and B are constants.

x	1.73	2.00	2.24	2.50	2.65	2.83
y	100	90	80	70	60	50

Show graphically that, for these values, the equations is approximately satisfied. Use the graph to estimate:

(a) the values A and B,

(b) the value of y when $x = 2.35$.

Solution 60

$$y = Ax^2 + B \qquad \qquad \text{... (1)}$$

x	1.73	2.00	2.24	2.50	2.65	2.83
x^2	2.99	4.00	5.02	6.25	7.02	8.01
y	100	90	80	70	60	50

In order to obtain a linear graph the values of x are squared as shown in the table above and the graph of y against x^2 is plotted.

Equation (1) is compared with the linear graph $y = mx + C$ where $m = A = $ gradient and $C = B = $ intercept. Appropriate scales are chosen, on the x-axis 1 cm = 1, on the y-axis 1 cm = 10. To find the intercept on the y-axis when $x = 0$, $y = B = 130$.

To find the gradient from the graph

$m = \frac{(130-20)}{(0-11.2)} = \frac{(110)}{(-11.2)} = -9.82.$

The equation (1) may be written

$y = -9.82x^2 + 130.$

(a) $A = -9.82$ and $B = 130$

(b) when $x = 2.35$, $x^2 = 5.52$, then $y = 75.9$.

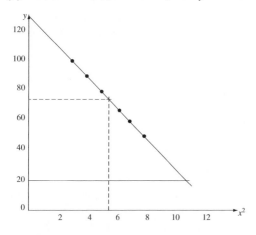

WORKED EXAMPLE 61

The table below gives corresponding values of x and y:

x	1.00	0.50	0.26	0.22	0.18
y	17.0	24.5	25.0	43.5	51.0

Verify graphically that these values of x and y satisfy approximately a relationship of the form $y = \frac{a}{x} + b$. From your graph obtain approximately values for a and b.

Solution 61

The equation $y = \frac{a}{x} + b$ is a non-linear one, when y is plotted against x, if this equation is compared with the linear equation $y = mx + c$, then we have to plot y against $\frac{1}{x}$. A new table is constructed.

x	1.00	0.50	0.26	0.22	0.18
$\frac{1}{x}$	1.00	2.00	3.85	4.55	5.56
y	17.0	24.5	35.0	43.5	51.0

y is plotted against $\frac{1}{x}$, a straight line is obtained as shown in the graph. The intercept on the y-axis is $b = 10$, and the gradient,

$a = \frac{(5.56 - 1.00)}{(51.1 - 17.0)} = \frac{(4.56)}{(34.0)} = 0.134.$

The equation may be written as

$y = \frac{0.134}{x} + 10.$

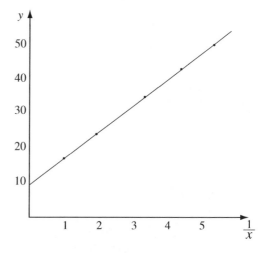

WORKED EXAMPLE 62

It is assumed that variables x and y satisfy a relationship of the form $yx = bx + c$.

Show graphically that the values of x and y given in the following table approximately support this assumption.

x	y	xy
−0.1	0.8	−0.08
0.1	−0.6	−0.06
0.3	−0.133	−0.04
0.4	−0.075	−0.03
0.6	0.017	−0.01
0.8	0.013	0.01

Plot a graph of xy against x to find approximate values of b and c. Draw an alternative linear graph and check the values of b and c.

Solution 62

The graph $xy = bx + c$ may be a linear one if xy is plotted against x, the gradient of the graph will be b and the intercept on the y-axis is c.

An alternative graph may be obtained if we re-arrange the equation.

$$xy = bx + c$$

dividing each term by x

$$y = b + \frac{c}{x} \text{ or } y = \frac{c}{x} + b$$

y is plotted against $\frac{1}{x}$, where, c is now the gradient and b the intercept on the y-axis. From the graph xy against x, the gradient,

$$b = (0.01 - \frac{(-0.08)}{(0.8 - (-0.1))}$$

$$= \frac{(0.01 + 0.08)}{(0.8 + 0.1)}$$

$$= \frac{(0.09)}{(0.90)}$$

$$= 0.1$$

when $x = 0$, $xy = c = -0.07$.

The graph may be written as $xy = 0.1x - 0.07$.

Plotting the graph of y against $\frac{1}{x}$, is a straight line.

y	$\frac{1}{x}$
0.8	−10
−0.6	10
−0.133	3.33
−0.075	2.50
−0.017	1.67
0.013	1.25

the gradient $= \frac{(0.013 - 0.8)}{(1.25 - (-10))}$

$$= \frac{(-0.787)}{(11.25)} = -0.07$$

the intercept $= 0.1$.

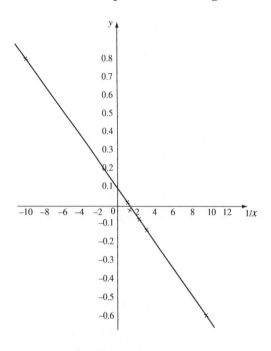

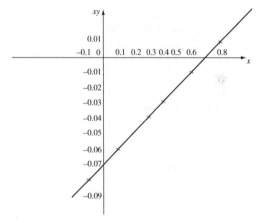

9.6 Recognizes the shapes of the curves with equations $x^2 + y^2 = a^2$;

$$\frac{x^2}{a^2} + \frac{y^2}{b^2} = 1;$$

$$\frac{x^2}{a^2} - \frac{y^2}{b^2} = 1;$$

$$xy = c^2.$$

The equation of a circle

Fig. 39 shows a circle with centre the origin, $(0, 0)$, and radius equal to a.

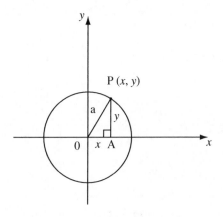

Fig. 39

Consider any point $P(x, y)$ on the circle, the y-coordinate is y and the x-coordinate is x, the right angled triangle 0AP gives the relationship $x^2 + y^2 = a^2$, using Pythagoras theorem. Therefore, the equation of a circle with $r = a$ and $C(0, 0)$ has an equation:

$$x^2 + y^2 = a^2 .$$

WORKED EXAMPLE 63

Write down the equation of a circle with a centre at the origin and radius equal to 3.

Solution 63

$x^2 + y^2 = 3^2.$

The equation of an ellipse.

The equation of an ellipse is given by

$\frac{x^2}{a^2} + \frac{y^2}{b^2} = 1.$

If $x = 0$, $y^2 = b^2$ or $y = \pm b$.
If $x = 0$, $x^2 = a^2$ or $x = \pm a$.

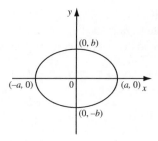

Fig. 40

If $a > b$

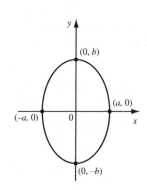

Fig. 41

If $b > a$

The ellipse has a centre at the origin and intersects the x-axis at $(a, 0)$, $(-a, 0)$ and the y-axis at

$(0, b)$, $(0, -b)$.

WORKED EXAMPLE 64

Sketch the following ellipses if

(i) $a = 2$ and $b = 3$

(ii) $a = 4$ and $b = 1$

and write down the corresponding equations.

Solution 64

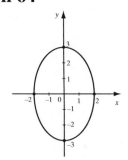

Fig. 42

$$\frac{x^2}{4} + \frac{y^2}{9} = 1$$

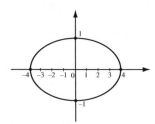

Fig. 43

$$\frac{x^2}{10} + \frac{y^2}{1} = 1.$$

WORKED EXAMPLE 65

Sketch the following curves:

(i) $3x^2 + 2y^2 = 6$
(ii) $9x^2 = 16y^2 = 144$.

State the values of the semi-axes in each case.

Solution 65

(i) $3x^2 + 2y^2 = 6$

dividing each term by 6

$$\frac{3x^2}{6} + \frac{2y^2}{6} = 1$$

$$\frac{x^2}{\frac{6}{3}} + \frac{y^2}{\frac{6}{2}} = 1$$

$$\frac{x^2}{2} + \frac{y^2}{3} = 1 \text{ or } \frac{x^2}{(\sqrt{2})^2} + \frac{y^2}{(\sqrt{3})^2} = 1$$

$a = \sqrt{2}$ and $b = \sqrt{3}$.

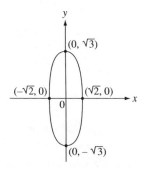

Fig. 44

(ii) $9x^2 + 16y^2 = 144$

dividing each term by 144

$$\frac{9x^2}{144} + \frac{16y^2}{144} = \frac{144}{144}$$

$$\frac{x^2}{\frac{144}{9}} + \frac{y^2}{\frac{144}{16}} = 1$$

$$\frac{x^2}{16} + \frac{y^2}{9} = 1 \quad \frac{x^2}{4^2} + \frac{y^2}{3^2} = 1$$

$a = 4, b = 3$

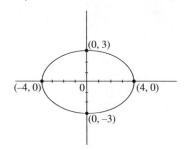

Fig. 45

The equation of a hyperbola

The equation of a hyperbola is given
$\frac{x^2}{a^2} - \frac{y^2}{b^2} = 1$.

If $x = 0$, $-\frac{y^2}{b^2} = 1$, $y^2 = -b^2$,

$y = \pm b\sqrt{-1}$ it does not exist since $\sqrt{-1}$ is not real.

If $y = 0$, $\frac{x^2}{a^2} = 1$, $\frac{x^2}{a^2} = 1$, $x^2 = a^2$, $x = \pm a$ this does exist.

Hence, the hyperbola intersects the x-axis.

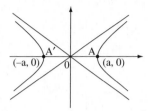

The vertices of the hyperbola are given by the sets of coordinates $A(a, 0)$, $A'(-a, 0)$.

Although b does not appear on the graph, the curvature of the graph must depend on the value of b.

If $a = b$, the asymptotes are perpendicular to each other rectangular hyperbola.

As asymptote is a line where the curve or curves tend to meet at infinity.

The equation of rectangular hyperbola.

The equation of a rectangular hyperbola is $xy = c^2$ the asymptotes are the axes.

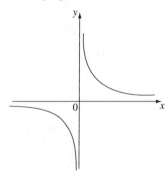

Where c is a constant.

Exercise 9

1. State whether the following quadratic functions have a minimum or a maximum.

   (i) $y = 2x^2 - 3x + 5$

   (ii) $y = 3x^2 - 4x - 7$

   (iii) $y = -x^2 - x - 1$

   (iv) $y = 1 - 3x + x^2$

   (v) $y = -9 + 5x - 3x^2$.

2. For the quadratic functions in question 1, state the coordinates of the graphs intersecting with the y-axis.

3. Sketch roughly the curves of the quadratic functions in question 1, given that the minimum or maximum occurs when
   $$x = -\frac{b}{2a}.$$

4. Determine the discriminant of each quadratic function in question 1
   $(D = b^2 - 4ac)$.

5. Draw the following hyperbolas:

   (i) $y = \frac{1}{x}$

   (ii) $y = -\frac{2}{x}$

   (iii) $xy = 3$

10

Uses graphs to determine values and establish power laws.

10.1 Uses logarithms to reduce laws of the type $y = ax^n$ to straight line form.

10.2 Tabulates values of log x and log y.

10.3 Plots a straight line graph to verify the relationship.

10.4 Uses the graph to determine values of the constants a and b.

Non linear to linear law.

$y = ax^n$ is a non linear function where x and y are variables a and n are constants.

Suppose that we have a set of values of x and corresponding values of y which satisfy approximately the relationship $y = ax^n$. If y is plotted against x, the graph will be a non linear one which cannot be used to determine the constants a and n, to make the above function linear, we can take logarithms to the base ten on both sides.

$y = ax^n$
$\log y = \log ax^n = \log a + n \log x$ or $\log y = n \log x + \log a$.

If this equation is compared with the linear equation $Y = mX + C$ then $\log y = Y, n = m$, $\log x = X$ and $\log a = C$ the non linear equation is made to a linear equation.

$$\log y = n \log x + \log a$$
$$\downarrow \quad \quad \downarrow \quad \downarrow \quad \quad \downarrow$$
$$Y \quad = m \quad X \ + \quad C.$$

WORKED EXAMPLE 66

The following table of values is thought to be connected by a law of the type: $y = ax^n$

x	y
5623	2.82
3162	2.51
1000	2.00
316	1.59
178	1.41
100	1.26
31.6	1.00
10	0.794
3.16	0.631

By plotting a graph of log y (vertical) against log x (horizontal), determine the value of the constants a and n to three significant figures.

Solution 66

$y = ax^n$

Taking logarithms to the base ten on both sides of the equation, we have:

$\log y = n \log x + \log a$. A new table of log y and log x is formed.

log x	log y
3.75	0.45
3.50	0.40
3.00	0.30
2.50	0.20
2.25	0.15
2.00	0.10
1.50	0
1.00	−0.10
0.5	−0.20

The graph of log y against log x is plotted which is a straight line.

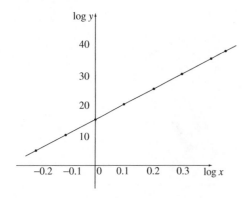

The gradient

$$= n = \left(\frac{0.5 - 3.75}{-0.20 - 0.45}\right) = \frac{-3.25}{-0.65} = 5.$$

If $\log x = 0$, $\log a = \log y = 1.5$ and therefore $a = 10^{1.5} = 31.6$. The law is

$y = 31.6x^5$, where

$a = 31.6$ and $n = 5$.

WORKED EXAMPLE 67

The following equations are non-linear:

(i) $y = ax^n$

(ii) $xy = a + bx$

(iii) $y = ax^{\frac{2}{3}} + b$.

State in each case which quantities should be plotted along the y-axis and which quantities along the x-axis in order to obtain straight line graphs.

Solution 67

(i) $y = ax^n$, $\log y = n \log x + \log a$, log y against log x is plotted.

(ii) $xy = a + bx$ $y = \dfrac{a}{x} + b$, y against $\dfrac{1}{x}$ is plotted.

(iii) $y = ax^{\frac{3}{2}} + b$, y against $x^{\frac{3}{2}}$ is plotted.

Exercises 10

1. The following equations are non-linear:

   (i) $y = ab^x$

   (ii) $T = T_0 e^{\mu\theta}$

   (iii) $y = \dfrac{A}{x^n}$

   State in each case which quantities should be plotted along the y-axis and which quantities along the x-axis in order to obtain straight line graphs.

2. The following table of values is thought to be connected by a law of the type.

   $y = ab^x$

x	1.50	2.50	3.15	4.00	4.75
y	1.00	3.09	6.31	16.6	39.8

By plotting a graph of log y (vertical), against x (horizontal), determine the value of the constant a and b to two signification figures.

3. T and θ are believed to be related by a law of the form: $T = T_0 e^{\mu\theta}$.

The following pairs of values have been obtained:

θ (radians)	T (kilograms)
5	66.7
10	181.3
15	492.7
20	1274.1
25	3641.0

Take 2 cm: 5 unit (for θ, with θ-axis parallel to the short edge of the paper).

For the $\ln T$ axis, parallel to the long edge of the paper, take 1 cm: 0.5 unit.

4. The following values of current and voltage were observed in a circuit.

I (amperes)	1	2	3	4	5
V (volts)	5	40	135	320	625

The values are connected by a law of the form $V = KI^n$.

Draw a graph of log V against log I and hence derive values of K and n.

State the law connecting I and V.

Assignments
Analytical Mathematics II

Phase Test 1 – $1\frac{1}{2}$ Hours

Attempt all questions.

1. Solve the quadratic equation $2x^2 - 7x - 3 = 0$ by using the formula.

   9 MARKS

2. Factorise $25x^2 - 20x + 4$

   15 MARKS

3. Solve the simulataneous equations

   $y = x^2 + 1.213x + 0.574$

   $y = 2.213x + 0.435.$

   15 MARKS

4. Determine the value of x

   (a) $\log_9 3 = x$

   (b) $\log_5 x = 5$

   (c) $\log_x 81 = 4$

   (d) Simplify $\log_5 25 - \log_5 5 + \log_8 8.$

   16 MARKS

5. $q = Q(1 - e^{-\frac{t}{CR}})$

   If $q = 0.01$, $Q = 0.015$, $C = 0.0001$, $R = 7000$, Find t.

   15 MARKS

6. Sketch the following graphs:

   (i) $y = \dfrac{4}{\sqrt{x}}$

   (ii) $y = \sqrt{x}$

   (iii) $\dfrac{x^2}{4} + \dfrac{y^2}{9} = 1.$

   15 MARKS

7. The following equations are non-linear:

   (i) $y = ax^n$

   (ii) $xy = m + cx$

   (iii) $y = a\sqrt{x} + b.$

   State in each case which quantities should be plotted along the y-axis and which quantities along the x-axis in order to obtain straight line graphs.

   15 MARKS

   TOTAL MARKS = 100 MARKS

Phase Test 2 – $1\frac{1}{2}$ Hours

Attempt all questions.

1. Solve the quadratic equation $2x^2 - 7x - 3 = 0$ by using the formula;

   $$x = \frac{-b \pm \sqrt{b^2 - 4ac}}{2a}$$

2. Factorise $2x^2 + 13x + 15$

   by splitting the middle term into two factors such that their sum is equal to $13x$ and their product is equal to $(2x^2)15$.

3. Factorise $x^2 - 3x + 2$ by completing the squares.

4. Solve the simultaneous equations:

   $y = 2x^2 - 5.3x + 1.25$

   $y = 2x - 1.$

5. Form the quadratic equations whose roots are:

$(-1, -3)$ and $\left(\dfrac{3}{4}, -\dfrac{1}{5}\right)$.

6. If $v = V(1 - e^{-\frac{t}{RC}})$ and;
   C = 100 μF
   R = 100 KΩ
   V = 500 volts.
   Determine t when $v = 50$ volts.

7. Determine the value of x

   (i) $\log_{27} 3 = x$

   (ii) $\log_{1000} x = 3$

   (iii) $\log_y x = 0$.

8. Sketch the graphs of $y = e^x$, $y = e^{2x}$ and $y = e^{-x}$, $y = e^{-2x}$ and one pair of axes.

Phase Test 3 – $1\frac{1}{2}$ Hours

Attempt all questions.

1. Solve the equation $x^2 + 3x - 7 = 0$.

2. Factorise $2x^2 + 5x - 3$.

3. Factorise $x^2 - 12x + 35$.

4. Solve the simultaneous equations:
   $y = -x + 5$
   $y = x^2 - 2x + 1$.

5. Form the quadratic equations whose roots are:

   $(-5, -4)$ and $\left(\dfrac{1}{2}, -\dfrac{3}{5}\right)$.

6. Determine the item t in the equations

   $i = 35e^{-\frac{t}{R}}$

   $L = 1$

   $R = 1$

   $i = 15$.

7. Determine the value of x:

   (i) $\log_{\frac{1}{5}} 5 = x$

   (ii) $\log x = 2$

   (iii) $\log_{\frac{1}{100}} x = 5$.

8. Draw the graph $y = e^{-x}$ for values of:

| x | -3 | -2 | -1 | 0 | 1 | 2 | 3 |

Phase Test 4 – $1\frac{1}{2}$ Hours

Attempt all questions.

1. Differentiate from first principles;
   $y = x + 2x^2$. **16 MARKS**

2. Find the gradient $y = \dfrac{3}{x} + \dfrac{1}{x^2} + \dfrac{2}{x^3}$.
   8 MARKS

3. Find the gradient
   $y = 3x^4 + 6x^3 - 5x^2 + 3x - 7$
   when $x = 0$
   10 MARKS

4. $y = -3\cos x$ what is $\dfrac{dy}{dx}$?
   6 MARKS

5. $y = 5\sin x$ what is $\dfrac{dy}{dx}$?
   6 MARKS

6. $\int \sin \dfrac{x}{5} dx$.
   6 MARKS

7. $\int(-\cos 3x)dx$.
   6 MARKS

8. $\int(\cos x + \sin x + e^x)dx$.
   10 MARKS

9. $\int_{1}^{3}(x^2 + 3x + 1)dx$.
   16 MARKS

10. $\int_{\frac{\pi}{2}}^{\pi}\left(\sin\dfrac{3\Phi}{2}\right)d\Phi$. **16 MARKS**

TOTAL MARKS = 100 MARKS

Solutions.

Phase Test 4

1. $y = x + 2x^2$ ...(1)

    let x be increased to $x + \delta x$ and y to $y + \delta y$

    $y + \delta y = (x + \delta x) + 2(x + \delta x)^2$ ...(2)

    (2) − (1)

    $\delta y = x + \delta x + 2x^2 + 4x\delta x + 2\delta x^2 - x - 2x^2$

    $\delta y = \delta x + 4x\delta x + 2\delta x^2$

    dividing each term by δx

    $\dfrac{\delta y}{\delta y} = 1 + 4x + 2\delta x$

    as $\delta x \to 0$ $\dfrac{\delta y}{\delta x} \to \dfrac{dy}{dx}$

    $\therefore \dfrac{dy}{dx} = 1 + 4x.$

2. $y = \dfrac{3}{x} + \dfrac{1}{x^2} + \dfrac{2}{x^3}$

    $= 3x^{-1} + x^{-2} + 2x^{-3}$

    $\dfrac{dy}{dx} = -3x^{-2} - 2x^{-3} - 6x^{-4}$

    $= -\dfrac{3}{x^2} - \dfrac{2}{x^3} - \dfrac{6}{x^4}.$

3. $y = 3x^4 + 6x^3 - 5x^2 + 3x - 7$

    $\dfrac{dy}{dx} = 12x^3 + 18x^2 - 10x + 3$

    when $x = 0$, $\dfrac{dy}{dx} = 3.$

4. $y = -3\cos x$

    $\dfrac{dy}{dx} = -3(-\sin x) = 3\sin x$

5. $y = 5\sin x$ $\dfrac{dy}{dx} = 5\cos x$

6. $\int \sin \dfrac{x}{5} dx = -\left(\cos \dfrac{x}{5}\right)\left(\dfrac{1}{5}\right) + c$

    $= -5\cos \dfrac{x}{5} + c.$

7. $\int -\cos 3x dx = \left(-\sin 3\dfrac{x}{3}\right) + c.$

Phase Test 5 – $1\frac{1}{2}$ Hours

Answer all questions.

1. Find the derivative of the function
    $y = 3x^3 - 5x^2 + 7x - 2.$

    10 MARKS

2. Determine the gradient for the functions;

    $y = x^2 - 2x + 1$ when (i) $x = 1$ and
    (ii) $x = -1$.

    10 MARKS

3. Differentiate $y = 3\sin x - 4\cos x$.

    10 MARKS

4. If $y = 3e^x - \dfrac{5}{x}$ what is $\dfrac{dy}{dx} = ?$

    10 MARKS

5. If $y = -3e^x + 5\cos x - 5\sin x + x^2$, determine $\dfrac{dy}{dx}$.

    10 MARKS

6. Integration:

   (i) $\int \sin x \, dx$

   (ii) $\int \cos x \, dx$

What is the significance of the arbitrary constant?

10 MARKS

7. $\int_{1}^{2} \left(\dfrac{1}{x^2} + x - x^3 \right) dx.$

10 MARKS

8. Determine the area under the curve;

$y = 5 \cos \theta$ between the limits $\theta = 0$ and $\theta = \dfrac{\pi}{2}$ radius. Sketch the function.

10 MARKS

9.   (i) $\int_{0}^{1} e^t \, dt$

    (ii) $\int_{0}^{\frac{\pi}{2}} - \sin x \, dx.$

10 MARKS

10.

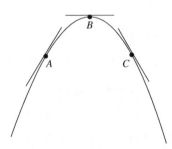

Fig. 66

Write down the sign of the gradients at A, B and C, indicating which is negative, which is positive and which is zero.

10 MARKS

TOTAL MARKS = 100 MARKS

Phase Test 6 – $1\frac{1}{2}$ Hours

Attempt all questions.

1. Determine the area under the graph of $y = 3x^3$ between $x = 1$ and $x = 2$.

15 MARKS

2. Evaluate the definite integral

$\int_{0}^{\frac{\pi}{2}} (3 \sin x + e^x - \cos x) dx.$

25 MARKS

3. Differentiate the following functions;

   (i) $y = 3x^3 - 2x^2 + x - 7$

   (ii) $y = 3 \cos x + \sin x = e^x.$

10 MARKS

4. Determine the gradients of the function at $x = \dfrac{\pi}{4}$

   (i) $y = 5 \sin x$

   (ii) $y = 4 \cos x.$

15 MARKS

5. Find the maximum or minimum value of the functions;

   (i) $y = x^2 - 3x + 1$

   (ii) $y = -x^2 - 5x + 2.$

25 MARKS

6. Differentiate from first principle;

$y = 5x.$

10 MARKS

TOTAL MARKS = 100 MARKS

Phase Test 7 – $1\frac{1}{2}$ Hours

Section A: Answer all the questions.

1. Write the following expression as a perfect square;

   $4x^2 - 20xy + 25y^2$.

2. Evaluate $(9999)^2 - (9998)^2$ without the use of the calculator, showing clearly the working.

3. A quadratic equation has roots -3 and -5. Determine the quadratic equation.

4. Solve using the formula, the quadratic equation;

   $4y^2 - 17y - 15 = 0$.

5. Factorise the quadratic expression

   $x^2 + 2x - 15$.

6. Determine the value of x

   $\log_{64} x = \frac{1}{6}$.

7. Determine the value of y

   $\log_y 625 = 4$.

8. Determine the value of z

   $\log_{10} 0.000001 = z$.

9. Simplify

   $\log_5 25 - 5 \log_5 5 - \log_5 1$.

10. Sketch the graphs $y = e^x$ and $y = e^{-x}$.

Section B: Answer all the questions.

1. The voltage v across a capacitor at time t seconds is given by;
   $v = V(1 - e^{-25t})$ volts
   (i) If $V = 200$, $t = 0.025$, calculate u.
   (ii) If $u = 50$, $V = 200$, determine the value of t.

2. The voltage v across a capacitor in series with a resistor was measured at various times t giving the following results.

t (s)	0	0.03	0.07	0.1	0.2
v (V)	100	74	50	37	13

(a) If related by the law $u = ae^{bt}$, plot a straight line graph, and determine values of a and b.

(b) Determine the value of t when $u = 80$ using the formula in (a.)

3. (a) If $y = 4x^3 - 48x$, find
   (i) The two values of x for which $\dfrac{dy}{dx} = 0$.
   (ii) The value of $\dfrac{dy}{dx}$ where $x = 1$.

   (b) Determine the area under the graph
   $y = \sin x$ between $x = 0$ and $x = \dfrac{3\pi}{4}$.

4. Determine the derivative of $y = 3x^2$ from first principles.

5. (i) $\int \left(\dfrac{4}{x^2} - \dfrac{1}{x^3} + x + 3x^2 \right) dx$

   (ii) $\int_1^2 e^x dx$ (iii) $\int_{\frac{\pi}{4}}^{\frac{\pi}{2}} \cos x \, dx$.

Phase Test 8 – $1\frac{1}{2}$ Hours

Section A: Answer all the questions.

1. For the cubic expression $y = x^3 - 3x^2 + 9x$

   (a) Obtain the indefinite integral.

   (b) Calculate the area between the curve, the x-axis and the ordinates at $x = 1$ and $x = 2$.

2. Differentiate;
   (i) $y = 5x^4 - 3x^2$
   (ii) $y = 3 \sin x^c + 4 \cos x^c$.

3. A current, I, is the sum of two components;
   $I = i_1 + i_2$
   Where $i_1 = 4 \sin(1000t)$ and
   $i_2 = 3 \cos(1000t)$

Draw a phasor diagram to show i_1, i_2 and I.

Express the resultant, I, in the form;

$I = I_{max} \sin(1000t + \Phi)$

Evaluating I_{max} and Φ.

4. T and θ are believed to be related by a law of the form;

$T = T_0\, e^{\mu\theta}$.

The following pairs of values have been obtained:

θ^c	T kg
4	55.65
$7\frac{3}{4}$	117.79
14	411.12
$20\frac{1}{4}$	1434.9
25	3710.3

By taking $\log s_e$ and plotting InT against θ, show that the law is obeyed, and determine the values of T_0 and μ.

Take 1 cm: 1 unit for θ, with θ-axis parallel to the long edge of the paper. For the InT-axis, parallel to the short edge of the paper, take 4 cms: 1 unit.

5. Two circles have radii R_1 mm, R_2 mm, where $R_2 = R_1 + 6$, and the area of the larger circle is $1.44 \times$ area of smaller circle.

Set up, and solve, a quadratic equation to find R_1 and R_2.

Phase Test 9 – $1\frac{1}{2}$ Hours

Section A: Answer all the questions.

1. (a) Factorise the expression $3x^2 + x - 10$.

   (b) Obtain the roots of the quadratic equations; $20x^2 + 19x - 273 = 0$.

2. By using the laws of logarithms, solve the following equations for x, without the use of log tables: $\log 4x^3 - 2\log 2x = \log 3x^2$.

3. Plot the values of $\log_{10} x$ and $\log_{10} y$, given in the table below, on the graph paper provided which includes axes and scales. If the relationship between x and y is known to be to the form $y = Ax^n$ where A and n are constants, use your graph to obtain the values of A and n.

$\log_{10} x$	$\log_{10} y$
0.3	−0.94
0.6	−0.88
1.0	−0.80
1.48	−0.71
1.9	−0.62

4. A sinusoidal current wave is given by;

$i = 20 \sin 50\dfrac{\pi}{3}t.$

(a) Calculate:

   (i) its frequency

   (ii) its period.

(b) Sketch ONE cycle of the current wave to a base of time, giving the more important values of current time.

5. (a) Differentiate the following with respect to x :

   (i) $y = 2x^3 - 6x^2 + 8x + 3$

   (ii) $y = 3 \sin x - 4 \cos x$.

   (b) (i) Obtain the indefinite integral $I = \int (3x^2 - 2x + 1)\mathrm{d}x$

   (ii) Determine the area under the curve $y = 5 \cos \theta$ between the limits $\theta = 0$ and $\theta = \dfrac{\pi}{2}$ radians.

Phase Test 10 – $1\frac{1}{2}$ Hours

Section A: Answer all the questions.

1. (a) Draw the graphs;

   (i) $y = \dfrac{1}{x}$ for $x = 100$, $x = 10, 1, 0.1, 0.01$

   (ii) $y = 4\sqrt{x}$ for $x = 1$, $x = 4$, $x = 16$.

(b) Write down the equations for

　(i)　　and　(ii) above.

2. (a) Draw the graph for the quadratic equation;

$y = (x - 1)(x + 3) = x^2 + 2x - 3$ for values of $x, -4, -3, -2, -1, 0, 1, 2$. Find the values of x when $y = 2$.

(b) The following equations are non-linear:

　(i) $y = ax^2 + b$

　(ii) $y = b\frac{1}{x} + a$

　(iii) $y = ax^n$ (or $\log y = n \log x + \log a$)

　State in each case which quantities should be plotted along the y-axis and which quantities along the x-axis in order to obtain straight line graphs.

3. (a) Differentiate from first principles the function $y = 5x^2$ explaining your steps clearly.

(b) Find the derivatives of the following functions.

　(i) $y = \dfrac{3}{x} - \dfrac{1}{x^2} + \dfrac{5}{x^3}$

　(ii) $y = 3x^5 - 7x^4 - 6x^3 + 3x^2 - x - 1$

　(iii) $y = -\cos x$.

4. (a) Evaluate the integrals;

　(i) $\int\limits_{1}^{3} x^3 \mathrm{d}x$

　(ii) $\int\limits_{0}^{1} x^{\frac{5}{3}} \mathrm{d}x$

　(iii) $\int\limits_{0}^{\frac{\pi}{4}} \sin x \mathrm{d}x$.

5. Find the area between the curve $y = \dfrac{1}{x^2}$, the x-axis and lines $x = 1$ and $x = 2$. Sketch a graph to illustrate your method.

Analytical Mathematics II
Solutions 1

1.   (i) $(1-2x)^2 = 1 - 4x + 4x^2$
   (ii) $(2+y)^2 = 4 + 4y + y^2$
   (iii) $(b+3c)^2 = b^2 + 6bc + 9c^2$
   (iv) $(3-x)^2 = 9 - 6x + x^2$
   (v) $(4x+5y)^2 = 16x^2 + 40xy + 25y^2$

2.   (i) $z^2 - 2az + a^2 = (z-a)^2$
   (ii) $1 + 2x + x^2 = (1+x)^2$
   (iii) $9x^2 + 6xy + y^2 = (3x+y)^2$.

3.   (i) $(a+b)^2 = a^2 + 2ab + b^2$
   (ii) $(a-b)^2 = a^2 - 2ab + b^2$
   (iii) $a^2 - b^2 = (a-b)(a+b)$.

4.   (i) $(96)^2 - (95)^2$
   $\qquad = (96-95)(96+95)$
   $\qquad = 1(191) = 191$
   (ii) $(101)^2 - (100)^2$
   $\qquad = (101-100)(101+100) = 201$
   (iii) $(199)^2 - (197)^2$
   $\qquad = (199-197)(199+197)$
   $\qquad = 2(396) = 792$.

5.   (i) $y^2 - 9^2 = 0,\ y^2 = 9^2,\ y = \pm 9$
   (ii) $4t^2 - 1 = 0,\ 4t^2 = 1,$
   $\qquad t^2 = \dfrac{1}{4},\ t = \pm\dfrac{1}{2}$
   (iii) $16x^2 - 9 = 0,\ 16x^2 = 9,$
   $\qquad x^2 = \dfrac{9}{16},\ x = \pm\dfrac{3}{4}$.

6.   (i) $x^2 + 3x + 2 = x^2 + 2x + x + 2$
   $\qquad = x(x+2) + (x+2)$
   $\qquad = (x+2)(x+1)$

(ii) $6x^2 + x - 1 = 6x^2 + 3x - 2x - 1$
$\qquad = 3x(2x+1) - (2x+1)$
$\qquad = (2x+1)(3x-1)$

(iii) $x^2 + 10x - 24$
$\qquad = x^2 + 12x - 2x - 24$
$\qquad = x(x+12) - 2(x+12)$
$\qquad = (x+12)(x-2)$

(iv) $x^2 - 2x - 80$
$\qquad = x^2 - 10x + 8x - 80$
$\qquad = x(x-10) + 8(x-10)$
$\qquad = (x-10)(x+8)$

(v) $x^2 - 4x + 3$
$\qquad = x^2 - 3x - x + 3$
$\qquad = x(x-3) - (x-3)$
$\qquad = (x-3)(x-1)$

(vi) $x^2 + 9x + 20$
$\qquad = x^2 + 5x + 4x + 20$
$\qquad = x(x+5) + 4(x+5)$
$\qquad = (x+5)(x+4)$

(vii) $x^2 - 6x + 9$
$\qquad = x^2 - 3x - 3x + 9$
$\qquad = x(x-3) - 3(x-3)$
$\qquad = (x-3)(x-3)$
$\qquad = (x-3)^2$

(viii) $9x^2 - 9x - 28$
$\qquad = 9x^2 - 21x + 12x - 28$
$\qquad = 3x(3x-7) + 4(3x-7)$
$\qquad = (3x-7)(3x+4)$

(ix) $5x^2 + 9x - 2$

$\quad = 5x^2 + 10x - x - 2$

$\quad = 5x(x + 2) - (x + 2)$

$\quad = (x + 2)(5x - 1)$

(x) $2x^2 - 3x - 9$

$\quad = 2x^2 - 6x + 3x - 9$

$\quad = 2x(x - 3) + 3(x - 3)$

$\quad = (x - 3)(2x + 3).$

7. (i) $x^2 - 2x + 1 = (x - 1)^2$

$\quad = x^2 - 2x + 1^2 - 1^2 + 1$

$\quad = (x - 1)^2 - 1 + 1$

$\quad = (x - 1)^2$

(ii) $x^2 - 3x - 4$

$\quad = x^2 - 3x + \dfrac{9}{4} - \dfrac{9}{4} - 4$

$\quad = \left(x - \dfrac{3}{2}\right)^2 - \dfrac{9}{4} - 4$

$\quad = \left(x - \dfrac{3}{2}\right)^2 - \dfrac{9}{4} - \dfrac{16}{4}$

$\quad = \left(x - \dfrac{3}{2}\right)^2 - \dfrac{25}{4}$

$\quad = \left(x - \dfrac{3}{2}\right)^2 - \left(\dfrac{5}{2}\right)^2$

$\quad = \left[\left(x - \dfrac{3}{2}\right) - \dfrac{5}{2}\right]$

$\qquad \left[\left(x - \dfrac{3}{2}\right) + \dfrac{5}{2}\right]$

$\quad = (x - 4)(x + 1)$

(iii) $x^2 - 2x = x^2 - 2x + 1^2 - 1^2$

$\quad = (x - 1)^2 - 1^2$

$\quad = [(x - 1) - 1][(x - 1) + 1]$

$\quad = x(x - 2)$

(iv) $x^2 + 5x = x^2 + 5x + \left(\dfrac{5}{2}\right)^2 - \left(\dfrac{5}{2}\right)^2$

$\quad = \left(x + \dfrac{5}{2}\right)^2 - \left(\dfrac{5}{2}\right)^2$

$\quad = \left[\left(x + \dfrac{5}{2}\right) - \dfrac{5}{2}\right]$

$\qquad \left[\left(x + \dfrac{5}{2}\right) + \dfrac{5}{2}\right]$

$\quad = x(x + 5)$

(v) $6x^2 - x - 1$

$\quad = 6\left(x^2 - \dfrac{x}{6} - \dfrac{1}{6}\right)$

$\quad = 6\left[x^2 - \dfrac{x}{6} + \left(\dfrac{1}{12}\right)^2 \right.$

$\qquad \left. - \left(\dfrac{1}{12}\right)^2 - \dfrac{1}{6}\right]$

$\quad = 6\left[\left(x - \dfrac{1}{12}\right)^2 - \dfrac{1}{144} - \dfrac{1}{6}\right]$

$\quad = 6\left[\left(x - \dfrac{1}{12}\right)^2 - \dfrac{1 + 24}{144}\right]$

$\quad = 6\left[\left(x - \dfrac{1}{12}\right)^2 - \left(\dfrac{5}{12}\right)^2\right]$

$\quad = 6\left[\left\{\left(x - \dfrac{1}{12}\right) - \dfrac{5}{12}\right\}\right.$

$\qquad \left.\left\{\left(x - \dfrac{1}{12}\right) + \dfrac{5}{12}\right\}\right]$

$\quad = 6\left(x - \dfrac{1}{2}\right)\left(x + \dfrac{4}{12}\right)$

$\quad = (2x - 1)(3x + 1).$

8. (i) $x = -3 \quad$ and $\quad x = -2$

$\quad x + 3 = 0, \qquad x + 2 = 0$

$\quad (x + 3)(x + 2) = 0$

$\quad x^2 + 3x + 2x + 6 = 0$

$\quad \mathbf{x^2 + 5x + 6 = 0}$

(ii) $x = 1 \quad$ and $\quad x = -4$

$\quad x - 1 = 0 \qquad x + 4 = 0$

$\quad (x - 1)(x + 4) = 0$

$\quad x^2 - x + 4x - 4 = 0$

$\quad \mathbf{x^2 + 3x - 4 = 0}$

(iii) $x = 2$ and $x = -3$

$x - 2 = 0 \qquad x + 3 = 0$

$(x - 2)(x + 3) = 0$

$x^2 - 2x + 3x - 6 = 0$

$\boldsymbol{x^2 + x - 6 = 0}$

(iv) $x = 5$ and $x = 6$

$x - 5 = 0 \qquad x - 6 = 0$

$(x - 5)(x - 6) = 0$

$x^2 - 5x - 6x + 30 = 0$

$\boldsymbol{x^2 + 11x + 30 = 0}$

(v) $x = \dfrac{1}{2}$ and $x = \dfrac{3}{4}$

$x - \dfrac{1}{2} = 0 \qquad x - \dfrac{3}{4} = 0$

$2x - 1 = 0 \qquad 4x - 3 = 0$

$(2x - 1)(4x - 3) = 0$

$8x^2 - 4x - 6x + 3 = 0$

$\boldsymbol{8x^2 - 10x + 3 = 0}$

(vi) $x = -\dfrac{3}{5}$ and $x = \dfrac{6}{7}$

$x + \dfrac{3}{5} = 0 \qquad x - \dfrac{6}{7} = 0$

$5x + 3 = 0 \qquad 7x - 6 = 0$

$(5x + 3)(7x - 6) = 0$

$35x^2 + 21x - 30x - 18 = 0$

$\boldsymbol{35x^2 - 9x - 18 = 0}$

(vii) $x = 2$ and $x = -4$

$x - 2 = 0 \qquad x + 4 = 0$

$(x - 2)(x + 4) = 0$

$x^2 - 2x + 4x - 8 = 0$

$\boldsymbol{x^2 + 2x - 8 = 0}$

(viii) $x = 3$ and $x = 3$

$x - 3 = 0 \qquad x - 3 = 0$

$(x - 3)(x - 3) = 0$

$x^2 - 3x - 3x + 9 = 0$

$\boldsymbol{x^2 - 6x + 9 = 0.}$

9. (i) $x^2 - 3x + 2 = 0$

$x = \dfrac{3 \pm \sqrt{9 - 8}}{2}$

$= \dfrac{3 \pm 1}{2}, x = 2 \text{ or } x = 1$

(ii) $x^2 + 3x + 2 = 0$

$x = \dfrac{-3 \pm \sqrt{9 - 8}}{2}$

$= \dfrac{-3 \pm 1}{2}, x = -2 \text{ or } x = -1$

(iii) $6x^2 + 5x + 1 = 0$

$x = \dfrac{-5 \pm \sqrt{25 - 24}}{12}$

$= \dfrac{-5 \pm 1}{12}$

$x = -\dfrac{1}{2} \text{ or } x = -\dfrac{1}{3}$

(iv) $x^2 - 8x + 15 = 0$

$x = \dfrac{8 \pm \sqrt{64 - 60}}{2}$

$= \dfrac{8 \pm 2}{2}, x = 5 \text{ or } x = 3$

(v) $x^2 + 5x + 6 = 0$

$x = \dfrac{-5 \pm \sqrt{25 - 24}}{2}$

$= \dfrac{-5 \pm 1}{2}, x = -3 \text{ or } x = -2$

(vi) $(x + 1)(x - 3) = x + 2$

$x^2 + x - 3x - 3 = x + 2$

$x^2 - 3x - 5 = 0$

$x = \dfrac{3 \pm \sqrt{9 + 20}}{2}$

$= \dfrac{3 \pm \sqrt{29}}{2},$

$x = 4.19 \text{ or } x = -1.19$

(vii) $x^2 - 0.02x - 0.03 = 0$

$x = \dfrac{0.02 \pm \sqrt{(0.02)^2 + 4 \times 0.03}}{2}$

$= \dfrac{0.02 \pm 0.347}{2}$

$x = 0.18 \text{ or } x = -0.16$

(viii) $x^2 + 7x - 5 = 0$

$$x = \frac{-7 \pm \sqrt{49 + 20}}{2}$$

$$= \frac{-7 \pm \sqrt{69}}{2}$$

$$= \frac{-7 \pm 8.31}{2}$$

$$x = 0.65 \text{ or } x = -7.66$$

(ix) $x^2 - 9x - 15 = 0$

$$x = \frac{9 \pm \sqrt{81 + 60}}{2}$$

$$= \frac{9 \pm 11.87}{2}$$

$$x = 10.4 \text{ or } x = -1.44.$$

(x) $\dfrac{x + 1}{3} + \dfrac{4}{x - 2} = 5$

$$\frac{(x + 1)(x - 2) + 12}{3(x - 2)} = 5$$

or $(x + 1)(x - 2) + 12$

$$= 15(x - 2)$$

$$x^2 - x - 2 + 12 = 15x - 30$$

$$x^2 - 16x + 40 = 0$$

$$x = \frac{16 \pm \sqrt{256 - 160}}{2}$$

$$= \frac{16 \pm \sqrt{96}}{2}$$

$$x = 12.9 \text{ or } x = 3.10$$

(xi) $\dfrac{1}{(x - 1)} + \dfrac{2}{(x + 2)} = 7$

$$\frac{x + 2 + 2x - 2}{(x - 1)(x + 2)} = 7$$

or $3x = 7(x^2 + x - 2)$

$$3x = 7x^2 + 7x - 14$$

or $7x^2 + 4x - 14 = 0$

$$x = \frac{-4 \pm \sqrt{16 + 4 \times 7 \times 14}}{14}$$

$$= \frac{-4 \pm 20.2}{14}$$

$$x = 1.16 \text{ or } x = -1.73$$

(xii) $0.3x^2 - 2.9x + 2.1 = 0$

$$x = \frac{2.9 \pm \sqrt{(2.9)^2 - 4 \times 0.3 \times 2.1}}{0.6}$$

$$= \frac{2.9 \pm 2.43}{0.6}$$

$$x = 8.88 \text{ or } x = 0.78$$

(xiii) $x^2 - 5 = 0$

$$x = \frac{0 \pm \sqrt{0 + 20}}{2} = \pm \frac{\sqrt{20}}{2}$$

$$x = \pm 2.24$$

(xiv) $x^2 - 3 = 0$

$$x = \frac{0 \pm \sqrt{0 + 12}}{2} = \pm \frac{\sqrt{12}}{2}$$

$$x = \pm 1.73$$

(xv) $(x - 7)(x + 8) = 0$

$$x^2 - 7x + 8x - 56 = 0$$

$$x^2 + x - 56 = 0$$

$$x = \frac{-1 \pm \sqrt{1 + 4 \times 56}}{2}$$

$$= \frac{-1 \pm 15}{2}$$

$$x = 7 \text{ or } x = -8$$

(xvi) $x^2 - 6x + 8.4375 = 0$

$$x = \frac{6 \pm \sqrt{36 - 4 \times 8.4375}}{2}$$

$$= \frac{6 \pm 1.5}{2}$$

$$x = 3.75 \text{ or } x = 2.25$$

(xvii) $x^2 + 2x + 0.4375 = 0$

$$x = \frac{-2 \pm \sqrt{4 - 4 \times 0.4375}}{2}$$

$$= \frac{-2 \pm 1.5}{2}$$

$$x = -0.25 \text{ or } x = -1.75$$

(xviii) $x^2 - 3.9x - 0.1975 = 0$

$$x = \frac{3.9 \pm \sqrt{(3.9)^2 + 4 \times 0.1975}}{2}$$

$$= \frac{3.9 \pm 4}{2}$$

$$x = 3.95 \text{ or } x = -0.05.$$

10. $y = (x + 5)(x + 3) = x^2 + 8x + 15$ is a quadratic expression, this is a curve which represents a parabola.

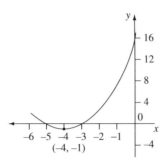

Fig. 49

Fig. 49 shows this curve with the appropriate pair of coordinates cutting the x-axis and y-axis. The minimum occurs at

$$x = -\frac{b}{2a} = -\frac{8}{2} = -4$$

$$y_{min} = (-4)^2 + 8(-4) + 15$$

$$= 16 - 32 + 15 = -1.$$

When $y = 0$, then the curve cuts the x-axis at two points

$$x^2 + 8x + 15$$

$$= (x + 5)(x + 3) = 0$$

$$x = -5, x = -3.$$

11. (i)

x	x^2	$-7x$	$+10$	y
0	0	0	10	10
1	1	-7	10	4
2	4	-14	10	0
3	9	-21	10	-2
4	16	-28	10	-2
5	25	-35	10	0
6	36	-42	10	4

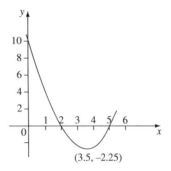

Fig. 50

$$y_{min} = 3.5^2 - 7(3.5) + 10 = -2.25$$

(ii)

x	$-x^2$	$-8x$	-7	y
-8	-64	64	-7	-7
-7	-49	56	-7	0
-6	-36	48	-7	5
-5	-25	40	-7	8
-4	-16	32	-7	9
-3	-9	24	-7	8
-2	-4	16	-7	5
-1	-1	8	-7	0
0	0	0	-7	-7

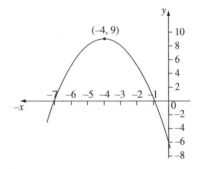

Fig. 51

$$y_{max} = -(-4)^2 - 8(-4) - 7$$

$$= -16 + 32 - 7 = 9$$

$$x = -\frac{b}{2a} = -\frac{8}{2} = -4.$$

When $y = 0$, $x^2 - 7x + 10 = 0$, there are two solutions $x = 2$ and $x = 5$, where the curve intersects the x-axis when $y = 0$, $-x^2 - 8x - 7 = 0$, there are two solutions $x = -7$ and $x = -1$, where the curve intersects the x-axis.

12. $s = \dfrac{1}{2}(u + v)t$ and substituting

$$v = u + at = \frac{1}{2}(u + u + at)t$$

$$= \frac{1}{2}(2u + at)t = ut + \frac{1}{2}at^2$$

therefore $s = ut + \dfrac{1}{2}at^2$.

This represents a quadratic equation in t, which can be written as:

$$\frac{1}{2}at^2 + ut - s = 0.$$

If $s = 15$, $u = 5$ and $a = 3$

$$\frac{3}{2}t^2 + 5t - 15 = 0$$

$$3t^2 + 10t - 30 = 0$$

$$t = \frac{-10 \pm \sqrt{100 + 360}}{6}$$

$$= \frac{-10 \pm 21.5}{6}$$

$t = 1.91$ s and $t = -5.25$ s the latter is negative and disregarded since it is meaningless. Therefore,

$t = 1.91$ s.

13.

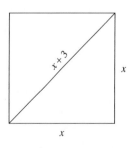

Fig. 52

$$(x + 3)^2 = x^2 + x^2 = x^2 + 6x + 9$$

$$x^2 - 6x - 9 = 0$$

$$x = \frac{6 \pm \sqrt{36 + 36}}{2} = \frac{6 \pm 8.49}{2}$$

$x = 7.24$ and $x = -1.25$ which is disregarded, therefore $x = 7.24$ units.

14.

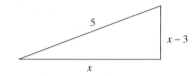

Fig. 53

$$x^2 + (x - 3)^2 = 5^2$$

$$x^2 + x^2 - 6x + 9 = 25$$

$$2x^2 - 6x - 16 = 0$$

$$x^2 - 3x - 8 = 0$$

$$x = \frac{3 \pm \sqrt{9 + 32}}{2} = \frac{3 \pm 6.4}{2}$$

$x = 4.7$ cm or $x = -1.7$ cm (which is disregarded).

Therefore the height is $x - 3 = 4.7 - 3$ $= 1.7$ cm.

15. (i) $y = 9x^2 - 7x - 25$

$$y = 2x + 3$$

$$9x^2 - 7x - 25 = 2x + 3$$

$$9x^2 - 9x - 28 = 0$$

$$x = \frac{9 \pm \sqrt{81 + 4 \times 9 \times 28}}{18}$$

$$= \frac{9 \pm 33}{18}$$

$x = 2.33$ or $x = -1.33$.

$$y = 2x + 3 = 2(2.33) + 3$$

$$y = 4.66 + 3 = 7.66$$

$y = 7.66$ when $x = 2.33$

$y = 2(-5) + 5 \quad y = -10 + 5$

$y = -5 \quad$ when $x = -5$

$y = 2(-4) + 5$

$y = -8 + 5 \quad y = -3$

when $x = -4$

(ii) $y = x^2 + 11x + 25 \quad y = 2x + 5$

$x^2 + 11x + 25 = 2x + 5$

$x^2 + 9x + 20 = 0$

$x = \dfrac{-9 \pm \sqrt{81 - 80}}{2} = \dfrac{-9 \pm 1}{2}$

$x = -5$ or $x = -4$.

(iii) $y = 9x^2 + 7x - 20 \quad y = 7x - 4$

$9x^2 + 7x - 20 - 7x + 4 = 0$

$9x^2 - 16 = 0$

or $(3x - 4)(3x + 4) = 0$

$x = \dfrac{4}{3}$ or $x = -\dfrac{4}{3}$.

$y = 7\left(\dfrac{4}{3}\right) - 4 = \dfrac{28}{3} - 4 = \dfrac{28}{3} - \dfrac{12}{3}$

$y = \dfrac{16}{3}$ when $x = \dfrac{4}{3}$

$y = 7\left(-\dfrac{4}{3}\right) - 4$

$= -\dfrac{28}{3} - 4 = -\dfrac{28}{3} - \dfrac{12}{3}$

$y = -\dfrac{40}{3}$ when $x = -\dfrac{4}{3}$

(iv) $y = 14x^2 - 25x + 1$

$y = +4x - 11$

$14x^2 - 25x + 1 = +4x - 11$

$14x^2 - 29x + 12 = 0$

$x = \dfrac{29 \pm \sqrt{(29)^2 - 4 \times 14 \times 12}}{28}$

$= \dfrac{29 \pm 13}{28}$

$x = 1.5$ or $x = 0.57$.

$y = 4x - 11 = 4(1.5) - 11$

$= 6 - 11 = -5$

$y = -5$ when $x = 1.5$

$y = 4x - 11 = 4(0.57) - 11$

$= 2.28 - 11$

$y = -8.72$ which $x = 0.57$

16. The area of a trapezium is given by the formula $\frac{1}{2}(a + b)h$, where a and b are the parallel lines $(a < b)$ and h is the distance between the parallel lines.

If $a = x, b = x + 5$ and $h = 2x$

$A = \dfrac{1}{2}(a + b)h = \dfrac{1}{2}(x + x + 5)2x$

$125 = (2x + 5)x = 2x^2 + 5x$

$2x^2 + 5x - 125 = 0$.

Apply the quadratic formula

$x = \dfrac{-5 \pm \sqrt{25 + 1000}}{4}$

$= \dfrac{-5 \pm 32.02}{4}$

$= 6.76$ m or -9.26 m.

The last answer is irrelevant root and it is disregarded.

The longer side $= x + 5 = 6.75 + 5 = 11.75$ m.

The distance $2x = 13.5$.

Check area $= A = \dfrac{1}{2}(6.75 + 11.75)13.5 = 125$ approximately.

Solutions 2

1. $\log_x y = n, \quad x^n = y.$

2. $Z^y = N, \quad \log_z N = y.$

3. $\log_{10} 0.00001$

$$0.00001 = \frac{1}{100,000}$$

$$= \frac{1}{(10)^5} = 10^{-5}$$

$$\log_{10} 10^{-5} = -5 \log_{10} 10 = -5.$$

4. $10^5 = 10 \times 10 \times 10 \times 10 \times 10 = 100,000.$

5. $\log_N N = 1.$

   By the definition the base N is raised to the result 1 and is equal to the number N.

   $N^1 = N.$

   When the base and number of a logarithm are the same then the result is equal to unity.

6. $\log_{10} 10 \times 10 \times 10 \times 10 \times 10$

$$= \log_{10} 10^5 = 5 \log_{10} 10 = 5$$

   Since $\log_{10} 10 = 1.$

7. $\log_{\frac{1}{2}} \frac{1}{2} = x$ by definition $\left(\frac{1}{2}\right)^x = \left(\frac{1}{2}\right)^1$

   therefore x is 1 and $\log_{\frac{1}{2}} \frac{1}{2} = 1.$

8. $\log_{10} \frac{1}{10^5} = -5$

   $\log_{10} 1 - \log_{10} 10^5 = 0 - 5 \log_{10} 10$

   $= -5 \times 1$

   $= -5.$

9. (i) $6^2 = 36, \log_6 36 = 2$

   (ii) $7^3 = 343, \log_7 343 = 3$

(iii) $\left(\frac{1}{2}\right)^{\frac{1}{2}} = \frac{1}{\sqrt{2}}$

$$\log_{\frac{1}{2}} \frac{1}{\sqrt{2}} = \frac{1}{2}$$

(iv) $9^3 = 729, \log_9 729 = 3.$

10. (i) $\log_3 x = y, 3^y = x$

    (ii) $\log_5 Z = N, 5^N = Z$

    (iii) $\log_b N = R, b^R = N$

    (iv) $\log_5 125 = 3, 5^3 = 125$

    (v) $\log_2 1024 = 10, 2^{10} = 1024.$

11. (i) $\log_2 x = 5, 2^5 = x = 32$

    (ii) $\log_{\frac{1}{2}} x = \frac{1}{2}, \left(\frac{1}{2}\right)^{\frac{1}{2}} = x = \frac{1}{\sqrt{2}}$

    (iii) $\log_x 512 = 9, x^9 = 512 \; x = 2$

    (iv) $\log_x 3^5 = 5, x^5 = 3^5$

    $x = 3$

    (v) $\log_3 \frac{1}{3} = x, 3^x = \frac{1}{3} = 3^{-1},$

    $x = -1$

12. (i) $\log_{100} 10 = x, 100^x = 10, x = \frac{1}{2}$

    (ii) $\log_{\frac{1}{2}} 2 = x, \left(\frac{1}{2}\right)^x = 2,$

    $(2^{-1})^x = 2, 2^{-x} = 2^1, x = -1$

    (iii) $\log_2 \frac{1}{2} = x, 2^x = \frac{1}{2} = 2^{-1},$

    $2^x = 2^{-1}, x = -1$

    (iv) $\log_1 1 = x, 1^x = 1^1, x = 1$

(v) $\log_{100} 1000 = x$, $100^x = 1000$,

$\quad 10^{2x} = 10^3$, $2x = 3$, $x = \dfrac{3}{2}$

(vi) $\log_{10} 10^{-23} = -23 \log_{10} 10$

$\quad = -23 \times 1 = -23$

(vii) $\log_3 \dfrac{1}{3^3} = \log_3 1 - \log_3 3^3$

$\quad = 0 - 3 \log_3 3 = -3$

(viii) $\log_M M = x$, $M^x - M^1$, $x = 1$.

13. $\log_{10} x = -\infty$, $10^{-\infty} = x$

$x = \dfrac{1}{10^\infty} = \dfrac{1}{\infty} = 0$.

Therefore as $x \to 0$ then $\log_{10} 0 \to -\infty$.

14. $\dfrac{1}{\infty} \to 0$, $\dfrac{1}{10} = 0.1$, $\dfrac{1}{100} = 0.01$,

$\dfrac{1}{1,000} = 0.001$, $\dfrac{1}{10^{100}} \to 0$

15. $\dfrac{1}{x} = \dfrac{1}{-\infty} = 0$

16. $\log_{\frac{1}{1000}} 1000 = x$, $\dfrac{1}{(1,000)^x}$

$= (1,000)^{-x} = (1,000)^1$, $x = -1$

17. $\log_b x - 2 \log_b x + \log_b x^5$

$\quad = \log_b x - \log_b x^2 + \log_b x^5 = \log_b \dfrac{x^1 x^5}{x^2}$

$\quad = \log_b x^4$.

18. $\sqrt{\log_{\frac{1}{x}} x - \log_x \dfrac{1}{x} + 2}$

$\quad = \sqrt{-1 + 1 + 2} = \sqrt{2}$

$\log_{\frac{1}{x}} x = y$, $\left(\dfrac{1}{x}\right)^y = x^1$,

$x^{-y} = x^1$, $y = -1$

$\log_{\frac{1}{x}} x = -1$

$\log_x \dfrac{1}{x} = z$, $x^z = \dfrac{1}{x} = x^{-1}$, $z = -1$

$\log_x \dfrac{1}{x} = -1$.

19. $\log_{10} 20 - \log_{10} 200 + \log_{10} 80 - \log_{10} 8$

$\quad = \log_{10} \dfrac{20}{200} \times \dfrac{80}{8}$

$\quad = \log_{10} 1 = 0$

20. $\log a - \log ab + \log b$

$\quad = \log \dfrac{ab}{ab} = \log 1 = 0$.

21. $\log Q^{\frac{1}{3}} P^{\frac{1}{4}} R^{\frac{1}{5}}$

$\quad = \left(\dfrac{1}{3}\right) \log Q + \left(\dfrac{1}{4}\right) \log P + \left(\dfrac{1}{5}\right) \log R$.

Solutions 3

1. $y = 5e^x$, $\dfrac{dy}{dx} = 5e^x$

   at $x = 1$, $\dfrac{dy}{dx} = 5e$

   at $x = 1$ $y = 5e$,

   at $x = 2$, $\dfrac{dy}{dx} = 5e^2$

   $y = 5e^x$

   at $x = 2$, $y = 5e^2$.

   Therefore the function at $x = 1$ is equal to the gradient at this point and similarly at $x = 2$.

2. $y = \dfrac{1}{2}e^x$, $\dfrac{dy}{dx} = \dfrac{1}{2}e^x$

   $= \dfrac{1}{2}e^{0.5} = 0.824$

3. $y = 4e^x$, $\dfrac{dy}{dx} = 4e^x = 4e^{0.1} = 4.42$

4. Graphs

   (i)

   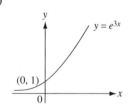

   (ii)

   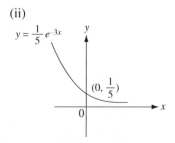

   (iii)

   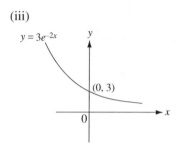

   Fig. 54

5. Graphs

   (i)   (ii)

   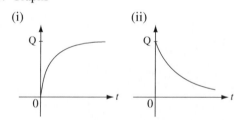

   Fig. 55

6 (a)

x	$y = 3e^x$	x	$y = 3e^x$
-2	0.406	0.2	3.66
-1.8	0.496	0.4	4.476
-1.6	0.606	0.6	5.466
-1.4	0.740	0.8	6.677
-1.2	0.904	1.0	8.155
-1.0	1.104	1.2	9.96
-0.8	1.345	1.4	12.17
-0.6	1.646	1.6	14.86
-0.4	2.011	1.8	18.15
-0.2	2.456	2.0	22.17
0	3		

The table shows the value of x at 0.2 unit intervals. The values of y are computed from the calculator and plotted against the corresponding values of x.

The graphs intersect at $x = 0$ and $y = 3$, that is, $A(0, 3)$.

(i) When $y = 15, x = 1.63$

$y = 10, x = 1.24$

$y = 5, x = 0.5$

(ii) When $x = -1.9, y = 0.5$

$x = -1.1, y = 1.0$

$x = 0.3, y = 4.1$

$x = 0.9, y = 7.5$

$x = 1.7, y = 16.5.$

The y-axis is the line of symmetry.

6 (b)

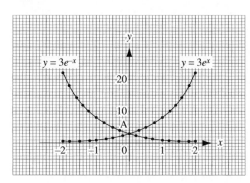

Fig. 56

7. (i) $32.5e^{-3.7}$

Shift →

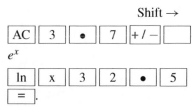

The answer $0.80351461 = 0.804$ approximately to three decimal places.

(ii) $7.5e^{3.1}$

Shift

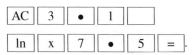

The answer $166.4846346 = 166$ approximately to three significant figures.

(iii) $25e^2$

Shift e^x

The answer is $184.7264025 = 185$ approximately to three significant figures.

(iv) $100e^{-3}$

Shift

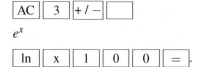

The answer is $4.978706837 = 4.98$ approximately to three significant figures.

(v) $-1000\,e^{\frac{3}{4}}$

Shift

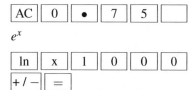

The number is $-2117.000017 = -2120$ to three significant figures.

8.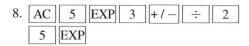

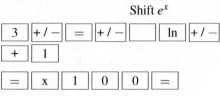

$$18.12692469 = 18.1 \text{ to three significant figures.}$$

9. $2 = Q(1 - e^{-\frac{(5 \times 10^{-3})}{(2)}})$

   $= Q(1 - e^{-2.5 \times 10^{-3}})$

   $= Q(1 - e^{-0.0025})$

   $Q = \dfrac{2}{(1 - e^{-0.0025})} = 801 \text{ coulombs.}$

Solutions 4/5

1. $\begin{pmatrix} a_{11} & a_{12} \\ a_{21} & a_{22} \end{pmatrix}$.

   This matrix has 2 rows and 2 columns.

   $$2 \quad \times \quad 2$$
   $$\uparrow \qquad\qquad \uparrow$$
   rows   columns

2. A 2×2 matrix represents two vectors:

   $$\begin{pmatrix} a_{11} \\ a_{21} \end{pmatrix} \quad \text{and} \quad \begin{pmatrix} a_{12} \\ a_{22} \end{pmatrix}$$

   where a_{11} is the x coordinate
   $\qquad a_{21}$ is the y coordinate

   similarly a_{12} is the x coordinate
   $\qquad\quad a_{22}$ is the y coordinates.

   A 2×1 matrix is $\begin{pmatrix} a_{11} \\ a_{21} \end{pmatrix}$.

   That is, two rows and one column.

3. $\mathbf{P} + \mathbf{Q} = \begin{pmatrix} -3 & -1 \\ -4 & -5 \end{pmatrix} + \begin{pmatrix} 2 & 2 \\ 3 & 4 \end{pmatrix}$

   $$= \begin{pmatrix} -1 & 1 \\ -1 & -1 \end{pmatrix}$$

   $\mathbf{Q} - \mathbf{P} = \begin{pmatrix} 2 & 2 \\ 3 & 4 \end{pmatrix} - \begin{pmatrix} -3 & -1 \\ -4 & -5 \end{pmatrix}$

   $$= \begin{pmatrix} 5 & 3 \\ 7 & 9 \end{pmatrix}.$$

4. (i) $\mathbf{A} + \mathbf{B} + \mathbf{C}$

   $$= \begin{pmatrix} 1 & 2 \\ 3 & 4 \end{pmatrix} + \begin{pmatrix} 5 & 6 \\ 7 & 8 \end{pmatrix} + \begin{pmatrix} 9 & 10 \\ 11 & 12 \end{pmatrix}$$

   $$= \begin{pmatrix} 15 & 18 \\ 21 & 24 \end{pmatrix}.$$

(ii) $2\mathbf{A} + 5\mathbf{B} - 3\mathbf{C}$

$$= 2 \begin{pmatrix} 1 & 2 \\ 3 & 4 \end{pmatrix} + 5 \begin{pmatrix} 5 & 6 \\ 7 & 8 \end{pmatrix}$$

$$- 3 \begin{pmatrix} 9 & 10 \\ 11 & 12 \end{pmatrix}$$

$$= \begin{pmatrix} 2 & 4 \\ 6 & 8 \end{pmatrix} + \begin{pmatrix} 25 & 30 \\ 35 & 40 \end{pmatrix}$$

$$- \begin{pmatrix} 27 & 30 \\ 33 & 36 \end{pmatrix}$$

$$= \begin{pmatrix} 27 & 34 \\ 41 & 48 \end{pmatrix} - \begin{pmatrix} 27 & 30 \\ 33 & 36 \end{pmatrix}$$

$$= \begin{pmatrix} 0 & 4 \\ 8 & 12 \end{pmatrix}.$$

5. $\mathbf{A} + \mathbf{B} = \begin{pmatrix} 1 & 0 \\ 2 & 3 \end{pmatrix} + \begin{pmatrix} 2 & 3 \\ 1 & a \end{pmatrix} = \begin{pmatrix} 3 & 3 \\ 3 & 6 \end{pmatrix}$

$$= \begin{pmatrix} 3 & 3 \\ 3 & 3+a \end{pmatrix} = \begin{pmatrix} 3 & 3 \\ 3 & 6 \end{pmatrix}$$

$$3 + a = 6$$
$$a = 3.$$

6. $\mathbf{A} + \mathbf{B} = \mathbf{B} + \mathbf{A}$ Associative

$$\mathbf{A} + \mathbf{B} = \begin{pmatrix} a_{11} & a_{12} \\ a_{21} & a_{22} \end{pmatrix} + \begin{pmatrix} b_{11} & b_{12} \\ b_{21} & b_{22} \end{pmatrix}$$

$$= \begin{pmatrix} a_{11} + b_{11} & a_{12} + b_{12} \\ a_{21} + b_{21} & a_{22} + b_{22} \end{pmatrix}$$

$$\mathbf{B} + \mathbf{A} = \begin{pmatrix} b_{11} & b_{12} \\ b_{21} & b_{22} \end{pmatrix} + \begin{pmatrix} a_{11} & a_{12} \\ a_{21} & a_{22} \end{pmatrix}$$

$$= \begin{pmatrix} a_{11} + b_{11} & a_{12} + b_{12} \\ a_{21} + b_{21} & a_{22} + b_{22} \end{pmatrix}$$

therefore $\mathbf{A} + \mathbf{B} = \mathbf{B} + \mathbf{A}$.

7. (i) $\mathbf{AB} = \begin{pmatrix} 3 & -3 \\ 5 & 2 \end{pmatrix} \begin{pmatrix} 1 & 2 \\ -2 & 1 \end{pmatrix}$

$= \begin{pmatrix} 3+6 & 6-3 \\ 5-4 & 10+2 \end{pmatrix}$

$= \begin{pmatrix} 9 & 3 \\ 1 & 12 \end{pmatrix}.$

(ii) $\mathbf{A}^2 = \begin{pmatrix} 3 & -3 \\ 5 & 2 \end{pmatrix} \begin{pmatrix} 3 & -3 \\ 5 & 2 \end{pmatrix}$

$= \begin{pmatrix} 9-15 & -9-6 \\ 15+10 & -15+4 \end{pmatrix}$

$= \begin{pmatrix} -6 & -15 \\ 25 & -11 \end{pmatrix}.$

(iii) $\mathbf{B}^2\mathbf{A} = \begin{pmatrix} 1 & 2 \\ -2 & 1 \end{pmatrix} \begin{pmatrix} 1 & 2 \\ -2 & 1 \end{pmatrix}$

$\begin{pmatrix} 3 & -3 \\ 5 & 2 \end{pmatrix}$

$= \begin{pmatrix} 1-4 & 2+2 \\ -2-2 & -4+1 \end{pmatrix}$

$\begin{pmatrix} 3 & -3 \\ 5 & 2 \end{pmatrix}$

$\mathbf{B}^2\mathbf{A} = \begin{pmatrix} -3 & 4 \\ -4 & -3 \end{pmatrix} \begin{pmatrix} 3 & -3 \\ 5 & 2 \end{pmatrix}$

$= \begin{pmatrix} -9+20 & 9+8 \\ -12-15 & 12-6 \end{pmatrix}$

$= \begin{pmatrix} 11 & 17 \\ -27 & 6 \end{pmatrix}.$

8. $\mathbf{MN} = \begin{pmatrix} 2 & 2 \\ 0 & 1 \end{pmatrix} \begin{pmatrix} -1 & 3 \\ 2 & 4 \end{pmatrix}$

$= \begin{pmatrix} -2+4 & 6+8 \\ 0+2 & 0+4 \end{pmatrix}$

$= \begin{pmatrix} 2 & 14 \\ 2 & 4 \end{pmatrix}$

$\mathbf{NM} = \begin{pmatrix} -1 & 3 \\ 2 & 4 \end{pmatrix} \begin{pmatrix} 2 & 2 \\ 0 & 1 \end{pmatrix}$

$= \begin{pmatrix} -2+0 & -2+3 \\ 4+0 & 4+4 \end{pmatrix}$

$= \begin{pmatrix} -2 & 1 \\ 4 & 8 \end{pmatrix}.$

9. $\mathbf{I}^3 = \begin{pmatrix} 1 & 0 \\ 0 & 1 \end{pmatrix} \begin{pmatrix} 1 & 0 \\ 0 & 1 \end{pmatrix} \begin{pmatrix} 1 & 0 \\ 0 & 1 \end{pmatrix}$

$= \begin{pmatrix} 1+0 & 0+0 \\ 0+0 & 0+1 \end{pmatrix} \begin{pmatrix} 1 & 0 \\ 0 & 1 \end{pmatrix}$

$= \begin{pmatrix} 1 & 0 \\ 0 & 1 \end{pmatrix} \begin{pmatrix} 1 & 0 \\ 0 & 1 \end{pmatrix} = \begin{pmatrix} 1 & 0 \\ 0 & 1 \end{pmatrix} = \mathbf{I}.$

$5\mathbf{I} = 5 \begin{pmatrix} 1 & 0 \\ 0 & 1 \end{pmatrix} = \begin{pmatrix} 5 & 0 \\ 0 & 5 \end{pmatrix}.$

10. (i) $\mathbf{A} + 3\mathbf{I} = \begin{pmatrix} 3 & 4 \\ 6 & 9 \end{pmatrix} + 3 \begin{pmatrix} 1 & 0 \\ 0 & 1 \end{pmatrix}$

$= \begin{pmatrix} 3 & 4 \\ 6 & 9 \end{pmatrix} + \begin{pmatrix} 3 & 0 \\ 0 & 3 \end{pmatrix}$

$= \begin{pmatrix} 6 & 4 \\ 6 & 12 \end{pmatrix}.$

(ii) $\mathbf{IA} = \begin{pmatrix} 1 & 0 \\ 0 & 1 \end{pmatrix} \begin{pmatrix} 3 & 4 \\ 6 & 9 \end{pmatrix}$

$= \begin{pmatrix} 3+0 & 4+0 \\ 0+6 & 0+9 \end{pmatrix} = \begin{pmatrix} 3 & 4 \\ 6 & 9 \end{pmatrix}.$

11. (i) $\begin{vmatrix} 2 & 3 \\ 1 & -2 \end{vmatrix}$

$= 2 \times (-2) - 1 \times 3$

$= -4 - 3 = -7$

(ii) $\begin{vmatrix} -1 & -1 \\ -1 & 2 \end{vmatrix}$

$= (-1)(2) - (-1)(-1)$

$= -2 - 1 = -3$

(iii) $\begin{vmatrix} -2 & 6 \\ 1 & 3 \end{vmatrix}$

$= (-2)(3) - 6 \times 1 = -6 - 6 = -12.$

12. (i) $xy - zt = \begin{vmatrix} x & z \\ t & y \end{vmatrix}$

(ii) $ab + cd = \begin{vmatrix} a & -c \\ d & b \end{vmatrix}$

(iii) $3 \times 2 - 5 \times 1 = \begin{vmatrix} 3 & 5 \\ 1 & 2 \end{vmatrix}.$

13. (i) $3I_1 - 5I_2 = 1$

$I_1 + I_2 = 11$

$3I_1 - 5I_2 - 1 = 0$

$I_1 + I_2 - 11 = 0$

$$\Delta_1 = \begin{vmatrix} -5 & -1 \\ 1 & -11 \end{vmatrix},$$

$$\Delta_2 = \begin{vmatrix} 3 & -1 \\ 1 & -11 \end{vmatrix}, \quad \Delta = \begin{vmatrix} 3 & -5 \\ 1 & 1 \end{vmatrix}$$

$$\frac{I_1}{\Delta_1} = -\frac{I_2}{\Delta_2} = \frac{1}{\Delta}, I_1 = \frac{\Delta_1}{\Delta}$$

$$= \frac{\begin{vmatrix} -5 & -1 \\ 1 & -11 \end{vmatrix}}{\begin{vmatrix} 3 & -5 \\ 1 & 1 \end{vmatrix}} = \frac{+56}{8} = 7$$

$$I_2 = -\frac{\Delta_2}{\Delta}$$

$$= -\frac{\begin{vmatrix} 3 & -1 \\ 1 & -11 \end{vmatrix}}{\begin{vmatrix} 3 & -5 \\ 1 & 1 \end{vmatrix}} = \frac{32}{8} = 4$$

$I_1 = 7, I_2 = 4.$

(ii) $-x + y = 9$ ... (1)

$-2x + 20y = 18$ ... (2)

rewriting (1) and (2) as

$-x + y - 9 = 0$

$-2x + 20y - 18 = 0$

$$\Delta_1 = \begin{vmatrix} 1 & -9 \\ 20 & -18 \end{vmatrix},$$

$$\Delta_2 = \begin{vmatrix} -1 & -9 \\ -2 & -18 \end{vmatrix},$$

$$\Delta = \begin{vmatrix} -1 & 1 \\ -2 & 20 \end{vmatrix}$$

$$\frac{x}{\Delta_1} = -\frac{y}{\Delta_2} = \frac{1}{\Delta}$$

$$x = \frac{\Delta_1}{\Delta}$$

$$= \frac{\begin{vmatrix} 1 & -9 \\ 20 & -18 \end{vmatrix}}{\begin{vmatrix} -1 & 1 \\ -2 & 20 \end{vmatrix}} = \frac{-18 + 180}{-20 + 2}$$

$$= \frac{162}{-18} = -9$$

$$y = -\frac{\Delta_2}{\Delta}$$

$$= -\frac{\begin{vmatrix} -1 & -9 \\ -2 & -18 \end{vmatrix}}{\begin{vmatrix} -1 & 1 \\ -2 & 20 \end{vmatrix}} = -\frac{(18 - 18)}{-20 + 2} = 0$$

$x = -9, y = 0.$

14. A singular matrix is a matrix whose determinant is zero.

$\begin{pmatrix} 3 & 5 \\ 3 & 5 \end{pmatrix}$ is a singular matrix.

Since $\begin{vmatrix} 3 & 5 \\ 3 & 5 \end{vmatrix} = 3 \times 5 - 3 \times 5 = 0.$

15.   (i) $A = \begin{pmatrix} 1 & 2 \\ 3 & 4 \end{pmatrix}$

Minors $= \begin{pmatrix} 4 & 3 \\ 2 & 1 \end{pmatrix}$

cofactors $= \begin{pmatrix} 4 & -3 \\ -2 & 1 \end{pmatrix}$

A^{*T} the transpose of the cofactors or the adjoint matrix.

$$\begin{pmatrix} 4 & -2 \\ -3 & 1 \end{pmatrix}$$

$$|A| = \begin{vmatrix} 1 & 2 \\ 3 & 4 \end{vmatrix} = 1 \times 4 - 2 \times 3 = -2$$

$$A^{-1} = \frac{1}{-2}\begin{pmatrix} 4 & -2 \\ -3 & 1 \end{pmatrix}$$

$$= \begin{pmatrix} -2 & 1 \\ \frac{3}{2} & -\frac{1}{2} \end{pmatrix}$$

$$A^{-1}A = \begin{pmatrix} -2 & 1 \\ \frac{3}{2} & -\frac{1}{2} \end{pmatrix}\begin{pmatrix} 1 & 2 \\ 3 & 4 \end{pmatrix}$$

$$= \begin{pmatrix} -2+3 & -4+4 \\ \frac{3}{2}-\frac{3}{2} & 3-2 \end{pmatrix}$$

$$= \begin{pmatrix} 1 & 0 \\ 0 & 1 \end{pmatrix} = I.$$

(ii) $A = \begin{pmatrix} -1 & 3 \\ 4 & 2 \end{pmatrix}$

Minors $= \begin{pmatrix} 2 & 4 \\ 3 & -1 \end{pmatrix}$

cofactors $= \begin{pmatrix} 2 & -4 \\ -3 & -1 \end{pmatrix}.$

The adjoint matrix or the transpose of the cofactors.

$$= A^{*T} \begin{pmatrix} 2 & -3 \\ -4 & 1 \end{pmatrix}$$

$$|A| = \begin{vmatrix} -1 & 3 \\ 4 & 2 \end{vmatrix} = -2 - 12 = -14$$

$$A^{-1} = \frac{A^{*T}}{|A|}$$

$$= \frac{\begin{pmatrix} 2 & -3 \\ -4 & -1 \end{pmatrix}}{-14}$$

$$A^{-1} = \begin{pmatrix} -\frac{1}{7} & \frac{3}{14} \\ \frac{2}{7} & \frac{1}{14} \end{pmatrix}$$

$$A^{-1}A = \begin{pmatrix} -\frac{1}{7} & \frac{3}{14} \\ \frac{2}{7} & \frac{1}{14} \end{pmatrix} \begin{pmatrix} -1 & 3 \\ 4 & 2 \end{pmatrix}$$

$$= \begin{pmatrix} \frac{1}{7} + \frac{6}{7} & \frac{-3}{7} + \frac{3}{7} \\ -\frac{2}{7} + \frac{2}{7} & \frac{6}{7} + \frac{1}{7} \end{pmatrix}$$

$$= \begin{pmatrix} 1 & 0 \\ 0 & 1 \end{pmatrix} = I.$$

(iii) $A = \begin{pmatrix} 2 & 5 \\ 6 & -2 \end{pmatrix}$

$$A^* = \begin{pmatrix} -2 & -6 \\ -5 & 2 \end{pmatrix}$$

$$A^{*T} = \begin{pmatrix} -2 & -5 \\ -6 & 2 \end{pmatrix}$$

$$|A| = \begin{vmatrix} 2 & 5 \\ 6 & -2 \end{vmatrix} = -4 - 30 = -34$$

$$A^{-1} = \frac{A^{*T}}{|A|}$$

$$= \frac{\begin{pmatrix} -2 & -5 \\ -6 & 2 \end{pmatrix}}{-34}$$

$$= \begin{pmatrix} \frac{1}{17} & \frac{5}{34} \\ \frac{+3}{17} & \frac{-1}{17} \end{pmatrix}$$

$$A^{-1}A = \begin{pmatrix} \frac{1}{17} & \frac{5}{34} \\ \frac{3}{17} & \frac{-1}{17} \end{pmatrix} \begin{pmatrix} 2 & 5 \\ 6 & -2 \end{pmatrix}$$

$$= \begin{pmatrix} \frac{2}{17} + \frac{15}{17} & \frac{5}{17} - \frac{5}{17} \\ \frac{6}{17} - \frac{6}{17} & \frac{15}{17} + \frac{2}{17} \end{pmatrix}$$

$$= \begin{pmatrix} 1 & 0 \\ 0 & 1 \end{pmatrix} = I.$$

16. (i) $3a - 5b = 1$
$a + b = 11$

$$\begin{pmatrix} 3 & -5 \\ 1 & 1 \end{pmatrix} \begin{pmatrix} a \\ b \end{pmatrix} = \begin{pmatrix} 1 \\ 11 \end{pmatrix}$$

$$A = \begin{pmatrix} 3 & -5 \\ 1 & 1 \end{pmatrix}$$

$$A^* = \begin{pmatrix} 1 & -1 \\ 5 & 3 \end{pmatrix}$$

$$A^{*T} = \begin{pmatrix} 1 & 5 \\ -1 & 3 \end{pmatrix}$$

$$|A| = 3 \times 1 + 5 \times 1 = 8$$

$$A^{-1} = \frac{A^{*T}}{|A|}$$

$$= \begin{pmatrix} \frac{1}{8} & \frac{5}{8} \\ -\frac{1}{8} & \frac{3}{8} \end{pmatrix}$$

$$A^{-1}A \begin{pmatrix} a \\ b \end{pmatrix} = A^{-1} \begin{pmatrix} 1 \\ 11 \end{pmatrix}$$

$$I \begin{pmatrix} a \\ b \end{pmatrix} = A^{-1} \begin{pmatrix} 1 \\ 11 \end{pmatrix}$$

$$\begin{pmatrix} a \\ b \end{pmatrix} = \begin{pmatrix} \frac{1}{8} & \frac{5}{8} \\ -\frac{1}{8} & \frac{3}{8} \end{pmatrix} \begin{pmatrix} 1 \\ 11 \end{pmatrix}$$

$$a = \frac{1}{8} + \frac{55}{8} = \frac{56}{8} = 7$$

$$b = -\frac{1}{8} + \frac{33}{8} = 4$$

$$a = 7$$

$$b = 4.$$

(ii) $-I_1 + I_2 = 9$
$-2I_1 + 20I_2 = 18$

$$\begin{pmatrix} -1 & 1 \\ -2 & 20 \end{pmatrix} \begin{pmatrix} I_1 \\ I_2 \end{pmatrix} = \begin{pmatrix} 9 \\ 18 \end{pmatrix}$$

$$A = \begin{pmatrix} -1 & 1 \\ -2 & 20 \end{pmatrix}$$

$$A^* = \begin{pmatrix} 20 & 2 \\ -1 & -1 \end{pmatrix}$$

$$A^{*T} = \begin{pmatrix} 20 & -1 \\ 2 & -1 \end{pmatrix}$$

$$A^{-1} = \frac{A^{*T}}{|A|}$$

$$= \frac{\begin{pmatrix} 20 & -1 \\ 2 & -1 \end{pmatrix}}{-20 + 2} = \begin{pmatrix} \frac{-20}{18} & \frac{1}{18} \\ -\frac{1}{9} & \frac{1}{18} \end{pmatrix}$$

$$A^{-1}A \begin{pmatrix} I_1 \\ I_2 \end{pmatrix} = A^{-1} \begin{pmatrix} 9 \\ 18 \end{pmatrix}$$

$$I \begin{pmatrix} I_1 \\ I_2 \end{pmatrix} = \begin{pmatrix} -\frac{10}{9} & \frac{1}{8} \\ \frac{-1}{9} & \frac{1}{18} \end{pmatrix} \begin{pmatrix} 9 \\ 18 \end{pmatrix}$$

$$\begin{pmatrix} I_1 \\ I_2 \end{pmatrix} = \begin{pmatrix} -10 + 1 \\ -1 + 1 \end{pmatrix} = \begin{pmatrix} -9 \\ 0 \end{pmatrix}$$

$$I_1 = -9 \qquad I_2 = 0.$$

Solutions 6

1. See Fig. A and Fig. B

$$\frac{\delta y}{\delta x} = \frac{9-4}{3-2} = \frac{5}{1} \text{ at } Q_1$$

$$\frac{\delta y}{\delta x} = \frac{6.25-4}{2.5-2} = \frac{2.25}{0.5} = 4.5 \text{ at } Q_2$$

$$\frac{\delta y}{\delta x} = \frac{4.41-4}{2.1-2} = \frac{0.41}{0.10} = 4.1 \text{ at } Q_3$$

As Q moves towards P, the gradient of the chord decreases to a limit of 4 as Q approaches P, that is, $\delta x \to 0$.

At P the gradient is the tangent, that is,
$$\frac{\delta y}{\delta x} \to \frac{dy}{dx} = 4 \qquad y = x^2$$

$$\frac{dy}{dx} = 2x, \text{ when } x = 2, \quad \frac{dy}{dx} = 4,$$

see graphs that follow.

2. $$\frac{dy}{dx} = \lim_{\delta x \to 0} \frac{\delta y}{\delta x}$$

$\delta x = 1$ at Q_1 $\qquad \delta x = 0.5$ at Q_2

$\delta x = 0.1$ at Q_3 $\qquad \delta x \to 0$ at Q_4

the gradient of the chord, $\frac{\delta y}{\delta x}$, tends towards the tangent at P, $\frac{dy}{dx}$.

3.

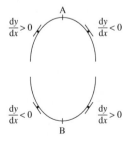

At the maximum, the gradient from positive changes to the negative.

At the minimum the gradient from negative changes to the positive.

A and B are the turning points where the gradient changes.

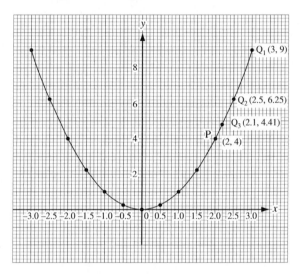

Fig. A

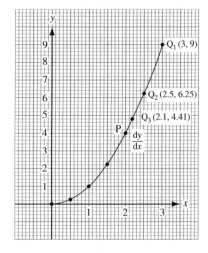

Fig. B

Solutions 7

1. (i) $y + \delta y = -5$ ... (1)

         $y = -5$ ... (2)

        (1) $-$ (2)

        $\delta y = -5 + 5 = 0$

        $\dfrac{\delta y}{\delta x} = 0, \dfrac{dy}{dx} = 0$ as $\delta x \to 0$.

        The derivative of $y = -5$, $\dfrac{dy}{dx} = 0$.

   (ii) $y = 2x, y + \delta y = 2(x + \delta x)$

        $\delta y = 2x + 2\delta x - 2x$

        $\delta y = 2\delta x$

        $\dfrac{\delta y}{\delta x} = 2$

        as $\delta x \to 0$, $\dfrac{\delta y}{\delta x} \to \dfrac{dy}{dx}$

        $\dfrac{dy}{dx} = 2$.

  (iii) $y = -3x^2$

        $y + \delta y = -3(x + \delta x)^2$

        $\delta y = -3x^2 - 6x\delta x - 3\delta x^2 + 3x^2$

        $\delta y = -6x\delta x - 3\delta x^2$

        $\dfrac{\delta y}{\delta x} = -6x - 3\delta x$

        as $\delta x \to 0, \dfrac{\delta y}{\delta x} \to \dfrac{dy}{dx}$

        $\dfrac{dy}{dx} = -6x$.

   (iv) $y = 4x^3, y + \delta y = 4(x + \delta x)^3$

             $= 4(x^2 + 3x^2\delta x + 3x\delta x^2 + \delta x^3)$

        $\delta y = 4x^3 + 12x^2\delta x + 12x\delta x^2$

             $+ 4\delta x^3 - 4x^3$

        $\delta y = 12x^2\delta x + 12x\delta x^2 + 4\delta x^3$

        $\dfrac{\delta y}{\delta x} = 12x^2 + 12x\delta x + 4\delta x^2,$

        as $\delta x \to 0, \dfrac{\delta y}{\delta x} \to \dfrac{dy}{dx}$

        $\dfrac{dy}{dx} = 12x^2$.

2. (i) $y = 3x^4, \dfrac{dy}{dx} = 12x^3$

   (ii) $y = 3x^2, \dfrac{dy}{dx} = 6x$

  (iii) $y = 3x^2 - 3x, \dfrac{dy}{dx} = 6x - 3$

   (iv) $y = x^2 + 3x + 5, \dfrac{dy}{dx} = 2x + 3$

   (v) $y = 4x^3 + 4x^2 + 4x + 5$

        $\dfrac{dy}{dx} = 12x^2 + 8x + 4$

   (vi) $y = \dfrac{3x^3}{4} - \dfrac{x^2}{2} - \dfrac{x}{5} + 5$

        $\dfrac{dy}{dx} = \dfrac{9x^2}{4} - x - \dfrac{1}{5}$

  (vii) $y = 4x^3 + 2x^2 + 20$

        $\dfrac{dy}{dx} = 12x^2 + 4x$

(viii) $y = 5x^6 - 3x^4 + x + 1$

        $\dfrac{dy}{dx} = 30x^5 - 12x^3 + 1$

   (ix) $y = x^3 - x^2 - x + 1$

        $\dfrac{dy}{dx} = 3x^2 - 2x - 1$

   (x) $y = 1.9 - 2.5x + 7.4x^2$

        $\dfrac{dy}{dx} = -2.5 + 14.8x$.

3. (i) $y = 4x^2$, $\dfrac{dy}{dx} = 8x$,

$x = 1$, $\dfrac{dy}{dx} = 8$

(ii) $y = 2x^3$, $\dfrac{dy}{dx} = 6x^2$,

$x = -2$, $\dfrac{dy}{dx} = 24$

(iii) $y = 3x - 5$, $\dfrac{dy}{dx} = 3$

(iv) $y = 5x^4 - 3x^3 + 2x^2 + 5x - 1$

$\dfrac{dy}{dx} = 20x^3 - 9x^2 + 4x + 5$

$x = 0$, $\dfrac{dy}{dx} = 5$

(v) $y = \dfrac{x^2}{3} - \dfrac{x}{5}$,

$\dfrac{dy}{dx} = \dfrac{2x}{3} - \dfrac{1}{5}$, $x = -\dfrac{1}{2}$,

$\dfrac{dy}{dx} = \dfrac{2}{3}\left(\dfrac{-1}{2}\right) - \dfrac{1}{5}$

$= -\dfrac{1}{3} - \dfrac{1}{5} = -\dfrac{8}{15}$

4. (i) $y = 3x$, $\dfrac{dy}{dx} = 3$

(ii) $y = -x^2$, $\dfrac{dy}{dx} = -2x$

(iii) $y = 4x^3$, $\dfrac{dy}{dx} = 12x^2$

(iv) $y = 5x^4$, $\dfrac{dy}{dx} = 20x^3$

(v) $y = \dfrac{x^4}{5}$, $\dfrac{dy}{dx} = \dfrac{4x^3}{5}$

(vi) $y = \left(\dfrac{1}{2}\right)x^{\frac{1}{2}}$,

$\dfrac{dy}{dx} = \dfrac{1}{4}x^{-\frac{1}{2}}$

(vii) $y = \left(-\dfrac{3}{4}\right)x^{\frac{3}{2}}$,

$\dfrac{dy}{dx} = \left(-\dfrac{3}{4}\right)\left(\dfrac{3}{2}\right)x^{\frac{1}{2}} = -\dfrac{9}{8}x^{\frac{1}{2}}$

(viii) $y = -\dfrac{1}{x}$, $y = -x^{-1}$,

$\dfrac{dy}{dx} = x^{-2} = \dfrac{1}{x^2}$

(ix) $y = \dfrac{1}{x^2} = x^{-2}$, $\dfrac{dy}{dx} = -2x^{-3} = -\dfrac{2}{x^3}$

(x) $y = 5\sqrt{x} = 5x^{+\frac{1}{2}}$,

$\dfrac{dy}{dx} = \dfrac{5}{2}x^{-\frac{1}{2}} = \dfrac{5}{2\sqrt{x}}$

(xi) $y = \dfrac{4}{\sqrt{x}} = 4x^{-\frac{1}{2}}$,

$\dfrac{dy}{dx} = -2x^{-\frac{3}{2}} = \dfrac{-2}{\sqrt{x^3}}$

(xii) $y = 5\sqrt[3]{x^2} = 5x^{\frac{2}{3}}$,

$\dfrac{dy}{dx} = \left(\dfrac{10}{3}\right)x^{-\frac{1}{3}} = \dfrac{10}{3x^{\frac{1}{3}}}$

(xiii) $y = 3x^3 + 2x^2 - 5x + 7$,

$\dfrac{dy}{dx} = 9x^2 + 4x - 5$

(xiv) $y = 5x^2 + 5x - \dfrac{3}{x}$,

$\dfrac{dy}{dx} = 10x + 5 + \dfrac{3}{x^2}$

(xv) $y = \sqrt{x} + \dfrac{1}{\sqrt{x}} = x^{\frac{1}{2}} + x^{-\frac{1}{2}}$,

$\dfrac{dy}{dx} = \left(\dfrac{1}{2}\right)x^{-\frac{1}{2}} - \left(\dfrac{1}{2}\right)x^{-\frac{3}{2}}$

(xvi) $s = 10 - 6t - 7t^2 + 2t^3$,

$\dfrac{ds}{dt} = -6 - 14t + 6t^2$

(xvii) $s = 4\pi r^2$, $\dfrac{ds}{dr} = 8\pi r$

(xviii) $A = \pi r^2$, $\dfrac{dA}{dr} = 2\pi r$

(xix) $s = \dfrac{3}{5}\sqrt{t} = \dfrac{3}{5}t^{\frac{1}{2}}$, $\dfrac{ds}{dt} = \dfrac{3}{10}t^{-\frac{1}{2}}$

(xx) $k = \dfrac{0.01}{T^2} = 0.01T^{-2}$,

$\dfrac{dk}{dT} = -0.02T^{-3}$.

5. $y = 3x^2 - 5x - 5$, $\dfrac{dy}{dx} = 6x - 5$, when

   $x = 1$, $\dfrac{dy}{dx} = 1$

   $x = -2$, $\dfrac{dy}{dx} = 6(-2) - 5 = -17$

6. $y = x^3 + x^2 - 5x + 7$

   $\dfrac{dy}{dx} = 3x^2 + 2x - 5$ when

   $x = 0$, $\dfrac{dy}{dx} = -5$,

   $x = 1$, $\dfrac{dy}{dx} = 3 + 2 - 5 = 0$,

   $x = 2$, $\dfrac{dy}{dx} = 3(2)^2 + 2(2) - 5 = 11$.

7. $y = 3x^2 + x - 5$

   $\dfrac{dy}{dx} = 6x + 1$

   (a) $\dfrac{dy}{dx} = 1 = 6x + 1$, $x = 0$

   (b) $\dfrac{dy}{dx} = 2 = 6x + 1$, $x = \dfrac{1}{6}$

   (c) $\dfrac{dy}{dx} = 0 = 6x + 1$, $x = -\dfrac{1}{6}$

8. (i) $y = 3\sin\theta$ $\quad \dfrac{dy}{d\theta} = 3\cos\theta$

   (ii) $y = -5\cos\theta$ $\quad \dfrac{dy}{d\theta} = +5\sin\theta$

9. (i) $t = 4\sin x$

   $\dfrac{dt}{dx} = 4\cos x$ $\quad$ when $x = 0$

   $\dfrac{dt}{dx} = 4\cos 0 = 4$ $\quad$ when $x = \dfrac{\pi}{4}$

   $\dfrac{dt}{dx} = 4\cos\dfrac{\pi}{4} = \dfrac{4}{\sqrt{2}}$

   when $x = \dfrac{\pi}{2}$

   $\dfrac{dt}{dx} = 4\cos\dfrac{\pi}{2} = 0$

(ii) $t = -5\cos x$

   $\dfrac{dt}{dx} = 5\sin x$

   when $x = 0$

   $\dfrac{dt}{dx} = 5\sin 0 = 5 \times 0 = 0$

   when $x = \dfrac{\pi}{4}$

   $\dfrac{dt}{dx} = 5\sin\dfrac{\pi}{4} = 5\dfrac{1}{\sqrt{2}} = \dfrac{5}{\sqrt{2}}$

   when $x = \dfrac{\pi}{2}$

   $\dfrac{dt}{dx} = 5\sin\dfrac{\pi}{2} = 5 \times 1 = 5$.

10. (i) $y = x^2 - 6x + 5$,

   $\dfrac{dy}{dx} = 2x - 6 = 0$,

   $x = 3$

(ii) $y = 4x^2 + 2x + 7$,

   $\dfrac{dy}{dx} = 8x + 2 = 0$,

   $x = -\dfrac{1}{4}$

(iii) $y = 6x^2 + 5$,

   $\dfrac{dy}{dx} = 12x = 0$,

   $x = 0$

(iv) $y = x^2 + 3x - 1$,

   $\dfrac{dy}{dx} = 2x + 3 = 0$,

   $x = -\dfrac{3}{2}$

(v) $y = \dfrac{1}{3}x^2 - 2x + 2$,

   $\dfrac{dy}{dx} = \dfrac{2}{3}x - 2 = 0$,

   $x = 3$.

Solutions 8

1. $\int ax^n dx = \dfrac{ax^{n+1}}{n+1} + c, n \neq -1.$

2. (i) $\int 3t^5 dt = \dfrac{3t^6}{6} + c = \dfrac{1}{2}t^6 + c$

   (ii) $\int 5y^4 dy = \dfrac{5y^5}{5} + c = y^5 + c$

   (iii) $\int -z^3 dz = \dfrac{-z^4}{4} + c$

   (iv) $\int 2x^2 dx = \dfrac{2x^3}{3} + c$

   (v) $\int -3y^3 dy = \dfrac{-3y^4}{4} + c$

3. (i) $\int x dx = \dfrac{x^2}{2} + c$

   (ii) $\int y dy = \dfrac{y^2}{2} + c$

   (iii) $\int z dz = \dfrac{z^2}{2} + c$

   (iv) $\int t dt = \dfrac{t^2}{2} + c$

   (v) $\int 3x^3 dx = \dfrac{3x^4}{4} + c$

   (vi) $\int z^{\frac{1}{4}} dx = \dfrac{4z^{\frac{5}{4}}}{5} + c$

   (vii) $\int (2t^2 - 3t) dt = \dfrac{2}{3}t^3 - \dfrac{3}{2}t^2 + c$

   (viii) $\int \dfrac{1}{x^3} dx = \int x^{-3} dx$

$$= \dfrac{x^{-2}}{-2} + c = -\dfrac{1}{2x^2} + c$$

   (ix) $\int \dfrac{1}{y^2} dy = \int y^{-2} dy = \dfrac{y^{-1}}{-1} + c$

$$= -\dfrac{1}{y} + c$$

(x) $\int x^{\frac{3}{4}} dx = \dfrac{4x^{\frac{7}{4}}}{7} + c.$

4. (i) $\int (2x^2 + 3x + 5)\, dx$

$$= \dfrac{2}{3}x^3 + \dfrac{3}{2}x^2 + 5x + c$$

   (ii) $\int \left(\dfrac{1}{x^2} + \dfrac{1}{x^3} - \dfrac{1}{x^4} \right) dx$

$$= \int \left(x^{-2} + x^{-3} - x^{-4} \right) dx$$

$$= -\dfrac{1}{x} - \dfrac{1}{2x^2} + \dfrac{1}{3x^3} + c.$$

5. (i) $\int \dfrac{1}{\sqrt{x}} dx = \int \dfrac{1}{x^{\frac{1}{2}}} dx = \int x^{-\frac{1}{2}} dx$

$$= \dfrac{x^{\frac{1}{2}}}{\frac{1}{2}} + c = 2\sqrt{x} + c.$$

   (ii) $\int \left(\sqrt{x} - \dfrac{1}{\sqrt{x}} \right) dx$

$$= \int \left(x^{\frac{1}{2}} - x^{-\frac{1}{2}} \right) dx$$

$$= \dfrac{2}{3}x^{\frac{3}{2}} - 2x^{\frac{1}{2}} + c.$$

6. (i) $\int 3 \sin x dx = -3 \cos x + c$

   (ii) $\int 5 \cos x dx = 5 \sin x + c.$

7. (i) $\int\limits_{1}^{2} (x^2 - 3x)\, dx = \left[\dfrac{x^3}{3} - \dfrac{3x^2}{2} \right]_{1}^{2}$

$$= \left[\dfrac{2^3}{3} - \dfrac{3}{2}2^2 \right] - \left[\dfrac{1}{3} - \dfrac{3}{2} \right]$$

$$= \left(\dfrac{8}{3} - 6 \right) - \left(\dfrac{2-9}{6} \right)$$

$$= \frac{8-18}{3} + \frac{7}{6} = -\frac{10}{3} + \frac{7}{6}$$

$$= -\frac{20}{6} + \frac{7}{6} = -\frac{13}{6}$$

$$\left(\frac{13}{6} \text{ square units}\right).$$

(ii) $\int_{-1}^{1} \left(-x^3 - 2x\right) dx$

$$= \left[\frac{-x^4}{4} - \frac{2x^2}{2}\right]_{-1}^{1}$$

$$= \left[-\frac{1}{4} - 1\right] - \left[-\frac{1}{4} - 1\right] = 0.$$

8. (i) $\int_{0}^{1} \left(ax^2 + bx + c\right) dx$

$$= \left[\frac{ax^3}{3} + \frac{bx^2}{2} + cx\right]_{0}^{1}$$

$$= \frac{a}{3} + \frac{b}{2} + c \text{ square units}.$$

(ii) $\int_{t=1}^{t=2} (3t - 5)dt = \left[\frac{3t^2}{2} - 5t\right]_{t=1}^{t=2}$

$$= (6 - 10) - \left(\frac{3}{2} - 5\right)$$

$$= -4 + 3.5 = 0.5 \text{ square units}.$$

9. (i)

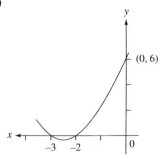

Fig. 57

(ii) $\int_{-3}^{-2} (x + 2)(x + 3)dx$

$$= \int_{-3}^{-2} (x^2 + 5x + 6)dx$$

$$= \left[\frac{x^3}{3} + \frac{5x^2}{2} + 6x\right]_{-3}^{-2}$$

$$= \left[\frac{(-2)^3}{3} + \frac{5}{2}(-2)^2 + 6(-2)\right]$$

$$\quad - \left[\frac{(-3)^3}{3} + \frac{5}{2}(-3)^2 + 6(-3)\right]$$

$$= \left(-\frac{8}{3} + 10 - 12\right) - (-9 + 22.5 - 18)$$

$$= \left(-2\frac{2}{3} - 2\right) + 4.5$$

$$= 0.167 \text{ square units}.$$

10. $\int_{4}^{5} (x - 4)(x - 5)dx$

$$= \int_{4}^{5} (x^2 - 9x + 20)dx$$

$$= \left[\frac{x^3}{3} - \frac{9}{2}x^2 + 20x\right]_{4}^{5}$$

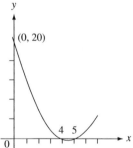

Fig. 58

$$= \left[\frac{5^3}{3} - \frac{9}{2}5^2 + 20(5)\right]$$

$$\quad - \left[\frac{4^3}{3} - \frac{9}{2}4^2 + 20(4)\right]$$

$$= (41.67 - 112.5 + 100) - (21.3 - 72 + 80)$$

$$= 29.17 - 29.3 = 0.13 \text{ square units}.$$

11. $\int 2x\,dx = \dfrac{2x^2}{2} + c = x^2 + c$

12. $\int 3x^2\,dx = \dfrac{3x^3}{3} + c = x^3 + c$

13. $\int 5x^3\,dx = \dfrac{5x^4}{4} + c$

14. $\int \dfrac{x^4}{4}\,dx = \dfrac{1}{20}x^5 + c$

15. $\int x^{\frac{1}{2}}\,dx = \dfrac{2}{3}x^{\frac{3}{2}} + c$

16. $\int -x^{\frac{3}{2}}\,dx = \dfrac{-x^{\frac{5}{2}}}{\frac{5}{2}} + c = -\dfrac{2}{5}x^{\frac{5}{2}} + c$

17. $\int \dfrac{1}{x^2}\,dx = \int x^{-2}\,dx = -\dfrac{1}{x} + c$

18. $\int 3\sqrt{x}\,dx = \int 3x^{\frac{1}{2}}\,dx$

$= \dfrac{3x^{\frac{3}{2}}}{\frac{3}{2}} + c = 2x^{\frac{3}{2}} + c$

19. $\int \dfrac{1}{\sqrt{x}}\,dx = \int x^{-\frac{1}{2}}\,dx$

$= \dfrac{x^{\frac{1}{2}}}{\frac{1}{2}} + c = 2x^{\frac{1}{2}} + c$

20. $\int 5\sqrt[3]{x}\,dx = \int 5x^{\frac{1}{3}}\,dx$

$= \dfrac{5x^{\frac{4}{3}}}{\frac{4}{3}} + c = \dfrac{15}{4}x^{\frac{4}{3}} + c$

21. $\int (2x^3 + 2x^2 + 5x + 2)\,dx$

$= \dfrac{2x^4}{4} + \dfrac{2x^3}{3} + \dfrac{5x^2}{2} + 2x + c$

$= \dfrac{1}{2}x^4 + \dfrac{2}{3}x^3 + \dfrac{5}{2}x^2 + 2x + c$

22. $\int_0^1 \left(\sqrt{x} + \dfrac{1}{\sqrt{x}} \right)\,dx$

$= \int_0^1 \left(x^{\frac{1}{2}} + x^{-\frac{1}{2}} \right)\,dx$

$= \left[\dfrac{x^{\frac{3}{2}}}{\frac{3}{2}} + \dfrac{x^{\frac{1}{2}}}{\frac{1}{2}} \right]_0^1 = \dfrac{2}{3} + 2 = 2\dfrac{2}{3}$ s.u

23. $\int_0^1 \left(10 + 6t + 7t^2 + 2t^3 \right)\,dt$

$= \left[10t + \dfrac{6t^2}{2} + \dfrac{7}{3}t^3 + \dfrac{2}{4}t^4 \right]_0^1$

$= 10 + 3 + \dfrac{7}{3} + \dfrac{1}{2}$

$= 15.8$ square units

24. $\int_1^2 \pi r^2\,dr = \left[\dfrac{\pi r^3}{3} \right]_1^2$

$= \left(\dfrac{\pi}{3} \right)2^3 - \dfrac{\pi}{3} = \dfrac{7\pi}{3}$ s.u.

25. $\int_1^3 0.2t^{1.2}\,dt = \left[\dfrac{0.2t^{2.2}}{2.2} \right]_1^3$

$= \dfrac{0.2}{2.2}3^{2.2} - \dfrac{0.2}{2.2} = 0.928$ s.u.

26. $\int_0^1 \dfrac{3}{5}\sqrt{t}\,dt = \int_0^1 \dfrac{3}{5}t^{\frac{1}{2}}\,dt = \left[\dfrac{3\,t^{\frac{3}{2}}}{5\,\frac{3}{2}} \right]_0^1 = \dfrac{2}{5}$ s.u.

27. $\int_1^2 \dfrac{0.1}{T^2}\,dT = \int_1^2 0.1T^{-2}\,dT$

$= \left[\dfrac{0.1T^{-1}}{-1} \right]_1^2$

$= \left[\dfrac{-0.1}{T} \right]_1^2$

$= \dfrac{-0.1}{2} + \dfrac{0.1}{1} = \dfrac{0.1}{2} = 0.05$ s.u.

Solutions 9

1. (i) Minimum since $a > 0$, $a = 2$

   (ii) minimum since $a > 0$, $a = 3$

   (iii) maximum since $a < 0$, $a = -1$

   (iv) minimum since $a > 0$, $a = 1$

   (v) maximum since $a < 0$, $a = -3$.

2. When $x = 0$

   (i) $y = 5$ $(0, 5)$

   (ii) $y = -7$ $(0, -7)$

   (iii) $y = -1$ $(0, -1)$

   (iv) $y = 1$ $(0, 1)$

   (v) $y = -9$ $(0, -9)$.

3. (i) $x = -\dfrac{b}{2a}$

      $= -\dfrac{(-3)}{2(2)} = \dfrac{3}{4}$

   (ii) $x = -\dfrac{b}{2a}$

      $= -\dfrac{4}{2(3)} = -\dfrac{2}{3}$

   (iii) $x = -\dfrac{b}{2a}$

      $= -\dfrac{(-1)}{2(-1)} = -\dfrac{1}{2}$

   (iv) $x = -\dfrac{b}{2a}$

      $= -\dfrac{(-3)}{2(1)} = \dfrac{3}{2}$

   (v) $x = -\dfrac{b}{2a}$

      $= -\dfrac{5}{2(-3)} = \dfrac{5}{6}$.

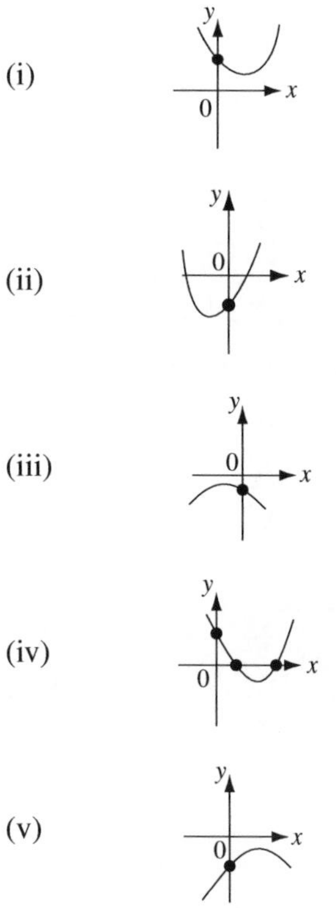

(i)

(ii)

(iii)

(iv)

(v)

Fig. 59

4. $D = b^2 - 4ac$

   (i) $b^2 - 4ac = (-3)^2 - 4(2)(5)$

             $= 9 - 40 = -31$

   (ii) $b^2 - 4ac = 4^2 - 4(3)(-7)$

             $= 16 + 84 = 100$

   (iii) $b^2 - 4ac = (-1)^2 - 4(-1)(-1)$

             $= 1 - 4 = -3$

   (iv) $b^2 - 4ac = (-3)^2 - 4(1)(1) = 9 - 4 = 5$

   (v) $b^2 - 4ac = 5^2 - 4(-3)(-9)$

             $= 25 - 108 = -83$.

5. (i) $y = \dfrac{1}{x}$

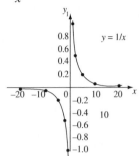

Fig. 60

x	1	2	5	10	20
y	1	0.5	0.2	0.1	0.05

When x tends to zero, y tends to positive infinity

x	y
−1	−1
−2	−0.5
−5	−0.2
−10	−0.1
−20	−0.05

when x tends to zero, y tends to negative infinity

(ii) $y = -\dfrac{2}{x}$

x	y
1	−2
2	−1
5	−0.4
10	−0.2
20	−0.1

x	−1	−2	−5	−10	−20
y	2	1	0.4	0.2	0.1

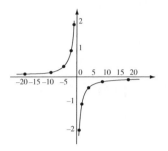

Fig. 61

(iii) $xy = 3$

$y = \dfrac{3}{x}$

x	1	3	6	15	30
y	3	1	0.5	0.2	0.1

When x tends to zero, y tends to the positive infinity.

x	−1	−3	−6	−15	−30
y	−3	−1	−0.5	−0.2	−0.1

When x tends to zero, y tends to the negative infinity.

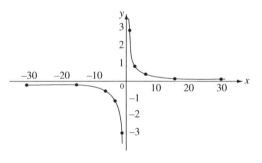

Fig. 62

It is observed from the above functions, when x is small, y is large and when y is small x is large, one variable is the reciprocal of the other variable and vice-versa.

Solutions 10

1. (i) $y = ab^x$

    Taking logarithms to the base ten, we have;

    $$\log y = \log ab^x$$
    $$= \log a + \log b^x$$
    $$= \log a + x \log b$$
    $$\log y = (\log b)x + \log a$$

    $\log y$ against x is plotted.

    (ii) $T = T_0 e^{\mu\theta}$

    Taking logarithms to the base e, we have;

    $$\log_e T = \log_e T_0 + \log_e e^{\mu\theta}$$
    $$\log_e T = \log_e T_0 + \mu\theta \log_e e$$
    $$\text{In}T = \mu\theta + \text{In}T_0$$

    InT against θ is plotted.

    (iii) $y = \dfrac{A}{x^n}$

    $$\log y = \log \frac{A}{x^n}$$
    $$\log y = \log A - \log x^n$$
    $$\log y = -n \log x + \log A$$

    $\log y$ against $\log x$ is plotted.

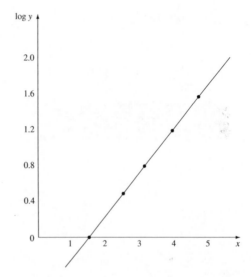

2. $y = ab^x$

    $$\log y = x \log b + \log a$$

    $\log y$ is plotted against x, so the following table is formed.

x	1.5	2.5	3.15	4	4.75
$\log y$	0	0.49	0.8	1.22	1.60

    The gradient $= \log b = \dfrac{(1.60 - 0)}{(4.75 - 1.5)}$

    $$= \frac{1.60}{3.25} = 0.49.$$

    When $\log y = 0, x = 1.5$

    $$0 = 1.5 \log b + \log a$$

$\log a = -1.5$

$\log b = -1.5(0.49) = -0.735$

$10^{-0.735} = a = 0.18.$

Therefore $y = 0.18(0.49)^x$ is the relationship connecting x and y.

3. $T = T_0 e^{\mu\theta}$

$\text{In}T = \text{In}T_0 e^{\mu\theta} = \text{In}T_0 + \text{In}e^{\mu\theta}$

$\quad = \mu\theta + \text{In}T_0$

Where $\text{In}e = 1$, $\text{In}T$ is plotted against θ from the table.

θ	5	10	15	20	25
InT	4.2	5.2	6.2	7.15	8.2

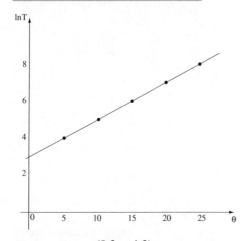

The gradient $= \dfrac{(8.2 - 4.2)}{(25 - 5)}$

$\quad = \dfrac{4}{20} = \dfrac{1}{5} = \mu = 0.2$

When $\theta = 0$, $\text{In}T = \text{In}T_0$, the intercept in the y-axis;

$\text{In}T_0 = 3.2$, $T_0 = e^{3.2} = 24.5$

The law relating T and θ is: $T = 24.5 e^{0.2\theta}$.

4. $V = KI^n$

$\log V$	$\log I$
0.699	0
1.602	0.301
2.130	0.477
2.505	0.602
2.796	0.699

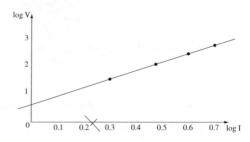

Gradient $= \dfrac{(2.796 - 0.699)}{(0.699 - 0)}$

$\quad = \dfrac{2.097}{0.699} = 3.$

If $\log I = 0$

$\log V = \log K = 0.699$

$K = 10^{0.699}$, $K = 5$, $V = 5I^3$.

Index
Analytical Mathematics II

i

Mathematics
for
Technicians

Algebra III

Anthony Nicolaides
B.Sc. (Eng.), C.Eng. M.I.E.T.

P.A.S.S. PUBLICATIONS
Private Academic & Scientific Studies Ltd

© A. Nicolaides
Second Edition 2009

ISBN-13   978-1-872684-52-9

Algebra III

First Published in Great Britain 1991 by Private Academic & Scientific Studies Ltd

P.A.S.S. PUBLICATIONS

Preface

This book covers adequately the following further Mathematics for Technicians:

- Exponential functions and natural logarithms, exponential growth and decay

- Complex numbers: addition, subtraction multiplication of a complex number in Cartesian form, vector representation of complex numbers, modulus and argument, polar representation of complex numbers, multiplication and division of complex numbers in polar form, polar to Cartesian form and vice versa, use of calculator.

- Trigonometric graphs: amplitude, period and frequency, graph sketching eg $\sin x$, $2\sin x$, $\frac{1}{2}\sin x$, $\sin 2x$, $\sin \frac{1}{2}x$ for values of x between 0 and $360°$; phase angle, phase difference, combination of two waves of the same frequency.

- Matrices and Determinants and Applications in solving equations of two unknowns.

- Binomial theorem $(1 + x)^n$ where n is positive, negative and fractional values.

The author was a course tutor for the National Diploma in Engineering for many years who encouraged students to go to Universities and many students obtained Engineering degrees in Electrical and Electronic Engineering. One particular success, an enthusiastic student, Anthony Robertson, who was admitted on the course with less than the required entry requirements obtained, a First class Honours Degree from Manchester University in Electronic Engineering.
Another success, Alex Yau who obtained 28 distinctions and four GCE A level in one year, he pursued his studies in University College in Civil Engineering, obtaining a Second Upper Honours Degree.

Anthony Nicolaides
B.Sc.(Eng.), C.Eng. M.I.E.T.

Contents

Algebra III

Mathematics III
ALGEBRA III

1

Exponential functions and natural logarithms.

1. Evaluates expressions involving exponentials and natural logarithms.

a. Defines natural (Naperian) logarithms.

The logarithm of a number N to the base e is equal to x, that is $\log_e N = x$ by the definition of a logarithm, the base e when it is raised to the power x gives the number N, that is $e^x = N$ remember that

$$e = 1 + \frac{1}{1!} + \frac{1}{2!} + \frac{1}{3!} + \frac{1}{4!} + \cdots .$$ to

infinite terms and this infinite series when it is summed up gives the number 2.7182818 to eight significant figures $\log_e N = \ln N$.

(iii) $\log_e 0.25 = -1.386$

(iv) $\log_e 2 = 0.693$.

Solution 1

(a)   (i) $e^{2.35} = 10.49$ $\log_e 10.49 = 2.35$

    (ii) $\ln 0.0498 = -3$

    (iii) $\ln 1.649 = \frac{1}{2}$

    (iv) $\ln 148.4 = 5$

    (v) $\ln 7.389 = 2$

(b)   (i) $e^{6.114} = 452$

    (ii) $e^{1.308} = 3.7$

    (iii) $e^{-1.386} = 0.25$

    (iv) $e^{0.693} = 2$.

WORKED EXAMPLE 1

(a) Express the following in logarithmic form:

    (i) $e^{2.35} = 10.49$

    (ii) $e^{-3} = 0.0498$

    (iii) $e^{\frac{1}{2}} = 1.65$

    (iv) $e^5 = 148.4$

    (v) $e^2 = 7.389$.

(b) Express the following in indicial form:

    (i) $\log_e 452 = 6.114$

    (ii) $\log_e 3.7 = 1.308$

WORKED EXAMPLE 2

(a) Express the following in logarithmic form:

    (i) $e^0 = 1$

    (ii) $e^1 = e$

    (iii) $e^{-1} = 0.368$

    (iv) $e^x = N$.

(b) Express the following in indicial form:

    (i) $\ln 23.75 = 3.168$

    (ii) $\ln 35,315 = 10.5$

    (iii) $\ln 1 = 0$.

Solution 2

(a) (i) $e^0 = 1$, hence $\ln 1 = 0$

(ii) $e^1 = 2.718$, hence $\ln 2.718 = 1$

(iii) $e^{-1} = 0.368$, hence $\ln 0.368 = -1$

(iv) $e^x = N$, hence $\ln N = x$.

(b) $\ln 23.75 = 3.168$, $e^{3.168} = 23.75$

$\ln 36,315 = 10.5$, $e^{10.5} = 35,315$

$\ln 1 = 0$, $= e^0 = 1$.

b. Determines natural (Naperian) logarithms from tables and by calculator.

The natural logarithm or hyperbolic logarithm, $\log_e N$ is denoted by $\ln N$ which is found on most scientific calculators.

It is very easy to determine the natural logarithm of any positive number by calculator. Press the 'ln' button and then the number.

$\boxed{\ln}$ $\boxed{2}$ $= \ln 2 = 0.6931471$,

$\ln 35 = 3.5553481$

$\ln 0.59 = -0.5276327$, check these answers on your calculator.

$\log_e 2 = \ln 2 = 0.6931471$

by definition $e^{0.6931471} = 1.999998$

$= 2$ approximately

$\log_e 0.59 = -0.5276327$

by definition

$e^{-0.5276327} = 0.59$

$\log_e 35 = 3.555348$

by definition $\quad e^{3.555348} = 35$.

To obtain the latter answers, we use, shift or '2nd button' and then the 'ln' button in order to obtain e^x.

▬▬▬▬▬▬

WORKED EXAMPLE 3

Practice with your calculator and find the logarithms to the base e of the following numbers:-

(i) 23.75   (ii) 2.95

(iii) 35,759   (iv) 267

(v) 0.999 and then inverse the procedure to obtain back the numbers.

Solution 3

(i) $\ln 23.75 = 3.1675825$

(ii) $\ln 2.95 = 1.0818052$

(iii) $\ln 35,759 = 10.484557$

(iv) $\ln 267 = 5.5872487$

(v) $\ln 0.999 = -1.0005003 \times 10^{-3}$.

It is observed that positive numbers below unity have negative logarithms and the logarithms of numbers above unity are positive and the logarithm of a negative number is not defined in the real world of numbers $\log_e(-1)$ is not defined and the calculator registers the symbol **E** or Maths Error on the display indicating that there is an error.

c. States the relationship between common and natural (Naperian) logarithms.

The logarithm of a number to the base 10 is called a common logarithm and it is denoted as $\log_{10} N$ or simply $\log N$. In this case the base 10 is implied, it is the only base that can be omitted.

What is the relationship between $\log_{10} N$ and $\log_e N$?

Let $y = \log_e N$

by definition $e^y = N \ldots (1)$

taking logarithms to the base 10 on both sides of the equation (1) we have

$$\log_{10} e^y = \log_{10} N$$

applying the rule that $\log a^n = n \log a$, we have

$$y \log_{10} e = \log_{10} N$$

$$y = \frac{\log_{10} N}{\log_{10} e} = \log_e N$$

$$\ln N = \frac{\log_{10} N}{\log_{10} e}.$$

$$\log N = \log_{10} e \log_e N$$

$$\log N = 0.4342944 \ln N \qquad \ldots (1)$$

the logarithm of the number N to the base 10 is expressed in terms of the logarithm of the number N to the base e.

From above $\ln N = \dfrac{\log N}{0.4342944}$

$\ln N = 2.3025851 \log N$ and therefore

the logarithm of the number N to the base e is expressed in terms of the logarithm of the number N to the base 10.

d. Uses natural (Naperian) logarithms to evaluate expressions arising in technological units.

Charging a capacitor.

The instantaneous value of voltage, v, or the voltage across a capacitor which is being charged through a resistor is given by the expression.

$$v = V(1 - e^{-\frac{t}{\tau}}) \qquad \text{where } \tau = RC.$$

WORKED EXAMPLE 4

If $v = 50$ volts, $V = 150$ volts and $\tau = 5$ ms determine the time taken t.

Solution 4

$$v = V(1 - e^{-\frac{t}{\tau}})$$

dividing both sides by V we have

$$\frac{v}{V} = 1 - e^{-\frac{t}{\tau}}$$

$$e^{-\frac{t}{\tau}} = 1 - \frac{v}{V}$$

$$e^{-\frac{t}{\tau}} = \frac{V - v}{V}$$

the reciprocal of each side $e^{\frac{t}{\tau}} = \frac{V}{V-v}$

taking logarithms on both sides to the base e, we have

$$\ln e^{\frac{t}{\tau}} = \ln \frac{V}{V - v}$$

$$\frac{t}{\tau} \ln e = \ln \frac{V}{V - v}$$

$$\frac{t}{\tau} = \ln \frac{V}{V - v}$$

since $\ln e = 1$, $\log_e e = 1$ or $e^1 = e$ by definition

$$t = \tau \ln \frac{V}{V - v} = 5 \times 10^{-3} \ln \frac{150}{150 - 50}$$

$$= 5 \times 10^{-3} \ln \frac{150}{100} = 5 \times 10^{-3} \ln 1.5$$

$$= 5 \times 10^{-3} \times 0.4054651$$

$$= 2.03 \times 10^{-3} = 2.03$$

$$\tau = 2.03 \text{ ms.}$$

Magnetising a coil

WORKED EXAMPLE 5

The instantaneous value of current i at $t = 1$ ms is 1 A, and the final value of current $I = 5$ A. Determine the time constant of the inductive circuit, given that $i = I(1 - e^{-\frac{t}{\tau}})$ where τ is the constant.

Solution 5

The growth of current is given by the equation

$$i = I(1 - e^{-\frac{t}{\tau}})$$

dividing both sides by I

$$\frac{i}{I} = 1 - e^{-\frac{t}{\tau}}$$

$$e^{-\frac{t}{\tau}} = 1 - \frac{i}{I}$$

$$e^{-\frac{t}{\tau}} = \frac{I - i}{I}$$

the reciprocal of each side $e^{\frac{t}{\tau}} = \frac{I}{I-i}$

taking logarithms on both sides to the base e, we have

$$\ln e^{\frac{t}{\tau}} = \ln \frac{I}{I - i}$$

$$\frac{t}{\tau} \ln e = \ln \frac{I}{I - i}$$

but $\ln e = 1$

$$t = \tau \ln \frac{I}{I - i}$$

$$\tau = \frac{t}{\ln \dfrac{I}{I - i}}$$

$$\tau = \frac{10^{-3}}{\ln \dfrac{5}{5 - 1}}$$

$$\tau = \frac{10^{-3}}{\ln 1.25} \qquad \tau = \frac{10^{-3}}{0.2231435}$$

$$\tau = 4.48 \times 10^{-3} \qquad \tau = 4.48 \text{ ms.}$$

e. Solves equation involving e^x and $\ln x$.

Let us consider an equation that contains terms such as e^x and e^{2x} such an equation is called an indicial or exponential equation.

WORKED EXAMPLE 6

Solve the equation $e^x + e^{-x} = 4$.

Solution 6

$$e^x + e^{-x} = 4$$

multiplying each term by e^x,

$$e^{2x} + e^0 - 4e^x = 0.$$

Applying the laws of indices

$$e^{2x} + e^0 - 4e^x = 0 \qquad e^{2x} - 4e^x + 1 = 0.$$

If we replace $y = e^x$, the resulting equation becomes a quadratic equation

$$y^2 - 4y + 1 = 0$$

$$y = \frac{4 \pm \sqrt{16 - 4}}{2}$$

$$= \frac{4 \pm \sqrt{12}}{2} = \frac{4 \pm 3.464}{2}$$

$$y = 3.732, \ y = 0.268$$
$$e^x = 3.732, \ \ln e^x = \ln 3.732, \ x = 1.317$$
$$e^x = 0.268, \ \ln e^x = \ln 0.268, \ x = -1.317.$$

WORKED EXAMPLE 7

Solve the logarithmic equation

$$\log_e x - \log_e \frac{1}{x + 1} = 2.$$

Solution 7

Applying the rule $\log A - \log B = \log \frac{A}{B}$ the equation can be written as

$$\log_e x - \log_e \frac{1}{x + 1} = 2$$

$$\log_e \frac{x}{\dfrac{1}{(x + 1)}} = 2$$

$$\log_e x(x + 1) = 2$$

by the definition of logarithm

$$e^2 = x(x + 1)$$
$$x^2 + x - e^2 = 0$$

$$x = \frac{-1 \pm \sqrt{1 + 4e^2}}{2}$$

$$= \frac{-1 \pm \sqrt{1 + 4 \times 7.3890561}}{2}$$

$$= \frac{-1 \pm 5.53}{2}$$

$$x = \frac{-1 + 5.53}{2}, x = \frac{-1 - 5.53}{2}.$$
$$x = 2.264 \text{ or } x = -3.264.$$

Exercises 1

1. From the calculator find
   (i) $\log_e 1.234$
   (ii) $\log_e 12.34$
   (iii) $\log_e 1234$.

2. Find the numbers whose natural logarithms are
   (i) 4.174   (ii) 9.21   (iii) −3.66.

3. The number of radioactive atoms present at a time $t = 0$, is N_0 and the number of radioactive atoms at the end of a time t, is N and these number related by the equation $N = N_0 e^{-\lambda t}$ where λ is the radioactivity decay constant.
   If $N = \frac{1}{2}N_0$ when $t = 1500$ years find the time when $N = \frac{1}{20}N_0$.

4. $e^{2x} - 5e^x + 6 = 0$ is an indicial or exponential equation by substituting $y = e^x$, solve the equation for y and hence find the values of x.

5. Solve the equation $6e^{2x} - 7e^x + 2 = 0$.

6. If $i = Ie^{-\frac{t}{5\times0.001}}$, $i = 3$ A, $I = 10$ A, determine t.

7. If $v = V(1 - e^{-\frac{t}{5\times0.001}})$
   if $t = 1 \times 10^{-3}$s, $V = 100$ volts, determine v.

8. (i) If $v = V(1 - e^{-\frac{t}{RC}})$ and $R = 1$ and $C = 5$, $v = 1$, $V = 10$ determine the value of t.

   (ii) If $t = 1$, $RC = 1$ what is v if $V = 100$.

9. Calculate correct to three significant figures:-
   (i) $\dfrac{e^{0.3} - e^{-0.3}}{2}$ (ii) $\dfrac{e^{0.5} + e^{-0.5}}{2}$

   (iii) $6(e^{0.8} - e^{-0.8})$.

10. If $\log_e x = 5.95$ find x.

2

Complex numbers.

Extends the number system to complex numbers.

a. Defines a complex number.
b. Plots complex numbers on an Argand diagram.
c. Determines the sum and difference of two complex numbers in the form $a + jb$, and relates results to Argand diagram.
d. Determines the product of two complex numbers in the form $a + jb$.
e. Defines the conjugate of a complex number.
f. Uses 2e and evaluates $\frac{Z_1}{Z_2}$.

2a. Definition of a complex number.

A complex number is a number which is not real. The square root of minus one, that is, $\sqrt{-1}$, is a complex number because there is no real number which can be multiplied by itself in order to give the answer of -1. The square roots of four, $\sqrt{4}$, however, are equal to ± 2 which are real numbers, because $2 \times 2 = 4$ or $(-2) \times (-2) = 4$.

Solving the quadratic equation $x^2 + x + 1 = 0$ we have

$$x = \frac{-1 \pm \sqrt{1 - 4 \times 1}}{2 \times 1}$$

$$= \frac{-1 \pm \sqrt{-3}}{2}$$

$$= -\frac{1}{2} \pm \frac{\sqrt{-3}}{2}.$$

The j-notation.

The roots are

$$x_1 = -\frac{1}{2} + \frac{\sqrt{-3}}{2} \quad \text{and} \quad x_2 = -\frac{1}{2} - \frac{\sqrt{-3}}{2}$$

$$\sqrt{-3} = \sqrt{-1}\sqrt{3} = j\sqrt{3}$$

where $\sqrt{-1} = j$ and the roots can be expressed in terms of j

$$x_1 = -\frac{1}{2} + j\frac{\sqrt{3}}{2} \text{ and}$$

$$x_2 = -\frac{1}{2} - j\frac{\sqrt{3}}{2} \text{ and better still}$$

$$Z_1 = -\frac{1}{2} + j\frac{\sqrt{3}}{2} \text{ and}$$

$$Z_2 = -\frac{1}{2} - j\frac{\sqrt{3}}{2}$$

where Z denotes impedance.

In general $Z = x + jy$, the real term of Z is x and the imaginary term of Z is y, Re $Z = x$ and Im $Z = y$.

2b. Plots complex numbers on an Argand diagram.

An Argand diagram is a pair of cartesian axes, the y-axis and the x-axis.

The x-axis is the real axis and the y-axis is the imaginary axis.

Fig. 1 Argand diagram

We can label the y axis by jy and the x-axis by x as shown in the diagram, Fig. 1.

$Z = x + jy$, x and y are real quantities which can be either positive or negative.

WORKED EXAMPLE 8

Plot the complex numbers on an Argand diagram.

  (i) $Z_1 = 3 + j4$

 (ii) $Z_2 = 3 - j4$

(iii) $Z_3 = -3 + j4$

(iv) $Z_4 = -3 - j4$.

Solution 8

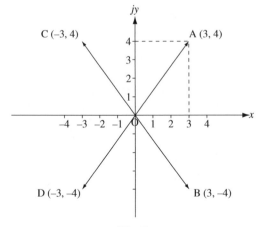

Fig. 2

Referring to Fig. 2.

We mark off three units along the positive x-axis and 4 units along the positive y-axis, the point **A** gives a pair of co-ordinates (3,4) and this is joined to the origin, **OA** represents the complex number Z_1, similarly **B**(3, −4) and **OB** represents the complex number Z_2, **OC** = Z_3 and **OD** = Z_4.

The argand diagram is very important diagram.

In order to locate the complex number in the correct quadrant and read off the position from the reference OX which is zero degrees, OY, the positive y-axis is $90° - OX$, the negative x-axis is $180°$ and OY, the negative y-axis is $270°$ all measured in an anti-clockwise direction. Complex numbers are vectors, that is, possess a magnitude and direction.

2c. Determines the sum and difference of two complex numbers in the form $a + jb$, and relates results to Argand diagram.

Consider two complex numbers

$Z_1 = x_1 + jy_1$ and $Z_2 = x_2 + jy_2$

to find the sum $Z_1 + Z_2$, we add the real terms separately and we add the imaginary terms separately

$$Z_1 + Z_2 = x_1 + jy_1 + x_2 + jy_2$$
$$= (x_1 + x_2) + j(y_1 + y_2).$$

The difference of the complex numbers is given

by $Z_1 - Z_2 = (x_1 + jy_1) - (x_2 + jy_2)$

$$= (x_1 - x_2) + j(y_1 - y_2).$$

The sum and difference can be easily found in the cartesian form of the complex number $(Z = x + jy)$.

To the vector sum or vector difference a parallelgram is formed as shown below in the worked example.

WORKED EXAMPLE 9

Find the sum $Z_1 + Z_2$ and the difference $Z_1 - Z_2$ of the two complex numbers $Z_1 = 2 + j5$ and $Z_2 = 4 + j2$.

 (i) Algebraically.

(ii) Vectorially or graphically on an Argand diagram.

Solution 9

(i) $Z_1 + Z_2 = 2 + j5 + 4 + j2 = 6 + j7$

(ii) $Z_1 - Z_2 = 2 + j5 - 4 - j2 = -2 + j3.$

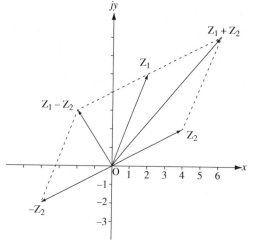

Fig. 3

2d. The product of two complex numbers.

If $Z_1 = x_1 + jy_1$ and

$Z_2 = x_2 + jy_2$ the product

$Z_1 Z_2 = (x_1 + jy_1)(x_2 + jy_2)$

$= x_1 x_2 + jy_1 x_2 + jx_1 y_2 + j^2 y_1 y_2$

$= (x_1 x_2 - y_1 y_2) + j(y_1 x_2 + x_1 y_2)$

where $j^2 = -1$.

WORKED EXAMPLE 10

Determine the products

(i) $Z_1 Z_2$ (ii) $Z_1 Z_3$

(iii) $Z_2 Z_3$ if $Z_1 = -3 - j4,$
$Z_2 = 2 - j3, Z_3 = -3 + j5.$

Solution 10

(i) $Z_1 Z_2 = (-3 - j4)(2 - j3)$

$= -6 - j8 + 9j + j^2 12$

$= -6 - 12 + j = -18 + j$

$\boxed{Z_1 Z_2 = -18 + j}$

(ii) $Z_1 Z_3 = (-3 - j4)(-3 + j5)$

$= 9 + j12 - j15 - j^2 20$

$= 9 + 20 - j3$

$\boxed{Z_1 Z_3 = 29 - j3}$

(iii) $Z_2 Z_3 = (2 - j3)(-3 + j5)$

$= -6 + j9 + j10 - j^2 15$

$\boxed{Z_2 Z_3 = 9 + j19}$.

2e. The conjugate of a complex number.

If $Z = x + jy$, Z^* or $\bar{Z}$ is the conjugate of Z ($Z^*(Z - \text{star})$) or ($\bar{Z}(\text{Zbar})\ \bar{Z}) = x - jy$.

The real term remains unaltered the imaginary term changes sign.

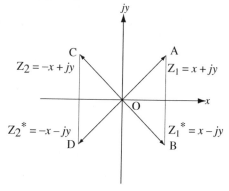

Fig. 4

The x-axis is used as a mirror in which we see the image of **A** is **B** a mirror image of **C** is **D** and vice-versa, the image mirror of $Z_1 = x - jy$ is $Z^* = x + jy$ and image mirror of $Z_2^* = -x - jy$ is $Z_2^{**} = -x + jy$.

The conjugate is used in the next topic in evaluating as quotient $\frac{Z_1}{Z_2}$.

2f Evaluates $\frac{Z_1}{Z_2}$ using the conjugate technique.

If $Z_1 = x_1 + jy_1$ and $Z_2 = x_2 + jy_2$,

the quotient $\dfrac{Z_1}{Z_2} = \dfrac{x_1 + jy_1}{x_2 + jy_2}$.

In order to divide two complex numbers we need to multiply the numerator and denominator by the conjugate of the denominator, which is $x_2 + jy_2$

$$\frac{Z_1}{Z_2} = \frac{(x_1 + jy_1)}{(x_2 + jy_2)} \times \frac{(x_2 - jy_2)}{(x_2 - jy_2)}$$

$$= \frac{x_1 x_2 + jy_1 x_2 - jx_1 y_2 + y_1 y_2}{x_2^2 - j^2 y_2^2}$$

$$= \frac{(x_1 x_2 + y_1 y_2) + j(y_1 x_2 - x_1 y_2)}{x_2^2 + y_2^2}$$

remember $(a+b)(a-b) = (a^2 - b^2)$ is the difference of squares also observe that the denominator is now a positive real quantity.

▬▬▬▬▬▬▬▬▬

WORKED EXAMPLE 11

If $Z_1 = -3 - j4$, $Z_2 = 2 - j3$, $Z_3 = -3 + j5$

Determine (i) $\dfrac{Z_1}{Z_2}$ (ii) $\dfrac{Z_2}{Z_1}$ (iii) $\dfrac{Z_2}{Z_3}$

(iv) $\dfrac{Z_3}{Z_1}$ using the conjugate technique.

Solution 11

(i) $\dfrac{Z_1}{Z_2} = \dfrac{-3 - 4j}{2 - 3j} \times \dfrac{2 + 3j}{2 + 3j}$

$$= \frac{-6 - 8j - 9j + 12}{4 + 9} = \frac{6}{13} - \frac{17}{13}j$$

(ii) $\dfrac{Z_2}{Z_1} = \dfrac{(2 - 3j)}{(-3 - 4j)} \times \dfrac{(-3 + 4j)}{(-3 + j4)}$

$$= \frac{-6 + 9j + 8j + 12}{(-3)^2 + 4^2} = \frac{6}{25} + \frac{17j}{25}$$

(iii) $\dfrac{Z_2}{Z_3} = \dfrac{(2 - 3j)}{(-3 + 5j)} \times \dfrac{-3 - 5j}{-j - 5j}$

$$= \frac{-6 + 9j - 10j + 15j^2}{(-3)^2 - j^2 25}$$

$$= \frac{-21 - 1j}{34}$$

(iv) $\dfrac{Z_3}{Z_1} = \dfrac{(-3 + 5j)}{(-3 - 4j)} \times \dfrac{(-3 + 4j)}{(-3 + 4j)}$

$$= \frac{9 - 15j - 12j - 20}{9 + 16}$$

$$= -\frac{11}{25} - \frac{27}{25}j.$$

Exercises 2

1. Write the following in complex number notation:

    (i) $\sqrt{-2}$ (ii) $\sqrt{-4}$

    (iii) $\sqrt{-8}$ (iv) $\sqrt{-16}$

    (v) $\sqrt{-27}$.

2. Determine whether the following quadratic equations have real or complex roots and find the roots

    (i) $3x^2 - x + 1 = 0$

    (ii) $x^2 - 4x + 8 = 0$

    (iii) $x^2 + 2x + 2 = 0$

    (iv) $-5x^2 + 7x + 5 = 0$

    (v) $-x^2 + x - 5 = 0$.

3. Express the following points of co-ordinates in the complex number form:

    (i) **A**$(1, 3)$

    (ii) **E**$(-1, 3)$

    (iii) **F**$(2, -4)$

    (iv) **J**$(-3, -4)$.

4. Express the following complex numbers in the form of points of coordinates:

    (i) $Z_1 = 3 + j4$

    (ii) $Z_2 = 3 - j4$

    (iii) $Z_3 = -3 + j4$

    (iv) $Z_4 = -3 - j4$.

5. Plot the complex numbers in (4) in an Argand diagram.

6. (i) If Re $Z = x$ and Im $Z = y$, write down the value of Z.

    (ii) If Re $Z = -3$ and Im $Z = 5$, write down the value of Z.

7. (a) Find the sum and difference of the vectors
$$E_1 = 20 + j30 \text{ and } E_2 = 10 + j15.$$

    (b) Find the product and the quotient of the complex numbers E_1 and E_2, that is, $E_1 E_2$ and $\frac{E_1}{E_2}$.

8. Express in the form $a + jb$ the following:-

    (i) $(3j)(5j)$

    (ii) $(4 - 5j)(1 + j)$

    (iii) $(1 + j)(1 - j)$

    (iv) $(4 + 3j)^2$

    (v) $(1 - j^2)^2$.

9. Express the following operations in the form $a + jb$:

If $Z_1 = 3 - 4j$, $Z_2 = 1 + j$, $Z_3 = 2 + 3j$

    (i) $Z_1 Z_2$ (ii) $Z_1 Z_3$ (iii) $Z_1 Z_2 Z_3$.

10. If a complex number $Z = x + jy$ and its conjugate $Z^* = x - jy$, show that

    (i) $ZZ^* = x^2 + y^2$ and (ii) $\left[\dfrac{1}{Z}\right]^* = \dfrac{1}{Z^*}$.

Modulus and argument of complex numbers

Understands the modulus, argument form of complex numbers.

a. Converts $a + jb$ into polar form and vice-versa. Relates j to an operator and shows that j can be regarded as $\sqrt{-1}$.

b. Defines the modulus and argument of a complex number.

c. Multiplies and divides complex numbers using the polar form.

d. Determines the square roots of a complex number.

3a/b. Polar form of a complex number.

Modulus

$$Z = x + jy$$

the modulus of Z is denoted $|Z|$ and means the magnitude of the complex number Z

$$|Z| = \sqrt{(x)^2 + (y)^2}$$

note that the real term is squared and the imaginary term (y) is squared and <u>not</u> the j.

The hypotenuse of the right angled triangle with sides x and y is the modulus of Z.

$$|Z| = \sqrt{x^2 + y^2} = r$$

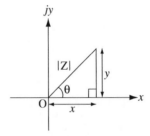

Fig. 5

Argument

The argument of Z is the angle of Z measured in an anti clockwise direction from the reference line $ox(0°)$ arg Z is the notation for the argument of Z $\tan\theta = \frac{y}{x}$ arg $Z = \theta = \tan^{-1}(\frac{y}{x})$ the inverse function of the tangent arg $Z = \theta = \tan^{-}1(\frac{y}{x})$.

To avoid error in evaluating the angle of the complex number, it is necessary to display the complex number on an Argand diagram.

$$Z = x + jy = r\cos\theta + jr\sin\theta$$

$$= r(\cos\theta + j\sin\theta).$$

The polar form of $Z = x + jy$ is $Z = r(\cos\theta + j\sin\theta)$, $\cos\theta + j\sin\theta$ can be replaced by the abbreviation $\angle\theta = \cos\theta + j\sin\theta$
$\angle-\theta = \cos\theta - j\sin\theta$.

Determine the moduli and arguments of the following complex numbers:

(i) $Z_1 = 3j$

(ii) $Z_2 = 5$

(iii) $Z_3 = -2 + j3$

(iv) $Z_4 = \cos \Phi - j \sin \Phi$.

Solution 12

(i) $Z_1 = 3j$ $|Z_1| = \sqrt{0 + 3^2} = 3$

$\arg Z_1 = \tan^{-1} \dfrac{3}{0} = 90°$

(ii) $Z_2 = 5$, $|Z_2| = 5$ $\arg Z_2 = 0°$

(iii) $Z_3 = -2 + j3$

$|Z_3| = \sqrt{(-2)^2 + 3^2} = \sqrt{4 + 9} = \sqrt{13}$

$\arg Z_3 = 180 - \tan^{-1} \dfrac{3}{2} = 123.7°$

(iv) $Z_4 = \cos \Phi - j \sin \Phi$

$|Z_4| = \sqrt{\cos^2 \Phi + (\sin \Phi)^2} = 1$

$\arg Z_4 = -\Phi$.

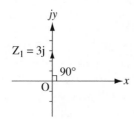

Fig. 6

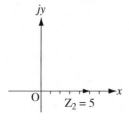

Fig. 7

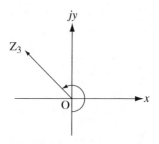

Fig. 8

Determine the polar forms of the complex numbers:

(i) $Z_1 = -3 + j4$

(ii) $Z_2 = 2 - j3$

(iii) $Z_3 = -3 + j5$.

Solution 13

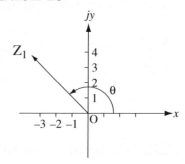

Fig. 9

(i) $|Z_1| = \sqrt{(-3)^2 + (4)^2}$

$= \sqrt{9 + 16} = 5$

$\arg Z_1 = 180° - \tan^{-1} \dfrac{4}{3}$

$= 126°52' = \theta$

$Z_1 = 5(\cos 126°52' + j \sin 126°52')$

$Z_1 = 5\underline{/126°52'}$.

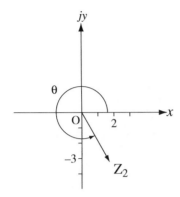

Fig. 10

$Z_2 = 2 - j3$

(ii) $|Z_2| = \sqrt{2^2 + (-3)^2} = \sqrt{13}$

$\arg Z_2 = 360° - \tan^{-1} \frac{3}{2}$

$= 360° - 56°18'35''$

$= 303°41'.$

$Z_2 = \sqrt{13}\underline{/303°41'}$

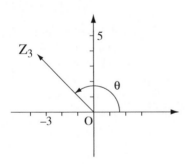

Fig. 11

(iii) $Z_3 = -3 + j5$

$|Z_3| = \sqrt{(-3)^2 + 5^2} = \sqrt{34}$

$\arg Z_3 = 180° - \tan^{-1} \frac{5}{3}$

$= 180° - 59°2'10'' = 120°57' = \theta$

$Z_3 = \sqrt{13}\underline{/120°57'}.$

3c Multiplication and division of complex numbers using polar form.

Multiplication of complex numbers using polar form.

$Z_1 = r_1\underline{/\theta_1} \qquad Z_2 = r_2\underline{/\theta_2}$

$Z_1 Z_2 = r_1 r_2 \underline{/\theta_1 + \theta_2}$

the moduli are multiplied and the arguments are added.

WORKED EXAMPLE 14

If $Z_1 = 3\underline{/45°}$, $Z_2 = 4\underline{/65°}$, $Z_3 = 5\underline{/90°}$.

Determines

(i) $Z_1 Z_3$ (ii) $Z_1 Z_2$ (iii) $Z_2 Z_3$

in (a) polar form and (b) cartesian form.

Solution 14

(a) (i) $Z_1 Z_3 = \left(3\underline{/45°}\right)\left(5\underline{/90°}\right)$

$= 15\underline{/135°}$

(ii) $Z_1 Z_2 = \left(3\underline{/45°}\right)\left(4\underline{/65°}\right)$

$= 12\underline{/110°}$

(iii) $Z_2 Z_3 = \left(4\underline{/65°}\right)\left(5\underline{/90°}\right)$

$= 20\underline{/155°}.$

(b) (i) $Z_1 Z_3 = (\cos 135° + j \sin 135°)$

$Z_1 Z_3 = -\frac{15}{\sqrt{2}} + \frac{15}{\sqrt{2}}j = -10.6 + 10.6j$

(ii) $Z_1 Z_2 = 12(\cos 110° + j \sin 110°)$

$= -4.1 + j11.3$

(iii) $Z_2 Z_3 = 20\underline{/155°}$

$= 20(\cos 155° + j \sin 155°)$

$Z_2 Z_3 = -18.1 + j8.45.$

Division of complex numbers using the polar form.

$$Z_1 = r_1\angle\theta_1 \qquad Z_2 = r_2\angle\theta_1$$

$$\frac{Z_1}{Z_2} = \frac{r_1\angle\theta_1}{r_2\angle\theta_2} = \frac{r_1}{r_2}\angle\theta_1 - \theta_2$$

$$\frac{Z_2}{Z_1} = \frac{r_2\angle\theta_2}{r_1\angle\theta_1} = \frac{r_2}{r_1}\angle\theta_2 - \theta_1.$$

The division is performed by dividing the moduli and substracting the arguments.

▬▬▬▬▬▬
WORKED EXAMPLE 15

If $Z_1 = 25\angle\frac{\pi}{3}$ $Z_2 = 5\angle\frac{\pi}{6}$ $Z_3 = 1\angle\frac{\pi}{4}$

Determine

(i) $\dfrac{Z_1}{Z_2}$ (ii) $\dfrac{Z_1}{Z_3}$ (iii) $\dfrac{Z_2}{Z_1}$ (iv) $\dfrac{Z_3}{Z_2}$

    in (a) polar form and in

        (b) cartesian form.

Solution 15

(a) (i) $\dfrac{Z_1}{Z_2} = \dfrac{25\angle\frac{\pi}{3}}{5\angle\frac{\pi}{6}} = 5\angle\frac{\pi}{3} - \frac{\pi}{6} = 5\angle\frac{\pi}{6}$

(ii) $\dfrac{Z_1}{Z_3} = \dfrac{25\angle\frac{\pi}{3}}{1\angle\frac{\pi}{4}} = 25\angle\frac{\pi}{3} - \frac{\pi}{4} = 25\angle\frac{\pi}{12}$

(iii) $\dfrac{Z_2}{Z_1} = \dfrac{5\angle\frac{\pi}{6}}{25\angle\frac{\pi}{3}} = \frac{1}{5}\angle\frac{\pi}{6} - \frac{\pi}{3} = \frac{1}{5}\angle-\frac{\pi}{6}$

(iv) $\dfrac{Z_3}{Z_2} = \dfrac{1\angle\frac{\pi}{4}}{5\angle\frac{\pi}{6}} = \frac{1}{5}\angle\frac{\pi}{4} - \frac{\pi}{6} = \frac{1}{5}\angle\frac{\pi}{12}.$

(b) (i) $\dfrac{Z_1}{Z_2} = 5\angle\frac{\pi}{6} = 5\left(\cos\frac{\pi}{6} + j\sin\frac{\pi}{6}\right)$

        $= 5(0.866 + j0.5) = 4.33 + j2.5$

(ii) $\dfrac{Z_1}{Z_3} = 25\angle\frac{\pi}{12} = 25(\cos\frac{\pi}{12} + j\sin\frac{\pi}{12})$

        $= 24.2 + j6.47$

(iii) $\dfrac{Z_2}{Z_1} = \frac{1}{5}\angle-\frac{\pi}{6}$

        $= 0.2\left(\cos\frac{\pi}{6} - j\sin\frac{\pi}{6}\right) = 0.173 - j0.1$

(iv) $\dfrac{Z_3}{Z_2} = \frac{1}{5}\angle\frac{\pi}{12} = 0.2\left(\cos\frac{\pi}{12} + j\sin\frac{\pi}{12}\right)$

        $= 0.193 + j0.052.$

3d. The square roots of a complex number.

Let $Z = x + jy$.

The square roots of this complex number are complex numbers, since $x + jy = (a + bj)^2$ then $\sqrt{x + jy} = \pm(a + jb)$ where a and b are real quantities, squaring up both sides.

$$x + jy = (a + jb)^2 = a^2 + j^2b^2 + 2jba$$
$$= a^2 - b^2 + j2ab.$$

Equating the real and imaginary terms, we have
$x = a^2 - b^2 \ldots (1)$ and $y = 2ab \ldots (2)$
substituting (2) in (1) we have $b = \frac{y}{2a}$,
$x = a^2 - (\frac{y}{2a})^2$.

$$x = a^2 - \frac{y^2}{4a^2}$$

$$4a^4 - 4a^2x - y^2 = 0$$

which is a quartic equation in a

$$a^2 = \frac{4x \pm \sqrt{16x^2 + 16y^2}}{8} = \frac{1}{2}x \pm \frac{1}{2}\sqrt{x^2 + y^2}$$

$$a = \pm\sqrt{\frac{1}{2}(x \pm \sqrt{x^2 + y^2})}$$

$$a = \pm\sqrt{\frac{1}{2}(x + \sqrt{x^2 + y^2})}$$

since the other value is not valid

$$a = \pm\sqrt{\frac{1}{2}(x - \sqrt{x^2 + y^2})}$$

$$b = \frac{y}{2a} = \frac{y}{2\left(\pm\sqrt{\frac{1}{2}\left(x + \sqrt{x^2 + y^2}\right)}\right)}$$

$$= \pm\frac{y}{2\sqrt{\frac{1}{2}\left(x + \sqrt{x^2 + y^2}\right)}}$$

otherwise a shall be a complex number.

The theory above seems to be somehow complex and tedious.

WORKED EXAMPLE 16

Determine the square roots of $3 + j4$.

Solution 16

Let $3 + j4 = (a + jb)^2 = a^2 - b^2 + j2ab$ where a and b are real.

Equating real and imaginary terms

$$a^2 - b^2 = 3 \qquad \ldots (1)$$

$$2ab = 4 \qquad \ldots (2)$$

From (2) $b = \dfrac{4}{2a} = \dfrac{2}{a}$ and substituting in (1)

$$a^2 - \frac{4}{a^2} = 3$$

or $a^4 - 3a^2 - 4 = 0$

solving for a^2,

$$a^2 = \frac{3 \pm \sqrt{9 + 16}}{2} = \frac{3 \pm 5}{2}$$

$a^2 = 4$ and $a^2 = -1$ the latter is not valid since a must be a real quantity, hence $a = \pm 2$ and $b = \pm 1$. If $a = 2$, $b = 1$, if $a = -2$, $b = -1$.

WORKED EXAMPLE 17

Determine the square roots of j.

Solution 17

Let $\sqrt{j} = \pm(a + jb)$, squaring up both sides, $j = a^2 - b^2 + j2ab$, equating real and imaginary terms, $a^2 - b^2 = 0$ and $2ab = 1$ or $b = \frac{1}{2a}$ but

$$a^2 - \frac{1}{(2a)^2} = 0, \quad 4a^4 = 1, \quad a^2 = \pm\frac{1}{2} \text{ only}$$

$a^2 = \dfrac{1}{2}$ is valid or $a = \pm\dfrac{1}{\sqrt{2}}$.

If $a = \dfrac{1}{\sqrt{2}}$, $b = \dfrac{1}{2}\sqrt{2} = \dfrac{\sqrt{2}}{2}\dfrac{\sqrt{2}}{\sqrt{2}} = \dfrac{1}{\sqrt{2}}$ and

if $a = -\dfrac{1}{\sqrt{2}}$, $b = \dfrac{1}{\frac{-2}{\sqrt{2}}} = -\dfrac{1}{\sqrt{2}}$.

Therefore $\sqrt{j} = \pm\left[\dfrac{1}{\sqrt{2}} + j\dfrac{1}{\sqrt{2}}\right]$.

The square roots of j are $\dfrac{1}{\sqrt{2}} + j\dfrac{1}{\sqrt{2}}$

and $-\dfrac{1}{\sqrt{2}} - \dfrac{j1}{\sqrt{2}}$.

Application of complex numbers in A.C. theory.

Applies complex numbers to a.c. quantities.

Identifies complex numbers with phasor quantities.

Solves simple a.c. circuit problems using complex numbers e.g. (a) R, L, and C in series combination (b) R, L, and C in parallel combination.

Identifies complex numbers with phasor quantities.

The current through a resistor and the voltage across a resistor are in phase.

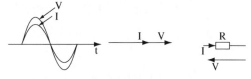

Fig. 12

$$R = \frac{V}{I} = \frac{V\angle 0°}{I\angle 0°} = \frac{V}{I}\angle 0°.$$

The current through a pure inductor and the voltage across the inductor are 90° out of phase, the current lags the voltage by 90°.

$$X_L = \frac{V_L}{I_L} = \frac{V_L\angle 90°}{I_L\angle 0°}$$

$$= \frac{V_L}{I_L}\angle 90° = \omega L\angle 90°.$$

Therefore X_L, the inductive reactance can be represented in complex numbers as

$$X_L = j\omega L.$$

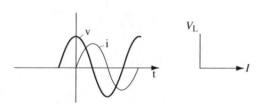

Fig. 13

The current through a capacitor and the voltage across the capacitor are 90° out of phase, the current leads the voltage by 90°.

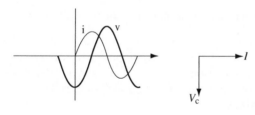

Fig. 14

$$X_c = \frac{V_c}{I} = -j\frac{V_c}{I} = -jX_c$$

$$= -j\frac{1}{\omega C}\frac{j}{j} = \frac{1}{j\omega C}$$

$$X_c = \frac{1}{j\omega C}.$$

Solves simple a.c. circuit problems using complex numbers.

(a) The impedance of the a.c. circuit can be written in complex numbers

$$Z = R + j\omega L + \frac{1}{j\omega C}$$

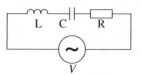

Fig. 15

$$V = 30\angle 30° \text{ volts}$$

$$f = 1000 \text{ Hz.}$$

WORKED EXAMPLE 18

If the supply voltage is given as $30\angle 30°$ volts and $R = 10 \ \Omega$, $C = 20 \ \mu F$, $L = 0.5$ H. Calculate the current in the circuit.

Solution 18

$$I = \frac{V}{Z} = \frac{30\angle 30°}{620.4\angle 89°5'} = 48.3\angle -59°5' \text{ mA}$$

$$Z = R + j2\pi fL + \frac{1}{j2\pi fC}$$

$$= 10 + j2\pi\,1000(0.5) + \frac{10^6}{j2\pi\,1000 \times 20}$$

$$Z = 10 + j628.3 - j7.96 = 10 + j620.34$$

$$|Z| = \sqrt{10^2 + (628.3 - 7.96)^2} = 620.4 \ \Omega$$

$$\arg Z = \tan^{-1}\frac{620.34}{10} = 89°5'.$$

WORKED EXAMPLE 19

A capacitor is connected in series with a resistor and the combination is connected across an a.c. supply voltage of $240\angle 0°$ volts.

If $C = 100 \ \mu F$, $R = 50 \ \Omega$ and $f = 50$ Hz. Determine the magnitude and argument of the impedance and hence calculate the current in polar form.

Solution 19

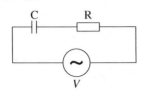

Fig. 16

$V = 240\angle 0°$ volts

$f = 50$ Hz

$Z = R + \dfrac{1}{j\omega C} = 50 + \dfrac{1}{2j\pi(50(100)\times 10^{-6}}$

$= 50 - 31.83j$

$|Z| = \sqrt{50^2 + (-31.83)^2} = 59.3\Omega$

$\arg Z = -\tan^{-1}\dfrac{31.83}{50} = -32.5°$

$Z = 59.3\angle -32.5°\,\Omega$

$I = \dfrac{V}{Z} = \dfrac{240\angle 0°}{59.3\angle -32.5°} = 4.05\angle 32.5°$ mA.

(b) To determine the Impedance of the A.C. Circuits.

(i) $Z = \dfrac{R(j\omega L)}{R + j\omega L}$

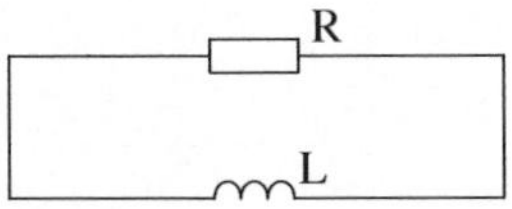

Fig. 17

(ii) $Z = \dfrac{R\left(\dfrac{1}{j\omega C}\right)}{R + \dfrac{1}{j\omega C}} = \dfrac{R}{j\omega CR + 1}$

$= \dfrac{R}{1 + j\omega CR}$

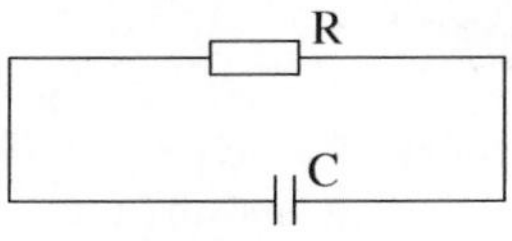

Fig. 18

(iii) $Z = \dfrac{(j\omega L)\left(\dfrac{1}{j\omega C}\right)}{j\omega L + \dfrac{1}{j\omega C}}$

$= \dfrac{j\omega L}{(j\omega L)(j\omega C) + 1} = \dfrac{j\omega L}{1 - \omega^2 LC}$

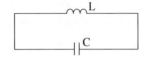

Fig. 19

(iv) $\dfrac{1}{Z} = \dfrac{1}{R} + j\omega C + \dfrac{1}{j\omega L}$

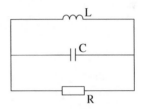

Fig. 20

(v) $\dfrac{1}{Z} = j\omega C + \dfrac{1}{R + j\omega L}$

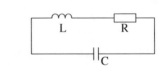

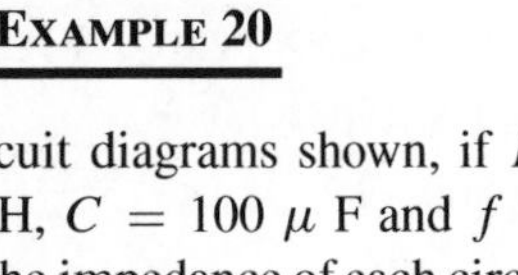

Fig. 21

WORKED EXAMPLE 20

For the circuit diagrams shown, if $R = 10\ \Omega$, $L = 50$ mH, $C = 100\ \mu$ F and $f = 100$ Hz, determine the impedance of each circuit in cartesian and polar forms.

Solution 20

(i) $Z = j\dfrac{R\omega L}{R + j\omega L}$

$= j\dfrac{(10)(2\pi 100)(0.05)}{10 + j2\pi 100(0.05)} = \dfrac{314.2j}{10 + 31.42j}$

$$Z = \frac{314.2j}{10 - 31.42j} \times \frac{10 - 31.42j}{10 - 31.42j}$$

$$= \frac{3142j + 9872.2}{100 + 987.2}$$

$$Z = \frac{9872.2}{1087.2} + j\frac{3142}{1087.2} = 9.08 + 2.89j$$

$$Z = (9.08 + j2.89)\Omega$$

$$|Z| = \sqrt{9.08^2 + 2.89^2} = 9.53\Omega$$

$$\arg Z = \tan^{-1}\frac{2.89}{9.08} = 17.7°$$

$$Z = 9.53\underline{/17.7°}\Omega.$$

(ii) $Z = \dfrac{R}{1 + j\omega CR}$

$$= \frac{10}{1 + j2\pi(100)100 \times 10^{-6}10}$$

$$= \frac{10}{1 + j0.628}$$

$$Z = \frac{10(1 - j0.628)}{(1 + j0.628)(1 - j0.628)}$$

$$= \frac{10}{1.39} - j\frac{6.28}{1.39} = 7.17 - j4.52$$

$$Z = (7.17 - j4.52)\Omega$$

$$|Z| = \sqrt{7.17^2 + (-4.52)^2} = 8.48$$

$$\arg Z = -\tan^{-1}\frac{4.52}{7.17} = -32.2°$$

$$Z = 8.48\underline{/-32.2°}\Omega.$$

(iii) $Z = \dfrac{j\omega L}{1 - \omega^2 LC}$

$$= \frac{j2\pi 100(0.05)}{1 - 4\pi^2 10{,}000 \times (0.05) \times 100 \times 10^{-6}}$$

$$= \frac{j2\pi 100(0.05)}{-0.974}$$

$$Z = -j\frac{31.4}{0.974} = -j32.3, \quad |Z| = 32.3,$$

$$\arg Z = \underline{/-90°}$$

$$Z = 32.3\underline{/-90°}\Omega.$$

(iv) $\dfrac{1}{Z} = \dfrac{1}{10} + j2\pi 100 \times 100 \times 10^{-6}$

$$+ \frac{1}{j2\pi 100 \times 0.05}\frac{j}{j}$$

$$\frac{1}{Z} = \frac{1}{10} + j0.0628 - j0.0318$$

$$\frac{1}{Z} = 0.1 + j0.031$$

$$Z = \frac{1}{0.1 + j0.031} \times \frac{0.1 - j0.031}{0.1 - j0.031}$$

$$= \frac{0.1 - j0.031}{0.1^2 + 0.031^2} = 9.12 - j2.83$$

$$|Z| = 9.55\ \Omega, \arg Z = \tan^{-1}-\frac{2.83}{9.12}$$

$$= \tan^{-1}-0.310 = -17.2°$$

$$\therefore Z = 9.55\underline{/-17.2°}\Omega.$$

(v) $\dfrac{1}{Z} = j2\pi 100 \times 100 \times 10^{-6}$

$$+ \frac{1}{10 + j2\pi 100 \times 0.05}$$

$$= j0.0628 + \frac{1}{10 + j31.4}$$

$$\frac{1}{Z} = \frac{j0.0628 - 0.0628 \times 31.4 + 1}{10 + j31.4}$$

$$= \frac{-0.972 + j0.628}{10 + j31.4}$$

$$Z = \frac{10 + j31.4}{-0.972 + j0.628}$$

$$= \frac{(10 + j31.4)(-0.972 - j0.628)}{(-0.972 + j0.628)(-0.972 - j0.628)}$$

$$Z = \frac{-9.72 - j30.5 - j6.28 + 19.72}{1.34}$$

$$= \frac{10}{1.34} - j\frac{36.78}{1.34} = 7.46 - j27.4$$

$$Z = (7.46 - j27.4)\Omega \quad |Z| = 28.4$$

$$\arg Z = -\tan^{-1}\frac{27.4}{7.46} = -74.8°$$

$$Z = 28.4\underline{/-74.8°}\Omega.$$

WORKED EXAMPLE 21

The r.m.s. voltage, V, is given by the complex number $V = 3 + j4$ and the r.m.s. current, I, is given by the complex number $I = 1 - j2$. Determine the moduli and arguments of V and I

and hence find the phase angle between V and I. If the power in the circuit is given by the expression $P = |I||V|\cos\phi$ where ϕ is the phase angle between V and I, find the power in watts.

Solution 21

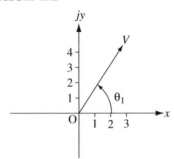

Fig. 22

$V = 3 + j4$

$|V| = \sqrt{3^2 + 4^2} = \sqrt{9 + 16} = \sqrt{25} = 5$

$\arg V = \tan^{-1}\frac{4}{3} = 53°7'48.3''$
$\qquad = 53.13° = \theta_1$

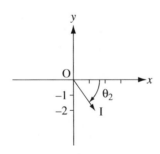

Fig. 23

$I = 1 - j2$

$|I| = \sqrt{1^2 + (-2)^2} = \sqrt{1 + 4} = \sqrt{5}$

$\arg I = -\tan^{-1}(\frac{2}{1}) = -63°26'5.8''$
$\qquad = -63.44° = -\theta_2$

$\phi = \text{phaseangle} = \theta_1 - (-\theta_2) = \theta_1 + \theta_2$
$\qquad = 53.13° + 63.44° = 116.57°$

$P = |I||V|\cos\phi = \sqrt{5}\,5\cos 116.57°$
$\qquad = \sqrt{55}(-0.4472908) = -5$

$P = 5W$ the power is positive.

Exercises 3

1. Calculate the modulus and the argument of the following complex numbers (in the range $-\pi \le \theta \le \pi$):-

    (i) $Z_1 = 1 + j\sqrt{3}$ (ii) $Z_2 = \sqrt{2} - j$

    (iii) $Z_3 = -1 + j\sqrt{3}$ (iv) $Z_4 = 2 - j3$

    (v) $Z_5 = -2 - 4j$.

2. Express in polar form the following:-

    (i) $Z_1 = 3 + 4j$ (ii) $Z_2 = 3 - 4j$

    (iii) $Z_3 = -3 - 4j$ (iv) $Z_4 = -3 + 4j$.

3. Express in cartesian form the following complex numbers:-

    (i) $Z_1 = 3\underline{/-30°}$ (ii) $Z_2 = 5\underline{/-\frac{\pi}{2}}$

    (iii) $Z_3 = 1\underline{/-180°}$ (iv) $Z_4 = 7\underline{/-\frac{4\pi}{3}}$

    (v) $Z_5 = 3\underline{/360°}$.

4. Express $Z = \dfrac{1 + 2j}{3 + 4j}$ in the form $x + jy$ and in the form $r\underline{/\theta}$.

5. A complex number Z has a modulus $\sqrt{2}$ and an argument of $\frac{\pi}{3}$. Write down this complex number in
    (i) the cartesian form
    (ii) the polar form.

6. (a) Mark in Argand diagram the points P_1 and P_2 which represent the two complex number $Z_1 = -1 - j$ and $Z_2 = 1 + j\sqrt{3}$.

    On the same diagram, mark the points P_3 and P_4 which represent $(Z_1 - Z_2)$ and $(Z_1 + Z_2)$ respectively.

    (b) Find the modulus and argument of
    (i) Z_1 (ii) Z_2 (iii) $Z_1 Z_2$
    (iv) Z_1/Z_2 (v) $\dfrac{Z_2}{Z_1}$.

7. If $Z_1 = 5\underline{/30°}$, $Z_2 = 7\underline{/50°}$,
    $Z_3 = 9\underline{/45°}$

Determine in polar form the following:-

(i) $Z_1 Z_2 Z_3$ (ii) $Z_1 Z_2$

(iii) $Z_3 Z_1$ (iv) $\dfrac{Z_2}{Z_3}$

(v) $\dfrac{Z_1 Z_2}{Z_3}$

and write down the corresponding cartesian form of the complex numbers.

8. Find the square roots of the following:-

(i) j (ii) $3 - j4$ (iii) $j - 2$.

9. The current and voltage in an a.c. circuit are given by $I = 3 + 4j$ and $V = 5 + j5$. Determine the moduli for I and V and hence find the phase angle between V and I.

If $P = |I||V|\cos\phi$, calculate P.

10. Find the impedances of the following circuits:-
(i) If $f = 50$ Hz

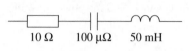

10 Ω   100 μΩ   50 mH

Fig. 24

(ii)

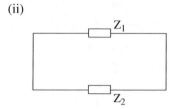

Fig. 25

If $Z_1 = 5 - j8$ and $Z_2 = 10 + j10$ in parallel and hence determine the magnitude of Z and its phase angle.

4

Polar Co-ordinates. Simple Curve Sketching.

4. Understands polar co-ordinates.

a. Defines polar coordinates, r and θ.

b. States the relationships between polar and cartesian coordinates.

c. Converts cartesian to polar coordinates and vice versa.

d. Plots graphs of functions defined in polar coordinates such as $r = a$, $\theta = \alpha$, $r = k\theta$, $r = 2a\cos\theta$.

a. Polar Co-ordinates.

A horizontal line is drawn from a fixed point 0 to the right as shown in Fig 26. The fixed point is called the **pole** and the line to the right of 0 is call the **initial line**.

O ———————————▶ INITIAL LINE

Fig. 26

The initial line is the reference line, which is rotated either clockwise or anti-clockwise, the clockwise angle is negative and the anti-clockwise angle is positive.

A line from the pole 0 is drawn at an algle θ (positive) to the initial line in an anti-clockwise direction as shown in Fig 27.

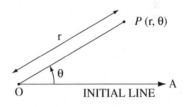

Fig. 27

The magnitude of **OP** $= r$ and in direction to the initial line is θ and therefore, the polar coordinates of **P** are (r, θ). Therefore, the position of a point **P** in a plane is fixed if the distance **OP**, r, and the angle θ are known.

b. Relationship between Polar and Cartesian Coordinates.

The cartesian coordinates may be expressed in terms of r and θ. (x, y), cartesian coordinates, and (r, θ), polar coordinates.

The cartesian coordinates of a point **P** is represented by **P**(x, y). The cartesian axes ox and oy intersect perpendicularly at a point O, called the origin. The point **P** is plotted as shown in Fig. 28, x units horizontally and y units vertically.

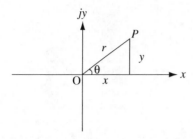

Fig. 28

Let **OP** $= r =$ the radius vector = the magnitude of **OP** and $\theta =$ the vectorial angle = the direction of **OP** with the **ox** axis (positive). Referring to Fig. 28, we have

$x = r \cos \theta$ and $y = r \sin \theta$

$r = x^2 + y^2 \quad \theta = \tan^{-1} \dfrac{y}{x}$

$(r, \theta) = \left[\sqrt{x^2 + y^2}, \tan^{-1} \dfrac{y}{x} \right].$

Therefore a curve given cartesian coordinates can be expressed in polar coordinates and vice-versa.

<hr>

WORKED EXAMPLE 22

Plot the following polar co-ordinate points:

  (i) $P_1(1, 30°)$ (ii) $P_2(2, 60°)$

 (iii) $P_3(3, \frac{\pi}{2})$ (iv) $P_4(-2, \frac{\pi}{4})$

  (v) $P_5(-1, -\dfrac{\pi}{2})$.

Solution 22

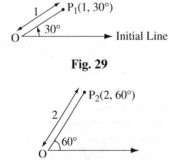

$P_1(1, 30°)$

Fig. 29

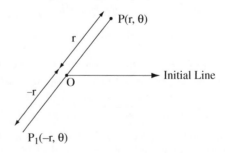

Fig. 30

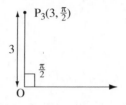

Fig. 31

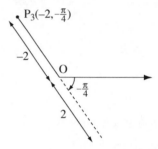

Fig. 32

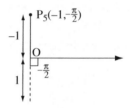

Fig. 33

Sign conventions.

If r is positive in the direction **OP** $(r > 0)$, then **OP′** $(-r, \theta)$ in the direction θ from the initial line. **Fig. 34** Illustrates this sign convention. A positive value of r is in the direction $\overrightarrow{\mathbf{OP}}$. A negative value r is in the direction $\overrightarrow{\mathbf{PO}}$ produced.

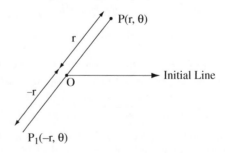

Fig. 34

c. To convert cartesian to polar co-ordinates.

$x = r \cos \theta$ and $y = r \sin \theta$

$$\frac{y}{x} = \frac{r \sin \theta}{r \cos \theta} = \tan \theta$$

$$\tan \theta = \frac{y}{x}$$

$$r = \sqrt{x^2 + y^2}.$$

WORKED EXAMPLE 23

To convert the following cartesian sets of co-ordinates to the corresponding polar sets of co-ordinates:-

(i) $\left[\frac{3}{\sqrt{2}}, \frac{3}{\sqrt{2}}\right]$ (ii) $(\sqrt{3}, 1)$ (iii) $(5, 0)$

(iv) $\left[\frac{7}{2}, -\frac{7\sqrt{3}}{2}\right]$ and (v) $(3.86, 1.04)$.

Solution 23

(i) $\tan \theta = \dfrac{y}{x} = \dfrac{3\sqrt{2}}{3\sqrt{2}} = 1$

and $\theta = \tan^{-1} 1 = \dfrac{\pi}{4}$

$$r = \sqrt{x^2 + y^2}$$

$$= \sqrt{\left(\frac{3}{\sqrt{2}}\right)^2 + \left(\frac{3}{\sqrt{2}}\right)^2}$$

$$= \sqrt{\left(\frac{9}{2}\right) + \left(\frac{9}{2}\right)} = \sqrt{9} = 3$$

$$r = 3$$

therefore $\left[\frac{3}{\sqrt{2}}, \frac{3}{\sqrt{2}}\right] \equiv \left[3, \frac{\pi}{4}\right]$

(ii) $\tan \theta = \dfrac{y}{x} = \dfrac{1}{\sqrt{3}}$ and

$$\theta = \tan^{-1} \frac{1}{\sqrt{3}} = \frac{\pi}{6}$$

therefore $(\sqrt{3}, 1) \equiv \left[2, \frac{\pi}{6}\right]$

(iii) $\tan \theta = \dfrac{y}{x}$ and $\theta = 0°$

$$r = \sqrt{x^2 + y^2} = \sqrt{5^2 + 0^2} = \sqrt{25} = 5$$

therefore $(5, 0) \equiv (5, 0°)$

(iv) $\tan \theta = \dfrac{y}{x} = \dfrac{-7\frac{\sqrt{3}}{2}}{\frac{7}{2}} = \sqrt{3}$ and

$$\theta = -\frac{\pi}{3}.$$

$$r = \sqrt{x^2 + y^2} = \sqrt{\left(\frac{7}{2}\right)^2 + \left(-7\frac{\sqrt{3}}{2}\right)^2}$$

$$= \sqrt{\frac{49}{4} + \frac{49 \times 3}{4}} = \sqrt{49} \quad r = 7$$

therefore $\left(\frac{7}{2}, \frac{-7\sqrt{3}}{2}\right) = \left(7, -\frac{\pi}{3}\right)$

(v) $\tan \theta = \dfrac{y}{x} = \dfrac{1.04}{3.86}$

$$= 0.26943 \text{ and } \theta = 15.079° = 15.1°$$

$$r = \sqrt{x^2 + y^2} = \sqrt{3.86^2 + 1.04^2}$$

$$= \sqrt{14.8996 + 1.0816} = 3.9976 \approx 4.0$$

therefore $(3.86, 1.04) \equiv (4, 15.1°)$.

To convert polar to cartesian co-ordinates.

$$x = r \cos \theta \qquad \ldots (1)$$

$$y = r \sin \theta \qquad \ldots (2)$$

It r and θ are known, these are substituted in the equations (1) and (2) above and the corresponding cartesian co-ordinates are found.

WORKED EXAMPLE 24

Find the corresponding cartesin co-ordinates to the sets of polar co-ordinates

(i) $\left(3, \frac{\pi}{4}\right)$ (ii) $\left(2, \frac{\pi}{6}\right)$ (iii) $(5, 0)$

(iv) $\left(7, -\frac{\pi}{3}\right)$ (v) $\left(4, \frac{\pi}{12}\right)$.

Solution 24

Fig. 35 shows the relationship between polar and cartesian

$$\cos \theta = \frac{x}{r} \text{ or } x = r \cos \theta = 3 \cos \frac{\pi}{4} = \frac{3}{\sqrt{2}}.$$

$$\sin \theta = \frac{y}{r} \text{ or } y = r \sin \theta = 3 \sin \frac{\pi}{4} = \frac{3}{\sqrt{2}}.$$

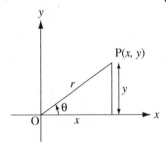

Fig. 35

therefore $\left[3, \dfrac{\pi}{4}\right] \equiv \left[\dfrac{3}{\sqrt{2}}, \dfrac{3}{\sqrt{2}}\right].$

(i) $x = r \cos \theta$

$= 2 \cos \dfrac{\pi}{6}$

$= 2 \dfrac{\sqrt{3}}{2} = \sqrt{3}$

$y = r \sin \theta = 2 \sin \dfrac{\pi}{6} = 2(\dfrac{1}{2}) = 1$

therefore $(2, \dfrac{\pi}{6})(\sqrt{3}, 1).$

(ii) $x = r \cos \theta = 5 \cos 0 = 5$

$y = r \sin \theta = 5 \sin 0 = 0$

therefore, $(5, 0^c) \equiv (5, 0)$

(iii) $x = r \cos \theta = 7 \cos \left(-\dfrac{\pi}{3}\right) = \dfrac{7}{2}.$

$y = r \sin \theta = 7 \sin \left(-\dfrac{\pi}{3}\right) = -7\dfrac{\sqrt{3}}{2}$

(iv) $x = r \cos \theta = 4 \cos \dfrac{\pi}{12} = 3.86$

$y = r \sin \theta = 4 \sin \dfrac{\pi}{12} = 1.04$

therefore $\left(4, \dfrac{\pi}{12}\right) = (3.86, 1.04).$

Remember that $\sin \dfrac{\pi}{4} = \cos \dfrac{\pi}{4} = \dfrac{1}{\sqrt{2}} = 0.707$

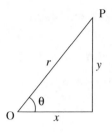

Fig. 36

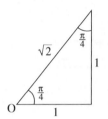

Fig. 37

$$\sin \frac{\pi}{6} = \frac{1}{2}$$

$$\cos \frac{\pi}{6} = \frac{\sqrt{3}}{2}$$

$$\cos 0° = 1$$

$$\sin 0° = 0.$$

$$\sin \left(\frac{-\pi}{3}\right) = \frac{\sqrt{3}}{2}$$

$$\cos \left(\frac{\pi}{3}\right) = \frac{1}{2}.$$

'Half-lines', the lengths are indefinite but the position of the line is at certain angle, defining the 'half-line'.

Therefore, the graph of $\theta = \alpha$ is a 'half-line' at the particular angle measured clockwise as negative and anti-clockwise as positive.

Graphs of $r = k\theta$

$r = k\theta$ denotes graphs of 'half-lines' where k is a constant and θ is a variable.

If $k = 1$

$\theta°$	3θ	θ^c	$r = \theta^c$	$r = 2\theta^c$
0	0	0	0	0
30	90	$\frac{\pi}{6}$	$\frac{\pi}{6}$	$\frac{\pi}{3}$
60	180	$\frac{\pi}{3}$	$\frac{\pi}{3}$	$\frac{2\pi}{3}$
90	270	$\frac{\pi}{2}$	$\frac{\pi}{2}$	π
120	360	$\frac{2\pi}{3}$	$\frac{2\pi}{3}$	$\frac{4\pi}{3}$
150	450	$\frac{5\pi}{6}$	$\frac{5\pi}{6}$	$\frac{5\pi}{3}$
180	540	π	π	2π
210	630	$\frac{7\pi}{6}$	$\frac{7\pi}{6}$	$\frac{7\pi}{3}$
240	720	$\frac{4\pi}{3}$	$\frac{4\pi}{3}$	$\frac{8\pi}{3}$
270	810	$\frac{3\pi}{2}$	$\frac{3\pi}{2}$	3π
300	900	$\frac{5\pi}{3}$	$\frac{5\pi}{3}$	$\frac{10\pi}{3}$
330	990	$\frac{11\pi}{6}$	$\frac{11\pi}{6}$	$\frac{11\pi}{3}$
360	1080	2π	2π	4π

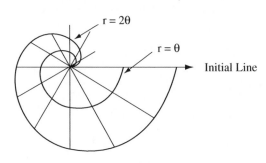

Fig. 38

d. Plots graphs of functions defined in polar co-ordinates such as

$r = a, \theta = d, r = k\theta, r = 2a\cos\theta$.

Graph of $r = \alpha$

$r = a$, the length of r is equal to 'a' for all the angles from $0°$ to 2π or $360°$, that means the

function $r = a$ in polar co-ordinates is a circle with the center at the pole and radius equal to 'a'.

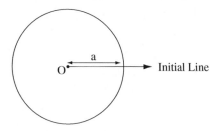

Fig. 39

Graph of $\theta = \alpha$

The polar equation of the initial line is $\theta = 0°$ in radians, or $\theta = 0°$ in degrees.

The polar equations of 'half-lines' are shown in **Fig. 40**

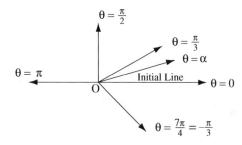

Fig. 40

All the lines drawn from the pole, 0 are drawn at the angles

$$\theta = 0^c, \quad \theta = \alpha, \quad \theta = \frac{\pi}{3}, \quad \theta = \frac{\pi}{2} \quad \theta = \pi$$

$\theta = \frac{7\pi}{4} = -\frac{\pi}{4}$, these are known as half lines.

Graph of $r = 2a\cos\theta$

θ	$r = 2a\cos\theta$	$\theta°$	$r = 2a\cos\theta$
0	$2a$	150	$-1.732a$
30	$1.732a$	180	$-2a$
60	a	210	$-1.732a$
90	0	240	$-a$
120	$-a$	270	0

$\theta°$	300	330	360
$r = 2a\cos\theta$	a	$1.732a$	$2a$

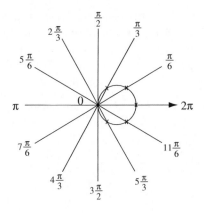

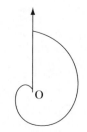

Fig. 44

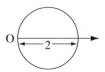

Fig. 45

Polar curve sketching.

To sketch the polar curves, it is advisable to tabulate values of θ in steps of 30° or $\frac{\pi}{6}$ in the range $0 \le \theta \le 2\pi$.

If r is a function of $\cos \theta$, the curve is symmetrical about the initial line $\theta = 0^c$ since $\cos(-\theta) = \cos \theta$ is an even function, so that values of θ up to and including π should only be recorded.

In general, the student is advised to think in degrees and work in radians.

WORKED EXAMPLE 25

Sketch the graphs defined by the polar coordinates

(i) $r = 2$

(ii) $\theta = \dfrac{\pi}{4}$

(iii) $r = 3\theta$

(iv) $r = 2 \cos \theta$ for one revolution.

Solution 25

Fig. 42

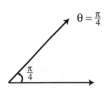

Fig. 43

Exercises 4

1. Plot the following polar co-ordinates:-

(i) $\mathbf{A}\left(1, \dfrac{\pi}{6}\right)$ (ii) $\mathbf{B}\left(-1, \dfrac{\pi}{6}\right)$

(iii) $\mathbf{C}\left(2, \dfrac{\pi}{3}\right)$ (iv) $\mathbf{D}\left(-2, \dfrac{\pi}{3}\right)$

(v) $\mathbf{E}\left(-3, -\dfrac{\pi}{4}\right)$ (vi) $\mathbf{F}\left(2, \dfrac{3\pi}{4}\right)$

(vii) $\mathbf{G}\left(\sqrt{2}, \dfrac{\pi}{8}\right)$ (viii) $\mathbf{H}\left(\sqrt{3}, 0^c\right)$

(ix) $\mathbf{I}\left(5, \pi^c\right)$ (x) $\mathbf{J}\left(-5, \dfrac{\pi}{2}\right)$.

2. Plot the following pairs of points and calculate the distances PQ in each case.

(i) $P\left(1, \dfrac{\pi}{6}\right)$, $Q\left(-1, \dfrac{\pi}{6}\right)$

(ii) $P(\sqrt{3}, 0^c)$, $Q(-\sqrt{3}, 0^c)$

(iii) $P(4, \tan^{-1} 1)$, $Q(-4, \tan^{-1} 1)$.

3. A triangle ABC has the following polar co-ordinates: **A** $(1,0)$, **B** $(2, \frac{\pi}{2})$ and **C** $(3, \pi)$. Find the area of the triangle ABC.

4. Find the polar equations of the following linear cartesian equations:-

(i) $\dfrac{x}{a} + \dfrac{y}{b} = 1$ (ii) $y = 3x - 5$

(iii) $y = -3x$ (iv) $y = x$

(v) $x = 5$ (vi) $y = 2$

(vii) $y = 0$ (viii) $y = x + 1$

(ix) $x = -5$.

5. Find the polar equations of the following cartesian curves:-

(i) $x^2 + y^2 = 1$ (ii) $x^2 + y^2 = 2^2$

(iii) $\dfrac{x^2}{3^2} + \dfrac{y^2}{4^2} = 1$ (iv) $\dfrac{x^2}{4^2} - \dfrac{y^2}{5^2} = 1$

(v) $yx = 5$ (vi) $y^2 = 4x$

(vii) $x^2 - 4y = 0$

(viii) $x^2 + y^2 - x - y - 1 = 0$

(ix) $y = \dfrac{1}{x}$.

6. Find the cartesian equations of the following polar equations:

(i) $r = 5\theta$ (ii) $r = -3\theta$

(iii) $r = 2\cos\theta$ (iv) $\theta = \dfrac{\pi}{4}$

(v) $\theta = \dfrac{\pi}{2}$ (vi) $r = 1$

(vii) $r = 2^2$.

7. Draw the graphs of the following polar curves:-

(i) $r = 5$ (ii) $r = 3\theta$

(iii) $r = 3\cos\theta$ (iv) $\theta = \dfrac{\pi}{3}$

(v) $\theta = -\dfrac{\pi}{2}$.

8. Why do we need the polar co-ordinate system? Illustrate your answer by considering an example in the cartesian co-ordinate system and an example in the polar co-ordinate system.

5

Matrices and determinants

Understands the notation of matrices and determinants.

(a) Recognises the notation for a matrix.
(b) Calculates the sum and difference of two matrices (2 × 2 only).
(c) Calculates the product of two matrices (2 × 2 only).
(d) Demonstrates that the product of two matrices is, in general non-commutative.
(e) Defines the unit matrix.
(f) Recognises the notation for a determinant.
(g) Evaluates a 2 × 2 determinant.

a. Notation of a matrix.

What is a matrix?

A matrix is an array of numbers enclosed by two brackets, such as the following examples:-

(i) $\begin{pmatrix} 2 & 3 \\ 1 & -2 \end{pmatrix}$

(ii) $\begin{pmatrix} 1 \\ 2 \end{pmatrix}$

(iii) $(2, -3)$.

(iv) $\begin{pmatrix} 1 & 2 & 3 \\ -1 & 2 & 4 \end{pmatrix}$

(v) $\begin{pmatrix} 1 & 2 \\ 3 & 4 \\ 5 & 6 \end{pmatrix}$

(vi) $\begin{pmatrix} 1 & 2 & 3 \\ 4 & 5 & 6 \\ 7 & 8 & 9 \end{pmatrix}$.

Each number is called an **element** of the matrix, the number of elements in (i) are four, in (ii) are two, in (iii) are two, in (iv) are six, in (v) are six, in (vi) are nine, in the above examples there are **rows** and **columns**.

(i) has two rows and two columns
(ii) has two rows and one column
(iii) has one row and two columns
(iv) has two rows and three columns
(v) has three rows and two columns and
(vi) has three rows and three columns.

The **order** of the matrix is denoted as follows:-

For (i) 2 × 2 the first two denotes the rows and the second two denotes the columns.

For (ii) 2 × 1 (two rows × one column)
For (iii) 1 × 2 (one row × two columns)
For (iv) 2 × 3 (two rows × three columns)
For (v) 3 × 2 (three rows × two columns)
For (vi) 3 × 3 (three rows × three columns).

Types of matrices

Example
(i) is a **square matrix**
(ii) is a **column matrix**
(iii) is a **row matrix**
(iv) is a **rectangular matrix**
(v) is a **rectangular matrix**
(vi) is a **square matrix** or a 3 **square matrix**.

In a square matrix like the last example, 1,5,9 are called its **diagonal elements**. The sum of the diagonal elements of a square matrix of example (iv) is called the **trace** of the matrix, that is, $1 + 5 + 9 = 15$ is the trace of the matrix.

Zero or Null Matrix.

$$\begin{pmatrix} 0 & 0 \\ 0 & 0 \end{pmatrix} \quad \text{and} \quad \begin{pmatrix} 0 & 0 & 0 \\ 0 & 0 & 0 \\ 0 & 0 & 0 \end{pmatrix}$$

are null matrices of order two and three respectively.

Diagonal matrix.

The matrix is a square matrix in which all the elements are zero except the diagonal elements.

$$\begin{pmatrix} 1 & 0 \\ 0 & 2 \end{pmatrix} \quad \text{and} \quad \begin{pmatrix} 1 & 0 & 0 \\ 0 & 2 & 0 \\ 0 & 0 & 3 \end{pmatrix}$$

are diagonal matrices of order two and three respectively. Note that a diagonal matrix runs from upper left to lower right.

Unit Matrix.

This is a diagonal matrix where all the diagonal elements are unity such as

$$\mathbf{I} = \begin{pmatrix} 1 & 0 \\ 0 & 1 \end{pmatrix} \quad \mathbf{I} = \begin{pmatrix} 1 & 0 & 0 \\ 0 & 1 & 0 \\ 0 & 0 & 1 \end{pmatrix}$$

of order two and three respectively. The unit matrix is denoted by the letter I.

Matrices are in general denoted by capital letters such as **A, B, C**.

b. To calculate the sum and difference of two matrices (2 × 2 only).

Addition of matrices.

$$\mathbf{A} = \begin{pmatrix} a_{11} & a_{12} \\ a_{21} & a_{22} \end{pmatrix}$$

where A denotes the 2×2 matrix with elements a_{11}, a_{12}, a_{21} and a_{22}. This is a general form of a 2×2 matrix. The subscripts denote the position of the elements, for example a_{11}, the first

subscript 1 denotes the first row and the second subscript 1 denotes the first column, a_{12}, the first subscript 1 denotes the first row and the second subscript 2 denotes the second column. Generally, the first subscript denotes the row and the second subscript denotes the column.

If $\mathbf{B} = \begin{pmatrix} b_{11} & b_{12} \\ b_{21} & b_{22} \end{pmatrix}$ and $\mathbf{A} = \begin{pmatrix} a_{11} & a_{12} \\ a_{21} & a_{22} \end{pmatrix}$ then

$$\mathbf{A} + \mathbf{B} = \begin{pmatrix} a_{11} & a_{12} \\ a_{21} & a_{22} \end{pmatrix} + \begin{pmatrix} b_{11} & b_{12} \\ b_{21} & b_{22} \end{pmatrix}$$

$$\mathbf{B} + \mathbf{A} = \begin{pmatrix} b_{11} & b_{12} \\ b_{21} & b_{22} \end{pmatrix} + \begin{pmatrix} a_{11} & a_{12} \\ a_{21} & a_{22} \end{pmatrix}$$

$$= \begin{pmatrix} b_{11} + a_{11} & b_{12} + a_{12} \\ b_{21} + a_{21} & b_{22} + a_{22} \end{pmatrix}.$$

Therefore, from the above $\mathbf{A} + \mathbf{B} = \mathbf{B} + \mathbf{A}$ and the addition of matrices is associative.

WORKED EXAMPLE 26

Find the sums of the following:-

   (i) **A + B**

   (ii) **B + A**

   (iii) **A + C**

   (iv) **B + C**.

If $\mathbf{A} = \begin{pmatrix} -1 & 2 \\ 3 & -1 \end{pmatrix}$,

$$\mathbf{B} = \begin{pmatrix} 3 & -4 \\ 2 & 1 \end{pmatrix}, \quad \mathbf{C} = \begin{pmatrix} 0 & -1 \\ -1 & 2 \end{pmatrix}$$

Solution 26

(i) $\mathbf{A} + \mathbf{B} = \begin{pmatrix} -1 & 2 \\ 3 & -1 \end{pmatrix} + \begin{pmatrix} 3 & -4 \\ 2 & 1 \end{pmatrix}$

$$= \begin{pmatrix} -1 + 3 & 2 - 4 \\ 3 + 2 & -1 + 1 \end{pmatrix}$$

$$= \begin{pmatrix} 2 & -2 \\ 5 & 0 \end{pmatrix}$$

(ii) $\mathbf{B} + \mathbf{A} = \begin{pmatrix} 3 & -4 \\ 2 & 1 \end{pmatrix} + \begin{pmatrix} -1 & 2 \\ 3 & -1 \end{pmatrix}$

$= \begin{pmatrix} 3-1 & -4+2 \\ 2+3 & 1-1 \end{pmatrix}$

$= \begin{pmatrix} 2 & -2 \\ 5 & 0 \end{pmatrix}$

note that $\mathbf{A} + \mathbf{B} = \mathbf{B} + \mathbf{A}$.

(iii) $\mathbf{A} + \mathbf{C} = \begin{pmatrix} -1 & 2 \\ 3 & -1 \end{pmatrix} + \begin{pmatrix} 0 & -1 \\ -1 & 2 \end{pmatrix}$

$= \begin{pmatrix} -1+0 & 2-1 \\ 3-1 & -1+2 \end{pmatrix}$

$= \begin{pmatrix} -1 & 1 \\ 2 & 1 \end{pmatrix}$

(iv) $\mathbf{B} + \mathbf{C} = \begin{pmatrix} 3 & -4 \\ 2 & 1 \end{pmatrix} + \begin{pmatrix} 0 & -1 \\ -1 & 2 \end{pmatrix}$

$= \begin{pmatrix} 3+0 & -4-1 \\ 2-1 & 1+2 \end{pmatrix}$

$= \begin{pmatrix} 3 & -5 \\ 1 & 3 \end{pmatrix}.$

Subtraction of matrices

$\mathbf{A} - \mathbf{B} = \begin{pmatrix} a_{11} & a_{12} \\ a_{21} & a_{22} \end{pmatrix} - \begin{pmatrix} b_{11} & b_{12} \\ b_{21} & b_{22} \end{pmatrix}$

$= \begin{pmatrix} a_{11} - b_{11} & a_{12} - b_{12} \\ a_{21} - b_{21} & a_{22} - b_{22} \end{pmatrix}$

$\mathbf{B} - \mathbf{A} = \begin{pmatrix} b_{11} - a_{11} & b_{12} - a_{12} \\ b_{21} - a_{21} & b_{22} - a_{22} \end{pmatrix}.$

We can see that the substraction is similar to the addition, the corresponding elements either substracted or added.

━━━━━━━━━━━━━━
WORKED EXAMPLE 27
━━━━━━━━━━━━━━

If $\mathbf{A} = \begin{pmatrix} 1 & -1 \\ 0 & 0 \end{pmatrix}$ $\mathbf{B} = \begin{pmatrix} 2 & 3 \\ -1 & -1 \end{pmatrix}$

$\mathbf{C} = \begin{pmatrix} 1 & 1 \\ 1 & 0 \end{pmatrix}$

Find

(i) $\mathbf{A} - \mathbf{B}$ (ii) $\mathbf{A} - \mathbf{C}$ (iii) $\mathbf{C} - \mathbf{B}$.

Solution 27

$\mathbf{A} - \mathbf{B} = \begin{pmatrix} 1 & -1 \\ 0 & 0 \end{pmatrix} + \begin{pmatrix} 2 & 3 \\ -1 & -1 \end{pmatrix}$

$= \begin{pmatrix} 1-2 & -1-3 \\ 0-(-1) & 0-(-1) \end{pmatrix}$

$= \begin{pmatrix} -1 & -4 \\ 1 & 1 \end{pmatrix}$

$\mathbf{A} - \mathbf{C} = \begin{pmatrix} 1 & -1 \\ 0 & 0 \end{pmatrix} - \begin{pmatrix} 1 & 1 \\ 1 & 0 \end{pmatrix}$

$= \begin{pmatrix} 1-1 & -1-1 \\ 0-1 & 0-0 \end{pmatrix}$

$= \begin{pmatrix} 0 & -2 \\ -1 & 0 \end{pmatrix}$

$\mathbf{C} - \mathbf{B} = \begin{pmatrix} 1 & 1 \\ 1 & 0 \end{pmatrix} - \begin{pmatrix} 2 & 3 \\ -1 & -1 \end{pmatrix}$

$= \begin{pmatrix} 1-2 & 1-3 \\ 1-(-1) & 0-(-1) \end{pmatrix}$

$= \begin{pmatrix} -1 & -2 \\ 2 & 1 \end{pmatrix}.$

What is the meaning of $2\mathbf{A}$ if $\mathbf{A} = \begin{pmatrix} 1 & 2 \\ 3 & 4 \end{pmatrix}$?

It means that each element is multiplied by 2.

$2\mathbf{A} = 2\begin{pmatrix} 1 & 2 \\ 3 & 4 \end{pmatrix} = \begin{pmatrix} 2 & 4 \\ 6 & 8 \end{pmatrix}$

━━━━━━━━━━━━━━
WORKED EXAMPLE 28
━━━━━━━━━━━━━━

If $\mathbf{A} = \begin{pmatrix} 1 & 0 \\ 1 & -1 \end{pmatrix}$ $\mathbf{B} = \begin{pmatrix} -3 & 5 \\ 2 & -1 \end{pmatrix}$

Find

(i) $3\mathbf{A} + \mathbf{B}$ (ii) $4\mathbf{B} - 2\mathbf{A}$.

Solution 28

(i) $3\mathbf{A} + \mathbf{B} = 3\begin{pmatrix} 1 & 0 \\ 1 & -1 \end{pmatrix} + \begin{pmatrix} -3 & 5 \\ 2 & -1 \end{pmatrix}$

$= \begin{pmatrix} 3 & 0 \\ 3 & -3 \end{pmatrix} + \begin{pmatrix} -3 & 5 \\ 2 & -1 \end{pmatrix}$

$$= \begin{pmatrix} 3-3 & 0+5 \\ 3+2 & -3-1 \end{pmatrix}$$

$$= \begin{pmatrix} 0 & 5 \\ 5 & -4 \end{pmatrix}$$

(ii) $4\mathbf{B} - 2\mathbf{A} = 4\begin{pmatrix} -3 & 5 \\ 2 & -1 \end{pmatrix} - 2\begin{pmatrix} 1 & 0 \\ 1 & -1 \end{pmatrix}$

$$= \begin{pmatrix} -12 & 20 \\ 8 & -4 \end{pmatrix} - \begin{pmatrix} 2 & 0 \\ 2 & -2 \end{pmatrix}$$

$$= \begin{pmatrix} -12-2 & 20-0 \\ 8-2 & -4-(-2) \end{pmatrix}$$

$$= \begin{pmatrix} -14 & 20 \\ 6 & -2 \end{pmatrix}.$$

c. Calculates the product of two matrices (2 × 2) only.

If $\mathbf{A} = \begin{pmatrix} a_{11} & a_{12} \end{pmatrix}$ $\mathbf{B} = \begin{pmatrix} b_{11} & b_{12} \\ b_{21} & b_{22} \end{pmatrix}$

$$\mathbf{AB} = \begin{pmatrix} \overrightarrow{a_{11} & a_{12}} \\ a_{21} & a_{22} \end{pmatrix} + \begin{pmatrix} \downarrow b_{11} & b_{12} \\ b_{21} & b_{22} \end{pmatrix}$$

To find the product of two matrices, the technique is different, the arrows shown above help a great deal, the results is

$$\mathbf{AB} = \begin{pmatrix} a_{11}b_{11} + a_{12}b_{21} & a_{11}b_{12} + a_{12}b_{22} \\ a_{21}b_{11} + a_{22}b_{21} & a_{21}b_{12} + a_{22}b_{22} \end{pmatrix}.$$

Observe that the elements of the tails of the arrows are multiplied and added to the product of the elements of the arrow heads.

Repeat for practice.

$$\mathbf{BA} = \begin{pmatrix} \overrightarrow{b_{11} & b_{12}} \\ b_{21} & b_{22} \end{pmatrix} + \begin{pmatrix} \downarrow a_{11} & a_{12} \\ a_{21} & a_{22} \end{pmatrix}$$

$$= \begin{pmatrix} b_{11}a_{11} + b_{12}a_{21} & b_{11}a_{12} + b_{12}a_{22} \\ b_{21}a_{11} + b_{22}a_{21} & b_{21}a_{12} + b_{22}a_{22} \end{pmatrix}.$$

WORKED EXAMPLE 29

If $\mathbf{A} = \begin{pmatrix} -1 & 2 \\ -2 & -3 \end{pmatrix}$ and $\mathbf{B} = \begin{pmatrix} 1 & 2 \\ 3 & 4 \end{pmatrix}$

Find (i) $\mathbf{AB}$ (ii) $\mathbf{BA}$.

Solution 29

(i) $\mathbf{AB} = \begin{pmatrix} \overrightarrow{-1 & 2} \\ -2 & 3 \end{pmatrix} \begin{pmatrix} 1 & 2 \\ 3\downarrow & 4 \end{pmatrix}$

$$= \begin{pmatrix} (-1)(1) + (2)(3) & (-1)(2) + (2)(4) \\ (-2)(1) + (-3)(3) & (-2)(2) + (-3)(4) \end{pmatrix}$$

$$= \begin{pmatrix} -1+6 & -2+8 \\ -2-9 & -4-12 \end{pmatrix} = \begin{pmatrix} 5 & 6 \\ -11 & 16 \end{pmatrix}$$

(ii) $\mathbf{BA} = \begin{pmatrix} \overrightarrow{1 & 2} \\ 3 & 4 \end{pmatrix} \begin{pmatrix} \downarrow -1 & 2 \\ -2 & -3 \end{pmatrix}$

$$= \begin{pmatrix} (1)(-1) + (2)(-2) & (1)(2) - (2)(3) \\ (3)(-1) + (4)(-2) & (3)(2) + (4)(-3) \end{pmatrix}$$

$$= \begin{pmatrix} -1-4 & 2-6 \\ -3-8 & 6-12 \end{pmatrix} = \begin{pmatrix} -5 & -4 \\ -11 & -6 \end{pmatrix}$$

Note that $\mathbf{AB}$ is not equal to $\mathbf{BA}$

$$\mathbf{AB} \neq \mathbf{BA}.$$

WORKED EXAMPLE 30

$\mathbf{A} = \begin{pmatrix} 3 & 7 \\ 5 & -6 \end{pmatrix}$, $\mathbf{B} = \begin{pmatrix} 1 & 0 \\ 0 & 1 \end{pmatrix}$,

$\mathbf{C} = \begin{pmatrix} 0 & 0 \\ 0 & 0 \end{pmatrix}$.

Find (i) $\mathbf{AB}$ (ii) $\mathbf{BA}$
(iii) $\mathbf{AC}$ (iv) $\mathbf{CB}$.

Solution 30

(i) $\mathbf{AB} = \begin{pmatrix} 3 & 7 \\ 5 & -6 \end{pmatrix} \begin{pmatrix} 1 & 0 \\ 0 & 1 \end{pmatrix}$

$$= \begin{pmatrix} 3 \times 1 + 3 \times 0 & 7 \times 0 + 7 \times 1 \\ 5 \times 1 + (-6) \times 0 & 5 \times 0 + (-6)(1) \end{pmatrix}$$

$$= \begin{pmatrix} 3 & 7 \\ 5 & -6 \end{pmatrix}$$

Note that $\mathbf{AB} = \mathbf{A}$.

(ii) $\mathbf{BA} = \begin{pmatrix} 1 & 0 \\ 0 & 1 \end{pmatrix} \begin{pmatrix} 3 & 7 \\ 5 & -6 \end{pmatrix}$

$= \begin{pmatrix} 1 \times 3 + 0 \times 5 & 1 \times 7 + 0(-6) \\ 0 \times 3 + 1 \times 5 & 0 \times 7 + 1(-6) \end{pmatrix}$

$= \begin{pmatrix} 3 & 7 \\ 5 & -6 \end{pmatrix}$

Note that $\mathbf{BA = A}$.

(iii) $\mathbf{AC} = \begin{pmatrix} 3 & 7 \\ 5 & -6 \end{pmatrix} + \begin{pmatrix} 0 & 0 \\ 0 & 0 \end{pmatrix}$

$= \begin{pmatrix} 3 \times 0 + 7 \times 0 & 3 \times 0 + 7 \times 0 \\ 5 \times 0 + (-6) \times 0 & 0 \times 7 + (-6) \times 0 \end{pmatrix}$

$= \begin{pmatrix} 0 & 0 \\ 0 & 0 \end{pmatrix}$

Note that $\mathbf{AC = C}$.

(iv) $\mathbf{CB} = \begin{pmatrix} 0 & 0 \\ 0 & 0 \end{pmatrix} \begin{pmatrix} 1 & 0 \\ 0 & 0 \end{pmatrix}$

$= \begin{pmatrix} 0 \times 1 + 0 \times 1 & 0 \times 0 + 0 \times 0 \\ 0 \times 1 + 0 \times 0 & 0 \times 0 + 0 \times 1 \end{pmatrix}$

$= \begin{pmatrix} 0 & 0 \\ 0 & 0 \end{pmatrix}$

Note that $\mathbf{CB = C}$.

d. Demonstrates that the product of two matrices is in general, non-commutative.

We have already demonstrated that $\mathbf{AB}$ is not equal to $\mathbf{BA}$, that is

$\mathbf{AB \neq BA}$.

If $\mathbf{A} = \begin{pmatrix} 1 & 2 \\ -2 & -1 \end{pmatrix}$ and $\mathbf{B} = \begin{pmatrix} 2 & 3 \\ 1 & 1 \end{pmatrix}$

$\mathbf{AB} = \begin{pmatrix} 1 & 2 \\ -2 & -1 \end{pmatrix} \begin{pmatrix} 2 & 3 \\ 1 & 1 \end{pmatrix}$

$= \begin{pmatrix} 1 \times 2 + 2 \times 1 & 1 \times 3 + 2 \times 1 \\ (-2) \times 2 + (-1)(1) & (-2)(3) + (-1)(1) \end{pmatrix}$

$= \begin{pmatrix} 4 & 5 \\ -5 & -7 \end{pmatrix}$

$\mathbf{BA} = \begin{pmatrix} 2 & 3 \\ 1 & 1 \end{pmatrix} \begin{pmatrix} 1 & 2 \\ -2 & -1 \end{pmatrix}$

$= \begin{pmatrix} 2 \times 1 + 3(-2) & 2 \times 2 + 3(-1) \\ 1 \times 1 + 1 \times (-2) & 1 \times 2 + (1)(-1) \end{pmatrix}$

$= \begin{pmatrix} -4 & 1 \\ -1 & 1 \end{pmatrix}$

therefore $\mathbf{AB \neq BA}$ and the product of two matrices is, in general, non commutative.

But we have seen that if $\mathbf{B}$ is a unit matrix and $\mathbf{A}$ is a matrix of different elements then $\mathbf{AB = A}$ and $\mathbf{BA = A}$, in this case $\mathbf{AB = BA}$.

e. Defines the unit matrix.

A unit matrix is a matrix whose diagonal elements are equal to 1

$$\mathbf{I} = \begin{pmatrix} 1 & 0 \\ 0 & 1 \end{pmatrix}$$

Any matrix that is pre- or post-multiplied by $\mathbf{I}$ is unaltered.

$\mathbf{AI = I}$, $\mathbf{A}$ is post multiplied by $\mathbf{I}$, $\mathbf{IA = I}$, $\mathbf{A}$ is pre-multiplied, $\mathbf{AI = IA = A}$.

f. Recognises the notation for a determinant.

A determinant is an array of elements enclosed by vertical lines such that

$$\begin{vmatrix} a & b \\ c & d \end{vmatrix}$$

and means that $ad - cb$

therefore $\begin{vmatrix} a & b \\ c & d \end{vmatrix} = ad - dc$

The number of rows is equal to the number of columns, 2×2 or 3×3 or 4×4, but we will restrict our work to 2×2.

a, b, c, d are called the elements of the determinant.

g. Evaluates a 2 × 2 determinant.

WORKED EXAMPLE 30

Evaluate the following determinants:

(i) $\begin{vmatrix} a & b \\ c & d \end{vmatrix}$ (ii) $\begin{vmatrix} -1 & -1 \\ -1 & -1 \end{vmatrix}$

(iii) $\begin{vmatrix} 1 & 2 \\ 3 & 4 \end{vmatrix}.$

Solution 31

(i) $\begin{vmatrix} a & b \\ c & d \end{vmatrix} = ad - cd$

(ii) $\begin{vmatrix} -1 & -1 \\ -1 & -1 \end{vmatrix}$

$= (-1)(-1) - (-1)(-1) = 1 - 1 = 0$

(iii) $\begin{vmatrix} 1 & 2 \\ 3 & 4 \end{vmatrix}$

$= 1 \times 4 - 3 \times 2 = 4 - 6 = -2.$

It is observed that if the rows are the same or if the columns are the same as in example (ii) the determinant is equal to zero.

WORKED EXAMPLE 32

Factorise $\begin{vmatrix} a & 1 \\ a^2 & 1 \end{vmatrix}.$

Solution 32

$\begin{vmatrix} a & 1 \\ a^2 & 1 \end{vmatrix} = a\begin{vmatrix} 1 & 1 \\ a & 1 \end{vmatrix} = a\Delta$

If $a = 1$ then $= \Delta = \begin{vmatrix} 1 & 1 \\ 1 & 1 \end{vmatrix} = 0$

and $a - 1$ is a factor

or $1 - a$ is a factor

therefore

$\begin{vmatrix} a & 1 \\ a^2 & 1 \end{vmatrix} = a\begin{vmatrix} 1 & 1 \\ a & 1 \end{vmatrix} = a(a - 1).$

Exercises 5

1. Write down the following matrices:

   (i) a 2 × 2 unit matrix.
   (ii) a 2 × 2 zero matrix.
   (iii) a 2 × 2 diagonal matrix.

2. Write down the following matrices:

   (i) a 3 × 1 column matrix.
   (ii) a 3 × 3 square matrix.
   (iii) a 1 × 3 row matrix.
   (iv) a 3 × 2 or 2 × 3 rectangular matrix.
   (v) a 3 × 3 unit matrix.
   (vi) a 3 × 3 diagonal matrix.
   (vii) a null 3 × 3 matrix.

3. If $\mathbf{A} = \begin{pmatrix} -1 & 2 \\ -3 & 3 \end{pmatrix}$, $\mathbf{B} = \begin{pmatrix} 1 & -2 \\ 3 & 5 \end{pmatrix}$, $\mathbf{C} = \begin{pmatrix} 0 & 1 \\ 1 & 0 \end{pmatrix}.$

   Find
   (i) $\mathbf{A} + \mathbf{B} + \mathbf{C}$
   (ii) $2\mathbf{A} - 3\mathbf{C} + 2\mathbf{B}$
   (iii) $5\mathbf{B} + 4\mathbf{A}$

4. If $\mathbf{A} = \begin{pmatrix} 6 & 7 \\ 8 & 9 \end{pmatrix}$ $\mathbf{B} = \begin{pmatrix} 10 & 11 \\ 12 & 13 \end{pmatrix}$ $\mathbf{C} = \begin{pmatrix} 0 & 1 \\ -1 & 0 \end{pmatrix}.$

   Find
   (i) $\mathbf{ABC}$
   (ii) $\mathbf{A}^2$
   (iii) $\mathbf{BC}$
   (iv) $\mathbf{AC}$
   (v) $\mathbf{CB}$.

5. Show that $\mathbf{AB} \neq \mathbf{BA}$ and $\mathbf{BC} \neq \mathbf{CB}$ if $\mathbf{A}$, $\mathbf{B}$, $\mathbf{C}$ are the matrices shown in exercise 4.

6. Are matrices associative or commutative? Give a simple example in each case to illustrate the associativity and commutativity.

7. What is a unit matrix and what is the effect of multiplying a matrix by unit matrix? Illustrate the answers with examples.

8. A vector $\begin{pmatrix} x \\ y \end{pmatrix}$ is a

   column matrix $\begin{pmatrix} x \\ y \end{pmatrix}$.

   If $\overrightarrow{OP} = \begin{pmatrix} 3 \\ 5 \end{pmatrix}$ and $\overrightarrow{OQ} = \begin{pmatrix} 2 \\ 7 \end{pmatrix}$.

   find the resultant of these two vectors by adding the ordered pairs vectorially and by adding the two matrices and verify that they are the same.

9. If $\mathbf{A} = \begin{pmatrix} 1 & b \\ a & 0 \end{pmatrix}$, $\mathbf{B} = \begin{pmatrix} -1 & 2 \\ 3 & 4 \end{pmatrix}$,

   $\mathbf{C} = \begin{pmatrix} 5 & 10 \\ -5 & 22 \end{pmatrix}$.

   Determine the values of a and b

   if $\mathbf{AB} = \mathbf{C}$.

   Explain the equality of a matrix.

10. Evaluate the determinants:

    (i) $\begin{vmatrix} a & b \\ a^2 & b^2 \end{vmatrix}$

    (ii) $\begin{vmatrix} 1 & 3 \\ 2 & 4 \end{vmatrix}$

    (iii) $\begin{vmatrix} a & 3 \\ 4 & a \end{vmatrix}$.

11. If the determinants are equal to zero, find the value of a, without evaluating

    (i) $\begin{vmatrix} a & 2 \\ a^2 & 4 \end{vmatrix}$

    (ii) $\begin{vmatrix} 3 & a \\ 9 & a^2 \end{vmatrix}$

    (iii) $\begin{vmatrix} 1 & a \\ a & 1 \end{vmatrix}$.

12. Factorise the determinants:

    (i) $\begin{vmatrix} 2x & 1 \\ 8x^2 & 2 \end{vmatrix}$

    (ii) $\begin{vmatrix} 2y & x \\ 4y^2 & x^2 \end{vmatrix}$.

6

Solutions of simultaneous equations

Solves simultaneous equations with two unknowns using matrices and determinants.

(a) Solves simultaneous linear equations with two unknowns using determinants.

(b) Describes the meaning of a determinant whose value is zero, and defines a singular matrix.

(c) Obtains the inverse of a 2×2 matrix.

(d) Solves simultaneous linear equations with two unknowns by means of matrices.

(e) Relates the use of matrices to simple technical problems.

Linear simultaneous equations with two unknowns.

Solve first of all the linear simultaneous equations using an algebraic method

$$3x - y = 9 \qquad \ldots(1)$$

$$-4x + 3y = -7 \qquad \ldots(2)$$

Multiply each term of equation (1) by 3

$$9x - 3y = 27 \qquad \ldots(3)$$

$$-4x + 3y = -7 \qquad \ldots(4)$$

adding these equations we have

$$5x = 20$$

$$x = 4$$

substituting $x = 4$ in equation (1)

$$3(4) - y = 9$$

$$12 - 9 = y$$

$$y = 3$$

therefore, using the elimination and substitution methods, we have found that the above equations are simultaneously verified by putting $x = 4$ and $y = 3$. The procedure shall be more complicated if we had to solve three unknowns or even more.

We are going to restrict ourselves to two unknowns and solve these equations by determinants and by matrices.

a. To solve simultaneous linear equations with two unknowns using determinants.

$$3x - y = 9$$

$$-4x + 3y = -7$$

Rewrite

$$3x - y - 9 = 0$$

$$-4x + 3y + 7 = 0$$

The array of numbers are

$$\begin{array}{ccc} 3 & -1 & -9 \\ -4 & 3 & 7 \end{array}$$

We can form three determinants Δ_1, Δ_2, and Δ where

$$\Delta = \begin{vmatrix} 3 & -1 \\ -4 & 3 \end{vmatrix} \qquad \Delta_1 = \begin{vmatrix} -1 & -9 \\ 3 & 7 \end{vmatrix}$$

$$\Delta_2 = \begin{vmatrix} 3 & -9 \\ -4 & 7 \end{vmatrix}.$$

Observe that in order to write, Δ, we delete the last column of the constants, in order to write Δ_1 we delete the first column, of the coefficients of x and in order to write Δ_2, we delete the second column of the coefficients of y.

Crammer's rule states:

$$\frac{x}{\Delta_1} = -\frac{y}{\Delta_2} = \frac{1}{\Delta}$$

$$x = \frac{\Delta_1}{\Delta} \quad \text{and} \quad y = -\frac{\Delta_2}{\Delta}$$

$$\Delta_1 = \begin{vmatrix} -1 & -9 \\ 3 & 7 \end{vmatrix}$$

$$= (-1)(7) - (3)(-9)$$

$$= -7 + 27 = 20$$

$$\Delta_2 = \begin{vmatrix} 3 & -9 \\ -4 & 7 \end{vmatrix}$$

$$= (3)(7) - (-4)(-9)$$

$$= 21 - 36 = -15$$

$$\Delta = \begin{vmatrix} 3 & -1 \\ -4 & 3 \end{vmatrix}$$

$$= (3)(3) - (-1)(-4) = 9 - 4 = 5$$

therefore $x = \dfrac{\Delta_1}{\Delta} = \dfrac{20}{5} = 4$

$$y = -\frac{\Delta_2}{\Delta} = -\frac{(-15)}{5} = 3$$

and the answers are the same as before but with a different method.

The use of determinants may be more tedious, but is a systematic method which can be adopted in solving any number of unknowns, it is a computer orientated method.

b. Describes the meaning of a determinant whose value is zero, and defines a singular matrix.

A singular matrix is a matrix whose determinant is zero.

If $\mathbf{M} = \begin{pmatrix} a_{11} & a_{12} \\ a_{21} & a_{22} \end{pmatrix}$ then $|\mathbf{M}| = 0$

$$\begin{vmatrix} a_{11} & a_{12} \\ a_{21} & a_{22} \end{vmatrix} = 0$$

$$a_{11}a_{22} - a_{21}a_{12} = 0$$

We have seen that when two rows or two columns of a determinant are the same, then the determinant is zero.

If the determinant is zero, then the solutions are not defined and therefore there are no solution.

c. Obtains the inverse of 2 × 2 matrix.

The inverse of a matrix.

We have seen how to add, to subtract and to multiply matrices, now we have to show how to divide two matrices.

Notation of the inverse matrix.

The inverse of a matrix A is denoted as A^{-1}.

To find the inverse matrix of A.

Step $\mathbf{IA^*} = \mathbf{A}$ star (read as)

$\mathbf{A^*}$ denotes the cofactors of the elements of the matrix $\mathbf{A}$.

If $\mathbf{A} = \begin{pmatrix} a_{11} & a_{12} \\ a_{21} & a_{22} \end{pmatrix}$

the elements are a_{11}, a_{12}, a_{21} and a_{22}.

The minor of the element a_{11} is found by deleting the new row containing a_{11} and deleting the column containing a_{11} thus the minor of a_{11} is a_{22}.

$$\begin{matrix} a_{11} & a_{12} \\ a_{21} & a_{22} \end{matrix}$$

The minor a_{12} is a_{21} since

$$\begin{matrix} a_{11} & a_{12} \\ a_{21} & a_{22} \end{matrix}$$

The minor of a_{21} is a_{12} since

$$\begin{matrix} a_{11} & a_{12} \\ a_{21} & a_{22} \end{matrix}$$

and the minor of a_{22} is a_{11} since

$$\begin{matrix} a_{11} & a_{12} \\ a_{21} & a_{22} \end{matrix}$$

The minors of $\mathbf{A}$ are $\begin{pmatrix} a_{22} & a_{21} \\ a_{12} & a_{11} \end{pmatrix}$.

The cofactor of $\mathbf{A}$ are found by writing plus and minus alternatively starting with a plus at the upper left.

Therefore $\mathbf{A}^* = \begin{pmatrix} a_{22} & -a_{21} \\ -a_{12} & a_{11} \end{pmatrix}$.

WORKED EXAMPLE 33

If $\mathbf{A} = \begin{pmatrix} 1 & -2 \\ 3 & -4 \end{pmatrix}$ find the $\mathbf{A}.^*$

Solution 33

$\mathbf{A}^* = \begin{pmatrix} -4 & -3 \\ 2 & 1 \end{pmatrix}$

Step II $(\mathbf{A}^*)^T$ Transpose of $\mathbf{A}^*$ that is the columns are written as rows and the rows as columns.

$(\mathbf{A}^*)^T = \begin{pmatrix} a_{22} & -a_{12} \\ -a_{21} & a_{11} \end{pmatrix}$

$(\mathbf{A}^*)^T$ is called the adjoint matrix of $\mathbf{A}$

Step III Finally to obtain the inverse matrix of $\mathbf{A}$, we divide the adjoint matrix of $\mathbf{A}$ by the determinant of $\mathbf{A}$.

$$\mathbf{A}^{-1} = \frac{(\mathbf{A}^*)^T}{|\mathbf{A}|}.$$

WORKED EXAMPLE 34

Find the inverse matrix of $\mathbf{A} = \begin{pmatrix} 3 & -1 \\ -4 & -3 \end{pmatrix}$.

Solution 34

Step I

The minors of $\mathbf{A} = \begin{pmatrix} -3 & -4 \\ -1 & 3 \end{pmatrix}$.

The cofactors of $\mathbf{A} = \mathbf{A}^* = \begin{pmatrix} -3 & 4 \\ 1 & 3 \end{pmatrix}$.

Step II

The adjoint matrix of $\mathbf{A}$ is $(\mathbf{A}^*)^T = \begin{pmatrix} -3 & 4 \\ 1 & 3 \end{pmatrix}$.

Step III

$$\mathbf{A}^{-1} = \frac{(\mathbf{A}^*)^T}{|\mathbf{A}|}$$

$$|\mathbf{A}| = \begin{vmatrix} 3 & -1 \\ -4 & -3 \end{vmatrix}$$

$$= (3)(-3) - (-1)(-4)$$
$$= -9 - 4 = -13$$

$$\mathbf{A}^{-1} = \frac{\begin{pmatrix} -3 & 1 \\ 4 & 3 \end{pmatrix}}{-13} = \begin{pmatrix} \frac{3}{13} & -\frac{1}{13} \\ \frac{-4}{13} & -\frac{3}{13} \end{pmatrix}.$$

WORKED EXAMPLE 35

If $\mathbf{A} = \begin{pmatrix} 3 & -1 \\ -4 & 3 \end{pmatrix}$ and $\mathbf{B} = \begin{pmatrix} \frac{3}{5} & \frac{1}{5} \\ \frac{4}{5} & \frac{3}{5} \end{pmatrix}$.

Find $\mathbf{AB}$.

Solution 35

$$\mathbf{AB} = \begin{pmatrix} 3 & -1 \\ -4 & 3 \end{pmatrix} \begin{pmatrix} \frac{3}{5} & \frac{1}{5} \\ \frac{4}{5} & \frac{3}{5} \end{pmatrix}$$

$$= \begin{pmatrix} \frac{9}{5} - \frac{4}{5} & \frac{3}{5} - \frac{3}{5} \\ -\frac{12}{5} + \frac{12}{5} & -\frac{4}{5} + \frac{9}{5} \end{pmatrix} = \begin{pmatrix} 1 & 0 \\ 0 & 1 \end{pmatrix}$$

$$\mathbf{AB} = \begin{pmatrix} 1 & 0 \\ 0 & 1 \end{pmatrix} = \mathbf{I} = \text{unit matrix.}$$

The use of finding the inverse matrix is to multiply the matrix $\mathbf{A}$ by its inverse and find that $(\mathbf{AA}^{-1} = \mathbf{I})$ it is equal to unit matrix.

d. Solves simultaneous linear equations with two unknowns by means of matrices.

Solve $\qquad 3x - y = 9$

$$-4x + 3y = -7$$

by means of matrices

In matrix form these two equations may be written as

$$\begin{pmatrix} 3 & -1 \\ -4 & 3 \end{pmatrix}\begin{pmatrix} x \\ y \end{pmatrix} = \begin{pmatrix} 9 \\ -7 \end{pmatrix}$$

Check by finding the product of the left hand side.

$$\begin{pmatrix} 3 & -1 \\ -4 & 3 \end{pmatrix}\begin{pmatrix} x \\ y \end{pmatrix} = \begin{pmatrix} 3x - y \\ -4x + 3y \end{pmatrix}$$

$\quad 2 \times 2 \qquad 2 \times 1 \qquad 2 \times 1$
$\qquad\qquad\qquad\qquad$ answer

Equating the matrices $\begin{pmatrix} 3x - y \\ -4x + 3y \end{pmatrix} = \begin{pmatrix} 9 \\ 7 \end{pmatrix}$

we have

$$3x - y = 9$$
$$-4x + 3y = -7$$

$$\mathbf{A}^{-1}\begin{pmatrix} 3 & -1 \\ -4 & 3 \end{pmatrix}\begin{pmatrix} x \\ y \end{pmatrix} = \mathbf{A}^{-1}\begin{pmatrix} 9 \\ -7 \end{pmatrix}.$$

If $\quad \mathbf{A} = \begin{pmatrix} 3 & -1 \\ -4 & 3 \end{pmatrix}$ then $\quad \mathbf{A}^{-1}\begin{pmatrix} \frac{3}{5} & \frac{1}{5} \\ \frac{4}{5} & \frac{3}{5} \end{pmatrix}$

premultiply each side above by $\mathbf{A}^{-1}$

$$\mathbf{A}^{-1}\begin{pmatrix} 3 & -1 \\ -4 & 3 \end{pmatrix}\begin{pmatrix} x \\ y \end{pmatrix} = \mathbf{A}^{-1}\begin{pmatrix} 9 \\ -7 \end{pmatrix}$$

$$I\begin{pmatrix} x \\ y \end{pmatrix} = \begin{pmatrix} \frac{3}{5} & \frac{1}{5} \\ \frac{4}{5} & \frac{3}{5} \end{pmatrix}\begin{pmatrix} 9 \\ -7 \end{pmatrix}$$

$$\begin{pmatrix} x \\ y \end{pmatrix} = \begin{pmatrix} \frac{27}{5} - \frac{7}{5} \\ \frac{36}{5} - \frac{21}{5} \end{pmatrix} = \begin{pmatrix} \frac{20}{5} \\ \frac{15}{5} \end{pmatrix}$$

$$\begin{pmatrix} x \\ y \end{pmatrix} = \begin{pmatrix} 4 \\ 3 \end{pmatrix}$$

$x = 4 \qquad y = 3.$

e. Relates the use of matrices to simple technical problems.

An example using h-parameters.

The hybrid parameters or h-parameters of a network are given in a matrix form as

$$\begin{pmatrix} h_{11} & h_{12} \\ h_{12} & h_{22} \end{pmatrix}$$

The input voltage and the output current of a network are expressed in terms of the input current and the output voltage

$$V_1 = I_1 h_{11} + h_{12}V_2$$
$$I_2 = I_1 h_{21} + h_{22}V_2$$

these equations can be written in matrix form as

$$\begin{pmatrix} V_1 \\ I_2 \end{pmatrix} = \begin{pmatrix} h_{11} & h_{12} \\ h_{21} & h_{22} \end{pmatrix}\begin{pmatrix} I_1 \\ V_2 \end{pmatrix}.$$

The a.c. equivalent circuit of an a.c. amplifier using h-parameters is given

$$v_{be} = h_{ie}i_b + h_{re}v_{ce}$$
$$i_c = h_{fe}i_b + h_{oe}v_{ce}$$

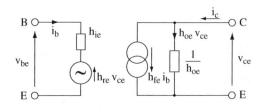

Fig. 46

An example using Kirchoff's laws

$$V_1 = I_1 r_1 + (I_1 + I_2)R_L$$

$$V_1 = I_1(r_1 + R_L) + I_2 R_L$$

$$V_2 = I_2 r_2 + (I_1 + I_2)R_L$$

$$V_2 = I_1 R_L + I_2(r_2 + R_L)$$

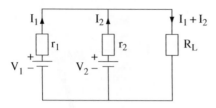

$$V_1 = I_1(r_1 + R_L) + I_2 R_L$$

$$V_2 = I_1 r_1 + I_2(r_2 + R_L)$$

These equations in matrix form are written

$$\begin{pmatrix} V_1 \\ V_2 \end{pmatrix} = \begin{pmatrix} r_1 + R_L & R_L \\ r_1 & r_2 + R_L \end{pmatrix} \begin{pmatrix} I_1 \\ I_2 \end{pmatrix}.$$

To find I_1 and I_2, we have to find first the inverse matrix of

$$\begin{pmatrix} r_1 + R_L & R_L \\ r_1 & r_2 + R_L \end{pmatrix} = \mathbf{M}$$

pre-multiplying by $\mathbf{M}^{-1}$

$$\mathbf{M}^{-1} \begin{pmatrix} V_1 \\ V_2 \end{pmatrix} = \mathbf{M}^{-1} \mathbf{M} \begin{pmatrix} I_1 \\ I_2 \end{pmatrix}$$

and hence I_1 and I_2 may be calculated.

Exercises 6

(1) Solve the following simultaneous linear equations:-

(i) $2x - y = 5$
$x + y = -7$

(ii) $-3x + 2y = 2$
$x - 3y = 5$

using the elimination and substitution method of algebra.

(2) Solve the simultaneous linear equations of question (1) using determinants.

(3) Write down the minors and hence the cofactors of the matrices:

(i) $A = \begin{pmatrix} 1 & 2 \\ 3 & 4 \end{pmatrix}$

and

(ii) $\mathbf{M} = \begin{pmatrix} -1 & -2 \\ -3 & 4 \end{pmatrix}$.

(4) Determine the adjoint matrices of 3(i) and 3(ii).

(5) Find the inverse matrices of the following

(i) $\begin{pmatrix} 2 & -1 \\ 2 & 1 \end{pmatrix}$

(ii) $\begin{pmatrix} -3 & 2 \\ 1 & -3 \end{pmatrix}$.

(6) Solve the simultaneous linear equations of question (1) using matrices.

(7) Determine the currents I_1 and I_2 of the network using

(i) Determinants.

(ii) Matrices.

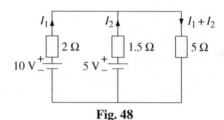

Fig. 48

(8) Determine

(i) $\dfrac{v_{ce}}{v_{be}}$

(ii) $\dfrac{i_c}{i_b}$ for the network

where $v_{ce} = -1000 i_c$.

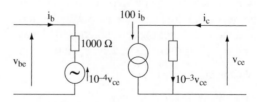

Fig. 49

7

Binomial theorem

Understands and uses the binomial theorem.

a. Expands expressions of the form $(a + x)^n$ for small positive integer n.

b. States the general form for the binomial coefficients for all positive integer n.

c. Expands expressions of the form $(1 + x)^n$ where n takes positive, negative or fractional values.

d. States the range of values of x for which the series is convergent.

e. Calculates the effect on the subject of a formula when one or more of the independent variables is subject to a small change or error.

Binomial expansion (Sir Isaac Newton 1642-1727).

BINOMIAL is an expression containing two terms from basic algebra we have learnt that the expansion $(a+b)^2 = (a+b)(a+b) = a^2+ab+ab+b^2$ and therefore $(a+b)^2 = a^2+2ab+b^2$, the student should remember this expansion, that is, the squared of the first term (a) plus twice the product of the first term (a) and second term (b) plus the squared of the second term (b), namely $(a + b)^2 = a^2 + 2ab + b^2$ there are three terms.

What is the expansion of $(a + b)^3$?

$$(a + b)^3 = (a + b)^2(a + b)$$
$$= (a^2 + 2ab + b^2)(a + b)$$

$$= a^3 + 2a^2b + ab^2 + a^2b + 2ab^2 + b^3$$

$(a + b)^3 = a^3 + 3a^2b + 3ab^2 + b^3$, there are four terms

The expansion of $a + b$ to a power greater than three can be found. The binomial expansion for $(1 + x)^n$ is stated:-

$$(1 + x)^n = 1 + nx + \frac{n(n - 1)}{1 \times 2}x^2$$

$$+ \frac{n(n - 1)(n - 2)}{1 \times 2 \times 3}x^3 + \ldots + x^n.$$

There are $n + 1$ terms if n is a positive integer, but there are infinite terms if n is not a positive integer and x lies between -1 and $+1$.

The binomial expansion for simple positive integer values of n and including the general x^r is given.

$$(1 + x)^n = 1 + nx + \frac{n(n - 1)}{1 \times 2}x^2$$

$$+ \frac{n(n - 1)(n - 2)}{1 \times 2 \times 3}x^3 + \ldots$$

$$+ \frac{\left(\begin{array}{c}n(n - 1)(n - 2) \\ \ldots [n - (r - 1)]\end{array}\right)x^r}{1 \times 2 \times 3 \times \ldots x^r} + \ldots + x^n$$

Note that 1×2 can be written as 2! (factorial two)

$1 \times 2 \times 3 = 3!$ (factorial three), $1 \times 2 \times 3 \times \ldots \times n = n!$ (factorial n). The above expansion can be written as

$$(1+x)^n = \frac{1x^0}{0!} + \frac{n}{1!}x^1$$

$$+ \frac{n(n-1)}{2!}x^2$$

$$+ \frac{n(n-1)(n-3)}{3!}x^3 + \dots$$

$$+ \frac{n(n-1)\dots[n-(r-1)]x^r}{r!}$$

$$+ \dots + \frac{n!x^n}{n!}$$

The following observations are made:-

1. The powers of x are in ascending order $0, 1, 2, \dots, n$.

2. The factorial number is the same as that of the power.

3. The coefficients of x^3 are three factors $n(n-1)(n-2)$ that of x^5 are $n(n-1)(n-2)(n-3)(n-4)$, five factors.

The expansion is written simply as:-

$$(1+x)^n = 1 + nx + \frac{n(n-1)}{2!}x^2$$

$$+ \frac{n(n-1)(n-2)}{3!}x^3 + \dots$$

$$+ \frac{n(n-1)\dots[n-(r-1)]x^r}{r!} + \dots + x^n.$$

Obtains the coefficients of the powers of x using Pascal's triangle.

Blaise Pascal (1623-1662). The following expansions are written by referring to the Pascal's triangle.

$$(1+x)^0 = 1$$

$$(1+x)^1 = 1 + x$$

$$(1+x)^2 = 1 + 2x + x^2$$

$$(1+x)^3 = 1 + 3x + 3x^2 + x^3$$

$$(1+x)^4 = 1 + 4x + 6x^2 + 4x^3 + x^4$$

$$(1+x)^5 = 1 + 5x + 10x^3 + 5x^4 + x^5$$

$$(1+x)^6 = 1 + 6x + 15x^2 + 20x^3 + 15x^4$$

$$+ 6x^5 + x^6$$

$$(1+x)^7 = 1 + 7x + 21x^2 + 35x^3 + 35x^4$$

$$+ 21x^5 + 7x^6 + x^7$$

$$(1+x)^8 = 1 + 8x + 28x^2 + 56x^3 + 70x^4$$

$$+ 56x^5 + 28x^6 + 8x^7 + x^8$$

$$(1+x)^9 = 1 + 9x + 36x^2 + 84x^3 + 126x^4$$

$$+ 126x^5 + 84x^6 + 36x^7 + 9x^8 + x^9$$

$$(1+x)^{10} = 1 + 10x + 45x^2 + 120x^3$$

$$+ 210x^4 + 252x^5 + 210x^6$$

$$+ 120x^7 + 45x^8 + 10x^9 + x^{10}.$$

Pascal's triangle.

```
                 1
               1   1
             1   2   1
           1   3   3   1
         1   4   6   4   1
       1   5  10  10   5   1
     1   6  15  20  15   6   1
   1   7  21  35  35  21   7   1
 1   8  28  56  70  56  28   8   1
1  9  36  84 126 126  84  36   9   1
1 10 45 120 210 252 210 120  45  10  1
```

The following can be observed from the above triangle:

1. We write ones along the sides of the triangle.

2. The first 1 is the answer to the expansion $(1+x)^0 = 1$, any number raised to the power nought is unity.

3. The second row are the coefficients of $(1+x)' = 1 + x$, the coefficient of x is unity and that of $x°$ is 1.

4. The third row shows the coefficients of the expansion $(1+x)^2 = 1 + 2x + x^2$, the coefficient of $x°$ is 1, the coefficient of x^1 is 2 and the coefficient of x^2 is unity.

5. The fourth row has coefficients 1, 3, 3 and 1, the 3 is derived by adding 1 and 2 from the third row as indicated by the upward arrows and so on. Pascal's triangle enables us to write down the binomial expansion upto the $n = 10$ without very much trouble for value of n greater than 10, Newton's expansion is much easier.

WORKED EXAMPLE 36

Expand $(1 + x)^4$, $(1 + x)^5$, $(1 + x)^6$, $(1 + x)^7$, $(1 + x)^8$, $(1 + x)^9$, $(1 + x)^{10}$ using Newton's expansion method.

Solution 36

$$(1 + x)^4 = 1 + 4x + \frac{4 \times 3}{1 \times 2}x^2 + \frac{4 \times 3 \times 2}{1 \times 2 \times 3}x^3$$

$$+ \frac{4 \times 3 \times 2 \times 1}{1 \times 2 \times 3 \times 4}x^4$$

$$= 1 + 4x + 6x^2 + 4x^3 + x^4$$

$$(1 + x)^5 = 1 + 5x + \frac{5 \times 4}{1 \times 2}x^2 + \frac{5 \times 4 \times 3}{1 \times 2 \times 3}x^3$$

$$+ \frac{5 \times 4 \times 3 \times 2}{1 \times 2 \times 3 \times 4}x^4 + x^5$$

$$= 1 + 5x + 10x^2 + 10x^3 + 5x^4 + x^5$$

$$(1 + x)^6 = 1 + 6x + \frac{6 \times 5}{1 \times 2}x^2 + \frac{6 \times 5 \times 4}{1 \times 2 \times 3}x^3$$

$$+ \frac{6 \times 5 \times 4}{1 \times 2 \times 3}x^4$$

$$+ \frac{6 \times 5 \times 4 \times 3}{1 \times 2 \times 3 \times 4}x^5 + x^6$$

$$= 1 + 6x + 15x^2 + 20x^3 + 20x^4$$

$$+ 15x^5 + x^6$$

$$(1 + x)^7 = 1 + 7x + 21x^2 + 35x^3 + 35x^4$$

$$+ 21x^5 + 7x^6 + x^7$$

$$(1 + x)^8 = 1 + 8x + \frac{8 \times 7}{1 \times 2}x^2 + \frac{8 \times 7 \times 6}{1 \times 2 \times 3}x^3$$

$$+ \frac{8 \times 7 \times 6 \times 5}{1 \times 2 \times 3 \times 4}x^4$$

$$+ \frac{8 \times 7 \times 6 \times 5 \times 4}{1 \times 2 \times 3 \times 4 \times 5}x^5$$

$$+ \frac{8 \times 7 \times 6 \times 5 \times 4 \times 3}{1 \times 2 \times 3 \times 4 \times 5 \times 6}x^6$$

$$+ \frac{8 \times 7 \times 6 \times 5 \times 4 \times 3 \times 2}{1 \times 2 \times 3 \times 4 \times 5 \times 6 \times 7}x^7 + x^8$$

$$= 1 + 8x + 28x^2 + 56x^3 + 70x^4 +$$

$$56x^5 + 28x^6 + 8x^7 + x^8$$

$$(1 + x)^9 = 1 + 9x + \frac{9 \times 8}{1 \times 2}x^2 + \frac{9 \times 8 \times 7}{1 \times 2 \times 3}x^3$$

$$+ \frac{9 \times 8 \times 7 \times 6}{1 \times 2 \times 3 \times 4}x^4$$

$$+ \frac{9 \times 8 \times 7 \times 6 \times 5}{1 \times 2 \times 3 \times 4 \times 5}x^5$$

$$+ \frac{9 \times 8 \times 7 \times 6 \times 5 \times 4}{1 \times 2 \times 3 \times 4 \times 5 \times 6}x^6$$

$$+ \frac{9 \times 8 \times 7 \times 6 \times 5 \times 4 \times 3}{1 \times 2 \times 3 \times 4 \times 5 \times 6 \times 7}x^7$$

$$+ \frac{(9 \times 8 \times 7 \times 6 \times 5 \times 4 \times 3 \times 2)}{(1 \times 2 \times 3 \times 4 \times 5 \times 6 \times 7 \times 8)}x^8 + x^9$$

$$= 1 + 9x + 36x^2 + 84x^3 + 126x^4 +$$

$$126x^5 + 84x^6 + 36x^7 + 9x^8 + x^9$$

$$(1 + x)^{10} = 1 + 10x + 45x^2 + 120x^3 +$$

$$210x^4 + 252x^5 + 210x^6 + 120x^7 +$$

$$45x^8 + 10x^9 + x^{10}.$$

Rewrites $(a + bx)^n = a^n(1 + z)^n$ where $z = \frac{b}{a}x$ and hence expands more general binomial expressions.

$$(a + bx)^n = \left[a(1 + \frac{b}{a}x)\right]^n = a^n\left(1 + \frac{b}{a}x\right)^n$$

$$= a^n(1 + z)^n$$

where $z = \frac{b}{a}x$.

WORKED EXAMPLE 37

Expand the following Binomial expressions:
  (i) $(x + 2y)^4$
  (ii) $(3x - 2y)^5$ using the above technique.

Solution 37

(i) $(x+2y)^4 = \left[x\left(1 + 2\dfrac{y}{x}\right)\right]^4 = x^4(1+z)^4$

where $z = 2\dfrac{y}{x}$

$(1 + z)^4 = 1 + 4z + 6z^2 + 4z^3 + z^4$

therefore $(x + 2y)^4 = x^4(1 + z)^4$

$$= x^4(1 + 4z + 6z^2 + 4z^3z^4)$$

$$= x^4\left[1 + 4\left(\frac{2y}{x}\right) + 6\left(\frac{2y}{x}\right)^2\right.$$

$$\left. + 4\left(\frac{2y}{x}\right)^3 + \left(\frac{2y}{x}\right)^4\right]$$

$$= x^4\left[1 + 8\frac{y}{x} + 24\frac{y^2}{x^2} + 32\frac{y^3}{x^3} + 16\frac{y^4}{x^4}\right]$$

$$= x^4 + 8yx^3 + 24y^2x^2 + 32y^3x + 16y^4$$

(ii) $(3x - 2y)^5 = \left[3x\left(1 - \dfrac{2y}{3x}\right)\right]^5$

$$= 3^5 x^5\left[1 + \left(\frac{-2y}{3x}\right)\right]^5$$

$(1+z)^5 = 1+5z+10z^2+10z^3+5z^4+z^5$

$$= 1 + 5\left(\frac{-2y}{3x}\right) + 10\left(\frac{-2y}{3x}\right)^2$$

$$+ 10\left(\frac{-2y}{3x}\right)^3 + 5\left(\frac{2y}{3x}\right)^4 + \left(\frac{-2y}{3x}\right)^5$$

$$= 1 - \frac{10y}{3x} + \frac{40}{9}\frac{y^2}{x^2} - \frac{80}{27}\frac{y^3}{x^3}$$

$$+ \frac{80}{81}\frac{y^4}{x^4} - \frac{32}{243}\frac{y^5}{x^5}$$

$(3x - 2y)^5$

$$= 243\, x^5\left(1 - \frac{10}{3}\frac{y}{x} + \frac{40}{9}\frac{y^2}{x^2}\right.$$

$$\left. - \frac{80}{27}\frac{y^3}{x^3} + \frac{80}{81}\frac{y^4}{x^4} - \frac{32}{243}\frac{y^5}{x^5}\right)$$

$$= 243x^5 - 810yx^4 + 1080y^2x^3$$

$$- 720x^2y^3 + 240y^4x - 32y^5.$$

Obtains the first few terms of the infinite expansions of $(1 + x)^n$ which pertain when n is other than a positive integer.

The expansion of $(1+x)^n$ when n is not a positive integer, is an infinite series of terms.

$$(1 + x)^n = 1 + nx + n(n - 1)\frac{x^2}{2!}$$

$$+ n(n - 1)(n - 2)\frac{x^3}{3!} + \dots$$

the values of x are small and lie between -1 and $+1$, that is,

$$-1 < x < 1.$$

WORKED EXAMPLE 38

Obtain the first five terms of the infinite series expansion of $\sqrt{\dfrac{1+x}{1-x}}$.

Solution 38

$$\sqrt{\frac{1+x}{1-x}} = \frac{(1+x)^{\frac{1}{2}}}{(1-x)^{\frac{1}{2}}} = (1+x)^{\frac{1}{2}}(1-x)^{-\frac{1}{2}}$$

where

$$(1 + x)^{\frac{1}{2}} = 1 + \frac{1}{2}x + \frac{1}{2}\left(\frac{1}{2} - 1\right)x^2\frac{1}{2!}$$

$$+ \frac{1}{2}\left(\frac{1}{2} - 1\right)\left(\frac{1}{2} - 2\right)x^3\frac{1}{3!}$$

$$+ \frac{1}{2}\left(\frac{1}{2} - 1\right)\left(\frac{1}{2} - 2\right)\left(\frac{1}{2} - 3\right)x^4\frac{1}{4!}$$

$$= 1 + \frac{1}{2}x - \frac{1}{8}x^2 + \frac{1}{16}x^3 - \frac{5}{128}x^4$$

$$(1-x)^{-\frac{1}{2}} = 1 + \left(-\frac{1}{2}\right)(-x) + \left(\frac{-1}{2} - 1\right)$$

$$\times (-x)^2 \frac{1}{2!} + \left(-\frac{1}{2}\right)\left(-\frac{1}{2}-1\right)\left(-\frac{1}{2}-2\right)$$

$$\times (-x)^3 \frac{1}{3!} + \left(-\frac{1}{2}\right)\left(-\frac{1}{2}-1\right)\left(-\frac{1}{2}-2\right)$$

$$\times \left(-\frac{1}{2} - 3\right)(-x)^4 \frac{1}{4!}$$

$$= 1 + \frac{1}{2}x + \frac{3}{8}x^2 + \frac{5}{16}x^3 + \frac{35}{128}x^4.$$

$$(1+x)^{\frac{1}{2}}(1-x)^{-\frac{1}{2}} = 1 + \frac{1}{2}x + \frac{3}{8}x^2 + \frac{5}{16}x^3$$

$$+ \frac{1}{2}x + \frac{1}{2}x^2 + \frac{3}{16}x^3 + \frac{5}{32}x^4 - \frac{1}{8}x^2 - \frac{1}{16}x^3$$

$$- \frac{3}{64}x^4 + \frac{1}{16}x^3 + \frac{1}{32}x^4 - \frac{5}{128}x^2$$

$$= 1 + x + \frac{1}{2}x^2 + \frac{1}{2}x^3 + \frac{13}{128}x^4.$$

WORKED EXAMPLE 39

Write down the first four terms in the binomial expansion of the following:-

(i) $(1-x)^{-2}$

(ii) $\left(1 + \frac{1}{3}x\right)^{-3}$

(iii) $(3-x)^{\frac{1}{2}}$.

Solution 39

(i) $(1-x)^{-2} = 1 + (-2)(-x)$

$$+ (-2)(-3)(-x)^2 \frac{1}{2}$$

$$+ (-2)(-3)(-4)(-x)^3 \frac{1}{2 \times 3}$$

$$= 1 + 2x + 3x^2 + 4x^3$$

(ii) $\left(1 + \frac{1}{3}x\right)^{-3} = 1 + (-3)\left(\frac{1}{3}x\right)$

$$+ (-3)(-4)\left(\frac{1}{3}x^2\right)\frac{1}{2}$$

$$+ (-3)(-4)(-5)\left(\frac{1}{3}x\right)^3 \frac{1}{1 \times 2 \times 3}$$

$$= 1 - x + \frac{2}{3}x^2 - \frac{10}{27}x^3$$

(iii) $(3-x)^{\frac{1}{2}} = 3^{\frac{1}{2}}\left(1 - \frac{x}{3}\right)^{\frac{1}{2}}$

$$= 3^{\frac{1}{2}}\left(1 + \left(\frac{1}{2}\right)\right)\left(-\frac{x}{3}\right)$$

$$+ \left(\frac{1}{2}\right)\left(-\frac{1}{2}\right)\left(-\frac{x}{3}\right)^2 \frac{1}{2}$$

$$+ \frac{1}{2}\left(-\frac{1}{2}\right)\frac{\left(-\frac{3}{2}\right)\left(-\frac{x}{3}\right)^3}{3!}$$

$$= 3^{\frac{1}{2}}\left(1 - \frac{x}{6} - \frac{1}{72}x^2 - \frac{1}{216}x^3\right).$$

Obtain similar expansions for $(a + bx)^n$ states the validity condition for such infinite expansions.

$$(a + bx)^n = \left[a\left[1 + \frac{bx}{a}\right]\right]^n$$

$$= a^n \left[1 + \frac{bx}{a}\right]^n = a^n(1+z)^n$$

where $z = \dfrac{bx}{a}$ and n is not a positive integer

$$(1+z)^n = 1 + nz + n(n-1)z^2 \frac{1}{2!}$$

$$+ n(n-1)(n-2)z^3 \frac{1}{3!} + \ldots$$

which is an infinite series of expansion.

WORKED EXAMPLE 40

Find the first four terms in the expansion $(3 - 2x)^{-2}$ as a series in ascending powers of x, and write down the first four terms in the expansion of $(3 + 2x)^{-2}$.

Find the range of values for which both the above expansions are valid.

Solution 40

$$(3 - 2x)^{-2} = 3^{-2}\left[1 - 2\frac{x}{3}\right]^{-2}$$

$$= \frac{1}{9}\left[1 - 2\frac{x}{3}\right]^{-2}$$

$$\left[1 - 2\frac{x}{3}\right]^{-2} = 1 + (-2)\left[-2\frac{x}{3}\right]$$

$$+ (-2)(-3)\left[-2\frac{x}{3}\right]^2\frac{1}{2!}$$

$$+ (-2)(-3)(-4)\left[-2\frac{x}{3}\right]^3\frac{1}{3!}$$

$$= 1 + \frac{4}{3}x + \frac{4}{3}x^2 + \frac{32}{27}x^3.$$

$$(3 - 2x)^{-2} = \frac{1}{9}\left[1 + \frac{4}{3}x + \frac{4}{3}x^2 + \frac{32}{27}x^3\right]$$

$$= \frac{1}{9} + \frac{4}{27}x + \frac{4}{27}x^2 + \frac{32}{243}x^3.$$

The expansion is valid for values of x such that

$$-1 < \frac{-2x}{3} < 1 \text{ from which } -1 < -\frac{2x}{3}$$

$$\text{and } \frac{-2x}{3} < 1$$

$$-1 < -2\frac{x}{3}, 1 > 2\frac{x}{3} \text{ or } x < \frac{3}{2}$$

$$-\frac{2x}{3} < 1, -2x < 3, \text{ or } x > -\frac{3}{2}$$

therefore $-\frac{3}{2} < x < \frac{3}{2}$, that is, x lies between

$-\frac{3}{2}$ and $\frac{3}{2}$.

$$(3 + 2x)^{-2} = \frac{1}{9} - \frac{4}{27}x + \frac{4}{27}x^2 - \frac{32}{243}x^3$$

the signs change from the previous expansion except the first term which remains at $\frac{1}{9}$.

This expansion is valid for values of x such that

$$-1 < \frac{2x}{3} < 1 \text{ or for } -\frac{3}{2} < x < \frac{3}{2}.$$

Therefore x lies between $-\frac{3}{2}$ and $\frac{3}{2}$ for both expansions.

Applies the binomial theorem to the calculation of certain roots to a desired degree of accuracy and to the simplification of certain formulae by first or second order approximations.

We have seen that the binomial theorem is

$$(1 + x)^n = 1 + nx + n(n - 1)x^2\frac{1}{2!}$$

$$+ n(n - 1)(n - 2)x^3\frac{1}{3!} + \ldots$$

an infinite series when n is not a positive integer and x lies between -1 and $+1$.

If $x < 1$ then we can approximate the

expansion $(1 + x)^n \approx 1 + nx + n(n - 1)\frac{x^2}{2}$

a second order approximate or further still to a first order approximation $(1 + x)^n = 1 + nx$.

WORKED EXAMPLE 41

Use the binomial theorem to find the value to five significant figures of

  (i) $(1.003)^{-\frac{1}{5}}$

  (ii) $(1.02)^{\frac{1}{4}}$

  (iii) $(1.0001)^{-\frac{1}{7}}$.

Solution 41

$$(i)(1.003)^{-\frac{1}{5}} = (1 + 0.003)^{-\frac{1}{5}}$$

$$= 1 + \left[-\frac{1}{5}\right](0.003)$$

$$+ \left[-\frac{1}{5}\right]\left[-\frac{1}{5} - 1\right](0.003)^2\frac{1}{2!}$$

$(1.003)^{-\frac{1}{5}} \approx 1 - \dfrac{1}{5}0.003$

$$+ \left[-\dfrac{1}{5}\right]\left[-\dfrac{6}{5}\right]0.000009\left[\dfrac{1}{2}\right]$$

$$= 1 - 0.0006 + \dfrac{6}{25 \times 2} \times 0.000009$$

$$= 1 - 0.0006 + 0.00000108$$

$$\approx 0.9994011 \approx 0.9994011 \text{ to five}$$
significant figures.

If we use $(1+x)^n \approx 1 + nx$

$$(1 + 0.003)^{-\frac{1}{5}} \approx 1 - \dfrac{1}{5}0.003$$

$$= 1 - 0.0006 = 0.9994$$

so in this case we used the first order approximation it would have been sufficient to obtain an accuracy to five significant figures.

If the answer were required to seven significant figures, we should take the second order approximation

$(1.003)^{-\frac{1}{5}} \approx 0.9994016 \approx 0.999402.$

The calculator gives $(1.003)^{-\frac{1}{5}} = 0.999401.$

Exercises 7

1. Write down the first three terms in the expansion, in ascending powers of x for the following binomial expressions:-

   (i) $(1 - 5x)^{-3}$

   (ii) $(1 + 3x)^{\frac{3}{4}}$

   (iii) $(1 - 4x)^{-\frac{1}{3}}$

   (iv) $(1 - x)^{\frac{1}{2}}$

   (v) $(1 + x)^{-\frac{1}{2}}.$

2. Find the first three non-zero terms in the expansions in ascending powers of x:

   (i) $(1 + px)^n$
   (ii) $(1 - px)^{-n}$
   (iii) $(1 + 3ax)^{-n}$
   (iv) $(1 - 2bx)^n$
   (v) $(1 - bx)^{+n}.$

3. Find the first three non-zero terms in the following expansions, in ascending powers of y:

   (i) $\sqrt{\dfrac{1 - y}{1 + y}}$

   (ii) $\dfrac{1}{\sqrt{1 - y^2}}$

   (iii) $\sqrt{9 + ay}$

   (iv) $\dfrac{1}{\sqrt{16 - by}}.$

4. Expand $(25 + x)^{\frac{1}{2}}$ in ascending powers of x up to and including the term in x^3.

5. Expand in ascending powers of x up to and including the term in x^3.

   (i) $(1 + 2x)^{\frac{1}{3}}$

   (ii) $(1 - 3x)^{-\frac{1}{5}}.$

   Given that $(1 + 2x)^{\frac{1}{3}} + 25(1 - 3x)^{-\frac{1}{5}}$

   $= a + bx + cx^2 + dx^3 + \ldots$, find the numerical values of $a, b, c,$ and d.

6. Find the coefficients of x^3 in the expansions:

   (i) $(1 + 2x)^{\frac{1}{2}}(1 - 3x)^{-\frac{1}{2}}$

   (ii) $(1 - x)^{-\frac{1}{2}}(1 + x)^{-\frac{1}{2}}$

   (iii) $\dfrac{1 - x}{(1 + x)^3}.$

7. Expand $(1 - 7x)^{-\frac{1}{3}}$ in ascending powers of x up to and including the terms in x^3.

8. Write down the term containing b^r in the binomial expansion of $(a + b)^n$ where n is a positive integer.

9. Write down the coefficient of x^{25} in the binomial expansion of $(1 - 3x)^{37}$.

10. The period T of a simple pendulum is given by the formula $T = 2\pi\sqrt{\dfrac{l}{g}}$ where l is the length of the pendulum and g is the acceleration due to gravity.

    It is required to calculate g from the formula above.

If errors of $+1\%$ in T and -0.5% in l are made, use the binomial expansions to determine the percentage error in the calculated value g, giving your answer correct to three decimal places.

11. It is required to determine l from the formula
$$f = k\frac{\sqrt{w}}{l}$$
If errors of -2% in l and $+1\%$ in w are made, use the binomial expansion, to find the percentage error in the calculated value of f. (Hint expand $(1+x)^{\frac{1}{2}}$ and $(1-2x)^{-1}$ in ascending powers of x up to and including the term in x^2).

12. Write down and simplify the first four terms in the expansion of $(1+x)^n$ in ascending powers of x when $n = 3$, $n = -3$ and when $n = -\frac{1}{3}$.

13. Find correct to 4 decimal places the values of

   (i) $\dfrac{1}{(1.005)^3}$ (ii) $\sqrt[3]{27.003}$

   (iii) $(1.05)^{\frac{1}{5}}$ (iv) $0.995^{-\frac{1}{3}}$.

14. Express (i) $(1+x)^{\frac{1}{2}}$ and (ii) $(1-x)^{-3}$ as series of ascending powers of x, in each case up to and including the term in x^2.

   Hence show that, if x is small
   $$\frac{(1+x)^{\frac{1}{2}}}{(1-x)^3} = 1 + \frac{7}{2}x + \frac{59}{8}x^2.$$

   Calculate the percentage change which occurs in the value of $\frac{w^{\frac{1}{2}}}{z^3}$ if w is increased by 1% and z is decreased by 1%.

15. Expand $(1+bx)^{-n}$ in ascending power of x up to and including the term in x^3. Given that the first four terms are $1 + 5x + 9x^2 + ax^3$, calculate the values of the constants a, b and n.

16. Find the term independent of x in the

   expansion of $\left[x - \dfrac{1}{x^2}\right]^5 \left[x + \dfrac{1}{x}\right]^9$.

17. Use the binomial Theorem to find the value, correct to five significant figures, of $(1.003)^{15}$.

18. Find the coefficient of x^4 in the expansion of $(3 - ax)^8$

   Find the coefficient of x^4 in the expansion of $(2a - x)^7$.

   If the two coefficients are equal find the non-zero value of a.

19. Expand $\left[1 + \dfrac{1}{3}x\right]^{-3}$ as far as the term in x^4. Hence, or otherwise, obtain the coefficient of x^4 in the expansion of $(1 - x - x^3)\left[1 + \dfrac{1}{3}x\right]^{-3}$, the values of x being such as to make the expansions valid.

20. Write down the first four terms in the binomial expansion of $(1 - x)^{-2}$.

21. Find the non-zero value of a if the coefficient of x^3 in the expansion of $(a - x)^5$ is equal to the coefficient of x^3 in the expansion of $(3 - ax)^7$.

8

The exponential function.

Uses the series expansion of the exponential function.

a. States the expansion of e^x in a power series.

b. Deduces the expansion of e^{-x}.

c. States that the expansions are convergent for all x.

d. Deduces the expansion of ae^{kx} where k is positive or negative.

e. Deduces the series for e and evaluates e four decimal places.

Exponential function is a constant raised to a variable x, that is, a^x is an exponential function where 'a' is, a constant and x is a variable, specifically when the constant e is raised to x.

a. The Expansion of e^x.

$$e^x = 1 + \frac{x}{1!} + \frac{x^2}{2!} + \frac{x^3}{3!} + \frac{x^4}{4!} + \frac{x^5}{5!} + \ldots + \frac{x^r}{r!} + \ldots$$

where $r!$ (read as r factorial).

FACTORIAL

$r! = 1 \times 2 \times 3 \times 4 \times \ldots (r-1)r$

$5! = 1 \times 2 \times 3 \times 4 \times 5$

$4! = 1 \times 2 \times 3 \times 4$

$3! = 1 \times 2 \times 3$

$2! = 1 \times 2$

$1! = 1$.

The first term of this power series is actually $\frac{x^o}{0!}$ where $x^0 = 1$ and $0! = 1$, to show that $0! = 1$, we have.

$r! = 1 \times 2 \times 3 \times \ldots (r-1)r = (r-1)! \, r$.

If $r = 1$, $\quad 1! = (1-1)! \, 1$

and therefore $1! = 0! = 1$.

This infinite series is called power series since the powers of x are increasing by $1, 0, 1, 2, 3, 4, \ldots$, the powers are ascending.

If $x = 1$ then

$$e^1 = 1 + \frac{1}{1!} + \frac{1}{2!} + \frac{1}{3!} + \frac{1}{4!} + \frac{1}{5!} + \ldots$$

$$= 1 + 1 + 0.5 + \frac{1}{6} + \frac{1}{24} + \frac{1}{120} + \frac{1}{720} + \ldots$$

If we sum all these terms to infinity e will be equal $e = 2.718281828$.

b. Deduces the expansion of e^{-x}.

If x is replaced by $-x$

$$e^{-x} = 1 + \frac{(-x)}{1!} + \frac{(-x)^2}{2!} + \frac{(-x)^3}{3!} + \frac{(-x)^4}{4!} + \ldots$$

$$= 1 - \frac{x}{1!} + \frac{x^2}{2!} - \frac{x^3}{3!} + \frac{x^4}{4!} + \ldots + (-1)^r \frac{x^r}{r!}$$

the general term of this expansion is $(-1)^r \dfrac{x^r}{r!}$

because if $r = 2$, then $(-1)^2 \dfrac{x^2}{2!}$, the third term

if $r = 3$ then $(-1)^3 \dfrac{x^3}{3!} = -\dfrac{x^3}{3!}$, the fourth term.

Then which is the fourth term.

c. States that the expansions are convergent for all x.

What is the difference between a convergent and divergent series?

The series $1+2+3+4+\ldots$ summed up to infinity gives a very large or infinite result, this is a divergent series, the series as it progresses it becomes greater and greater, therefore it diverges.

The series
$$1+1+\frac{1}{2}+\frac{1}{6}+\frac{1}{24}+\frac{1}{120}+\frac{1}{720}+\frac{1}{5040}+\ldots$$
as it progresses it becomes smaller and, therefore it converges, that is, the sum of the infinite terms is finite. Therefore the expansions of e^x are convergent for all x.

d. Deduces, the expansions of ae^{kx} where k is positive or negative.

The expansion of ae^{kx} can be similarly stated

$$ae^{kx} = a\left(1 + \frac{kx}{1!} + \frac{(kx)^2}{2!} + \frac{(kx)^3}{3!} + \ldots\right)$$

$$= a\left(1 + \frac{kx}{1!} + \frac{k^2x^2}{2!} + \frac{k^3x^3}{3!} + \ldots\right).$$

If $k = 2, a = 3$

$$3e^{2x} = 3\left(1 + \frac{2x}{1!} + \frac{4x^2}{2!}\left(\frac{4^2}{2!}\right) + \frac{8x^3}{3!} + \ldots\right).$$

If $k = -3, a = 3$

$$3e^{-3x} = 3\left(1 - \frac{3x}{1!} + \frac{9x^2}{2!} - \frac{27x^3}{3!} + \frac{81x^4}{4!} + \ldots\right).$$

e. Deduces the series for e and evaluates e to four decimal places.

$$e^1 = 1 + \frac{1}{1!} + \frac{1}{2!} + \frac{1}{3!} + \frac{1}{4!} + \frac{1}{5!} + \ldots$$

$$e^1 = 1 + 1 + 0.5 + 0.1666666 + 0.0416666$$

$$+ 0.0083333333 + 0.00133888889$$

$$+ 0.000198412 + \ldots$$

$$= 2.7182539 \approx 2.7183.$$

Taking eight terms gives approximately 2.7183 correct to 4 decimal places. The value of e lies between 2 and 3.

The irrational number e.

The number e is not a rational number, that is, it cannot be expressed exactly as a ratio. Such as $\frac{N}{D}$ where N and D are integer numbers. The number e is an irrational a number like $\sqrt{2}, \sqrt{3}, \pi$.

WORKED EXAMPLE 42

Determine the values of the following exponential functions:-

(i) e^{-2} (ii) e^3

(iii) $e^{\frac{1}{4}}$, correct to four decimal places by considering 10 terms of the expansion.

Solution 42

(i) $e^{-2} = 1 + \frac{(-2)}{1} + \frac{(-2)^2}{2!} + \frac{(-2)^3}{3!}$

$$+ \frac{(-2)^4}{4!} + \frac{(-2)^5}{5!} + \frac{(-2)^6}{6!}$$

$$+ \frac{(-2)^7}{7!} + \frac{(-2)^8}{8!} + \frac{(-2)^9}{9!}$$

$$= 1 - 2 + 2 - 1.3333333$$

$$+ 0.66666666 - 0.26666666$$

$$+ 0.0888888 - 0.0253968 + 6.349263$$

$$\times 10^{-3} - 1.4109347 \times 10^{-3}$$

$$= 0.135097 \approx 0.1351.$$

In calculating the above, we perform the calculation as follows:

for example $\frac{(-2)^7}{7!}$ is performed as follows: For the CASIO fx991 MS calculator: ON, $(-2)7 \div 7! = -0.0253968$, that is, press ON, $((-1), 2,),\hat{} 7, \div 7$ shift $x! = -0.0253968$, similarly for all the other numbers, adding up the terms give 0.135097 and correct to four decimal places the answer for $e^{-2} = 0.1351$.

The value of e^{-2} is obtained by shift $\ln(-)2, = 0.1353352$ (directly).

(ii) $e^3 = 1 + \dfrac{3}{1!} + \dfrac{3^2}{2!} + \dfrac{3^3}{3!} + \dfrac{3^4}{4!} + \dfrac{3^5}{5!} + \dfrac{3^6}{6!}$

$\quad + \dfrac{3^7}{7!} + \dfrac{3^8}{8!} + \dfrac{3^9}{9!}$

$\quad = 1 + 3 + 4.5 + 4.5 + 3.375$

$\quad\quad + 2.025 + 1.0125 + 0.4339285$

$\quad\quad + 0.1627232 + 0.054241$

$\quad = 20.063393 \text{ or } 20.0634$

correct to four decimal places.

e^3 directly is found, shift $\ln 3\ =\ $ is 20.085537.

(iii) $e^{\frac{1}{4}} = 1 + \dfrac{\frac{1}{4}}{1!} + \dfrac{(\frac{1}{4})^2}{2!} + \dfrac{(\frac{1}{4})^3}{3!} + \dfrac{(\frac{1}{4})^4}{4!}$

$\quad + \dfrac{(\frac{1}{4})^5}{5!} + \dfrac{(\frac{1}{4})^6}{6!} + \dfrac{(\frac{1}{4})^7}{7!} + \dfrac{(\frac{1}{4})^8}{8!} + \dfrac{(\frac{1}{4})^9}{9!}$

$\quad = 1 + \dfrac{1}{4} + \dfrac{1}{32} + \dfrac{1}{384} + \dfrac{1}{6144}$

$\quad + \dfrac{1}{122880}$ negligible terms

$\quad = 1.2840251 \text{ or } 1.2840 \text{ correct to four}$

decimal places $e^{\frac{1}{4}} = 1.2840254$ by

pressing shift $\ln 0.25$.

WORKED EXAMPLE 43

Write down the first five terms of the expansions of the following exponential functions without evaluating.

(i) $e^{\frac{1}{2}}$ (ii) $e^{-\frac{1}{2}}$ (iii) $e^{\frac{1}{3}}$

(iv) $e^{\frac{1}{5}}$ (v) e^5.

Solutions 43

(i) $e^{\frac{1}{2}} = 1 + \dfrac{\frac{1}{2}}{1!} + \dfrac{(\frac{1}{2})^2}{2!} + \dfrac{(\frac{1}{2})^3}{3!} + \dfrac{(\frac{1}{2})^4}{4!}$

$\quad = 1 + \dfrac{1}{2 \times 1!} + \dfrac{1}{2^2 \times 2!}$

$\quad + \dfrac{1}{2^3 \times 3!} + \dfrac{1}{2^4 \times 4!}$

(ii) $e^{-\frac{1}{2}} = 1 + \dfrac{(\frac{-1}{2})}{1!} + \dfrac{(\frac{-1}{2})^2}{2!} + \dfrac{(\frac{-1}{2})^3}{3!} + \dfrac{(\frac{-1}{2})^4}{4!}$

$\quad = 1 - \dfrac{1}{2 \times 1!} + \dfrac{1}{2^2 \times 2!} - \dfrac{1}{2^3 \times 3!}$

$\quad + \dfrac{1}{2^4 \times 4!}$

(iii) $e^{\frac{1}{3}} = 1 + \dfrac{\frac{1}{3}}{1!} + \dfrac{(\frac{1}{3})^2}{2!} + \dfrac{(\frac{1}{3})^3}{3!} + \dfrac{(\frac{1}{3})^4}{41!}$

$\quad = 1 + \dfrac{1}{3 \times 1!} + \dfrac{1}{3^2 \times 2!}$

$\quad + \dfrac{1}{3^3 \times 3!} + \dfrac{1}{3^4 \times 4!}$

(iv) $e^{\frac{1}{5}} = 1 + \dfrac{\frac{1}{5}}{1!} + \dfrac{[\frac{1}{5}]^2}{2!} + \dfrac{[\frac{1}{5}]^3}{3!} + \dfrac{[\frac{1}{5}]^4}{4!}$

$\quad = 1 + \dfrac{1}{5 \times 1!} + \dfrac{1}{5^2 \times 2!}$

$\quad + \dfrac{1}{5^3 \times 3!} + \dfrac{1}{5^4 \times 4!}$

(v) $e^5 = 1 + \dfrac{5}{1!} + \dfrac{5^2}{2!} + \dfrac{5^3}{3!} + \dfrac{5^4}{4!}$.

WORKED EXAMPLE 44

Determine the series for

(i) $\cosh 2x = \dfrac{e^{2x} + e^{-2x}}{2}$ and

(ii) $\sinh 3x = \dfrac{1}{2}(e^{3x} - e^{-3x})$ by writing 5 terms for each expansion.

Solution 44

(i) $\cosh 2x = \dfrac{e^{2x} + e^{-2x}}{2}$

$\quad = \dfrac{1}{2}\left[1 + \dfrac{2x}{1} + \dfrac{(2x)^2}{2!} + \dfrac{(2x)^3}{3!} + \dfrac{(2x)^4}{4!} \right]$

$\quad + \dfrac{1}{2}\left[1 - \dfrac{2x}{1!} + \dfrac{(2x)^2}{2!} - \dfrac{(2x)^3}{3!} + \dfrac{(2x)^4}{4!} \right]$

$\quad = \dfrac{1}{2}\left[2 + \dfrac{2(2x)^2}{2!} + \dfrac{2(2x)^4}{4!} \right]$

$\quad \cosh 2x = 1 + \dfrac{(2x)^2}{2!} + \dfrac{(2x)^4}{4!}$.

(ii) $\sinh 3x = \dfrac{1}{2}(e^{3x} - e^{-3x})$

$$= \frac{1}{2}\left[1 + \frac{3x}{1!} + \frac{(3x)^2}{2!} + \frac{(3x)^3}{3!} + \frac{(3x)^4}{4!}\right]$$

$$-\frac{1}{2}\left[1 - \frac{3x}{1!} + \frac{(3x)^2}{2!} - \frac{(3x)^3}{3!} + \frac{(3x)^4}{4!}\right]$$

$$\sinh 3x = \frac{1}{2}\left[2\frac{3x}{1} + 2\frac{(3x)^3}{3!}\right]$$

$$= 3x + \frac{(3x)^3}{3!}.$$

Exercise 8

1. Write down the first five terms for the expansion e^x.

2. Write down the first five terms for the expansion e^{-x}.

3. Write down the first five terms for the expansion e^{-1} and hence evaluate correct to five significant figures.

4. Write down the first five terms for the following expansions:

    (i) e (ii) $\dfrac{1}{e}$ (iii) $\dfrac{1}{e^2}$

    (iv) $\dfrac{1}{2}\left[e + \dfrac{1}{e}\right]$ (v) $\dfrac{1}{2}\left[e - \dfrac{1}{e}\right]$.

5. Determine the following expansions:

    (i) $2e^{3x}$

    (ii) $3e^{-2x}$

    (iii) $5e^{-x}$

    (iv) $4e^{\frac{x}{2}}$

    (v) $e^{-\frac{3}{2}x}$ as far as the x^5.

6. Find correct to four significant figures, the values of

    (i) $e^{0.55}$

    (ii) $e^{-3.5}$

    (iii) $e^{0.02}$ by considering eight terms.

7. Find the first three terms of the series $\dfrac{e^x - e^{-x}}{e^x}$.

8. How many terms are there in the expansion e^x? is the expansion convergent or divergent? Explain.

9. What is the special property of the exponential function e^x?

10. If x increases how does $y = e^x$ change?

9

Graphs of trigonometric or circular functions of sine and cosine.

Sketches graphs of functions involving sine, cosine.

a. States the approximations $\sin x \approx \tan x \approx x$ and $\cos x \approx 1 - \dfrac{x^2}{2}$ for small x.

b. Sketches graphs of $\sin A$, $\sin 2A$, $2\sin A$, $\sin \dfrac{A}{2}$, $\cos A$, $\cos 2A$, $\cos A \cos 2A$ for values of A between $0°$ and $360°$.

c. Sketches graphs of $\sin^2 A$, $\cos^2 A$, for values of A between $0°$ and $360°$.

d. Sketches graphs of the functions in 9b and 9c where A is replaced by ωt.

e. Defines and identifies amplitude and frequency.

f. Defines angular velocity ω in rad/s and period T as $\dfrac{2\pi}{\omega}$.

States the approximations $\sin x \approx x$, **$\tan x \approx x$ and $\cos x \approx 1 - \dfrac{x^2}{2}$ for small x.**

The series expansion for $\sin x$ is given as $\sin x = \dfrac{x}{1!} - \dfrac{x^3}{3!} + \dfrac{x^5}{5!} - \dots$ where x is expressed in radians. For small values of x, this expansion is approximated $\sin x \approx x$.

We take only the first term as the other terms are extremely small and are negligible.

Find the value of $\sin x$ when x is
  (i) $1°$ (ii) $0.5°$
  (iii) $10'$ (iv) $1'$.

Solution 45

These angles in degrees must be first expressed in radians. If $x°$ is expressed in degrees then x^c in radians is given by $x^c = \dfrac{\pi x^0}{180}$

(i) $x^c = \dfrac{\pi 1}{180} = 0.0174532^c$

  $\sin 0.0174532^c = 0.0174523$

(ii) $x^c = \dfrac{\pi \frac{1}{2}}{180} = 0.0087266^c$

  $\sin 0.0087266^c = 0.00872266$

(iii) $x^c = \dfrac{\pi \frac{10}{60}}{180} = 2.9088821 \times 10^{-3}$

  $\sin 2.9088821 \times 10^{-3} = 2.908878$

(iv) $x^c = \dfrac{\pi \frac{1}{60}}{180} = 2.9088821 \times 10^{-4}$

  $\sin 2.9088821 \times 10^{-4} = 2.908882 \times 10^{-4}$.

This illustrates clearly that if x is very small and it is expressed in radians then $\sin x \approx x$.

similarly $\tan x \approx x$.

The series expansion for $\cos x$ is given by

$$\cos x = 1 - \frac{x^2}{2} + \frac{x^4}{4!} - \frac{x^6}{6!} + \dots$$

If x is very small, this can be approximated to

$$\cos x \approx 1 - \frac{x^2}{2}.$$

Defines angular velocity ω in radians per second and period T as $\dfrac{2\pi}{\omega}$.

Angular velocity.

Consider a particle orbiting in a circular path with an angular velocity, ω in radians per second. If the particle turns an angle, θ, as shown in the diagrams and takes t seconds, the angular velocity is given $\omega = \frac{\theta}{t}$.

Fig. 50

Some examples possessing angular velocity, wheel of a car rotating a shaft is rotating, a sine wave.
The angle, $\theta = \omega t$, θ is measured in radians, ω in radians per second and t in seconds.
The angular velocity, $\omega = 2\pi f$, where f is the frequency in hertz.
The periodic time, T, is the time taken to trace one complete cycle $T = \dfrac{1}{f} = \dfrac{2\pi}{\omega}$

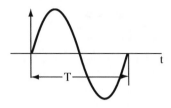

Fig. 51

period or periodic time.

Defines and identifies amplitude and frequency.

THE FREQUENCY, f, is the number of cycles which are traced in one second

$$f = \frac{1}{T}.$$

If $f = 50$ Hz, that is, 50 complete cycles are traced in one second.

To plot graphs of trigonometric functions.

A sinewave is represented trigonometrically by the equation $y = A \sin \omega t$ where A is the amplitude or the maximum or the peak value of the wave, ω is the angular velocity or angular frequency with which the wave displaces and t is the time at any point on the sinewave.

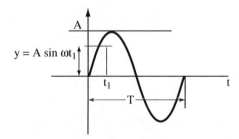

Fig. 52

At $t = t_1$, $y = A \sin \omega \, t_1$.
Plot the graph $y = 5 \sin 2\pi 1000 t$ against t, where $t = \frac{\theta}{\omega}$.

Draw the following trigonometric functions:

(i) $y = 2 \sin \omega t$

(ii) $y = 2 \sin(\omega t + \dfrac{\pi}{6})$

(iii) $y = 2 \sin(\omega t - \dfrac{\pi}{3})$

on the same time axis by taking points at intervals of $\omega t = \dfrac{\pi}{6}$, displaying $-2\pi \leq \omega t \leq 2\pi$. (two cycles).

State the amplitude of each waveform, and whether it lags or leads.

Determine the co-ordinates of the points on the y-axis and x-axis where the curves meet and the points of their intersections in the range $(0 \leq \omega t \leq 2\pi)$.

Solution 46

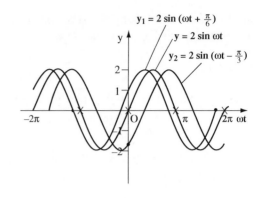

Fig. 53

The amplitude of each waveform is 2.

The sinewave $y = 2 \sin \omega t$ is a reference wave form it begins at the origin, $y = 2 \sin(\omega t + \frac{\pi}{6})$ leads the wave $y = 2 \sin \omega t$ by $\frac{\pi}{6}$ and $y = 2 \sin(\omega t - \frac{\pi}{3})$ lags the wave $y = 2 \sin \omega t$ by $\frac{\pi}{3}$.

When $\omega t = 0$ the curves cut the y-axis

$y = 0$ when $\omega t = 0$

$\theta^c = \omega t$	$\sin \omega t$	$y = 2 \sin \omega t$	$y_1 = 2 \sin\left(\omega t + \frac{\pi}{6}\right)$	$y_2 = 2 \sin\left(\omega t - \frac{\pi}{3}\right)$
0	0	0	1.000	−1.732
$\frac{\pi}{6}$	0.500	1.000	1.732	−1.000
$\frac{\pi}{3}$	0.866	1.732	2.000	0
$\frac{\pi}{2}$	1.000	2.000	1.732	1.000
$\frac{2\pi}{3}$	0.866	1.732	1.000	1.732
$\frac{5\pi}{6}$	0.500	1.000	0	2.000
π	0	0	−1.000	1.732
$\frac{7\pi}{6}$	−0.500	−1.000	−1.732	1.000
$\frac{4\pi}{3}$	−0.866	−1.732	−2.000	0
$\frac{3\pi}{2}$	−1.000	−2.000	−1.732	−1.000
$\frac{5\pi}{3}$	−0.866	−1.732	−1.000	−1.732
$\frac{11\pi}{6}$	−0.500	−1.000	0	−2.000
2π	0	0	1.000	−1.732

$y_1 = 1$ when $\omega t = 0$

$y_2 = -1.732$ when $\omega t = 0.$

When $y = 0$, the curves cut the x-axis from the table, when

$y = 0, \quad \omega t = 0, \pi, 2\pi$

$y_1 = 0, \quad \omega t = \dfrac{5\pi}{6}, \dfrac{11\pi}{6}$

$y_2 = 0, \quad \omega t = \dfrac{2\pi}{3}, \dfrac{5\pi}{3}.$

To find the intersections of the sinewaves, we solve the simultaneous equations.

$y = 2 \sin \omega t$

$y_1 = 2 \sin \left(\omega t + \dfrac{\pi}{6} \right)$

when $y = y_1$,

$2 \sin \omega t = 2 \sin \omega t \cos \dfrac{\pi}{6} + 2 \sin \dfrac{\pi}{6} \cos \omega t$

$2 \sin \omega t = 2 \sin \omega t \dfrac{\sqrt{3}}{2} + 2 \left(\dfrac{1}{2} \right) \cos \omega t.$

$(2 - \sqrt{3}) \sin \omega t = \cos \omega t$

$\tan \omega t = \dfrac{1}{2 - \sqrt{3}}$

$\tan \omega t = 3.732$

$\omega t = 75° = \dfrac{5\pi}{12}$

and $\omega t = 255° = \dfrac{17\pi}{12}.$

The above curves intersect at $\frac{5\pi}{12}$ and $\frac{17\pi}{12}$ giving the corresponding values in y of 1.93 and -1.93. The co-ordinates of intersecting in the range $0 \le \omega t \le 2\pi$ are shown at $A \left(\frac{5\pi}{12}, 1.93 \right)$ and at $B \left(\frac{17\pi}{12}, -1.93 \right)$.

The intersections of the two curves $y = 2 \sin \omega t$ and $y_2 = 2 \sin(\omega t - \frac{\pi}{3})$ are found by solving these equations simultaneously when $y = y_2$

$2 \sin \omega t = 2 \sin(\omega t - \frac{\pi}{3})$

$2 \sin \omega t = 2 \sin \omega t \cos \frac{\pi}{3} - 2 \sin \frac{\pi}{3} \cos \omega t$

$\qquad = 2(\sin \omega t) \left(\dfrac{1}{2} \right) - 2 \left(\dfrac{\sqrt{3}}{2} \right) \cos \omega t$

$2 \sin \omega t = \sin \omega t = \sqrt{3} \cos \omega t$

$\sin \omega t = -\sqrt{3} \cos \omega t$

$\tan \omega t = -\sqrt{3}$

$\omega t = \dfrac{2\pi}{3}, \dfrac{5\pi}{3}.$

The co-ordinates are at $C \left(\dfrac{2\pi}{3}, \sqrt{3} \right)$ and at $D \left(\dfrac{5\pi}{3}, -\sqrt{3} \right).$

The co-ordinates of the intersections of the curves
$y_1 = 2 \sin(\omega t + \frac{\pi}{6})$ and $y_2 = 2 \sin(\omega t - \frac{\pi}{3}).$
When $y_1 = y_2$, $2 \sin(\omega t + \frac{\pi}{6}) = 2 \sin(\omega t - \frac{\pi}{3})$
or $\sin \omega t \cos \frac{\pi}{6} + \sin \frac{\pi}{6} \cos \omega t = \sin \omega t \cos \frac{\pi}{3} - \sin \frac{\pi}{3} \cos \omega t$ or

$\dfrac{\sqrt{3}}{2} \sin \omega t + \dfrac{1}{2} \cos \omega t = \dfrac{1}{2} \sin \omega t - \dfrac{\sqrt{3}}{2} \cos \omega t$

$\left(\dfrac{1}{2} + \dfrac{\sqrt{3}}{2} \right) \cos \omega t = \dfrac{1}{2} \sin \omega t - \dfrac{\sqrt{3}}{2} \sin \omega t$

$\left(\dfrac{1 + \sqrt{3}}{2} \right) \cos \omega t = \dfrac{1 - \sqrt{3}}{2} \sin \omega t$

$\tan \omega t = \dfrac{1 + \sqrt{3}}{1 - \sqrt{3}}$

$\qquad = \dfrac{2.732}{-0.732} = -3.7322$

$\omega t = 180° - 75° = 105° = \dfrac{7\pi}{12}$

and $\omega t = \dfrac{19\pi}{12}.$

The co-ordinates are at $E \left(\dfrac{7\pi}{12}, 1.93 \right)$ and at $F \left(\dfrac{19\pi}{12}, 1.93 \right).$

Plot on the same graph

(i) $\sin \dfrac{1}{2}\omega t$

(ii) $\sin \omega t$

(iii) $\sin 2\, \omega t$

(iv) $\sin 3\, \omega t$

$\theta^c = \omega t$	$\sin \frac{\omega t}{2}$	$\sin \omega t$	$\sin 2\omega t$	$\sin 3\omega t$
0	0	0	0	0
$\frac{\pi}{6}$	0.259	0.5	0.866	1
$\frac{\pi}{3}$	0.5	0.866	0.866	0
$\frac{\pi}{2}$	0.707	1	0	1
$\frac{2\pi}{6}$	0.866	0.866	−0.866	0
π	1	0	0	0
$\frac{7\pi}{6}$	0.966	−0.5	0.866	−1
$\frac{4\pi}{3}$	0.866	−0.866	0.866	0
$\frac{3\pi}{2}$	0.707	−1	0	1
$\frac{5\pi}{3}$	0.5	−0.866	−0.866	0
$\frac{11\pi}{6}$	0.259	−0.5	−0.866	−1
2π	0	0	0	0

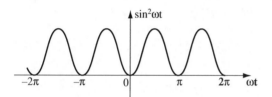

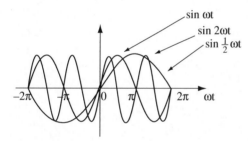

For $\sin \dfrac{\omega t}{2}$ half cycle is drawn $0 \le \omega t \le 2\pi$.

For $\sin \omega t$ full cycle is drawn $0 \le \omega t \le 2\pi$.

For $\sin 2\omega t$ two full cycles are drawn $0 \le \omega t \le 2\pi$.

For $\sin 3\omega t$ three full cycles are drawn $0 \le \omega t \le 2\pi$.

Plot on the same graph

  (i) $\cos \dfrac{1}{2}\omega t$ (ii) $\cos \omega t$

 (iii) $\cos 2\omega t$ (iv) $\cos 3\omega t$.

For $\sin \dfrac{1}{2}\omega t$ half cycle is drawn $0 \le \omega t \le 2\pi$.

For $\cos \omega t$ full cycle is drawn $0 \le \omega t \le 2\pi$.

For $\cos 2\omega t$ two full cycles is drawn $0 \le \omega t \le 2\pi$.

For $\cos 3\omega t$ three full cycle is drawn $0 \le \omega t \le 2\pi$.

Plot on the same graph

  (i) $\cos \dfrac{1}{2}\omega t$ (ii) $\cos \omega t$

 (iii) $\cos 2\omega t$ (iv) $\cos 3\omega t$

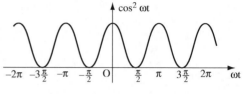

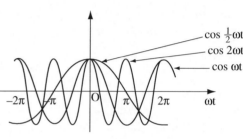

Fig. 54

For $\cos \dfrac{\omega t}{2}$ half cycle is drawn $0 \le \omega t \le 2\pi$.

For $\cos \omega t$ full cycles is drawn $0 \le \omega t \le 2\pi$.

For $\cos 2\omega t$ two full cycles are drawn $0 \le \omega t \le 2\pi$.

For $\cos 3\omega t$ three full cycles are drawn $0 \le \omega t \le 2\pi$.

To plat $\sin^2 \omega t$ and $\cos^2 \omega t$ for two cycle $-2\pi \le \omega t \le 2\pi$.

The graphs are shown plotted

$\theta^c = \omega t$	$\sin \omega t$	$\sin^2 \omega t$	$\cos^2 \omega t$
0	0	0	1
$\frac{\pi}{6}$	0.5	0.25	0.75
$\frac{\pi}{3}$	0.866	0.75	0.25
$\frac{\pi}{2}$	1	1	0
$\frac{2\pi}{3}$	0.866	0.75	0.25
$\frac{5\pi}{6}$	0.5	0.25	0.75
π	0	0	0
$\frac{7\pi}{6}$	−0.5	0.25	0.75
$\frac{4\pi}{3}$	−0.866	0.75	0.25
$\frac{3\pi}{2}$	−1	1	0
$\frac{5\pi}{3}$	−8.866	0.75	0.25
$\frac{11\pi}{6}$	−1.5	0.25	0.75
2π	0	0	1

Exercises 9

1. Convert the following angles in degrees to the corresponding angles in radians.

 (i) $5°$ (ii) $2°$ (iii) $15'$

 (iv) $5'$ (v) $2'$.

2. Convert the following angles in radians to the corresponding angles in degrees:

 (i) 0.05^c (ii) 0.5^c

 (iii) 0.00015^c (iv) 1^c.

3. Find the approximate values of the following trigonometric or circular functions:

 (i) $\sin 1.5'$ (ii) $\sin 0.05^c$

 (iii) $\sin 0.75°$ (iv) $\tan 0.5°$

 (v) $\cos 1'$ (vi) $\cos 0.75°$

 (vii) $\cos 25'$.

4. A sinewave is represented trigonometrically by the equation.

$$y = 30 \sin 31420t.$$

 Determine:
 (i) the amplitude of the wave
 (ii) the frequency (Hz)
 (iii) the period (s)
 (iv) the angular velocity (rad/s).

5. The angles of a sinewave are given in degrees as 0, 30, 60, 90, 120, 150, 180, 210, 240, 270, 300, 330, 360. Write down the corresponding values of time t, in terms of π and the angular velocity, ω.

6. Sketch the following graphs:-

 (i) $\sin \omega t$ (ii) $\sin 2\omega t$

 (iii) $1.5 \sin \omega t$ (iv) $\sin \frac{\omega t}{2}$

 (v) $\sin^2 \omega t$ in the range $-2\pi \le \omega t \le 2\pi$.

7. Sketch the following graphs:-

 (i) $\cos \omega t$ (ii) $\cos 2\omega t$

 (iii) $1.5 \cos \omega t$ (iv) $\cos \frac{\omega t}{2}$

 (v) $\cos^2 \omega t$.

8. Sketch the following graphs against t:

 (i) $\sin \omega t$ (ii) $\sin 2\omega t$

 (iii) $2 \sin \omega t$ (iv) $\sin \frac{\omega t}{2}$

 (v) $\sin^2 \omega t$.

9. Sketch the following graphs against t:

 (i) $\cos \omega t$ (ii) $\cos 2\omega t$

 (iii) $2 \cos \omega t$ (iv) $\cos \frac{\omega t}{2}$

 (v) $\cos^2 \omega t$.

10. Sketch the following graphs on the same base for comparison:

 (a) (i) $\sin x$
   (ii) $\sin 2x$
   (iii) $\sin \frac{x}{2}$

 (b) (i) $\cos x$
   (ii) $\cos 2x$
   (iii) $\cos \frac{x}{2}$.

10

Resultant of waves

Combines sinewaves.

a. Determines the single wave resulting from a combination of two waves of the same frequency using phasors and/or a graphical method.
b. Defines the term phase angle.
c. Measures the amplitude and phase angle of the resultant wave in 10a.
d. Determines graphically the single wave resulting from a combination of two waves, within the limitations of 10b and 10c.
e. Shows that the resultant of two sine waves of different frequencies gives rise to a non-sinusoidal, periodic function.

Compound formulae.

$\sin(A + B) = \sin A \cos B + \cos A \sin B$ the expansion of the compound angles.
If $B = -B$
$\sin(A - B) = \sin A \cos(-B) + \cos A \sin(-B)$
$\sin(A - B) = \sin A \cos B - \cos A \sin B$
$\cos(-B) = \cos B$ even function
$\sin(-B) = -\sin B$ odd function

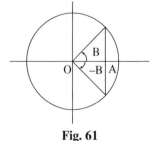

Fig. 61

$\cos B = OA \quad \cos(-B) = OA$ therefore
$\cos B = \cos(-B)$
Even function

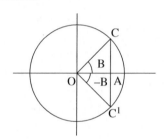

Fig. 62

$\sin B = AC \quad \sin(-B) = AC'$ but $AC' = -AC$
therefore $\sin(-B) = -\sin B$.

Odd function

$\cos (A + B) = \cos A \cos B - \sin A \sin B$

if $B = -B$

$\cos(A - B) = \cos A \cos(-B) - \sin A \sin(-B)$
$\cos(A - B) = \cos A \cos B + \sin A \sin B$.

Phase angle.

The trigonometric or circular function $y = R \sin(\omega t \pm \alpha)$ plot the functions:

If $y = 5 \sin(2\pi 10^3 t + \frac{\pi}{6})$ and
$y = 5 \sin(2\pi 10^3 t - \frac{\pi}{3})$

where $R = 5$ the amplitude, $\omega = 2\pi 10^3$ radians, $f = 1000$ Hz, $\alpha = \frac{\pi}{6}$ and $\alpha = -\frac{\pi}{3}$ the phase angles.

When the phase angle is plus the sinewave leads and when the phase angle is minus the sine wave lags.

Leading waveform means that the peak is reached before and lagging waveform means that the peak is reached after. This is illustrated.

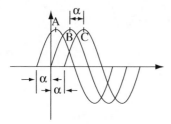

Fig. 63

B is the reference waveform, starts at the origin
C lags B by an angle α
A leads B by an angle α.

Draw the following waveforms:-

$y_1 = 3 \sin \omega t$
$y_2 = 5 \sin(\omega t + \frac{\pi}{6})$
$y_3 = 4 \sin(\omega t - \frac{\pi}{3})$

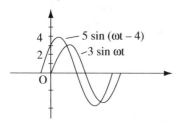

Fig. 64

Phase angle leading and lagging.

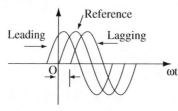

Fig. 65

Reference waveform $y = R \sin \omega t$.

Leading the reference waveform

$y = R \sin(\omega t + \alpha)$.

Lagging the reference waveform

$y = R \sin(\omega t - \alpha)$.

$R \sin(\omega t + \alpha)$ to be expressed in the form $a \cos \omega t + b \sin \omega t$.

Using $\sin(A + B) = \sin A \cos B + \cos A \sin B$, we expand

$R \sin(\omega t + \alpha) = R \sin \omega t \cos \alpha + R \sin \cos \omega t$.

WORKED EXAMPLE 47

Express $3 \sin(\omega t + \frac{\pi}{3})$ in the form $a \cos \omega t + b \sin \omega t$.

Solution 47

$3 \sin(\omega t + \frac{\pi}{3}) = 3 \sin \omega t \cos \frac{\pi}{3} + 3 \sin \frac{\pi}{3} \cos \omega t$

$$= \sin \omega t + 3 \frac{\sqrt{3}}{2} \cos \omega t.$$

WORKED EXAMPLE 48

To express $\frac{3}{2} \sin \omega t + \frac{3\sqrt{3}}{2} \cos \omega t$ in the form $R \sin(\omega t + \alpha)$.

Solution 48

$\frac{3}{2} \sin \omega t + \frac{3\sqrt{3}}{2} \cos \omega t$

$$= R \sin \omega t \cos \alpha + R \sin \alpha \cos \omega t.$$

Equating the coefficients of $\sin \omega t$, we have

$R \cos \alpha = \frac{3}{2}$ hence $\cos \alpha = \dfrac{\frac{3}{2}}{R}$.

Equating the coefficients of $\cos \omega t$, we have

$R \sin \alpha = \dfrac{3\sqrt{3}}{2}$

hence $\sin \alpha = \dfrac{3\frac{\sqrt{3}}{2}}{R}$.

Forming a right angled triangle

$$\tan \alpha = \frac{3\frac{\sqrt{3}}{2}}{\frac{3}{2}} = \sqrt{3} \quad \alpha = \frac{\pi}{3}$$

$$R^2 = \left(\frac{3}{2}\right)^2 + \left(\frac{3\sqrt{3}}{2}\right)^2 = \frac{9}{4} + \frac{27}{4} = \frac{36}{4}$$

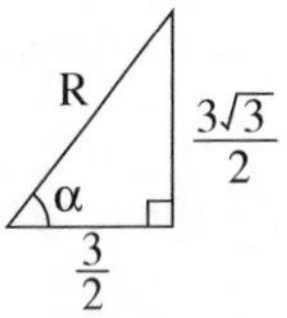

Fig. 66

$R^2 = 9$ and $\boxed{R = 3}$

$a \cos \omega t + b \sin \omega t = R \sin(\omega t \pm \alpha)$

$\qquad = R \sin \omega t \cos \alpha + R \sin \alpha \cos \omega t$

$a = R \sin \alpha$

$b = R \cos \alpha \quad a^2 + b^2 = R^2 \quad \tan \alpha = \frac{a}{b}$

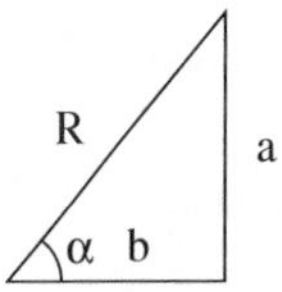

Fig. 67

Alternating voltages and currents.

Alternating voltages and currents can be expressed trigonometrically.

WORKED EXAMPLE 49

An alternating voltage is given by the expression $v = 100 \sin(3142t + \frac{\pi}{3})$.

Draw the above waveform for two cycles.

Calculate:

  (i) the peak value of the voltage

  (ii) the frequency

  (iii) the angular velocity

  (iv) the periodic time

  (v) the instantaneous value of the voltage when $t = 0.5$ ms.

Solution 49

The waveform is plotted as shown in the diagram.

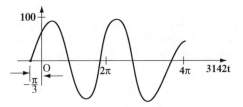

  (i) Peak value of the voltage = 100 volts.

  (ii) $\omega = 2\pi f = 3142$
       $f = 500$ Hz

  (iii) $\omega = 3142$ radians/second

  (iv) $T = \frac{1}{f} = \frac{1}{500} = 2$ ms

  (v) $v = 100 \sin(3142 \times 0.5 \times 10^{-3} + \frac{\pi}{3})$
     $= 100 \sin(2.6181976^c)$
     $= 50$ volts.

The total angle $3142t + \frac{\pi}{3}$ should be expressed in radians.

WORKED EXAMPLE 50

An instantaneous current is given by the expression
$i = 50 \sin(3142t - \frac{\pi}{6})$ mA.
Calculate:

  (i) the frequency

  (ii) the amplitiude

  (iii) the instantaneous value after 0.1 ms.

Solution 50

  (i) $\omega = 2\pi f = 3142$

     $f = \frac{3142}{2\pi} = 500$ Hz

  (ii) 50 mA

  (iii) $i = 50 \sin(3142 \times 0.1 \times 10^{-3} - \frac{\pi}{6})$ mA
     $i = 50 \sin(-0.2093987)$ mA
     $= 10.4$ mA.

WORKED EXAMPLE 51

A sinusoidal alternating voltage has the equation

$v = 141.4 \sin(377t + \frac{\pi}{2})$ volts.

Determine

(i) the peak value

(ii) the angular velocity

(iii) the periodic time

(iv) the frequency

(v) the instantaneous voltage
when $t = 2.5$ ms.

Solution 51

(i) 141.4 volts

(ii) $\omega = 377$ radians/second

(iii) $T = \dfrac{1}{f} = \dfrac{1}{60} = 0.0167\text{s} = 16.7$ ms

(iv) $2\pi f = 377 \quad f = 60$ Hz

(v) $v = 141.4 \sin\left(377 \times 2.5 \times 10^{-3} + \frac{\pi}{2}\right)$
$= 83.1$ volts.

WORKED EXAMPLE 52

The voltages across three components in a circuit can be expressed as:

$v_1 = 35 \sin \omega t$, $v_2 = 50 \sin(\omega t + \frac{\pi}{3})$,

$v_3 = 70 \sin(\omega t - \frac{\pi}{2})$.

Determine the resultant total voltage across the circuit and express it in the form
$v_R = v_m \sin(\omega t \pm \theta)$.

Solution 52

$v = 35 \sin \omega t + 50 \sin(\omega t + \frac{\pi}{3}) + 70 \sin(\omega t - \frac{\pi}{2})$

$v = 35 \sin \omega t + 50 \sin \omega t \cos \frac{\pi}{3} + 50 \sin \frac{\pi}{3} \cos \omega t$

$\quad + 70 \sin \omega t \cos \frac{\pi}{2} - 70 \sin \frac{\pi}{2} \cos \omega t$

$v = 35 \sin \omega t + 50 \sin \omega t \left(\frac{1}{2}\right) + 50\frac{\sqrt{3}}{2} \cos \omega t$

$\quad + 70 \sin \omega t (0) - 70 \cos \omega t$

$v = 35 \sin \omega t + 25 \sin \omega t + 25\sqrt{3} \cos \omega t$
$\quad - 70 \cos \omega t$

$v = 60 \sin \omega t - 26.7 \cos \omega t = R \sin(\omega t - \alpha)$

$v = 60 \sin \omega t - 26.7 \cos \omega t \equiv R \sin \omega t \cos \alpha$
$\quad - R \sin \alpha \cos \omega t$

The coefficients of $\sin \omega t$ are equal

$60 = R \cos \alpha \qquad \ldots (1)$

The coefficients of $\cos \omega t$ are equal

$-26.7 = -R \sin \alpha \qquad \ldots (2)$

From (1) $\quad \cos \alpha = \dfrac{60}{R}$.

From (2) $\quad \sin \alpha = \dfrac{26.7}{R}$.

Constructing a right angled triangle

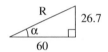

Fig. 68

$R^2 = 60^2 + 26.7^2 = 4312.89 \quad R = 65.7$

$\tan \alpha = \dfrac{26.7}{60}$ or

$\alpha = 23°59' = 0.4186881^c \approx 0.42^c$.

$v_R = 65.7 \sin(\omega t) - 0.42^c$.

Adding two sine waves of the same frequency.

The following examples will illustrate the effect.

(a) if $y_1 = 3 \sin \omega t \quad y_2 = 4 \sin \omega t$

The resultant
$y = y_1 + y_2$
$= 3 \sin \omega t + 4 \sin \omega t = 7 \sin \omega t$.

The resultant sinewave is another sinewave with different amplitude.

(b) if $y_1 = 3 \sin \omega t \quad y_2 = 4 \sin(\omega t + \frac{\pi}{3})$

$y = y_1 + y_2 = 3 \sin \omega t + 4 \sin(\omega t + \frac{\pi}{3})$

$= 3 \sin \omega t + 4 \sin \omega t \cos \frac{\pi}{3}$

$\quad + 4 \sin \frac{\pi}{3} \cos \omega t$

$$= 3\sin\omega t + 2\sin\omega t + 2\sqrt{3}\cos\omega t$$
$$= 5\sin\omega t + 2\sqrt{3}\cos\omega t$$
$$= R\sin(\omega t + \alpha)$$
$$= R\sin\omega t\cos\alpha + R\sin\alpha\cos\omega t$$

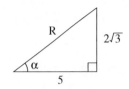

Fig. 69

$$5 = R\cos\alpha \text{ and } R\sin\alpha = 2\sqrt{3}$$
$$R^2 = (2\sqrt{3})^2 + 5^2, \ R = \sqrt{12+25} = \sqrt{37}$$
$$\tan\alpha = \frac{2\sqrt{3}}{5} \quad \alpha = \tan^{-1}\frac{2\sqrt{3}}{5} = 34.72°$$
$$y = \sqrt{37}\sin(\omega t + 34.72°)$$

the amplitude is different to the other amplitudes and the sinewave is leading the individual sinewaves by an angle of 34.72°.

Therefore adding sinewaves or cosine waves of the same frequency, the resultant is a sinewave which is displaced by an angle α either leading or lagging of different amplitudes.

Adding two sinewaves of different frequency

$$y_1 = \sin\omega t \qquad y_2 = 4\sin 2\omega t$$

The resultant $y = y_1 + y_2 = 3\sin\omega t + 4\sin 2\omega t$
$$= 3\sin\omega t + 8\sin\omega t\cos\omega t$$

which is a non-sinusoidal waveform which is called complex waveform.

$y = \sin\omega t + \dfrac{1}{2}\sin 2\omega t$ gives the waveform

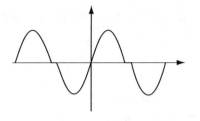

Complex Wave

Fig. 70

Complex Wave.

The resultant of the waveforms

$$y = 0.5\sin x + 0.5\sin 2x + 0.5\sin 3x$$

is shown in the graph.

Exercises 10

1. Sketch $y_1 = 3\sin x$ and $y_2 = 4\sin x$ and hence obtain $y_1 + y_2$.

2. Sketch $y_1 = 2\sin 2x$ and $y_2 = \sin(2x + \dfrac{\pi}{3})$ and hence combine the waveforms.

3. Find the resultant waveform
$$y = 2\sin x + 3\sin 2x.$$

4. Find the resultant curve
$$y = \sin\frac{\theta}{2} + \sin\theta + \sin 2\theta.$$

5. Write down the equation of two waveforms, one has amplitude 5 and leads by 30° and the other has amplitude 12 and lag by 90°.

Algebra III Solutions
Solution 1

1. (i) $\log_e 1.234 = 0.21$

    (ii) $\log_e 12.34 = 2.51$

    (iii) $\log_e 1234 = 7.12$

    in three significant figures.

2. (i) $\log_e N = 4.174$

    $e^{4.174} = N = 64.98$

    (ii) $\log_e N = 9.21$

    $e^{9.21} = N = 9997$

    (iii) $\log_e N = -3.66$

    $e^{-3.66} = N = 0.0257$

    in four significant figures.

3. $N = No\, e^{-\lambda t}$

    when $t = 1500$ years

    $\frac{1}{2}No = No\, e^{-\lambda 1500}$

    $\frac{1}{2} = e^{-1500\lambda}$

    $e^{1500\lambda} = 2$

    taking logarithms to the base e on both sides

    $\ln e^{1500\lambda} = \ln 2$

    $1500\lambda \ln e = \ln 2$

    $\lambda = \dfrac{\ln 2}{1500} = 4.621 \times 10^{-4}$

    $\frac{1}{20}No = No\, e^{-4.621 \times 10^4 t}$

    $\frac{1}{20} = e^{-4.621 \times 10^{-4} t}$

    $20 = e^{4.621 \times 10^{-4} t}$

    $\ln 20 = 4.621 \times 10^{-4} t \ln e$

    $t = \dfrac{\ln 20}{4.621 \times 10^{-4}}$

    $\tau = 6483$ years.

4. $e^{2x} - 5e^x + 6 = 0 \qquad\qquad \dots (1)$

    $y = e^x$ squaring both sides $y^2 = (e^x)^2$ or

    $y^2 = e^{2x}$ since $(e^x)(e^x) = e^{2x}$.

    Equation (1) is now written in terms of y

    $y^2 - 5y + 6 = 0$

    $y = \dfrac{5 \pm \sqrt{25 - 24}}{2}$

    $= \dfrac{5 \pm 1}{2}$

    $y = \dfrac{5 + 1}{2}$ and $y = \dfrac{5 - 1}{2}$

    $y = 3$ and $y = 2$

    therefore $e^x = 3$, to find x, we must take logs to the base e on both sides

    $\ln e^x = \ln 3$

    $x \ln e = \ln 3$

    $x = \ln 3$

    $x = 1.0986123$

    $x \approx 1.099$

    also $e^x = 2$

    $\ln e^x = 2$

    $x = \ln 2$

    $x = 0.693$

    Therefore the solutions of equation (1) are $x = 0.693$ and 1.099.

5. $6e^{2x} - 7e^x + 2 = 0$

Let $W = e^x$ then $e^{2x} = W^2$

$6W^2 - 7W + 2 = 0$

$W = \dfrac{7 \pm \sqrt{49 - 4 \times 6 \times 2}}{12}$

$= \dfrac{7 \pm \sqrt{49 - 48}}{12} = \dfrac{7 \pm 1}{12}$

$W = \frac{2}{3}$ or $W = \frac{1}{2}$

$e^x = \frac{2}{3}$ or $e^x = \frac{1}{2}$

taking logs

$\ln e^x = \ln \frac{2}{3}$ $\qquad \ln e^x = \ln \frac{1}{2}$

$x = \ln \frac{2}{3}$ $\qquad x = \ln \frac{1}{2}$

$x = -0.405$ $\qquad x = -0.693$.

6. $i = I e^{-\frac{t}{5 \times 0.001}}$

$3 = 10 e^{-\frac{t}{5 \times 0.001}}$

$e^{-\frac{t}{5 \times 0.001}} = 0.3$

$e^{\frac{t}{5 \times 0.001}} = \dfrac{1}{0.3}$

$\dfrac{t}{5 \times 0.001} \ln e = \ln \dfrac{1}{0.3}$

$t = 5 \times 0.001 \times \ln \dfrac{1}{0.3}$

$\qquad = 5 \times 0.001 \times 1.203972804$

$\qquad = 6.02$ ms to 3 s.f.

7. $v = V(1 - e^{-\frac{t}{5 \times 0.001}})$

$\qquad = 100\left(1 - e^{-\frac{1 \times 10^{-3}}{5 \times 0.001}}\right)$

$\qquad = 100(1 - e^{-0.2})$

$= 100(1 - 0.818730753)$

$= 18.1$ volts to 3 s.f.

8. (i) $v = V\left(1 - e^{-\frac{t}{RC}}\right)$

$1 = 10\left(1 - e^{-\frac{t}{5}}\right)$

$\dfrac{1}{10} = 1 - e^{-\frac{t}{5}}$

$e^{-0.2t} = 1 - 0.1 = 0.9$

$e^{0.2t} = \dfrac{1}{0.9}$

$0.2t = \ln \dfrac{1}{0.9} = 0.105360575$

$t = 0.526802578 = 0.527$ s to 3 s.f.

(ii) $v = V\left(1 - e^{-\frac{t}{RC}}\right)$

$\qquad = 100\left(1 - e^{-\frac{1}{1}}\right)$

$\qquad = 100\left(1 - e^{-1}\right)$

$\qquad = 100 \times 0.63212058$

$\qquad = 63.2$ volts to 3 s.f.

9. (i) $\dfrac{e^{0.3} - e^{-0.3}}{2}$

$= \dfrac{1.349858808 - 0.740818}{2}$

$= 0.304520293 = 0.305$ to 3 s.f.

(ii) $\dfrac{e^{0.5} + e^{-0.5}}{2}$

$= \dfrac{1.648721271 + 0.0606530659}{2}$

$= 1.127625965$

$= 1.13$ to 3 s.f.

Solution 2

1.   (i) $\sqrt{-2} = \sqrt{(-1)(2)}$

            $= \sqrt{-1}\sqrt{2} = j\sqrt{2}$

  (ii) $\sqrt{-4} = \sqrt{(-1)(4)} = \sqrt{-1}\sqrt{4} = j2$

  (iii) $\sqrt{-8} = \sqrt{(-1)(8)} = \sqrt{-1}\sqrt{8}$

             $= j\sqrt{8} = j2\sqrt{2}$

  (iv) $\sqrt{-16} = \sqrt{(-1)(16)}$

              $= \sqrt{-1}\sqrt{16} = j4$

  (v) $\sqrt{-27} = \sqrt{(-1)(27)}$

             $= \sqrt{-1}\sqrt{27} = j3\sqrt{3}.$

2.   (i) $3x^2 - x + 1 = 0$

      using $x = \dfrac{-b \pm \sqrt{b^2 - 4ac}}{2a}$

      $x = \dfrac{-(-1) \pm \sqrt{(-1)^2 - 4(3)(1)}}{2 \times 3}$

      $= \dfrac{1 \pm \sqrt{1 - 12}}{6} = \dfrac{1 \pm \sqrt{-11}}{6}$

      $x = \dfrac{1}{6} \pm j\dfrac{\sqrt{11}}{6}$ complex roots.

  (ii) $x^2 - 4x + 8 = 0$ using the quadratic formula

      $x = \dfrac{-(-4) \pm \sqrt{(-4)^2 - 4 \times 1 \times 8}}{2 \times 1}$

      $= \dfrac{4 \pm \sqrt{16 - 32}}{2} = \dfrac{4 \pm \sqrt{-16}}{2}$

      $x = 2 \pm j2$ complex roots.

  (iii) $x^2 + 2x + 2 = 0$ using the quadratic formula

      $x = \dfrac{-2 \pm \sqrt{2^2 - 4 \times 1 \times 2}}{2}$

      $= \dfrac{-2 \pm \sqrt{4 - 8}}{2} = \dfrac{2}{2} \pm \dfrac{\sqrt{-4}}{2}$

      $x = -1 \pm j1$ complex roots.

  (iv) $-5x^2 + 7x + 5 = 0$ using the quadratic formula

      $x = \dfrac{-7 \pm \sqrt{7^2 - 4(-5)(5)}}{2 \times (-5)}$

      $= \dfrac{-7 \pm \sqrt{49 + 100}}{-10}$

      $= \dfrac{-7 \pm \sqrt{149}}{-10}$

      $x = \dfrac{-7}{-10} \pm \dfrac{\sqrt{149}}{-10} = \dfrac{7}{10} \pm \dfrac{12.2}{-10}$

      $= 0.7 \mp 1.22$ real roots.

  (v) $-x^2 + x - 5 = 0$ using the quadratic formula

      $x = \dfrac{-1 \pm \sqrt{1 - 4(-1)(-5)}}{2 \times (-1)}$

      $= \dfrac{-1 \pm \sqrt{1 - 20}}{-2} = \dfrac{-1 \pm \sqrt{-19}}{-2}$

      $x = \dfrac{-1}{-2} \pm j\dfrac{4.36}{-2}$

      $x = 0.5 \mp j2.18$ complex roots.

3.   (i) $A(1, 3), x = 1$ and $y = 3$

      then $Z_A = 1 + j3$

  (ii) $E(-1, 3), x = -1$ and $y = 3$

      then $Z_E = -1 + j3$

  (iii) $F(2, -4), x = 2$ and $y = -4$

      then $Z_F = 2 - j4$

(iv) $J(-3, -4)$, $x = -3$ and $y = -4$

then $Z_J = -3 - j4$

where $Z = x + jy$.

4. (i) $Z_1 = 3 + j4$, $P_1(3, 4)$

(ii) $Z_2 = 3 - j4$, $P_2(3, -4)$

(iii) $Z_3 = -3 + j4$, $P_3(-3, 4)$

(iv) $Z_4 = -3 + -j4$, $P_4(-3, -4)$.

5.

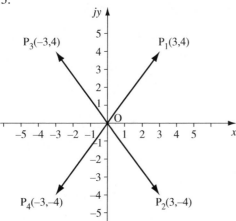

Fig. 71

6. (i) Re $Z = x$ and Im $Z = y$,

then $Z = x + jy$

(ii) Re $Z = -3$ and Im $Z = 5$,

then $Z = -3 + j5$.

7. (a) $E_1 = 20 + j30$ and $E_2 = 10 + j15$

$E_1 + E_2 = (20 + j30) + (10 + j15)$

$= (20 + 10) + j(30 + 15)$

$E_1 + E_2 = 30 + j45$

add the real terms separately and add the imaginary terms separately.

$E_1 - E_2 = (20 + j30) - (10 + j15)$

$= 20 + j30 - 10 - j15$

$= (20 - 10) + j(30 - 15)$

$E_1 - E_2 = 10j + 15$.

(b) $E_1 E_2 = (20 + j30)(10 + j15)$

$= 20 \times 10 + 20j15 + j30 \times 10 + j30 \times j15$

$= 200 + j300 + j300 + j^2 450$

$= (200 - 450) + j600 = -250 + j600$.

Multiplying numerator and denominator by the conjugate of the denominator.

$$\frac{E_1}{E_2} = \frac{20 + j30}{10 + j15}$$

$$= \frac{20 + j30}{10 + j15} \times \frac{10 - j15}{10 - j15}$$

$$\frac{E_1}{E_2} = \frac{(20 + j30)(10 - j15)}{(10 + j15)(10 - j15)}$$

remember $(a + b)(a - b) = (a^2 - b^2)$

$$= \frac{200 + j300 - j300 - j^2 450}{100 - (-1)225}$$

$$= \frac{650}{100 + 225}$$

$$= \frac{650}{325} = 2.$$

8. (i) $(3j)(5j) = 15j^2$

$= -15 = -15 + j0$

(ii) $(4 - 5j)(1 + j) = 4 - 5j + 4j - 5j^2$

$= 4 + 5 - j = 9 - j$

(iii) $(1 + j)(1 - j) = 1^2 - j^2 = 1 + 1 = 2$

(iv) $(4 + 3j)^2 = 4^2 + (3j)^2 + 2(4)(3j)$

$= 16 + 9j^2 + 24j$

$= 16 - 9 + 24j = 7 + 24j$

(v) $(1 - j^2)^2 = 1^2 + (-j^2)^2 + 2(1)(-j^2)$

$= 1 + [-(-1)]^2 + 2(-(-1))$

$= 1 + 1 + 2 = 4$.

9. (i) $Z_1 Z_2 = (3 - 4j)(1 + j)$

$= 3 - 4j + 3j - 4j^2$

$= 3 + 4 - j = 7 - j$

(ii) $Z_1 Z_3 = (3 - 4j)(2 + 3j)$
$$= 6 - 8j + 9j - 12j^2$$
$$= 6 + 12 + j = 18 + j$$

(iii) $Z_1 Z_2 Z_3 = (3 - 4j)(1 + j)(2 + 3j)$
$$= (7 - j)(2 + j3)$$
$$= 14 - 2j + 21j - 3j^2$$
$$= 14 + 3 + 19j = 17 + 19j.$$

10. (i) $ZZ^* = (x + jy)(x - jy)$
$$= (x^2 - j^2 y^2) = x^2 + y^2$$

(ii) $\left(\dfrac{1}{Z}\right)^* = \left(\dfrac{1}{x + jy}\right)^*$

$$= \left(\frac{x - jy}{(x + jy)(x - jy)}\right)^*$$

$$= \left(\frac{x - jy}{x^2 + y^2}\right)^*$$

$$= \frac{x}{x^2 + y^2} + j\frac{y}{x^2 + y^2}$$

$$\frac{1}{Z^*} = \frac{1}{x - jy} \times \frac{x + jy}{x + jy} = \frac{x + jy}{x^2 + y^2}$$

$$= \frac{x}{x^2 + y^2} + j\frac{y}{x^2 + y^2}$$

therefore $\left(\dfrac{1}{Z}\right)^* = \dfrac{1}{Z^*}.$

Solution 3

1. (i) $Z_1 = 1 + j\sqrt{3}$

    $|Z_1| = \sqrt{1^2 + (\sqrt{3})^2} = \sqrt{1+3} = 2$

    $\arg Z_1 = \tan^{-1} \dfrac{\sqrt{3}}{1}$

    (ii) $Z_2 = \sqrt{2} - j$

    $|Z_2| = \sqrt{(2)^2 + (-1)^2}$
    $= \sqrt{4+1} = \sqrt{5}$

    $\arg Z_2 = -\tan^{-1} \dfrac{1}{\sqrt{2}}$

    (iii) $Z_3 = 1 + j\sqrt{3}$

    $|Z_3| = \sqrt{(-1)^2 + (\sqrt{3})^2}$
    $= \sqrt{1+3} = 2$

    $\arg Z_3 = 180° - \tan^{-1} \sqrt{3}$

    (iv) $Z_4 = 2 + j3$

    $|Z_4| = \sqrt{(2)^2 + (3)^2}$
    $= \sqrt{4+9} = \sqrt{13}$

    $\arg Z_4 = \tan^{-1} \dfrac{3}{2}$

    (v) $Z_5 = -2 - 4j$

    $|Z_5| = \sqrt{(-2)^2 + (-4)^2}$
    $= \sqrt{4+16} = 4.47$

    $\arg Z_5 = -\left[180° - \tan^{-1} \dfrac{4}{2}\right].$

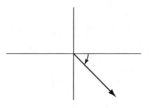

Fig. 73(ii)

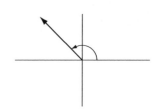

Fig. 74(iii)

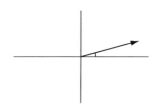

Fig. 75(iv)

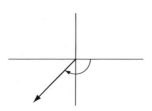

Fig. 76(v)

2. (i) $Z_1 = 3 + 4j$

    $|Z_1| = \sqrt{(3)^2 + (4)^2}$
    $= \sqrt{9+16} = \sqrt{25} = 5$

    $\arg Z_1 = \tan^{-1} \dfrac{4}{3} = \theta_1 = 53.13°$

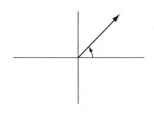

Fig. 72(i)

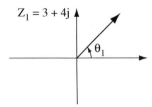

$Z_1 = 3 + 4j$

Fig. 77

(ii) $Z_2 = 3 - 4j$

$|Z_2| = \sqrt{(3)^2 + (-4^2)}$

$\quad = \sqrt{9 + 16} = \sqrt{25} = 5$

$\arg Z_2 = \tan^{-1} \frac{4}{3}$

$\quad = \theta_2 = -53.13°$

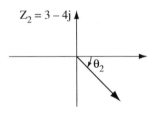

$Z_2 = 3 - 4j$

Fig. 78

(iii) $Z_3 = -3 - 4j$

$|Z_3| = \sqrt{(-3)^2 + (-4)^2}$

$\quad = \sqrt{9 + 16} = \sqrt{25} = 5$

$\arg Z_3 = [180° - 53.13°]$

$\quad = -126.87°$

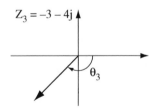

$Z_3 = -3 - 4j$

Fig. 79

(iv) $Z_4 = -3 + 4j$

$|Z_4| = \sqrt{(-3)^2 + (4)^2}$

$\quad = \sqrt{9 + 16} = \sqrt{25} = 5$

$\arg Z_4 = 180° - \tan^{-1} \frac{4}{3} = 126.87°.$

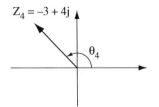

$Z_4 = -3 + 4j$

Fig. 80

3. (i) $Z_1 = 3\angle{-30°}$

$\quad = 3(\cos 30° - j \sin 30°)$

$\quad = 3(0.866 - j0.5)$

$Z_1 = 2.598 - j1.5$

(ii) $Z_2 = 5\angle{-\frac{\pi}{2}}$

$\quad = 5(\cos \frac{\pi}{2} - j \sin \frac{\pi}{2})$

$\quad = 5(0 - j1)$

$Z_2 = -j5$

(iii) $Z_3 = 1\angle{-180°}$

$\quad = 1(\cos 180° - j \sin 180°)$

$\quad = 1(-1 - j0)$

$Z_3 = -1$

(iv) $Z_4 = 7\angle{\frac{4\pi}{3}}$

$\quad = 7(\cos \frac{4\pi}{3} + j \sin \frac{4\pi}{3})$

$Z_4 = 7(-0.5 - j0.866)$

$\quad = -3.5 - j6.062$

$Z_4 = -3.5 - j6.062$

(v) $Z_5 = 3\angle{360°}$

$\quad = 3(\cos 360° + j \sin 360°)$

$\quad = 3(1 + j0) = 3.$

5. $|Z| = \sqrt{2}$ and $\arg Z = \frac{\pi}{3}$

(i) $Z = \sqrt{2}\angle{\frac{\pi}{3}}$

$\quad = \sqrt{2}(\cos \frac{\pi}{3} + j \sin \frac{\pi}{3})$

$\quad = \sqrt{2}(0.5 + j0.866)$

$Z = 0.707 + j1.225$

(ii) $Z = \sqrt{2}\angle{\frac{\pi}{3}}$

$\quad = \sqrt{2}(\cos \frac{\pi}{3} + j \sin \frac{\pi}{3})$

6.

(a)

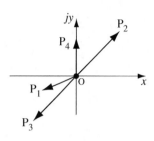

Fig. 81

$Z_1 = -1 - j \qquad Z_2 = 1 + j\sqrt{3}$

$Z_1 - Z_2 = -1 - j - 1 - j\sqrt{3} = -2 - j2.732$

$Z_1 - Z_2 = -2 - j2.732$

$Z_1 + Z_2 = -1 - j + 1 + j\sqrt{3} = j0.732.$

(b) (i) $Z_1 = -1 - j$

$\qquad |Z_1| = \sqrt{(-1)^2 + (1)^2}$
$\qquad \quad = \sqrt{1 + 1} = \sqrt{2}$

$\qquad \arg Z_1 = 180° + \tan^{-1} 1$
$\qquad \qquad \quad = 180° + 45° = 225° = \theta$

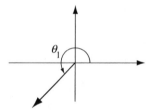

Fig. 82

(ii) $Z_2 = 1 + j\sqrt{3}$

$\qquad |Z_2| = \sqrt{1 + (\sqrt{3})^2} = \sqrt{4} = 2$

$\qquad \arg Z_2 = \tan^{-1} \dfrac{\sqrt{3}}{1} = \theta_2 = 60°$

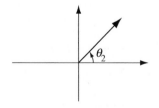

Fig. 83

(iii) $Z_1 Z_2 = \sqrt{2}\angle 225° \, 2\angle 60°$

$\qquad \quad = 2\sqrt{2}\angle 285°$

$\qquad |Z_1 Z_2| = 2\sqrt{2} \quad \arg Z_1 Z_2 = 285°$

(iv) $\dfrac{Z_1}{Z_2} = \dfrac{\sqrt{2}\angle 225°}{2\angle 60°} = \dfrac{\sqrt{2}}{2}\angle 165°$

$\qquad \left|\dfrac{Z_1}{Z_2}\right| = \dfrac{\sqrt{2}}{2} \quad \arg \dfrac{Z_1}{Z_2} = 165°$

(v) $\dfrac{Z_2}{Z_1} = \dfrac{2\angle 60°}{\sqrt{2}\angle 225°} = \dfrac{2}{\sqrt{2}}\angle{-165°}$

$\qquad \arg \dfrac{Z_2}{Z_1} = -165°$

$\qquad \left|\dfrac{Z_2}{Z_1}\right| = 2\sqrt{2}\dfrac{\sqrt{2}}{\sqrt{2}} = \sqrt{2}.$

7. $Z_1 = 5\angle 30°, \ Z_2 = 7\angle 50°, \ Z_3 = 9\angle{-45°}$

(i) $Z_1 Z_2 Z_3 = 5\angle 30° \, 7\angle 50° \, 9\angle{-45°}$

$\qquad \quad = 315\angle{30° + 50° - 45°}$

$\qquad Z_1 Z_2 Z_3 = 315\angle 35°$

(ii) $Z_1 Z_2 = 5\angle 30° \, 7\angle 50°$

$\qquad \quad = 35\angle{30° + 50°} = 35\angle 80°$

(iii) $Z_3 Z_1 = 9\angle{-45°} \, 5\angle 30°$

$\qquad \quad = 45\angle{-15°}$

(iv) $\dfrac{Z_2}{Z_3} = \dfrac{7\angle 50°}{9\angle{-45°}} = 0.778\angle 95°$

(v) $Z_1 Z_2 / Z_3 = 35\angle 80° / 9\angle{-45°}$

$\qquad \quad = \dfrac{35}{9}\angle{80° - 45°} = 3.89\angle 125°.$

The cartesian form

(i) $Z_1 Z_2 Z_3 = 315\angle 35°$

$\qquad \quad = 315(\cos 35° + j \sin 35°)$

$\qquad Z_1 Z_2 Z_3 = 315(0.819 + j0.574)$

$\qquad \quad = 258 + j181$

(ii) $Z_1 Z_2 = 35\underline{/80°}$

$\qquad = 35(\cos 80° + j \sin 80°)$

$\qquad = 35(0.174 + j0.985)$

$Z_1 Z_2 = 6.09 + j34.5$

(iii) $Z_3 Z_1 = 45\underline{/-15°}$

$\qquad = 45(\cos 15° - j \sin 15°)$

$\qquad = 45(0.966 - j0.259)$

$Z_3 Z_1 = 43.5 - j11.7$

(iv) $\dfrac{Z_2}{Z_3} = 0.778\underline{/95°}$

$\qquad = 0.778(\cos 95° + j \sin 95°)$

$\qquad = 0.778(-0.0872 + j0.996)$

$\qquad = -0.0678 + j0.775$

(v) $\dfrac{Z_1 Z_2}{Z_3} = 3.89\underline{/125°}$

$\qquad = 3.89(\cos 125° + j \sin 125°)$

$\qquad = 3.89(-0.574 + j0.819)$

$\qquad = -2.23 + j3.19.$

8. (i) $\sqrt{j} = \pm(a + jb)$ squaring up both sides where a and b are real numbers $j = a^2 + j^2 b^2 + j2ab$ $= a^2 - b^2 + j2ab$ equating real and imaginary terms $0 = a^2 - b^2$ or $a^2 = b^2$ or $a = \pm b$, $1 = 2ab$, if $a = b$, $1 = 2a^2$ or $a = \pm\dfrac{1}{\sqrt{2}}$

if $a = -b$,

$1 = 2ab = -2b^2 \quad b = \pm\left(-\dfrac{1}{\sqrt{2}}\right)$

which are complex numbers and are disregarded.

Therefore $\sqrt{j} = \pm(a + ja)$

$= \pm a(1 + j) = \mp\dfrac{1}{\sqrt{2}}(1 + j)$ that is

the square roots of $\sqrt{j}$ are $\dfrac{1}{\sqrt{2}} + \dfrac{1}{\sqrt{2}}j$

and $-\dfrac{1}{\sqrt{2}} - \dfrac{1}{\sqrt{2}}j.$

(ii) Let $\sqrt{3 - j4} = \pm(a + jb)$

squaring up both sides

$3 - j4 = (a^2 + j^2 b^2 + j2ab)$

$= a^2 - b^2 + j2ab$ equating real and imaginary terms $3 = a^2 - b^2$ and $-4 = 2ab$ or $a = -\dfrac{2}{b}$

$3 = \left(-\dfrac{2}{b}\right)^2 - b^2 = \dfrac{4}{b^2} - b^2$

multiplying each term by b^2

$3b^2 = 4 - b^4$ or $b^4 + 3b^2 - 4 = 0.$

Let $b^2 = W$

$W^2 + 3W - 4 = 0$ applying the quadratic formula

$W = \dfrac{-3 \pm \sqrt{9 - 4(1) \times (-4)}}{2}$

$\qquad = \dfrac{-3 \pm \sqrt{9 + 16}}{2} = -\dfrac{3 \pm 5}{2}$

$W = 1$ or $W = -4$

$b^2 = 1$ or $b = \pm 1$

$a = -\dfrac{2}{b} = -\dfrac{2}{1}$ or $a = -\dfrac{2}{-1} = 2$

$a = -2$ when $b = 1$ and $a = 2$ when $b = -1$

therefore $\sqrt{3 - j4} = \pm(-2 + j)$

the square roots of $3 - j4$ are $-2 + j$, and $2 - j$.

(iii) $\sqrt{j - 2} = \pm(1 + jb)$ squaring up both sides

$j - 2 = a^2 - b^2 + j2ab$ equating real and imaginary terms $a^2 - b^2 = -2$ and $1 = 2ab$ or $a = \dfrac{1}{2b}$.

$\left(\dfrac{1}{2b}\right)^2 - b^2 = -2$ or $\dfrac{1}{4b^2} - b^2 = -2$

multiplying each term by b^2,

$\dfrac{1}{4} - b^4 = -2b^2$ or

$b^4 - 2b^2 - \dfrac{1}{4} = 0 \quad 4b^4 - 8b^2 - 1 = 0$

applying the quadratic formula

$$b^2 = \frac{8 \pm \sqrt{64 + 4 \times 4}}{2 \times 4}$$

$$b^2 = \frac{8 \pm \sqrt{16 \times 5}}{8}$$

$$= \frac{8 \pm 4\sqrt{5}}{8}$$

$$= 1 \pm \frac{1}{2}\sqrt{5}$$

$b^2 = 1 \pm 1.118034$ which is $b^2 = 2.118334$
or $b^2 = -0.118034$ the latter is invalid,

$$b^2 = 2.1183034, \quad b = \pm 1.46$$

$$a = \frac{1}{2(1.46)} = 0.343 \quad \text{if} \quad b = 1.46$$

$$a = -0.343 \quad \text{if} \quad b = -1.46$$

therefore $\sqrt{j - 2} = \pm(0.343 + j1.46)$ and
the square roots of $j - 2$ are $0.343 + j1.46$
and $-0.343 - j1.46$.

9. $I = 3 + j4 \quad |I| = \sqrt{3^2 + 4^2} = 5$
$\arg I = \tan^{-1}\frac{4}{3} = 53.13°$

$V = 5 + j5 \quad |V| = \sqrt{5^2 + 5^2} = 7.07$,
$\arg V = \tan^{-1}\frac{5}{5} = 45°$

the phase angle between V and I is
$53.13° - 45°$ or $8.13°$, and
$P = |I||V|\cos\phi = 5 \times 7.07 \times \cos 8.13°$
and $P = 34.994 \approx 35W$.

10. (i) $X_c = \dfrac{1}{2\pi f C}$

$$= \frac{1}{2\pi\, 50\, 100 \times 10^{-6}} = 31.8\ \Omega$$

$X_L = 2\pi f L$

$$= 2\pi\, 50 \times 50 \times 10^{-3} = 15.71\ \Omega$$

$Z = R + jX_L - jX_c$

$$= 10 + j15.71 - j31.8$$

$|Z| = \sqrt{10^2 + (15.71 - 31.8)^2}$

$$= 18.9\ \Omega$$

$\arg Z = -\tan^{-1}\dfrac{31.8 - 15.71}{10}$

$$= -\tan^{-1}(3.18 - 1.571)$$

$$= -58.14°.$$

(ii) $Z = \dfrac{Z_1 Z_2}{Z_1 + Z_2}$

$$= \frac{(5 - j8)(10 + j10)}{5 - j8 + 10 + j10}$$

$$= \frac{-50 - j80 + j50 + 80}{15 + j2}$$

$$= \frac{30 - j30}{15 + j2}$$

$|Z| = \dfrac{\sqrt{130^2 + (-30)^2}}{\sqrt{15^2 + 2^2}}$

$$= \frac{133.4}{15.1} = 8.815\,\Omega$$

$\arg Z = \arg(130 - j30)$
$\qquad - \arg(15 + j2)$
$\qquad = -12.99° - 7.595°$
$\qquad = -20.6°.$

Solution 4

1.

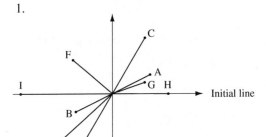

Fig. 84

2.

(i) $PQ = 1 + 1 = 2$

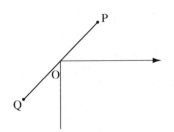

Fig. 85

(ii) $PQ = \sqrt{3} + \sqrt{3} = 2\sqrt{3}$

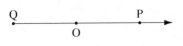

Fig. 86

(iii) $PQ = 4 + 4 = 8$

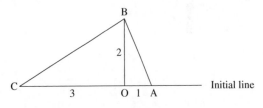

Fig. 87

3.

Area $\triangle ABC = \dfrac{1}{2}(2)(1 + 3) = 4$ square units.

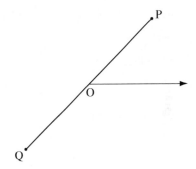

Fig. 88

4. (i) $\dfrac{x}{a} + \dfrac{y}{b} = 1$

$\sin \theta = \dfrac{y}{r}$ and $\cos \theta = \dfrac{x}{r}$

$y = r \sin \theta$ and $x = r \cos \theta$

$\dfrac{r \cos \theta}{a} + \dfrac{r \sin \theta}{b} = 1$

$r = \dfrac{ab}{b \cos \theta + a \sin \theta}$

(ii) $y = 3x - 5$

$\quad x = r\cos\theta$ and $y = r\sin\theta$

$\quad r\sin\theta = 3r\cos\theta - 5$

$\quad r(\sin\theta - 3\cos\theta) = -5$

$\quad r = \dfrac{5}{3\cos\theta - \sin\theta}$

(iii) $y = -3x$

$\quad r\sin\theta = -3r\cos\theta$

$\quad \sin\theta = -3\cos\theta$

$\quad \tan\theta = -3$

$\quad \theta = \tan^{-1}(-3)$

(iv) $y = x$

$\quad r\sin\theta = r\cos\theta$

$\quad \tan\theta = 1$

$\quad \tan^{-1}1 = \frac{\pi}{4}$

(v) $x = 5 \qquad r\cos\theta = 5$

$\quad r = \dfrac{5}{\cos\theta}$

(vi) $y = 2 \qquad r\sin\theta = 2$

$\quad r = \frac{2}{\sin\theta}$

(vii) $y = 0$

$\quad r\sin\theta = 0 \quad$ or $\quad \theta = 0°$

(viii) $y = x + 1$

$\quad r\sin\theta = r\cos\theta + 1$

$\quad r(\sin\theta - \cos\theta) = 1$

$\quad r = \dfrac{1}{\sin\theta - \cos\theta}$

(ix) $x = -5$

$\quad r\cos\theta = -5$

$\quad r = -\frac{5}{\cos\theta}.$

5. (i) $x^2 + y^2 = 1$

$\quad r^2\cos^2\theta + r^2\sin^2\theta = 1$

$\quad r^2(\cos^2\theta + \sin^2\theta) = 1$

(ii) $x^2 + y^2 = 2^2 \qquad r = 2$

(iii) $\dfrac{x^2}{3^2} + \dfrac{y^2}{4^2} = 1$

$\quad \dfrac{r^2\cos^2\theta}{3^2} + \dfrac{r^2\sin^2\theta}{4^2} = 1$

$\quad 16r^2\cos^2\theta + 9r^2\sin^2\theta = 144$

(iv) $\dfrac{x^2}{4^2} - \dfrac{y^2}{5^2} = 1$

$\quad \dfrac{r^2\cos\theta}{16} - \dfrac{r^2\sin^2\theta}{25} = 1$

$\quad 25r^2\cos^2\theta - 16r^2\sin^2\theta = 400$

(v) $yx = 5$

$\quad r\sin\theta r\cos\theta = 5$

$\quad r^2 = \dfrac{5}{\sin\theta\cos\theta}$

(vi) $y^2 = 4x \qquad r^2\sin^2\theta = 4r\cos\theta$

$\quad r = \dfrac{4\cos\theta}{\sin^2\theta} = 4\cos\theta\,\mathrm{cosec}^2\theta$

(vii) $x^2 - 4y = 0,$

$\quad r^2\cos^2\theta - 4r\sin\theta = 0$

(viii) $x^2 + y^2 - x - y - 1 = 0$

$\quad r^2\cos^2\theta + r^2\sin^2\theta$

$\quad\quad -r\cos\theta - r\sin\theta - 1 = 0$

$\quad r^2(\cos^2\theta + \sin^2\theta)$

$\quad\quad = r(\cos\theta + \sin\theta)$

$\quad r = \cos\theta + \sin\theta$

(xi) $y = \frac{1}{x}$

$\quad r\sin\theta = \dfrac{1}{r\cos\theta}$

$\quad r^2 = \dfrac{1}{\sin\theta\cos\theta}.$

6. (i) $r = 5\theta \qquad r = \sqrt{x^2 + y^2}$

$\quad \theta = \tan^{-1}\frac{y}{x}$

$\quad \sqrt{x^2 + y^2} = 5\tan^{-1}\frac{y}{x}$

(ii) $r = -3\theta$

$\boxed{\sqrt{x^2 + y^2} = -3\tan^{-1}\dfrac{y}{x}}$

(iii) $r = 2\cos\theta \qquad r^2 = 2x$

$\quad x^2 + y^2 = 2x$

(iv) $\theta = \dfrac{\pi}{4}$

$\tan^{-1}\dfrac{y}{x} = \dfrac{\pi}{4}$ $\dfrac{y}{x} = \tan\dfrac{\pi}{4} = 1$

$\boxed{y = x}$

(v) $\theta = \dfrac{\pi}{2}$

$\tan^{-1}\dfrac{y}{x} = \dfrac{\pi}{2}$ $\tan\dfrac{\pi}{2} = \dfrac{y}{x}$

$y = x\tan\dfrac{\pi}{2}$ $\dfrac{y}{\tan\frac{\pi}{2}} = x$

$\boxed{x = 0}$

(vi) $r = 1$

$\sqrt{x^2 + y^2} = 1$ $x^2 + y^2 = 1$

(vii) $r = 2^2$ $\sqrt{x^2 + y^2} = 4$

$\boxed{x^2 + y^2 = 4^2.}$

7.   (i) $r = 5$

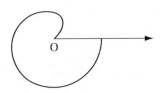

The radius of the circle is 5 and the centre is the pole.

(ii) $r = 3\theta$

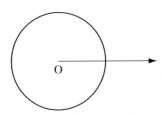

If $\theta = 0, r = 0$ $\theta = \frac{\pi}{3}, r = \pi$

$\theta = \frac{\pi}{2}, r = \frac{3\pi}{2}$

$\theta = \pi, r = 3\pi$ and $\theta = 2\pi, r = 6\pi$

(iii) $r = 3\cos\theta$

θ	$\cos\theta$	$3\cos\theta$
0°	1	3
30°	0.866	2.598
60°	0.5	1.5
90°	0	0
120°	−0.866	−2.598
150°	0.866	−2.598
180°	1	3

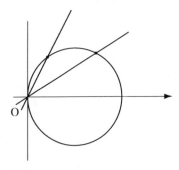

(iv) $\theta = \dfrac{\pi}{3}$

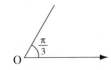

(v) $\theta = -\dfrac{\pi}{2}$

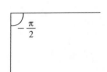

8. From the above examples, it can be seen that some functions in cartesian co-ordinate system are easy to be drawn and some functions in polar co-ordinate system are easy to be drawn.

Examples

(a) $y = x$ or $\theta = \frac{\pi}{2}$ is a straight line through the origin for $y = x$ and $\theta = \frac{\pi}{2}$ is a straight line drawn from the pole at 90°.

(b) $y = \frac{1}{x}$ or $yx = 1$ is a simple cartesian curve, the rectangular hyperbola

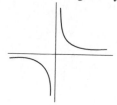

but the corresponding polar curve is

$$r^2 = \frac{1}{\sin\theta \cos\theta}$$

which is rather difficult to recognise, a table needs to be constructed for various angles and the corresponding values of r to be calculated.

(c) $r = 3\theta$ is an archimediam spiral which is easy to be drawn, but the corresponding cartesian form is $\sqrt{x^2 + y^2} = 3\tan^{-1}\frac{y}{x}$ which would be rather very difficult to interpret.

Solution 5

1. (i) $\begin{pmatrix} 1 & 0 \\ 0 & 1 \end{pmatrix}$ unit matrix 2×2

    (ii) $\begin{pmatrix} 0 & 0 \\ 0 & 0 \end{pmatrix}$ zero matrix 2×2

    (iii) $\begin{pmatrix} 3 & 0 \\ 0 & -2 \end{pmatrix}$ diagonal matrix 2×2.

2. (i) $\begin{pmatrix} a \\ b \\ c \end{pmatrix}$ 3×1 column matrix

    (ii) $\begin{pmatrix} 1 & 2 & 3 \\ 4 & 5 & 6 \\ 7 & 8 & 9 \end{pmatrix}$ 3×3 square matrix

    (iii) $\begin{pmatrix} a & b & c \end{pmatrix}$ 1×3 row matrix

    (iv) $\begin{pmatrix} a & d \\ b & e \\ c & f \end{pmatrix}$

      3×2 rectangular matrix

      $\begin{pmatrix} a & b & c \\ d & e & f \end{pmatrix}$

      2×3 rectangular matrix

    (v) $\begin{pmatrix} 1 & 0 & 0 \\ 0 & 1 & 0 \\ 0 & 0 & 1 \end{pmatrix}$ 3×3 unit matrix

    (vi) $\begin{pmatrix} a & 0 & 0 \\ 0 & b & 0 \\ 0 & 0 & c \end{pmatrix}$

      3×3 diagonal matrix

    (viii) $\begin{pmatrix} 0 & 0 & 0 \\ 0 & 0 & 0 \\ 0 & 0 & 0 \end{pmatrix}$

      3×3 Null matrix.

3. $\mathbf{A} = \begin{pmatrix} -1 & 2 \\ -3 & 3 \end{pmatrix}$ $\mathbf{B} = \begin{pmatrix} 1 & -2 \\ 3 & 5 \end{pmatrix}$

$\mathbf{C} = \begin{pmatrix} 0 & 1 \\ 1 & 0 \end{pmatrix}$.

(i) $\mathbf{A} + \mathbf{B} + \mathbf{C}$

$= \begin{pmatrix} -1 & 2 \\ -3 & 3 \end{pmatrix} + \begin{pmatrix} 1 & -2 \\ 3 & 5 \end{pmatrix}$

$\quad + \begin{pmatrix} 0 & 1 \\ 1 & 0 \end{pmatrix}$

$= \begin{pmatrix} -1+1+0 & 2-2+1 \\ -3+3+1 & 3+5+0 \end{pmatrix}$

$= \begin{pmatrix} 0 & 1 \\ 1 & 8 \end{pmatrix}$.

(ii) $2\mathbf{A} - 3\mathbf{C} + 2\mathbf{B}$

$= 2\begin{pmatrix} -1 & 2 \\ -3 & 3 \end{pmatrix} - 3\begin{pmatrix} 0 & 1 \\ 1 & 0 \end{pmatrix}$

$\quad + 2\begin{pmatrix} 1 & -2 \\ 3 & 5 \end{pmatrix}$

$= \begin{pmatrix} -2 & 4 \\ -6 & 6 \end{pmatrix} - \begin{pmatrix} 0 & 3 \\ 3 & 0 \end{pmatrix}$

$\quad + \begin{pmatrix} 2 & -4 \\ 6 & 10 \end{pmatrix}$

$= \begin{pmatrix} -2-0+2 & 4-3-4 \\ -6-3+6 & 6-0+10 \end{pmatrix}$

$= \begin{pmatrix} 0 & -3 \\ -3 & 16 \end{pmatrix}$.

(iii) $5\mathbf{B} + 4\mathbf{A}$

$= 5\begin{pmatrix} 1 & -2 \\ 3 & 5 \end{pmatrix} + 4\begin{pmatrix} -1 & 2 \\ -3 & 3 \end{pmatrix}$

$= \begin{pmatrix} 5 & -10 \\ 15 & 25 \end{pmatrix} + \begin{pmatrix} -4 & 8 \\ -12 & 12 \end{pmatrix}$

$= \begin{pmatrix} 5-4 & -10+8 \\ 15-12 & 25+12 \end{pmatrix}$

$= \begin{pmatrix} 1 & -2 \\ 3 & 37 \end{pmatrix}$.

4. $A = \begin{pmatrix} 6 & 7 \\ 8 & 9 \end{pmatrix}$ $B = \begin{pmatrix} 10 & 11 \\ 12 & 13 \end{pmatrix}$

$C = \begin{pmatrix} 0 & 1 \\ -1 & 0 \end{pmatrix}$

(i) $AB = \begin{pmatrix} 6 & 7 \\ 8 & 9 \end{pmatrix} \begin{pmatrix} 10 & 11 \\ 12 & 13 \end{pmatrix}$

$= \begin{pmatrix} 60 + 84 & 66 + 91 \\ 80 + 108 & 88 + 117 \end{pmatrix}$

$= \begin{pmatrix} 144 & 157 \\ 188 & 205 \end{pmatrix}$

$ABC = \begin{pmatrix} 144 & 157 \\ 188 & 205 \end{pmatrix} \begin{pmatrix} 0 & 1 \\ -1 & 0 \end{pmatrix}$

$= \begin{pmatrix} -157 & 144 \\ -205 & 188 \end{pmatrix}$

(ii) $A^2 = AA = \begin{pmatrix} 6 & 7 \\ 8 & 9 \end{pmatrix} \begin{pmatrix} 6 & 7 \\ 8 & 9 \end{pmatrix}$

$= \begin{pmatrix} 36 + 56 & 42 + 63 \\ 48 + 72 & 56 + 81 \end{pmatrix}$

$= \begin{pmatrix} 92 & 105 \\ 120 & 137 \end{pmatrix}$

(iii) $BC = \begin{pmatrix} 10 & 11 \\ 12 & 13 \end{pmatrix} \begin{pmatrix} 0 & 1 \\ -1 & 0 \end{pmatrix}$

$= \begin{pmatrix} 10 \times 0 + 11(-1) & 10 + 11(0) \\ 12 \times 1 + 13(-1) & 12 \times 1 + 13(0) \end{pmatrix}$

$= \begin{pmatrix} -11 & 10 \\ -13 & 12 \end{pmatrix}$

(iv) $AC = \begin{pmatrix} 6 & 7 \\ 8 & 9 \end{pmatrix} \begin{pmatrix} 0 & 1 \\ -1 & 0 \end{pmatrix}$

$= \begin{pmatrix} 6 \times 0 + 7(-1) & 6 \times 1 + 7(0) \\ 8(0) + 9(-1) & 8 \times 1 + 9(0) \end{pmatrix}$

$= \begin{pmatrix} -7 & 6 \\ -9 & 8 \end{pmatrix}$

(v) $CB = \begin{pmatrix} 0 & 1 \\ -1 & 0 \end{pmatrix} \begin{pmatrix} 10 & 11 \\ 12 & 13 \end{pmatrix}$

$= \begin{pmatrix} 12 & 13 \\ -10 & -11 \end{pmatrix}$.

5. $AB = \begin{pmatrix} 144 & 157 \\ 188 & 205 \end{pmatrix}$

$BA \begin{pmatrix} 10 & 11 \\ 12 & 13 \end{pmatrix} \begin{pmatrix} 6 & 7 \\ 8 & 9 \end{pmatrix}$

$= \begin{pmatrix} 60 + 88 & 70 + 99 \\ 72 + 104 & 84 + 117 \end{pmatrix}$

$= \begin{pmatrix} 148 & 169 \\ 176 & 201 \end{pmatrix}$

therefore $AB \neq BA$.

$BC = \begin{pmatrix} -11 & 10 \\ -13 & 12 \end{pmatrix}$

$CB = \begin{pmatrix} 0 & 1 \\ -1 & 0 \end{pmatrix} \begin{pmatrix} 10 & 11 \\ 12 & 13 \end{pmatrix}$

$= \begin{pmatrix} 12 & 13 \\ -10 & -11 \end{pmatrix}$

therefore $BC \neq CB$.

6. $A + B = B + A$ using the examples of question 5

$A + B = \begin{pmatrix} 6 & 7 \\ 8 & 9 \end{pmatrix} + \begin{pmatrix} 10 & 11 \\ 12 & 13 \end{pmatrix}$

$= \begin{pmatrix} 16 & 18 \\ 20 & 22 \end{pmatrix}$

$B + A = \begin{pmatrix} 10 & 11 \\ 12 & 13 \end{pmatrix} + \begin{pmatrix} 6 & 7 \\ 8 & 9 \end{pmatrix}$

$= \begin{pmatrix} 16 & 18 \\ 20 & 22 \end{pmatrix}$

therefore $A + B = B + A$ the matrices are associative.

In question five, we have seen that $AB \neq BA$ and $BC \neq CB$ therefore matrices are not commutative.

7. A unit matrix is a diagonal matrix whose elements are one.

$I = \begin{pmatrix} 1 & 0 \\ 0 & 1 \end{pmatrix}$ $A = \begin{pmatrix} 1 & -2 \\ 3 & -4 \end{pmatrix}$

$IA = \begin{pmatrix} 1 & 0 \\ 0 & 1 \end{pmatrix} \begin{pmatrix} 1 & -2 \\ 3 & -4 \end{pmatrix}$

$= \begin{pmatrix} 1 & -2 \\ 3 & -4 \end{pmatrix}$.

Matrix **A** is unaltered when it is premultiplied by a unit matrix

$$\mathbf{AI} = \begin{pmatrix} 1 & -2 \\ 3 & -4 \end{pmatrix} \begin{pmatrix} 1 & 0 \\ 0 & 1 \end{pmatrix}$$

$$= \begin{pmatrix} 1 & -2 \\ 3 & -4 \end{pmatrix}$$

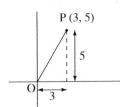

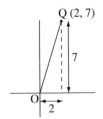

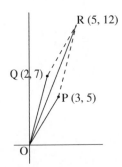

Matrix **A** is unaltered when it is post multiplied by a unit matrix

$$\overrightarrow{OP} + \overrightarrow{OQ} = \begin{pmatrix} 3 \\ 5 \end{pmatrix} + \begin{pmatrix} 2 \\ 7 \end{pmatrix}$$

$$= \begin{pmatrix} 3+2 \\ 5+7 \end{pmatrix} = \begin{pmatrix} 5 \\ 12 \end{pmatrix}$$

$$\overrightarrow{OR} = \begin{pmatrix} 5 \\ 12 \end{pmatrix}$$

9. $\mathbf{A} = \begin{pmatrix} 1 & b \\ a & 2 \end{pmatrix}$ $\mathbf{B} = \begin{pmatrix} -1 & 2 \\ 3 & 4 \end{pmatrix}$

$$\mathbf{AB} = \begin{pmatrix} 1 & b \\ a & 2 \end{pmatrix} \begin{pmatrix} -1 & 2 \\ 3 & 4 \end{pmatrix}$$

$$= \begin{pmatrix} -1+3b & 2+4b \\ -a+6 & 2a+8 \end{pmatrix}$$

$$\mathbf{C} = \begin{pmatrix} 5 & 10 \\ -1 & 22 \end{pmatrix}$$

AB = C

therefore the corresponding elements are equal

$$-1 + 3b = 5 \Rightarrow 3b = 6 \Rightarrow b = 2$$
$$2 + 4b = 10 \Rightarrow 4b = 8 \Rightarrow b = 2$$
$$-a + b = -5 \Rightarrow -a = -7 \Rightarrow a = 7$$
$$2a + 8 = 22 \Rightarrow 2a = 14 \Rightarrow a = 7$$
$$a = 7 \text{ and } b = 2.$$

10.   (i) $\begin{vmatrix} a & b \\ a^2 & b^2 \end{vmatrix} = a \begin{vmatrix} 1 & b \\ a & b^2 \end{vmatrix}$

$$= ab \begin{vmatrix} 1 & 1 \\ a & b \end{vmatrix}$$

$$= ab(b-a)$$

      factorising

  (ii) $\begin{vmatrix} 1 & 3 \\ 2 & 4 \end{vmatrix} = 1 \times 4 - 2 \times 3$

$$= 4 - 6 = -2$$

  (iii) $\begin{vmatrix} a & 3 \\ 4 & a \end{vmatrix} = a^2 - 12.$

11.   (i) $\begin{vmatrix} a & 2 \\ a^2 & 4 \end{vmatrix} = a \begin{vmatrix} 1 & 2 \\ a & 4 \end{vmatrix}$

$$= 2a \begin{vmatrix} 1 & 1 \\ a & 2 \end{vmatrix}$$

If the two columns are equal the determinant is zero, therefore $a = 2$.

  (ii) $\begin{vmatrix} 3 & a \\ 9 & a^2 \end{vmatrix} = 3 \begin{vmatrix} 1 & a \\ 3 & a^2 \end{vmatrix}$

$$= 3a \begin{vmatrix} 1 & 1 \\ 3 & a \end{vmatrix}$$

therefore $a = 3$ and the columns are the same and hence the Δ is zero.

  (iii) $\begin{vmatrix} 1 & a \\ a & 1 \end{vmatrix}$ If $a = 1$ then the $\Delta = 0$.

12. (i) $\begin{vmatrix} 2x & 1 \\ 8x^2 & 2 \end{vmatrix} = 2x \begin{vmatrix} 1 & 1 \\ 4x & 2 \end{vmatrix}$

$= 2x(2 - 4x)$

(ii) $\begin{vmatrix} 2y & x \\ 4y^2 & x^2 \end{vmatrix} = 2 \begin{vmatrix} y & x \\ 2y^2 & x^2 \end{vmatrix}$

$\begin{vmatrix} 2y & x \\ 4y^2 & x^2 \end{vmatrix} = 2y \begin{vmatrix} 1 & x \\ 2y & x^2 \end{vmatrix}$

$= 2yx \begin{vmatrix} 1 & 1 \\ 2y & x \end{vmatrix}$

$= 2yx(x - 2y).$

Solution 6

1. (i) $2x - y = 5$ ... (1)

    $x + y = -7$ ... (2)

    Adding equations (1) and (2)

    $3x = -2$ or $x = -\frac{2}{3}$

    substituting $x = -\frac{2}{3}$ in (2)

    $-\frac{2}{3} + y = -7$ or

    $y = -7 + \frac{2}{3} = -6\frac{1}{3} = -\frac{19}{3}$

    therefore $x = -\frac{2}{3}$ and $y = -\frac{19}{3}$.

    (ii) $-3x + 2y = 2$ ... (1)

    $x - 3y = 5$ ... (2)

    multiply (2) by 3, we have

    $3x - 9y = 15$ ... (3)

    equations (1) and (3) are

    $-3x + 2y = 2$ ... (3)

    $3x - 9y = 15$ ... (4)

    adding equations (3) and (4)

    $-7y = 17$ or $y = -\frac{17}{7}$

    substituting $y = -\frac{17}{7}$ in equation (2)

    $x - 3\left(-\frac{17}{7}\right) = 5$ or

    $x = 5 - \frac{51}{7} = \frac{35 - 51}{7}$

    $x = -\frac{16}{7}$

    therefore $x = -\frac{16}{7}$ and $y = -\frac{17}{7}$.

2. (i) $2x - y = 5$

    $x + y = -7$

    using Crammer's rule

$$\frac{x}{\Delta_1} = -\frac{y}{\Delta_2} = \frac{1}{\Delta}$$

where $\Delta_1 = \begin{vmatrix} -1 & -5 \\ 1 & 7 \end{vmatrix}$

$= -7 + 5 = -2$

$\Delta_2 = \begin{vmatrix} 2 & -5 \\ 1 & 7 \end{vmatrix} = 14 + 5 = 19$

$\Delta = \begin{vmatrix} 2 & -1 \\ 1 & 1 \end{vmatrix} = 2 + 1 = 3$

$\frac{x}{\Delta_1} = \frac{1}{\Delta}$ or $x = \frac{\Delta_1}{\Delta} = -\frac{2}{3}$

$\frac{y}{\Delta_2} = -\frac{1}{\Delta}$ or $y = -\frac{\Delta_2}{\Delta} = -\frac{19}{3}$

therefore $x = -\frac{2}{3}$ and $y = -\frac{19}{3}$.

(ii) $-3x + 2y = 2$

$x - 3y = 5$

Using Crammer's rule

$$\frac{x}{\Delta_1} = -\frac{y}{\Delta_2} = \frac{1}{\Delta}$$

where $\Delta_1 = \begin{vmatrix} 2 & -2 \\ -3 & -5 \end{vmatrix}$

$\Delta_2 = \begin{vmatrix} -3 & -2 \\ 1 & -5 \end{vmatrix}$

$\Delta = \begin{vmatrix} -3 & 2 \\ 1 & -3 \end{vmatrix}$

$\Delta_1 = -10 - 6 = -16$,

$\Delta_2 = 15 + 2 = 17$, $\Delta = 9 - 2 = 7$

$x = \frac{\Delta_1}{\Delta} = -\frac{16}{7}$ and

$y = -\frac{\Delta_2}{\Delta} = -\frac{17}{7}$ and therefore

$x = -\frac{16}{7}$ and $y = -\frac{17}{7}$.

3. (i) $\mathbf{A} = \begin{pmatrix} 1 & 2 \\ 3 & 4 \end{pmatrix}$

the minors are $\begin{pmatrix} 4 & 3 \\ 2 & 1 \end{pmatrix}$

and the corresponding cofactors are
$\begin{pmatrix} 4 & -3 \\ -2 & 1 \end{pmatrix}$

(ii) $\mathbf{M} = \begin{pmatrix} -1 & -2 \\ -3 & 4 \end{pmatrix}$

the minors are $\begin{pmatrix} 4 & -3 \\ -2 & -1 \end{pmatrix}$ and

hence the cofactors are $\begin{pmatrix} 4 & 3 \\ 2 & -1 \end{pmatrix}$.

4. (i) $\mathbf{A} = \begin{pmatrix} 1 & 2 \\ 3 & 4 \end{pmatrix}$

$\mathbf{A}^* = \begin{pmatrix} 4 & -3 \\ -2 & 1 \end{pmatrix}$

$(\mathbf{A}^*)^T$ adjoint matrix

$\qquad = \begin{pmatrix} 4 & -2 \\ -3 & 1 \end{pmatrix}$

(ii) $\mathbf{M} = \begin{pmatrix} -1 & -2 \\ -3 & 4 \end{pmatrix}$

$\mathbf{M}^* = \begin{pmatrix} 4 & 3 \\ 2 & -1 \end{pmatrix}$

$(\mathbf{M}^*)^T$ = the transpose of the cofactors

$\qquad$ = adjoint matrix = $\begin{pmatrix} 4 & 2 \\ 3 & -1 \end{pmatrix}$.

5. (i) $\mathbf{A} = \begin{pmatrix} 2 & -1 \\ 2 & 1 \end{pmatrix}$

$(\mathbf{A}^*)^T = \begin{pmatrix} 1 & 1 \\ -2 & 2 \end{pmatrix}$

$|\mathbf{A}| = \begin{pmatrix} 2 & -1 \\ 2 & 1 \end{pmatrix} = 2 + 2 = 4$

$\mathbf{A}^{-1} = \dfrac{(\mathbf{A}^*)^T}{|\mathbf{A}|} = \dfrac{1}{4}\begin{pmatrix} 1 & 1 \\ -2 & 2 \end{pmatrix}$

$\qquad = \begin{pmatrix} \dfrac{1}{4} & \dfrac{1}{4} \\ -\dfrac{1}{2} & \dfrac{1}{2} \end{pmatrix}$

(ii) $\mathbf{B} = \begin{pmatrix} -3 & 2 \\ 1 & -3 \end{pmatrix}$

$\mathbf{B}^* = \begin{pmatrix} -3 & -1 \\ -2 & -3 \end{pmatrix}$

$(\mathbf{B}^*)^T \begin{pmatrix} -3 & -2 \\ -1 & -3 \end{pmatrix}$

$|\mathbf{B}| = \begin{vmatrix} -3 & 2 \\ 1 & -3 \end{vmatrix} = 9 - 2 = 7$

$\mathbf{B}^{-1} = \dfrac{(\mathbf{B}^*)^T}{|\mathbf{B}|} = \dfrac{1}{7}\begin{pmatrix} -3 & -2 \\ -1 & -3 \end{pmatrix}$

$\qquad = \begin{pmatrix} -\dfrac{3}{7} & -\dfrac{2}{7} \\ -\dfrac{1}{7} & -\dfrac{3}{7} \end{pmatrix}$.

6. (i) $2x - y = 5$

$x + y = -7$

In matrix form

$\begin{pmatrix} 2 & -1 \\ 1 & 1 \end{pmatrix}\begin{pmatrix} x \\ y \end{pmatrix} = \begin{pmatrix} 5 \\ -7 \end{pmatrix}$

If $\mathbf{A} = \begin{pmatrix} 2 & -1 \\ 1 & 1 \end{pmatrix}$

$\mathbf{A}^* = \begin{pmatrix} 1 & -1 \\ 1 & 2 \end{pmatrix}$

$(\mathbf{A}^*)^T = \begin{pmatrix} 1 & 1 \\ -1 & 2 \end{pmatrix}$

$|\mathbf{A}| = \begin{vmatrix} 2 & -1 \\ 1 & 1 \end{vmatrix} = 2 + 1 = 3$

$\mathbf{A}^{-1} = \dfrac{(\mathbf{A}^*)^T}{|\mathbf{A}|} = \begin{pmatrix} \dfrac{1}{3} & \dfrac{1}{3} \\ -\dfrac{1}{3} & \dfrac{2}{3} \end{pmatrix}$

$\mathbf{A}^{-1}\mathbf{A} = \begin{pmatrix} \dfrac{1}{3} & \dfrac{1}{3} \\ -\dfrac{1}{3} & \dfrac{2}{3} \end{pmatrix}\begin{pmatrix} 2 & -1 \\ 1 & 1 \end{pmatrix}$

$\qquad = \begin{pmatrix} \dfrac{2}{3}+\dfrac{1}{3} & -\dfrac{1}{3}+\dfrac{1}{3} \\ -\dfrac{2}{3}+\dfrac{2}{3} & \dfrac{1}{3}+\dfrac{2}{3} \end{pmatrix}$

$\qquad = \begin{pmatrix} 1 & 0 \\ 0 & 1 \end{pmatrix} = \mathbf{I}$

$$\begin{pmatrix} \dfrac{1}{3} & \dfrac{1}{3} \\ -\dfrac{1}{3} & \dfrac{2}{3} \end{pmatrix} \begin{pmatrix} 2 & -1 \\ 1 & 1 \end{pmatrix} \begin{pmatrix} x \\ y \end{pmatrix}$$

$$= \begin{pmatrix} \dfrac{1}{3} & \dfrac{1}{3} \\ -\dfrac{1}{3} & \dfrac{2}{3} \end{pmatrix} \begin{pmatrix} 5 \\ -7 \end{pmatrix}$$

$$\begin{pmatrix} x \\ y \end{pmatrix} = \begin{pmatrix} \dfrac{5}{3} & -\dfrac{7}{3} \\ -\dfrac{5}{3} & -\dfrac{14}{3} \end{pmatrix}$$

$$= \begin{pmatrix} -\dfrac{2}{3} \\ -\dfrac{19}{3} \end{pmatrix}$$

$$x = -\frac{2}{3} \text{ and } y = -\frac{19}{3}.$$

(ii) $-3x + 2y = 2$

$x - 3y = 5$

in matrix form

$$\begin{pmatrix} -3 & 2 \\ 1 & -3 \end{pmatrix} \begin{pmatrix} x \\ y \end{pmatrix} = \begin{pmatrix} 2 \\ 5 \end{pmatrix}.$$

Let $\mathbf{B} = \begin{pmatrix} -3 & 2 \\ 1 & -3 \end{pmatrix}$,

$$\mathbf{B}^{-1} = \begin{pmatrix} -\dfrac{3}{7} & -\dfrac{2}{7} \\ -\dfrac{1}{7} & -\dfrac{3}{7} \end{pmatrix}.$$

See solution 5 (ii)

$$\mathbf{B}^{-1}\mathbf{B} \begin{pmatrix} -\dfrac{3}{7} & -\dfrac{2}{7} \\ -\dfrac{1}{7} & -\dfrac{3}{7} \end{pmatrix} \begin{pmatrix} -3 & 2 \\ 1 & -3 \end{pmatrix}$$

$$= \begin{pmatrix} \dfrac{9}{7} - \dfrac{2}{7} & -\dfrac{6}{7} + \dfrac{6}{7} \\ \dfrac{3}{7} - \dfrac{3}{7} & -\dfrac{2}{7} + \dfrac{9}{7} \end{pmatrix}$$

$$\begin{pmatrix} -\dfrac{3}{7} & -\dfrac{2}{7} \\ -\dfrac{1}{7} & -\dfrac{3}{7} \end{pmatrix} \begin{pmatrix} -3 & 2 \\ 1 & -3 \end{pmatrix}$$

$$\begin{pmatrix} x \\ y \end{pmatrix} = \begin{pmatrix} -\dfrac{3}{7} & -\dfrac{2}{7} \\ -\dfrac{1}{7} & -\dfrac{3}{7} \end{pmatrix} \begin{pmatrix} 2 \\ 5 \end{pmatrix}.$$

$$\begin{pmatrix} x \\ y \end{pmatrix} = \begin{pmatrix} -\dfrac{6}{7} & -\dfrac{10}{7} \\ -\dfrac{2}{7} & -\dfrac{15}{7} \end{pmatrix}$$

$$= \begin{pmatrix} -\dfrac{16}{7} \\ -\dfrac{17}{7} \end{pmatrix}$$

and therefore $x = -\dfrac{16}{7}$ and $y = -\dfrac{17}{7}$.

7. Using Kirchhoff's Law

$10 = 2I_1 + 5I_1 + 5I_2$

$\boxed{10 = 7I_1 + 5I_2}$

$5 = 1.5I_2 + 5I_1 + 5I_2$

$\boxed{5 = 5I_1 + 6.5I_2}$

(i) $7I_1 + 5I_2 = 10$

$5I_1 + 6.5I_2 = 5$

by Crammer's rule.

$$\frac{I_1}{\Delta_1} = -\frac{I_2}{\Delta_2} = \frac{1}{\Delta}$$

$$\Delta_1 = \begin{vmatrix} 5 & -10 \\ 6.5 & -5 \end{vmatrix} = -25 + 65 = 40$$

$$\Delta_2 = \begin{vmatrix} 7 & -10 \\ 5 & -5 \end{vmatrix} = -35 + 50 = 15$$

$$\Delta = \begin{vmatrix} 7 & 5 \\ 5 & 6.5 \end{vmatrix} = 45 - 25 = 20$$

$$I_1 = \frac{\Delta_1}{\Delta} = \frac{40}{20} = 2 \text{ A}$$

$$I_2 = -\frac{\Delta_2}{\Delta} = -\frac{15}{20} = -0.75 \text{ A}.$$

(ii) In matrix form

$$\begin{pmatrix} 7 & 5 \\ 5 & 6.5 \end{pmatrix} = \begin{pmatrix} I_1 \\ I_2 \end{pmatrix} = \begin{pmatrix} 10 \\ 5 \end{pmatrix}$$

$$\mathbf{A} = \begin{pmatrix} 7 & 5 \\ 5 & 6.5 \end{pmatrix} \quad \mathbf{A}^* = \begin{pmatrix} 6.5 & -5 \\ -5 & 7 \end{pmatrix}$$

$$(\mathbf{A}^*)^{\mathrm{T}} = \begin{pmatrix} 6.5 & -5 \\ -5 & 7 \end{pmatrix}$$

$$\mathbf{A}^{-1} = \frac{(\mathbf{A}^*)^{\mathrm{T}}}{|\mathbf{A}|} = \frac{\begin{pmatrix} 6.5 & -5 \\ -5 & 7 \end{pmatrix}}{\begin{pmatrix} 7 & 5 \\ 5 & 6.5 \end{pmatrix}}$$

$$= \frac{\begin{pmatrix} 6.5 & -5 \\ -5 & 7 \end{pmatrix}}{20}$$

$$= \begin{pmatrix} \dfrac{6.5}{20} & \dfrac{5}{20} \\ \dfrac{5}{20} & \dfrac{7}{20} \end{pmatrix}$$

$$\mathbf{A}^{-1}\mathbf{A} = \begin{pmatrix} 0.325 & -0.25 \\ -0.25 & 0.35 \end{pmatrix}$$

$$\begin{pmatrix} 7 & 5 \\ 5 & 6.5 \end{pmatrix} = \begin{pmatrix} 1 & 0 \\ 0 & 1 \end{pmatrix}$$

$$\mathbf{I}\begin{pmatrix} I_1 \\ I_2 \end{pmatrix}$$

$$= \begin{pmatrix} 0.325 & -0.25 \\ -0.25 & 0.35 \end{pmatrix}\begin{pmatrix} 10 \\ 5 \end{pmatrix}$$

$$= \begin{pmatrix} 2 \\ -0.75 \end{pmatrix}$$

$$\begin{pmatrix} I_1 \\ I_2 \end{pmatrix} = \begin{pmatrix} 2 \\ -0.75 \end{pmatrix}$$

$I_1 = 2\,\mathrm{A}$ and $I_2 = -0.75\,\mathrm{A}$.

8. From the network, we have

$$v_{\mathrm{be}} = i_b 1000 + 10^{-4}v_{\mathrm{ce}} \qquad \ldots(1)$$
$$i_c = 100i_b + 10^{-3}v_{\mathrm{ce}} \qquad \ldots(2)$$
$$v_{\mathrm{be}} = i_b 1000 + 10^{-4}v_{\mathrm{ce}} \qquad \ldots(3)$$
$$\frac{v_{\mathrm{ce}}}{-1000} = 100i_b + 10^{-3}v_{\mathrm{ce}} \qquad \ldots(4)$$

eliminate i_b by multiplying (4) by 10

$$v_{\mathrm{be}} = 1000i_b + 10^{-4}v_{\mathrm{ce}}$$
$$-\frac{v_{\mathrm{ce}}}{100} = 1000i_b + 10^{-2}v_{\mathrm{ce}}$$
$$v_{\mathrm{be}} + \frac{v_{\mathrm{ce}}}{100} = (10^{-4}v_{\mathrm{ce}} - 10^{-2}v_{\mathrm{ce}})$$
$$v_{\mathrm{be}} = 10^{-4}v_{\mathrm{ce}} - 10^{-2}v_{\mathrm{ce}} - 10^{-2}v_{\mathrm{ce}}$$
$$\frac{v_{\mathrm{ce}}}{v_{\mathrm{be}}} = \frac{1}{-(0.02 - 0.0001)}$$
$$= -50.3$$
$$\frac{v_{\mathrm{ce}}}{v_{\mathrm{be}}} = -50.3.$$

(ii) $\dfrac{i_c}{i_b}$ can be found as follows

$$i_c = 100i_b + 10^{-3}(-1000i_c)$$
$$i_c(1+1) = 100i_b$$
$$\frac{i_c}{i_b} = \frac{100}{2} = 50.$$

Solution 7

1. (i) $(1 - 5x)^{-3} = 1 + (-3)(-5x)$

$\qquad + (-3)(-4)(-5x)^2 \frac{1}{2}$

$\qquad = 1 + 15x + 150x^2.$

(ii) $(1 + 3x)^{\frac{3}{4}} = 1 + \frac{3}{4}(3x)$

$\qquad + \left(\frac{3}{4}\right)\left(-\frac{1}{4}\right)(3x)^2 \frac{1}{2}$

$\qquad = 1 + \frac{9}{4}x - \frac{27}{32}x^2.$

(iii) $(1 - 4x)^{-\frac{1}{3}} = 1 + \left(-\frac{1}{3}\right)(-4x)$

$\qquad + \left(-\frac{1}{3}\right)\left(-\frac{4}{3}\right)(-4x)^2 \frac{1}{2}$

$\qquad = 1 + \frac{4}{3}x + \frac{32}{9}x^2.$

(iv) $(1 - x)^{\frac{1}{2}} = 1 + \frac{1}{2}(-x)$

$\qquad + \left(\frac{1}{2}\right)\left(-\frac{1}{2}\right)(-x)^2 \frac{1}{2}$

$\qquad = 1 - \frac{1}{2}x - \frac{1}{8}x^2.$

(v) $(1 + x)^{-\frac{1}{2}} = 1 + \left(-\frac{1}{2}\right)x$

$\qquad + \left(-\frac{1}{2}\right)\left(-\frac{3}{2}\right)x^2 \frac{1}{2}$

$\qquad = 1 - \frac{1}{2}x + \frac{3}{8}x^2.$

2. (i) $(1 + px)^n = 1 + npx + n(n-1)p^2x^2 \frac{1}{2}.$

(ii) $(1 - px)^{-n} = 1 + (-n)(-px)$

$\qquad + (-n)(-n - 1)(-px)^2 \frac{1}{2}$

$\qquad = 1 + npx + \frac{1}{2}n(n + 1)p^2x^2.$

(iii) $(1 + 3ax)^{-n} = 1 + (-n)(3ax)$

$\qquad + (-n)(-n - 1)(3ax)^2 \frac{1}{2}$

$\qquad = 1 - 3anx + \frac{9}{2}n(n + 1)a^2x^2.$

(iv) $(1 - 2bx)^n = 1 + n(-2bx)$

$\qquad + n(n - 1)(-2bx)^2 \frac{1}{2}$

$\qquad = 1 - 2nbx + 2n(n - 1)b^2x^2.$

(v) $(1 - bx)^n = 1 + n(-bx)$

$\qquad + n(n - 1)(-bx)^2 \frac{1}{2}.$

3. (i) $\dfrac{\sqrt{1 - y}}{\sqrt{1 + y}} = (1 - y)^{\frac{1}{2}}(1 + y)^{-\frac{1}{2}}$

$\qquad = \left[1 + \frac{1}{2}(-y) + \frac{1}{2}\left(-\frac{1}{2}\right)(-y)^2 \frac{1}{2}\right]$

$\qquad \times \left[1 - \frac{1}{2}y + \left(-\frac{1}{2}\right)\left(-\frac{3}{2}\right)(y)^2 \frac{1}{2}\right]$

$\qquad = \left(1 - \frac{1}{2}y - \frac{1}{8}y^2\right)\left(1 - \frac{1}{2}y + \frac{3}{8}y^2\right)$

$\qquad = 1 - \frac{1}{2}y + \frac{3}{8}y^2 - \frac{1}{2}y + \frac{1}{4}y^2 - \frac{1}{8}y^2$

$\qquad = 1 - y + \frac{1}{2}y^2.$

(ii) $\dfrac{1}{\sqrt{1 - y^2}} = (1 - y^2)^{-\frac{1}{2}}$

$\qquad = 1 + \left(-\frac{1}{2}\right)(-y^2)$

$$+\left(-\frac{1}{2}\right)\left(-\frac{3}{2}\right)(-y^2)^2\frac{1}{2}$$

$$= 1 + \frac{1}{2}y^2 + \frac{3}{8}y^4.$$

(iii) $\sqrt{9+ay} = \sqrt{9\left(1+\frac{ay}{9}\right)}$

$$= 3\left(1+\frac{ay}{9}\right)^{\frac{1}{2}}$$

$$= 3\left(1+\frac{1}{2}\frac{ay}{9} + \frac{1}{2}\left(-\frac{1}{2}\right)\left(\frac{ay}{9}\right)^2\right)$$

$$= 3 + \frac{1}{6}ay - \frac{1}{216}a^2y^2.$$

(iv) $\dfrac{1}{\sqrt{16-by}} = (16-by)^{-\frac{1}{2}}$

$$= 16^{-\frac{1}{2}}\left(1-\frac{by}{16}\right)^{-\frac{1}{2}}$$

$$= \frac{1}{4}\left(1+\left(-\frac{1}{2}\right)\left(-\frac{by}{16}\right)\right.$$

$$\left.+\left(-\frac{1}{2}\right)\left(-\frac{3}{2}\right)\left(\frac{by}{16}\right)^2\frac{1}{2}\right)$$

$$= \frac{1}{4} + \frac{by}{128} + \frac{3b^2}{8192}y^2.$$

4. $(25+x)^{\frac{1}{2}} = 5(1+\frac{x}{25})^{\frac{1}{2}}$

$$= 5\left(1+\frac{1}{2}\frac{x}{25} + \frac{1}{2}\left(-\frac{1}{2}\right)\left(\frac{x}{25}\right)^2\frac{1}{2}\right)$$

$$= 5 + \frac{x}{10} - \frac{x^2}{1000}.$$

5. (i) $(1+2x)^{\frac{1}{3}} = 1 + \frac{1}{3}(2x)$

$$+\frac{1}{3}\left(-\frac{2}{3}\right)(2x)^2\frac{1}{2}$$

$$+\frac{1}{3}\left(-\frac{2}{3}\right)\left(-\frac{5}{3}\right)(2x^3)\frac{1}{3!}$$

$$= 1 + \frac{2}{3}x - \frac{4}{9}x^2 + \frac{40}{81}x^3.$$

(ii) $(1-3x)^{\frac{1}{5}} = 1 + \left(-\frac{1}{5}\right)(-3x)$

$$+\left(-\frac{1}{5}\right)\left(-\frac{6}{5}\right)(-3x)^2\frac{1}{2}$$

$$+\left(-\frac{1}{5}\right)\left(-\frac{6}{5}\right)\left(-\frac{11}{5}\right)(-3x)^3\frac{1}{3!}$$

$$= 1 + \frac{3}{5}x + \frac{27}{25}x^2 + \frac{297}{125}x^3.$$

$(1+2x)^{\frac{1}{3}} + 25(1-3x)^{-\frac{1}{5}}$

$$= a + bx + cx^2 + dx^3 + \ldots$$

$$1 + \frac{2}{3}x - \frac{4}{9}x^2 + \frac{40}{81}x^3 + 25$$

$$+15x + 27x^2 + \frac{297}{5}x^3$$

$$= a + bx + cx^2 + dx^3$$

equating coefficients

$$a = 26, \; b = \frac{2}{3} + 15 = \frac{47}{3},$$

$$c = -\frac{4}{9} + 27 = \frac{239}{9}$$

and $\quad d = \dfrac{40}{81} + \dfrac{297}{5}$

$$= \frac{200 + 24057}{405} = \frac{24257}{405}$$

$$\boxed{a = 26} \quad \boxed{b = \frac{47}{3}} \quad \boxed{b = \frac{239}{9}}$$

$$\boxed{b = \frac{24257}{405}}$$

6. (i) $(1+2x)^{\frac{1}{2}}(1-3x)^{-\frac{1}{2}} = [1+\left(\frac{1}{2}\right)(2x)$

$$+\left(\frac{1}{2}\right)\left(-\frac{1}{2}\right)(2x)^2\frac{1}{2}$$

$$+\left(\frac{1}{2}\right)\left(-\frac{1}{2}\right)\left(-\frac{3}{2}\right)(2x)^3\frac{1}{3!}]$$

$$\times\left[1+\left(-\frac{1}{2}\right)(-3x) + \left(-\frac{1}{2}\right)\right.$$

$$\times\left(-\frac{3}{2}\right)(-3x)^2\frac{1}{2} + \left(-\frac{1}{2}\right)\left(-\frac{3}{2}\right)$$

$$\left.\times\left(-\frac{5}{2}\right)(-3x)^3\frac{1}{3!}\right]$$

The coefficient of x^3

$$\left(-\frac{1}{2}\right)\left(-\frac{3}{2}\right)\left(-\frac{5}{2}\right)(-3)^3\frac{1}{3!}$$

$$+\left(\frac{1}{2}\right)(2)\left(-\frac{1}{2}\right)\left(-\frac{3}{2}\right)(-3)^2\frac{1}{2}$$

$$+\left(\frac{1}{2}\right)\left(-\frac{1}{2}\right)(2)^2\frac{1}{2}\times\left(-\frac{1}{2}\right)(-3)$$

$$+\left(\frac{1}{2}\right)\left(-\frac{1}{2}\right)\left(-\frac{3}{2}\right)(2)^3\frac{1}{3!}$$

$$=\frac{135}{16}+\frac{27}{8}-\frac{3}{4}+\frac{1}{2}=\frac{185}{16}$$

(ii) $(1-x)^{-\frac{1}{2}}(1+x)^{-\frac{1}{2}}$

$$=[(1-x)(1+x)]^{-\frac{1}{2}}=(1-x^2)^{-\frac{1}{2}}$$

$$=1+\left(-\frac{1}{2}\right)(-x^2)$$

$$+\left(-\frac{1}{2}\right)\left(-\frac{3}{2}\right)(x^2)^2\frac{1}{2}$$

$$=1+\frac{1}{2}x^2+\frac{3}{8}x^4$$

there is no x^3 term, therefore the coefficient of x^3 is zero.

(iii) $\dfrac{1-x}{(1+x)^3}=(1-x)(1+x)^{-3}$

$$=(1-x)\Big[1+(-3)x+(-3)(-4)x^2$$

$$\times\frac{1}{2}+(-3)(-4)(-5)\frac{x^3}{3\times2}\Big]$$

the coefficient of x^3

$$(-3)(-4)(-5)\frac{1}{2\times3}-(-3)(-4)\frac{1}{2}$$

$$=-10-6=-16.$$

7. $(1-7x)^{-\frac{1}{3}}=1+\left(-\frac{1}{3}\right)(-7x)$

$$+\left(-\frac{1}{3}\right)\left(-\frac{4}{3}\right)(-7x)^2\frac{1}{2}$$

$$+\left(-\frac{1}{3}\right)\left(-\frac{4}{3}\right)\left(-\frac{7}{3}\right)(-7x)^3\frac{1}{3!}$$

$$=1+\frac{7}{3}x+\frac{98}{9}x^2+\frac{4802}{81}x^3.$$

8. $(a+b)^n=a^n+na^{n-1}b+\dfrac{n(n-1)}{2!}a^{n-2}$

$$+\ldots+n(n-1)(n-2)\ldots$$

$$(n-r+1)a^{n-r}\frac{b^r}{r!}+\ldots+b^n.$$

The term containing b^r is

$$n(n-1)(n-2)\ldots(n-r+1)\frac{b^r}{r!}.$$

9. The coefficient of x^{25} in the expansion $(1-3x)^{37}$ is

$$^{37}C_{25}(-3)^{25}=\frac{37!}{25!\,12!}(-3)^{25}.$$

10. $g'=\dfrac{4\pi^2l'}{(T')^2}=4\pi^2\dfrac{\left(l-\dfrac{0.5l}{100}\right)}{\left(T+\dfrac{1}{100}T\right)^2}$

$$=\frac{4\pi^2l}{T^2}\frac{(1-0.005)}{(1+0.01)^2}$$

$$=g(1-0.0005)(1+0.01)^{-2}$$

$$=g(1-0.005)(1-2\times0.01)$$

$$+(-2)(-3)\left((0.01)^2\frac{1}{2}\right)$$

$$=g(1-0.005)(1-0.02+0.0003)$$

$$=g\,0.995\times0.9803=g\,0.9753985$$

$$=g(1-0.0246).$$

The error in g is -0.0246 or -2.46%.

11. $f=\dfrac{k\sqrt{w}}{l}=kw^{\frac{1}{2}}l^{-1}=f'=k(w')^{\frac{1}{2}}(l')^{-1}$

where $w'=w+0.01w$, $l'=l-0.02l$

$$f'=kw^{\frac{1}{2}}(1+0.01)^{\frac{1}{2}}l^{-1}(1-0.02)^{-1}$$

$$=f(1+0.01)^{\frac{1}{2}}(1-0.02)^{-1}$$

$$=f\left(1+\frac{0.01}{2}+\left(\frac{1}{2}\right)\left(-\frac{1}{2}\right)(0.01)^2\frac{1}{2}\right)$$

$$\left(1+(-1)(-0.02)+(-1)(-2)\frac{(-0.02)^2}{2}\right)$$

$$=f\left(1+0.005-\frac{0.0001}{8}\right)$$

$$\times(1+0.02+0.0004)$$

$= 1.025489245 f$

$= \left(1 + \dfrac{2.55}{100}\right) f$

$+2.25\%$ the percentage error in the calculated value of f.

12. $(1 + x)^n = 1 + nx + \dfrac{1}{2}n(n - 1)x^2$

$\quad + \dfrac{n(n - 1)(n - 2)}{1 \times 2 \times 3}x^3$

$= 1 + nx + \dfrac{1}{2}n(n - 1)x^2$

$\quad + \dfrac{n(n - 1)(n - 2)}{6}x^3$

$(1 + x)^3 = 1 + 3x + 3x^2 + x^3$

If $n = -3$

$\quad (1 + x)^{-3} = 1 - 3x + 6x^2 - 10x^3$

If $n = -\dfrac{1}{3}$

$(1 + x)^{-\frac{1}{3}} = 1 - \dfrac{1}{3}x$

$\quad + \dfrac{1}{2}\left(-\dfrac{1}{3}\right)\left(-\dfrac{4}{3}\right)x^2$

$\quad + \left(\dfrac{1}{3}\right)\left(-\dfrac{4}{3}\right)\left(-\dfrac{7}{3}\right)\dfrac{x^3}{1 \times 2 \times 3}$

$= 1 - \dfrac{1}{3}x + \dfrac{2}{9}x^2 - \dfrac{14}{81}x^3.$

13. (i) $\dfrac{1}{(1.005)^3} = (1 + 0.005)^{-3}$

$\quad = 1 + (-3)(0.005)$

$\quad + (-3)(-4)(0.005)^2\dfrac{1}{2}$

$\quad = 1 - 0.015 + 0.00015$

$\quad \approx 0.9852$

(ii) $27.003^{\frac{1}{3}} = (27 + 0.003)^{\frac{1}{3}}$

$\quad = 3\left(1 + \dfrac{0.003}{27}\right)^{\frac{1}{3}} \approx 3\left(1 + \dfrac{1}{3}\right.$

$\quad \left.\dfrac{0.001}{9} + \dfrac{1}{3}\left(-\dfrac{2}{3}\right)\left(\dfrac{0.001}{9}\right)^2\dfrac{1}{2}\right)$

$\approx 3\left(1 + \dfrac{0.001}{27} + \dfrac{0.00001}{729}\right)$

$\approx 3 + \dfrac{0.001}{9} = 3.0001$

(iii) $(1.05)^{\frac{1}{5}} = (1 + 0.05)^{\frac{1}{5}}$

$\approx 1 + \dfrac{1}{5}0.05 + \dfrac{1}{5}\left(-\dfrac{4}{5}\right)(0.05)^2\dfrac{1}{2}$

$= 1 + 0.01 - \dfrac{4}{50}0.0025 \approx 1.0098$

(iv) $0.995^{-\frac{1}{3}} = (1 - 0.005)^{-\frac{1}{3}}$

$\approx 1 + \dfrac{1}{3}0.005 - \dfrac{1}{3}\left(-\dfrac{2}{3}\right)0.005^2 \times \dfrac{1}{2}$

$\approx 1.0017.$

14. (i) $(1 + x)^{\frac{1}{2}} = 1 + \dfrac{1}{2}x + \dfrac{1}{2}\left(-\dfrac{1}{2}\right)x^2\dfrac{1}{2}$

$\quad = 1 + \dfrac{1}{2}x - \dfrac{1}{8}x^2$

(ii) $(1 - x)^{-3} = 1 + (-3)(-x)$

$\quad + (-3)(-4)(-x)^2\left(\dfrac{1}{2}\right)$

$\quad = 1 + 3x + 6x^2$

$\dfrac{(1 + x)^{\frac{1}{2}}}{(1 - x)^3} = (1 + x)^{\frac{1}{2}}(1 - x)^{-3}$

$= \left(1 + \dfrac{1}{2}x - \dfrac{1}{8}x^2\right)(1 + 3x + 6x^2)$

$= 1 + 3x + 6x^2 + \dfrac{1}{2}x + \dfrac{3}{2}x^2 - \dfrac{1}{8}x^2$

$= 1 + \dfrac{7}{2}x + 7\dfrac{3}{8}x^2$

$= 1 + \dfrac{7}{2}x + \dfrac{59}{8}x^2.$

$w^{\frac{1}{2}}\dfrac{\left(1 + \dfrac{1}{100}\right)^{\frac{1}{2}}}{z^3\left(1 - \dfrac{1}{100}\right)^3}$

$= \dfrac{w^{\frac{1}{2}}}{z^3}\left(1 + \dfrac{1}{100}\right)^{\frac{1}{2}}\left(1 - \dfrac{1}{100}\right)^{-3}$

$$= \frac{w^{\frac{1}{2}}}{z^3}\left(1 + \frac{7}{2}\frac{1}{100} + \frac{59}{8}\frac{1}{100^2}\right)$$

$$= \frac{w^{\frac{1}{2}}}{z^3}(1 + 0.03574).$$

The percentage change in $\dfrac{w^{\frac{1}{2}}}{z^3}$ is $+3.57\%$

15. $(1 + bx)^{-n} = 1 + (-n)(bx)$

$$+(-n)(-n-1)(bx^2)\frac{1}{2}$$

$$+(-n)(-n-1)(-n-2)(bx)^3\frac{1}{3!}$$

$$= 1 - nbx + n(n+1)$$

$$\frac{b^2x^2}{2} - n(n+1)(n+2)\frac{b^3x^3}{3!}$$

$$1 + 5x + 9x^2 + ax^3.$$

Equating coefficients we have:

for x, $-nb = 5$ ... (1)

for x^2, $\dfrac{n(n+1)b^2}{2} = 9$ ... (2)

for x^3,

$$\frac{-n(n+1)(n+2)}{6}b^3 = a \qquad \dots (3)$$

From (1), $b = -\dfrac{5}{n}$ and substituting this

value in (2), $n(n+1)\left(-\dfrac{5}{n}\right)^2 = 18$

$$\frac{(n+1)}{n} = \frac{18}{25}$$

$$1 + \frac{1}{n} = \frac{18}{25}$$

$$\boxed{n = -\frac{25}{7}}$$

$$b = -\frac{5}{n} = \frac{-5}{-25/7} = \frac{7}{5}$$

$$\boxed{b = \frac{7}{5}}$$

$$a = \frac{(-n)(n+1)(n+2)b^3}{6}$$

$$= \frac{\left(\frac{25}{7}\right)\left(-\frac{18}{7}\right)\left(-\frac{11}{7}\right)\left(\frac{7}{5}\right)^3}{6}$$

$$= \frac{25 \times 18 \times 11 \times 7^3}{7^3 \times 125 \times 6} = \frac{33}{5}$$

16. $\left(x - \dfrac{1}{x^2}\right)^5 \left(x + \dfrac{1}{x}\right)^9$

$$= x^5\left(1 - \frac{1}{x^3}\right)^5 x^9\left(1 + \frac{1}{x^2}\right)^9$$

$$= x^{14}\left(1 - \frac{1}{x^3}\right)^5\left(1 + \frac{1}{x^2}\right)^9$$

$$= x^{14}\left(1 - \frac{5}{x^3} + \frac{10}{x^6} - \frac{10}{x^9} + \right)$$

$$\left(1 + \frac{9}{x^2} + \frac{36}{x^4} + \frac{84}{x^6} + \frac{126}{x^8}\right.$$

$$\left. + \frac{126}{x^{10}} + \frac{84}{x^{12}} + \frac{36}{x^{14}} + \right).$$

The term independent of x is

$$x^{14}\frac{36}{x^{14}} + \frac{x^{14} \times 10 \times 126}{x^6 x^6} + \frac{5 \times 9x^{14}}{x^{14}}$$

$$= 36 + 1260 + 45 = 1341.$$

17. $(1.003)^{15} = (1 + 0.003)^{15}$

$$\approx 1 + 15 \times 0.003 + \frac{15 \times 14}{2} \times 0.003^2$$

$$+ \frac{15 \times 14 \times 13}{1 \times 2 \times 3} \times 0.003^3$$

$$= 1 + 0.045 + 0.000882 + 1.2285 \times 10^{-5}$$

$$= 1.0459 \text{ to 5 s.f.}$$

18. $(3 - ax)^8 = 3^8\left(1 - \dfrac{ax}{3}\right)^8$

the coefficient of x^4 is

$$3^8 \times \frac{8 \times 7 \times 6 \times 5}{1 \times 2 \times 3 \times 4}\left(-\frac{a}{3}\right)^4$$

$$(2a - x)^7 = (2a)^7\left[1 - \frac{x}{2a}\right]^7$$

the coefficient of x^4 is

$$(2a)^7 \times \frac{7 \times 6 \times 5 \times 4}{1 \times 2 \times 3 \times 4}\left(-\frac{1}{2a}\right)^4$$

$$\frac{3^8 \times 8 \times 7 \times 6 \times 5}{1 \times 2 \times 3 \times 4} \times \frac{a^4}{81}$$

$$= \frac{2^7 \times a^7 \times 7 \times 6 \times 5 \times 4}{1 \times 2 \times 3 \times 4 \times 2^4 \times 9^4}$$

$$\frac{8 \times 3^8 \times a^4}{81} = \frac{2^7 \times a^3 \times 4}{2^4}$$

$$\Rightarrow a = \frac{2^7 \times 4 \times 81}{16 \times 8 \times 3^8}$$

$$= \frac{128 \times 4}{16 \times 8 \times 81}$$

$$a = \frac{4}{81}.$$

19. $\left[1 + \frac{1}{3}x\right]^{-3} = 1 + (-3)\left(\frac{1}{3}x\right)$

$$+ \frac{(-3)(-4)}{1 \times 2}\left(\frac{1}{3}x\right)^2$$

$$+ \frac{(-3)(-4)(-5)}{1 \times 2 \times 3}\left(\frac{1}{3}x\right)^3$$

$$+ \frac{(-3)(-4)(-5)(-6)}{1 \times 2 \times 3 \times 4}\left(\frac{1}{3}x\right)^4$$

$$= 1 - x + \frac{2}{3}x^2 - \frac{10}{27}x^3 + \frac{15}{81}x^4$$

$$(1 - x - x^3)\left[1 + \frac{1}{3}x\right]^{-1} = (1 - x - x^3)$$

$$\times (1 - x + \frac{2}{3}x^2 - \frac{10}{27}x^3 + \frac{15}{81}x^4).$$

The coefficient of x^4

$$\frac{15}{81} + \frac{10}{27} + 1 = \frac{15}{81} + \frac{30}{81} + \frac{1}{81}$$

$$= \frac{126}{81} = \frac{42}{27} = \frac{14}{9}$$

$$-1 < \frac{1}{3}x < 1 \text{ or } \left(\frac{1}{3}x\right) < 1 \text{ or } x < 3.$$

20. $(1 - x)^{-2} = 1 + (-2)(-x)$

$$+ \frac{(-2)(-3)}{1 \times 2}(-x)^2 + \frac{(-2)(-3)(-4)}{1 \times 2 \times 3}(-x)^3$$

$$= 1 + 2x + 3x^2 + 4x^3$$

let $y = \dfrac{x^2}{1 - x}$

$$(1 + 2y + 3y^2 + 4y^3)$$

$$\left[1 + 2\left(\frac{x^2}{1 - x}\right) + 3\left(\frac{x^2}{1 - x}\right)^2 \right.$$

$$\left. + 4\left(\frac{x^2}{1 - x}\right)^3\right]$$

$$(a - x)^5 = a^5\left(1 - \frac{x}{a}\right)^5$$

the coefficient of x^3 is

$$a^5 \times \frac{5 \times 4 \times 3}{1 \times 2 \times 3}\left(-\frac{1}{a}\right)^3$$

$$(3 - ax)^7 = 3^7\left(1 - \frac{ax}{3}\right)^7$$

the coefficient of x^3 is

$$3^7 \times \frac{7 \times 6 \times 5}{1 \times 2 \times 3}\left(-\frac{a}{3}\right)^3$$

$$a^5 \times \frac{5 \times 4 \times 3}{1 \times 2 \times 3}\left(-\frac{1}{a}\right)^3$$

$$= 3^7 \times \frac{7 \times 6 \times 5}{1 \times 2 \times 3}\left(-\frac{a}{3}\right)^3$$

$$-a^2 10 = \frac{-3^7 \times 35a^3}{27}$$

$$a = \frac{10 \times 27}{3^7 \times 35} = \frac{10 \times 27}{81 \times 27 \times 35}$$

$$= \frac{10}{81 \times 35}$$

$$a = \frac{2}{7 \times 81} = \frac{2}{567}.$$

Solution 8

1. $e^x = 1 + \dfrac{x}{1!} + \dfrac{x^2}{2!} + \dfrac{x^3}{3!} + \dfrac{x^4}{4!}.$

2. $e^{-x} = 1 - \dfrac{x}{1!} + \dfrac{x^2}{2!} - \dfrac{x^3}{3!} + \dfrac{x^4}{4!}.$

3. $e^{-1} = 1 - \dfrac{1}{1!} + \dfrac{1^2}{2!} - \dfrac{1^3}{3!} + \dfrac{1^4}{4!}$

$\quad = 1 - 1 + \dfrac{1}{2} - \dfrac{1}{6} + \dfrac{1}{24} = 0.375.$

4.   (i) $e = 1 + \dfrac{1}{1!} + \dfrac{1}{2!} + \dfrac{1}{3!} + \dfrac{1}{4!}$

  (ii) $e^{-1} = \dfrac{1}{e} = 1 - 1 + \dfrac{1}{2} - \dfrac{1}{6} + \dfrac{1}{24}$

  (iii) $\dfrac{1}{e^2} = e^{-2} = 1 - \dfrac{2}{1!} + \dfrac{2^2}{2!} - \dfrac{2^3}{3!} + \dfrac{2^4}{4!}$

  (iv) $\dfrac{1}{2}\left(e + \dfrac{1}{e}\right) = \dfrac{1}{2}\left(1 + 1 + \dfrac{1}{2} + \dfrac{1}{6}\right.$

$\qquad\qquad \left. + \dfrac{1}{24} + 1 - 1 + \dfrac{1}{2} - \dfrac{1}{6} + \dfrac{1}{24}\right)$

$\qquad = \dfrac{1}{2}\left(2 + 1 + \dfrac{1}{12}\right)$

$\qquad = \dfrac{1}{2}\left(3 + \dfrac{1}{12}\right) = \dfrac{3}{2} + \dfrac{1}{24} = 1.542$

  (v) $\dfrac{1}{2}\left(e - \dfrac{1}{e}\right) = \dfrac{1}{2}\left(1 + 1 + \dfrac{1}{2} + \dfrac{1}{6}\right.$

$\qquad\qquad \left. + \dfrac{1}{24} - 1 + 1 - \dfrac{1}{2} + \dfrac{1}{6} - \dfrac{1}{24}\right)$

$\qquad = \dfrac{1}{2}\left(2 + \dfrac{1}{3}\right) = 1 + \dfrac{1}{6} = \dfrac{7}{6}.$

5.   (i) $2e^{3x} = 2\left(1 + \dfrac{3x}{1!} \times \dfrac{(3x)^2}{2!}\right.$

$\qquad\qquad \left. + \dfrac{(3x)^3}{3!} + \dfrac{(3x)^4}{4!} + \dfrac{(3x)^5}{5!}\right)$

$\qquad = 2\left(1 + 3x + \dfrac{9}{2}x^2 + \dfrac{9}{2}x^3\right.$

$\qquad\qquad \left. + \dfrac{27}{8}x^4 + \dfrac{81}{40}x^5\right)$

$\qquad = 2 + 6x + 9x^2 + 9x^3 + \dfrac{27}{4}x^4 + \dfrac{81}{20}x^5$

  (ii) $3e^{-2x} = 3\left(1 + \dfrac{(-2x)}{1!} + \dfrac{(-2x)^2}{2!}\right.$

$\qquad\qquad \left. + \dfrac{(-2x)^3}{3!} + \dfrac{(-2x)^4}{4!} + \dfrac{(-2x)^5}{5!}\right)$

$\qquad = 3\left(1 - 2x + 2x^2 - \dfrac{4}{3}x^3\right.$

$\qquad\qquad \left. + \dfrac{2}{3}x^4 - \dfrac{4}{15}x^5\right)$

$\qquad = 3 - 6x + 6x^2 - 4x^3 + 2x^4 - \dfrac{4}{5}x^5$

  (iii) $5e^{-x} = 5\left(1 - x + \dfrac{x^2}{2} - \dfrac{x^3}{6}\right.$

$\qquad\qquad \left. + \dfrac{x^4}{24} - \dfrac{x^5}{120}\right)$

$\qquad = 5 - 5x + \dfrac{5}{2}x^2 - \dfrac{5}{6}x^3 + \dfrac{5}{24}x^4 - \dfrac{1}{24}x^5$

  (iv) $4\left(1 + \dfrac{\left(\frac{x}{2}\right)}{1!} + \dfrac{\left(\frac{x}{2}\right)^2}{2!}\right.$

$\qquad\qquad \left. + \dfrac{\left(\frac{x}{2}\right)^3}{3!} + \dfrac{\left(\frac{x}{2}\right)^4}{4!} + \dfrac{\left(\frac{x}{2}\right)^5}{5!}\right)$

$\qquad = 4\left(1 + \dfrac{1}{2}x + \dfrac{1}{8}x^2 + \dfrac{1}{48}x^3\right.$

$$+\frac{1}{384}x^4 + \frac{1}{3840}x^5\Big) = 4e^{\frac{x}{2}}$$

$$= 4 + 2x + \frac{1}{2}x^2 + \frac{1}{12}x^3$$

$$+\frac{1}{96}x^4 + \frac{1}{960}x^5.$$

(v) $e^{-\frac{3}{2x}} = 1 - \frac{3}{2}\frac{x}{1!} + \frac{9}{4}\frac{x^2}{2!}$

$$-\frac{27}{8}\frac{x^3}{3!} + \frac{81}{16}\frac{x^4}{4!} - \frac{243x^5}{32}$$

$$= 1 - \frac{3}{2}x + \frac{9}{8}x^2 - \frac{9}{16}x^3$$

$$+\frac{27}{128}x^4 - \frac{81}{1280}x^5.$$

6. (i) $e^{0.55} = 1 + \frac{0.55}{1} + \frac{0.55^2}{2} + \frac{0.55^3}{6}$

$$+\frac{0.55^4}{24} + \frac{0.55^5}{120} + \frac{0.55^6}{720} + \frac{0.55^7}{5040}$$

$$= 1 + 0.55 + 0.15125 + 0.0277291$$

$$+ 0.0038127604 + 0.00041940365+$$

$$0.000038445334 + 0.0000030207048$$

$$= 1.7332527$$

= 1.733 to four significant figures from the calculator $e^{0.55}$

= 1.733253 = 1.733 to four significant figures.

(ii) $e^{-3.5} = 1 - 3.5 + \frac{3.5^2}{2} - \frac{3.5^3}{6} + \frac{3.5^4}{24}$

$$-\frac{3.5^5}{120} - \frac{3.5^7}{5040} + \frac{3.5^8}{8!}$$

$$= 1 - 3.5 + 6.125 - 7.1458333$$

$$+ 6.2526042 - 4.3768229$$

$$+ 2.5531467 - 1.2765734$$

$$+ 0.5585008$$

= 0.1850224 = 0.185 to four significant figures, note that we have taken nine terms instead of eight terms since

the answer for eight terms is negative and equal to -0.3734784 but $e^{-3.5} = \frac{1}{e^{3.5}}$ is greater than zero.

(iii) $e^{0.02} = 1 + \frac{0.02}{1} + \frac{0.02^2}{2!} + \frac{0.02^3}{6}$

$$+\frac{0.02^4}{24} + \frac{0.02^5}{120} + \frac{0.02^6}{720} + \frac{0.02^7}{5040}$$

$$= 1 + 0.02 + 0.0002 + 1.3333$$

$$\times 10^{-6} + 6.6666 \times 10^{-9}+ \text{small}$$

$$= 1.0202013 = 1.020 \text{ to four signifi-}$$
cant figures

From the calculator

$e^{0.02} = 1.0202013.$

7. Find the first three terms of the series

$$\frac{e^x - e^{-x}}{e^x} = \frac{e^x}{e^x} - \frac{e^{-x}}{e^x} = 1 - e^{-2x}$$

$$e^{-2x} = 1 - 2x + \frac{(2x)^2}{2} - \frac{(2x)^3}{6}$$

$$= 1 - 2x + 2x^2 - \frac{4}{3}x^3.$$

Therefore the first three terms of the series

$$1 - e^{-2x} = 1 - \Big(1 - 2x + 2x^2 - \frac{4}{3}x^3\Big)$$

$$= 2x - 2x^2 + \tfrac{4}{3}x^3.$$

8. In the expansion of e^x there are infinite number of terms.

The terms converge, that is, they become smaller and smaller.

9. The special property of the exponential function e^x is that the gradient of any point is the same as the function.

$$y = e^x \quad \text{and} \quad \frac{dy}{dx} = e^x.$$

10. If x increases, then $y = e^x$ increases abruptly.

If $x = 1$, $y = 2.718$ $x = 2$, $y = 7.389$

$x = 3$, $y = 20.086$ $x = 4$, $y = 54.598.$

Solution 9

1.   (i) 180° are equivalent to π radians,

      $x°$ are equivalent $\dfrac{x\pi}{180}$ radians.

      $5° \equiv \left(\dfrac{5\pi}{180}\right)^{\text{c}} = 0.0872664^{\text{c}}$

  (ii) $2° \equiv \left(\dfrac{2\pi}{180}\right) = 0.0349065^{\text{c}}$

  (iii) $15' \equiv \left(\dfrac{15}{60}\right)\dfrac{\pi}{180}$

      radians $= 4.3633231 \times 10^{-3}$ radians

  (iv) $5' = 4.3633231 \times 10^{-3}$

      $= 1.454441 \times 10^{-3}$ radians

  (v) $2' = \dfrac{2}{5}\,1.454441 \times 10^{-3}$

      $= 5.817764 \times 10^{-4}$ radians.

2.   (i) π radians are equivalent to 180°

      x radians are equivalent $\dfrac{180x}{\pi}$ degrees

      $0.05^{\text{c}} = \dfrac{180}{\pi}0.05 = 2.87°$

  (ii) $0.5^{\text{c}} = \dfrac{180}{\pi}0.5 = 28.7°$

  (iii) $0.00015^{\text{c}} = \dfrac{180}{\pi}0.000115$

      $= 8.5943669 \times 10^{-3}$ degrees

      $= 0.515662$ minutes

      $= 31$ seconds

  (iv) $1^{\text{c}} = \dfrac{180}{\pi} \times 1 = 57.3°$.

3.   (i) $\sin 1.5' = \sin\left(\dfrac{1.5}{60}\dfrac{\pi}{180}\right)^{\text{c}}$

      $\approx \dfrac{1.5}{60}\dfrac{\pi}{180} = 4.36 \times 10^{-4}$

  (ii) $\sin 0.05^{\text{c}} \approx 0.05$

  (iii) $\sin 0.75° = \sin\left(\dfrac{0.75\pi}{180}\right)^{\text{c}}$

      $\approx \dfrac{0.75\pi}{180} = 0.0131$

  (iv) $\tan 0.5° = \tan\left(\dfrac{0.5\pi}{180}\right)^{\text{c}}$

      $\approx \dfrac{0.5\pi}{180} = 8.73 \times 10^{-3}$

  (v) $\cos 1' = \cos\left(\dfrac{1}{60°}\right)$

      $\cos\left(\dfrac{1}{60}\dfrac{\pi}{180}\right) \approx 1 - \left(\dfrac{\pi}{60} \times 180\right)^{2}\dfrac{1}{2}$

      $= 0.9999999$

  (vi) $\cos 0.75° = \cos\left(\dfrac{0.75\pi}{180}\right)$

      $\approx 1 - \left(\dfrac{0.75\pi}{180}\right)^{2}\dfrac{1}{2}$

      $\cos 0.75° = 0.9999143$

  (vii) $\cos 25' = \cos\left(\dfrac{25}{60}\right)°$

      $= \cos\left(\dfrac{25}{60}\dfrac{\pi}{180}\right)$

      $\approx 1 - \left(\dfrac{25}{60}\dfrac{\pi}{180}\right)^{2}\dfrac{1}{2}$

      $\cos 25' = 0.9999735$.

4. $y = 30 \sin 31420t$

   (i) the amplitude is 30

   (ii) the frequency is found from
$2\pi f = 31420$

      therefore $f = \dfrac{31420}{2\pi} = 5000$ Hz

   (iii) the period $T = \dfrac{1}{f} = \dfrac{1}{5000} = 0.2$ ms

   (iv) ω = angular velocity
      = 31420 radians/sec.

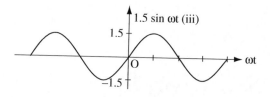

1.5 sin ωt (iii)

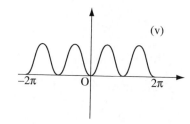

(v)

5. $\omega t = \theta$

$\theta°$	θ^c	t
0	0	0
30	$\frac{\pi}{6}$	$\frac{\pi}{6\omega}$
60	$\frac{\pi}{3}$	$\frac{\pi}{3\omega}$
90	$\frac{\pi}{2}$	$\frac{\pi}{2\omega}$
120	$\frac{2\pi}{3}$	$\frac{2\pi}{3\omega}$
150	$\frac{5\pi}{6}$	$\frac{5\pi}{6\omega}$
180	π	$\frac{\pi}{\omega}$
210	$\frac{7\pi}{6}$	$\frac{7\pi}{6\omega}$
240	$\frac{4\pi}{3}$	$\frac{4\pi}{3\omega}$
270	$\frac{3\pi}{2}$	$\frac{3\pi}{2\omega}$
300	$\frac{5\pi}{3}$	$\frac{5\pi}{3\omega}$
330	$\frac{11\pi}{6}$	$\frac{11\pi}{6\omega}$
360	2π	$\frac{2\pi}{\omega}$

$t = \dfrac{\theta}{\omega}$.

7.

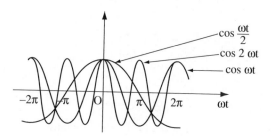

$\cos \frac{\omega t}{2}$

$\cos 2\,\omega t$

$\cos \omega t$

8. Similar to the above (6).

9. Similar to the above (7).

10.

  (a) (i)

$\sin x$

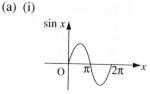

  (ii)

$\sin 2x$

6.

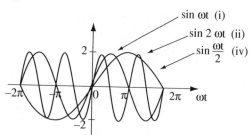

sin ωt (i)

sin 2 ωt (ii)

$\sin \frac{\omega t}{2}$ (iv)

(iii)

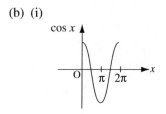

(ii)

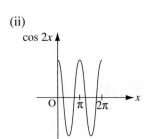

(b) (i)

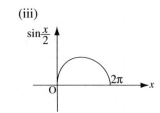

(iii)

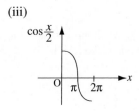

Solution 10

1. Sketch $y_1 = 3\sin x$ and $y_2 = 4\sin x$ on the same graph and add the instantaneous values, the result will be sinusoidal $y_1 + y_2 = 7\sin x$

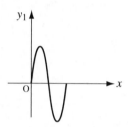

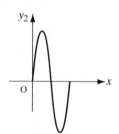

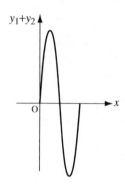

The frequencies are the same.

2. Sketch $y_1 = 2\sin 2x$ and

$y_2 = \sin(2x + \frac{\pi}{3})$

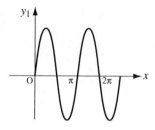

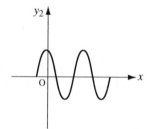

The frequencies are the same and phase angles different.

$$y_1 + y_2 = 2\sin 2x + \sin 2x \cos \frac{\pi}{3}$$
$$+ \sin \frac{\pi}{3} + \cos 2x$$

$$= 2\sin 2x + \frac{1}{2}\sin 2x + \frac{\sqrt{3}}{2}\cos 2x$$

$$= \frac{3}{2}\sin 2x + \frac{\sqrt{3}}{2}\cos 2x$$

the resultant waveform will be sinusoidal.

3.

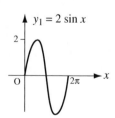

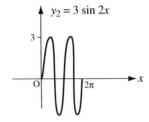

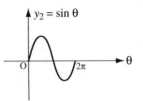

The resultant waveform will be complex wave as the two waves are of different frequencies.

4. $y = \sin \dfrac{\theta}{2} + \sin \theta + \sin 2\theta$

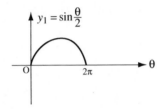

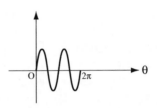

The resultant wave is complex, add the instantaneous values at $\theta = 0, \frac{\pi}{2}, \pi, \frac{3\pi}{2}, 2\pi$.

5. $y = 5 \sin(x + 30°)$ leads

$y = 12 \sin(x - 90°)$ lags.

Index
Algebra III

Mathematics
for
Technicians

Calculus III

Anthony Nicolaides
B.Sc. (Eng.), C. Eng. M.I.E.T.

P.A.S.S. PUBLICATIONS
Private Academic & Scientific Studies Ltd

© A. Nicolaides
Second Edition 2009

ISBN-13   978-1-872684-64-2

Calculus III

First Published in Great Britain 1991 by Private Academic & Scientific Studies Ltd

P.A.S.S. PUBLICATIONS

Preface

This book covers adequately the following:

Differentiation:

- The derivatives of the following functions: e^x, $\sin x$, $\cos x$, $\ln x$, x^n and there applications

- The derivatives of the sums, products quotients, function of a function (chain series)

- Numerical values of differential coefficients, second derivatives, turning points (maximum and minimum) or stationary values

- Applications; charging of a capacitor, discharging of a capacitor, growth of current through a coil.
    - Volume of a rectangular box.
    - Maximum power transfer theorem
    - Other Applications

Integration: review of standard integrals, indefinite integrals, definite integrals eg area under the curve, mean and RMS values; numerical eg trapezoidal, mid-ordinate and Simpson's rule.

The author was a full time senior lecturer and the course organiser for the BTEC National Diploma in Engineering.

Anthony Nicolaides
B.Sc.(Eng.), C.Eng. M.I.E.T.

Contents
Calculus III

CALCULUS III

1

The exponential function and its derivative.

$y = e^x$

is the exponential function, a constant value, in particular $e = 2.718281828$, is raised to the exponent x, which is a variable the expansion series is $e^x = 1 + \frac{x}{1!} + \frac{x^2}{2!} + \frac{x^3}{3!} + \cdots$ an exponential function e^x is shown.

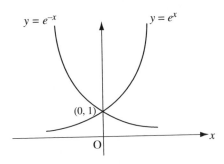

Fig. 1

The exponential function passes from ($x = 0$, $y = 1$) and increases abruptly as shown, that is, as x increases, y increases steeply. This function is a unique function with a special property of the exponential function, is the same as the function itself, that is,

If $y = e^x$, $\frac{dy}{dx} = e^x$

$$e^x = 1 + \frac{x}{1!} + \frac{x^2}{2!} + \frac{x^3}{3!} + \cdots$$

$$\frac{d}{dx}(e^x) = 0 + 1 + 2\frac{x}{2!} + 3\frac{x^2}{3!} + \cdots$$

hence $\frac{d}{dx}(e^x) = 1 + \frac{x}{1!} + \frac{x^2}{2!} + \frac{x^3}{3!} \cdots$

since $\quad \dfrac{2}{2!} = \dfrac{2}{1 \times 2} = \dfrac{1}{1!}$,

$\dfrac{3}{3!} = \dfrac{3}{1 \times 2 \times 3}$

$\quad = \dfrac{1}{1 \times 2} = \dfrac{1}{2!}$,

and so on.

The derivatives of the functions $\sin x$, $\cos x$, $\ln x$, e^x, x^n and its uses.

The derivatives of these functions are as follows:-

$y = \sin x \qquad \dfrac{dy}{dx} = \cos x$

$y = \cos x \qquad \dfrac{dy}{dx} = -\sin x$

$y = \ln x \qquad \dfrac{dy}{dx} = \dfrac{1}{x}$

$y = e^x \qquad \dfrac{dy}{dx} = e^x$

$y = x^n \qquad \dfrac{dy}{dx} = nx^{n-1}$.

The gradient at any point of the curve of Fig. 2 is $\frac{dy}{dx} = \cos x$, the gradient is positive, at **A**, zero at **B** and negative at **C**.

1

The gradient at any point of the curve of Fig. 3 is $\dfrac{dy}{dx} = -\sin x$.

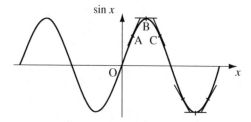

Fig. 2

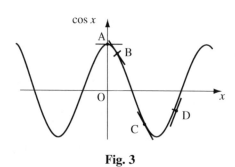

Fig. 3

The gradient at **A** of Fig. 3 is zero, the gradients at **B** and **C** are negative, the gradient at **D** is positive.

The gradient at any point of the curve of Fig. 4 is $\dfrac{dy}{dx} = \dfrac{1}{x}$ which is always positive since x is defined as a positive quantity.

The gradient at any point of the curve of Fig. 5 is $\dfrac{dy}{dx} = e^x$.

For any real value of x, the gradient is positive, since e raised to any power, is positive.

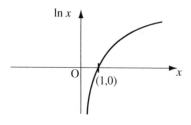

Fig. 4

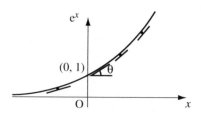

Fig. 5

The graph shows the gradients are positive since the angle θ is less than $90°$ and $\tan \theta$ is positive.

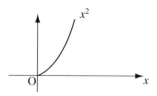

Fig. 6

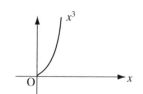

Fig. 7

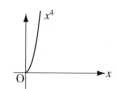

Fig. 8

The family of curves of $y = x^n$ as n increases from 1 to 4 are shown.

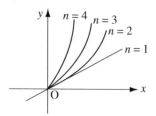

Fig. 9

As n increases the curve becomes steeper and steeper when $y = x^n$ $\frac{dy}{dx} = nx^{n-1}$.

If n is positive then the gradient is positive provided x is positive.

Evaluation of the derivatives at given points of the functions $\sin x$, $\cos x$, $\ln x$, e^x and x^n.

WORKED EXAMPLE 1

Referring to the Fig 2 of the sinewave graph $y = \sin x$.

Find the derivatives at $x = 0$, $x = \frac{\pi}{4}$, $x = \frac{\pi}{2}$, $x = \frac{5\pi}{6}$, $x = \pi$, $x = \frac{5\pi}{4}$, $x = \frac{3\pi}{2}$, $x = \frac{5\pi}{3}$.

Solution 1

$\frac{dy}{dx} = \cos x$ the gradient at any point of the curve

when

$x = 0$, $\quad \frac{dy}{dx} = \cos 0 = 1$, the gradient is 1,

$\qquad$ or $\tan \frac{\pi}{4} = 1$ $\quad 45°$ inclination

$\qquad$ to the horizontal

$x = \frac{\pi}{4}$, $\quad \frac{dy}{dx} = \cos \frac{\pi}{4} = 0.707$

$x = \frac{\pi}{2}$, $\quad \frac{dy}{dx} = \cos \frac{\pi}{2} = 0$ that is the

$\qquad$ gradient is horizontal

$x = \frac{5\pi}{6}$, $\quad \frac{dy}{dx} = \cos \frac{5\pi}{6} = -0.866$

$x = \pi$, $\quad \frac{dy}{dx} = \cos \pi = -1$

$x = \frac{5\pi}{4}$, $\quad \frac{dy}{dx} = \cos \frac{5\pi}{4} = -0.707$

$x = \frac{5\pi}{3}$, $\quad \frac{dy}{dx} = \cos \frac{5\pi}{3} = 0.5$.

WORKED EXAMPLE 2

Referring to the Fig. 3 of the cosine wave graph $y = \cos x$.

Find the derivatives at $x = 0$, $x = \frac{\pi}{6}$, $x = \frac{\pi}{2}$, $x = \frac{3\pi}{4}$, $x = \pi$, $x = \frac{4\pi}{3}$, $x = \frac{3\pi}{2}$, $x = \frac{7\pi}{4}$, $x = 2\pi$.

Solution 2

$y = \cos x$ $\qquad \frac{dy}{dx} = -\sin x$

at $x = 0$ $\qquad \frac{dy}{dx} = -\sin 0 = 0$

at $x = \frac{3\pi}{4}$ $\qquad \frac{dy}{dx} = -\sin \frac{3\pi}{4} = -\frac{1}{\sqrt{2}}$

at $x = \frac{\pi}{6}$ $\qquad \frac{dy}{dx} = -\sin \frac{\pi}{6} = -\frac{1}{2}$

at $x = \pi$ $\qquad \frac{dy}{dx} = \sin \pi = 0$

at $x = \frac{\pi}{2}$ $\qquad \frac{dy}{dx} = -\sin \frac{\pi}{2} = -1$

at $x = \frac{4\pi}{3}$ $\qquad \frac{dy}{dx} = -\sin \frac{3\pi}{2} = 1$

at $x = \frac{7\pi}{4}$ $\qquad \frac{dy}{dx} = -\sin \frac{7\pi}{4}$

$\qquad\qquad\qquad = -\left[-\frac{1}{\sqrt{2}}\right] = \frac{1}{\sqrt{2}}$

at $x = 2\pi$ $\qquad \frac{dy}{dx} = -\sin 2\pi = 0$.

WORKED EXAMPLE 3

Referring to the Fig. 4 of the graph $y = \ln x$. Find the derivatives at $x = 0.1, 0.5, 1, 2, 3, 5, 10$.

Solution 3

$y = \ln x$ $\qquad \frac{dy}{dx} = \frac{1}{x}$

at $\quad x = 0.1$ $\qquad \frac{dy}{dx} = \frac{1}{0.1} = 10$

$x = 0.5$ $\qquad \frac{dy}{dx} = \frac{1}{0.5} = 2$

$x = 1$ $\qquad \frac{dy}{dx} = \frac{1}{1} = 1$

$x = 3$ $\qquad \frac{dy}{dx} = \frac{1}{3}$

$x = 5$ $\qquad \frac{dy}{dx} = \frac{1}{5}$

$x = 10$ $\qquad \frac{dy}{dx} = \frac{1}{10}$.

The gradients for the range of values $0 < x < \infty$ are positive, this information indicates that the graph increases rapidly from $x > 0$ as shown and there are no turning points, that is there are neither maximum or minimum points.

WORKED EXAMPLE 4

Referring to the Fig. 5 of the graph, $y = e^x$. Find the derivatives at $x = -5, -3, -1, 0, 0.1, 1, 2, 3$.

Solution 4

The function $y = e^x$ has a first derivative of $\dfrac{dy}{dx} = e^x$

at $x = -5$, $\dfrac{dy}{dx} = e^{-5} = 0.006674$

at $x = -3$, $\dfrac{dy}{dx} = e^{-3} = 0.0498$

at $x = 1$, $\dfrac{dy}{dx} = e^{-1} = 0.368$

at $x = 0$, $\dfrac{dy}{dx} = e^0 = 1$

at $x = 0.1$, $\dfrac{dy}{dx} = e^{0.1} = 1.105$

at $x = 1$, $\dfrac{dy}{dx} = e^1 = 2.7183$

at $x = 2$, $\dfrac{dy}{dx} = e^2 = 7.389$

at $x = 3$, $\dfrac{dy}{dx} = e^3 = 20.09$.

The gradients become steeper and steeper as x increases steadily.

WORKED EXAMPLE 4

Referring to the Fig. 6 of the graph of $y = x^n$ or more specifically $y = x^2$ and $y = x^3$ find the derivatives at $x = 0, 1, 2, 3$.

Solution 5

$y = x^2$ $\dfrac{dy}{dx} = 2x$

at $x = 0$ $\dfrac{dy}{dx} = 0$

$x = 1$ $\dfrac{dy}{dx} = 2$

$x = 2$ $\dfrac{dy}{dx} = 4$

$y = x^3$ $\dfrac{dy}{dx} = 3x^2$

$x = 0$ $\dfrac{dy}{dx} = 0$

$x = 1$ $\dfrac{dy}{dx} = 3$

$x = 2$ $\dfrac{dy}{dx} = 12$

$x = 3$ $\dfrac{dy}{dx} = 27$.

Exercises 1

1. Sketch the following trigonometric functions:
   (i) $y = \sin x$ (ii) $y = \cos x$
   in the specified range $-2\pi \leq x \leq 2\pi$.

2. Sketch the following exponential and logarithmic functions:

   (i) $y = e^x$ (ii) $y = e^{-x}$
   (iii) $y = 3e^{-x}$ (iv) $y = \ln x$
   (v) $y = 2 \ln x$ (vi) $y = 3 \ln x$
   (vii) $5 \ln x$.

3. Sketch the family of curves:-
   (i) $y = 3x^2$ (ii) $y = 5x^3$
   (iii) $y = 2x^4$.

4. Write down the derivatives of the following functions:-
   (i) $y = 5e^x$ (ii) $y = -\sin x$
   (iii) $y = \cos x$ (iv) $y = \ln x$
   (v) $y = 5x^3$ (vi) $y = x^4$.

5. Evaluate the gradients of the functions.
   (i) $y = \sin x$
   (ii) $y = \cos x$ at $x = 0, \dfrac{\pi}{5}, \dfrac{\pi}{7}, \pi$.

6. Evaluate the gradients of the functions
   (i) $\ln x$ (ii) e^x at $x = 0.5, 1.5, 3.5, 5$.

7. Comment on the sign of the gradients of the trigonometric functions, $\sin x$ and $\cos x$.

8. Comment on the sign of the gradients of (i) $\ln x$ (ii) e^x (iii) e^{-x}. Is there any restriction on the value of x?

9. Sketch the graphs of (i) $y = x^2$, (ii) $y = x^3$, (iii) $y = x^4$ on the same graph for the range $-2 \leq x \leq 2$.

10. Evaluate the derivatives of the following algebraic functions:-

   (i) $y = 3x$

   (ii) $y = x^2$

   (iii) $y = 3x^3$ at $x = -1, 0, 2, -3$.

2

Differentiates sums, products and quotients uses function of a function rule.

a. States the basic rules for the derivatives of sum, product, quotient and function of a function.

b. Determines the derivatives of various combinations of any two of ax^n, $\sin ax$, $\cos ax$, $\ln ax$, e^{ax}.

c. Evaluates the derivatives in 2b at given points.

Derivative of sum or difference

Let y be given as $y = f(x) + g(x) - p(x)$ where $f(x)$, $g(x)$ and $p(x)$ are three different functions of x.

The derivative of these functions is distributive across addition and subtraction

$$\frac{dy}{dx} = \frac{d}{dx}f(x) + \frac{d}{dx}g(x) - \frac{d}{dx}p(x)$$
$$= f'(x) + g'(x) - p'(x).$$

The notation $f(x)$.

If $y = f(x)$, it means that y is a function of x.

The notation $f'(x)$, $f''(x)$, $f'''(x)$

$\dfrac{dy}{dx} = f'(x)$ $f'(x)$ is the derivative of $f(x)$.

$\dfrac{d}{dx}\{f(x) + g(x) - p(x)\}$

$\qquad = \dfrac{d}{dx}f(x) + \dfrac{d}{dx}g(x) - \dfrac{d}{dx}p(x)$

$\qquad = f'(x) + g'(x) - p'(x)$

$f''(x)$ is the derivative of $f'(x)$

$f'''(x)$ is the derivative of $f''(x)$

$f'(x)$, $f''(x)$ and $f'''(x)$ are the first, second and third derivatives of $f(x)$.

The derivatives of $\sin ax$ and $\cos ax$

$y = \sin ax$

Let $u = ax$ $\dfrac{du}{dx} = a$

$y = \sin u$ $\dfrac{dy}{du} = \cos u$

$\dfrac{dy}{dx} = \dfrac{dy}{du} \times \dfrac{du}{dx} = a \cos u = a \cos ax$

$\dfrac{dy}{dx} = a \cos ax.$

$y = \cos ax$ let $u = ax$ $\dfrac{du}{dx} = a$

$y = \cos u$ $\dfrac{dy}{du} = -\sin u$

$\dfrac{dy}{dx} = \dfrac{dy}{du} \times \dfrac{du}{dx} = a(-\sin u) = -a \sin u$

$\dfrac{dy}{dx} = -a \sin ax.$

If $a = 1$

the rate of change of $\sin x$, is $\dfrac{d}{dx}(\sin x) = \cos x$

the rate of change of $\cos x$, is

$\qquad \dfrac{d}{dx}(\cos x) = -\sin x.$

Therefore $\dfrac{d}{dx}(\sin x) = \cos x$

$$\dfrac{d}{dx}(\sin ax) = a\cos ax$$

$$\dfrac{d}{dx}(\cos x) = -\sin x$$

$$\dfrac{d}{dx}(\cos ax) = -a\sin ax.$$

The derivatives of $\ln ax$ and e^{ax}.

The derivatives of $\ln ax$ and e^{ax} are stated:

$$\dfrac{d}{dx}(\ln ax) = \dfrac{a}{ax} = \dfrac{1}{x}$$

$$\text{since } u = ax,\ \dfrac{du}{dx} = a$$

$$\dfrac{d}{dx}(\ln u) = \dfrac{1}{u} = \dfrac{1}{ax}$$

$$\dfrac{d}{dx}(\ln ax) = a \times \dfrac{1}{ax} = \dfrac{1}{x}$$

$$\dfrac{d}{dx}e^{ax} = ae^{ax} \qquad \text{since } u = ax \quad \dfrac{du}{dx} = a$$

$$\dfrac{d}{dx}(e^y) = e^u = e^{ax},$$

$$\dfrac{d}{dx}e^{ax} = ae^{ax}.$$

WORKED EXAMPLE 6

Differentiate the following functions with respect to x.

(i) $\sin 3x$ (ii) $\sin \dfrac{1}{3}x$

(iii) $\sin\left(-\dfrac{2}{3}x\right)$ (iv) $\cos(-x)$

(v) $\cos 5x$ (vi) $2\cos(-3x)$

(vii) $\sin \dfrac{x}{2} - \cos \dfrac{3}{2}x$

(viii) $3\cos 7x - \dfrac{1}{2}\sin 5x$

(ix) $-3\cos 3x + 3\sin 3x$

(x) $\sin x + 2\cos x - 3\sin 3x + 2\cos 2x.$

Solution 6

(i) $y = \sin 3x \qquad \dfrac{dy}{dx} = 3\cos 3x$

(ii) $y = \sin\dfrac{1}{3}x \qquad \dfrac{dy}{dx} = \dfrac{1}{3}\cos\dfrac{1}{3}x$

(iii) $y = \sin\left(-\dfrac{2}{3}x\right)$

$$\dfrac{dy}{dx} = -\dfrac{2}{3}\cos\left(-\dfrac{2}{3}x\right) = -\dfrac{2}{3}\cos\dfrac{2}{3}x$$

note that $\cos\left(-\dfrac{2}{3}x\right)$ is an even function **i.e.** the cosine of the positive or negative angle is positive.

(iv) $y = \cos(-x)$

$$\dfrac{dy}{dx} = -\sin(-x)(-1)$$

$$= +\sin(-x) = -\sin x$$

$$y = \cos(x) \qquad \dfrac{dy}{dx} = -\sin x$$

note that $\sin(-x)$ is an odd function **i.e.** the sine of the positive angle is positive, the sine of the negative angle is negative.

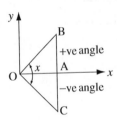

Fig. 10

$\mathbf{AB} = \sin x = +ve \qquad$ **ODD**
$\mathbf{AC} = \sin(-x) = -ve \qquad$ **FUNCTION**

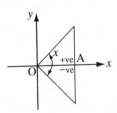

Fig. 11

$\cos x = \mathbf{OA} = positive$

$\cos(-x) = \mathbf{OA} = positive$

                          EVEN FUNCTION

(v) $y = \cos 5x \quad \dfrac{dy}{dx} = -5\sin 5x$

(vi) $y = 2\cos(-3x) = 2\cos 3x$

$$\frac{dy}{dx} = -2 \times 3 \sin 3x = -6 \sin 3x$$

(vii) $y = \sin \dfrac{1}{2}x - \cos \dfrac{3}{2}x,$

$$\frac{dy}{dx} = \frac{1}{2}\cos\frac{1}{2}x - \frac{3}{2}\left(-\sin\frac{3}{2}x\right)$$

$$= \frac{1}{2}\cos\frac{1}{2}x + \frac{3}{2}\sin\frac{3}{2}x.$$

(viii) $y = 3\cos 7x - \dfrac{1}{2}\sin 5x$

$$\frac{dy}{dx} = -21\sin 7x - \frac{5}{2}\cos 5x.$$

(ix) $y = -3\cos 3x + 3\sin 3x$

$$\frac{dy}{dx} = +9\sin 3x + 9\cos 3x.$$

(x) $y = \sin x + 2\cos x - 3\sin 3x + 2\cos 2x$

$$\frac{dy}{dx} = \cos x - 2\sin x - 9\cos 3x - 4\sin 2x.$$

WORKED EXAMPLE 7

(i) $\dfrac{d}{dx}(3\ln 3x)$ (ii) $\dfrac{d}{dy}\left(\dfrac{1}{5}\ln\dfrac{1}{5}y\right)$

(iii) $\dfrac{d}{dz}(\ln 7z)$ (iv) $\dfrac{d}{dt}\left(e^{-\frac{1}{3}t}\right)$

(v) $\dfrac{d}{dx}(e^{3x})$ (vi) $\dfrac{d}{du}(e^{3u})$

(vii) $\dfrac{d}{dx}(\ln x - e^x)$ (viii) $\dfrac{d}{dt}(-3\ln 3t + e^{-5t})$

(ix) $\dfrac{d}{dx}(\sin x - \cos 2x + \ln\dfrac{1}{3}x - e^{-4x})$

(x) $\dfrac{d}{dx}(5\cos 3x + 3\ln 4x + 5e^{5x}).$

Solution 7

(i) $\dfrac{d}{dx}(3\ln 3x) = \dfrac{3 \times 3}{3x} = \dfrac{3}{x}$

(ii) $\dfrac{d}{dy}\left(\dfrac{1}{5}\ln\dfrac{1}{5}y\right) = \dfrac{1}{5y}$

(iii) $\dfrac{d}{dz}(\ln 7z) = \dfrac{1}{z}$ or

$\dfrac{d}{dz}(\ln 7 + \ln z)$

$$= \frac{d}{dz}(\ln 7) + \frac{d}{dz}\ln z$$

$$= 0 + \frac{1}{z} = \frac{1}{z}$$

(iv) $\dfrac{d}{dt}\left(e^{-\frac{1}{3}t}\right) = -\dfrac{1}{3}e^{-\frac{1}{3}t}$

(v) $\dfrac{d}{dx}(e^{3x}) = 3e^{3x}$

(vi) $\dfrac{d}{du}(e^{3u}) = 3e^{3u}$

(vii) $\dfrac{d}{dx}(\ln x - e^x) = \dfrac{1}{x} - e^x$

(viii) $\dfrac{d}{dt}(-3\ln 3t + e^{-5t}) = -\dfrac{3}{t} - 5e^{-5t}$

(ix) $\dfrac{d}{dx}[\sin x - \cos 2x + \ln\dfrac{1}{3}x - e^{-4x}]$

$$= \cos x + 2\sin 2x + \frac{1}{x} + 4e^{-4x}$$

(x) $\dfrac{d}{dx}(5\cos 3x + 3\ln 4x + 5e^{5x})$

$$= -15\sin 3x + \frac{3}{x} + 25e^{5x}.$$

Evaluates the derivatives at a point of the function $\sin x$.

In the previous work, we have learnt to find the derivatives of the functions at any point, **i.e.** the gradient of the functions at any point.

Fig. 12 shows a sinewave and the gradients at different values of x.

It is now required to find the derivatives or the gradients of functions at specific values of the function.

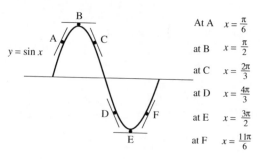

At A	$x = \frac{\pi}{6}$
at B	$x = \frac{\pi}{2}$
at C	$x = \frac{2\pi}{3}$
at D	$x = \frac{4\pi}{3}$
at E	$x = \frac{3\pi}{2}$
at F	$x = \frac{11\pi}{6}$

Fig. 12

Evaluate the derivative of the following functions when $x = \frac{\pi}{3}$:
  (i) $y = \sin 2x$
  (ii) $y = 3\cos 3x$
  (iii) $y = \sin x - \cos 2x$.

Solution 8

(i) $y = \sin 2x$ $\frac{dy}{dx} = 2\cos 2x$ the gradient at any point of x, but at $x = \frac{\pi}{3}$

$$\frac{dy}{dx} = 2\cos\left(2\frac{\pi}{3}\right) = 2\left(-\frac{1}{2}\right) = -1$$

(ii) $y = 3\cos 3x$
$$\frac{dy}{dx} = -9\sin 3x \text{ at } x = \frac{\pi}{3},$$
$$\frac{dy}{dx} = -9\sin\frac{3\pi}{3}$$
$$= -9\sin\pi = -9(0) = 0$$

(iii) $y = \sin x - \cos 2x$
$$\frac{dy}{dx} = \cos x + 2\sin 2x \quad \text{at } x = \frac{\pi}{3}$$
$$\frac{dy}{dx} = \cos\frac{\pi}{3} + 2\sin 2(\frac{\pi}{3})$$
$$= \frac{1}{2} + 2\frac{\sqrt{3}}{2}$$
$$= \frac{1 + 2\sqrt{3}}{2}$$
$$= 0.5 + 1.732 = 2.232.$$

Determine the values of the derivatives at the points shown adjacent to each function.

  (i) $y = 2\cos 2x - \sin x \quad (x = \frac{\pi}{2})$
  (ii) $y = e^{3x} - \ln x \quad (x = 0.5)$
  (iii) $y = e^{-2x} + \ln 7x \quad (x = 1)$
  (iv) $y = 3\sin x - \cos\frac{5}{2}x + e^{\frac{x}{2}} \quad (x = \frac{\pi}{4})$
  (v) $y = \cos 5x - \frac{1}{5}\ln 3x + e^{-4x} \quad (x = 1)$

Solution 9

(i) $\frac{dy}{dx} = -4\sin 2x - \cos x \quad$ at $x = \frac{\pi}{2}$
$$\frac{dy}{dx} = -4\sin 2(\frac{\pi}{2}) - \cos\frac{\pi}{2}$$
$$= -4\sin\pi - \cos\frac{\pi}{2} = 0$$

(ii) $y = e^{3x} - \ln x, \quad \frac{dy}{dx} = 3e^{3x} - \frac{1}{x}$
$$= 3e^{1.5} - \frac{1}{0.5} = 11.45$$

(iii) $y = e^{-2x} + \ln 7x \quad \frac{dy}{dx} = -2e^{-2x} + \frac{1}{x}$
at $x = 1$, $\frac{dy}{dx} = -2e^{-2} + 1 = 0.729$

(iv) $y = 3\sin x - \cos\frac{5}{2}x + e^{\frac{x}{2}}$
$$\frac{dy}{dx} = 3\cos x + \frac{5}{2}\sin\frac{5}{2}x + \frac{1}{2}e^{\frac{x}{2}}$$
when $x = \frac{\pi}{4}$
$$\frac{dy}{dx} = 3\cos\frac{\pi}{4} + \frac{5}{2}\sin\frac{5}{2}\left(\frac{\pi}{4}\right) + \frac{1}{2}e^{\frac{1}{2}\frac{\pi}{4}}$$
$$= 3(0.707) + \frac{5}{2}\sin\frac{5\pi}{8} + \frac{1}{2}e^{\frac{\pi}{8}}$$
$$= 2.121 + 2.31 + 0.741 = 5.17$$

(v) $y = \cos 5x - \frac{1}{5}\ln 3x + e^{-4x}$
$$\frac{dy}{dx} = -5\sin 5x - \frac{1}{5x} - 4e^{-4x}$$
at $x = 1$
$$\frac{dy}{dx} = -5\sin 5^c - \frac{1}{5} - 4e^{-4}$$
$$= -4.795 - 0.2 - 0.0733 = -5.07.$$

States that the derivative measures the rate of change of a function.

The derivative of a function is denoted by $\frac{dy}{dx}$ or $f'(x)$, this also is called the gradient of the function or the slope of the tangent at a point on the curve or the tangent of the angle.

Let $f(x)$ be a curve, at **P** a tangent is drawn, the gradient of this tangent is said to be the gradient of the curve at **P**.

The derivative at $\mathbf{P}(x_1, y_1)$ is denoted as shown $f'(x_1)$ and it is the rate of change of function at that point.

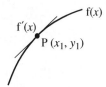

Fig. 13

$f'(x_1)$ = derivative of $f(x)$ at $\mathbf{P}$ or
$\frac{dy}{dx}$ = gradient of the curve at P
is derived from the equation of the curve and is called the underivative of y with respect to x or the rate of change of y with respect to x.

States that the gradient of a curve at a given point is given by the corresponding value of the derivative.

The gradient of the tangent at $\mathbf{P}(x_1, y_1)$ is the derivative of the function at $\mathbf{P}(x_1, y_1)$

$$\frac{dy}{dx} = f'(x_1).$$

This can be illustrated by a worked example.

WORKED EXAMPLE 10

(a) Find the derivative of the function $y = 3x^3 - 2x^2 + x + 1$ and hence determine the gradient at $x = 1$ and $x = \frac{1}{2}$.

(b) Show that the gradient of the function is always positive. Verify that $\frac{dy}{dx} > 0$ if $x = -1$.

Solution 10

(a) $f(x) = y = 3x^3 - 2x^2 + x + 1$

$\frac{dy}{dx} = 9x^2 - 4x + 1$ this is the derivative of the function y or $f(x)$.

i.e. the gradient at any point, but at $x = 1$,
$\frac{dy}{dx} = 9(1)^2 - 4(1) + 1 = 6$ the gradient

at $x = 1$ is $\frac{dy}{dx} = 6$

the gradient at $x = \frac{1}{2}$ is

$$\frac{dy}{dx} = 9\left(\frac{1}{2}\right)^2 - 4\left(\frac{1}{2}\right) + 1 = \frac{5}{4}$$

(b) $\frac{dy}{dx} = 9x^2 - 4x + 1$

$$= 9\left(x^2 - \frac{4}{9}x + \frac{1}{9}\right)$$

$$= 9\left[\left(x - \frac{2}{9}\right)^2 - \frac{4}{81} + \frac{1}{9}\right]$$

$$= 9\left[\left(x - \frac{2}{9}\right)^2 + \frac{5}{9}\right]$$

$$= 9\left(x - \frac{2}{9}\right)^2 + 5$$

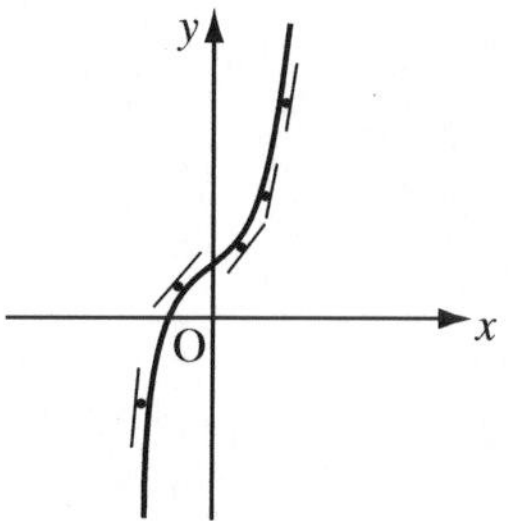

Fig. 14

therefore $\frac{dy}{dx}$ is always positive since $\left(x - \frac{2}{9}\right)^2$ is positive since it is squared and plus 5 will be positive.

The function $f(x)$ is roughly sketched in **Fig. 14** which shows that the gradient at any point is positive.

$\frac{dy}{dx} = 9x^2 - 4x + 1$

$$= 9(-1)^2 - (4)(-1) + 1$$

$$= 9 + 4 + 1 = 14.$$

WORKED EXAMPLE 11

Find the derivatives of the following sums:-

(i) $f(x) = 5x^2 - 7x - 2$

(ii) $g(x) = 3x^3 + 5x + x^{-2} + x^{-3}$

(iii) $\dfrac{d}{dx}\{f(x) - g(x)\}$.

Solution 11

(i) $f(x) = 5x^2 - 7x - 2$,

$$f'(x) = \frac{d}{dx}(5x^2) - \frac{d}{dx}(7x) - \frac{d}{dx}(2)$$

$$f'(x) = 10x - 7.$$

(ii) $g(x) = 3x^3 + 5x + x^{-2} + x^{-3}$

$$g'(x) = \frac{d}{dx}(3x^3) + \frac{d}{dx}(5x)$$

$$+ \frac{d}{dx}(x^{-2}) + \frac{d}{dx}x^{(-3)}$$

$$= g'(x) = 9x^2 + 5 - 2x^{-3} - 3x^{-4}$$

$$= 9x^2 + 5 - \frac{2}{x^3} - \frac{3}{x^4}.$$

(iii) $\dfrac{d}{dx}\{f(x) - g(x)\}$

$$= \frac{d}{dx}\{5x^2 - 7x - 2$$
$$- (3x^3 + 5x + x^{-2} + x^{-3})\}$$

$$= 10x - 7 - 9x^2 - 5 + 2x^{-3} + 3x^{-4}$$

$$= 10x - 7 - 9x^2 - 5 + \frac{2}{x^3} + \frac{3}{x^4}$$

$$= -9x^2 + 10x - 12 + \frac{2}{x^3} + \frac{3}{x^4}$$

alternatively

but $g'(x) = 9x^2 + 5 - \dfrac{2}{x^3} - \dfrac{3}{x^4}$

and $f'(x) = 10x - 7$

$$\frac{d}{dx}\{f(x) - g(x)\}$$

$$= f'(x) - g'(x)$$

$$= 10x - 7 - 9x^2 - 5 + \frac{2}{x^3} + \frac{3}{x^4}$$

$$= -9x^2 + 10x - 12 + \frac{2}{x^3} + \frac{3}{x^4}.$$

The positive and negative gradient of a curve.

Consider the two curves shown in Fig. 15 and Fig. 16.

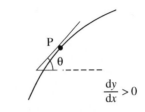

$$\frac{dy}{dx} > 0$$

Fig. 15

$$\frac{dy}{dx} < 0$$

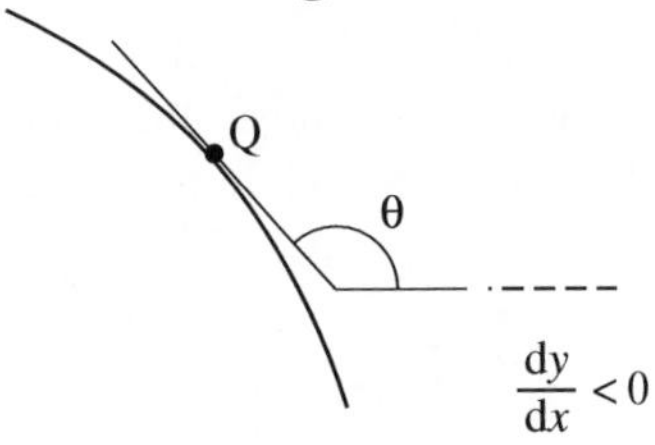

Fig. 16

What is a positive gradient?

Consider the right angled triangle where θ is less than 90°.

The gradient of **AB** is the tangent of the angle θ, $\tan\theta$ = gradient.

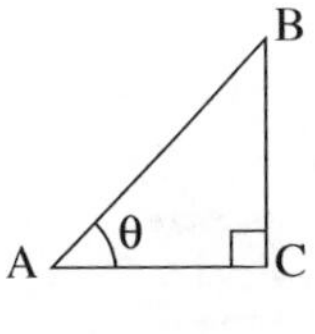

Fig. 17

If θ is less than 90° $\tan\theta$ is positive, therefore the gradient at **P** is positive, since the tangent of the angle θ is positive (θ is less than 90°).

If θ is greater than 90° and less than 180° as shown in the Fig. 16, the tangent is negative.

Therefore, the gradient at **P**, $\dfrac{dy}{dx} > 0$ (positive)

and the gradient at **Q**, $\dfrac{dy}{dx} < 0$ (negative).

Derivative of a product.

Differentiating an algebraic product such as $y = (1 + x^2)(2x - 1)$, we can first multiply the factors of the product and then differentiate

$$y = (1 + x^2)(2x - 1) = 2x + 2x^3 - 1 - x^2$$

$$\frac{dy}{dx} = 2 + 6x^2 - 2x = 6x^2 - 2x + 2$$

applying the basic rule $y = ax^n$, $\frac{dy}{dx} = anx^{n-1}$.
What happens if we require the derivative of a product such as $y = x \cdot \sin x$, where one factor is an algebraic function and the other factor is a trigonometric function?

We require the rule for a product of a function. If $y = uv$, differentiating with respect to x we have
$\frac{dy}{dx} = \frac{du}{dx} v + u \frac{dv}{dx}$ where u and v are functions of x

$$\boxed{\frac{dy}{dx} = \frac{du}{dx} v + u \frac{dv}{dx}}$$ The product rule.

WORKED EXAMPLE 12

Differentiate the function $y = x \sin x$.

Solution 12

$$\frac{d}{dx}(x \sin x) = \frac{dx}{dx} \sin x + x \frac{d}{dx}(\sin x)$$

$$\frac{dy}{dx} = \sin x + x \cos x.$$

WORKED EXAMPLE 13

Differentiate $y = (1 + x^2)(2x - 1)$

Solution 13

$$\frac{d}{dx} = \left[\frac{dy}{dx}(1 + x^2) \right](2x - 1)$$
$$+ (1 + x^2)\frac{d}{dx}(2x - 1)$$

where $u = 1 + x^2$ and $v = 2x - 1$

$$\frac{dy}{dx} = 2x(2x - 1) + (1 + x^2)2$$
$$= 4x^2 - 2x - 2x + 2 + 2x^2$$
$$= 6x^2 - 4x + 2.$$

WORKED EXAMPLE 14

Differentiate the following functions using the product rule:-

(i) $x \sin 2x$ (ii) $\cos 2x \sin 3x$

(iii) xe^{-3x} (iv) $e^{5x} \cos 4x$

(v) $e^{2x} \cos 3x$ (vi) $e^{3x} \log_e 3x$

(vii) $\sin 5x \log_e x$ (viii) $5 \cos 3x \ln x$

(ix) $e^{2x} \ln x \cos x$ (x) $e^{-x} \ln x \sin x$.

Solution 14

(i) $\frac{d}{dx}(x \sin 2x) = 1 \sin 2x + x(2 \cos 2x)$
$$= \sin 2x + 2x \cos 2x$$

(ii) $\frac{d}{dx}(\cos 2x \sin 3x)$
$$= -2 \sin 2x \sin 3x + (\cos 2x)3 \cos 3x$$
$$= -2 \sin 2x \sin 3x + 3 \cos 2x \cos 3x$$

(iii) $\frac{d}{dx}(xe^{-3x}) = 1.e^{-3x} + x(-3e^{-3x})$
$$= e^{-3x} - 3xe^{-3x}$$

(iv) $\frac{d}{dx}(e^{5x} \cos 4x)$
$$= 5e^{5x} \cos 4x + e^{5x}(-4 \sin 4x)$$
$$= 5e^{5x} \cos 4x - 4e^{5x} \sin 4x$$

(v) $\frac{d}{dx}(e^{2x} \cos 3x)$
$$= 2e^{2x} \cos 3x + e^{2x}(-3 \sin 3x)$$
$$= 2e^{2x} \cos 3x - 3e^{2x} \sin 3x$$

(vi) $\frac{d}{dx}(e^{3x} \log_e 3x) = 3e^{3x} \log_e 3x + e^{3x}\frac{1}{x}$

(vii) $\frac{d}{dx}(\sin 5x \log_e x)$
$$= 5 \cos 5x \log_e x + (\sin 5x)\frac{1}{x}$$

(viii) $\frac{d}{dx}(5 \cos 3x \ln x)$
$$= 5(-3 \sin 3x) \ln x + (5 \cos 3x)\frac{1}{x}$$
$$= -15 \sin 3x \ln x + \frac{5}{x} \cos 3x$$

(ix) $\dfrac{d}{dx}(e^{2x} \ln x \cos x)$

$= 2e^{2x} \ln x \cos x + e^{2x} \dfrac{1}{x} \cos x$

$\qquad + e^{2x} \ln x(-\sin x)$

$= 2e^{2x} \ln x \cos x + \dfrac{e^{2x}}{x} \cos x$

$\qquad - e^{2x} \ln x \sin x$

(x) $\dfrac{d}{dx}(e^{-x} \ln x \sin x)$

$= -e^{-x} \ln x \sin x + e^{-x} \dfrac{1}{x} \sin x$

$\qquad + e^{-x} \ln x \cos x$

$= -e^{-x} \ln x \sin x + \dfrac{e^{-x} \sin x}{x}$

$\qquad + e^{-x} \ln x \cos x.$

Derivative of a quotient.

Differentiating a quotient such as $y = \dfrac{3x^2 - 5x}{2x}$, we can first divide each term by $2x$ and then differentiate the simplied result.

$y = \dfrac{3x^2 - 5x}{2x} = \dfrac{3x^2}{2x} - \dfrac{5x}{2x}$

$y = \dfrac{3}{2}x - \dfrac{5}{2}, \quad \dfrac{dy}{dx} = \dfrac{3}{2}.$

What happens if we require the derivative of a quotient which is more complicated or the numerator is an algebraic function and the denominator is a trigonometric function. We require the rule for a quotient

$y = \dfrac{u}{v}.$

Differentiating both sides with respect to x, where u and v are functions of x as before:

The quotient Rule.

$$\boxed{\dfrac{dy}{dx} = \dfrac{\dfrac{du}{dx}v - u\dfrac{dv}{dx}}{v^2}}$$

Use the quotient rule to find the derivative of

$y = \dfrac{3x^2 - 5x}{2x}.$

Solution 15

$y = \dfrac{u}{v}$ where $u = 3x^2 - 5x$ and $v = 2x$

$\dfrac{du}{dx} = 6x - 5$ and $\dfrac{dv}{dx} = 2$

substituting these derivatives in the quotient rule

formula we have

$\dfrac{dy}{dx} = \dfrac{(6x - 5)2x - (3x^2 - 5x)2}{(2x)^2}$

$\qquad = \dfrac{12x^2 - 10x - 6x^2 + 10x}{4x^2}$

$\qquad = \dfrac{6x^2}{4x^2} = \dfrac{3}{2}.$

Differentiate the following functions:-

(i) $y = \dfrac{\sin x}{x}$ (ii) $y = \dfrac{\cos x}{x^2}$

(iii) $y = \dfrac{1}{\sin x}$ (iv) $y = \dfrac{\cos x}{\sin x}$

(v) $y = \dfrac{\sin x}{\cos x}$ (vi) $y = \dfrac{1}{\cos x}$

(vii) $y = \dfrac{(1 + x^2)}{2 \sin x}$ (viii) $y = \dfrac{5 \cos x}{(1 + 3x^2)}.$

Solution 16

(i) $y = \dfrac{\sin x}{x}$ $u = \sin x, v = x$

$\dfrac{du}{dx} = \cos x$ and $\dfrac{dv}{dx} = 1$

$\dfrac{dy}{dx} = \dfrac{x \dfrac{d}{dx}(\sin x) - \sin x \dfrac{d}{dx}(x)}{x^2}$

$\qquad = \dfrac{x \cos x - \sin x}{x^2}$

(ii) $y = \dfrac{\cos x}{x^2}$

$\dfrac{dy}{dx} = \dfrac{x^2(-\sin x) - 2x \cos x}{x^4}$

$\qquad = \dfrac{x(-\sin x) - 2 \cos x}{x^3}$

(iii) $y = \dfrac{1}{\sin x}$ $u = 1, v = \sin x,$

$$\dfrac{du}{dx} = 0, \dfrac{dv}{dx} = \cos x$$

$$\dfrac{dy}{dx} = \dfrac{(0)\sin x - 1\cos x}{\sin^2 x} = -\dfrac{\cos x}{\sin^2 x}$$

(iv) $y = \dfrac{\cos x}{\sin x}, u = \cos x \quad \dfrac{du}{dx} = -\sin x$

$$v = \sin x \quad \dfrac{dv}{dx} = \cos x$$

$$\dfrac{dy}{dx} = \dfrac{(-\sin x)\sin x - \cos x \cos x}{\sin^2 x}$$

$$= -\dfrac{\sin^2 x + \cos^2 x}{\sin^2 x} = -\dfrac{1}{\sin^2 x}$$

(v) $y = \dfrac{\sin x}{\cos x}, u = \sin x, v = \cos x$

$$\dfrac{du}{dx} = \cos x, \quad \dfrac{dv}{dx} = -\sin x$$

$$\dfrac{dy}{dx} = \dfrac{\cos x \cdot \cos x - \sin x(-\sin x)}{\cos^2 x}$$

$$= \dfrac{\cos^2 x + \sin^2 x}{\cos^2 x}$$

$$\dfrac{dy}{dx} = \dfrac{1}{\cos^2 x}$$

(vi) $y = \dfrac{1}{\cos x}$ $u = 1, v = \cos x$

$$\dfrac{du}{dx} = 0. \quad \dfrac{dv}{dx} = -\sin x$$

$$\dfrac{dy}{dx} = \dfrac{(0)\cos(x)1 - 1(-\sin x)}{\cos^2 x}$$

$$= \dfrac{\sin x}{\cos^2 x}$$

(vii) $y = \dfrac{1+x^2}{2\sin x}, u = 1 + x^2 \quad \dfrac{du}{dx} = 2x$

$$v = 2\sin x \quad \dfrac{dv}{dx} = 2\cos x$$

$$\dfrac{dy}{dx} = \dfrac{(2x)(2\sin x) - (1+x^2)(2\cos x)}{(2\sin x^2)}$$

$$= \dfrac{4x\sin x - 2(1+x^2)\cos x}{4\sin^2 x}$$

$$= \dfrac{2x\sin x - (1+x^2)\cos x}{2\sin^2 x}$$

(viii) $y = \dfrac{5\cos x}{(1+3x^2)}$ $u = 5\cos x \ v = 1+3x^2$

$$\dfrac{dy}{dx} = -5\sin x \qquad \dfrac{dv}{dx} = 6x$$

$$\dfrac{dy}{dx} = \dfrac{(5\sin x)(1+3x^2) - 5\cos x(6x)}{(1+3x^2)^2}$$

$$= -5\dfrac{[\sin x(1+3x^2) + 6x\cos x]}{(1+3x^2)^2}.$$

Function of a Function.

Consider the function $y = (1+x^2)^{15}$.

What is the derivative of this function?

$y = (1+x^2)^{15}$.

Simplify this function by changing the variable: let $u = 1 + x^2$, then the function becomes $y = u^{15}$ and the rate change of y with respect to u is: (found as follows:)

$$\dfrac{dy}{du} = 15u^{14}$$

but we require $\dfrac{dy}{dx} = \dfrac{dy}{du}\dfrac{du}{dx}$ which can be written as $\dfrac{\frac{dy}{du}}{\frac{dx}{du}} = \dfrac{dy}{du}\dfrac{du}{dx}$ and is called function of a function, $u = 1 + x^2$ and so we can find the derivative of u with respect to x $\dfrac{du}{dx} = 2x$.

The derivative of $y = (1+x^2)^{15}$ is therefore

$$\dfrac{dy}{dx} = \left[\dfrac{dy}{du}\right]\left[\dfrac{du}{dx}\right]$$

$$= (15u^{14})(2x) = 15(1+x^2)^{14}(2x)$$

and therefore $\dfrac{dy}{dx} = 30x(1+x^2)^{14}$. Observe that the derivative must be expressed in terms of x.

Therefore, in order to find the derivative of a complicated function, we first simplify it to an expression which can easily be differentiated. The method will be illustrated by a few worked examples.

▬▬▬▬▬▬

WORKED EXAMPLE 17

Use the method of function of a function to find the derivatives of the following functions:-

(i) $y = (1 + x^5)^5$ (ii) $y = \sin^3 2x$

(iii) $y = e^{-\frac{1}{x}}$

Solution 17

(i) $y = (1 + x^5)^5$

Let $u = 1 + x^5$ therefore $\dfrac{du}{dx} = 5x^4$ $y = u^5$

$\dfrac{dy}{du} = 5u^4$

$\dfrac{dy}{dx} = \dfrac{dy}{du}\dfrac{du}{dx}$

$= (5u^4)(5x^4) = 5(1 + x^5)^4 5x^4$

$\boxed{\dfrac{dy}{dx} = 25x^4(1 + x^5)^4}$

(ii) $y = \sin^3 2x$ let $u = 2x$, $\dfrac{du}{dx} = 2$

$y = \sin^3 u$ let $v = \sin u$ $\dfrac{dv}{du} = \cos u$

$y = v^3$ $\dfrac{dy}{dv} = 3v^2$

$\dfrac{dy}{dx} = \dfrac{dy}{dv} \times \dfrac{dv}{du} \times \dfrac{du}{dx} = (-v^2) \times (\cos u) \times (2)$

$= 6v^2 \cos u = 6 \sin^2 u \cos u$

$= 6 \sin^2 2x \cos 2x$

$\boxed{\dfrac{dy}{dx} = 6 \sin^2 x \cos 2x}$

This example was a little more complicated than the previous one, the method used was extended to function of a function of a function. We have obtained three separate derivatives whose product was $\frac{dy}{dx}$ and it was expressed in terms of x.

(iii) $y = e^{-\frac{1}{x}}$ let $u = -\dfrac{1}{x} = -x^{-1}$ then

$y = e^u$ $\dfrac{du}{dx} = +1x^{-2} = \dfrac{1}{x^2}$

$\dfrac{dy}{du} = e^u$

therefore $\dfrac{dy}{dx} = \dfrac{dy}{du}\dfrac{du}{dx} = e^u \dfrac{1}{x^2} = \dfrac{1}{x^2}e^{-\frac{1}{x}}$

$\boxed{\dfrac{dy}{dx} = \dfrac{1}{x^2}e^{-\frac{1}{x}}}$

Exercises 2

1. Find the derivatives of the following products.

(i) $x^2 \sin x$ (ii) $x \cos x$

(iii) $\sin x \cos x$ (iv) $\sin x \ln x$

(v) $\cos x \ln x$ (vi) $x \ln x$

(vii) $e^x \ln x$ (viii) $x^2 \ln x$

(ix) $e^x \sin x$ (x) $x^3 \ln x$

(xi) xe^x (xii) $x^n \ln x$.

2. Find the derivatives of the following functions:-

(i) $y = e^x - \cos x + \sin x - \ln x$

(ii) $y = x + e^x + \sin x + \cos x + \ln x$

(iii) $y = e^t + \sin t + \ln t - 5 \cos t$

(iv) $y = 3e^t - \cos t + 4 \ln t$

(v) $y = 5 \cos t - 7 \ln t$.

3. Find the value of $\dfrac{dy}{dx}$ of the following functions:-

(i) $y = \ln xe^{3x}$

(ii) $y = \cos 3x - \sin 5x$

(iii) $y = 3x^5 - \cos 4x$

(iv) $y = e^{-3x} \cos 5x + \sin 4x$

(v) $y = \sin 2x \cos 3x$.

4. Determine the values of $\dfrac{dy}{dx}$ at $x = \dfrac{\pi}{2}$.

(i) $y = \cos 3x - \sin 5x$

(ii) $y = \sin 2x \cos 3x$

(iii) $y = e^{-3x} \cos 5x + \sin 4x$.

5. Differentiate the following functions with respect to x.

(i) $y = 3e^{-3x} + 5 \cos 2x$

(ii) $y = -e^{-x} + 3e^x$

(iii) $y = 4(e^x - e^{-x})$

(iv) $y = \sin x \cos 2x$

(v) $y = -\ln x^2 + \dfrac{1}{x^3}$

(vi) $y = e^{-2x} + \cos 2x$

(vii) $y = 3e^{-x} \ln x - \cos(-x)$

(viii) $y = \sin 3x \cos 5x$

(ix) $y = e^{-3x} \cos 4x - e^{-x} \sin x$

(x) $y = 5 \sin x \ln \dfrac{1}{x}$.

6. Find $\dfrac{dy}{dx}$ at $x = \pi$ for the functions of exercise 1.

7. Find $\dfrac{dy}{dx}$, at $x = \dfrac{\pi}{2}$ for the functions of exercise 2 (i), (ii).

8. Find the values of the derivatives of exercise 3, when (a) $x = \dfrac{\pi}{2}$ and when (b) $x = \dfrac{\pi}{4}$.

9. Determine $\dfrac{dy}{dx}$ at $x = 0$ of exercise 5, except the logarithmic functions which are not defined.

10. If $y = 3 \sin^2 3x$, determine $\dfrac{dy}{dx}$ by the method of function of a function.

11. If $y = e^{-\frac{1}{t}}$, find $\dfrac{dy}{dt}$ by the method of function of a function.

12. If $y = e^{-\ln x}$, find $\dfrac{dy}{dx}$ by the method of function of a function.

13. Differentiate the following quotient functions:-

(i) $y = \dfrac{\sin x}{\ln x}$ (ii) $y = \dfrac{x^2}{\cos x}$

(iii) $y = \dfrac{1 - \sin 2x}{1 + \sin 2x}$ (iv) $y = \dfrac{1 + \tan x}{x^3}$

(v) $y = \dfrac{1 - x^2}{1 + x}$

and simplify as far as it is possible.

14. Find the gradients of the functions:

(i) $y = x^2$ (ii) $y = x \sec x$

(iii) $y = \dfrac{x}{\sin x}$ (iv) $y = e^{x^2}$

(v) $y = e^{3x} \cos 2x$ (vi) $y = \sin^2 x$

(vii) $y = \cos^2 2x$ (viii) $y = \dfrac{1 + x}{1 - x}$

(ix) $y = \dfrac{e^{2x}}{1 + 2x}$ (x) $y = \dfrac{1 - e^x}{1 + e^x}$.

Differentiates functions of the forms in 1 which are mathematical models of practical problems.

Charging of a Capacitor.

The Growth of the Voltage and Charge Across a Capacitor.

A capacitor C is connected in series with a resistor R and the combination is applied across a d.c. supply in series with a switch, **S** as shown in Fig. 18, the capacitor is assumed to be uncharged.

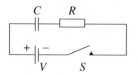

Fig. 18

when the switch, **S**, is closed, the current is initially maximum and equal to $I = \dfrac{V}{R}$ since the potential difference across C is zero (uncharged capacitor).

The potential difference across C after t seconds is an exponential function as shown

Let $\tau = RC = $ time <u>constant</u> in seconds and V is also a constant, the d.c. supply.

$$v_c = V - Ve^{-\frac{t}{RC}} \text{ or } v_c = V - Ve^{-\frac{t}{\tau}}$$

The rate of change of v_c with respect to time or the derivative of v_c with respect to time is $\dfrac{dv_c}{dt}$

$$\frac{dv_c}{dt} = \frac{d}{dt}(V) - \frac{d}{dt}\left(Ve^{-\frac{t}{\tau}}\right)$$

$$= 0 - \left(-\frac{1}{\tau}\right)e^{-\frac{t}{\tau}}$$

$$\frac{dv_c}{dt} = \frac{V}{\tau}e^{\frac{t}{\tau}}$$

$$\frac{d}{dt}(V) = 0 \qquad \text{since } V \text{ is a constant}$$

$\dfrac{d}{dt}(Ve^{-\frac{t}{\tau}})$ is found by the function of a function method.

Let $w = -\dfrac{t}{\tau}$ and $u = Ve^w$ and the corresponding derivatives are

$\dfrac{dw}{dt} = \dfrac{1}{\tau}$ and $\dfrac{du}{dw} = Ve^w$ therefore

$\dfrac{du}{dt} = \left(\dfrac{du}{dw}\right)\left(\dfrac{dw}{dt}\right) = (Ve^w)\left(-\dfrac{1}{\tau}\right)$

$= Ve^{-\frac{t}{\tau}}\left(-\dfrac{1}{\tau}\right)$

$\dfrac{du}{dt} = \dfrac{V}{\tau}e^{-\frac{t}{\tau}}.$ $\boxed{\dfrac{dv_c}{dt} = \dfrac{V}{\tau}e^{-\frac{t}{\tau}}}$

the rate of change of the potential difference across C with respect to time at any time t.

When $t = 0$, $\dfrac{dv_c}{dt} = \dfrac{V}{\tau}$ (1) where $e^0 = 1$ the initial rise of voltage

$\boxed{\left(\dfrac{dv_c}{dt}\right)_{t=0} = \dfrac{V}{\tau}}$

To appreciate the above, it is best to draw a graph of v_c against time and determine the gradients at different times t.

WORKED EXAMPLE 18

Draw a graph to scale for v_c against t.

Take $V = 10$ volts, $R = 1\,K\Omega$, $C = 100\,\mu F$ therefore $\tau = RC = 10^3 \times 100 \times 10^{-6} = 10^{-1} = 0.1$ s and consider the following times $t\,(s) = 0$, $0.01, 0.02, 0.04, 0.06, 0.1, 0.15, 0.2, 0.5, 1$.

Find the gradients at $t = 0, 0.1, 0.5, 1$ and 2s.

Solution 18

$t(s)$	$e^{-\frac{t}{0.1}}$	$1 - e^{-\frac{t}{0.1}}$	$v_c = 10 \times (1 - e^{-\frac{t}{0.1}})$
0	1	0	0
0.01	0.905	0.095	0.95
0.02	0.819	0.181	1.81
0.04	0.670	0.330	3.30
0.06	0.549	0.451	4.51
0.1	0.368	0.632	6.32
0.15	0.223	0.777	7.77
0.20	0.135	0.865	8.65
0.50	0.007	0.993	9.93
1.00	0.00005	0.99995	9.999

A graph of v_c against t is drawn.

$\dfrac{dv_c}{dt} = \dfrac{V}{\tau}e^{-\frac{t}{\tau}}$ the gradient at any time t.

At $t = 0$, $\dfrac{dv_c}{dt} = \dfrac{V}{\tau} = \dfrac{10}{0.1} = 100$ volts/s

at $t = 0.1$s, $\dfrac{dv_c}{dt} = 100e^{-\frac{0.1}{0.1}} = 36.8$ volts/s

at $t = 0.5$s, $\dfrac{dv_c}{dt} = 100e^{-5} = 0.674$ volts/s

at $t = 1$s, $\dfrac{dv_c}{dt} = 100e^{-10} = 4.54$ mV/s

at $t = 2$s, $\dfrac{dv}{dt} = 100e^{-20} = 2.06 \times 10^{-7}$ V/s

$= 0.206\,\mu$V/s.

The rate of changes of v_c with respect to t are as shown above and are represented by the tangents at the various times indicated. It is observed that the rate of change of v_c with respect to t is very high initially and very low finally as indicated by the values, initially the rate of rise of voltage is 100 V/s and finally 0.206 μV/s, the latter is a very small quantity and it may be neglected, since at this time the curve flattens.

These gradients are drawn at $t = 0, t = 0.1$ s and $t = 0.3$ s.

The curve tends to the final value of 10 V and the gradient tends to zero.

Discharging of a Capacitor.

Decay of Current, Voltage and Charge.

When C is fully charged, the switch S_1 is opened and the switch S_2 is closed as shown on Fig. 19.

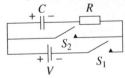

Fig. 19

At this instant, the circuit appears to be as shown in Fig. 20.

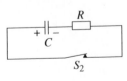

Fig. 20

The current in the circuit flows in the opposite direction as shown and after t seconds, the current is given by the equation.

$$i = -Ie^{-\frac{t}{\tau}}$$

Where $I = \dfrac{V}{R}$, $\tau = RC$ and t, i are variable quantities. Immediately after closing the switch S_2, the current is

$$I = \frac{10}{1\,\text{K}\Omega}$$
$$= 10\,\text{mA}.$$

Fig. 21

The graph of i against t is drawn for time.

$t(s)$	$e^{-\frac{t}{\tau}}$	$i = -Ie^{-\frac{t}{\tau}}$ (mA)
0	1	−10
0.01	0.905	−9.05
0.02	0.819	−8.19
0.03	0.741	−7.41
0.05	0.607	−6.07
0.1	0.368	−3.68
0.2	0.135	−1.35
0.3	0.05	−0.50

The curve rises from -10 mA at $t = 0$ to approximately 0 mA at t equal to a few seconds.

The rate of change of current with respect to t is found as follows:-

$$i = -Ie^{-\frac{t}{\tau}} \qquad \frac{di}{dt} = -I\left[-\frac{1}{\tau}\right]e^{-\frac{t}{\tau}}$$

$$\frac{di}{dt} = +\frac{I}{\tau}e^{-\frac{t}{\tau}}.$$

It is observed that this gradient is positive.

The initial rise of current is found by substituting $t = 0$ in the expression $\dfrac{di}{dt} = \dfrac{I}{\tau}e^{-\frac{t}{\tau}}$.

At $t = 0$, $\quad \dfrac{di}{dt} = \dfrac{I}{\tau}e^{-\frac{t}{\tau}}e^0 = 10I = 10 \times 10$

$$\frac{di}{dt} = 100\,\text{mA/s}$$

at $t = 0.05$ s,
$$\frac{di}{dt} = 10Ie^{-\frac{0.05}{0.1}} = 10Ie^{0.5}100 \times 0.607$$
$$= 60.7\,\text{mA/s}$$

at $t = 0.1$ s, $\quad \dfrac{di}{dt} = 100e^{-1} = 36.8\,\text{mA/s}$

at $t = 1$ s,

$$\frac{di}{dt} = 100e^{-10} = 100 \times 4.54 \times 10^{-5}$$
$$= 4.54 \times 10^{-3}\,\text{mA/s} = 4.54\,\text{mA/s}$$

at $t = 2$ s,

$$\frac{di}{dt} = 100e^{-20} = 100 \times 2.06 \times 10^{-9}$$
$$= 206\,\text{pA/s} = 206\,\text{pA/s}$$

an extremely small rise in current which is substantially zero, that is the gradient is horizontal.

The gradients at $t = 0$, $t = 0.1$ s, $t = 0.2$ s and $t = 0.3$ s are shown on the graph.

Growth of current through a coil.

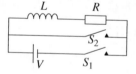

Fig. 22

When the switch, S_1 is after t seconds, the differential equation is given by $V = L\frac{di}{dt} + iR$ and the solution of this differential equation is given by $(i = I(1 - e^{-\frac{t}{R}})$, a similar expression to that for the growth of voltage across the capacitor.

$$i = I(1 - e^{-\frac{t}{\tau}}) \quad \text{where } \tau = \frac{L}{R}$$

I and τ are constants, i and t are variables.

If i is plotted against t we obtain a graph as shown, similar to that we have obtained previously.

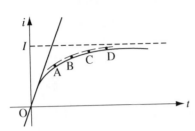

Fig. 23

The gradient at any point on the curve may be found by differentiating i with respect to t.

$$i = I(1 - e^{-\frac{t}{\tau}}) = I - Ie^{-\frac{t}{\tau}}$$

$$\frac{di}{dt} = 0 - I[-\frac{1}{\tau}]e^{-\frac{t}{\tau}} = \frac{I}{\tau}e^{-\frac{t}{\tau}}$$

$$\frac{di}{dt} = \frac{I}{\tau}e^{-\frac{t}{\tau}}$$

the gradient is positive at **O**, **A**, **B**, **C** and **D**. The initial rate of rise of current is given when $t = 0$.

At $t = 0$, $\dfrac{di}{dt} = \dfrac{I}{\tau}$ or $\left(\dfrac{di}{dt}\right)_{t=0} = \dfrac{I}{\tau}$.

WORKED EXAMPLE 19

Given that the current through the coil as a function of t is $i = I(I - e^{-\frac{t}{\tau}})$.

Calculate I for $t = 0, 0.1, 0.5, 1, 5,$ and 10 ms, if $L = 50$ mH, $R = 10\Omega$, $V = 10$ volts.

Determine the gradients at the above times.

Solution 19

$$\tau = \frac{L}{R} = \frac{50\,\text{mH}}{10} = 5\,\text{ms}$$

$$I = \frac{V}{R} = \frac{10}{10} = 1\,\text{A}$$

$$i = 1\left(1 - e^{-\frac{t}{5 \times 10^{-3}}}\right)$$

At $t = 0$ ms $i = I = 1$ A

$$t = 0.1\,\text{ms}\quad i = 1 - e^{-\frac{0.1 \times 10^{-3}}{5 \times 10^{-3}}}$$

$$= 1 - 0.9801986 = 19.8\,\text{mA}$$

$t = 0.5$ ms

$$i = 1 - e^{-\frac{0.5}{5}} = 1 - e^{-\frac{1}{10}} = 1 - 0.9048374$$
$$= 95.2\,\text{mA}$$

$t = 1$ ms

$$i = 1 - e^{-0.2} = 181\,\text{mA}$$

$t = 5$ ms

$$i = 1 - e^{-1} = 632\,\text{mA}$$

$t = 10$ ms

$$i = 1 - e^{-2} = 865\,\text{mA}.$$

The gradient is found by differentiating the expression $i = I(1 - e^{-\frac{t}{\tau}})$ multiplying out

$$i = I - Ie^{-\frac{t}{\tau}}$$

$$\frac{di}{dt} = -I[-\frac{1}{\tau}]e^{-\frac{t}{\tau}}$$

$$\frac{di}{dt} = \frac{I}{\tau}e^{-\frac{t}{\tau}}$$

the gradient at any time t.

At $t = 0$, $\dfrac{di}{dt} = \dfrac{1}{5 \times 10^{-3}}e^{-\frac{0}{\tau}} = \dfrac{1}{5 \times 10^{-3}} \times 1$

$= 0.2 \times 10^3$ A/s $= 200$ A/s the initial rate of rise of current is 200 **A**, at $t = 0.1$ ms,

$$\frac{di}{dt} = \frac{1}{5 \times 10^{-3}}e^{-\frac{0.1\,\text{ms}}{5\,\text{ms}}} = \frac{e^{-0.02}}{5 \times 10^{-3}}$$

$$= 200e^{-0.02} = 196\,\text{A/s}$$

at $t = 0.5$ ms $\dfrac{di}{dt} = 200e^{-0.1} = 181$ A/s

at $t = 1$ ms $\dfrac{di}{dt} = 200e^{-0.2} = 163.7$ A/s

at $t = 5$ ms $\dfrac{di}{dt} = 200e^{-1} = 73.6$ A/s

at $t = 10$ ms $\dfrac{di}{dt} = 200e^{-2} = 27.1$ A/s.

3

Determines and evaluates second derivatives.

a. States the notation for second derivatives as $\dfrac{d^2y}{dx^2}$ and similar form e.g. $\dfrac{d^2x}{dt^2}$

b. Determines the second derivative by applying 3a to the simplified result of a first differentiation.

c. Evaluates a second derivative determined in 3b at a given point.

d. State that $\dfrac{dx}{dt}$ and $\dfrac{d^2x}{dt^2}$ express velocity and acceleration in the x direction.

e. Calculates velocity and acceleration at a given time from an equation for displacement expressed in terms of time using 3d.

Notation for second derivatives.

We have seen previously that the notation for the first derivative is $\frac{dy}{dx}$, read as 'dee y by dee x' the gradient at a point of a curve

$$\lim_{\delta x \to 0} \frac{\delta y}{\delta x} = \frac{dy}{dx} = \text{the derivative of } y \text{ with}$$

respect to x or the differential coefficient of y with respect to x and the process of obtaining $\dfrac{dy}{dx}$ above y is given as a function of x is called differentiation.

Differentiating now $\frac{dy}{dx}$ results in the new notation

$$\frac{d}{dx}\left(\frac{dy}{dx}\right) \text{ or } \frac{d}{dx}\left(\frac{dy}{dx}\right) = \frac{d^2y}{dx^2}.$$

The rate of change of the first derivative.

What is the significance of $\dfrac{d^2y}{dx^2} = \dfrac{d}{dx}\left(\dfrac{dy}{dx}\right)$?

The rate of change of the gradient with respect to x is the second derivative, $\dfrac{d^2y}{dx^2}$.

The expression $\dfrac{d}{dx}\left(\dfrac{dy}{dx}\right)$ is written $\dfrac{d^2y}{dx^2}$ and is called the second differential coefficient of y with respect to x.

Similarly we can obtain higher derivatives:

$$\frac{d}{dx}\left(\frac{d^2y}{dx^2}\right) = \frac{d^3y}{dx^3} = \text{third derivative}$$

$$\frac{d}{dx}\left(\frac{d^3y}{dx^3}\right) = \frac{d^4y}{dx^4} = \text{fourth derivative.}$$

$$\frac{d}{dx}\left(\frac{d^{n-1}y}{dx^{n-1}}\right) = \frac{d^ny}{dx^n} = n^{\text{th}} \text{ derivative.}$$

If x is a function of t then the first derivative is denoted as $\dfrac{dx}{dt}$ and the second derivative is denoted as $\dfrac{d}{dt}\left(\dfrac{dx}{dt}\right) = \dfrac{d^2x}{dt^2}.$

WORKED EXAMPLE 20

Determine the first and second derivatives for the following functions:-

(i) $y = 3x^2 - 5x + 7$ (ii) $x = t - 6t^2 + 7t^3$

(iii) $u = 3v^2 + 5v - 1$ (iv) $w = 3z^2 - z - 4$.

Solution 20

(i) $\dfrac{dy}{dx} = 6x - 5$ $\dfrac{d^2y}{dx^2} = 6$

(ii) $\dfrac{dx}{dt} = 1 - 12t + 21t^2$

$\dfrac{d^2x}{dt^2} = -12 + 42t$

(iii) $\dfrac{du}{dv} = 6v + 5$ $\dfrac{d^2u}{dv^2} = 6$

(iv) $\dfrac{dw}{dz} = 6z - 1$ $\dfrac{d^2w}{dz^2} = 6$.

WORKED EXAMPLE 21

Determine the second derivatives of the following functions and simplify.

(i) $y = \dfrac{3x^2 - 1}{x + 1}$ (ii) $y = e^x + \sin x$

(iii) $y = e^{-x} \cos 2x$

(iv) $y = 3 \sin 2x - 5 \cos 2x$

(v) $y = \sin^2 x$.

Solution 21

(i) $y = \dfrac{3x^2 - 1}{x + 1}$ applying the quotient rule

$\dfrac{dy}{dx} = \dfrac{6x(x + 1) - (3x^2 - 1)(1)}{(x + 1)^2}$

$= \dfrac{6x^2 + 6x - 3x^2 + 1}{(x + 1)^2}$

$= \dfrac{3x^2 + 6x + 1}{(x + 1)^2}$

$\dfrac{d^2y}{dx^2} = \dfrac{\{(6x + 6)(x + 1)^2 \\ -(3x^2 + 6x + 1)2(x + 1)\}}{(x + 1)^4}$

$= \dfrac{(6x + 6)(x + 1) - 2(3x^2 + 6x + 1)}{(x + 1)^3}$

by dividing numerator and

denominator by $x + 1$

$\dfrac{d^2y}{dx^2} = \dfrac{6x^2 + 6x + 6x + 6 - 6x^2 - 12x - 2}{(x + 1)^3}$

$= \dfrac{4}{(x + 1)^3}$

the simplified form of the second derivative

is $\dfrac{d^2y}{dx^2} = \dfrac{4}{(x + 1)^3}$

(ii) $y = e^x + \sin x$

$\dfrac{dy}{dx} = e^x + \cos x$ $\dfrac{d^2y}{dx^2} = e^x - \sin x$

(iii) $y = e^{-x} \cos 2x$

$\dfrac{dy}{dx} = -e^{-x} \cos 2x + e^{-x}(-2 \sin 2x)$

$\dfrac{dy}{dx} = -e^{-x} \cos 2x - 2e^{-x} \sin 2x$

$\dfrac{d^2y}{dx^2} = -(-e^{-x}) \cos 2x$

$- e^{-x}(-2 \sin 2x) - 2(-e^{-x}) \sin 2x$

$- 2e^{-x}(2 \cos 2x)$

$= e^{-x} \cos 2x + 2e^{-x} \sin 2x$

$+ 2e^{-x} \sin 2x - 4e^{-x} \cos 2x$

$\dfrac{d^2y}{dx^2} = 4e^{-x} \sin 2x - 3e^{-x} \cos 2x$

(iv) $y = 3 \sin 2x - 5 \cos 2x$

$\dfrac{dy}{dx} = 6 \cos 2x - 5(-2 \sin 2x)$

$= 6 \cos 2x + 10 \sin 2x$

$\dfrac{d^2y}{dx^2} = -12 \sin 2x + 20 \cos 2x$.

Velocity and acceleration expressed as derivative.

The v velocity is the rate of change of displacement, x, with respect to time, t

$$v = \frac{dx}{dt}$$

The acceleration is the rate of change of velocity, v, with respect to time, t

$$a = \frac{dv}{dt} = \frac{d}{dt}\left(\frac{dx}{dt}\right)$$

$$a = \frac{d^2x}{dt^2}$$

The first derivative is the velocity and the second derivative is the acceleration.

$$v = \frac{dx}{dt} \text{ and } a = \frac{d^2x}{dt^2}.$$

Calculation of velocity and acceleration at a given time.

This is best illustrated with a worked example.

WORKED EXAMPLE 22

A body is moving along a straight line and its distance x metres from a fixed point on the line after a time t seconds is given by $x = 2t^3 - 3t^2 + 4t + 5$.
Find
(i) the velocity of the body after t second
(ii) the velocity of the body at $t = 0$
(iii) the velocity of the body after 5 seconds from the start
(iv) the acceleration at the start and after 2 seconds
(v) the displacements after 2 s, 3 s, and 5 s.

Solution 22

(i) $\frac{dx}{dt} = v = 6t^2 - 6t + 4$ after t seconds

(ii) $v = 4$ m/s at $t = 0$

(iii) $v = 6(5)^2 - 6(5) + 4$

$= 150 - 30 + 4 = 124$ m/s

(iv) $a = \frac{dv}{dt} = \frac{d^2s}{dt^2} = 12t - 6$ at t time

$a = 12(0) - 6 = -6$ m/s^2 at the start

$a = 12(2) - 6 = 18$ m/s^2 after 2 seconds

(v) $x = 2t^3 - 3t^2 + 4t + 5$

$x = 2(2)^3 - 3(2)^2 + 4(2) + 5$

$= 16 - 12 + 8 + 5 = 17$ m

$x = 2(3)^3 - 3(3)^2 + 4(3) + 5$

$= 54 - 27 + 12 + 5 = 44$ m

$x = 2(5)^3 - 3(5)^2 + 4(5) + 5$

$= 250 - 75 + 20 + 5$

$= 200$ m.

WORKED EXAMPLE 23

If the distance s metres of a body moves after t seconds is given by $s = 30t^2 - 3t + 5$ find:

(i) Its velocity after 3 seconds.

(ii) Its acceleration.

(iii) The distance the body has travelled before coming to rest.

(iv) The time when the velocity is 57 m/s.

(v) The velocity after 10 seconds.

Solution 23

(i) $s = 30t^2 - 3t + 5$

$\frac{ds}{dt} = 60t - 3$ the velocity at time t and

when $t = 3$

$v = \frac{ds}{dt} = 60 \times 3 - 3$

$= 180 - 3 = 177$ m/s

(ii) $a = \frac{dv}{dt} = \frac{d^2s}{dt^2} = 60$ m/s^2

(iii) $v = \dfrac{ds}{dt} = 0 \quad 60t - 3 = 0 \quad t = \frac{1}{20}$ s

$s = 30t^2 - 3t + 5$

$= 30\left(\dfrac{1}{20}\right)^2 - 3\dfrac{1}{20} + 5$

$= \dfrac{30}{400} - \dfrac{3}{20} + 5$

$= \dfrac{30 - 60 + 2000}{400} = \dfrac{1970}{400}$

$s = \dfrac{197}{40} = 4.93$ m

(iv) $v = 60t - 3 = 57$

$60t = 57 + 3 \quad t = 1$ s

(v) $v = 60t - 3$

$= 60(10) - 3 = 600 - 3 = 597$ m/s.

WORKED EXAMPLE 24

A body is falling freely from rest under gravity ($g = 9.81$ m/s^2), the distance, s metre travelled is given by the expression $s = 20t^2$. where t is the time in seconds.

Find

(i) The velocity after t seconds.

(ii) The velocity after 1 second.

(iii) The time taken for the body to fall 1500 m.

(iv) The acceleration.

Solution 24

$s = 20t^2$

(i) $v = \dfrac{ds}{dt} = 40t$

(ii) $v = 40$ m/s

(iii) $1500 = 20t^2$

$t = \sqrt{\dfrac{1500}{20}} = 8.66$ s

(iv) $a = \dfrac{dv}{dt} = \dfrac{d^2s}{dt^2} = 40$ m/s^2.

Exercise 3

1. Find $\dfrac{d^2y}{dx^2}$ for the following functions:-

   (i) $y = 3\sin 2x - 5\cos 2x$

   (ii) $y = 3x^3 - 2x^2 + x - 1$

   (iii) $y = 4e^{-2x} - 5e^{3x}$

   (iv) $y = e^{3x} - \cos 3x + \sin 3x$

   (v) $y = 5\ln x + x\sin 2x$.

2. Determine the first and second derivatives of the following functions:-

   (i) $x = 5t^5 - 4t^4 + 3t^3 - 2t^2 + t - 1$

   (ii) $x = \sin t - \cos t$

   (iii) $x = e^t \sin 2t$

   (iv) $x = \dfrac{e^{2t}}{(1+t)}$

   (v) $x = e^{\sin t}$.

3. Define velocity and acceleration and determine the velocity and acceleration for the functions in exercise 2 at $t = 0$.

4. Determine the second derivatives for the following functions:-

   (i) $y = \dfrac{x^2 + 1}{x - 1}$

   (ii) $y = x^2 \sin x$

   (iii) $y = \dfrac{\cos x}{e^{3x}}$

   (iv) $y = \dfrac{\ln x}{(1 + x)^2}$

   (v) $y = \dfrac{e^x}{1 + x}$.

5. Evaluate the second derivatives for the functions at $x = \frac{\pi}{2}$.

   (i) $y = \sin x \cos 2x$

   (ii) $y = e^x \tan \dfrac{x}{2}$

   (iii) $y = x^2 \ln x$

   (iv) $y = 5\cos 3x - 4\sin 4x$.

6. Determine $\dfrac{d^2 y}{dx^2}$ for $y = 3\cos 5kx$
   where k is a constant and at $x = \dfrac{\pi}{k}$.

7. What is the significance of $\dfrac{dy}{dx}$ and $\dfrac{d^2 y}{dx^2}$ of a function? Illustrate your answers clearly with the aid of sketches.

8. Find the second derivative for the function $y = e^x \sin 2x$.

9. Find the second derivative of the function $y = e^{-2x} \cos x$.

10. A particle moves s m in time t seconds given by the relation $s = 3t^3 - t^2 + t + 7$. Find the velocity and the acceleration of the particle after 5 seconds.

11. Find the $\dfrac{d^2 y}{dx^2}$ of the following quotients:-

    (i) $\dfrac{1 + \cos \theta}{\sin \theta}$ (ii) $\dfrac{\sin x}{e^{2x}}$ (iii) $\cot x$.

12. If $i = I_m \sin(2\pi f t - \dfrac{\pi}{3})$ determine $\dfrac{d^2 i}{dt^2}$.

13. If $v = V_m \cos(2\pi f t + \dfrac{\pi}{6})$ determine $\dfrac{d^2 v}{dt^2}$.

14. The volume of a sphere is given as $V = \dfrac{4}{3}\pi R^3$, find $\dfrac{d^2 V}{dR^2}$.

15. The volume of a cone is given as $V = \dfrac{1}{3}\pi r^2 h$ and $h = 3r$, find $\dfrac{d^2 V}{dr^2}$.

4

Determines the position and nature of the turning points of the graph of a quadratic or cubic function.

a. Defines a turning point of a graph.

b. Determines the derivative of the function of the graph concerned involving functions in 1b.

c. Determines the value of x (the independent variable) at the turning points using 4a and 4b.

d. Evaluates y (the dependent variable) corresponding to the values in 4c.

e. Determines the nature of the turning points by consideration of the gradient on either side of the point.

f. Determines and evaluates the second derivative of the function at the turning points.

g. Determines the nature of the turning points by the sign of the second derivative.

h. Solves problems involving maximum relevant to the technology and science.

i. Eliminates one independent variable using a constraint equation in functions such as $V = \pi r^2 h$.

The position and nature of the turning point of the graph of a quadratic or cubic function.

The quadratic function.

$$y = \mathrm{f}(x) = ax^2 + bx + c.$$

The quadratic function is a parabola with either a maximum or minimum as shown in Fig. 24 and Fig. 25.

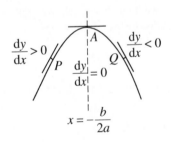

Fig. 24

Let us examine the various gradients shown on the graphs of Fig. 24 and Fig. 25.

The gradient at P is positive, that is, $\frac{dy}{dx} > 0$

25

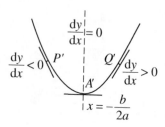

Fig. 25

The gradient at Q is negative, that is, $\frac{dy}{dx} < 0$.

The gradient at A is zero, that is $\frac{dy}{dx} = 0$.

Similarly the gradient at P' is negative, that is, $\frac{dy}{dx} < 0$.

The gradient at Q' is positive, that is $\frac{dy}{dx} > 0$.

The gradient at A' is zero, that is $\frac{dy}{dx} = 0$.

We have observed that the gradients at the maximum and at the minimum are zero.

a. Turning point.

Referring to Fig. 24, the gradient at **P** is positive to the left of **A** and at **Q** to the right of **A** is negative, the point where the gradient changes from positive to negative is called the turning point or the stationary point. Similarly referring to Fig. 25 the gradient to the left of **A** is negative and the gradient to the right of **A'** is positive, the point where the gradient changes from negative to positive, is called the turning point or the stationary point.

b. To determine the derivative of the function of the graph.

The quadratic function $f(x) = ax^2 + bx + c$

the gradient $\frac{dy}{dx} = f'(x) = 2ax + b$.

The cubic function

$$f(x) = ax^3 + bx^2 + cx + d$$

the gradient $\frac{dy}{dx} = f'(x) = 3ax^2 + 2bx + c$.

c. To determine the independent variable at the turning points.

For turning points $\frac{dy}{dx} = 0$, therefore for the quadratic $2ax + b = 0$ or $\boxed{x = -\frac{b}{2a}}$ or where the turning point occurs, which is either a maximum or a minimum.

For the cubic function $f(x) = ax^3 + bx^2 + cx + d$ for turning points $f'(x) = 3ax^2 + 2bx + c = 0$ which may be solved by using the

quadratic formula $x = \dfrac{-b \pm \sqrt{b^2 - 4ac}}{2a}$

thus $x = \dfrac{-2b \pm \sqrt{4b^2 - 4(3a)c}}{6a}$

giving two points.

The following examples illustrate the previous points.

WORKED EXAMPLE 25

Determine the gradient of the quadratic function $y = f(x) = x^2 - 4x + 3$ and hence find the value of x at which the turning point occurs.

Solution 25

$f'(x) = 2x - 4$ the gradient at any point of x.

For turning points, $f'(x) = 0$

therefore $\frac{dy}{dx} = 2x - 4 = 0$

$x = 2$ the point where the turning or stationary point occurs.

d. Evaluate y for the value of x found.

When $x = 2$

$$y = 2^2 - 4(2) + 3 = 4 - 8 + 3 = -1$$

therefore when $x = 2$, $y = -1$.

e. Determine the nature of the turning points by considering the gradient on either side of $x = 2$.

Find the gradient at $x = 1.9$ and the gradient at $x = 2.1$, that is, at a point slightly below the value of $x = 2$ and at a point slightly above the value of $x = 2$.

The gradient $\quad \dfrac{dy}{dx} = 2x - 4$

at $x = 1.9$, $\dfrac{dy}{dx} = 2(1.9) - 4 = 3.8 - 4 = -0.2$

at $x = 2.1$, $\dfrac{dy}{dx} = 2(2.1) - 4 = 4.2 - 4 = +0.2$

Therefore, the gradient before $x = 2$ is negative and after $x = 2$ is positive and the turning point must be a minimum.

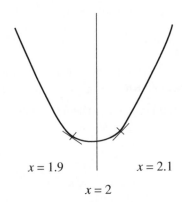

$x = 1.9 \qquad\qquad x = 2.1$

$x = 2$

Fig. 26

f. Determine and evaluate the second derivative of the function at the turning points.

If $y = x^2 - 4x + 3$ the first derivative of the function $\frac{dy}{dx} = 2x - 4$

the second derivative of the function $\frac{d^2y}{dx^2} = 2$.

The second derivative is positive therefore the rate of change of the gradient is positive and the turning point must be a minimum, the gradual changes from the negative value to the positive value.

We have performed two tests in order to establish the nature of the turning point, the former in (e) was more tedious than the latter in (f).

g. The sign of the second derivative establishes the nature of the turning point.

The second derivative of the function $y = f(x)$ is $\frac{d^2y}{dx^2}$.

If $\frac{d^2y}{dx^2} > 0$, the rate of change of the gradient with respect to x is positive,

therefore the function has a minimum.

If $\frac{d^2y}{dx^2} < 0$ the rate of change of the gradient with respect to x is negative therefore the function has a maximum. If $\frac{d^2y}{dx^2} = 0$, the rate of change of the gradient with respect to x is zero, therefore the function has neither a maximum nor a minimum. The turning point is called a point of <u>inflexion</u>, where the rate of change of the gradient with respect to x does not change, the gradient before the point of inflexion may be negative and therefore be also negative after the point of inflexion or the gradient before the point of inflexion may be positive and therefore be also positive after the point of inflexion. This is illustrated in the two diagrams of Fig. 27 and Fig. 28.

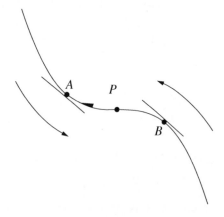

Fig. 27

Point of inflexion at P at A and at B the gradients are negative.

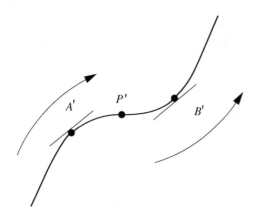

Fig. 28

Point of inflexion at P' at A' and at B' the gradients are positive.

The gradient at P is not necessarily zero. The curved parts before the point of inflexion may be concave and after the point of inflexion may be convex or vice-versa as shown by the curved arrows.

To find the point of inflexion of a function the second derivative is found and by making it zero, x is found when the point or points of inflexion occur.

WORKED EXAMPLE 26

Determine the maximum or minimum values of the following functions:-

(i) $y = x^2 + 4x + 8$

(ii) $y = x^2 - 4x + 7$

(iii) $y = -x^2 - 6x + 7$

(iv) $y = -x^2 + 6x - 8.$

Solution 26

(i) $y = x^2 + 4x + 8$, $\frac{dy}{dx} = 2x + 4$, $\frac{dy}{dx} = 0$

for turning points, $2x + 4 = 0$ or $x = -2.$

The second derivative $\frac{d^2y}{dx^2} = 2$ it is positive and the function has a minimum at $x = -2.$

$y_{min} = (-2)^2 + 4(-2) + 8 = 4.$

The turning point has coordinates $(-2, 4)$ when $x = 0, y = 8$, that is, the curve cuts the y axis at $(0, 8)$.

(ii) $y = x^2 - 4x + 7$, $\frac{dy}{dx} = 2x - 4$, $\frac{dy}{dx} = 0$ for turning point, $2x - 4 = 0$, $x = 2$, $\frac{d^2y}{dx^2} = 2$ it is positive and the function has a minimum at $x = 2$

$y_{min} = (2)^2 - 4(2) + 7$

$= 4 - 8 + 7 = 3.$

The turning point has coordinates $(2, 3)$ when $x = 0, y = 7.$

(iii) $y = -x^2 - 6x - 7$ $\quad \frac{dy}{dx} = -2x - 6$

$\frac{dy}{dx} = 0$ for turning point

$-2x - 6 = 0 \qquad x = -3$

$\frac{d^2y}{dx^2} = -2$, it is negative and the function has a maximum at $x = -3.$

The turning point has coordinates $(-3, 2)$

$y_{max} = -(-3)^2 - 6(-3) - 7$

$= -9 + 18 - 7 = 2$

when $x = 0, y = -7$, the curve intersects the y axis at $(0, -7).$

(iv) $y = -x^2 + 6x - 8$ $\quad \frac{dy}{dx} = -2x + 6$

$\frac{dy}{dx} = 0$ for turning point

$-2x + 6 = 0 \quad x = 3$

$\frac{d^2y}{dx^2} = -2$ it is negative and the function has a maximum at $x = 3$

$y_{max} = -(3)^2 + 6(3) - 8$

$= -9 + 18 - 8 = 1.$

The turning point has coordinates $(3, 1)$ and the curve cuts the y-axis when $x = 0$, at $y = -8.$

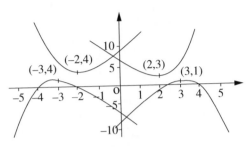

Fig. 29

WORKED EXAMPLE 27

Determine the stationary points on the following curves and distinguish between them.

(i) $y = x^3 + 2x^2 - 11x - 12$

(ii) $y = x^3 - x$.

Sketch the graphs and indicate the turning points.

Solution 27

(i) $y = x^3 + 2x^2 - 11x - 12$

the gradient at any point is found by differentiating,

$$\frac{dy}{dx} = 3x^2 + 4x - 11.$$

For turning points or stationary points or maximum and minimum $\frac{dy}{dx} = 0$ therefore $3x^2 + 4x - 11 = 0$ applying the quadratic formula

$$x = \frac{-4 \pm \sqrt{16 + 132}}{6} = \frac{-4 \pm \sqrt{148}}{6}$$

$$x = \frac{-4 \pm 12.2}{6}, \quad x = \frac{-4 - 12.2}{6} \quad \text{or}$$

$$x = \frac{-4 + 12.2}{6}$$

$$x = -2.69 \text{ or } x = 1.37.$$

There are two turning points one is maximum and the other is minimum but which is which?

The second derivative indicates the nature of the turning point

$$\frac{d^2y}{dx^2} = 6x + 4.$$

When $x = -2.69$, then

$$\frac{d^2y}{dx^2} = 6(-2.69) + 4 = -12.14$$

it is negative and there at $x = -2.69$ there is a maximum,

$$y_{max} = (-2.69)^3 + 2(-2.69)^2$$
$$-11(-2.69) - 12$$
$$= -19.5 + 14.47 + 29.59 - 12$$
$$= 12.56$$

When $x = 1.37$,
$\frac{d^2y}{dx^2} = 6(1.37) + 4 = 12.22$ it is positive and therefore at $x = 1.37$ there is a minimum,

$$y_{min} = 1.37^3 + 2(1.37)^2$$
$$-11(1.37) - 12$$
$$= 2.57 + 3.75 - 12$$
$$y_{min} = -20.78$$

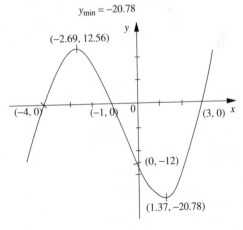

Fig. 30

(ii) $y = x^3 - x$

$$\frac{dy}{dx} = 3x^2 - 1 \quad \frac{dy}{dx} = 0 \quad 3x^2 - 1 = 0$$

$$x = \pm\frac{1}{\sqrt{3}}, \quad x = \frac{1}{\sqrt{3}} \text{ and } x = -\frac{1}{\sqrt{3}}$$

$$\frac{d^2 y}{dx^2} = 6x \quad \text{when } x = \frac{1}{\sqrt{3}},$$

$$\frac{d^2 y}{dx^2} = \frac{6}{\sqrt{3}} > 0 \text{ min}$$

$$\frac{d^2 y}{dx^2} = 6x \quad \text{when } x = -\frac{1}{\sqrt{3}},$$

$$\frac{d^2 y}{dx^2} = -\frac{6}{\sqrt{3}} < 0, \text{ max.}$$

$$y_{\min} = \left(\frac{1}{\sqrt{3}}\right)^3 - \frac{1}{\sqrt{3}} = -0.385$$

$$y_{\max} = \left(-\frac{1}{\sqrt{3}^3}\right) - \left(-\frac{1}{\sqrt{3}}\right) = 0.385.$$

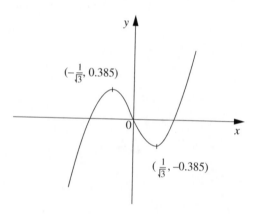

$(-\frac{1}{\sqrt{3}}, 0.385)$

$(\frac{1}{\sqrt{3}}, -0.385)$

Fig. 31

In the above examples, the cubic equations had two turning points, one maximum and one minimum. But note that <u>not</u> all cubic functions have a maximum or a minimum.

Investigate the cubic equation $y = x^3 + 3x + 5$ the first derivative gives us the gradient of the function, $\frac{dy}{dx} = 3x^2 + 3$. This gradient is always positive, so that there are no maxima or minima.

The second derivative, $\frac{d^2 y}{dx^2} = 6x$, this derivative is zero at $x = 0$, therefore $\frac{d^2 y}{dx^2} = 0$ there is a point of inflexion at $x = 0$ when $x = 0$, $y = 5$.

A rough sketch of the cubic function gives the graph of Fig. 32.

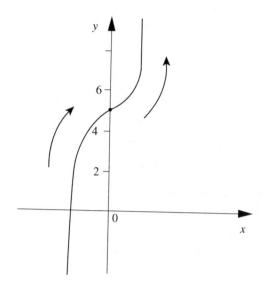

Fig. 32 Point of inflexion

It is observed that $x = 0$, the curve changes from a concave to a convex shape as shown.

Investigate the cubic equation

$$y = -x^3 + 2x^2 + 3 \qquad \frac{dy}{dx} = -3x^2 + 4x$$

$$\frac{dy}{dx} = 0 = -3x^2 + 4x = x(4 - 3x) = 0$$

$$x = 0 \quad \text{and } x = \frac{4}{3} \quad \frac{d^2 y}{dx^2} = -6x + 4$$

when $x = 0$ $\frac{d^2 y}{dx^2} = 4$ it has a minimum at this point

when $x = \frac{4}{3}$ $\frac{d^2 y}{dx^2} = -6\left[\frac{4}{3}\right] + 4 = -4$ it has a maximum at this point.

The graph is shown in Fig. 33a.

h/i. Applications of differentiation using first and second derivatives.

WORKED EXAMPLE 28

A cardboard of 1 square metre is given and it is required to construct an open box of maximum volume by cutting from each corner equal squares and the ends are turned up as shown. Determine the height of the box and the maximum volume in litres.

Fig. 33 and Fig. 34 show the cardboard and open box respectively.

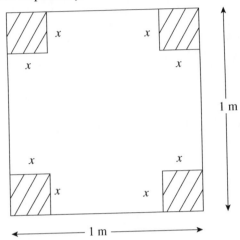

Fig. 33

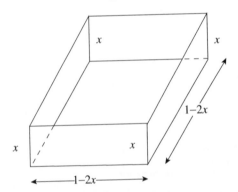

Fig. 34

Solution 28

$V = (1 - 2x)^2 x$

$V = (1 - 4x + 4x^2)x = x - 4x^2 + 4x^3$

$V = 4x^3 - 4x^2 + x \qquad \dfrac{dV}{dx} = 12x^2 - 8x + 1.$

For maximum volume, $\dfrac{dV}{dx} = 0$

$12x^2 - 8x + 1 = 0$

$x = \dfrac{8 \pm \sqrt{64 - 48}}{24} = \dfrac{8 \pm 4}{24}$

$x = \dfrac{1}{2} \text{ m or } x = \dfrac{1}{6} \text{ m}$

obviously if we take $x = \frac{1}{2}$, there will be nothing left, $x = \frac{1}{6}$ m is the answer for maximum volume. This can be checked by taking the second derivative.

$$\frac{d^2 V}{dx^2} = 24x - 8$$

If $x = \dfrac{1}{6}, \quad \dfrac{d^2 V}{dx^2} = 24\left[\dfrac{1}{6}\right] - 8 = -4$

it is maximum

$$V_{max} = 4\left(\frac{1}{6}\right)^3 - 4\left(\frac{1}{6}\right)^2 + \frac{1}{6}$$

$$= \frac{4}{216} - \frac{4}{36} + \frac{1}{6}$$

$$= \frac{4 - 24 + 36}{216}$$

$$V_{max} = \frac{16}{216} = \frac{2}{27}$$

$$x = \frac{1}{6} \text{ m} \quad \text{and}$$

$$V_{max} = \frac{2}{27} \text{ m}^3 = \frac{2000}{27} \text{ litres}$$

$$V_{max} = 74.074 \text{ or } V_{max} = 74\frac{2}{27} \text{ litres.}$$

WORKED EXAMPLE 29

To prove the maximum power transfer theorem!

A source of e.m.f., E, and internal resistance, r is connected across a variable load, R. Determine the condition between the internal resistance r and the external load R so that maximum power is dissipated in R.

Solution 29

The current through R is given $I = \frac{E}{r+R}$ the power dissipated in R is $P = I^2 R$

$$P = \left(\frac{E}{r+R}\right)^2 R \qquad P = \frac{E^2}{(r+R)^2} R$$

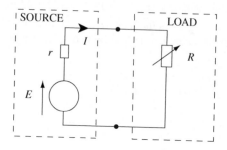

Fig. 35

in this expression P and R are the two variables, E and r are constants. It is required to find the rate of change of the power, P, with respect to the resistance, R, using the

quotient rule
$$\dfrac{\dfrac{du}{dx}v - \dfrac{dv}{dx}u}{v^2}$$

$$\frac{dP}{dR} = \frac{E^2(r+R)^2 - 2(r+R)E^2R}{(r+R)^4}$$

dividing numerator and denominator by $(r+R)$

$$= \frac{E^2(r+R) - 2E^2R}{(r+R)^3} = \frac{E^2r - E^2R}{(r+R)}$$

$$= \frac{E^2(r-R)}{r+R}.$$

For maximum power $\dfrac{dP}{dR} = 0$

$$\frac{E^2(r+R) - 2E^2R}{(r+R)^3} = 0$$

$$E^2(r+R) - 2E^2R = 0$$

$$(r+R) - 2R = 0$$

$$r+R = 2R$$

$$\boxed{R = r}$$

$$P = \frac{E^2r}{(r+r)^2} = \frac{E^2r}{4r^2} = \frac{E^2}{4r}$$

$$\boxed{P_{\max} = \frac{E^2}{4r}.}$$

The second derivative must be negative

$$\frac{d^2P}{dR^2} = \frac{\left\{\left[E^2 - 2E^2\right](r+R)^3 - \left[E^2(r+R) - 2RE^2\right]3(r+R)^2\right\}}{(r+R)^6}$$

simplifying

$$\frac{d^2P}{dR^2} = \frac{-E^2(r+R) - 3E^2(r+R) + 6E^2R}{(r+R)^4}$$

$$= \frac{-4E^2(r+R) + 6E^2R}{(r+R)^4}$$

$$\frac{d^2P}{dR^2} = \frac{-4E^2r + 2E^2R}{(r+R)^4}$$

$$= -\frac{2E^2r}{(r+R)^4}$$

$$= -\frac{2E^2r}{(r+r)^4}$$

$$= -\frac{E^2}{8r^3} \quad \text{if } r = R.$$

WORKED EXAMPLE 30

A cylindrical container, closed at both ends, contains a volume $24\pi\,\mathrm{m}^3$. Given that the total external surface area is a minimum.

Calculate:

  (i) The base radius

  (ii) the height

  (iii) the minimum surface area.

Solution 30

The surface area is given $S = 2\pi r^2 + 2\pi rh$ where r is the base radius and h is its height.

The volume of the cylindrical container
$$V = \pi r^2 h, \quad \pi r^2 h = 24\pi \quad h = \frac{24}{r^2}$$

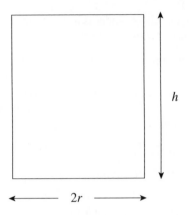

Fig. 36

the volume was given so that we know the relationship between its height, h, and base radius, r.

$S = 2\pi r^2 + 2\pi rh$.

substituting $h = \dfrac{24}{r^2}$ in this equation

$S = 2\pi r^2 + 2\pi r \cdot \dfrac{24}{r^2}$

$S = 2\pi r^2 + \dfrac{48\pi}{r} = 2\pi r^2 + 48\pi r^{-1}$

$S = 2\pi r^2 + 48\pi r^{-1}$ differentiating S with respect to r

$\dfrac{dS}{dr} = 4\pi r + (-1)48\pi r^{-2}$

$\dfrac{dS}{dr} = 4\pi r - \dfrac{48\pi}{r^2} = 4\pi r - 48\pi r^{-2}$.

For maximum or minimum surface area $\dfrac{dS}{dr} = 0$

$4\pi r - \dfrac{48\pi}{r^2} = 0 \quad 4\pi r = \dfrac{48\pi}{r^2} \quad r^3 = 12$

$r = \sqrt[3]{12} = 12^{\frac{1}{3}} = 2.29$ m

The second derivative

$\dfrac{d^2 S}{dr^2} = 4\pi - 48(-2)\pi r^{-3}$

$= 4\pi + \dfrac{96\pi}{r^3}$

this is certainly positive, therefore, the surface

area is minimum for $r = \sqrt[3]{12}$

and $h = \dfrac{24}{r^2} = \dfrac{24}{\left(12^{\frac{1}{3}}\right)^2} = \dfrac{24}{12^{\frac{2}{3}}} \quad h = 4.58$ m.

$S_{\min} = 2\pi r^2 + 2\pi rh$

$\quad = 2\pi \left(12^{\frac{1}{3}}\right)^2 + 2\pi \left(12^{\frac{1}{3}}\right)(4.58)$

$\quad = 32.95 + 65.9 = 98.85$

$\quad = 98.9$ m^2.

WORKED EXAMPLE 31

The length of the arc s is given by $s = r\theta$. The area of the triangle **ABO**, $\Delta_1 = \frac{1}{2}r^2 \sin\theta$.

The area of the sector **ABO** is $\Delta_2 = \frac{1}{2}r^2\theta$.

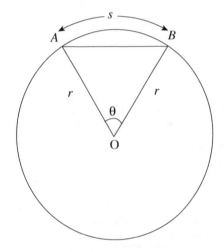

Fig. 37

Express the area of the triangle and sector in terms of s.

Find the maximum area of the triangle Δ assuming r is constant and s is variable.

Verify that the area is maximum.

What is the area of the sector for this condition?

Solution 31

$\Delta_1 = \dfrac{1}{2}r^2 \sin\theta = \dfrac{1}{2}r^2 \sin\left[\dfrac{s}{r}\right]$

for maximum area $\dfrac{d\Delta_1}{ds} = 0$

$$\frac{d\Delta_1}{ds} = \frac{1}{2}r^2\left(\frac{1}{r}\right)\cos\left(\frac{s}{r}\right) = 0$$

$$\frac{1}{2}r\cos\frac{s}{r} = 0 \quad \text{or } \cos\frac{s}{r} = 0$$

but $\cos\dfrac{\pi}{2} = 0 \quad \cos\dfrac{s}{r} = \cos\dfrac{\pi}{2}$

therefore $s = r\dfrac{\pi}{2}$

the second derivative

$$\frac{d^2\Delta_1}{ds^2} = -\frac{1}{2}r^2\left[\frac{1}{r}\right]\left[\frac{1}{r}\right]\sin\frac{s}{r}$$

or $\dfrac{d^2\Delta_1}{ds^2} = -\dfrac{1}{2}\sin\dfrac{s}{r} = -\dfrac{1}{2}\sin r\dfrac{\pi}{2}\dfrac{1}{r}$

$$= -\frac{1}{2}\sin\frac{\pi}{2} = -\frac{1}{2}$$

which is negative and indicates that Δ_1 is a maximum

$$\Delta_1 \max = \frac{1}{2}r^2\sin\left(\frac{s}{r}\right)$$

$$= \frac{1}{2}r^2\sin\left(r\frac{\frac{\pi}{2}}{r}\right) = \frac{1}{2}r^2$$

$$\Delta_2 = \frac{1}{2}r^2\theta = \frac{1}{2}r^2\frac{s}{r}$$

$$= \frac{1}{2}rs = \frac{1}{2}r.r\frac{\pi}{2} = \frac{r^2\pi}{4}.$$

WORKED EXAMPLE 32

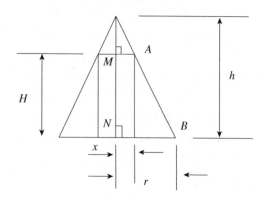

Fig. 38

A right circular cylinder is to be cut from a right circular solid cone as shown.

If x is the radius of the cylinder, find an expression for the volume, V, of the cylinder in terms of x, r and h, hence find the maximum volume of the cylinder as x varies, if $r = 3$ m and $h = \frac{3}{4\pi}$ m

Solution 32

The volume of the cylinder is given
$V = \pi x^2 \times$ height.

The height of the cylinder found from the similar right angled triangles **OMA** and **ONB** from which we have,

$$\frac{x}{r} = \frac{OM}{ON} = \frac{h - \text{height of cylinder}}{h}$$

$$\frac{x}{r} = \frac{h}{h} - \frac{\text{height of the cylinder}}{h} = 1 - \frac{H}{h} = \frac{x}{r}$$

height of the cylinder $= \left[1 - \dfrac{x}{r}\right]h = H$

$$V = \pi x^2\left[1 - \frac{x}{r}\right]h = \pi x^2 h - \pi\frac{x^3 h}{r}$$

differentiating V with respect to x

$$\frac{dV}{dx} = 2\pi x h - \frac{3\pi h}{r}x^2$$

this derivative is zero fox maximum or minimum.

$$2\pi x h - \frac{3\pi h}{r}x^2 = 0, \ 2\pi x h = \frac{3\pi h x^2}{r}, x = \frac{2r}{3}.$$

The second derivative, $\dfrac{d^2V}{dx^2} = 2\pi h - \dfrac{6\pi h}{r}x.$

If $x = \frac{2r}{3}$

$$\frac{d^2V}{dx^2} = 2\pi h - \frac{6\pi h}{r}\frac{2r}{3} = 2\pi h - 4\pi h = -2\pi h$$

which is a negative quantity and therefore the volume is a maximum when

$$x = \frac{2r}{3}.$$

$$V_{\max} = \pi\left[\frac{2r}{3}\right]^2\left[1 - \frac{\frac{2r}{3}}{r}\right]h = \frac{4}{9}\pi r^2\left(\frac{h}{3}\right)$$

$$V_{\max} = \frac{4}{27}\pi r^2 h = \frac{4}{27}\pi 3^2\left(\frac{3}{4\pi}\right) = 1 \text{ m}^3.$$

WORKED EXAMPLE 33

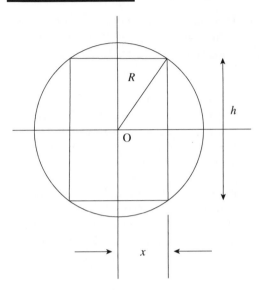

Fig. 39

A right circular cylinder is to be cut from a solid sphere of radius R as shown in the diagram.

Show that V, the volume of the cylinder is given by:-

$$V = 2\pi x^2 (R^2 - x^2)^{\frac{1}{2}}$$

where x is the radius of the cylinder. Find the maximum of the cylinder if x varies and assume that $\frac{d^2 V}{dx^2}$ is negative, that is, no need to find the second derivative.

Solution 33

Let h be the height of the cylinder then by using Pythagoras we obtain

$$\frac{1}{2}h = \sqrt{R^2 - x^2}$$

or $\quad h = 2\sqrt{R^2 - x^2}.$

The volume of the cylinder
$$V = \pi x^2 h = 2\pi x^2 \sqrt{R^2 - x^2}$$

$$\frac{dV}{dx} = 2\pi (2x)\sqrt{R^2 - x^2}$$
$$+ 2\pi x^2 \frac{1}{2}(R^2 - x^2)^{-\frac{1}{2}}(-2x)$$

for turning points $\dfrac{dV}{dx} = 0$

$$4\pi x (R^2 - x^2)^{\frac{1}{2}} = 2\pi x^3 (R^2 - x^2)^{-\frac{1}{2}}$$

$$2(R^2 - x^2) = x^2 \quad R = \sqrt{\frac{3x}{2}}$$

$$V_{max} = 2\pi \frac{2}{3}R^2 \left[R^2 - \frac{2}{3}R^2 \right]^{\frac{1}{2}}$$

$$= \frac{4}{3}\pi R^2 \left[\frac{1}{3}R^2 \right]^{\frac{1}{2}} \quad V_{max} = \frac{4\pi}{3\sqrt{3}}R^3.$$

Exercises 4

1. With the aid of the gradient, explain the meaning of the turning point or stationary point.

   What is the significance of $\dfrac{d}{dx}\left(\dfrac{dy}{dx}\right)$ being

   (a) positive   (b) negative   (c) zero.

2. Determine the turning points of the functions:-

   (i) $y = 2x^2 - 3x - 5$

   (ii) $y = -3x^2 - 2x + 1$

   (iii) $y = x^3 + 2x^2 - x + 1$

   (iv) $y = 2x^3 - 4x^2 - 3x - 5.$

3. Determine the nature of the turning points of the functions in exercise 2.

4. Find the points of inflexion of the curves

   (i) $y = x^3 + 2x^2 - x + 1$

   (ii) $y = 2x^3 - 4x^2 - 3x - 5.$

5. Determine the maximum and minimum values of the quadratic functions:-

   (i) $y = 2x^2 + 2x + 2$

   (ii) $y = 2x^2 - 2x + 4$

   (iii) $y = -x^2 - 3x - 4$

   (iv) $y = -x^2 + 5x - 5.$

6. The sum of two numbers is 144, find the numbers such that their product is maximum.

7. An open rectangular tank with a square base is to contain 500 m³ of liquid. If the side of the base is y metres show that the total surface area S of metal is given by
$S = y^2 + \frac{2000}{y}$.

Find the dimensions of the tank for a minimum surface area.

8. The power P given to the load R by the

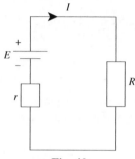

Fig. 40

generator of internal resistance r and e.m.f. E is given by $P = IE - I^2r$.

Determine the value of the current I for maximum power when $E = 12\,\text{V}$ and $r = 0.9\,\Omega$. Calculate the value of the maximum power for this current.

9. A closed box is to have a volume of 150 m³ and the length of the square base is x m while that of the depth is h m. Determine the dimensions of the box so that the surface area shall be a minimum.

10. An open tank is to be made from rectangular sheet of metal 15 m by 25 m. Equal squares are cut from each of the corners and the sides are bent up to form the tank. Determine the maximum volume of the tank.

Integration

5. Integrate trignometric and exponential functions.

a. Determines indefinite integrals of functions involving $\sin ax$, $\cos ax$, e^{ax}.

b. Evaluates definite integrals involving $\sin ax$, $\cos ax$, e^{ax}.

Revision.

Differentiation is the process of obtaining the derivative of a function. Integration is the reverse process of differentiation.

If the function $y = x^2$

$$\frac{dy}{dx} = 2x$$

$$dy = 2x\,dx$$

integrating both sides of this equation

$$\int dy = \int 2x\,dx \quad y = 2\frac{x^2}{2} + c \quad y = x^2 + c$$

so the integration of $2x$ is the function x^2 and the differentiation of x^2 is $2x$.

If $f(x)$ is a given function, it is required to find $F(x)$ such that $F'(x) = f(x)$. The process of finding $F(x)$ from $f(x)$ is called integration. $\int f(x)dx = F(x)$.

Determines Indefinite Integrals of Simple Algebraic Functions.

$\frac{d}{dx}(x^n) = nx^{n-1}$, and hence $\int nx^{n-1}dx = x^n$.

The indefinite integral of simple algebraic function

$$\int ax^n dx = a\frac{x^{n+1}}{n + 1} + \text{arbitrary constant.}$$

To integrate ax^n with respect to x, we write 'a' multiply by x, raised to a power equal to n plus 1, divided by the power, $n + 1$, and add an arbitrary constant

$$\int ax^n dx = \frac{ax^{n+1}}{n + 1} + c \quad (n \neq -1).$$

This arbitrary constant should appear in every indefinite integral.

Note that $\frac{d}{dx}(\log_e x) = \frac{1}{x}$ and therefore $\int \frac{1}{x}dx = \log_e x + c$.

WORKED EXAMPLE 34

$$\int 3x^4 dx = 3\frac{x^{4+1}}{4 + 1} + c = \frac{3}{5}x^5 + c.$$

Recognises the need to include an arbitary constant of integration.

Integrating the function $y = 2x^3$ with respect to x is shown by the indefinite integral,

$$\int 2x^3 dx = \frac{2x^4}{4} + c.$$

Sketching the graph, $y = 2x^3$ for positive value of x when $x = 0$, $y = 0$ when $x = 1$, $y = 2$ when $x = 2$, $y = 16$.

37

The area under the curve is given by the indefinite integral, $\int 2x^3 dx = \frac{2}{4}x^4 + c$, $y = \frac{1}{2}x^4 + c$ where c is an arbitrary constant since, we did not specify between which limits the area is required.

$$\frac{dy}{dx} = \frac{4}{2}x^3 = 2x^3 \text{ the constant disappeared.}$$

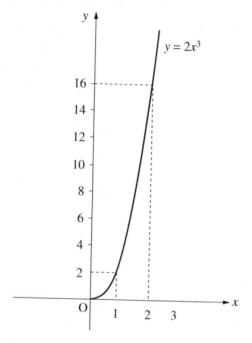

Fig. 41

Defines $\int_b^a y dx$ as the area under the curve between ordinates at $x = a$ and $x = b$.

$\int_a^b y dx$ is a definite integral since we are specifying that the area under the curve required is between the upper limit b and the lower limit a. The elemental area of the strip is $y dx$ and this is summed up between the limits.

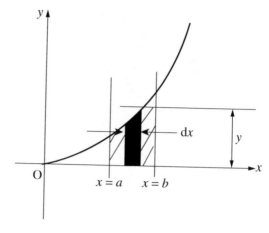

Fig. 42

Evaluates $\int_a^b y dx$ by $[\Phi(x)]_a^b = [\Phi(b)] - [\Phi(a)]$ for simple algebraic functions, where $\Phi(x)$ is the indefinite integral of $y(x)$.

If the integral of y is, $\Phi(x)$, we substitute x for b, the upper limit first, and the function become $\Phi(b)$ which represents $x = b$ and then subtract the area under curve, $\Phi(a)$ between $x = 0$ and $x = a$.

$$\int_a^b y dx = [\Phi(x)]_a^b = [\Phi(b) + c] - [\Phi(a) + c]$$

$= \Phi(b) - \Phi(a)$ and therefore the arbitrary constant chosen is cancelled. This value indicated by the hatched area under the curve.

Determines areas by applying the definite integral for simple algebraic function.

Evaluate the definite integral

$$\int_1^2 (3x^2 - 5x + 1)dx = \left[3\frac{x^3}{3} - \frac{5}{2}x^2 + x\right]_1^2$$

$$= \left[2^3 - \frac{5}{2}(2)^2 + 2\right] - \left[1^3 - \frac{5}{2}(1) + 1\right]$$

$$= (8 - 10 + 2) - \left[1 - \frac{5}{2} + 1\right] = \frac{1}{2}.$$

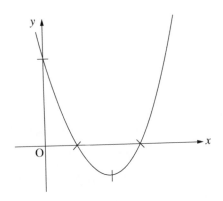

Fig. 43

━━━━━━━━━━━━━━
WORKED EXAMPLE 35
━━━━━━━━━━━━━━

Determine the definite integrals:

(i) $\int_2^3 (x^4 + 5)dx$

(ii) $\int_0^2 \left[\dfrac{x^3 + x}{x} \right] dx$

(iii) $\int_3^4 \left[3\sqrt{x} - \dfrac{1}{\sqrt{x}} \right] dx.$

Solution 35

(i) $\int_2^3 (x^4 + 5)dx = \left[\dfrac{x^5}{5} + 5x \right]_2^3$

$= \left[\dfrac{3^5}{5} + 5(3) \right] - \left[\dfrac{2^5}{5} + 5(2) \right]$

$= \left[\dfrac{243}{5} + 15 \right] - \left[\dfrac{32}{5} + 10 \right]$

$= \dfrac{318}{5} - \dfrac{82}{5} = \dfrac{236}{5} = 47.2$

(ii) $\int_0^2 \left[\dfrac{x^3 + x}{x} \right] dx = \int_0^2 \left[\dfrac{x^3}{x} + \dfrac{x}{x} \right] dx$

$= \int_0^2 (x^2 + 1)dx$

$= \left[\dfrac{x^3}{3} + x \right]_0^2 = \left[\dfrac{8}{3} + 2 \right] - [0]$

$= \dfrac{14}{3} = 4\dfrac{2}{3}$

(iii) $\int_3^4 \left(3\sqrt{x} - \dfrac{1}{\sqrt{x}} \right) dx$

$= \int_3^4 \left(3x^{\frac{1}{2}} - x^{-\frac{1}{2}} \right) dx$

$= \left[\dfrac{3x^{\frac{3}{2}}}{\frac{3}{2}} - \dfrac{x^{\frac{1}{2}}}{\frac{1}{2}} \right]_3^4$

$= \left[2(4)^{\frac{3}{2}} - 2(4)^{\frac{1}{2}} \right] - \left[2(3)^{\frac{3}{2}} - 2(3)^{\frac{1}{2}} \right]$

$= \left[2(2^2)^{\frac{3}{2}} - 4 \right] - \left[2(3\sqrt{3}) - 2\sqrt{3} \right]$

$= (16 - 4) - 4\sqrt{3} = 12 - 4\sqrt{3} = 5.07.$

Integrates trigonometric and exponential functions.

Determines graphically that the integral of cos θ between specific limits is sin θ.

$\int_0^{\frac{\pi}{2}} \cos \theta d\theta = [\sin \theta]_0^{\frac{\pi}{2}}$

$= \left[\sin \dfrac{\pi}{2} \right] - [\sin 0] = 1$

$\int_{\frac{\pi}{2}}^{\frac{3\pi}{2}} \cos \theta d\theta = [\sin \theta]_{\frac{\pi}{2}}^{\frac{3\pi}{2}}$

$= [\sin 3\tfrac{\pi}{2}] - [\sin \tfrac{\pi}{2}]$

$= -1 - 1.$

$= -2.$

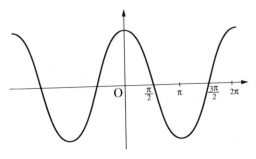

Fig. 44

The area under the curve between 0 and $\frac{\pi}{2}$ is 1 square unit and it is positive, shown here above the x-axis. The area between $\frac{\pi}{2}$ and $3\frac{\pi}{2}$ is −2 square units, and it is negative since the area is below the x-axis.

The area between $\theta = 0$ and $\theta = 2\pi$, it is obviously zero, since the area above the $x-$axis cancels the area below the $x-$axis

$$\int_0^{2\pi} \cos\theta d\theta = [\sin\theta]_0^{2\pi}$$
$$= [\sin 2\pi] - [\sin 0] = 0 - 0 = 0.$$

Determines indefinite integrals of functions involving $\sin ax$, $\cos ax$, e^{ax}.

$$\int \sin ax dx = -\frac{\cos ax}{a} + c,$$
$$\int \cos ax dx = \frac{\sin ax}{a} + c, \int e^{ax} dx = \frac{e^{ax}}{a} + c.$$

The derivative of $-\cos ax$ is $a\sin ax$ and when it is divided by a, then the derivative of $\frac{-\cos ax}{a}$ is $\sin ax$.

The derivative of $\sin ax$ is $a\cos ax$ and when it is divided by a, then the derivative of $\frac{a\sin ax}{a}$ is $\cos ax$.

The derivative of e^{ax} is ae^{ax} and when it is divided by a, then the derivative of $\frac{e^{ax}}{a}$ is e^{ax}.

Evaluates definite integrals involving $\sin ax$, $\cos ax$, e^{ax}.

▬▬▬
WORKED EXAMPLE 36
▬▬▬

Examples in evaluating definite integrals.

$$\int_0^{\frac{\pi}{2}} \sin 2x dx = \left[-\frac{\cos 2x}{2}\right]_0^{\frac{\pi}{2}}$$
$$= \left[-\frac{\cos 2(\frac{\pi}{2})}{2}\right] - \left[\frac{\cos 2(0)}{2}\right]$$
$$= -\frac{\cos\pi}{2} + \frac{\cos 0}{2} = \frac{-(-1)}{2} + \frac{1}{2}$$
$$= \frac{1}{2} + \frac{1}{2} = 1$$

$$\int_0^{\frac{\pi}{2}} 3\cos 6\Phi d\Phi = \left[3\frac{\sin 6\Phi}{6}\right]_0^{\frac{\pi}{2}}$$
$$= \left[\frac{1}{2}\sin 6\frac{\pi}{2}\right] - \left[\frac{1}{2}\sin 0\right] = 0$$

$$\int_0^1 e^{3x} dx = \left[\frac{e^{3x}}{3}\right]_0^1 = \frac{e^{3(1)}}{3} - \frac{e^{3(0)}}{3} = \frac{e^3}{3} - \frac{1}{3}$$
$$= \frac{e^3 - 1}{3} = 6.36$$

$$\int_0^2 (1 + 3e^{0.5x}) dx = \left[x + \frac{3e^{0.5x}}{0.5}\right]_0^2$$
$$= [2 + 6e^1] - [6]$$
$$= 2 + 6e - 6 = 6e - 4 = 12.3$$

$$\int_{0.5}^1 \left(e^{\frac{x}{3}} - e^{-\frac{x}{3}}\right) dx = \left[\frac{e^{\frac{x}{3}}}{\frac{1}{3}} - \frac{e^{-\frac{x}{3}}}{-\frac{1}{3}}\right]_{0.5}^1$$

$$= [3e^{\frac{1}{3}} + 3e^{-\frac{1}{3}}] - [3e^{\frac{1}{6}} + 3e^{-\frac{1}{6}}]$$
$$= [4.187 + 2.1496] - [3 \times 1.18 + 3 \times 0.8465]$$
$$= 6.3366 - 6.08 = 0.26.$$

c. Defines the Mean and Root Mean Square values of functions over a given range.

d. Evaluates the Mean and Root Mean Square values of simple periodic functions.

Mean Value

The rectangle shown in Fig.45 has a base, b and a height, h.

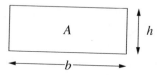

Fig. 45

The mean value over the base is obviously, h, the height is uniform throughout this base length.

If the area A is known and the base width is b, then the mean value or height may be found.

$$A = bh \qquad h = \frac{A}{b}$$

by dividing the area, A, by the base width.

In order to determine the mean value of a half-wave of a sinusoidal waveform, we divide the area of the half 'sinewave' by the base, π.

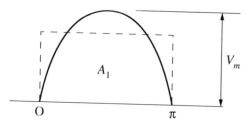

Fig. 46

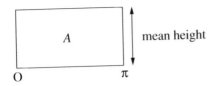

Fig. 47

Mean value = $\dfrac{\text{area of the half sinewave}}{\text{the base}}$.

The area of the half sinewave can be found by integration between the limits 0 and π

$\int_0^\pi V_m \sin\theta\, d\theta$

where the instantaneous value of the sinewave is given by $v = V_m \sin\theta$ and V_m is the peak or maximum value of the waveform.

Mean value $= \dfrac{\int_0^\pi V_m \sin\theta\, d\theta}{\pi} = \dfrac{V_m[-\cos\theta]_0^\pi}{\pi}$

$= \dfrac{V_m}{\pi}[-\cos\pi - (-\cos 0)]$

$= \dfrac{V_m}{\pi}[-(-1) + 1] = \dfrac{V_m 2}{\pi} = 0.637 V_m$.

The mean value or the average value of the voltage of a sinewave over half a cycle is $0.637 V_m$.

The mean value or the average value of the voltage or current of a sinewave over a complete cycle is 0 since the positive area cancels the negative area.

Mean value $= \dfrac{\int_0^{2\pi} V_m \sin\theta\, d\theta}{2\pi}$

$= \dfrac{V_m[-\cos\theta]_0^{2\pi}}{2\pi}$

$= \dfrac{V_m}{2\pi}[-\cos 2\pi - (-\cos 0)]$

$= \dfrac{V_m}{2\pi}(-1 + 1) = 0$.

WORKED EXAMPLE 37

Find the mean values of the waveforms whose shapes for one cycle are as shown:-

(i)

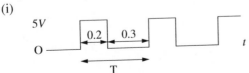

Fig. 48

(ii)

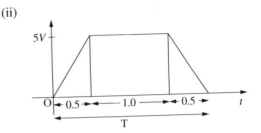

Fig. 49

Solution 37

(i) The area over one cycle $= 5 \times 0.2 = 1.0$.

The mean value $= \dfrac{\text{The area over one cycle}}{\text{the time taken}}$

$= \dfrac{1.0}{0.2 + 0.3} = 2V$

(ii) The area of one complete cycle

$= \dfrac{1}{2}(1.0 + 2.0)5 = 7.5$

$=$ the area of the trapezium.

The mean value $= \dfrac{7.5}{2} = 3.75V$.

Root Mean Square (R.M.S.)

To determine and define the Root Mean Square value of a sinewave.

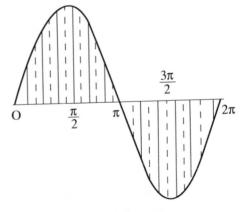

Fig. 50

Divide the base into twelve equal intervals of width $\frac{\pi}{6}$, the mean height between 0 and $\frac{\pi}{6}$ is $\frac{\pi}{12}$.

The r.m.s. value of $i = I_m \sin \omega t$ over one complete cycle can be found by integration

$$\frac{1}{2\pi} \int_0^{2\pi} i^2 d(\omega t) = \text{Mean squares}$$

$$\sqrt{\frac{1}{2\pi} \int_0^{2\pi} i^2 d(\omega t)} = \text{Root Means squares}$$

but $i = I_m \sin \omega t \int_0^{2\pi} I_m^2 \sin^2 \omega t d(\omega t)$

$$= I_m^2 \int_0^{2\pi} \sin^2 \omega t d(\omega t)$$

to evaluate this definite integral we need to substitute $\sin^2 \omega t$ in terms of the double angle $\cos 2\omega t$

$\cos(A + B) = \cos A \cos B - \sin A \sin B$,

if $B = A$

$\cos(A + A) = \cos A \cos A - \sin A \sin A$

$\cos 2A = \cos^2 A - \sin^2 A$

but $\sin^2 A + \cos^2 A = 1 \Rightarrow 1 - \sin^2 A = \cos^2 A$

$\cos 2A = 1 - \sin^2 A - \sin^2 A$

$\cos 2A = 1 - 2\sin^2 A$

$2\sin^2 A = 1 - \cos 2A$

$$\sin^2 A = \frac{1 - \cos 2A}{2}$$

therefore $\sin^2 \omega t = \dfrac{1 - \cos 2\omega t}{2}$

$$\frac{I_m^2}{2} \int_0^{2\pi} (1 - \cos 2\omega t) d(\omega t)$$

$$= \frac{I_m^2}{2} \left[\omega t - \frac{\sin 2\omega t}{2} \right]_0^{2\pi}$$

$$= \frac{I_m^2}{2} \left[2\pi - \frac{\sin 4\pi}{2} - 0 \right]$$

$$= \pi I_m^2.$$

Let $i = I_m \sin \omega t$ where i is the instantaneous value of the current, I_m is the peak value ω is the angular velocity and t is the time. Note that i and t are the variables.

ωt		$\sin \omega t$	
$\frac{\pi}{12}$	15°	0.259	i_1
$\frac{3\pi}{12}$	45°	0.707	i_2
$\frac{5\pi}{12}$	75°	0.966	i_3
$\frac{7\pi}{12}$	105°	0.966	i_4
$\frac{9\pi}{12}$	135°	0.707	i_5
$\frac{11\pi}{12}$	165°	0.259	i_6
$\frac{13\pi}{12}$	195°	−0.259	i_7
$\frac{15\pi}{12}$	225°	−0.707	i_8
$\frac{17\pi}{12}$	255°	−0.966	i_9
$\frac{19\pi}{12}$	285°	−0.966	i_{10}
$\frac{21\pi}{12}$	315°	−0.707	i_{11}
$\frac{23\pi}{12}$	345°	−0.259	i_{12}

Mean squares

$$= \frac{\left(\begin{array}{c} i_1^2 + i_2^2 + i_3^2 + i_4^2 + i_5^2 + i_6^2 + i_7^2 \\ +i_8^2 + i_9^2 + i_{10}^2 + i_{11}^2 + i_{12}^2 \end{array} \right)}{12}$$

$$= \frac{\left(\begin{array}{c} (0.259)^2 + (0.707)^2 + (0.966)^2 \\ +(0.966)^2 + (0.707)^2 + (0.259)^2 \\ +(-0.259)^2 + (-0.707)^2 \end{array} \right)}{12}$$

$$+ \frac{\left(\begin{array}{c} (-0.966)^2 + (-0.966)^2 \\ +(-0.707)^2 + (-0.259)^2) \end{array} \right)}{12}$$

$$= \frac{4 \times 0.259^2 + 4 \times 0.707^2 + 4 \times 0.966^2}{12} I_m^2$$

$$= \frac{0.259^2 + 0.707^2 + 0.966^2}{3} I_m^2 = 0.5 I_m^2$$

Mean squares $= \dfrac{1}{2} I_m^2$ R.M.S. $= I_m \sqrt{\dfrac{1}{2}} = \dfrac{I_m}{\sqrt{2}}$

$$\boxed{I = \frac{I_m}{\sqrt{2}}}$$

$$\sqrt{\frac{I_m^2}{2\pi} [\pi]} = \frac{I_m}{\sqrt{2}} = \text{R.M.S.} \quad I = \frac{I_m}{\sqrt{2}}$$

What is the R.M.S. value over a half cycle?

$$\sqrt{\frac{1}{\pi}\int_0^\pi i^2 d\,(\omega t)} = (I_m)\sqrt{\frac{1}{\pi}\frac{\pi}{2}} = \frac{I_m}{\sqrt{2}}$$

$$\frac{1}{2}\int_0^\pi (1-\cos 2\omega t)$$

$$= \frac{1}{2}\left[\omega t - \frac{\sin^2 \omega t}{2}\right]_0^\pi = \frac{1}{2}\pi.$$

Therefore the R.M.S. value of this function over any given range is the same.

WORKED EXAMPLE 38

To find the R.M.S. value of a saw-tooth waveform

$V_m = 5$ Volts

$T = 1$ s

Fig. 51

At time, t, the voltage is v. $\dfrac{v}{t} = \dfrac{V_m}{T}$

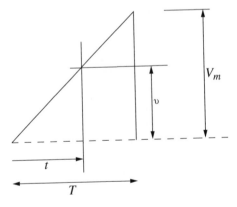

V_m

v

t

T

Fig. 52

$$v = \frac{V_m}{T}t$$

$$\text{R.M.S.} = \sqrt{\frac{1}{T}\int_0^T v^2 dt} = \sqrt{\frac{1}{T}\int_0^T \left[\frac{V_m}{T}t\right]^2 dt}$$

$$\text{R.M.S.} = \sqrt{\frac{1}{T}\int_0^T \frac{V_m^2 t^2}{T^2}dt}$$

$$= \sqrt{\frac{1}{T^3}\left[V_m^2 \frac{t^3}{3}\right]_0^T} = \sqrt{\frac{V_m^2 T^3}{3T^3}}$$

$$v = \frac{V_m}{\sqrt{3}}.$$

WORKED EXAMPLE 39

A current is given by $i = \dfrac{10I_m}{T^2}(Tt - t^2)$ from $t = 0$ to $t = T$. Find an expression for the r.m.s. value from 0 to T where I_m and T are constants.

Solution 39

$$\int_0^T i^2 dt = \frac{100I_m^2}{T^4}\int_0^T (Tt - t^2)^2 dt$$

$$= \frac{100I_m^2}{T^4}\int_0^T (T^2 t^2 - 2Tt^3 + t^4)dt$$

$$= \frac{100I_m^2}{T^4}\left[T^2\frac{t^3}{3} - 2T\frac{t^4}{4} + \frac{t^5}{5}\right]_0^T$$

$$= \frac{100I_m^2}{T^4}\left[\frac{T^5}{3} - \frac{T^5}{2} + \frac{T^5}{5}\right]$$

$$= \frac{100I_m^2}{T^4}\left[\frac{10T^5 - 15T^3 + 6T^5}{30}\right]$$

$$= \frac{100I_m^2}{T^4}\frac{T^5}{30}$$

$$= \frac{10}{3}TI_m^2$$

$$\text{R.M.S.} = \sqrt{\frac{1}{T}\int_0^T i^2 dt}$$

$$= \sqrt{\frac{1}{T}\frac{10}{3}TI_m^2}$$

$$= I_m\sqrt{\frac{10}{3}}.$$

Exercise 5

Evaluate

1. $\int_0^{\frac{\pi}{2}} \sin 2x dx$

2. $\int_0^{\frac{\pi}{4}} \cos 4x dx$

3. $\int_{\frac{\pi}{4}}^{\frac{\pi}{2}} \sin \frac{1}{2}x\,dx$

4. $\int_0^{2\pi} \cos 3x\,dx$

5. $\int_0^{\frac{\pi}{4}} \left[\sin 3x - \cos \frac{x}{3} - e^{-\frac{x}{3}} \right] dx$

6. $\int_0^{\frac{3\pi}{2}} \sin \omega t\,d(\omega t)$

7. $\int_{\frac{\pi}{6}}^{\frac{\pi}{3}} \cos 2\omega t\,d(\omega t)$

8. $\int_0^1 \dfrac{e^{-v} + e^v}{2}\,dv$

9. $\int_0^1 \dfrac{e^u - e^{-u}}{2u}\,du$

10. $\int_0^{2\pi} [\sin 2y - \cos(-2y)]\,dy.$

11. Determine the mean values of the following:-

    (i) $y = \sin 2x$ between $x = 0$ and $x = \dfrac{\pi}{2}.$

    (ii) $y = 2 \sin \dfrac{x}{2}$ between $x = 0$ and $x = \pi.$

    (iii) $y = \sin 3t$ between $t = 0$ and $t = \dfrac{\pi}{2}.$

    (iv) $y = 1 + 2 \sin \theta$ between $\theta = 0$ and $\theta = \pi.$

    (v) $y = e^{2x}$ between $x = 0$ and $x = 2.$

12. If $v = 200 \sin \omega t$, $i = 200 \sin(\omega t + \frac{\pi}{6})$. Find the mean values for each quantity from $t = 0$ to $\frac{\pi}{\omega}.$

13. If $v = 3 + 4 \cos \omega t$, find the r.m.s. value from $t = 0$ to $\dfrac{2\pi}{\omega}.$

14. Evaluate

    (i) $\int_0^{\frac{\pi}{3}} \cos(2x - \frac{\pi}{6})\,dx$

    (ii) $\int_1^2 (e^{3x} - e^{-3x})\,dx$

    (iii) $\int_0^{\frac{\pi}{2}} \left[1 - \sin(2x - \frac{\pi}{6}) \right] dx.$

15. Find the mean value of $\cos^2 \omega t$ between $t = 0$ and $t = \frac{2\pi}{\omega}.$

6

Uses numerical integration formulae to evaluate definite integral.

a. Derives the trapezoidal and mid-ordinate rules for numerical integration.

b. Derives Simpson's rule over two intervals to integrate a function defines either analytically or tabular or graphical form.

Derivation of the trapezoidal rule.

The graph of the function $y = e^x$ from $x = 0$ to $x = 1$ is shown.

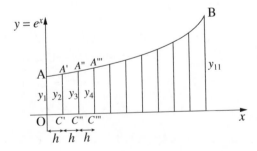

Fig. 53

The boundary of the area is **OABC**. The base width **OC** is divided into equal intervals, either odd or even, it does not matter in the final evalu-

ation. For convenience, let us divide **OC** into ten equal intervals of h width for eleven ordinates are drawn as shown, that is, 10 intervals correspond to $10 + 1 = 11$ ordinates if $x = 0$ then $y_1 = e^0 = 1$, if $x = 0.1$ they $y = e^{0.1} = 1.1052$, if $x = 0.2$ then $y_3 = e^{0.2} = 1.2214$, if $x = 0.3$ then $y_4 = e^{0.3} = 1.3499$, and so on until $x = 1$ when then $y_{11} = e^1 = 2.7183$.

The area of the trapezium $AA'C'O$ is given by the formula

$\frac{1}{2}(y_1 + y_2)h$, the area of the trapezium $A'A''C''C$ is

$\frac{1}{2}(y_2 + y_3)h$, the area of the trapezium $A''A'''C'''C''$

is $\frac{1}{2}(y_3 + y_4)h$, and so on.

Summing up all these areas, we have

$$\frac{1}{2}(y_1 + y_2)h + \frac{1}{2}(y_2 + y_3)h + \frac{1}{2}(y_3 + y_4)h$$
$$+ \ldots + \frac{1}{2}(y_{10} + y_{11})h$$
$$= \frac{h}{2}(y_1 + y_2 + y_2 + y_3 + y_3 + \ldots + y_{10}$$
$$+ y_{10} + y_{11})$$

For 11 ordinates or 10 intervals.

45

$$= \frac{h}{2}[y_1 + 2y_2 + 2y_3 + \ldots + 2y_{10} + y_{11}]$$

$$= \frac{h}{2}[y_1 + y_{11} + 2(y_2 + y_3 + y_4 + \ldots + y_{10})].$$

Derivation of the midordinate rule.

Considering again the same example of the exponential function $y = e^x$ from $x = 0$ to $x = 1.0$ for nine intervals and base width $h = 0.1$ we have:-

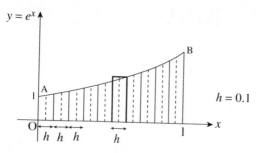

$h = 0.1$

Fig. 54

There are ten intervals, eleven ordinates, and ten mid-ordinates.

To find the first mid-ordinate $y_{1m} = \frac{1}{2}(y_1 + y_2)$ the second mid-ordinate

$y_{2m} = \frac{1}{2}(y_2 + y_3)$, $y_{3m} = \frac{1}{2}(y_3 + y_4)$ and so on

$y_{10m} = \frac{1}{2}(y_{10} + y_{11})$.

The approximate area of $OAA'C'$ = area of the rectangle = $y_{1m} \times h$.

The total area is the sum of the 10 rectangles.

Area = $y_{1m}h + y_{2m}h + y_{3m}h + \ldots + y_{10m}h$

$= h(y_{1m} + y_{2m} + \ldots + y_{10m})$.

Area = the sum of the mid-ordinates × interval width.

The above two rules, that is the trapezoidal and mid-ordinate rules are used to find certain areas approximately.

We have seen that definite integrals are used to evaluate areas exactly but certain definite integrals can be found approximately by using the above rules illustrated.

Certain definite integrals are however difficult to evaluate, but they can be evaluated approximately by using the rules above.

Definite integrals such as $\int_0^{\frac{\pi}{4}} \sqrt{\sin x}\,dx$ and $\int_0^1 e^{x^2}\,dx$ can be evaluated by the numerical methods of trapezoidial and mid-ordinate rules.

▬▬▬▬

WORKED EXAMPLE 40

Evaluate approximately the integral $\int_0^1 e^x dx$ by using

(i) the trapezoidal rule

(ii) the mid-ordinate rule with ten equal intervals.

What is the exact value of the integral?

Solution 40

(i) $\int_0^1 e^x dx \approx \frac{h}{2}[y_1 + y_{11} + 2(y_2 + y_3 + y_4$

$\qquad\qquad + y_5 + y_6 + y_7 + y_8 + y_9 + y_{10})]$

$h = \frac{1 - 0}{10} = \frac{\text{upperlimit} - \text{lower}}{\text{number of intervals}} = 0.1$

$y_1 = e^0 = 1 \qquad\qquad y_6 = e^{0.5} = 1.649$

$y_2 = e^{0.1} = 1.105 \qquad y_7 = e^{0.6} = 1.822$

$y_3 = e^{0.2} = 1.221 \qquad y_8 = e^{0.7} = 2.014$

$y_4 = e^{0.3} = 1.35 \qquad y_9 = e^{0.8} = 2.226$

$y_5 = e^{0.4} = 1.492 \qquad y_{10} = e^{0.9} = 2.460$

$\qquad\qquad\qquad\qquad\quad y_{11} = e^1 = 2.718$

$\int_0^1 e^x \approx \frac{0.1}{2}[1 + 2.718 + 2(1.105 + 1.221$

$\qquad + 1.35 + 1.492 + 1.649 + 1.822$

$\qquad + 2.014 + 2.226 + 2.460)]$

$\qquad = 0.05(3.718 + 30.678) = 1.7198$

(ii) $\int_0^1 e^x dx \approx$ the sum of the mid-ordinates
$\times$ the interval width

$= (y_{1m} + y_{2m} + y_{3m} + \ldots + y_{10m})h$

$= (1.0525 + 1.163 + 1.2855 + 1.421$

$+ 1.5705 + 1.7355 + 1.918 + 2.15$

$+ 2.3443 + 2.589) \times 0.1$

$= 17.198 \times 0.1 = 1.7198$

where $y_{1m} = \dfrac{1}{2}(y_1 + y_2)$ and so on.

$\int_0^1 e^x dx = [e^x]_0^1 = e^1 - e^0$

$= 2.7182818 - 1 = 1.7182818$ exactly.

The trapezoidal rule in evaluating definite integral is given by

$\int_a^b y dx \approx \dfrac{h}{2}[y_1 + 2(y_2 + y_3 + y_4$

$+ \ldots + y_{n-1}) + y_n]$.

The base of the area is $b - a$, this is divided into equal number or odd or even strips where the ordinates are denoted by $y_1, y_2, y_3, \ldots y_n$, and h is the width of the interval.

The mid-ordinate rule in evaluating a definite integral is given by

$\int_a^b y dx \approx h(y_{1m} + y_{2m} + y_{3m} + \ldots + y_{nm})$

where $y_{1m} = \dfrac{1}{2}(y_1 + y_2)$ the mid-ordinate of the ordinates y_1 and y_2.

WORKED EXAMPLE 41

Evaluate to three decimal places using the trapezoidal rule the following definite integrals:-

(i) $\int_1^2 \log_{10} x dx$ (ii) $\int_0^{\frac{\pi}{4}} \sqrt{\sin x} dx$

using 10 intervals or 11 ordinates.

Solution 41

(i) $\int_1^2 (\log_{10} x) dx = \dfrac{0.1}{2}[0 + 0.30103$

$+ 2(0.0414 + 0.07918 + 0.11394$

$+ 0.146128 + 0.17609 + 0.20412$
$+ 0.23045 + 2.55273 + 2.78754)$

x	y	y
1	log 1	0
1.1	log 1.1	0.0414
1.2	log 1.2	0.07918
1.3	log 1.3	0.11394
1.4	log 1.4	0.146128
1.5	log 1.5	0.17609
1.6	log 1.6	0.20412
1.7	log 1.7	0.23045
1.8	log 1.8	0.255273
1.9	log 1.9	0.278754
2.0	log 2.0	0.30103

$\int_1^2 \log_{10} x dx \approx 0.05[0.30103$
$+ 2 \times 0.2787536]$

$= 0.0964511$

$= 0.097.$

(ii)

$x°$	$\sin x°$	$\sqrt{\sin x}$
0	0	0
4.5	0.078459	0.28011
9.0	0.15643	0.39552
13.5	0.23345	0.48316
18	0.30902	0.55589
22.5	0.38268	0.61861
27	0.45399	0.67379
31.5	0.522498	0.72284
36	0.58779	0.76667
40.5	0.64945	0.80588
45	0.707107	0.840896

$h = 4.5° = 0.0785398^c$

$$\int_0^{\frac{\pi}{4}} \sqrt{\sin x}\,dx \approx \frac{0.0785398}{2}[0 + 0.840896$$

$$+ 2(0.28011 + 0.39552$$

$$+ 0.48316 + 0.55589$$

$$+ 0.61861 + 0.67379$$

$$+ 0.72284 + 0.76667$$

$$+ 0.80588)]$$

$$= 0.0392699(0.840896 + 10.60494)$$
$$= 0.4494768 \approx 0.449.$$

c. Deduces the general form of Simpson's rule 2n equal intervals.

Simpson's rule for evaluating approximate integrals.

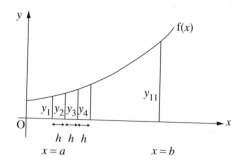

Fig. 55

Consider the area under the curve of a function $f(x)$ is required to be found between the limits $x = a$ and $x = b$.

The interval is $(b-a)$, this is divided into an even number of equal parts, h, therefore there are odd numbers of ordinates. If we take 15 ordinates then h is found by dividing the interval by 14.

d. States the approximate error in using Simpson's rule.

e. Evaluates definite integrals using Simpson's rule.

Simpson's rule

$$\int_{x=a}^{x=b} f(x)dx = \frac{h}{3}[y_1 + 4y_2 + 2y_3 + 4y_4$$

$$+ 2y_5 + \ldots + 4y_{n-1} + y_n]$$

$$= \frac{h}{3}[y_1 + y_n + 4(y_2 + y_4 + y_6$$

$$+ \ldots + y_{n-1} + 2(y_3 + y_5$$

$$+ y_7 + \ldots + y_{n-2}).$$

The exact value of the definite integral

$$\int_0^{\frac{\pi}{2}} \sin x\,dx = \Big[-\cos x\Big]_0^{\frac{\pi}{2}}$$

$$= \Big[-\cos \frac{\pi}{2}\Big] - \Big[-\cos 0\Big]$$

$$= 0 + 1 = 1\text{square unit.}$$

What is the approximate value of this area by applying Simpson's rule?

Use (a) five ordinates   (b) seven ordinates

$$\int_0^{\frac{\pi}{2}} \sin x\,dx = \frac{h}{3}[y_1 + y_5 + 4(y_2 + y_4) + 2y_3]$$

(a)

x	$\sin x$	
0	0	y_1
$\frac{\pi}{8}$	0.383	y_2
$\frac{\pi}{4}$	0.707	y_3
$3\frac{\pi}{8}$	0.924	y_4
$\frac{\pi}{2}$	1	y_5

$$\int_0^{\frac{\pi}{2}} \sin x\,dx \approx \frac{\frac{\pi}{8}}{3}[0 + 1 + 4(0.383$$

$$+ 0.924) + 2 \times 0.707]$$

$$= 0.131[1 + 5.228$$

$$+ 1.414] = 1.001 \approx 1.00.$$

where $h = \frac{\pi}{8}$.

(b) $\displaystyle\int_0^{\frac{\pi}{2}} \sin x \, dx \approx \frac{h}{3}[y_1 + y_7 + 4(y_2 + y_4$

$+ y_6) + 2(y_3 + y_5)]$

x	y
0	0
$\frac{\pi}{12}$	0.259
$\frac{\pi}{6}$	0.5
$\frac{\pi}{4}$	0.707
$\frac{\pi}{3}$	0.866
$\frac{5\pi}{12}$	0.966
$\frac{\pi}{2}$	1

where $h = \frac{\pi}{12}$

$\displaystyle\int_0^{\frac{\pi}{2}} \sin x \, dx \approx \frac{\pi}{36}[0 + 1 + 4(0.259$

$+ 0.707 + 0.966)$

$+ 2(0.5 + 0.866)]$

$= 0.0873(1 + 7.728$

$+ 2.732) = 1.000.$

WORKED EXAMPLE 42

Evaluate

(i) $\int_0^{\frac{1}{2}} \dfrac{dx}{\sqrt{1-x^2}}$ using Simpson's rule with 9 ordinates

(ii) $\int_0^{\frac{1}{2}} \dfrac{dx}{1+x^2}$ using Simpson's rule with 5 ordinates.

Solution 42

(i) 9 Ordinates or 8 intervals

$h = \dfrac{\frac{1}{2} - 0}{8} = \dfrac{1}{16}$

x	y
0	1
$\frac{1}{16}$	1.0019589
$\frac{2}{16}$	1.0079053
$\frac{3}{16}$	1.0180556
$\frac{4}{16}$	1.0327956
$\frac{5}{16}$	1.0527227
$\frac{6}{16}$	1.0787198
$\frac{7}{16}$	1.1120769
$\frac{1}{2}$	1.1547

where $y = \dfrac{1}{\sqrt{1-x^2}}$

$\displaystyle\int_0^{\frac{1}{2}} \frac{dx}{\sqrt{1-x^2}} \approx \frac{h}{3}[y_1 + y_4 + 4(y_2 + y_4 + y_6$

$+ y_8) + 2(y_3 + y_5 + y_7)]$

$= \dfrac{\frac{1}{16}}{3}[1 + 1.1547 + 4(1.002$

$+ 1.0181 + 1.0527$

$+ 1.1121) + 2(1.01 + 1.033$

$+ 1.079)]$

$= 0.02083[1 + 1.1547$

$+ 16.739 + 6.244] = 0.5236.$

(ii) $\int_0^{\frac{1}{2}} \dfrac{dx}{1+x^2} \approx \dfrac{h}{3}[y_1 + y_5 + 4(y_2 + y_4) + 2y_3]$

x	y
0	1
$\frac{1}{8}$	0.9846
$\frac{1}{4}$	0.941
$\frac{3}{8}$	0.8767
$\frac{1}{2}$	0.8

$$y = \frac{1}{1+x^2} \text{ and } h = \frac{1}{8}$$

$$\int_0^{\frac{1}{2}} \frac{dx}{1+x^2} \approx \frac{\frac{1}{8}}{3}[1 + 0.8 + 4(0.9846$$

$$+ 0.8767) + 2 \times 0.941]$$

$$= 0.04167(1.8 + 7.4412$$

$$+ 1.882) = 0.464.$$

Exercise 6

1. Find the area under the curve $y = 3x^2 + 2x + 1$ between $x = -3$ and $x = 2$ using

   (i) integration

   (ii) the trapezoidal rule with 5 intervals

   (iii) Simpson's rule with 11 ordinates

   (iv) the mid-ordinate rule with 10 intervals.

   Ans. (i) 35 square units

   (ii) 37.5 square units

   (iii) 36 square units

   (iv) 35.625 square units.

2. Evaluate approximately the area $\int_0^1 \frac{dx}{(1+x^2)^{\frac{1}{2}}}$

   using (i) Simpson's rule with 4 intervals.

   (ii) the trapezoidal rule with 6 ordinates.

   Comment about the number of ordinates and intervals in using these two rules.

   (Ans. (i) 0.881 (ii) 0.880).

3. Find approximately the definite integral $\int_1^2 10^x dx$ using Simpson's rule with eleven ordinates.

   (Ans. 32.72).

4. If the radius of a circle is 14 cm, determine the area of the circle by considering 15 ordinates when the centre is at the origin, for the area of one quarter of the circle and then multiplying the result by 4. Use Simpson's rule

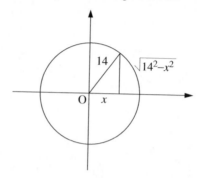

   Check this approximate area with the formula πr^2.

   What is the percentage error?
   Determine $\int_0^{14} \sqrt{14^2 - x^2} dx$ exactly.
   (Ans. 153.51, 153.94).

5. Find the approximate values of the integral $\int_0^\pi \sqrt{\sin x} dx$ using 10 intervals and employing

   (i) Trapezoidal Rule

   (ii) Simpson's rule.

   (Ans. (i) 2.323 (ii) 2.369).

6. Find the approximate values of the integral $\int_2^5 \ln x \, dx$ for 5 ordinates using Simpson's rule.

   (Ans. 3.661).

7

Determines the functions which satisfy the equation of the type $\frac{dy}{dx} = f(x)$ given the boundary conditions, where $f(x)$ is a simple polynomial function.

a. Determines and sketches a family of curves given their derivative, for a simple polynomial function.

b. Determines a particular curve of the family by specifying a point on it. Defines a boundary condition.

c. Solves differential equations of the type $\frac{dy}{dx} = f(x)$ given a boundary condition.

Differential equations.

(a) The equation of a straight line $y = mx + c$, the

gradient of the line is given by $\frac{dy}{dx} = m$.

Therefore a family of straight lines are obtained having the same gradient, that is, the lines are parallel.

If $x = 0$, $y = c$ the intercept of these lines.

The equation $\frac{dy}{dx} = m$ is a simple differential equation since it contains a differential coefficient, $\frac{dy}{dx}$.

If $m = 2$ then $\frac{dy}{dx} = 2$.

To solve this differential equation, we proceed as follows:-

$$dy = 2dx \quad \int dy = \int 2dx \quad y = 2x + c.$$

(b) If $x = 0$, $y = c$ and taking various values of c such as 0, 1, 2, 3, 4 a family of straight lines are drawn as shown.

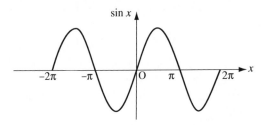

Expanding the idea of the differential equation to $\frac{dy}{dx} = x \quad dy = xdx$ integrating both sides

$$\int dy = \int xdx \quad y = \frac{x^2}{2} + c.$$

If $x = 0$, $y = c$ and taking various values for c such as 1, 2, 3 and 4 we have another family of curves, this type are parabolas.

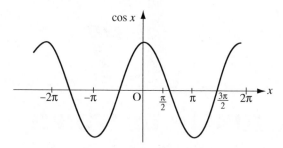

Solution of differential equations.

(c) The differential equation of the form
$\dfrac{dy}{dx} = f(x)$.

If $f(x) = 4x^3 + 3x^2 + 2x + 1$.

WORKED EXAMPLE 43

Solve the equation $\dfrac{dy}{dx} = 4x^3 + 3x^2 + 2x + 1$.

Solution 43

$$\dfrac{dy}{dx} = 4x^3 + 3x^2 + 2x + 1$$

$$dy = (4x^3 + 3x^2 + 2x + 1)dx$$

integrating both sides

$$\int dy = \int (4x^3 + 3x^2 + 2x - 1)dx$$

$$y = 4\dfrac{x^4}{4} + 3\dfrac{x^3}{3} + 2\dfrac{x^2}{2} + x + c$$

$$y = x^4 + x^3 + x^2 + x + c.$$

Therefore, the general solution is given with an arbitrary constant. In order to determine the arbitrary constant we must know the boundary conditions.

Boundary conditions.

If $y = 0$ when $x = 1$ then $0 = 1 + 1 + 1 + 1 + c$ therefore $c = -4$ and the particular solution of the differential equation is
$y = x^4 + x^3 + x^2 + x - 4.$

WORKED EXAMPLE 44

Determine the value of y in terms of x when the boundary conditions are stated adjacent each differential equation.

(i) $\dfrac{dy}{dx} = 5x^2 - 6x + 7$

   $y = 2$ when $x = -1$

(ii) $\dfrac{dy}{dx} = -3x^5 + x^4 - x^3 - 2x^2 + x - 5$

   $y = 1$ when $x = 1.$

Solution 44

(i) $\dfrac{dy}{dx} = 5x^2 - 6x + 7$

   $$dy = (5x^2 - 6x + 7)dx$$

   integrating both sides

   $$\int dy = \int (5x^2 - 6x + 7)dx$$

   $$y = 5\dfrac{x^3}{3} - 6\dfrac{x^2}{2} + 7x + c \text{ the general}$$
   solution when $x = -1$ then $y = 2$.

   Substitute these values in the general solution

   $$2 = -\dfrac{5}{3} - 3 - 7 + c$$

   $$c = 2 + 7 + 3 + \dfrac{5}{3} = 13\dfrac{2}{3}$$

   therefore the particular solution is given

   $$y = \dfrac{5}{3}x^3 - 3x^2 + 7x + 13\dfrac{2}{3}.$$

(ii) $\dfrac{dy}{dx} = -3x^5 + x^4 - x^3 - 2x^2 + x - 5$

   $$dy = (-3x^5 + x^4 - x^3 - 2x^2 + x - 5)dx$$

   integrating both sides

   $$\int dy = \int (-3x^5 + x^4 - x^3 - 2x^2 + x - 5)dx$$

$$y = -\frac{3}{6}x^6 + \frac{1}{5}x^5 - \frac{1}{4}x^4 - \frac{2}{3}x^3$$
$$+ \frac{1}{2}x^2 - 5x + c$$

$$1 = -\frac{1}{2} + \frac{1}{5} - \frac{1}{4} - \frac{2}{3} + \frac{1}{2} - 5 + c$$

$$c = \frac{360 - 12 + 15 + 40}{60}$$

$$c = \frac{403}{60}$$

$$y = -\frac{1}{2}x^6 + \frac{1}{5}x^5 - \frac{1}{4}x^4 - \frac{2}{3}x^3 + \frac{1}{2}x^2$$

$$-5x + \frac{403}{60}.$$

Exercise 7

1. The gradient of a function is given by $\frac{dy}{dx} = 3x^2 - 5x + 7$. Determine the function y, given that the boundary conditions $y = 0$ when $x = 1$.

2. Determine the value of y in terms of x when the boundary conditions are stated adjacent each differential equation.

    (i) $\frac{dy}{dx} = -3x - 1 \quad y = 1$ when $x = 1$

    (ii) $\frac{dy}{dx} = -5 \quad y = 0$ when $x = 5$.

3. The gradient of a curve is given by $\frac{dy}{dx} = 3e^{-5x}$. Determine the function given that $y = 3$, $y = 0$.

4. The gradient of a trigonometric function is given by $\frac{dy}{dx} = 3\sin 5x - 5\cos 3x$. Determine the differential equation when $x = \frac{\pi}{2}, y = 2$.

5. Solve the differential equation $\frac{dy}{dx} = 3\cos 3x - 5\sin 2x + 3e^{3x} + 5$, by finding first the general solution and then the particular solution having the boundary conditions $y = 2$ when $x = 0$.

First order differential equations of the form $\dfrac{dQ}{dt} = kQ$.

Derives first order differential equations of the form $\frac{dQ}{dt} = kQ$ from suitable rate of change problems and shows that their solutions are of the form Ae^{kT}.

a. Differentiates $Q = Ae^{kt}$.

b. Verifies that $Q = Ae^{kt}$ satisfies $\frac{dQ}{dt} = kQ$ by substitution.

c. Derives equations of the form $\frac{dQ}{dt} = kQ$ from problems arising in technology or science units, e.g. radioactive decay.

d. Solves the derived equation in 8c using 8b and a boundary condition.

Charging a capacitor.

A capacitor is charged via a resistor R by applying a d.c. voltage across the combination in series.

After closing the switch S_2, at time t the differential equation is

$$iR + \frac{1}{C}\int i\,dt = V \qquad \ldots (1)$$

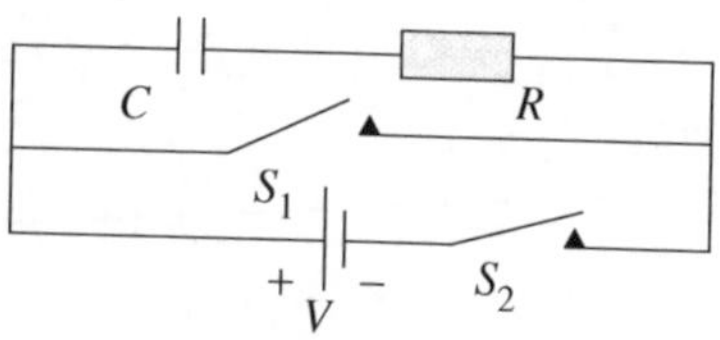

Fig. 56

since $i = C\frac{dv}{dt}$ separating the variables i, and v in the latter equation (1)

or $i\,dt = C\,dv$ integrating both sides $v = \int \frac{i}{C}\,dt$

the voltage across C after t seconds is

$$v = \frac{1}{C}\int i\,dt.$$

Differentiating equation (1) with respect to time

$$R\frac{di}{dt} + \frac{i}{C} = 0$$

$$\frac{di}{dt} = -\frac{i}{RC}, \quad \frac{di}{i} = -\frac{dt}{RC} \text{ integrating both sides}$$

$$\int \frac{di}{i} = -\int \frac{dt}{RC} \quad \ln i = -\frac{t}{RC} + \text{constant}.$$

At $t = 0$, constant $= \ln I$ since $i = I$

$$\ln i = -\frac{t}{RC} + \ln I \quad \ln \frac{i}{I} = -\frac{t}{RC}$$

$$e^{-\frac{t}{RC}} = \frac{i}{I}$$

$$i = Ie^{-\frac{t}{RC}}$$

$$\frac{di}{dt} = -\frac{I}{RC}e^{-\frac{t}{RC}}$$

$$v = \frac{1}{C}\int i\,dt = \frac{1}{C}\int Ie^{-\frac{t}{RC}}\,dt$$

$$= \frac{I}{C} \times \left(\frac{e^{-\frac{t}{RC}}}{-\frac{1}{RC}}\right) + \text{constant}$$

$$v = -IRe^{-\frac{t}{RC}} + \text{constant}.$$

At $t = 0$, $v = 0$, constant $= IR = V$

$v = IRe^{-\frac{t}{RC}} + V$

$v = -Ve^{-\frac{t}{RC}} + V = V(1 - e^{-\frac{t}{RC}})$

$v = V(1 - e^{-\frac{t}{RC}})$.

Discharging of a capacitor.

Open switch S_1 and close switch S_2 the current flows in the opposite direction.

$V = IR$ $i = -Ie^{-\frac{t}{RC}}$.

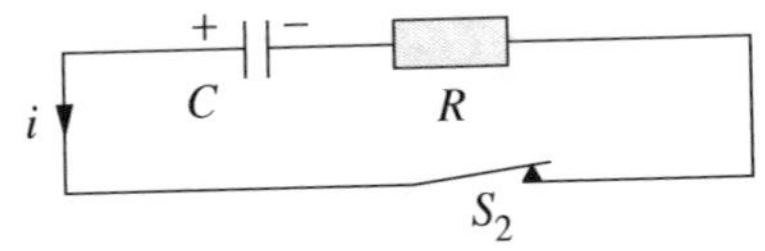

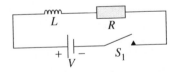

Fig. 57

The boundary conditions.

At the instant of closing the switch S_2 the potential difference across C is V and that across R is zero, immediately after closing the switch S_2, the current flows in the opposite direction to the charging current.

$$\frac{di}{dt} = -I\left(-\frac{1}{RC}\right)e^{-\frac{t}{RC}} = \frac{I}{RC}e^{-\frac{t}{RC}}.$$

Magnetising a coil.

$L\frac{di}{dt} + iR = V$ given that $i = 0$

when $t = 0$ $L\frac{di}{dt} = V - iR$

Fig. 58

$\frac{Ldi}{V - iR} = dt$ $\int \frac{Ldi}{V - iR} = \int dt$

$\frac{L \ln(V - iR)}{-R} = t + \text{constant}.$

$i = 0$ when $t = 0$ $\frac{L \ln V}{-R} = \text{constant}$

$-\frac{L}{R}\ln(V - iR) = t - \frac{L}{R}\ln V$

$\frac{L}{R}\ln V - \frac{L}{R}\ln(V - iR) = t$

$\frac{L}{R}\ln\frac{V}{V - iR} = t$ $\ln\frac{V}{V - iR} = t\frac{R}{L}$

$e^{t\frac{R}{L}} = \frac{V}{V - iR}$

$\frac{V - iR}{V} = e^{-\frac{t}{\tau}}$ where $\tau = \frac{L}{R}$.

$V - iR = Ve^{-\frac{t}{\tau}}$ $iR = V - Ve^{-\frac{t}{\tau}}$

$i = \frac{V}{R}(1 - e^{-\frac{t}{\tau}})$ $i = I(1 - e^{-\frac{t}{\tau}})$.

Radio activity decay.

The number of atoms disintegrating per second, $\frac{dN}{dt}$, is directly proportional to the number of atoms, N, present at that instant hence

$$\frac{dN}{dt} = -\lambda N$$

where λ is the radioactivity decay constant. Thus, if N_0 is the number of radioactive atoms present at a time $t = 0$, and N is the number at the end of a time t we have by integration

$$\int_{N_0}^{N} \frac{dN}{N} = -\lambda \int_0^1 dt$$

$[\ln N]_{N_0}^{N} = -\lambda t + c$ $\ln N - \ln N_0 = -\lambda t + c$.

At $t = 0$, $N = N_0$, $\ln\frac{N}{N_0} = -\lambda t$ $e^{-\lambda t} = \frac{N}{N_0}$

$$\boxed{N = N_0 e^{-\lambda t}}$$

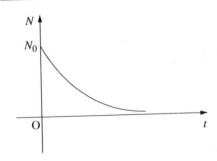

Fig. 59

WORKED EXAMPLE 45

Solve the equation $\dfrac{dy}{dx} = xy$.

Solution 45

$\dfrac{dy}{dx} = xy \qquad \dfrac{dy}{y} = x\,dx \qquad$ integrating both sides

$\ln y = \dfrac{x^2}{2} + c$

$\log_e y = \dfrac{x^2}{2} + c \qquad y = e^{\frac{x^2}{2}+c}$

$y = e^c e^{\frac{x^2}{2}} \qquad y = ke^{\frac{x^2}{2}}$.

WORKED EXAMPLE 46

Show that $y = a\sin(nx + \alpha)$ is a solution of the differential equation

$\dfrac{d^2y}{dx^2} + n^2y = 0$.

Solution 46

$y = a\sin(nx + \alpha) \qquad \dfrac{dy}{dx} = an\cos(nx + \alpha)$

$\dfrac{d^2y}{dx^2} = an[-n\sin(nx+\alpha)] = -an^2\sin(nx+\alpha)$

L.H.S. $= \dfrac{d^2y}{dx^2} + n^2y = n^2a\sin(nx + \alpha)$

$\qquad -an^2\sin(nx+\alpha) = n^2y - n^2y = 0$

R.H.S. $= 0$ therefore L.H.S. $=$ R.H.S. and
$\dfrac{d^2y}{dx^2} + n^2y = 0$.

WORKED EXAMPLE 47

If $q = Q(1 - e^{-\frac{t}{\tau}})$ show that

$\dfrac{dq}{dt} = Ie^{-\frac{t}{\tau}} \qquad \tau = RC$

where $Q = CV$, $V = IR$ and I, R, V, C, Q, are constants.

What is the rate of change of charge when $V = 200$ volts?

$R = 10{,}000\ \Omega$, $C = 10\ \mu F$ and $t = 1$ ms.

Solution 47

$q = Q - Qe^{-\frac{t}{\tau}}$

$\dfrac{dq}{dt} = -Q\left(-\dfrac{1}{\tau}\right)e^{-\frac{t}{\tau}}$

$\qquad = \dfrac{Q}{\tau}e^{-\frac{t}{\tau}} = \dfrac{CV}{RC}e^{-\frac{t}{\tau}}$

$\qquad = \dfrac{V}{R}e^{-\frac{t}{\tau}} = Ie^{-\frac{t}{\tau}}$.

$\dfrac{dq}{dt} = \dfrac{200}{10{,}000}e^{-\frac{0.001}{10{,}000 \times 10 \times 10^{-6}}}$

$\qquad = 0.02e^{-0.01}$

$\qquad = 0.0198$ C/s.

WORKED EXAMPLE 48

The rate of fall of temperature of a body at a temperature θ above the ambient temperature is given by the differential equation.

$\dfrac{d\theta}{dt} = -k\theta$

where k is a constant.

Solve the above differential equation given that $\theta = 45°C$ when $t = 0$

$\dfrac{d\theta}{\theta} = -k$

$\int \dfrac{d\theta}{\theta} = -\int k\,dt$

$\ln\theta = -kt + $ constant

when $t = 0$, $\theta = 45°C \quad \ln 45 = $ constant
$\ln\theta = -kt + \ln 45$

$\ln\dfrac{\theta}{45} = -kt \qquad e^{-kt} = \dfrac{\theta}{45}$

$\theta = 45e^{-kt} \qquad \theta = \theta_0 e^{-kt}$

where $\theta_0 = 45°C$.

If $\theta = 35°C$ after 30 s, determine the value of k.

$\theta = 45e^{-k30} = 35$

$e^{-k30} = \dfrac{35}{45}$ or $e^{k30} = \dfrac{45}{35}$

$k = \dfrac{1}{30} \ln \dfrac{45}{35}$

$\qquad = 8.38 \times 10^{-3}$.

Exercise 8

1. Solve the differential equation
   $\dfrac{di}{dt} = 5i$ given that $i = 5$ A at $t = 0$.

2. The instantaneous charge on a capacitor is given by the equation $q = Qe^{-\frac{t}{RC}}$ find the value of $\frac{dq}{dt}$ when $Q = 50$ mC, $R = 10\ k\Omega$, $C = 100\ \mu F$, and $t = 1$ ms.

3. Solve the differential equation
   $\frac{dy}{dx} = xe^y$, $y = 0$, $x = 1$.

4. Solve the differential equation
   $\dfrac{dy}{dx} = yx^3$, $x = 0$, $y = 1$.

5. Solve the differential equation
   $\dfrac{d\theta}{dt} = -k\theta$, given that $\theta = 38°$ when $t = 0$. If $\theta = 25°$ after 1 minute, determine the value of k, and express θ in terms of t.

6. After closing switch S_2, in Fig. 56 the differential equation t second afterwards is given by $V = iR + \frac{1}{C} \int i \, dt \ldots (1)$ where V, R, and C are constants.

   Differentiate the differential equation (1) with respect to t and hence derive an expression $i = Ie^{-\frac{t}{RC}}$ giving the boundary conditions, at $t = 0$, $i = I$.

7. The current through a capacitor is $i = C\frac{dv}{dt}$, solve the differential equation given that $i = Ie^{-\frac{t}{RC}}$ and the initial conditions, $t = 0$, $v = 0$.

Calculus III Assignments

Assignment 1

1. Differentiate with respect to x and evaluate

    (a) $y = 2x^3 + 3x^2 + x + 4$ at $x = 2$

    (b) $y = 3e^{3x}$ at $x = 1.5$ and 0

    (c) $y = \sin 3x + \cos 3x$ at $x = \dfrac{\pi}{2}$.

    14 marks

2. Differentiate with respect to x <u>four</u> of the following:-

    (a) $2 \sin x \log_e x$ (b) $e^{-2x} \cdot x^3$

    (c) $\dfrac{x^2 + x}{2x^2 + 1}$ (d) $\dfrac{\cos 2x}{e^{3x}}$

    (e) $(2x^3 + 3x^2 + x)^4$.   32 marks

    Note: If $y = u \cdot v$ then $\dfrac{dy}{dx} = v\dfrac{du}{dx} + u\dfrac{dv}{dx}$.

    If $y = \dfrac{u}{v}$ then $\dfrac{dy}{dx} = \dfrac{v\frac{du}{dx} - u\frac{dv}{dx}}{v^2}$.

3. Obtain $\dfrac{dy}{dx}$ and $\dfrac{d^2 y}{dx^2}$ at $x = 2.5$ for the following:

    (a) $y = 3x^3 + 3x - 2$

    (b) $\dfrac{x^2 e^{2x} + 3x^2 + 2}{x^2}$.   20 marks

4. Given $y = e^{-x}x$, show that

    $$\dfrac{d^2 y}{dx^2} + \dfrac{dy}{dx} + \dfrac{y}{x} = 0.$$ 10 marks

5. A body moves, s metres in t seconds so that $s = 2t - 2t^2 + 3t^3$. Calculate the velocity of the body when $t = 2$. Obtain the formula for the acceleration and calculate the time t when the acceleration is zero.   10 marks

6. A closed cylindrical can of radius r cm and height h cm holds 400 cm^3 when full. Show that the area of metal to make the can is $A = 2\pi r^2 + \frac{800}{r}$.

    Find $\dfrac{dA}{dr}$ and calculate the value of r which makes A a minimum.   14 marks

    Total 100

Assignment 1 solution

1. (a) $y = 2x^3 + 3x^2 + x + 4$

   $\dfrac{dy}{dx} = 6x^2 + 6x + 1$

   at $x = 2$

   $\dfrac{dy}{dx} = 6(2)^2 + 6(2) + 1$

   $= 24 + 12 + 1 = 37$ 4 marks

   (b) $y = 3e^{3x}$

   $\dfrac{dy}{dx} = 9e^{3x}$

   at $x = 1.5$, $\dfrac{dy}{dx} = 9e^{4.5} = 810$ to 3 s.f.

   at $x = 0$, $\dfrac{dy}{dx} = 9e^0 = 9$ 5 marks

   (c) $y = \sin 3x + \cos 3x$

   $\dfrac{dy}{dx} = 3\cos 3x - 3\sin 3x$

   at $x = \frac{\pi}{2}$

   $\dfrac{dy}{dx} = 3\cos \frac{3\pi}{2} - 3\sin \frac{3\pi}{2}$

   $= 0 - 3(-1) = 3.$ 5 marks

2. (a) $y = 2\sin x \log_e x$

   $\dfrac{dy}{dx} = 2\cos x \log_e x + 2\sin x \left(\frac{1}{x}\right)$

   $= 2\cos x \log_e x + \dfrac{2\sin x}{x}$

   (b) $y = e^{-2x} x^3$

   $\dfrac{dy}{dx} = -2e^{-2x} \cdot x^3 + e^{-2x} 3x^2$

   $= 3x^2 e^{-2x} - 2x^3 e^{-2x}$

   (c) $y = \dfrac{x^2 + x}{2x^2 + 1}$

   $\dfrac{dy}{dx} = \dfrac{\begin{array}{c}(2x+1)(2x^2+1)\\ -(x^2+x)(4x)\end{array}}{(2x^2+1)^2}$

   $= \dfrac{4x^3 + 2x^2 + 2x + 1 - 4x^3 - 4x^2}{(2x^2+1)^2}$

   $= \dfrac{-2x^2 + 2x + 1}{(2x^2+1)^2}$

   (d) $y = \dfrac{\cos 2x}{e^{3x}}$

   $\dfrac{dy}{dx} = \dfrac{(-2\sin 2x)e^{3x} - (\cos 2x)3e^{3x}}{(e^{3x})^2}$

   $= -\dfrac{2\sin 2x + 3\cos 2x}{e^{3x}}$

   (e) $y = (2x^3 + 3x^2 + x)^4$

   $\dfrac{dy}{dx} = 4(2x^3 + 3x^2 + x)^3 \times (6x^2 + 6x + 1).$

3. (a) $y = 3x^3 + 3x - 2$

   $\dfrac{dy}{dx} = 9x^2 + 3$ at $x = 2.5$,

   $\dfrac{dy}{dx} = 9(2.5)^2 + 3 = 59.25$

   $\dfrac{d^2y}{dx^2} = 18x$ at $x = 2.5$,

   $\dfrac{d^2y}{dx^2} = 18(2.5) = 45$

   (b) $y = \dfrac{x^2 e^{2x} + 3x^2 + 2}{x^2} = e^{2x} + 3 + 2x^{-2}$

   $\dfrac{dy}{dx} = 2e^{2x} - 4x^{-3} = 2e^{2x} - \dfrac{4}{x^3}$,

   at $x = 2.5$,

   $\dfrac{dy}{dx} = 2e^5 - \dfrac{4}{2.5^3} = 297$ to 3 s.f.

$$\frac{d^2y}{dx^2} = 4e^{2x} + 12x^{-4} = 4e^{2x} + \frac{12}{x^4}$$

$$= 4e^5 + \frac{12}{2.5^4}$$

$$= 593.6526364 + 0.3072$$

$$= 594 \text{ to } 3 \text{ s.f.}$$

4. $y = e^{-x}x,$

$$\frac{dy}{dx} = -e^{-x}x + e^{-x}.1$$

$$= -xe^{-x} + e^{-x}$$

$$\frac{d^2y}{dx^2} = -e^{-x} - x(-e^{-x}) - e^{-x}$$

$$= -2e^{-x} + xe^{-x}$$

$$= e^{-x}(x - 2)$$

$$\frac{d^2y}{dx^2} + \frac{dy}{dx} + \frac{y}{x} = -2e^{-x} + xe^{-x} - xe^{-x}$$

$$+ e^{-x} + \frac{e^{-x}x}{x} = 0$$

$$\therefore \frac{d^2y}{dx^2} + \frac{dy}{dx} + \frac{y}{x} = 0.$$

5. $s = 2t - 2t^2 + 3t^3$

$$\frac{ds}{dt} = 2 - 4t + 9t^2$$

at $t = 2$

$$v = \frac{ds}{dt} = 2 - 4(2) + 9(2)^2$$

$$= 2 - 8 + 36 = 30 \text{ m/s}$$

$$a = \frac{d^2s}{dt^2} = -4 + 18t$$

when $a = 0$

$$18t - 4 = 0 \Rightarrow t = \frac{4}{18} = \frac{2}{9} \text{ s.}$$

6. Surface area of can is $\pi r^2 + \pi r^2 + 2\pi rh$

$$A = 2\pi r^2 + 2\pi rh$$

$$V = \pi r^2 h \Rightarrow h = \frac{V}{\pi r^2} = \frac{400}{\pi r^2}$$

$$A = 2\pi r^2 + 2\pi r \frac{400}{\pi r^2}$$

$$= 2\pi r^2 + \frac{800}{r} = 2\pi r^2 + 800r^{-1}.$$

$$\frac{dA}{dr} = 4\pi r - 800r^{-2}$$

$$\frac{dA}{dr} = 0$$

$$4\pi r - 800r^{-2} = 0$$

$$4\pi r - 800r^{-2}$$

$$r^3 = \frac{800}{4\pi} \Rightarrow r = \sqrt[3]{\frac{800}{4\pi}} = 3.99 \text{ cm}$$

to 3 s.f. for A to be minimum.

Assignment 2

1. Find $\dfrac{dy}{dx}$ if

   (a) $y = 4x^3 + 6x^2 + 10x$ 3 marks

   (b) $y = \sqrt{x} - \dfrac{1}{\sqrt{x}}$.   3 marks

   Express the answer with positive indices only.

2. Find $\dfrac{dy}{dx}$ if

   (a) $y = (x^2 - x)^9$ 4 marks

   (b) $y = \sqrt{1 - 5x^3}$.   4 marks

3. Find

   (a) $\dfrac{d}{d\theta}(\sin 7\theta)$ 2 marks

   (b) $\dfrac{d}{d\theta}(\cos 4\theta)$ 2 marks

   (c) $\dfrac{d}{d\theta}\left(\cos 2\theta - \dfrac{3\pi}{2}\right)$.   2 marks

4. If $y = \log_e(x^2 + 5)$ determine the value of $\dfrac{dy}{dx}$ if $x = 1$.   5 marks

5. A curve is given in the form $y = 3\sin 2\theta - 5\tan\theta$ where θ is in radians. Find the gradient of the curve at the point where θ has a value equivalent to $34°$.   6 marks

6. Differentiate with respect to x:-

   (a) $x^3 \sin 2x$ 5 marks

   (b) $(x^2 + 1)\log_e x$.   5 marks

7. Find   (a) $\dfrac{d}{dm}\left(\dfrac{e^{2m}}{m + 3}\right)$.   6 marks

   Find   (b) $\dfrac{d}{d\theta}(\tan\theta)$.   6 marks

8. A body moves s metres in t seconds where $s = t^3 - 3t^2 - 3t + 8$.

   Find
   (a) its velocity at the end of 3 seconds;   3 marks

   (b) a value for t for which its velocity is zero;   6 marks

   (c) its acceleration at the end of 2 seconds.   3 marks

9. A curve has the equation $y = 10 + 3x - 2x^2$

   (a) Calculate the value of the gradient of this curve when $x = 6$.   5 marks

   (b) Determine the value of x which gives the maximum value of y.   5 marks

   (c) Determine the maximum value of y.   5 marks

   Total 80

Assignment 2 solution

1. (a) $y = 4x^3 + 6x^2 + 10x$

   $\dfrac{dy}{dx} = 12x^2 + 12x + 10$ 3 marks

   (b) $y = \sqrt{x} - \dfrac{1}{\sqrt{x}} = x^{\frac{1}{2}} - x^{-\frac{1}{2}}$

   $\dfrac{dy}{dx} = \dfrac{1}{2}x^{-\frac{1}{2}} + \dfrac{1}{2}x^{-\frac{3}{2}}$

   $= \dfrac{1}{2x^{\frac{1}{2}}} + \dfrac{1}{2x^{\frac{3}{2}}}$ 3 marks.

2. (a) $y = (x^2 - x)^9$

   $\dfrac{dy}{dx} = 9(x^2 - x)^8(2x - 1)$ 4 marks

   (b) $y = \sqrt{1 - 5x^3} = (1 - 5x^3)^{\frac{1}{2}}$

   $\dfrac{dy}{dx} = \dfrac{1}{2}(1 - 5x^3)^{-\frac{1}{2}}(-15x^2)$

   $= -\dfrac{15x^2}{2(1 - 5x^3)^{\frac{1}{2}}}$

   $= -\dfrac{15x^2}{2\sqrt{1 - 5x^3}}.$ 4 marks

3. (a) $\dfrac{d}{d\theta}(\sin 7\theta) = 7\cos 7\theta$ 2 marks

   (b) $\dfrac{d}{d\theta}(\cos 4\theta) = -4\sin 4\theta$ 2 marks

   (c) $\dfrac{d}{d\theta}\left(\cos 2\theta - \dfrac{3\pi}{2}\right) = -2\sin 2\theta$

       2 marks.

4. $y = \log_e(x^2 + 5)$

   $\dfrac{dy}{dx} = \dfrac{1}{x^2 + 5} \times 2x$

   if $x = 1$, $\dfrac{dy}{dx} = \dfrac{1}{1 + 5} \times 2(1) = \dfrac{2}{6} = \dfrac{1}{3}$

       5 marks.

5. $y = 3\sin 2\theta - 5\tan\theta$

   $\dfrac{dy}{dx} = 6\cos 2\theta - 5\sec^2\theta$

   $= 6\cos 68° - 5\sec^2 34°$

   $= 2.247639561 - 7.274808696$

   $= -5.03$ to 3 s.f.   6 marks.

6. (a) $y = x^3\sin 2x$

   $\dfrac{dy}{dx} = 3x^2\sin 2x + x^3(2\cos 2x)$

   $= 3x^2\sin 2x + 2x^3\cos 2x$ 5 marks

   (b) $y = (x^2 + 1)\log_e^x$

   $\dfrac{dy}{dx} = 2x\log_e^x + \dfrac{(x^2 + 1)}{x}$ 6 marks

7. (a) $\dfrac{d}{dm}\left(\dfrac{e^{2m}}{m + 3}\right)$

   $= \dfrac{2e^{2m}(m + 3) - e^{2m}}{(m + 3)^2}$

   $= \dfrac{e^{2m}(2(m + 3) - 1)}{(m + 3)^2}$

   $= \dfrac{e^{2m}(2m + 5)}{(m + 3)^2}$ 6 marks.

   (b) $\dfrac{d}{d\theta}(\tan\theta) = \sec^2\theta.$ 6 marks

8. (a) $s = t^3 - 3t^2 - 3t + 8$

   $\dfrac{ds}{dt} = 3t^2 - 6t - 3 = v$

   at $t = 3$

   $v = 3(3)^2 - 6(3) - 3$

   $= 27 - 18 - 3 = 6$ m/s;   3 marks

(b) $a = \dfrac{d^2s}{dt^2} = 6t - 6$

at $t = 2$

$a = 6(2) - 6 = 6 \text{ m/s}^2$ 6 marks.

9. (a) $y = 10 + 3x - 2x^2$

$\dfrac{dy}{dx} = 3 - 4x$

when $x = 6$

$\dfrac{dy}{dx} = 3 - 4(6) = 3 - 24 = -21$

5 marks.

(b) $\dfrac{dy}{dx} = 3 - 4x = 0$ for maximum value

$4x = 3 \qquad x = \dfrac{3}{4}$ 5 marks.

(c) $y_{max} = 10 + 3\left(\dfrac{3}{4}\right) - 2\left(\dfrac{3}{4}\right)^2$

$= 10 + \dfrac{9}{4} - \dfrac{18}{16}$

$= 10 + \dfrac{9}{4} - \dfrac{9}{8}$

$= 10 + \dfrac{9}{8}$

$y_{max} = 11\dfrac{1}{8}$ 5 marks.

80 marks.

Assignment 3

1. Evaluate the gradients of the function
   $y = 3 \cos x$ at $x = \frac{\pi}{6}$ and $x = \frac{7\pi}{4}$ and
   $x = 3\pi$.   5 marks

2. Evaluate the gradients of the function
   $y = e^{-3x}$ at $x = 3$, $x = 2$, $x = 0.5$.
                                                  5 marks

3. Determine the gradient of the function
   $y = 5 \ln 2x$.   5 marks

4. Sketch the graphs $y = x^2$, $y = x^3$, $y = x^4$
   on the same graph for the range $-2 \le x \le 2$.
                                                  5 marks

5. (i) $\dfrac{d}{dx}(3 \ln 5x)$ (ii) $\dfrac{d}{dt}\left(e^{-\frac{t}{3}}\right)$.
                                                  5 marks

6. Sketch the graph $y = x^3 - 2x^2 + x + 1$.

   You may take the derivative to help you find
   some information.

   What is the sign of the gradient?
                                                  15 marks

7. Differentiate

   (i) $y = \dfrac{\sin x}{1 + 3x^2}$

   (ii) $y = \cos 2x \sin 3x$.   10 marks

8. A cell of e.m.f., E, and internal resistance, r,
   is connected across a load, R.

   Write down an expression of I in terms of
   E, r, and R.   5 marks

   (a) Write down an expression for the power
       in the load ($P = I^2 R$) in terms of E, r
       and R.   5 marks

   (b) Find $\dfrac{dP}{dR}$ and $\dfrac{d^2 P}{dR^2}$ hence find the max-
       imum power dissipation in R.
                                                  10 marks

   (c) What is the condition?

9. Determine the turning point of
   $y = -x^2 - 6x - 7$.   15 marks

10. A body is falling freely from rest under
    gravity ($g = 9.81$ m/s^2), the distance
    s metres travelled s is given by the expression
    $s = 20t^2$, where t is the time in seconds.

    Find
    (i) the velocity after t seconds   5 marks
    (ii) the velocity after 1 second   5 marks
    (ii) the time taken for the body to fall
         1500 m.   5 marks
                                             _____
                                             100 marks

Assignment 3 solution

1. $y = 3\cos x$

$$\frac{dy}{dx} = -3\sin x$$

when $x = \dfrac{\pi}{6}$,

$$\frac{dy}{dx} = -3\sin\frac{\pi}{6} = -\frac{3}{2}$$

when $x = \dfrac{7\pi}{4}$,

$$\frac{dy}{dx} = -3\sin\frac{7\pi}{4} = -3\left(-\frac{1}{\sqrt{2}}\right) = \frac{3}{\sqrt{2}}$$

$$= 3 \times 0.707 = 2.121$$

when $x = 3\pi$,

$$\frac{dy}{dx} = -3\sin 3\pi = 0. \qquad \text{5 marks}$$

2. $y = e^{-3x}$

$$\frac{dy}{dx} = -3e^{-3x}$$

when $x = 3$,

$$\frac{dy}{dx} = -3e^{-9} = -0.00037$$

when $x = 2$,

$$\frac{dy}{dx} = -3e^{-6} = -0.00744$$

when $x = 0.5$,

$$\frac{dy}{dx} = -3e^{-1.5} = -0.669. \qquad \text{15 marks}$$

3. $y = 5\ln 2x$

$$\frac{dy}{dx} = 5 \times \frac{1}{2x} \times 2 = \frac{5}{x}$$

$$\frac{dy}{dx} = \frac{5}{x} \qquad \text{5 marks}$$

4.

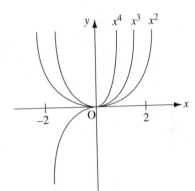

5 marks

5. (i) $\dfrac{d}{dx}(3\ln 5x) - \dfrac{3}{5}$

 (ii) $\dfrac{d}{dt}(e^{-\frac{t}{3}}) = -\dfrac{1}{3}e^{-\frac{t}{3}}.$ 10 marks

6. $y = x^3 - 2x^2 + x + 1$

$$\frac{dy}{dx} = 3x^2 - 4x + 1$$

$$\frac{d^2y}{dx^2} = 6x - 4$$

$$\frac{dy}{dx} = 0 \text{ for maximum or minimum}$$

$$3x^2 - 4x + 1 = 0$$

$$x = \frac{4 \pm \sqrt{16 - 4 \times 1 \times 3}}{6}$$

$$= \frac{4 \pm 2}{6}$$

$$x = 1 \text{ or } x = \frac{1}{3}$$

$$\frac{d^2y}{dx^2} = 6x - 4$$

65

when $x = 1$, $\dfrac{d^2y}{dx^2} = 2$ minimum

when $x = \dfrac{1}{3}$, $\dfrac{d^2y}{dx^2} = -2$ maximum

when $x = 1$, $y_{min} = 1 - 2 + 1 + 1 = 1$

when $x = \dfrac{1}{3}$,

$$y_{max} = \left(\dfrac{1}{3}\right)^3 - 2\left(\dfrac{1}{3}\right)^2 + \dfrac{1}{3} + 1$$

$$= \dfrac{1}{27} - \dfrac{2}{9} + \dfrac{1}{3} + 1$$

$$= \dfrac{1 - 6 + 9 + 27}{27} = \dfrac{31}{27} = 1\dfrac{4}{27}$$

$A\left(\dfrac{1}{3}, 1\dfrac{4}{27}\right)$

$B(1, 1)$ 15 marks

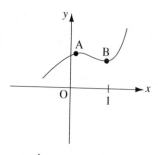

7. (i) $y = \dfrac{\sin x}{1 + 3x^2}$

$$\dfrac{dy}{dx} = \dfrac{(\cos x)(1 + 3x^2) - (\sin x)(6x)}{(1 + 3x^2)^2}$$

$$= \dfrac{(1 + 3x^2)\cos x - 6x \sin x}{(1 + 3x^2)^2}$$

(5 marks)

(ii) $y = \cos 2x \sin 3x$

$$\dfrac{dy}{dx} = (-2\cos 2x)(\sin 3x)$$
$$+ (\cos 2x)3(\cos 3x)$$

$$= -2\cos 2x \sin 3x - 3\cos 2x \cos 3x.$$

(5 marks)

8.

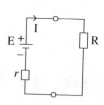

$$I = \dfrac{E}{r + R}$$

(a) $P = I^2R = \left(\dfrac{E}{r + R}\right)^2 R = \dfrac{E^2R}{(r + R)^2}$

(b) $\dfrac{dP}{dR} = \dfrac{E^2(r + R)^2 - E^2R2(r + R)}{(r + R)^4}$

$$= \dfrac{E^2}{(r + R)^2} - \dfrac{2E^2R}{(r + R)^3}$$

$$= E^2(r + R)^{-2} - 2E^2R(r + R)^{-3}$$

$$\dfrac{d^2P}{dR^2} = -2E^2(r + R)^{-3} - 2E^2(r + R)^{-3}$$
$$- 2E^2R[-3(r + R)^{-4}]$$

$$= -4E^2(r + R)^{-3} + 6E^2R(r + R)^{-4}$$

$\dfrac{dP}{dR} = 0$ for maximum power

$$\dfrac{E^2}{(r + R)^2} = \dfrac{2E^2R}{(r + R)^3}$$

$r + R = 2R \Rightarrow \boxed{R = r}$ the condition

$$P_{max} = E^2R = \left(\dfrac{E}{2R}\right)^2 R = \dfrac{E^2R}{4R^2} = \dfrac{E^2}{4R}.$$

(20 marks)

9. $y = -x^2 - 6x - 7$

$$\dfrac{dy}{dx} = -2x - 6$$

$-2x - 6 = 0$ for turning point

$x = -3$

$$\dfrac{d^2y}{dx^2} = -2 \text{ maximum}$$

$$y_{max} = -(-2)^2 - 6(-2) - 7$$

$$= -4 + 12 - 7 = 1$$

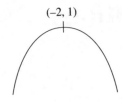

(−2, 1)

15 marks

10. $s = 10t^2$

(i) $\dfrac{ds}{dt} = 20t$ the velocity after t seconds

(ii) $\dfrac{ds}{dt} = 20(1) = 20$ m/s

(iii) $s = 1500 = 10t^2$

$t = \sqrt{150} = 12.2$ s to 3 s.f.   15 marks

100 marks

Calculus III Solutions

Solution 1

1. (i) $y = \sin x$

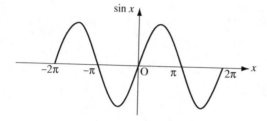

Fig. 60

    (ii) $y = \cos x$

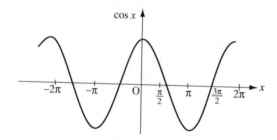

Fig. 61

2. (i) $y = e^x$

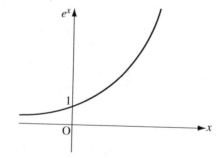

Fig. 62

(ii) $y = e^{-x}$

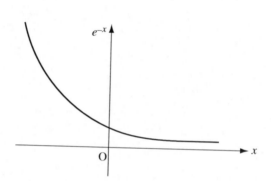

Fig. 63

(iii) $y = 3e^{-x}$

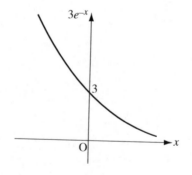

Fig. 64

(iv) $y = \ln x$

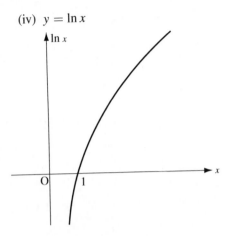

Fig. 65

(v) $y = 2 \ln x$

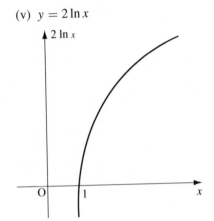

Fig. 66

(vi) $y = 3 \ln x$

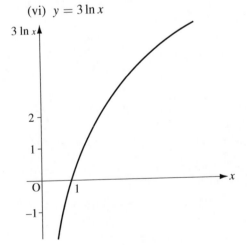

Fig. 67

(vii) $y = 5 \ln x$

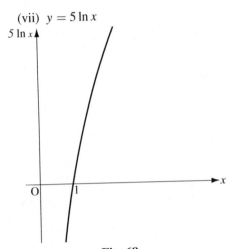

Fig. 68

3. (i) $y = 3x^2$

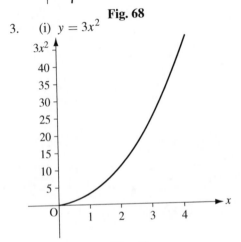

Fig. 69

(ii) $y = 5x^3$

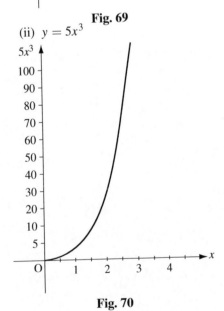

Fig. 70

(iii) $y = 2x^4$

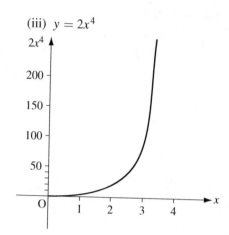

Fig. 71

4. (i) $y = 5e^x$ $\dfrac{dy}{dx} = 5e^x$

   (ii) $y = -\sin x$ $\dfrac{dy}{dx} = -\cos x$

   (iii) $y = \cos x$ $\dfrac{dy}{dx} = -\sin x$

   (iv) $y = \ln x$ $\dfrac{dy}{dx} = \dfrac{1}{x}$

   (v) $y = 5x^3$ $\dfrac{dy}{dx} = 15x^2$

   (vi) $y = x^4$ $\dfrac{dy}{dx} = 4x^3$.

5. (i) $y = \sin x$ $\dfrac{dy}{dx} = \cos x$

   at $x = 0$, $\dfrac{dy}{dx} = \cos 0 = 1$

   at $x = \dfrac{\pi}{5}$, $\dfrac{dy}{dx} = \cos \dfrac{\pi}{5} = 0.809$

   at $x = \dfrac{\pi}{7}$, $\dfrac{dy}{dx} = \cos \dfrac{\pi}{7} = 0.901$

   at $x = \pi$, $\dfrac{dy}{dx} = \cos \pi = -1$.

   (ii) $y = \cos x$ $\dfrac{dy}{dx} = -\sin x$

   at $x = 0$, $\dfrac{dy}{dx} = -\sin 0 = 0$

at $x = \dfrac{\pi}{5}$, $\dfrac{dy}{dx} = -\sin \dfrac{\pi}{5} = -0.588$

at $x = \dfrac{\pi}{7}$, $\dfrac{dy}{dx} = -\sin \dfrac{\pi}{7} = -0.433$

at $x = \pi$, $\dfrac{dy}{dx} = -\sin \pi = 0$.

6. (i) $y = \ln x$ $\dfrac{dy}{dx} = \dfrac{1}{x}$

   at $x = 0.5$, $\dfrac{dy}{dx} = \dfrac{1}{0.5} = 2$

   at $x = 1.5$, $\dfrac{dy}{dx} = \dfrac{1}{1.5} = 0.667$

   at $x = 3.5$, $\dfrac{dy}{dx} = \dfrac{1}{3.5} = 0.286$

   at $x = 5$, $\dfrac{dy}{dx} = \dfrac{1}{5} = 0.2$.

   (ii) $y = e^x$ $\dfrac{dy}{dx} = e^x$

   at $x = 0.5$, $\dfrac{dy}{dx} = e^{0.5} = 1.649$

   at $x = 1.5$, $\dfrac{dy}{dx} = e^{1.5} = 4.482$

   at $x = 3.5$, $\dfrac{dy}{dx} = e^{3.5} = 33.1$

   at $x = 5$, $\dfrac{dy}{dx} = e^5 = 148.4$.

7. $y = \sin x$, the gradients are positive when $-\dfrac{\pi}{2} < x < \dfrac{\pi}{2}$, the gradients are negative when $\dfrac{\pi}{2} < x < \dfrac{3\pi}{2}$

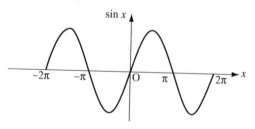

the gradients are negative when $-\dfrac{3\pi}{2} < x < -\dfrac{\pi}{2}$

the gradients are positive when $-2\pi < x < \dfrac{-3\pi}{2}$,

and when $\dfrac{3\pi}{2} < x < 2\pi$.

The gradients are zero at $x = -\frac{3\pi}{2}$, $-\frac{\pi}{2}, \frac{\pi}{2}, \frac{3\pi}{2}$.

$y = \cos x$

The gradients are positive in the ranges $-2\pi < x < -\pi$.

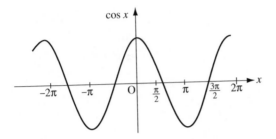

and $0 < x < -\pi$.

The gradients are negative in the ranges $-\pi < x < 0$ and $\pi < x < 2\pi$.

The gradients are zero when $x = -2\pi, -\pi$, $0, \pi$ and 2π.

8. The gradients of the logarithmic function $y = \ln x \left(\frac{dy}{dx} = \frac{1}{x}\right)$ are always positive since x must be positive in order that $\ln x$ is defined. At $x = 0$ is not defined.

The gradients of the exponential function $y = e^x$ are always positive since $\frac{dy}{dx} = e^x$ for any value of x positive, negative or zero.

The gradients of $y = e^{-x}$ are similarly all negative since $\left(\frac{dy}{dx} = -e^{-x} = -\frac{1}{e^x}\right)$.

9. (i) $y = x^2$

x	−2	−1	0	1	2
y	4	1	0	1	4

(ii) $y = x^3$

x	−2	−1	0	1	2
y	−8	−1	0	1	8

(iii) $y = x^4$

x	−2	−1	0	1	2
y	16	1	0	1	16

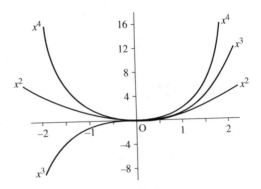

Fig. 72

10. (i) $y = 3x \qquad \frac{dy}{dx} = 3$

for all values of x

(ii) $y = x^2 \qquad \frac{dy}{dx} = 2x$

at $x = -1$, $\quad \frac{dy}{dx} = -2$

at $x = 0$, $\quad \frac{dy}{dx} = 0$

at $x = 1$, $\quad \frac{dy}{dx} = 2$

at $x = 2$, $\quad \frac{dy}{dx} = 4$

at $x = -3$, $\quad \frac{dy}{dx} = -6$

(iii) $y = 3x^3 \qquad \frac{dy}{dx} = 9x^2$

at $x = -1$, $\quad \frac{dy}{dx} = 9$

at $x = 0$, $\quad \frac{dy}{dx} = 0$

at $x = 1$, $\quad \frac{dy}{dx} = 9$

at $x = 2$, $\quad \frac{dy}{dx} = 36$

at $x = -3$, $\quad \frac{dy}{dx} = 81.$

Solution 2

1.   (i) $y = x^2 \sin x$

$$\frac{dy}{dx} = (2x)\sin x + x^2(\cos x)$$

$$= 2x \sin x + x^2 \cos x$$

(ii) $y = x \cos x$

$$\frac{dy}{dx} = (1)\cos x + x(-\sin x)$$

$$= \cos x - x \sin x$$

(iii) $y = \sin x \cos x$

$$\frac{dy}{dx} = (\cos x)\cos x + \sin x(-\sin x)$$

$$= \cos^2 x - \sin^2 x$$

(iv) $y = \sin x \ln x$

$$\frac{dy}{dx} = (\cos x)\ln x + \sin x \left(\frac{1}{x}\right)$$

$$= \cos x \ln x + \frac{\sin x}{x}$$

(v) $y = \cos x \ln x$

$$\frac{dy}{dx} = (-\sin x)\ln x + \cos x \left(\frac{1}{x}\right)$$

$$= -\sin x \ln x + \frac{\cos x}{x}$$

(vi) $y = x \ln x$

$$\frac{dy}{dx} = (1)\ln x + x \left(\frac{1}{x}\right) = \ln x + 1$$

(vii) $y = e^x \ln x$

$$\frac{dy}{dx} = (e^x)\ln x + e^x \left(\frac{1}{x}\right)$$

$$= e^x \ln x + \frac{e^x}{x}$$

(viii) $y = x^2 \ln x$

$$\frac{dy}{dx} = 2x \ln x + x^2 \left(\frac{1}{x}\right)$$

$$= 2x \ln x + x$$

(ix) $y = e^x \sin x$

$$\frac{dy}{dx} = (e^x)\sin x + e^x(\cos x)$$

$$= e^x \sin x + e^x \cos x$$

(x) $y = x^3 \ln x$

$$\frac{dy}{dx} = (3x^2)\ln x + x^3 \left(\frac{1}{x}\right)$$

$$= 3x^2 \ln x + x^2$$

(xi) $y = xe^x$

$$\frac{dy}{dx} = (1)e^x + x(e^x) = e^x + xe^x$$

(xii) $y = x^n \ln x$

$$\frac{dy}{dx} = (nx^{n-1})\ln x + x^n \left(\frac{1}{x}\right)$$

$$= nx^{n-1} \ln x + x^{n-1}.$$

2.   (i) $y = e^x - \cos x + \sin x - \ln x$

$$\frac{dy}{dx} = e^x + \sin x + \cos x - \frac{1}{x}$$

(ii) $y = x + e^x + \sin x + \cos x + \ln x$

$$\frac{dy}{dx} = 1 + e^x + \cos x - \sin x + \frac{1}{x}$$

(iii) $y = e^t + \sin t + \ln t - 5 \cos t$

$$\frac{dy}{dt} = e^t + \cos t + \frac{1}{t} + 5 \sin t$$

(iv) $y = 3e^t - \cos t + 4 \ln t$

$$\frac{dy}{dt} = 3e^t + \sin t + \frac{4}{t}$$

(v) $y = 5\cos t - 7\ln t$

$$\frac{dy}{dt} = -5\sin t - \frac{7}{t}.$$

3. (i) $y = \ln x e^{3x} \quad y = u \cdot v$

where $u = \ln x$ and $v = e^{3x}$

$$\frac{du}{dx} = \frac{1}{x} \quad \frac{dv}{dx} = 3e^{3x}$$

$$\frac{dy}{dx} = \left(\frac{1}{x}\right)e^{3x} + \ln x(3e^{3x})$$

$$= \frac{e^{3x}}{x} + 3e^{3x}\ln x$$

(ii) $y = \cos 3x - \sin 5x$

$$\frac{dy}{dx} = -3\sin 3x - 5\cos 5x$$

(iii) $y = 3x^5 - \cos 4x$

$$\frac{dy}{dx} = 3(5x^4) - (-4\sin 4x)$$

$$= 15x^4 + 4\sin 4x$$

(iv) $y = e^{-3x}\cos 5x + \sin 4x$

$$\frac{dy}{dx} = (-3e^{-3x})\cos 5x$$

$$+ e^{-3x}(-5\sin 5x) + 4\cos 4x$$

$$= -3e^{-3x}\cos 5x - 5e^{-3x}\sin 5x$$

$$+4\cos 4x$$

(v) $y = \sin 2x \cos 3x$

$$\frac{dy}{dx} = (2\cos 2x)\cos 3x$$

$$+ \sin 2x(-3\sin 3x)$$

$$= 2\cos 2x \cos 3x - 3\sin 2x \sin 3x.$$

4. (i) $y = \cos 3x - \sin 5x$

$$\frac{dy}{dx} = -3\sin 3x - 5\cos 5x$$

at $x = \frac{\pi}{2}$

$$\frac{dy}{dx} = -3\sin\left(3\frac{\pi}{2}\right) - 5\cos\left(5\frac{\pi}{2}\right)$$

$$\boxed{\sin\frac{3\pi}{2} = -1}$$

and $\frac{dy}{dx} = -3(-1) = 3.$

(ii) $y = \sin 2x \cos 3x$

$$\frac{dy}{dx} = (2\cos 2x)\cos 3x$$

$$+ \sin 2x(-3\sin 3x)$$

$$= 2\cos 2x \cos 3x - 3\sin 2x \sin 3x$$

at $x = \frac{\pi}{2}$

$$2\cos \pi \cos 3\frac{\pi}{2} - 3\sin \pi \sin 3\frac{\pi}{2}$$

$$\cos \pi = -1, \quad \cos 3\frac{\pi}{2} = 0$$

$$\frac{dy}{dx} = 2\cos 2\left(\frac{\pi}{2}\right)\cos 3\left(\frac{\pi}{2}\right)$$

$$-3\sin 2\left(\frac{\pi}{2}\right)\sin 3\left(\frac{\pi}{2}\right)$$

$$\sin \pi = 0, \sin\frac{3\pi}{2} = -1$$

$$\frac{dy}{dx} = 2(-1)(0) - 3(0)(-1)$$

$$= 0 - 0 = 0$$

(iii) $y = e^{-3x}\cos 5x + \sin 4x$

$$\frac{dy}{dx} = (-3e^{-3x})\cos 5x$$

$$+ e^{-3x}(-5\sin 5x) + 4\cos 4x$$

$$= -3e^{-3x}\cos 5x - 5e^{-3x}\sin 5x$$

$$+4\cos 4x$$

at $x = \frac{\pi}{2}$

$$\frac{dy}{dx} = -3e^{-\frac{3\pi}{2}}\cos\frac{5\pi}{2}$$

$$-5e^{-\frac{3\pi}{2}}\sin\frac{5\pi}{2} + 4\cos\frac{4\pi}{2}$$

$$\cos\frac{5\pi}{2} = 0 \quad \sin\frac{5\pi}{2} = 1$$

$$\cos 2\pi = 1$$

$$\frac{dy}{dx} = -3e^{-\frac{3\pi}{2}}(0) - 5e^{-\frac{3\pi}{2}}(1) + 4(1)$$

$$= -5e^{-\frac{3\pi}{2}} + 4$$

$$= -5(8.983291 \times 10^{-3}) + 4$$

$$= 3.9551.$$

5.   (i) $y = 3e^{-3x} + 5\cos 2x$

$$\frac{dy}{dx} = 3(-3e^{-3x}) + 5(-2\sin 2x)$$

$$= -9e^{-3x} - 10\sin 2x$$

(ii) $y = e^{-x} + 3e^x, \quad \dfrac{dy}{dx} = e^{-x} + 3e^x$

(iii) $y = 4(e^x - e^{-x}) = 4e^x - 4e^{-x}$

$$\frac{dy}{dx} = 4e^x - 4(-e^{-x})$$

$$= 4e^x + 4e^{-x}$$

(iv) $y = \sin x \cos 2x$

$$\frac{dy}{dx} = (\cos x)\cos 2x$$

$$+ \sin x(-2\sin 2x)$$

$$= \cos x \cos 2x - 2\sin x \sin 2x$$

(v) $y = -\ln x^2 + \dfrac{1}{x^3} = -\ln x^2 + x^{-3}$

Let $u = -\ln x^2 = -\ln W$

where $W = x^2$

$$\frac{du}{dW} = -\frac{1}{W} \qquad \frac{dW}{du} = 2x$$

$$\frac{du}{dx} = \frac{du}{dW} \cdot \frac{dW}{dx} = \left(-\frac{1}{W}\right)(2x)$$

$$= \left(-\frac{1}{x^2}\right)(2x) = -\frac{2}{x}$$

$$\frac{dy}{dx} = \left(-\frac{2}{x}\right) - 3x^{-4} = -\frac{2}{x} - \frac{3}{x^4}$$

(vi) $y = e^{-2x} + \cos 2x$

$$\frac{dy}{dx} = -2e^{-2x} + (-2\sin 2x)$$

$$= -2e^{-2x} - 2\sin 2x$$

(vii) $y = 3e^{-x}\ln x - \cos(-x)$

$$\frac{dy}{dx} = 3(-e^x)\ln x + 3e^{-x}\left(\frac{1}{x}\right)$$

$$-(-\sin(-x)(-1))$$

$$= -3e^{-x}\ln x + \frac{3e^{-x}}{x} - \sin(-x)$$

$$= -3e^{-x}\ln x + \frac{3e^{-x}}{x} + \sin x$$

Note

$\cos(-x) = \cos x$ an even function.

Alternatively

$\sin(-x) = -\sin x$ an odd function.

$$y = 3e^{-x}\ln x - \cos(-x)$$

$$= 3e^{-x}\ln x - \cos x$$

$$\frac{dy}{dx} = -3e^{-x}\ln x + \frac{3e^{-x}}{x} + \sin x.$$

(viii) $y = \sin 3x \cos 5x$

$$\frac{dy}{dx} = (3\cos 3x)\cos 5x$$

$$+ \sin 3x(-5\sin 5x)$$

$$= 3\cos 3x \cos 5x$$

$$-5\sin 3x \sin 5x$$

(ix) $y = e^{-3x}\cos 4x - e^{-x}\sin x$

$$\frac{dy}{dx} = (-3e^{-3x})\cos 4x$$

$$+e^{-3x}(-4\sin 4x)$$

$$-(-e^{-x}\sin x) - e^{-x}\cos x$$

$$= -3e^{-3x}\cos 4x - 4e^{-3x}\sin 4x$$

$$+e^{-x}\sin x - e^{-x}\cos x$$

(x) $y = 5\sin x \ln \dfrac{1}{x}$

$$\frac{dy}{dx} = (5\cos x)\ln\frac{1}{x}$$

$$+5\sin x \left(\frac{1}{\frac{1}{x}}\right)(-x^{-2})$$

$$= 5\cos x \ln\frac{1}{x} - 5\frac{\sin x}{x}.$$

Note

$$u = \ln \frac{1}{x} \qquad W = \frac{1}{x} = x^{-1}$$

$$u = \ln W \qquad \frac{dW}{dx} = -x^{-2} = -\frac{1}{x^2}$$

$$\frac{du}{dW} = \frac{1}{W}$$

$$\frac{du}{dx} = \frac{du}{dW} \cdot \frac{dW}{dx} = \frac{1}{W}\left(-\frac{1}{x^2}\right)$$

$$\frac{dy}{dx} = \frac{1}{\frac{1}{x}}\left(-\frac{1}{x^2}\right) = -\frac{1}{x}$$

the derivative of $\ln \frac{1}{x}$ is $-\frac{1}{x}$.

6. The derivatives of exercise 1 are:-

(i) $\dfrac{dy}{dx} = 2x \sin x + x^2 \cos x$ at $x = \pi$,

$$\frac{dy}{dx} = -\pi^2 = -9.87$$

(ii) $\dfrac{dy}{dx} = \cos x - x \sin x$ at $x = \pi$,

$$\frac{dy}{dx} = -1$$

(iii) $\dfrac{dy}{dx} = \cos^2 x - \sin^2 x$ at $x = \pi$,

$$\frac{dy}{dx} = 1$$

(iv) $\dfrac{dy}{dx} = \cos x \ln x + \dfrac{\sin x}{x}$ at $x = \pi$,

$$\frac{dy}{dx} = -\ln \pi = -1.15$$

(v) $\dfrac{dy}{dx} = -\sin x \ln x + \dfrac{\cos x}{x}$ at $x = \pi$,

$$\frac{dy}{dx} = -\frac{1}{\pi} = -0.318$$

(vi) $\dfrac{dy}{dx} = \ln x + 1$,   at $x = \pi$,

$$\frac{dy}{dx} = \ln \pi + 1 = 2.145$$

(vii) $\dfrac{dy}{dx} = e^x \ln x + \dfrac{e^x}{x}$,   at $x = \pi$,

$$\frac{dy}{dx} = e^\pi \ln \pi + \frac{e^\pi}{\pi} = 33.86$$

(viii) $\dfrac{dy}{dx} = 2x \ln x + \dfrac{x^2}{x}$,   at $x = \pi$,

$$\frac{dy}{dx} = 2\pi \ln \pi = 39.5$$

(ix) $\dfrac{dy}{dx} = e^x \sin x + e^x \cos x$,   at $x = \pi$,

$$\frac{dy}{dx} = -e^\pi = -23.14$$

(x) $\dfrac{dy}{dx} = 3x^2 \ln x + x^2$,   at $x = \pi$,

$$\frac{dy}{dx} = 3\pi^2 \ln \pi + \pi^2 = 43.8$$

(xi) $\dfrac{dy}{dx} = e^x + xe^x$,   at $x = \pi$,

$$\frac{dy}{dx} = e^\pi + \pi e^\pi = 95.84$$

(xii) $\dfrac{dy}{dx} = nx^{n-1} \ln x + x^{n-1}$,   at $x = \pi$,

$$\frac{dy}{dx} = n\pi^{n-1} \ln \pi.$$

7. The derivatives of 2 (i) and 2 (ii) are:-

(i) $\dfrac{dy}{dx} = e^x + \sin x + \cos x - \dfrac{1}{x}$

(ii) $\dfrac{dy}{dx} = 1 + e^x + \cos x - \sin x + \dfrac{1}{x}$

at $x = \dfrac{\pi}{2}$

(i) $\dfrac{dy}{dx} = e^{\frac{\pi}{2}} + \sin \dfrac{\pi}{2} + \cos \dfrac{\pi}{2} - \dfrac{1}{\frac{\pi}{2}}$

$$= e^{\frac{\pi}{2}} + 1 + 0 - \frac{2}{\pi}$$

$$= 4.81 + 1 - 0.637 = 5.173$$

(ii) $\dfrac{dy}{dx} = 1 + e^{\frac{\pi}{2}} + \cos \dfrac{\pi}{2} - \sin \dfrac{\pi}{2} + \dfrac{2}{\pi}$

$$= 1 + 4.81 + 0 - 1 + 0.637 = 5.447$$

8. The derivatives of exercise 3 are:-

(i) $\dfrac{dy}{dx} = \dfrac{e^{3x}}{x} + 3e^{3x}\ln x$

(ii) $\dfrac{dy}{dx} = -3\sin 3x - 5\cos 5x$

(iii) $\dfrac{dy}{dx} = 15x^4 + 4\sin 4x$

(iv) $\dfrac{dy}{dx} = -3e^{-3x}\cos 5x$
$-5e^{-3x}\sin 5x + 4\cos 4x$

(v) $\dfrac{dy}{dx} = 2\cos 2x\cos 3x$
$-3\sin 2x\sin 3x.$

(a)

(i) $\dfrac{dy}{dx} = \dfrac{e^{\frac{3\pi}{2}}}{\frac{\pi}{2}} + 3e^{\frac{3\pi}{2}}\ln\dfrac{\pi}{2}$

$= 2\dfrac{e^{\frac{3\pi}{2}}}{\pi} + 3e^{\frac{3\pi}{2}}\ln\dfrac{\pi}{2}$

$= 70.87 + 333.95(0.4515827)$

$= 221.7$

(ii) $\dfrac{dy}{dx} = -3\sin 3\dfrac{\pi}{2} - 5\cos 5\dfrac{\pi}{2} = 3$

(iii) $\dfrac{dy}{dx} = 15\left(\dfrac{\pi}{2}\right)^4 + 4\sin 4\dfrac{\pi}{2} = 91.3$

(iv) $\dfrac{dy}{dx} = -3e^{-\frac{3\pi}{2}}\cos\dfrac{5\pi}{2}$
$-5e^{-\frac{3\pi}{2}}\sin 5\dfrac{\pi}{2}$
$= 4\cos\dfrac{4\pi}{2}$
$= -0.045 + 4 = 3.955$

(v) $\dfrac{dy}{dx} = 2\cos\dfrac{2\pi}{2}\cos\dfrac{3\pi}{2}$
$-3\sin\dfrac{2\pi}{2}\sin\dfrac{3\pi}{2}$
$= -2(0) - 3(0)(-1) = 0.$

(b)

(i) $\dfrac{dy}{dx} = \dfrac{e^{\frac{3\pi}{4}}}{\frac{\pi}{4}} + 3e^{\frac{3\pi}{4}}\ln\dfrac{\pi}{4}$
$= 13.43 - 7.65 = 5.78$

(ii) $\dfrac{dy}{dx} = -3\sin 3\dfrac{\pi}{4} - 5\cos 5\dfrac{\pi}{4}$
$= -3\dfrac{1}{\sqrt{2}} - 5\left(-\dfrac{1}{\sqrt{2}}\right)$
$= -\dfrac{3}{\sqrt{2}} + \dfrac{5}{\sqrt{2}} = \dfrac{2}{\sqrt{2}}\dfrac{\sqrt{2}}{\sqrt{2}} = 1.414$

(iii) $\dfrac{dy}{dx} = 15\left(\dfrac{\pi}{4}\right)^4 + 4\sin 4\dfrac{\pi}{4} = 5.71$

(iv) $\dfrac{dy}{dx} = -3e^{\frac{-3\pi}{4}}\cos 5\dfrac{\pi}{4}$
$-5e^{\frac{-3\pi}{4}}\sin 5\dfrac{\pi}{4} + 4\cos\dfrac{4\pi}{4}$
$= -3(0.0947802)(-0.707)$
$-5(0.0947802)(-0.707) - 4$
$= 0.2 + 0.3351 - 4 = -3.47$

(v) $\dfrac{dy}{dx} = 2\cos 2\dfrac{\pi}{4}\cos 3\dfrac{\pi}{4}$
$-3\sin 2\dfrac{\pi}{4}\sin 3\dfrac{\pi}{4}$
$= 2(0)(-0.707) - 3(1)(0.707)$
$= -2.121.$

9.

(i) $\dfrac{dy}{dx} = -9e^{-3x} - 10\sin 2x,$
$x = 0, \quad \dfrac{dy}{dx} = -9$

(ii) $\dfrac{dy}{dx} = e^{-x} + 3e^x, \quad x = 0,$
$\dfrac{dy}{dx} = 1 + 3 = 4$

(iii) $\dfrac{dy}{dx} = 4e^x + 4e^{-x},$
$x = 0, \quad \dfrac{dy}{dx} = 4 + 4 = 8$

(iv) $\dfrac{dy}{dx} = \cos x \cos 2x - 2 \sin x \sin 2x,$

$\quad x = 0, \quad \dfrac{dy}{dx} = 1$

(vi) $\dfrac{dy}{dx} = -2e^{-2x} - 2 \sin 2x$

$\quad$ at $x = 0, \quad \dfrac{dy}{dx} = -2 - 0 = -2$

(viii) $\dfrac{dy}{dx} = 3 \cos 3x \cos 5x$

$\qquad -5 \sin 3x \sin 5x \quad$ at $x = 0$

$\qquad = 3 \cos 0 \cos 0 - 5 \sin 0 \sin 0 = 3$

(ix) $\dfrac{dy}{dx} = -3e^{-3x} \cos 4x - 4e^{-3x} \sin 4x$

$\qquad + e^{-x} \sin x - e^{-x} \cos x$ at $x = 0$

$\quad \dfrac{dy}{dx} = -3(1)(1) - 4(1)(0) + 1(0)$

$\qquad -(1)(1) = -3 - 1 = -4.$

10. $y = 3 \sin^2 3x$ simplify by replacing $W = 3x$

$\quad y = 3 \sin^2 W \qquad \dfrac{dW}{dx} = 3$

$\quad$ simplify by replacing $\sin W = u$

$\quad \dfrac{du}{dW} = \cos W$

$\quad y = 3u^2$

$\quad \dfrac{dy}{du} = 3(2u) = 6u$

$\quad \dfrac{dy}{dx} = \dfrac{dy}{du} \dfrac{du}{dW} \dfrac{dW}{dx} = 6u(\cos W)(3)$

$\qquad = 18 \sin W \cos 3x$

$\qquad = 18 \sin 3x \cos 3x$

$\quad \dfrac{dy}{dx} = 18 \sin 3x \cos 3x.$

11. $y = e^{-\frac{1}{t}}$

$\quad$ Let $u = -\dfrac{1}{t} = -t^{-1},$

$\quad \dfrac{du}{dt} = t^{-2} = \dfrac{1}{t^2} \quad y = e^u$

$\dfrac{dy}{du} = e^u \qquad \dfrac{dy}{dt} = \dfrac{dy}{du} \dfrac{du}{dt}$

$\qquad = e^u \dfrac{t}{t^2} = \dfrac{1}{t^2} e^{-\frac{1}{t}}$

$\dfrac{dy}{dt} = \dfrac{1}{t^2} e^{-\frac{1}{t}}$

12. $y = e^{-\ln x}$

$\quad$ Let $u = -\ln x, \qquad \dfrac{du}{dx} = -\dfrac{1}{x}$

$\quad y = e^u \qquad \dfrac{dy}{du} = e^u$

$\quad \dfrac{dy}{dx} = \dfrac{dy}{du} \dfrac{du}{dx}$

$\qquad = e^u \left(-\dfrac{1}{x}\right) = e^{-\ln x} \left(-\dfrac{1}{x}\right)$

$\quad \dfrac{dy}{dx} = -\dfrac{1}{x} e^{-\ln x}.$

13. $\quad$ (i) $y = \dfrac{\sin x}{\ln x}$

$\quad \dfrac{dy}{dx} = \dfrac{(\cos x) \ln x - \sin x \left(\dfrac{1}{x}\right)}{(\ln x)^2}$

$\qquad = \dfrac{\cos x \ln x - \dfrac{\sin x}{x}}{(\ln x)^2}$

$\quad$ (ii) $y = \dfrac{x^2}{\cos x}$

$\quad \dfrac{dy}{dx} = \dfrac{2x \cos x - x^2(-\sin x)}{\cos^2 x}$

$\qquad = \dfrac{2x \cos x + x^2 \sin x}{\cos^2 x}$

$\quad$ (iii) $y = \dfrac{1 - \sin 2x}{1 + \sin 2x}$

$\quad \dfrac{dy}{dx} = \dfrac{\{(-2 \cos 2x)(1 + \sin 2x) \\ -(1 - \sin 2x)(2 \cos 2x)\}}{(1 + \sin 2x)^2}$

$\qquad = \dfrac{\{-2 \cos 2x - 2 \cos 2x \sin 2x \\ -2 \cos 2x + 2 \sin 2x \cos 2x\}}{(1 + \sin 2x)^2}$

$\qquad = -\dfrac{4 \cos 2x}{(1 + \sin 2x)^2}$

(iv) $y = \dfrac{1 + \tan x}{x^3}$

$\dfrac{dy}{dx} = \dfrac{(\sec^2 x)x^3 - (1 + \tan x)(3x^2)}{x^6}$

$= \dfrac{x^3 \sec^2 x - 3x^2(1 + \tan x)}{x^6}$

where $\dfrac{d}{dx}(\tan x) = \sec^2 x$

(v) $y = \dfrac{1 - x^2}{1 + x}$

$= \dfrac{(1 - x)(1 + x)}{(1 + x)}$

$= 1 - x$

$\dfrac{dy}{dx} = -1.$

14.

(i) $y = x^2 \qquad \dfrac{dy}{dx} = 2x$

(ii) $y = x \sec x$

$\dfrac{dy}{dx} = (1) \sec x + x \sec x \tan x$

$= \sec x + x \sec x \tan x$

(iii) $y = \dfrac{x}{\sin x}$

$\dfrac{dy}{dx} = \dfrac{1 . \sin x - x \cos x}{\sin^2 x}$

$= \dfrac{\sin x - x \cos x}{\sin^2 x}$

(iv) $y = e^{x^2}$

$\dfrac{dy}{dx} = 2x . e^{x^2}$

(v) $y = e^{3x} \cos 2x$

$\dfrac{dy}{dx} = 3e^{3x} \cos 2x - 2e^{3x} \sin 2x$

(vi) $y = \sin^2 x \qquad \dfrac{dy}{dx} = 2 \sin x \cos x$

(vii) $y = \cos^2 2x$

$\dfrac{dy}{dx} = -4 \cos 2x \sin 2x$

(viii) $y = \dfrac{1 + x}{1 - x}$

$\dfrac{dy}{dx} = \dfrac{(1 - x) - (1 + x)(-1)}{(1 - x^2)}$

$= \dfrac{2}{(1 - x)^2}$

(ix) $y = \dfrac{e^{2x}}{1 + 2x}$

$\dfrac{dy}{dx} = \dfrac{2e^{2x}(1 + 2x) - e^{2x}(2)}{(1 + 2x)^2}$

$= \dfrac{2e^{2x} + 4e^{2x}x - 2e^{2x}}{(1 + 2x)^2}$

$= \dfrac{4xe^{2x}}{(1 + 2x)^2}.$

(x) $y = 1 - e^x$

$\dfrac{dy}{dx} = \dfrac{(-e^x)(1 + e^x) - (1 - e^x)(e^x)}{(1 + e^x)^2}$

$\dfrac{dy}{dx} = \dfrac{-e^x - e^{2x} - e^x + e^{2x}}{(1 + e^x)^2}$

$= \dfrac{-2e^x}{(1 + e^x)^2}.$

Solution 3

1. (i) $y = 3\sin 2x - 5\cos 2x$

$$\frac{dy}{dx} = 6\cos 2x + 10\sin 2x$$

$$\frac{d^2y}{dx^2} = -12\sin 2x + 20\cos 2x$$

(ii) $y = 3x^3 - 2x^2 + x - 1$

$$\frac{dy}{dx} = 9x^2 - 4x + 1$$

$$\frac{d^2y}{dx^2} = 18x - 4$$

(iii) $y = 4e^{-2x} - 5e^{3x}$

$$\frac{dy}{dx} = -8e^{-2x} - 15e^{3x}$$

$$\frac{d^2y}{dx^2} = 16e^{-2x} - 45e^{3x}$$

(iv) $y = e^{3x} - \cos 3x + \sin 3x$

$$\frac{dy}{dx} = 3e^{3x} + 3\sin 3x + 3\cos 3x$$

$$\frac{d^2y}{dx^2} = 9e^{3x} + 9\cos 3x - 9\sin 3x$$

(v) $y = 5\ln x + x\sin 2x$

$$\frac{dy}{dx} = \frac{5}{x} + \sin 2x + 2x\cos 2x$$

$$\frac{d^2y}{dx^2} = -\frac{5}{x^2} + 2\cos 2x + 2\cos 2x$$
$$-4x\sin 2x.$$

2. (i) $x = 5t^5 - 4t^4 + 3t^3 - 2t^2 + t - 1$

$$\frac{dx}{dt} = 25t^4 - 16t^3 + 9t^2 - 4t + 1$$

$$\frac{d^2x}{dt^2} = 100t^3 - 48t^2 + 18t - 4$$

(ii) $x = \sin t - \cos t \quad \dfrac{dx}{dt} = \cos t + \sin t$

$$\frac{d^2x}{dt^2} = -\sin t + \cos t$$

(iii) $x = e^t \sin 2t$

$$\frac{dx}{dt} = e^t \sin 2t + e^t 2\cos 2t$$

$$\frac{d^2x}{dt^2} = e^t \sin 2t + 2e^t \cos 2t$$
$$+2e^t \cos 2t - 4e^t \sin 2t$$
$$= -3e^t \sin 2t + 4e^t \cos 2t$$

(iv) $x = \dfrac{e^{2t}}{1+t}$

$$\frac{dx}{dt} = \frac{2e^{2t}(1+t) - e^{2t} \cdot 1}{(1+t)^2}$$

$$= \frac{2e^{2t}}{(1+t)^2}(1+t) - \frac{e^{2t}}{(1+t)^2}$$

$$= \frac{2e^{2t}}{1+t} - \frac{e^{2t}}{(1+t)^2}$$

$$\frac{d^2y}{dt^2} = \frac{4e^{2t}(1+t) - 2e^{2t}}{(1+t)^2}$$

$$-\frac{2e^{2t}(1+t)^2 - e^{2t}2(1+t)}{(1+t)^4}$$

$$= \frac{4e^{2t}}{(1+t)} - \frac{2e^{2t}}{(1+t)^2}$$
$$-\frac{2e^{2t}}{(1+t)^2} + \frac{2e^{2t}}{(1+t)^3}$$

(v) $x = e^{\sin t} \quad \dfrac{dx}{dt} = \cos t\, e^{\sin t}$

$$\frac{d^2x}{dt^2} = -\sin t\, e^{\sin t} + \cos^2 t\, e^{\sin t}.$$

3. (i) $v = \dfrac{dx}{dt} = 25t^4 - 16t^3 + 9t^2 - 4t + 1$

at $t = 0$ $v = 1$ m/s

$a = \dfrac{d^2x}{dt^2} = 100t^3 - 48t^2 + 18t - 4$

$a = -4$ m/s^2

(ii) $v = \dfrac{dx}{dt} = \cos t + \sin t$

at $t = 0$ $v = 1$ m/s

$a = \dfrac{d^2x}{dt^2} = -\sin t + \cos t$

$= 1$ m/s^2

(iii) $v = \dfrac{dx}{dt} = e^t \sin 2t + 2e^t \cos 2t$

at $t = 0$ $v = 2$ m/s

$a = \dfrac{d^2x}{dt^2} = -3e^t \sin 2t + 4e^t \cos 2t$

at $t = 0$ $a = 4$ m/s^2

(iv) $v = \dfrac{dx}{dt} = \dfrac{2e^{2t}}{1+t} - \dfrac{e^{2t}}{(1+t)^2}$

at $t = 0$ $v = 2 - 1 = 1$ m/s

$a = \dfrac{d^2x}{dt^2} = \dfrac{4e^{2t}}{1+t} - \dfrac{2e^{2t}}{(1+t)^2}$

$\qquad - \dfrac{2e^{2t}}{(1+t)^2} + \dfrac{2e^{2t}}{(1+t)^3}$

$\qquad = 4 - 2 - 2 + 2$

$a = 2$ m/s^2.

(v) $v = \dfrac{dx}{dt} = \cos t e^{\sin t}$

at $t = 0$ $v = 1$ m/s

$a = \dfrac{d^2x}{dt^2} = -\sin t e^{\sin t} + \cos^2 t e^{\sin t}$

$a = 1$ m/s^2.

$a = \dfrac{d^2x}{dt^2} = -\sin t e^{\sin t} + \cos^2 t e^{\sin t}$

$a = 1$ m/s^2.

4. (i) $y = \dfrac{x^2 + 1}{x - 1}$

$\dfrac{dy}{dx} = \dfrac{2x(x-1) - (x^2+1)(1)}{(x-1)^2}$

$\qquad = \dfrac{2x^2 - 2x - x^2 - 1}{(x-1)^2}$

$\qquad = \dfrac{x^2 - 2x - 1}{(x-1)^2}$

$\dfrac{dy}{dx} = \dfrac{x^2 - 2x - 1}{(x-1)^2}$

$\dfrac{d^2y}{dx^2} = \dfrac{\{(2x-2)(x-1)^2 - (x^2-2x-1)2(x-1)\}}{(x-1)^4}$

$\qquad = \dfrac{2}{x-1} - \dfrac{2(x^2-2x-1)}{(x-1)^3}$

$\dfrac{d^2y}{dx^2} = \dfrac{2}{x-1} - \dfrac{2(x^2-2x-1)}{(x-1)^3}$

(ii) $y = x^2 \sin x$

$\dfrac{dy}{dx} = 2x \sin x + x^2 \cos x$

$\dfrac{d^2y}{dx^2} = 2 \sin x + 2x \cos x$

$\qquad\qquad +2x \cos x - x^2 \sin x$

$\qquad = 2 \sin x + 4x \cos x - x^2 \sin x$

(iii) $y = \dfrac{\cos x}{e^{3x}}$

$\dfrac{dy}{dx} = \dfrac{-\sin x e^{3x} - \cos x (3e^{3x})}{e^{6x}}$

$\qquad = -e^{3x} \dfrac{(\sin x + 3 \cos x)}{e^{6x}}$

$\qquad = -\dfrac{\sin x + 3 \cos x}{e^{3x}}$

$\dfrac{d^2y}{dx^2} = \dfrac{\{-(\cos x - 3 \sin x)e^{3x}}{e^{6x}}$
$\qquad\qquad\qquad +(\sin x + 3 \cos x)3e^{3x}\}$

$\qquad = \dfrac{3 \sin x + 9 \cos x - \cos x + 3 \sin x}{e^{3x}}$

$\qquad = \dfrac{6 \sin x + 8 \cos x}{e^{3x}}$

$\dfrac{d^2y}{dx^2} = \dfrac{6 \sin x + 8 \cos x}{e^{3x}}$

(iv) $y = \dfrac{\ln x}{(1+x)^2}$ $y = \ln x(1+x)^{-2}$

$\dfrac{dy}{dx} = \dfrac{1}{x}(1+x)^{-2} + \ln x[-2(1+x)^{-3}]$

$\quad = \dfrac{(1+x)^{-2}}{x} - 2(1+x)^{-3}\ln x$

$\quad = x^{-1}(1+x)^{-2} - 2(1+x)^{-3}\ln x$

$\dfrac{d^2y}{dx^2} = -x^{-2}(1+x)^{-2} + x^{-1}$

$\quad \times [-2(1+x)^{-3}] + 6(1+x)^{-4}\ln x$

$-2(1+x)^{-3}\dfrac{1}{x} = -\dfrac{1}{x^2(1+x)^2}$

$-\dfrac{2}{x(1+x)^3} + \dfrac{6\ln x}{(1+x)^4} - \dfrac{2}{x(1+x)^3}$

(v) $y = \dfrac{e^x}{1+x}$ $y = e^x(1+x)^{-1}$

$\dfrac{dy}{dx} = e^x(1+x)^{-1}$

$\quad + e^x[-(1+x)^{-2}] = \dfrac{e^x}{1+x} - \dfrac{e^x}{(1+x)^2}$

$\dfrac{dy}{dx} = e^x(1+x)^{-1} - e^x(1+x)^{-2}$

$\dfrac{d^2y}{dx^2} = e^x(1+x)^{-1} + e^x[-(1+x)^{-2}]$

$\quad - e^x(1+x)^{-2} - e^x[-2(1+x)^{-3}]$

$\quad = \dfrac{e^x}{1+x} - \dfrac{e^x}{(1+x)^2}$

$\quad \quad - \dfrac{e^x}{(1+x)^2} + \dfrac{2e^x}{(1+x)^3}$

$\quad = \dfrac{e^x}{1+x} - \dfrac{2e^x}{(1+x)^2} + \dfrac{2e^x}{(1+x)^3}.$

5.   (i) $y = \sin x \cos 2x$

$\dfrac{dy}{dx} = \cos x \cos 2x - 2\sin x \sin 2x$

$\dfrac{d^2y}{dx^2} = -\sin x \cos 2x$

$\quad - 2\cos x \sin 2x - 2\cos x \sin 2x$

$\quad - 2\sin x(2\cos 2x)$

$\dfrac{d^2y}{dx^2} = -\sin x \cos 2x$

$\quad -2\cos x \sin 2x - 2\cos x \sin 2x$

$\quad -4\sin x \cos 2x$ at $x = \pi/2$

$\dfrac{d^2y}{dx^2} = -\sin\dfrac{\pi}{2}\cos 2\left(\dfrac{\pi}{2}\right)$

$\quad -2\cos\dfrac{\pi}{2}\sin 2\left(\dfrac{\pi}{2}\right)$

$\quad -2\cos\left(\dfrac{\pi}{2}\right)\sin 2\left(\dfrac{\pi}{2}\right)$

$\quad -4\sin\dfrac{\pi}{2}\cos 2\left(\dfrac{\pi}{2}\right)$

$\quad = -1(-1) - 2(0)(0) - 2(0)(0)$

$\quad -4(1)(-1) = 1 + 4 = 5$

$\dfrac{d^2y}{dx^2} = 5$

(ii) $y = e^x \tan\dfrac{x}{2}$

$\dfrac{dy}{dx} = e^x \tan\dfrac{x}{2} + e^x\dfrac{1}{2}\sec^2\dfrac{x}{2}$

$\dfrac{d^2y}{dx^2} = e^x \tan\dfrac{x}{2} + e^x\dfrac{1}{2}\cdot\sec^2\dfrac{x}{2}$

$\quad + \dfrac{e^x}{2}\sec^2\dfrac{x}{2} + \dfrac{e^x}{2}2\sec^2\dfrac{x}{2}\tan\dfrac{x}{2}$

at $x = \dfrac{\pi}{2}$,

$\dfrac{d^2y}{dx^2} = e^{\frac{\pi}{2}}\tan\dfrac{\pi}{4} + \dfrac{1}{2}e^{\frac{\pi}{2}}\sec^2\dfrac{\pi}{4}$

$\quad + \dfrac{1}{2}e^{\frac{\pi}{2}}\sec^2\dfrac{\pi}{4}\sec^2\dfrac{\pi}{4}\tan\dfrac{\pi}{4}$

$\quad = e^{\frac{\pi}{2}} + e^{\frac{\pi}{2}} + e^{\frac{\pi}{2}} + e^{\frac{\pi}{2}}\times 2\times 1$

$\quad = 5e^{\frac{\pi}{2}} = 24.05$

(iii) $y = x^2\ln x$ $\dfrac{dy}{dx} = 2x\ln x + x^2\dfrac{1}{x}$

$\quad = 2x\ln x + x$

$\dfrac{d^2y}{dx^2} = 2\ln x + 2x\dfrac{1}{x} + 1$

$\dfrac{d^2y}{dx^2} = 2\ln x + 3$

at $x = \dfrac{\pi}{2}$

$\dfrac{d^2y}{dx^2} = 2\ln\dfrac{\pi}{2} + 3 = 3.903$

$$\frac{d^2y}{dx^2} = 3.903$$

(iv) $y = 5\cos 3x - 4\sin 4x$

$$\frac{dy}{dx} = -15\sin 3x - 16\cos 4x$$

$$\frac{d^2y}{dx^2} = -45\cos 3x + 64\sin 4x$$

at $x = \dfrac{\pi}{2}$

$$\frac{d^2y}{dx^2} = -45\cos 3\left(\frac{\pi}{2}\right)$$

$$+64\sin 4\left(\frac{\pi}{2}\right)$$

$$= 0.$$

6. $y = 3\cos 5kx \qquad \dfrac{dy}{dx} = -15k\sin 5kx$

$$\frac{d^2y}{dx^2} = -75k^2\cos 5kx$$

at $x = \dfrac{\pi}{k}$

$$\frac{d^2y}{dx^2} = -75k^2\cos 5k\left(\frac{\pi}{k}\right)$$

$$= -75k^2\cos 5\pi = 75k^2.$$

7. $\dfrac{dy}{dx}$ is the gradient of a function at any point x, $\dfrac{d^2y}{dx^2}$ is the rate of change of the gradient with respect to x at any point x.

$\dfrac{dy}{dx}$ can be positive, negative or zero

$\dfrac{d^2y}{dx^2}$ can be positive, negative or zero

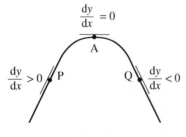

Fig. 73

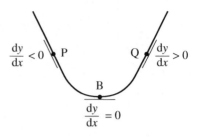

Fig. 74

$\dfrac{d^2y}{dx^2} < 0$ if the function has a maximum

$\dfrac{d^2y}{dx^2} > 0$ if the function has a minimum.

8. $y = e^x \sin 2x$

$$\frac{dy}{dx} = e^x \sin 2x + 2e^x \cos 2x$$

$$\frac{d^2y}{dx^2} = e^x \sin 2x + 2e^x \cos 2x$$

$$+2e^x \cos 2x - 2 \times 2e^x \sin 2x$$

$$= e^x \sin 2x + 4e^x \cos 2x - 4e^x \sin 2x$$

$$= 4e^x \cos 2x - 3e^x \sin 2x.$$

9. $ye^{-2x}\cos x$

$$\frac{dy}{dx} = -2e^{-2x}\cos x + e^{-2x}(-\sin x)$$

$$\frac{d^2y}{dx^2} = 4e^{-2x}\cos x + 2e^{-2x}\sin x$$

$$+2e^{-2x}\sin x - e^{-2x}\cos x$$

$$= 3e^{-2x}\cos x + 4e^{-2x}\sin x.$$

10. $s = 3t^3 - t^2 + t + 7$

$$\frac{ds}{dt} = 9t^2 - 2t + 1 = v \text{ at } t = 5,$$

$$v = 225 - 10 + 1 = 116 \text{ m/s}$$

$$\frac{d^2s}{dt^2} = 18t - 2 = a$$

at $t = 5$ $a = 90 - 2 = 88 \text{ m/s}^2$.

11. (i) $y = \dfrac{1 + \cos\theta}{\sin\theta}$

$$\frac{dy}{d\theta} = \frac{\{(-\sin\theta)(\sin\theta) -(1+\cos\theta)\cos\theta\}}{\sin^2\theta}$$

$$= \frac{(-\sin^2\theta) - \cos\theta - \cos^2\theta}{\sin^2\theta}$$

$$= -\frac{(\sin^2\theta + \cos^2\theta) + \cos\theta}{\sin^2\theta}$$

$$= -\frac{1 + \cos\theta}{\sin^2\theta}$$

$$\frac{d^2y}{d\theta^2} = \frac{\sin\theta\sin^2\theta +(1+\cos\theta)2\sin\theta\cos\theta}{\sin^4\theta}$$

$$= \frac{\sin^2\theta}{\sin^3\theta} + \frac{2(1+\cos\theta)\cos\theta}{\sin^3\theta}$$

$$= \frac{1}{\sin\theta} + \frac{2\cos\theta}{\sin^3\theta}(1+\cos\theta)$$

(ii) $y = \dfrac{\sin x}{e^{2x}}$

$$\frac{dy}{dx} = \frac{\cos x e^{2x} - \sin x(2e^{2x})}{e^{4x}}$$

$$= \frac{\cos x - 2\sin x}{e^{2x}}$$

$$\frac{d^2y}{dx^2} = \frac{(-\sin x - 2\cos x)e^{2x} -(\cos x - 2\sin x)2e^{2x}}{e^{4x}}$$

$$= \frac{-\sin x - 2\cos x - 2\cos x + 4\sin x}{e^{2x}}$$

$$= \frac{3\sin x - 4\cos x}{e^{2x}}$$

(iii) $y = \cot\theta \quad y = \dfrac{\cos\theta}{\sin\theta}$

$$\frac{dy}{d\theta} = \frac{-\sin\theta\sin\theta - \cos\theta\cos\theta}{\sin^2\theta}$$

$$= -\frac{(\sin^2\theta + \cos^2\theta)}{\sin^2\theta}$$

$$= -\frac{1}{\sin^2\theta} = -\text{cosec}^2\theta$$

$$\frac{dy}{d\theta} = -\text{cosec}^2\theta$$

$$\frac{d^2y}{d\theta^2} = -2\text{cosec}\theta(-\text{cosec}\theta\cot\theta)$$

$$= 2\text{cosec}^2\theta\cot\theta.$$

12. If $i = I_m \sin\left(2\pi ft - \dfrac{\pi}{3}\right)$

$$\frac{di}{dt} = 2\pi f I_m \cos\left(2\pi ft - \frac{\pi}{3}\right)$$

$$\frac{d^2i}{dt^2} = -4\pi^2 f^2 I_m \sin\left(2\pi ft - \frac{\pi}{3}\right).$$

13. $v = V_m \cos\left(2\pi ft + \dfrac{\pi}{6}\right)$

$$\frac{dv}{dt} = -2\pi f V_m \sin\left(2\pi ft + \frac{\pi}{6}\right)$$

$$\frac{d^2v}{dt^2} = -4\pi^2 f^2 V_m \cos\left(2\pi ft + \frac{\pi}{6}\right).$$

14. $V = \dfrac{4}{3}\pi R^3 \quad \dfrac{dV}{dR} = 4\pi R^2$

$$\frac{d^2V}{dR^2} = 8\pi R.$$

15. $V = \dfrac{1}{3}\pi r^2 h = \dfrac{1}{3}\pi r^2(3r) \quad V = \pi r^3$

$$\frac{dV}{dr} = 3\pi r^2 \quad \frac{d^2V}{dr^2} = 6\pi r.$$

Solution 4

1. Referring to Fig. 73, page 15 of the solutions, the gradient to the left of the peak is positive, $\frac{dy}{dx} > 0$, that is, the tangent of the angle is positive and the angle to the horizontal is less $90°$, the gradient to the right of the peak point **A** is negative, $\frac{dy}{dx} < 0$, that is, the tangent of the angle is negative and the angles to the horizontal is more than $90°$ and less than $180°$. The gradient at **P** is positive, the gradient at **Q** is negative and the gradient at **A** is zero, $\frac{dy}{dx} = 0$, the change of the gradient from **P** to **Q** via **A** is negative, that is, $\frac{d}{dx}\left(\frac{dy}{dx}\right) = \frac{d^2y}{dx^2} < 0$ and shows clearly that the turning point is a <u>maximum</u>.

Referring to Fig. 74, page 15 of the solutions, the gradient at P' is negative and that at Q' is positive $\frac{d}{dx}\left(\frac{dy}{dx}\right) = \frac{d^2y}{dx^2} > 0$ and shows clearly that the turning point is minimum. If $\frac{d}{dx}\left(\frac{dy}{dx}\right) = 0$, that is, the turning point is neither a maximum or a minimum, it is a point of inflection.

In general, for a turning point, the gradient, $\frac{dy}{dx} = 0$.

2. (i) $y = 2x^2 - 3x - 5$

$$\frac{dy}{dx} = 4x - 3 \text{ the gradient at any point of } x$$

$\frac{dy}{dx} = 0$, gives the turning point

$$4x - 3 = 0 \text{ or } x = \frac{3}{4}$$

when $x = \frac{3}{4}$,

$$y = 2\left(\frac{3}{4}\right)^2 - 3\left(\frac{3}{4}\right) - 5$$

$$y = \frac{18}{16} - \frac{9}{4} - 5 = -6.125$$

the turning point has coordinates

$$\left(\frac{3}{4}, -6\frac{1}{8}\right)$$

(ii) $y = -3x^2 - 2x + 1$

$$\frac{dy}{dx} = -6x - 2$$

$$\frac{dy}{dx} = 0 \text{ for turning points}$$

$$-6x - 2 = 0 \qquad x = -\frac{1}{3}$$

$$y = -3\left(-\frac{1}{3}\right)^2 - 2\left(-\frac{1}{3}\right) + 1$$

$$= -\frac{3}{9} + \frac{2}{3} + 1 = 1\frac{1}{3}$$

the turning point is $\left(-\frac{1}{3}, \frac{4}{3}\right)$.

(iii) $y = x^3 + 2x^2 - x + 1$

$$\frac{dy}{dx} = 3x^2 + 4x - 1$$

$$\frac{dy}{dx} = 0 \text{ for turning points}$$

$$3x^2 + 4x - 1 = 0$$

$$x = \frac{4 \pm \sqrt{16 + 12}}{6} = \frac{-4 \pm \sqrt{28}}{6}$$

$$x = 0.215$$

$$y = (0.215)^3 + 2(0.215)^2$$
$$-0.215 + 1 = 0.887$$

$$x = -1.549$$

$$y = (-1.549)^3 + 2(-1.549)^2$$
$$-(-1.549) + 1 = 3.631$$

The turning points are $(0.215, 0.887)$ and $(-1.549, 3.631)$.

(iv) $y = 2x^3 - 4x^2 - 3x - 5$

$$\frac{dy}{dx} = 6x^2 - 8x - 3$$

$\dfrac{dy}{dx} = 0$ for turning points

$$6x^2 - 8x - 3 = 0$$

$$x = \frac{8 \pm \sqrt{64 + 72}}{12}$$

$$= \frac{\sqrt{8 \pm \sqrt{136}}}{12}$$

$$x = 1.639$$

$$y = 2(1.639)^3 - 4(1.639)^2$$
$$-3(1.639) - 5 = -11.86$$

$$x = -0.305$$

$$y = 2(-0.305)^3 - 4(-0.305)^2$$
$$-3(-0.305) - 5 = -4.52$$

The turning points are
$(1.639, -11.86)$ and $(-0.305, -4.52)$.

3. (i) The gradient of the function $y = 2x^2 - 3x - 5$ is $\frac{dy}{dx} = 4x - 3$, the turning point occurs at the point $\left(\frac{3}{4}, -6\frac{1}{8}\right)$ where $\frac{dy}{dx} = 0$. The second derivative establishes whether the function has a maximum or a minimum.

$\dfrac{d^2y}{dx^2} = 4$ this is positive and indicates that the function has a minimum. At $x = \frac{3}{4}$, the minimum occurs $y_{min} = -6\frac{1}{8}$.

(ii) $\dfrac{dy}{dx} = -6x - 2 = 0$ for turning point

$\dfrac{d^2y}{dx^2} = -6$ this is negative and indicates that a maximum occurs at $x = -\frac{1}{3}$.

(iii) $\dfrac{dy}{dx} = 0$ giving turning points at
$x = 0.215 \quad x = -1.549$

$$\frac{d^2y}{dx^2} = 6x + 4$$

if $x = 0.215$

$\dfrac{d^2y}{dx^2} = 6(0.215) + 4 = 5.29$ thus

the point $(0.215, 0.887)$ is a minimum.

If $x = -1.549$,

$$\frac{d^2y}{dx^2} = 6(-1.549) + 4 = -5.29$$

thus the point $(-1.549, 3.631)$
is a maximum.

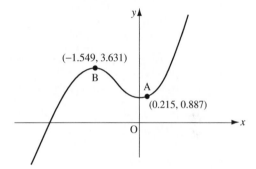

Fig. 75

Finding the minimum and maximum points, the curve is sketched as shown Fig. 75.

(iv) $\dfrac{dy}{dx} = 0$ for turning points

$x = 1.639$ and $x = -0.305$

$$\frac{d^2y}{dx^2} = 12x - 8 \quad \text{if } x = 1.639$$

$$\frac{d^2y}{dx^2} = 12(1.639) - 8 = 11.7$$

if $x = -0.305$,

$$\frac{d^2y}{dx^2} = 12(-0.305) - 8$$
$$= -11.7 \text{ maximum.}$$

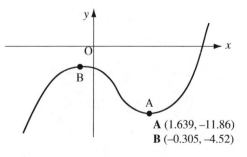

A $(1.639, -11.86)$
B $(-0.305, -4.52)$

Fig. 76

4. (i) $y = x^3 + 2x^2 - x + 1$

$$\frac{dy}{dx} = 3x^2 + 4x - 1$$

$$\frac{d^2y}{dx^2} = 6x + 4$$

The point of inflexion occurs when

$$\frac{d^2y}{dx^2} = 0$$

$$6x + 4 = 0 \quad x = -\frac{2}{3}$$

$$y = \left(-\frac{2}{3}\right)^3 + 2\left(-\frac{2}{3}\right)^2 - \left(-\frac{2}{3}\right) + 1$$

$$= -0.296 + 0.889 + 0.667 + 1 = 2.26.$$

The point of inflexion occurs at $(-\frac{2}{3}, 0.926)$.

(ii) $y = 2x^3 - 4x^2 - 3x - 5$

$$\frac{dy}{dx} = 6x^2 - 8x - 3$$

$$\frac{d^2y}{dx^2} = 12x - 8$$

The point of inflexion occurs when

$$\frac{d^2y}{dx^2} = 0 \quad 12x - 8 = 0 \quad x = \frac{2}{3}.$$

$$y = 2\left(\frac{2}{3}\right)^3 - 4\left(\frac{2}{3}\right)^2 - 3\left(\frac{2}{3}\right) - 5$$

$$= \frac{16}{27} - \frac{16}{9} - 7 = \frac{16 - 48 - 189}{27}$$

$$= -\frac{221}{27} = -8.185.$$

The point of inflexion is $(\frac{2}{3}, -8.185)$.

5. (i) $y = 2x^2 + 2x + 2 \quad \frac{dy}{dx} = 4x + 2 = 0$
for turning points

$$x = -\frac{1}{2} \quad \frac{d^2y}{dx^2} = 4 \text{ minimum}$$

$$y = 2\left(-\frac{1}{2}\right)^2 + 2\left(-\frac{1}{2}\right) + 2$$

$$= 2 \times \frac{1}{4} - 1 + 2 = \frac{3}{2}.$$

Therefore $\left(-\frac{1}{2}, \frac{3}{2}\right)$ are the coordinates of the minimum point.

(ii) $y = 2x^2 - 2x + 4$

$$\frac{dy}{dx} = 4x - 2 = 0$$

for turning points $x = \frac{1}{2}$

$$\frac{d^2y}{dx^2} = 4 \text{ minimum point}$$

$$y_{min} = 2\left(\frac{1}{2}\right)^2 - 2\left(\frac{1}{2}\right) + 4$$

$$= \frac{1}{2} - 1 + 4 = \frac{7}{2}.$$

The coordinates of the minimum are $\left(\frac{1}{2}, \frac{7}{2}\right)$.

(iii) $y = -x^2 - 3x - 4$

$$\frac{dy}{dx} = -2x - 3 = 0 \text{ for turning points}$$

$$x = -\frac{3}{2}$$

$$\frac{d^2y}{dx^2} = -2 \text{ maximum point}$$

$$y_{max} = -\left(-\frac{3}{2}\right)^2 - 3\left(-\frac{3}{2}\right) - 4$$

$$= -\frac{9}{4} + \frac{9}{2} - 4$$

$$= \frac{9}{4} - 4 = -\frac{7}{4}.$$

The coordinates of the maximum are $\left(-\frac{3}{2}, -\frac{7}{4}\right)$.

(iv) $y = -x^2 + 5x - 5$

$$\frac{dy}{dx} = -2x + 5 = 0 \text{ for turning points,}$$

$$x = \frac{5}{2}$$

$$\frac{d^2y}{dx^2} = -2 \text{ maximum point}$$

$$y_{max} = -\left(\frac{5}{2}\right)^2 + 5\left(\frac{5}{2}\right) - 5$$

$$= -\frac{25}{4} + \frac{25}{2} - 5$$

$$= \frac{25}{4} - 5 = \frac{5}{4}.$$

The coordinates of the maximum are $\left(\frac{5}{2}, \frac{5}{4}\right)$.

6. Let x and y be the numbers

$$x + y = 144 \qquad y = 144 - x$$

the product of the numbers are $x(144 - x)$.

Let $p = x(144 - x) = 144x - x^2$

$$\frac{dp}{dx} = 144 - 2x = 0 \text{ for turning points}$$

$$x = 72$$

$$\frac{d^2 p}{dx^2} = -2 \text{ maximum.}$$

Therefore the numbers are 72 and 72.

7. The surface area of the open rectangular tank is made up of the square base and four rectangular sides, $S = $ surface area $=$ area of base $+$ area of sides

$$S = y^2 + 4yh \quad \text{where } h \text{ is the height.}$$

The volume of the tank, $V = 500 \text{ m}^3$

$$500 = hy^2 \text{ or } h = \frac{500}{y^2}$$

and therefore

$$S = y^2 + 4y\frac{500}{y^2} = y^2 + \frac{2000}{y}.$$

To find the minimum surface area, we differentiate S with respect to y,

$$S = y^2 + 2000y^{-1}$$

$$\frac{dS}{dy} = 2y - 2000y^{-2}.$$

For minimum or maximum surface area, $\frac{dS}{dy} = 0$

$$2y - 2000y^{-2} = 0 \quad 2y = 2000y^{-2}$$

$$2y^3 = 2000 \quad y^3 = 1000 \quad y = 1000^{\frac{1}{3}}$$

the second derivative $\frac{d^2 S}{dy^2} = 2 + 4000y^{-3}$ which is always positive, and therefore the surface is minimum when $y = 1000^{\frac{1}{3}}$.

Therefore,

$$S_{min} = (1000^{\frac{1}{3}})^2 + \frac{2000}{1000^{\frac{1}{3}}}$$

$$= 100 + \frac{2000}{10}$$

$$= 100 + 200 = 300 \text{ m}^2$$

$$y = 1000^{\frac{1}{3}} = 10, \quad h = \frac{500}{y^2} = \frac{500}{100} = 5$$

$$y = 10 \text{ m and } h = 5 \text{ m.}$$

8. $P = IE - I^2 r \qquad \frac{dP}{dI} = E - 2Ir$

$$\frac{dP}{dI} = 0 \text{ for maximum power}$$

$$E - 2Ir = 0,$$

$$I = \frac{E}{2r} = \frac{12}{1.8} = 6.67 \quad I = 6.67 \text{ A}$$

$$P_{max} = 6.67 \times 12 - 6.67^2(0.9)$$

$$= 80.04 - 40.04 = 40 \text{ watts.}$$

9. Volume of the box $= x^2 h = 150$ where h is the height of the box, x is the length

$$S = x^2 + x^2 + 4xh = 2x^2 + 4x\frac{150}{x^2} =$$

$$2x^2 + \frac{600}{x}, \text{ the surface area of the closed box.}$$

$$S = 2x^2 + 600x^{-1} \qquad \frac{dS}{dx} = 4x - 600x^{-2}$$

$$\frac{dS}{dx} \text{ is zero for maximum or minimum}$$

$$\frac{dS}{dx} = 4x - \frac{600}{x^2} = 0$$

$$4x^3 = 600 \quad x^3 = 150$$

$$x = 150^{\frac{1}{3}} = 5.313 \text{ m}$$

$$h = \frac{150}{x^2} = \frac{150^1}{150^{\frac{2}{3}}}$$

$$= 150^{\frac{1}{3}} = 5.313 \text{ m}$$

in three decimal places.

10. Let x be the side of the squares which are to be cut. The base of the tank has an area $(25 - 2x)$, $(15 - 2x)$ and the volume of the tank is

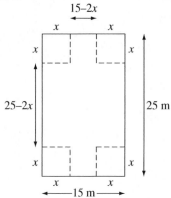

Fig. 77

$V = (25 - 2x)(15 - 2x)x$

$ = (375 - 30x - 50x + 4x^2)x$

$ = 375x - 30x^2 - 50x^2 + 4x^3$

$V = 4x^3 - 80x^2 + 375x.$

Differentiating with respect to x, we have

$\dfrac{dV}{dx} = 12x^2 - 160x + 375$

$\dfrac{dV}{dx} = 0$ for minimum or maximum

$12x^2 - 160x + 375 = 0$

$x = \dfrac{160 \pm \sqrt{160^2 - 4 \times 12 \times 375}}{2 \times 12}$

$ = \dfrac{160 \pm \sqrt{25600 - 18000}}{24}$

$ = \dfrac{160 \pm 87.18}{24}, \quad x = 10.3 \text{ or } x = 3.03$

$\dfrac{d^2V}{dx^2} = 24x - 160$

if $x = 10.3$, $\quad \dfrac{d^2V}{dx^2} = 87.2 > 0$

If $x = 3.03$, $\quad \dfrac{d^2V}{dx^2} = -87.3 < 0$,
the latter gives a maximum.

$V_{max} = (25 - 2 \times 3.03)(15 - 2 \times 3.03) \times 3.03$

$\phantom{V_{max}} = 4 \times 3.03^3 - 80 \times 3.03^2 + 375 \times 3.03$

$\phantom{V_{max}} = 111.27 - 734.47 + 1136.25$

$V_{max} = 513.1 \text{ cubic units.}$

Solution 5

1. $\int_0^{\frac{\pi}{2}} \sin 2x\,dx = \left[\dfrac{-\cos 2x}{2}\right]_0^{\frac{\pi}{2}}$

$= \left[\dfrac{-\cos \pi}{2}\right] - \left[\dfrac{-\cos 0}{2}\right]$

$= \dfrac{-(-1)}{2} + \dfrac{1}{2} = \dfrac{1}{2} + \dfrac{1}{2} = 1.$

2. $\int_0^{\frac{\pi}{4}} \cos 4x\,dx = \left[\dfrac{\sin 4x}{4}\right]_0^{\frac{\pi}{4}}$

$= \left[\dfrac{\sin \pi}{4}\right] - \left[\dfrac{\sin 0}{4}\right]$

$= 0 - 0 = 0.$

3. $\int_{\frac{\pi}{4}}^{\frac{\pi}{2}} \sin \frac{1}{2}x\,dx = \left[\dfrac{-\cos \frac{1}{2}x}{\frac{1}{2}}\right]_{\frac{\pi}{4}}^{\frac{\pi}{2}}$

$= \left[-2\cos \dfrac{\pi}{4}\right] - \left[-2\cos \dfrac{\pi}{8}\right]$

$= \dfrac{-2}{\sqrt{2}} + 2(0.9238795) = 0.4335.$

4. $\int_0^{2\pi} \cos 3x\,dx = \left[\dfrac{\sin 3x}{3}\right]_0^{2\pi}$

$= \left[\dfrac{\sin 6\pi}{3}\right] - \left[\dfrac{\sin 0}{3}\right] = 0 - 0 = 0.$

5. $\int_0^{\frac{\pi}{4}} \left(\sin 3x - \cos \dfrac{1}{3}x - e^{-\frac{x}{3}}\right) dx$

$= \left[\dfrac{-\cos 3x}{3} - \dfrac{\sin \frac{1}{3}x}{\frac{1}{3}} - \dfrac{e^{-\frac{x}{3}}}{-\frac{1}{3}}\right]_0^{\frac{\pi}{4}}$

$= \left[\dfrac{-\cos \frac{3\pi}{4}}{3} - 3\sin \dfrac{\pi}{3 \times 4} + 3e^{-\frac{1}{3}\cdot\frac{\pi}{4}}\right]$

$\qquad - \left[-\dfrac{\cos 0}{3} - 3\sin 0 + 3e^0\right]$

$= \left[\dfrac{1}{3\sqrt{2}} - 3 \times 0.2588 + 3 \times 0.7696654\right]$

$\qquad - \left[-\dfrac{1}{3} + 3\right]$

$= 0.2357378 - 0.7765$

$\qquad + 2.3089962 - 2.67$

$= -0.902.$

6. $\int_0^{\frac{3\pi}{2}} \sin \omega t\,d(\omega t) = \left[\dfrac{-\cos \omega t}{1}\right]_0^{\frac{3\pi}{2}}$

$= \left[\dfrac{-\cos \frac{3\pi}{2}}{1}\right] - [-\cos 0] = 1.$

7. $\int_{\frac{\pi}{6}}^{\frac{\pi}{3}} \cos 2\omega t\,d(\omega t) = \left[\dfrac{\sin 2\omega t}{2}\right]_{\frac{\pi}{6}}^{\frac{\pi}{3}}$

$= \left[\dfrac{\sin 2(\frac{\pi}{3})}{2}\right] - \left[\dfrac{\sin \frac{\pi}{3}}{2}\right]$

$= 0.433 - 0.433 = 0.$

8. $\int_0^1 \dfrac{e^{-v} + e^v}{2}\,dv = \dfrac{1}{2}\left[\dfrac{e^{-v}}{-1} + \dfrac{e^v}{1}\right]_0^1$

$= \dfrac{1}{2}\left[\dfrac{e^{-1}}{-1} + e\right] - \dfrac{1}{2}[-e^0 + e^0]$

$= \dfrac{1}{2}\left(e - \dfrac{1}{e}\right) - \dfrac{1}{2}(0)$

$= \dfrac{1}{2}\left(e - \dfrac{1}{e}\right) = 1.175.$

9. $\int_0^1 \dfrac{e^u - e^{-u}}{2}\,du = \left[\dfrac{e^u + e^{-u}}{2}\right]_0^1$

$= \dfrac{e^1 + e^{-1}}{2} - \dfrac{e^0 + e^0}{2}$

$= 1.54 - 1 = 0.54.$

10. $\int_0^{2\pi} [\sin 2y - \cos(-2y)]dy$

$= \left[\dfrac{-\cos 2y}{2} - \dfrac{\sin 2y}{2} \right]_0^{2\pi}$

$= \left[\dfrac{-\cos 4\pi}{2} - \dfrac{\sin 4\pi}{2} \right] - \left[-\dfrac{1}{2} - \dfrac{0}{2} \right]$

$= -\dfrac{1}{2} + \dfrac{1}{2} = 0.$

11. (i) $\dfrac{1}{\frac{\pi}{2}} \int_0^{\frac{\pi}{2}} \sin 2x \, dx = \dfrac{2}{\pi} \left[-\dfrac{\cos 2x}{2} \right]_0^{\frac{\pi}{2}}$

$= \dfrac{2}{\pi} \left[-\dfrac{\cos \pi}{2} + \dfrac{\cos 0}{2} \right]$

$= \dfrac{2}{\pi} \left[\dfrac{1}{2} + \dfrac{1}{2} \right] = \dfrac{2}{\pi} = 0.637$

(ii) $\dfrac{1}{\pi} \int_0^{\pi} 2 \sin \dfrac{1}{2}x \, dx$

$= \dfrac{1}{\pi} \left[\dfrac{-2 \cos \frac{1}{2}x}{\frac{1}{2}} \right]_0^{\pi}$

$= \dfrac{1}{\pi} \left[-4 \cos \dfrac{\pi}{2} + 4 \cos 0 \right]$

$= \dfrac{4}{\pi} = 1.273$

(iii) $\dfrac{1}{\frac{\pi}{2}} \int_0^{\frac{\pi}{2}} \sin 3t \, dt = \dfrac{2}{\pi} \left[\dfrac{-\cos 3t}{3} \right]_0^{\frac{\pi}{2}}$

$= \dfrac{2}{\pi} \left[\dfrac{-\cos 3(\frac{\pi}{2})}{3} + \dfrac{\cos 0}{3} \right]$

$= \dfrac{2}{3\pi} = 0.2122$

(iv) $\dfrac{1}{\pi} \int_0^{\pi} (1 + 2 \sin \theta) d\theta$

$= \dfrac{1}{\pi} [\theta - 2 \cos \theta]_0^{\pi}$

$= \dfrac{1}{\pi} [\pi - 2 \cos \pi - 0 + 2 \cos 0]$

$= \dfrac{1}{\pi} [\pi + 2 + 2] = 1 + \dfrac{4}{\pi} = 2.273$

(v) $\dfrac{1}{2} \int_0^2 e^{2x} dx = \dfrac{1}{2} \left[\dfrac{e^{2x}}{2} \right]_0^2$

$= \dfrac{1}{2} \left[\dfrac{e^4}{2} - \dfrac{e^0}{2} \right] = \dfrac{1}{4}e^4 - \dfrac{1}{4} = 13.4.$

12. $\dfrac{1}{\frac{\pi}{\omega}} \int_0^{\frac{\pi}{\omega}} 200 \sin \omega t \, dt$

$= \dfrac{\omega}{\pi} \left[\dfrac{-200 \cos \omega t}{\omega} \right]_0^{\frac{\pi}{\omega}}$

$= \dfrac{\omega}{\pi} \left[\dfrac{-200 \cos \pi}{\omega} \right] = \dfrac{\omega}{\pi} \left[\dfrac{-200 \cos 0}{\omega} \right]$

$= \dfrac{\omega}{\pi} \times \dfrac{200}{\omega} + \dfrac{200}{\pi} = \dfrac{400}{\pi}$

$\dfrac{1}{\frac{\pi}{\omega}} \int_0^{\frac{\pi}{\omega}} 200 \sin(\omega t + \dfrac{\pi}{6}) dt$

$= \dfrac{\omega}{\pi} \left[\dfrac{-200 \cos(\omega t + \frac{\pi}{6})}{\omega} \right]_0^{\frac{\pi}{\omega}}$

$= \dfrac{\omega}{\pi} \left[-\dfrac{200 \cos(\pi + \frac{\pi}{6})}{\omega} \right]$

$\quad - \dfrac{\omega}{\pi} \left[-\dfrac{200 \cos(\pi + \frac{\pi}{6})}{\omega} \right]$

$= -\dfrac{200}{\pi} \left(-\dfrac{\sqrt{3}}{2} \right) + \dfrac{200}{\pi} \dfrac{\sqrt{3}}{2} = \dfrac{200}{\pi} \sqrt{3}.$

13. $\sqrt{\dfrac{\omega}{2\pi} \int_0^{\frac{2\pi}{\omega}} (3 + 4 \cos \omega t)^2 dt}$

$= \sqrt{\dfrac{\omega}{2\pi} \int_0^{\frac{2\pi}{\omega}} (9 + 24 \cos \omega t + 16 \cos^2 \omega t) dt}$

$= \sqrt{\dfrac{\omega}{2\pi} \left[9t + 24 \dfrac{\sin \omega t}{\omega} + 16 \left(\dfrac{\sin 2\omega t}{4\omega} + \dfrac{1}{2}t \right) \right]_0^{\frac{2\pi}{\omega}}}$

where $\cos 2\omega t = 2 \cos^2 \omega t - 1$

or $\dfrac{\cos 2\omega t + 1}{2} = \cos^2 \omega t$

$= \dfrac{\omega}{2\pi} \left[9 \dfrac{2\pi}{\omega} + \dfrac{24}{\omega} \sin 2\pi + \dfrac{16}{4\omega} \sin 2(2\pi) + \dfrac{2\pi}{2\omega} 16 \right]$

$= \sqrt{9 + \dfrac{16}{2}} = \sqrt{17} = 4.12.$

14. (i) $\int_0^{\frac{\pi}{3}} \cos(2x - \frac{\pi}{6})dx$

$$= \left[\frac{\sin(2x - \frac{\pi}{6})}{2} \right]_0^{\frac{\pi}{3}}$$

$$= \left[\frac{\sin\left(2\frac{\pi}{3} - \frac{\pi}{6}\right)}{2} \right]$$

$$- \left[\frac{\sin\left(-\frac{\pi}{6}\right)}{2} \right]$$

$$= \frac{\sin\frac{\pi}{2}}{2} + \frac{1}{4} = \frac{3}{4}$$

(ii) $\int_1^2 (e^{3x} - e^{-3x})dx = \left[\frac{e^{3x}}{3} + \frac{e^{-3x}}{3} \right]_1^2$

$$= \left[\frac{e^6}{3} + \frac{e^{-6}}{3} \right] - \left[\frac{e^3}{3} + \frac{e^{-3}}{3} \right]$$

$$= 134.5 - 6.71 = 127.8$$

(iii) $\int_0^{\frac{\pi}{2}} [1 - \sin(2x - \frac{\pi}{6})]dx$

$$= \left[x + \frac{\cos(2x - \frac{\pi}{6})}{2} \right]_0^{\frac{\pi}{2}}$$

$$= \left[\frac{\pi}{2} + \frac{\cos(\pi - \frac{\pi}{6})}{2} \right]$$

$$- \left[\frac{\cos(-\frac{\pi}{6})}{2} \right]$$

$$= \frac{\pi}{2} - \frac{\sqrt{3}}{4} - \frac{\sqrt{3}}{4}$$

$$= \frac{\pi}{2} - \frac{\sqrt{3}}{2} = \frac{\pi - \sqrt{3}}{2}.$$

15. $\frac{1}{\frac{2\pi}{\omega}} \int_0^{\frac{2\pi}{\omega}} \cos^2 \omega t \, dt$

$$= \frac{\omega}{2\pi} \left[\int_0^{\frac{2\pi}{\omega}} \frac{\cos 2\omega t + 1}{2} dt \right]$$

$$\cos 2\omega t = 2\cos^2 \omega t - 1 \text{ or}$$

$$\cos^2 \omega t = \frac{\cos 2\omega t + 1}{2}$$

$$= \frac{\omega}{2\pi} \left[\frac{\sin 2\omega t}{4\omega} + \frac{1}{2}t \right]_0^{2\frac{\pi}{\omega}}$$

$$= \frac{\omega}{2\pi} \left[\frac{\sin 4\pi}{4\omega} + \frac{1}{2}\frac{2\pi}{\omega} \right]$$

$$= \frac{\omega}{2\pi}\frac{\pi}{\omega} = \frac{1}{2}.$$

16. $\sqrt{\frac{\omega}{2\pi} \int_1^{\frac{2\pi}{\omega}} V_m^2 \sin^2 \omega t \, dt}$

$$= \sqrt{\frac{V_m^2 \omega}{2\pi} \int_0^{\frac{2\pi}{\omega}} \frac{1 - \cos 2\omega t}{2} dt}$$

$$\cos 2\omega t = 1 - 2\sin^2 \omega t$$

$$2\sin^2 \omega t = 1 - \cos^2 \omega t$$

$$\sin^2 \omega t = \frac{1 - \cos 2\omega t}{2}$$

$$= V_{\max}\sqrt{\frac{\omega}{2\pi} \left[\frac{1}{2}t - \frac{\sin 2\omega t}{4\omega} \right]_0^{\frac{2\pi}{\omega}}}$$

$$= V_{\max}\sqrt{\frac{\omega}{2\pi} \left(\frac{\pi}{\omega} - \frac{\sin 4\pi}{4\omega} \right)}$$

$$= \frac{V_{\max}}{\sqrt{2}}.$$

Solution 6

1.

(i) $\int_{-3}^{2} (3x^2 + 2x + 1)dx$

$$= \left[3\frac{x^3}{3} + 2\frac{x^2}{2} + x \right]_{-3}^{2}$$

$$= [2^3 + 2^2 + 2] - [(-3)^3 + (-3)^2 + (-3)]$$

$$= 14 + 21 = 35 \text{ square units.}$$

(ii) $\int_{-3}^{2} (3x^2 + 2x + 1)dx$

$$\approx \frac{h}{2}[y_1 + 2(y_2 + y_3 + y_4 + y_5) + y_6]$$

$$= \frac{1}{2}[22 + 2(9 + 2 + 1 + 6) + 17]$$

$$= 37.5 \text{ square units}$$

$$h = \frac{2 - (-3)}{5}$$

$$= \frac{5}{5} = 1 \text{ the width of the interval}$$

$$y = 3x^2 + 2x + 1$$

y_1 occurs at $x = -3$

$y_1 = 3(-3)^2 + 2(-3) + 1$

$\quad = 27 - 6 + 1 = 22$

y_2 occurs at $x = -2$

$y_2 = 3(-2)^2 + 2(-2) + 1 = 12 - 4 + 1 = 9$

y_3 occurs at $x = -1$

$y_3 = 3(-1)^2 + 2(-1) + 1 = 3 - 2 + 1 = 2$

y_4 occurs at $x = 0$

$y_4 = 3(0)^2 + 2(0) + 1 = 1$

y_5 occurs at $x = 1$

$y_5 = 3(1)^2 + 2(1) + 1 = 6$

y_6 occurs at $x = 2$

$y_6 = 3(2)^2 + 2(2) + 1 = 17.$

(iii) $\int_{-3}^{2} (3x^2 + 2x + 1)dx$

$$\approx \frac{h}{3}[y_1 + 4(y_2 + y_4 + y_6 + y_8 + y_{10})$$

$$+ 2(y_3 + y_5 + y_7 + y_9) + y_{11}]$$

$$h = \frac{2 - (-3)}{10} = \frac{5}{10} = \frac{1}{2} \text{ the width of}$$

the interval 11 ordinates correspond to 10 intervals.

y_1	-3
y_2	$-\frac{5}{2}$
y_3	-2
y_4	$-\frac{3}{2}$
y_5	-1
y_6	$-\frac{1}{2}$
y_7	0
y_8	$\frac{1}{2}$
y_9	1
y_{10}	$\frac{1}{2}$
y_{11}	2

$$h = \frac{1}{2} = -\frac{5}{2} - (-3) = \frac{1}{2}$$

$$y = 3x^2 + 2x + 1$$

$y_1 = 3(-3)^2 + 2(-3) + 1$

$\quad = 27 - 6 + 1 = 22$

$y_2 = 3(-\frac{5}{2})^2 + 2(-\frac{5}{2}) + 1 = 14.75$

$y_3 = 3(-2)^2 + 2(-2) + 1 = 9$

$y_4 = 3(-1\frac{1}{2})^2 + 2(-1\frac{1}{2}) + 1 = 4.75$

$y_5 = 3(-1)^2 + 2(-1) + 1 = 2$

$y_6 = 3(-\frac{1}{2})^2 + 2(-\frac{1}{2}) + 1 = 0.75$

$y_7 = 3(0)^2 + 2(0) + 1 = 1$

$y_8 = 3(\frac{1}{2})^2 + 2(\frac{1}{2}) + 1 = 2.75$

$y_9 = 3(1)^2 + 2(1) + 1 = 6$

$y_{10} = 3(1\frac{1}{2})^2 + 2(1\frac{1}{2}) + 1 = 10.75$

$y_{11} = 3(2)^2 + 2(2) + 1 = 17$

$\int_{-3}^{2}(3x^2 + 2x + 1)dx$

$\approx \frac{\frac{1}{2}}{3}[22 + 17 + 4(14.75 + 4.75 + 0.75$

$+ 2.75 + 10.75) + 2(9 + 2 + 1 + 6)]$

$= \frac{1}{6}[39 + 4 \times 33.75 + 2 \times 18]$

$= \frac{210}{6}$

$= 35$ square units.

(iv) $\int_{-3}^{2}(3x^2 + 2x + 1)dx \approx$ the sum of the mid ordinates x the interval width

$= (y_{1m} + y_{2m} + y_{3m} + \ldots + y_{10m})h$

From above,

$y_{1m} = \frac{y_1 + y_2}{2} = \frac{22 + 14.75}{2} = 18.375$

$y_{2m} = \frac{14.75 + 9}{2} = 11.875$

$y_{3m} = \frac{9 + 4.75}{2} = 6.875$

$y_{4m} = \frac{4.75 + 2}{2} = 3.375$

$y_{5m} = \frac{2 + 0.75}{2} = 1.375$

$y_{6m} = \frac{0.75 + 1}{2} = 0.875$

$y_{7m} = \frac{1 + 2.75}{2} = 1.875$

$y_{8m} = \frac{2.75 + 6}{2} = 4.375$

$y_{9m} = \frac{6 + 10.75}{2} = 8.375$

$y_{10m} = \frac{10.75 + 17}{2} = 13.875$

$\int_{-3}^{2}(3x^2 + 2x + 1)dx$

$\approx \frac{1}{2}(18.375 + 11.875 + 6.875$

$+ 3.375 + 1.375 + 0.875 + 1.875$

$+ 4.375 + 8.375 + 13.875)$

$h = \frac{2 - (-3)}{10} = \frac{1}{2} = \frac{1}{2} \times 71.25$

$= 35.625$ square units.

2. (i) $\int_{0}^{1} \frac{dx}{(1 + x^2)^{\frac{1}{2}}}$

$\approx \frac{h}{3}[y_1 + 4(y_2 + y_4) + 2y_3 + y_5]$

4 intervals are equivalent to five ordinates y_1, y_2, y_3, y_4 and y_5, and the approximate formula for Simpson's rule is as above.

$y = \frac{1}{(1 + x^2)^{\frac{1}{2}}}$

To find $h = \frac{1 - 0}{4} = 0.25$

x 0, 0.25, 0.5, 0.75, 1.00

$y_1 = \frac{1}{(1 + 0)^{\frac{1}{2}}} = 1$ when $x = 0$

$y_2 = \frac{1}{(1 + 0.25^2)^{\frac{1}{2}}} = 0.97$

when $x = 0.25$

$y_3 = \frac{1}{(1 + 0.5^2)^{\frac{1}{2}}} = 0.894$ when $x = 0.5$

$y_4 = \frac{1}{(1 + 0.75^2)^{\frac{1}{2}}} = 0.8$ when $x = 0.75$

$y_5 = \frac{1}{(1 + 1^2)^{\frac{1}{2}}} = 0.707$ when $x = 1$

$\int_{0}^{1} \frac{dx}{(1 + x^2)^{\frac{1}{2}}}$

$\approx \frac{0.25}{3}[1 + 4(0.97 + 0.8)$

$+ 2 \times 0.894 + 0.707]$

$= 0.08333(1 + 7.08 + 1.788 + 0.707)$

$= 0.083333 \times 10.575 = 0.881.$

(ii) $\int_0^1 \dfrac{dx}{(1+x^2)^{\frac{1}{2}}}$

$\approx \dfrac{h}{2}[y_1 + 2(y_2 + y_3 + y_4 + y_5) + y_6]$

six ordinates are equivalent to
five intervals

$h = \dfrac{1-0}{5} = 0.2$

x 0, 0.2, 0.4, 0.6, 0.8, 1.0

$y = \dfrac{1}{(1+x^2)^{\frac{1}{2}}}$

$y_1 = 1$ when $x = 0$

$y_2 = \dfrac{1}{(1+0.2^2)^{\frac{1}{2}}} = 0.9806$

when $x = 0.2$

$y_3 = \dfrac{1}{(1+0.4^2)^{\frac{1}{2}}} = 0.9285$

when $x = 0.4$

$y_4 = \dfrac{1}{(1+0.6^2)^{\frac{1}{2}}} = 0.8575$

when $x = 0.6$

$y_5 = \dfrac{1}{(1+0.8)^2{}^{\frac{1}{2}}} = 0.7809$

when $x = 0.8$

$y_6 = \dfrac{1}{(1+1)^{\frac{1}{2}}} = 0.7071$ when $x = 1$

$\int_0^1 \dfrac{dx}{(1+x^2)^{\frac{1}{2}}}$

$\approx \dfrac{0.2}{2}[1 + 2(0.9806 + 0.9285$

$+ 0.8575 + 0.7809) + 0.7071]$

$= 0.1(1 + 7.095 + 0.7071) = 0.880.$

To apply Simpson's rule, we must have an odd number of ordinates or even number of intervals and to apply the trapezoidal rule, the number of ordinates can be either odd or even and the number of intervals can be either even or odd respectively.

3. $\int_1^2 10^x dx$

$\approx \dfrac{h}{3}[y_1 + 4(y_2 + y_4 + y_6 + y_8 + y_{10})$

$+ 2(y_3 + y_5 + y_7 + y_9) + y_{11}]$

$h = \dfrac{2-1}{10} = 0.1$

$y = 10^x$

x 1, 1.1, 1.2, 1.3, 1.4, 1.5, 1.6, 1.7, 1.8, 1.9, 2.0

$y_1 = 10^1 = 10$ $(x = 1)$

$y_2 = 10^{1.1} = 12.589$ $(x = 1.1)$

$y_3 = 10^{1.2} = 15.849$ $(x = 1.2)$

$y_4 = 10^{1.3} = 19.9526$ $(x = 1.3)$

$y_5 = 10^{1.4} = 25.114$ $(x = 1.4)$

$y_6 = 10^{1.5} = 31.623$ $x = 1.5$

$y_7 = 10^{1.6} = 39.811$ $x = 1.6$

$y_8 = 10^{1.7} = 50.119$ $x = 1.7$

$y_9 = 10^{1.8} = 63.096$ $x = 1.8$

$y_{10} = 10^{1.9} = 79.433$ $x = 1.9$

$y_{11} = 10^2 = 100.000$ $x = 2.0$

$\int_1^2 10^x dx$

$\approx \dfrac{0.1}{3}[10 + 4(1.2589 + 1.9953$

$+ 31.623 + 50.119 + 79.433)$

$+ 2(1.5849 + 2.5119$

$+ 39.811 + 63.096) + 100]$

$= 0.03333(10 + 657.72 + 214 + 100)$

$= 32.72.$

4. Consider an elemental strip of height y and width dx.

The elemental area $= y dx$.

The area of the first quadrant of circle, or the area of one quarter of the circle is given by the integral.

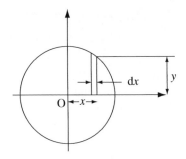

Fig. 78

$$\int_0^{14} y\,dx = \int_0^{14} \sqrt{14^2 - x^2}\,dx$$

$$\int_0^{14} \sqrt{14^2 - x^2}\,dx \approx \frac{h}{3}[y_1 + 4(y_2 + y_4 + y_6$$
$$+ y_8 + y_{10} + y_{12} + y_{14})]$$
$$+ 2(y_3 + y_5 + y_7 + y_9$$
$$+ y_{11} + y_{13}) + y_{15}$$

15 ordinates are 14 intervals

$$h = \frac{14 - 0}{14} = \frac{14}{14} = 1 \text{ cm using Simpson's rule.}$$

x 0, 1, 2, 3, 4, 5, 6, 7, 8, 9, 10, 11, 12, 13, 14

$y = \sqrt{14 - x^2}$

$y_1 = 14$

$y_2 = \sqrt{14^2 - 1^2} = 13.964$

$y_3 = \sqrt{14^2 - 2^2} = 13.856$

$y_4 = \sqrt{14^2 - 3^2} = 13.675$

$y_5 = \sqrt{14^2 - 4^2} = 13.416$

$y_6 = \sqrt{14^2 - 5^2} = 13.077$

$y_7 = \sqrt{14^2 - 6^2} = 12.649$

$y_8 = \sqrt{14^2 - 7^2} = 12.124$

$y_9 = \sqrt{14^2 - 8^2} = 11.489$

$y_{10} = \sqrt{14^2 - 9^2} = 10.724$

$y_{11} = \sqrt{14^2 - 10^2} = 9.798$

$y_{12} = \sqrt{14^2 - 11^2} = 8.660$

$y_{13} = \sqrt{14^2 - 12^2} = 7.211$

$y_{14} = \sqrt{14^2 - 13^2} = 5.196$

$- y_{15} = \sqrt{14^2 - 14^2} = 0$

$$\int_0^{14} \sqrt{14^2 - x^2}\,dx$$

$$\approx \frac{1}{3}[14 + 4(13.964 + 13.675 + 13.077$$
$$+ 12.124 + 10.724) + 8.660 + 5.196$$
$$+ 2(13.856 + 13.416 + 12.649 + 11.489$$
$$+ 9.798 + 7.211) + 0]$$

$$= \frac{1}{3}(14 + 309.68 + 136.68) = 153.51 \text{ cm}^2$$

Total area $= 4 \times 153.51 = 614.02 \text{ cm}^2$

Area of a circle is $\pi 14^2 = 615.8 \text{ cm}^2$.

The percentage error

$$= \frac{(615.8 - 614.62) \times 100}{615.8}$$

$$= 0.289\% \approx 0.3\%.$$

Alternative method by integration

Let $x = 14 \sin\theta$, If $x = 14$, $\sin\theta = 1$ or $\theta = \dfrac{\pi}{2}$

$$\frac{dx}{d\theta} = 14\cos\theta \quad x = 0, \sin\theta = 0 \text{ or } \theta = 0$$

the new limits are $0, \frac{\pi}{2}$

$$\int_0^{14} \sqrt{14^2 - x^2}\,dx$$

$$= \int_0^{\frac{\pi}{2}} \sqrt{14^2 - 14^2 \sin^2\theta}\, 14\cos\theta\,d\theta$$

$$= 14^2 \int_0^{\frac{\pi}{2}} \cos^2\theta\,d\theta$$

$$\cos 2\theta = 2\cos^2\theta - 1 \text{ or}$$

$$\frac{\cos 2\theta + 1}{2} = \cos^2\theta$$

$$= 14^2 \int_0^{\frac{\pi}{2}} \frac{\cos 2\theta + 1}{2}\,d\theta$$

$$= 14^2 \left[\frac{\sin 2\theta}{4} + \frac{\theta}{2}\right]_0^{\frac{\pi}{2}}$$

$$= 14^2 \frac{\pi}{4} = 153.94 \text{ cm}^2 \text{ exact.}$$

5. (i) $\displaystyle\int_0^{\pi} \sqrt{\sin x}\,dx$

$$\approx \frac{h}{2}[y_1 + 2(y_2 + y_3 + y_4 + y_5 + y_6$$
$$+ y_7 + y_8 + y_9 + y_{10}) + y_{11}]$$

$$= \frac{\pi}{20}[0 + 2(2 \times 0.55589 + 2 \times 0.76667$$

$$+ 2 \times 0.89945 + 0$$

$$+ 2 \times 0.97522 + 2 \times 1)]$$

$$= \frac{\pi}{10} \times 14.78892 = 2.323 \text{ square units.}$$

x	$y = \sqrt{\sin x}$
0	0
$\frac{\pi}{10}$	0.55589
$\frac{2\pi}{10}$	0.767
$\frac{3\pi}{10}$	0.89945
$\frac{4\pi}{10}$	0.97522
$\frac{5\pi}{10}$	1
$\frac{6\pi}{10}$	0.97522
$\frac{7\pi}{10}$	0.89945
$\frac{8\pi}{10}$	0.76667
$\frac{9\pi}{10}$	0.55589
π	0

(ii) $\displaystyle\int_0^\pi \sqrt{\sin x}\, dx$

$$\approx \frac{\frac{\pi}{10}}{3}[0 + 4(0.5589 + 0.89945$$

$$+ 1 + 0.89945 + 0.55589)$$

$$+ 2(0.76667 + 0.97522$$

$$+ 0.97522 + 0.76667)]$$

$$= \frac{\pi}{30}[15.65476 + 6.96756]$$

$$= \underline{2.369} \text{ square units.}$$

6.

x	$y = \ln x$
2	0.693
$2\frac{3}{4}$	1.0116
$3\frac{1}{2}$	1.2528
$4\frac{1}{4}$	1.4469
5	1.6094

$$h = \frac{5 - 2}{4} = \frac{3}{4}$$

$$\int_2^5 \ln x\, dx \approx \frac{h}{3}[y_1 + 4y_2 + 2y_3 + 4y_4 + y_5]$$

$$= \frac{\frac{3}{4}}{3}[0.693 + 4(1.0116) + 2(1.2528)$$

$$+ 4(1.4469) + 1.6094]$$

$$= \frac{1}{4}[0.693 + 4.0464 + 2.5056$$

$$+ 5.7876 + 1.6094]$$

$$= 3.6605 = \underline{3.661} \text{ square units.}$$

Solution 7

1. $\dfrac{dy}{dx} = 3x^2 - 5x + 7$ $dy = (3x^2 - 5x + 7)dx$

integrating both sides of this equation we have

$\int dy = \int (3x^2 - 5x + 7)dx$

$y = 3\dfrac{x^3}{3} - 5\dfrac{x^2}{2} + 7x + c$ the general solution.

Employing the boundary conditions

$y = 0, x = 1$

$0 = 1 - \dfrac{5}{2} + 7 + c$ $c = \dfrac{5}{2} - 8 = -\dfrac{11}{2}$

therefore the function solution is

$y = x^3 - \dfrac{5}{2}x^2 + 7x - \dfrac{11}{2}$, which is the particular solution.

2. (i) $\dfrac{dy}{dx} = -3x - 1$

$dy = (-3x - 1)dx$

integrating both sides

$\int dy = \int (-3x - 1)dx$

$y = -3\dfrac{x^2}{2} - x + c$, the general solution

when $x = 1, y = 1$

$1 = -\dfrac{3}{2} - 1 + c$ $c = 2 + \dfrac{3}{2} = \dfrac{7}{2}$

therefore $y = -\dfrac{3}{2}x^2 - x + \dfrac{7}{2}$ is the particular solution.

(ii) $\dfrac{dy}{dx} = -5$

$dy = -5dx$ integrating both sides

$\int dy = -\int 5dx$

$y = -5x + c$ general solution

$0 = -25 + c$

$c = 25$ therefore $y = -5x + 25$, is the particular solution.

3. $\dfrac{dy}{dx} = 3e^{-5x}$

$dy = 3e^{-5x}dx$ integrating both sides

$\int dy = \int 3e^{-5x}dx$ $y = \dfrac{3e^{-5x}}{-5} + c$,

the general solution

when $x = 0, y = 3$ $3 = -\dfrac{3}{5}e^0 + c$

$c = 3 + \dfrac{3}{5} = \dfrac{18}{5}$ the particular solution is given

$y = -\dfrac{3}{5}e^{-5x} + \dfrac{18}{5}$.

4. $\dfrac{dy}{dx} = 3\sin 5x - 5\cos 3x$

$dy = (3\sin 5x - 5\cos 3x)dx$

integrating both sides

$\int dy = \int (3\sin 5x - 5\cos 3x)dx$

$y = -\dfrac{3}{5}\cos 5x - \dfrac{5}{3}\sin 3x + c$

when $x = \frac{\pi}{2}, y = 2$

$2 = -\dfrac{3}{5}\cos 5(\frac{\pi}{2}) - \dfrac{5}{3}\sin 3(\frac{\pi}{2}) + c$

$c = 2 + \dfrac{5}{3}\sin \frac{3\pi}{2} = 2 - \dfrac{5}{3} = \dfrac{1}{3}$,

$\cos \frac{5\pi}{2} = 0$

therefore $y = -\dfrac{3}{5}\cos 5x - \dfrac{5}{3}\sin 3x + \dfrac{1}{3}$.

5. $\dfrac{dy}{dx} = 3\cos 3x - 5\sin 2x + 3e^{3x} + 5$

$\int dy = \int (3\cos 3x - 5\sin 2x + 3e^{3x} + 5)dx$

$y = \sin 3x + \dfrac{5}{2}\cos 2x + e^{3x} + 5x + c$

general solution when $x = 0$, $y = 2$

$2 = \dfrac{5}{2} + 1 + c \qquad c = -\dfrac{3}{2}$

$y = \sin 3x + \dfrac{5}{2}\cos 2x + e^{3x} + 5x - \dfrac{3}{2}.$

Solution 8

1. $\dfrac{di}{dt} = 5i$ separating the variables $\dfrac{di}{i} = 5dt$

   integrating both sides $\int \dfrac{di}{i} = \int 5dt$

   $\ln i = 5t + c \quad \ln 5 = 0 + c \quad c = \ln 5$

   therefore $\ln i = 5t + \ln 5$

   $\ln i - \ln 5 = 5t \quad \ln \frac{i}{5} = 5t$

   by the definition of a logarithm

   $e^{5t} = \dfrac{i}{5} \quad i = 5e^{5t}.$

2. $q = Qe^{-\frac{t}{RC}}$

   $\dfrac{dq}{dt} = Q\left[-\dfrac{1}{RC}\right]e^{-\frac{t}{RC}} = -\dfrac{Q}{RC}e^{-\frac{t}{RC}}$

   $= -\dfrac{50 \times 10^{-3}}{10 \times 10^3 \times 100 \times 10^{-6}}e^{-\frac{10^{-3}}{10 \times 10^3 \times 100 \times 10^{-6}}}$

   $= -\dfrac{50}{1000}e^{-\frac{1}{1000}}$

   $= -0.05 \times 0.999 \approx -0.05.$

3. $\dfrac{dy}{dx} = xe^y \quad \dfrac{dy}{e^y} = xdx$

   integrating both sides

   $\int \dfrac{dy}{e^y} = \int xdx \quad \int e^{-y}dy = \int xdx$

   $\dfrac{e^{-y}}{-1} = \dfrac{x^2}{2} + c \quad e^{-y} = -\dfrac{x^2}{2} + k$

   $e^0 = -\dfrac{1}{2} + k \quad 1 = -\dfrac{1}{2} + k$

   $k = \dfrac{3}{2} \quad e^{-y} = -\dfrac{x^2}{2} + \dfrac{3}{2}.$

4. $\dfrac{dy}{dx} = yx^3 \quad \dfrac{dy}{y} = x^3dx$

   integrating both sides $\int \dfrac{dy}{y} = \int x^3dx$

   $\ln y = \dfrac{x^4}{4} + c \quad \ln 1 = 0 + c$

   $c = 0$ therefore $\boxed{y = e^{\frac{x^4}{4}}}$

5. $\dfrac{d\theta}{dt} = -k\theta \quad \dfrac{d\theta}{\theta} = -kdt$

   $\ln \theta = -kt + c$

   $\ln 38 = -k(0) + c \quad c = \ln 38$

   $\ln \theta - \ln 38 = -kt$

   $\ln \dfrac{\theta}{38} = -kt \quad e^{-kt} = \dfrac{\theta}{38}$

   $\theta = 38e^{-kt}$

   $25 = 38e^{-k60} \quad e^{k60} = \dfrac{38}{25}$

   $k60 = \ln \frac{38}{25} \quad k = \dfrac{1}{60}\ln \frac{38}{25}$

   $k = 6.98 \times 10^{-3}$

   therefore $\theta = 38e^{-6.98 \times 10^{-3}t}.$

6. $V = iR + \dfrac{1}{C}\int idt \ldots (1)$

   $\dfrac{di}{dt}R + \dfrac{i}{C} = 0 \quad t = 0$ when $i = I$

   $\dfrac{di}{dt} = -\dfrac{i}{RC}$

   $\dfrac{di}{i} = -\dfrac{dt}{RC}$

   $\int \dfrac{di}{i} = \int -\dfrac{dt}{RC}$

   $\ln i = -\dfrac{t}{RC} + k$ (constant)

   at $t = 0$, constant $= k = \ln I$

$$\ln i = -\frac{t}{RC} + \ln I$$

$$\ln \frac{i}{I} = -\frac{t}{RC}$$

$$i = Ie^{-\frac{t}{RC}}.$$

7. $i = C\dfrac{\mathrm{d}v}{\mathrm{d}t} = Ie^{-\frac{t}{RC}},$

$C\mathrm{d}v = Ie^{-\frac{t}{RC}}\,\mathrm{d}t$, integrating both sides

$$Cv = \frac{Ie^{-\frac{t}{RC}}}{\frac{1}{RC}} + \text{constant},$$

$$v = -IRe^{-\frac{t}{RC}} + \text{constant}$$

$$t = 0,\, v = 0,\, V = \text{constant},$$

$$v = V(1 - e^{-\frac{t}{RC}}).$$

Index
Calculus III

i